Manfred Brauneck and ITI Germany (eds.)
Independent Theatre in Contemporary Europe

Theatre Studies | Volume 80

Manfred Brauneck and ITI Germany (eds.)
Independent Theatre in Contemporary Europe
Structures – Aesthetics – Cultural Policy

[transcript]

Supported by the International Balzan Prize Foundation

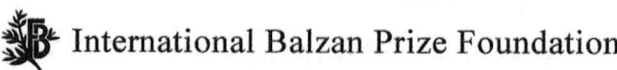 International Balzan Prize Foundation

 An electronic version of this book is freely available, thanks to the support of libraries working with Knowledge Unlatched. KU is a collaborative initiative designed to make high quality books Open Access for the public good. The Open Access ISBN for this book is 978-3-8394-3243-3

Bibliographic information published by the Deutsche Nationalbibliothek
The Deutsche Nationalbibliothek lists this publication in the Deutsche Nationalbibliografie; detailed bibliographic data are available in the Internet at http://dnb.d-nb.de

© 2017 transcript Verlag, Bielefeld

All rights reserved. No part of this book may be reprinted or reproduced or utilized in any form or by any electronic, mechanical, or other means, now known or hereafter invented, including photocopying and recording, or in any information storage or retrieval system, without permission in writing from the publisher.

Cover layout: Kordula Röckenhaus, Bielefeld
Cover illustration: »Tetralogia – Una Vision de Colombia«, Athanor Danza/ Companhia Alvaro Restrepo, Kampnagel Hamburg, 2002, Photo: Friedemann Simon
Proofread by Anna Galt, Esther Geyer, Anne John, Claudia Jones, Rachael McGill, Rahel Schöppenthau und Lisenka Sedlacek
Translated by Rhonda Farr, Rachael McGill, William Wheeler
Typeset by Justine Haida, Bielefeld
Printed and bound in Great Britain by Marston Book Services Ltd, Oxfordshire
Print-ISBN 978-3-8376-3243-9
PDF-ISBN 978-3-8394-3243-3

Dear readers

The International Balzan Prize Foundation promotes culture and science, and supports initiatives that serve the ideals of humanity, peace and fraternity. In 2010, for the first time, the foundation awarded its prize to a theatre researcher. Professor Manfred Brauneck, of Hamburg, was honoured with the *Premio Balzan* for his life's work. In accordance with the prize regulations, Professor Brauneck donated half of the prize money to a research project for promising academics. He asked the German Centre of the International Theatre Institute, of which he is a long-standing member, to manage this project; its aim was to complement Brauneck's own studies in theatre history with an examination of structural changes to European theatre since the beginning of the 1990s. The context is a Europe experiencing change through the creation of the European Union, which has influenced international production, networking, digitalisation, project-based work and hybridisation of forms, as well as leading to the economisation of more and more areas of life and the commercialisation of the public sphere. The research project *The Role of Independent Theatre in European Contemporary Theatre: Studies on Structural and Aesthetic Changes* was developed together with four young researchers and four mentors: Professor Gabriele Brandstetter, Freie Universität Berlin, Dr. Barbara Müller-Wesemann, Zentrum für Theaterforschung der Universität Hamburg, Professor Günther Heeg, Universität Leipzig and Professor Wolfgang Schneider, Universität Hildesheim. A series of symposia and colloquia allowed the collaborators to survey the field of research and undertake an expansive discussion about working methods. The setting of both a regional focus and a limit to the practices to be described was of crucial importance.

The Institute for Theatre Studies at the University of Leipzig then organised a symposium as part of the festival euro-scene Leipzig 2012. The symposium was entitled *Art and Life: Metamorphoses in (Eastern) European Independent Theatre*. Experts from artistic and scientific disciplines and participants discussed questions around current structures and developments in the performing arts in Eastern Europe.

In March 2013, the *Post-Migrant Perspectives on European Theatre* conference took place at the Goethe Institute in London. Using the starting point of the national scenes in Germany, Great Britain, the Netherlands and Sweden, the conference members contemplated the effects of European migrant societies and the special role of post-migrant theatre artists from the artistic, scientific and cultural/political perspectives. The exchange also served to open up new perspectives and networks for a Post-Migrant Theatre in Europe.

The current volume presents the studies that were completed under the auspices of the research project; each asking their own questions, they approach the various areas of contemporary theatre and dance in field-specific as well as multi-disciplinary ways. The authors investigate the interaction between the changing means of production and distribution as well as the changing dialectics of content versus form; in order to do so, they interview numerous artists.

This expansive research initiative, the first to take on an international approach, is a prominent project for the International Theatre Institute. It assists in understanding the work of theatre professionals and the role of theatre as public benefit, as well as serving to strengthen the preservation of cultural diversity in the face of the increasing global economic pressures of recent decades. We would like to thank Professor Manfred Brauneck for this initiative, for his critical and thoughtful guidance and for his faith in the work of the authors as well as that of the ITI.

Andrea Zagorski, Dr. Thomas Engel
ITI Germany

Table of Contents

Dear readers

Manfred Brauneck
Preface | 13

Petra Sabisch
For a Topology of Practices
A Study on the Situation of Contemporary and Experimental Dance, Choreography and Performance Art in Europe (1990-2013) | 43
Introduction | 43
1. On the Situation of International Independent Dance, Choreography and Performance Art in Europe | 50
    1.1 Current State of Research | 50
    1.2 Critique and Formulation of the Problem | 75
    1.3 Why Practices? On Methods | 90
    1.4 On the Method of this Study | 98
2. Practices: Case Studies | 101
    2.1 *Special Issue/Edition Spéciale* in Aubervilliers and elsewhere (2011-2012) | 101
    2.2 The Festival *In-Presentable* in Madrid (2003-2012) | 110
    2.3 *The Double Lecture Series*, Stockholm (28.9.-2.10.2011) | 122
    2.4 *Performing Arts Forum* (PAF, St. Erme, France, since 2005) | 131
    2.5 *sommer.bar* (Berlin 2006-2011) | 144
3. Conclusion in the Form of a Prolegomenon | 155
Literature and Sources | 157

Andrea Hensel
Independent Theatre in the Post-Socialist Countries of Eastern Europe
New Forms of Production and Creativity in Theatre Aesthetics | 185
1. Introduction | 185
2. Independent Theatre after the Political Upheavals of 1989/1991 | 188
    2.1 Former Socialist People's Republics | 191
    2.2 Post-Yugoslavian States | 207
    2.3 Post-Soviet States | 219
    2.4 Excursus: The Independent Dance Scene | 224
3. Conditions for Artistic Work | 228
    3.1 Cultural Policies and Funding | 228
    3.2 Production and Presentation Conditions | 232
    3.3 Training | 235
    3.4 International Networking | 237
4. Exemplary Analyses | 240
    4.1 The Independent Groups *DramAcum* and *TangaProject* – Romania | 241
    4.2 *Romania! Kiss me!* – Romania | 245
    4.3 *Reasons to be Happy* – Slovenia | 248
    4.4 *They Live (in Search of Text Zero)* – Serbia | 251
    4.5 *Lili Handel* – Bulgaria/The Netherlands/Belgium | 254
    4.6 *Szutyok* – Hungary | 257
    4.7 *Magnificat* – Poland | 259
    4.8 *Mŕtve duše* – Slovakia | 261
5. Summary and Outlook | 262
Literature and Sources | 266

Henning Fülle
A Theatre for Postmodernity in Western European Theaterscapes | 275
A New Theatre Arising from the Crisis of Modernity? | 275
Some Historical Background: Theatre as Art | 279
Theaterschrift – Reflection and Impulses for a Theatre of Postmodernity | 282
Scenography – 'The Written Space' | 287
Worldliness and Aesthetic Exploration | 288
Dramaturgy of the New Theatre | 291
Acting – Performance | 293
Theaterscapes and New Theatre in Europe – Cultural-Political Situations and Impulses | 296
Model Structures: the Netherlands and Belgium | 298
Theatre (almost) Without the State: Great Britain | 302

Theatre Culture as a Service to the Social Welfare State –
Sweden, Norway, Denmark | 304
Professionals and Amateurs – Finland | 307
Cultural Modernisation of the 'Grande Nation' – France | 308
Theatre as the Edification of Civil Society – Switzerland | 311
Austria, a Cultural State | 312
Theatreland Italy | 314
Post-Postmodernism? | 315
Literature and Sources | 317

Azadeh Sharifi
Theatre and Migration
Documentation, Influences and Perspectives in European Theatre | 321
1. Introduction | 321
   1.1 Position in the Context | 321
   1.2 Theoretical Contextualisation in Existing Discourses | 323
   1.3 Historical Turning Points of Migration | 329
   1.4 Overview of the Research | 332
   1.5 On My Own Behalf | 333
2. Overview of the Countries | 334
   2.1 Germany | 334
   2.2 Austria | 340
   2.3 Switzerland | 343
   2.4 The Netherlands | 345
   2.5 France | 348
   2.6 Great Britain | 352
   2.7 Sweden | 355
   2.8 Italy | 358
3. Excursus: Minority Theatre | 365
   3.1 Theoretical Considerations | 365
   3.2 Roma in the European Societies and the Theatre of the Roma | 366
   3.3 German-Sorbian Folk Theatre Bautzen | 369
   3.4 Bimah – Jewish Theatre Berlin | 370
   3.5 Minority Theatre and Postmigrant Theatre | 371
4. Structural Changes | 372
   4.1 Cultural and Political Measures as Exemplified by the Arts Council and its Programme of Cultural Diversity | 374
   4.2 Structural Changes in State Theatres | 378
   4.3 Institutionalisation and Independent Structures | 380
   4.4 Professional Training | 383

5. Aesthetic Trends and Influences on the European Theatre | 388
   5.1 Metaphor of Migration, Metaphors of Displacement | 390
   5.2 Postmigrant Perspectives in Theatre | 395
   5.3 Formats of Empowerment: Documentary Theatre | 399
   5.4 Influences on Aesthetic Discourses | 400
6. Prospects for a European Theatre | 403
   6.1 Theatre and Migration: From the Independent Scene to Institutionalisation | 403
   6.2 Postmigrant Perspectives for European Theatre | 405
Literature and Sources | 407

Tine Koch
Independent Children's Theatre in Europe since 1990
Developments – Potentials – Perspectives | 417
1. Introduction | 417
   1.1 Objectives | 417
   1.2 Methodological Procedure | 418
   1.3 Source Material | 418
   1.4 Working Definition of the Term "Independent Theatre Scene" | 420
   1.5 Limitations of the Study: "Independent Children's Theatre in Europe"? | 421
   1.6 Excursus: Poland and Russia – "No Practice" | 422
2. Manifestations, Discourses, Developments | 425
   2.1 Structural Emancipation of (Independent) Children's Theatre | 425
   2.2 Independent Children's Theatre in Europe is Today … Cultural Education! | 437
   2.3 Independent Children's Theatre in Europe Today is also… "A Theatre for Early Years!" | 445
   2.4 Independent Children's Theatre in Europe Today is… Interdisciplinary! | 450
   2.5 Dance Theatre for Children: The Ideal Way to Arts Education? | 453
   2.6 Interim Conclusion I: Risks Involved in the Developments Outlined | 462
3. Critical Reflections on the Circumstances | 468
   3.1 Precarious Production and Presentation Conditions | 469
   3.2 Economisation | 480
   3.3 Paradoxical Funding Criteria | 488
   3.4 Interim Conclusion II: Possibilities and Limitations of the Independent Scene | 495

4. Conclusion: Five Demands on Cultural Policy Makers | 500
    4.1 End the Inadequate Financing
of Independent Children's Theatre! | 500
    4.2 Revamp and Revise Impedimentary Funding Criteria! | 501
    4.3 More Venues and Production Houses
for Independent Children's Theatre! | 502
    4.4 No Disproportionate Preferential Treatment
for Participative Formats! | 504
    4.5 Fight the Usurpation of Art and Culture by the Mechanisms
of the Market Economy! | 506
Literature and Sources | 510

Matthias Rebstock
Varieties of Independent Music Theatre in Europe | 523
1. Terms and Structures | 527
    1.1 What Does 'Music Theatre' Mean? | 527
    1.2 'Frei' or 'Independent'? | 531
    1.3 Genres and Discourses | 533
    1.4 Protagonists and Structures | 537
2. Lines of Innovation in the Field of Independent Music Theatre | 547
    2.1 Working Processes | 547
    2.2 Other Places and Spaces | 550
    2.3 Other Forms and Formats | 554
    2.4 Interactivity and Intermediality | 557
    2.5 Embodied and Disembodied Voices | 560
    2.6 Musician as Performer | 563
    2.7 Conceptualisation, Interrogation of Reality, Research | 564
    2.8 Opera as Material | 567
3. Conclusion | 569
Literature and Sources | 570

Wolfgang Schneider
Towards a Theatrical Landscape
Funding the performing arts: cultural policy considerations | 575
    Planning and Developing Theatre | 577
    Theatrical Collaboration: a European Tendency | 579
    Theatre and Interculturality | 581
    Children and Young People's Theatre | 583
    Independent Theatre Needs Cultural Policy | 585
    Theatre Funding: European Comparisons | 588

Models of Theatre Development Planning | 591
The Top Ten of Independent Theatre Funding | 593
Literature and Sources | 596

Authors | 599

Preface

Manfred Brauneck

> 'Truth in the theatre is always on the move'
> (Peter Brook: *The Empty Space*. 1968)

Independent theatre takes place outside the established institutions, the repertory theatres or, as Otto Brahm called them, the "permanent stages". It emerged as an alternative and in opposition to such theatres. In most European countries, it still represents a separate theatre culture, in its beginnings – in the 1960s – a preponderantly politically virulent, and sometimes even a subcultural sphere. Yet it always calls for contemporaneity and explores new paths, even transcending boundaries and conventions.[1]

---

1 | In English-speaking countries, this realm of the theatre is referred to as "independent theatre". Furthermore, the expression "fringe theatre" also exists in English. It appeared in connection with the Edinburgh Festival of Music and Drama when on the fringe of this festival a large number of small, independent, experimental theatre groups put on a kind of alternative programme: "amusing and anarchistic" (Brian McMaster). This gave rise to the extraordinarily popular Edinburgh Festival Fringe. The term "underground theatre" originated in the 1960s. It refers to a theatre which regards itself as oppositional in a rather diffuse sense, independent and subversive; garish and obscene in its aesthetic means.

Unlike the term "Freies Theater" – *Théâtre Libre, Teatro Libero, Teatro Livre* – the term "independent theatre" primarily accentuates the distance to the commercially run theatres, to the theatre business as it functioned on the West End stages in London in the 1950s. Later the attribute "independent" was also used by the film industry and referred to a comparable distinction between the production structures of the big Hollywood studios and those of small film companies. Equally important are the American terms "Off-Broadway theatre" and "Off-Off-Broadway theatre". They are collective names for a trend which distanced itself from the commercialisation of the New York Broadway theatre in favour of more experimental and also political aspirations, above all with new production structures. The term "Freies Theater" includes the broad spectrum of meanings of all these terms, but – owing to the historical context – also refers to the resistance to censorship and other

Since these beginnings, independent theatre has undergone distinct changes: structurally, in its artistic orientation and its social positioning. This transformation had its roots in the changed circumstances of the times – the decades after 1980/90 – not least also in the new generation and life experiences of people currently working in the theatrical field, which are so unlike those of the early years. This is also true of the audience of the independent theatre. Since the upheavals in the former socialist countries in the 1990s, independent theatre has been concerned with reorganising itself in public theatre life after a difficult time characterised by government interference and censorship. Also in those European countries in which, up until the middle of the 1970s, dictatorships were in place, in Portugal, Spain and Greece, independent theatre existed under specific conditions, and its history took its own particular course there. In all European countries, the relationship of the independent theatres to the repertory theatres has changed in recent decades. Even if most of the "permanent stages" reacted to the changed circumstances differently during the same period, some underwent a comparably profound change.

Venues of the independent theatre – inasmuch as it exists as a theatre sphere in its own right – are, for the most part, not typical theatre buildings, but 'alternative venues': abandoned factory buildings or something similar, usually buildings rededicated to this purpose yet still showing traces of their original use, and these vestiges of past use characterise the aesthetics of these locations as well as the audience's sense of space and view to the happenings on stage. Much has been eliminated – even in the 'production houses' and 'culture factories' which have since emerged – for example, the tiered pricing and with it the seating hierarchy. Thus, the independent theatre responds to the audience's expectations of a 'different theatre' even in its artistic form, which allows the unwieldy, the cumbersome and the imperfect, and which tries out the unusual and experiments, exposing the audience to its experiments and challenging it as it goes along. In the beginnings of the independent theatre movement, the 'stage' and the audience shared – even in the socialist countries or in the countries under authoritarian regimes – a largely common political, oppositional attitude. In Spain and Portugal, student theatre groups were the nucleus of an independent, oppositional theatre movement. Today, this connection can be seen in a much more differentiated and open way.

---

state repression. In the following English translation, the internationally used term "independent theatre" has been adopted. However, all these terms make clear that this realm of the theatre can only be adequately understood in the context of the entirety of the theatre-cultural structures and traditions of the individual countries.

There is no doubt, however, that the independent theatre offers young people the possibility of pursuing their inclination to work in the theatre even if they have not completed the professional training required for an engagement at a "permanent stage" (i.e. an ensemble theatre). Yet, this is in no way the rule, since the circumstances of the independent theatre in the individual European countries are too different. Even the differences among the independent theatre groups in the training standard of those people working there are considerable. In general, an increasing professionalisation can be observed in this scene which has taken place in many countries in the last two or three decades. Of course, for many young artists, actors or directors – often job entrants coming directly from drama school – work in the independent theatre can be a springboard for a career at a repertory theatre.

Independent theatre seeks contact with the audience. In some of its formats, the boundary between observing and participating has disappeared. In the 1960/70s, performances of independent groups – 'in the West' – occasionally took place in factory halls or in front of the gates to factories, in hospitals, in retirement homes or even in prisons, on the street, in parks – in places where one would not expect to find the conventional sort of theatre. Mobility was always a principle of the work of independent groups. Some of these performances were in the tradition of the "Arbeitertheater", theatre for working-class audiences, or the Soviet-Russian agitprop collective of the 1920/30s. Some independent groups found orientation in these traditions and saw themselves as a spearhead in the fight for political enlightenment.

Today, the audience of the independent theatre comes largely from social circles which regard themselves in the broadest sense as 'progressive', which are interested in specific social problems, but, above all, which are open for the work of young artists. A part of the audience presumably belongs to an academic milieu, as is generally the case with spoken theatre and which is also primarily dealt with here. And it is usually younger people and, as is often said, those young in spirit who attend the performances of independent theatre groups. Some of the older spectators were more or less close to the protest movements in the 1960/70s in whose context the international independent theatre movement emerged. A younger generation will discover its own life experiences, its own language, its own music and its own world of imagery in the theatre of the independent scene. The venues at which these performances take place are often quite familiar to younger spectators.

Since then, independent theatre has become a part of the public theatre scene in virtually all European countries. Ever since the 1980/90s, it has been an established part of the European theatre culture, a result of the social and cultural change since the last decades of the twentieth century. In countries in which a traditional (state or municipal) theatre scene no longer or hardly exists today, the independent theatre or independent productions account for practically all of the public theatre life. Independent theatre is predominantly a phenomenon in the cultural life of larger cities, linked through a brisk touring scene which provides an essential economic basis for most independent groups. Independent theatre is often bound by its emancipatory claim to an alternative scene which distances it from mainstream society.

Thus, most independent theatre groups have adopted a critical stance to the prevailing cultural sector in their own societies, especially in countries in which there is a state-funded or municipal theatre whose prominent stages receive media coverage. The criticism of the 'independents' is also aimed at the ambition of these theatres and their spokespeople of being paramount in representing theatre per se – as an institution – in its cultural and educational significance, and ultimately as a supposedly indispensable bastion of high culture. The predominantly young artists working in independent theatre are apparently of one mind in this criticism.

The criticism of the independent theatres is not only directed at the circumstances in the public theatre sector, but at the artistic orientation of the state and repertory theatres. The independent theatres tend to generalise when implying that the established theatres demonstrate an overall resistance to innovation. It was precisely the stage and theatre directors of the "permanent stages" in the 1970/80s who caused a furore with their productions, broke any number of taboos and cast aside traditional conventions. Some of these stages strove at this time to achieve a politically motivated reinterpretation of the "Volksstück" genre, with which the repertory theatre tried to establish a greater proximity to the current reality of those social classes which were usually not the focus of their traditional programmes. City districts were innovatively used for productions, and prominent ensembles performed in working-class neighbourhoods. In some European countries, public policies on culture addressed this problem. This primarily involved the dismantling of centralised structures in the theatre (mainly in France); Jack Lang also concerned government participation in the funding of public theatre and independent groups. These considered themselves to be in a kind of pioneering role with regard to such reform efforts. Quite rightly, the independents saw a reflection of those social structures in the conventions of mainstream theatre which abetted the exclusion of social groups from public cultural life.

The theatre-cultural circumstances in (at that time) socialist countries, or in countries governed by dictatorships until the middle of the 1970s, were fundamentally different from those in the democratically governed countries in Europe.

In this regard, the spectrum of artistic directions which could be found in the work of the independent theatre was extraordinarily diverse. It reflects the change which many groups in the independent scene have undergone since the last decades of the twentieth century and since the beginning of the twenty-first century. This spectrum reaches – in principle, in the initial period, the 1960s/70s – from the adaptation of the political aesthetics of the Brecht theatre, from Erwin Piscator's inflammatory documentarism, a fallback on the theatre movement for the working class in the 1920/30s, from the street theatre, the political cabaret and subversive varieties of clown theatre, the 'happening', as well as the many different directions of the US-American theatre movement referred to as *Theater der Erfahrung [theatre of experience]* (e.g., Jens Heilmeyer or Pea Fröhlich). In the 1980s/90s, independent theatre finally underwent a course correction which, to a large extent, followed the general development of the theatre at the end of this century. The growing professionalism in the independent scene addressed the new developments in spoken theatre: experimental multimedia projects which prioritized artistic intentions over the political statements of previous decades, the entire range of post-dramatic directions, and new performative formats. However, the commitment to specific social groups, such as migrants, the jobless or other minorities, remained a characteristic of the independent theatre throughout the entire course of its history, as did the work in the collective, which is still the prevailing production form of most groups in the independent scene.

If a certain depolitisation of this realm of theatre can be observed today in comparison with the early years, this reflects (somewhat seismographically) the zeitgeist of the last decades – a finding which probably applies to the development of the theatre in general.

The independent (and most likely, every) theatre wants an active audience and decides, wherever the spatial circumstances allow, for theatrical arrangements which avoid a rigid vis à vis of stage and audience. In this respect, the possibilities provided by alternative venues are greater than the standardised spatial arrangements in conventional theatres whose architecture largely prescribes an arrangement in which stage and audience face each other.

Above all, the independent theatre creates production conditions which make it largely independent of government subsidies, but also of commercial constraints, and in this way allow it to maintain a certain autonomy. At least, that was the original idea of the independents. The general tendency is to defy performance bans. Accordingly, the work for the artists in the independent scene is sometimes risky, especially under dictatorships or totalitarian/autocratic regimes, especially when their work deals with political issues.

As far as the social conditions of artists working in the independent scene are concerned, their situation is predominantly precarious in free societies which are subject to the regulative requirements of the market. This is true for almost all European countries, especially those in the former Eastern bloc, which since the 1990s had to cope with the transformation from a planned to a market economy, which has also massively affected the cultural sector.

Furthermore, in some of these countries, the independent theatre is still exposed to government repression.

Most independent artists must pursue some sort of secondary employment for a living. Only a tiny minority of independents are able to earn a living through their work in the theatre. This situation is aggravated not least by their readiness to relinquish habitual patterns in their artistic practice, and their disinclination to comply with the representational forms generally expected by the established stages. Socio-political regulation of the sphere of artistic creation serves in many cases to exclude artists from the independent scene, or to marginalise this entire theatrical sector.

From the perspective of those working in this realm, the independent theatre's claim to freedom may indeed be primarily a claim to artistic freedom, a personally motivated claim, as well as a socially critical and often a political claim. Thus, the impulses which move the independents are also quite diverse. For young people, work in the independent scene is a way of life, although not necessarily one which will be pursued for an entire lifetime. It is a decision in favour of collective working, largely free of hierarchies, together with like-minded persons, usually in a group which is homogeneous with regard to age structure and which shares the same political and artistic perceptions and mind-set. This may be considered the rule, and it is also true for groups whose members are of different cultural and ethnic origin. Prominent international ensembles such as that of Peter Brook or Eugenio Barba practised this artistic multiculturalism right from the start and often used the ethnic characteristics of the actors as a productive moment in their artistic work, and in doing so jarred the traditional role expectations of the audience. Perhaps this was also a reason why they became role models for many independent theatre groups.

That the independents' claim to freedom is not only restricted to the artistic realm has long been noted by their critics. This may well be one reason why the relationship between official cultural-political institutions and the independent theatre is still strained despite all official declarations to the effect that its social significance has never been questioned (at least openly). In their view, the independents cannot really be integrated into those concepts of theatre culture which are particularly relevant when allocating the public funds available for the theatres, even if the requirements of the large, cost-intensive repertory theatres are not at all comparable to those of the flat operating structures of the independent groups. Not without good reason, the more flexible production structures of the independent theatre or the free productions are frequently the subject of discussion – as in Germany – when it comes to considering a fundamental reform of the theatre systems, not least for reasons stemming from the pressure of fiscal policy plans. In the Netherlands, independent groups are virtually the sole remaining representatives of public theatre – especially after the massive political-cultural cutbacks by the Dutch Parliament in 2011.

The political-cultural relationship with the independent theatre – also with respect to professional reviews of its theatre productions – is apparently challenging with regard to an understanding of theatre which is oriented toward allegedly indispensable, traditional artistic standards and a more or less politically and ideologically neutral concept of culture. As a consequence of an extensive liberalisation of social life, the potential for provocation in most performances by independent theatre groups is, however, rather small, especially for its audience. A resonance which goes beyond these circles will most likely not be realised. In that, the independent theatre today hardly differs from the "permanent stages".

Quite the reverse is true of the public perception of the theatre as an institution in the central Western European countries in the 1960/70s. In these early years, the independent theatre was driven by the dynamics of an international protest movement which questioned the fundamental values of Western industrial societies, including their understanding of culture. Most independent groups considered themselves part of this political movement and were quite willing to hazard the consequences of a break with the traditional cultural structures. The independent theatre also helped to ensure that the boundaries between different art forms became more permeable or were even blurred (e.g., the boundaries which had separated the theatre and the fine arts). The relationship between art and everyday life was also under discussion; new forms of production and communication were tested. Even if developments in the fine arts were almost a decade ahead of those in the theatre, the direction they took was the same. New visual and hybrid genres emerged whose action character shared an interface with the theatre. Although they were of the same ephemeral nature, they also contributed to change in the theatre. The theatre adapted more and more developments from the field of the fine arts, above all when conceiving new space for performances. Essential to these new stage aesthetics was the reception of performance art, object and action art, pop art, happenings and those media interdisciplinary hybrid forms which have led to a kind of 'theatricalisation' of the fine arts. From its outset, this movement had an international dimension.

The Documenta 6 (1977) in Kassel presented an overview of the developments in performance art in the 1970s. In 1979, parallel to the festival, Theater der Nationen, an exhibition conceived by stage designers, took place in Hamburg with the title *Inszenierte Räume*. It dealt with the interaction of theatre and fine arts and with "boundaries and transitions" (Ivan Nagel). Even though these developments did not take place directly in connection with the independent theatre, they strongly contributed to accelerating a process in which boundaries between art forms were becoming blurred or even obliterated. If a more or less stable consensus had existed up to the 1950s as to what art – what theatre as art – was, and what importance art and theatre should have for society, this consensus was revoked in connection with these dramatic changes, almost all aesthetic paradigms were scrutinised, and the social function of art was redefined and expanded. The fine arts played a leading role in this regard. The developments in the theatre were able to absorb the dissolution of aesthetic norms, a process already underway, and could profit from a creative atmosphere tempered by a break with tradition and characterised by innovation and rebellion.

In the theatre, the mimetic art tradition, which had long been the theatre's true reference to reality, and likewise many of the traditional artistic standards had already been abandoned in the first third of the twentieth century by the theatre of the historical avant-gardes. A process of deliterarisation and depsychologisation of the theatre and acting had already commenced around 1900. The avant-garde continued this process more radically.

The figurine and finally the 'performer' replaced that type of actor who played his role either empathetically or by commenting on it in 'epic' distance. Dadaists and futurists had consistently alarmed the middle classes in independent productions and called their artefacts Antikunst. It was an art not meant to last forever which, above all, was also unfit for exploitation by the 'culture business'. The history of the reception of avant-garde art soon indicated that this provocation strategy had proven to be ineffective. After only a few years, their artefacts not only found their way into the museums, where they were admired as devotionalia of a rebellious time, but also onto the international art market.

Although these developments in the first third of the twentieth century pursued artistic intentions and reacted to the circumstances of a time which had little to do with the concrete political approach of the independent theatre movement in the 1960/70s, the independents regarded themselves as a 'second avant-garde'. Many groups in the independent theatre movement in the 1960/70s could identify with the provocative actions of their historical predecessors and the radical cultural criticism in the manifests of Antonin Artaud, a cult figure of avant-garde theatre in the context of French surrealism.

The Living Theatre, which was founded in New York at the beginning of the 1950s by the stage designer Julian Beck and the actress Judith Malina (a former assistant of Erwin Piscator in his Dramatic Workshop at the New York New School for Social Research), was one of the first theatre collectives and also inspired later developments in Europe. It was theatre which not only rendered a fundamental criticism of the 'American way of life', but practiced a new way of life that celebrated the union of *Life, Revolution and Theatre* in a collective effort, with a radical call for freedom. The Living Theatre ranked among the most prominent theatre collectives in the New York Off-Off-Broadway scene and preoccupied the police force and the courts virtually from the outset.

If the early (up until approximately 1963), rather escapist productions of the Living Theatre did not really reckon with much audience attendance, the

Bread & Puppet Theatre (under this name since 1965) of Peter Schumann manifested a new direction of political folk theatre in its street actions in 1961 with its spectacular, over-dimensionally large stick puppets. In the 1960s, both theatre collectives – The Living Theatre (for the first time in 1963) and Schumann's theatre ensemble (for the first time in 1968) went on tour in Europe. In the middle of the 1950s, Joseph Papp showed his experimental Shakespeare productions on a provisional stage mounted on a wagon in New York parks (including Central Park) and regarded these open-air events (with free admission) as a new form of political folk theatre. Since 1960, this project has been subsidised by the City of New York as the New York Shakespeare Festival.

Throughout the years, the Open Theatre, founded by Joseph Chaikin in 1963, was the Off-Off- Broadway groups which most rigourously pursued a clear political line. In the 1960s, this theatre collective performed his productions, which were directed against the military commitment of the United States in Vietnam, in Europe as well.

The LaMama Experimental Theatre Club, founded by Ellen Stewart in New York in 1964, emerged as the centre of the discussion concerning the upheavals in different artistic genres, especially in the theatre, at the beginning of the 1970s, and this mainly because of international workshops there under directors who were key figures in the independent scene in Europe – such as the Polish directors Jerzy Grotowski and Tadeusz Kantor, but also Peter Brook, Eugenio Barba and the Romanian director Andrei Şerban – but also because of the work of artists from more than 70 countries. LaMama was, above all, a forum for young playwrights. Starting in 1965, Ellen Stewart toured Europe every year with her Repertory Troupe. Branches of LaMama were established in Amsterdam, London, Munich, Spoleto and in Paris.

In 1977, the Squat Theatre, which had been founded in Budapest in 1969 by Peter Halász and Anna Koos under the name Kassák-Theatre, moved to New York. It was a theatre collective whose anarchistic environments suspended the differentiation between art and everyday life and which performed at countless festivals in Europe to "realise the theatre which lies beyond art" (Squat Theatre). From the end of the 1970s, the two Californian workers' theatre collectives San Francisco Mime Troupe (founded in 1959) and the Teatro Campesino (founded in 1965 in the wake of a farm workers' strike) went on tour in Europe.

It was the first time in the history of European theatre that this theatre received significant impulses from the reception of US-American theatre developments, comparable to pop art, which was the most important contribution made by the United States to fine arts in the twentieth century. This, too, was a rebellion of the young against the generation of their parents, a frontal attack on their taste and their cultural standards.

Eventually, in the second half of the 1960s – intensified by the escalation of the student demonstrations in Paris in 1968 – a wave of independent theatre groups with a predominantly political orientation was set in motion. With his Teatr 13 Rzędów, which had already been founded in Opole in 1959, Grotowski relocated to Wrocław in 1965, where he established himself as the Teatr Laboratorium, which was dedicated to the research of theatre and acting. Projects such as *The Constant Prince* (based on Calderón and Słowacki; the first version was performed in 1965) and *Apokalypsis cum Figuris* (1968/69), as well as Grotowski's text, *Ku teatrowi ubogiemu*, which was published in Polish in 1965 and first appeared in English (*Towards a Poor Theatre*) in 1969, had a tremendous impact on the independent scene and revolutionised its understanding of theatre. It enhanced the components of independent theatre – which until then had been mostly political – with the aspect of "experience", an existential transgression of borders in the "total act" which Grotowski demanded from his actors. In international tours, almost annually from 1966 to 1970, and in countless workshops, Grotowski and his key staff propagated the idea of the "poor theatre", communicated its spiritual conceptual world, and introduced its acting techniques. From the beginning of the 1970s, Grotowski was showered with official honours as one of the most influential theatre artists of his time.

In 1956, Tadeusz Kantor founded the Teatr Cricot 2 in Krakow and, as a theatre director and professional painter, continued in the tradition of the Cricot theatre of the 1930s. Like its predecessor, the Cricot 2 was an experimental theatre whose hermetic aesthetics were strongly influenced by Kantor's own artwork, the happening, pop art and surrealism. Even though Kantor's theatre represented one of the most distinguished positions in the theatre of the twentieth century, its theatre work ultimately had no direct effect on the independent theatre movement. Kantor's legacy was, however, a new interpretation of the theatre as an autonomous world of sensory images and the uncompromising subjectivity of his artistic work.

Eugenio Barba's Odin Teatret was originally founded as an amateur theatre group in Oslo, Norway. In 1966, he moved it to Holstebrø, Denmark following a study trip to Kerala, India. He managed it at the new Denmark location under the name Nordisk Teaterlaboratorium and it was sponsored by local municipal authorities. Barba's work initially focused on researching Far Eastern acting techniques.

The emergence of these theatre laboratories – geographically far away from the political focal points of these years – did not necessarily have to do with the political protest movements at the end of this decade, yet their concepts and working methods were virtually 'soaked up' by the international independent theatre scene in Europe and in the United States because a radical concept of freedom was immanent to their ideas of the theatre: an alternative concept to the Western understanding of theatre and acting. Whereas Kantor had conceived his Theatre of Death in a confrontation with the main directions of avant-garde art in the twentieth century while also falling back on the ritual masques from the mythical origin of European theatre, Grotowski and Barba, and later also Peter Brook, believed to have discovered a new basis for the art of theatre in Far Eastern spirituality and in the suspension of the dualism of body and spirit so typical for Western thinking. It was necessary to study this and to experiment with it in an artistic context. And in any case, followers of the independent theatre movement firmly believed that the theatre was a place where new experiences could be made.

One of the most radical cases against the Western "written tradition" was made by Richard Schechner with his Performance Group, founded in New York in 1967. Schechter's staging of *Dionysos in '69*, a free adaptation of Euripides' *Bacchae* (first performed in 1968), was a group performance which probably most consistently and exclusively relied on the human body as a medium for staged, ritual and therapeutic techniques. Schechner also staged the productions of his Environment Theatre on a tour of Europe and was invited with his *Performance Group* to perform at the International Theatre Festival (BITEF) in Belgrade, Yugoslavia.

Such theses called the Western style of literary-dramatic theatre into question and were taken by independent groups as an inspiration for a theatre deemed authentic, for a theatre which, from its general approach, was primarily one thing: transcultural. The fact that this course de-substantiated the original political commitment of the independent theatre movement corresponded with the development which the international protest movements took towards the end of the 1970s. The war which the United States had waged in Vietnam, the central point of departure for all political protests in these years, ended in 1975. The political commitment which had also artistically inspired the independent theatre movement was significantly reduced and replaced by an ideologically more or less open alternative movement.

The theatre cooperative of Ariane Mnouchkine, the Théâtre du Soleil (Theatre of the Sun), has existed in Paris since 1964. Originally, Mnouchkine directed a student theatre (as of 1960) influenced by Jean-Paul Sartre's concept of a "théâtre populaire". After extensive travels in East Asia (1963) during which Mnouchkine studied the traditional Indian and Japanese theatre, the Kathakali, the Nō and the Kabuki, the Théâtre du Soleil took on more distinct contours. Mnouchkine also oriented herself in her programme toward the tradition of the French folk theatre, as did Planchon in his "people's theatre factory" (Simone Seym) in Villeurbanne, a working class district in Lyon, both of them with great success. Jean Vilar, the most dedicated representative of the new, 'national people´s theatre' in France, coined the idea that the theatre is a public utility like "gas, water or electricity".

Peter Brook, who broke with traditional theatre in 1970 with his production of Shakespeare's *A Midsummer Night's Dream* (still in Stratford, England), founded the Centre International de la Création Théâtrale in Paris in 1968, which was renamed the Centre International de Recherches Théâtrales in 1970 and which became a centre of applied theatre research. Brook's book *The Empty Space* (1968), in which a concept of theatre is described which frees itself from all decorative aspects, detaches itself from any moralising gesture, and only concentrates on the actors, became the 'bible' of the independent theatre movement.

In the Federal Republic of Germany, Rainer Werner Fassbinder founded the Antiteater (1968) as the successor to the Action Theater. Fassbinder's theatre collective was among the earliest independent theatre groups founded in Germany. The radical, culturally critical statements of Artaud and the fundamental opposition of the New York Living Theatre provided the first orientation for his own theatre work. Likewise, the revolutionary theatre collective Rote Rübe was founded in Munich in 1970 after having originated from a LaMama workshop; in the same year, the Freie Theater München emerged, which celebrated a life free of all bourgeois taboos in spectacular street actions. Shortly thereafter, however, West Berlin became the centre of the independent scene and home to the Theatermanufaktur (founded in 1972), which mainly staged political-historical subject matter.

In Italy, the director Luca Ronconi and his group Teatro Libero staged *L'Orlando Furioso* (based on the romance epic of the same name by Ludovico Ariosto) in 1968/69 at the Festival of the Two Worlds in Spolto. In this production, the boundaries between all the art forms were obliterated to achieve a spectacular environment in the tradition of the Italian "Jahrmarkt-Theater" or popular theatre. After the festival in Spoleto, this production was performed in many public places in Italy and subsequently on a tour of Europe and in the US. It was also the year in which the very popular Italian actor, playwright and director Dario Fo took leave of his previous regular audience, the "enlightened bourgeoisie" (Dario Fo), for whom he had long performed as a comedian and satirist. Together with his wife, the actress Franca Rame, Fo founded the theatre collective La Nuova Scena in 1968. In 1970, he changed the name of the collective to La Comune, worked for the goals of the communist party in Italy, and mainly performed in factories and working-class districts of the cities in the north of the country. Fo regarded this theatre work as satirical-political popular theatre. It was a theatre of provocations, but also of improvisation in the style of the travelling folk in the Middle Ages, the "giulari". Fo changed course significantly with respect to his early years. In the following decade, Italy was plagued by a wave of terrorist attacks. The kidnapping and murder of the conservative politician Aldo Moro by the Red Brigades in1978 was a trauma in recent Italian history.

In 1970, the theatre collective Het Werkteater was founded in Amsterdam. The Shaffyteater and the Mickeryteater, both also in Amsterdam, were venues used by independent theatre groups from all around the world. In particular, the Mickery was a communication forum for the theatre developments of that time in New York (LaMama), London (The People Show, The Pip Simmons Theatre Group) and the Japanese underground-theatre (Terayama Shujis Tenjo Sajiki). The Brazilian director Augusto Boal attracted a lot of attention in the independent scene in the 1970s as the founder of the Theatre of the Oppressed, whose subversive acting techniques had been developed in Latin America. From 1976, the director lived in Europe and taught these forms of political theatre in many workshops. Henry Thorau documented Boal's experiments with the so-called "Invisible Theatre", with which Boal experimented in France and Italy in 1978.

The independent theatre of this time was predominantly political theatre and advocated radical-socialist, and sometimes anarchist, ideas. Most groups favoured a new form of political popular theatre that was meant to be (in the sense of Bertolt Brecht) entertaining and realistic without being too 'folksy'. Brecht's theatre aesthetics were primarily accepted in their experimental aspects: the epic structures and the dialectics of presentation and commentary. Jean-Paul Sartre, the most prominent figure and visionary of the left-wing protest movement in Europe, declared "truth" and "radicalism" to be the essential characteristics of intellectual social criticism.

A brief retrospective: The word "free" appears in European theatre history for the first time at the end of the nineteenth century in the names of two theatres: the Théâtre Libre in Paris, which was founded in 1887 by André Antoine, an employee of a Paris gas company and devoted member of an amateur theatre group, and the Freie Bühne in Berlin (1889), where the writer Otto Brahm was the driving force of this private theatre society. Both theatre groups opted out of the existing theatre conventions in their countries. Jacob Grein, an impresario and theatre critic, founded the Independent Theatre Society, in London in 1891, which was a private theatre society pursuing goals similar to those of the "free" or "independent" stages in Paris and Berlin. The performances of these three groups did not, of course, take place in "alternative venues". In Paris, Antoine founded his own theatre. In Berlin, the society Freie Bühne rented smaller private theatres for its performances, as did the Independent Theatre Society in London. In the first year, the performances of the Society could be seen mainly in the Royalty Theatre.

The wish to be free or independent was at this time a declaration of war – not only on the field of art, but on the political circumstances of the times and the economic constraints of the theatre operations in the commercial theatres, whose owners were all private persons who mostly opposed any sort of innovations since they might threaten the commercial success of their "businesses". Especially in Germany, there was a heated discussion in the nineteenth and early twentieth centuries in which the "Geschäftstheater" (commercial theatre) was confronted with the demand of reformers for a largely government subsidised "Kulturtheater" (culture theatre) – such were the controversial labels. However, this was also a time in which public communication, particularly the theatre, was subject to control by organs of government authority. Politics and art formed a fatal alliance whose functioning was to be ensured by censorship. Thus, it was the primary aim of the "free" stages and the "independents" to elude the censorship laws by assuming the status of a society or club and declaring their performances as private events. However, in France and Germany this meant constant conflict between the author or theatre operator and the regulatory authorities: the police and the courts. Also, most conservative theatre critics joined ranks with the opponents of free and independent theatre makers. Freeing himself from the constraints of the "commercial theatre" was the main aim of Grein's Independent Theatre Society – and this in the highly commercialised London theatre scene, which had almost entirely isolated itself from the continental European developments since this type of theatre supposedly would not 'pay off'.

The artistic focus was on naturalism, the modernity of that time, and realistic performing arts. It was important to gain acceptance for the plays of Henrik Ibsen, Leo Tolstoy, Émile Zola and Gerhart Hauptmann on European stages. These authors and their followers fought to make theatre contemporary once again, to bring "truth" to the stage. Around 1880/90, this was the slogan of a group of young authors in Germany. Furthermore, the new dramatic art had established itself along the boundary between science and art. This was also considered by progressive minds to be modern in those decades marked by a limitless faith in science. The French critic and author Émile Zola had signaled the direction for this development: Writers should "experiment" in the same manner as natural scientists.

The battle lines were drawn: on the one side stood those who had pledged themselves to the fight for modernity; on the other side, the traditionalists who were determined to shield the realm of art from any kind of reference to contemporary issues, especially political ones (at that time this mainly meant "social issues"). These were the subject of the naturalistic plays. Conservative political parties saw the road to revolution and anarchy paved by these plays. Conservative critics simply refused to accept the artistic character of this direction. "Tendenzkunst" ("trend art") was their battle cry. The conflicts escalated to the point that naturalism even became an issue in the French parliament (1894, in connection with anarchism debates), the German Reichstag (1894, in connection with a plot to overthrow the government), and at the party convention of the German Social Democrats in Gotha (1896). However, for the latter, the new dramatic art was not radical or militant enough; it lacked the positive heroism which the great classic dramas seemed to impart.

In order to better understand the independent theatre from the last third of the twentieth century until today, these comments on the early history of the independents around 1890 may be helpful, even though the political and the socio-historical circumstances have changed radically since then. Today, censorship is also a thing of the past (at least in the history books). The European countries settled these issues in very different ways and with a certain time lag. In England, censorship lasted into the 1960s. Since the 1930s, dictatorships have introduced more serious forms of state repression to "bring the cultural realm in their sphere of influence into line", as it was called in the jargon of the NS dictatorship – in the end, to subjugate it to the dictates of their political doctrine.

In the years around 1890, when the wish to be free was mainly related to those circumstances which existed in the theatre, one thing became clear: the interest of naturalistic authors to bring not only "social issues" to the stage, but a new idea of man. The focus was placed on the dependence of man on those elementary factors which biology and sociology had only just discovered: inherited psycho-pathological dispositions and the seemingly compulsive influence of the milieu, the social environment of individuals. Both reflected current materialistic schools of thought and diametrically opposed the idealistic conception of man on which classical literary tradition was based. There also seemed to be a certain partisanship among naturalist writers for those persons on the fringe of society or for those living in psychological impoverishment – or victims of that "Lebenslüge" (sham existence) which Henrik Ibsen had diagnosed as the prevailing state of the bourgeois society at the end of this century.

A situation which in the broadest sense was comparable to this one emerged under this aspect in the first decades after the Second World War. Both victors and vanquished had suppressed the trauma of the catastrophes of war more than they had tried to come to terms with it. In countries which had come under Soviet-Russian control, a socialist new beginning was propagated and violently enforced under the control and direction of the communist parties. The tendency in Western European societies to more or less pick up and continue where they had left off before the war was obvious with the re-establishment of the old circumstances. In countries in which fascist governments were in power, the change of system generally went quite smoothly. The re-education campaign of the Americans in West Germany and in Austria was of little consequence. After the material and psychological devastations of the war, the European humanist tradition was invoked. Plays which dealt with tolerance and enlightened humanity dominated the programmes of the big theatres in the years immediately following the war.

The protests of the young which were soon to be heard in these post-war years were directed against the attitude of the war generation, especially against that of the 'fathers', against their suppression of guilt and shared responsibility. In France and in the Netherlands, the subject of collaboration with the German occupation force divided the nation. In the 1950s in England, the frustration of a young generation and their protest against materialism and the hollowness of middle-class conventions found expression in the theatre of the Angry Young Men. Soon thereafter, a far more devastating moral analysis of British society was articulated in the plays of Edward Bond. In the Federal Republic of Germany, the documentary theatre of the 1960s posed the question of guilt and responsibility for the annihilation of the Jews and 'investigated' the circumstances to ascertain the perpetrators of the NS crimes. These plays were also concerned with bringing a truth to the stage which had long been suppressed. However, these were positions of political and moral social criticism which were indeed presented in the repertories of the "permanent stages" of Western Europe and not in the independent scene. The ferocity of the debates which then came to light was a sign that the time was ripe for fundamental changes and an intensification of the conflict between the generations. These irritations spread to wide circles of bourgeois society. The psychoanalyst Alexander and Margarete Mitscherlich referred to these findings in a book about West German post-war society entitled *Inability to Mourn* (1967). Ultimately, the political morals were on the line.

Similar developments with respect to the direction and radicalism of social criticism took place in Japan, which had undergone a process of adaptation to the Western industrial societies since the middle of the nineteenth century. At the end of the 1960s, an extremely radical theatre scene emerged there which was "alternative" in its aesthetic manifestations and described by the term "Angura" ("underground"). The image which many young people had of the situation in Japanese society was triggered by this movement. In terms of content, it largely reflected the statements of the protest movements in Europe and the United States. One of the most prominent representatives of this direction was Terayama Shuji. Terayama showed his shocking theatrical installations with the group Tenjo Sajiki in the United States and Europe and spread his idea of a subversive theatre in many workshops in the independent scene. It was a radical, alternative concept to Brecht's epic theatre of enlightenment. According to Terayama, theatre is the "only place where lawlessness is tolerated".

The rise of the international protest movement in the 1960s had its origins in the intellectual milieu of the universities of California; in the United States, that country where the interaction of capitalism, imperialism and racism in public life, in the justice system and in the political realm seemed to be particularly blatant and where, at the beginning of the 1960s, it escalated in a series of militant protest actions. Historical cornerstones for the emergence of these protests were the racially motivated unrest in some of the large cities in the United States which led to solidarity among and a radical politisation of social minorities, the war waged by the United States in Southeast Asia, and the political murders in the years 1963 (J. F. Kennedy), 1965 (Malcolm X, spokesman of the Black Muslim movement) and 1968 (Dr Martin Luther King Jr and Robert Kennedy), which shook the world. In Europe, the escalation of the student revolts in Paris in May 1968 was a signal to initiate a fundamental criticism not only of the universities where this protest began, but of the authoritarian structures in post-war Western societies. A multitude of newly founded student theatres followed in the wake of these protests. In Paris and Los Angeles, the streets were on fire. In 1968, Warsaw Pact troops, which had already put down a popular uprising in Hungary in 1956, marched into Prague – a centre of budding liberalisation under Soviet control – occupied the city, and put an abrupt end to the "Prague Spring". In the Federal Republic of Germany, the extra-parliamentary opposition became more radical: in 1967, there were mass demonstrations when the Shah of Persia visited Berlin, in which a student was shot; in 1968, thousands demonstrated against the adoption of the so-called "Notstandsgesetze" or emergency laws; and mass demonstrations took place in West Berlin. An assassination attempt on the spokesman of the extra-parliamentary opposition, Rudi Dutschke, was the culmination of these sometimes civil-war-like conflicts; however, this was only a preface to the "German Autumn of 1977", when the terrorist attacks of the RAF rocked the rule of law in the Federal Republic. The activists of the protest movements in the 1960/70s used the revolutions in Cuba and Vietnam, but mainly the cultural revolution in China, as models. Mao Tse-tung, Ho Chi Minh and Che Guevara were celebrated as pioneers and heroes of the revolution.

From the outset, many of these protest actions had strongly theatrical, even poetic characteristics. The slogan of the French student revolts – "Fantasy for Power!" – described an attitude which called for a complete release of creative forces: in politics, on the street and in art. Werner Hofmann has already pointed out the "happening character" of France's May. 1972 Joseph Beuys explained at the Dokumenta 5 in Kassel, Germany, that "everyone is an artist". In their happenings, Beuys and Wolf Vostel propagated the unity of art, politics and life as a total work of art.

An early indication of a looming course correction of the original political protest movement was the pop music festival in Woodstock, New York, in August 1969, at which more than 500,000 young people came together to celebrate peace, music and love: "Fuck the system!" was the slogan of a new alternative counter-culture. The aim of these youth protests was always to shatter the supposed affirmative relationship between art and society. The social philosopher Herbert Marcuse, who was teaching in California, had provided his intellectual following with the catchwords. In this context, being free always referred to the approach to life represented by a younger generation. The scandalous performance of the Living Theatre at the Avignon Festival and the statement made by the New York group – its "unconditional *No* to the present society" – was one of the theatre highlights in this politically turbulent year (1968).

The countless independent theatre groups which had emerged in the meantime in the United States, in Western Europe and – as a kind of subculture – in some countries under Soviet influence, articulated their political protest and demanded a new kind of art: an "art for everyone". First and foremost, they were concerned with justifying new lifestyles which were to be antiauthoritarian more than anything else. A cramped striving for authenticity was the main aim of art and life. The understanding of the completed artwork which had long served as the focus of art-theoretical discourses seemed to have become obsolete.

A new stage was set in the history of European theatre in connection with these developments and their ideological environment: the intensive artistic and theoretical preoccupation of some directors with non-European, mainly Far Eastern theatre cultures. For the first time, European theatre acquired a global dimension.

The beginnings of this development could already be observed around 1900 and in the first third of the twentieth century when the ensemble of Kawakami Otojiro presented traditional Japanese theatre in a series of guest performances in the United States and in Europe. Developments in dance and the fine arts in Europe also profited from these guest performances, which imparted a picture of an entirely different concept of art extending far beyond the world of theatre. Around 1910-12, Vsevolod Meyerhold discovered the estranging effects of East Asian acting techniques in connection with his "conditional theatre". And Bertolt Brecht indicated the proximity of Chinese dramatic art to his own estrangement or defamiliarization theatre. His verdict that the Western actors were, without exception, dilettantes because they would only reproduce a repertoire of expressions known to them from their everyday life – whereas Chinese and Japanese actors were required to learn a strictly codified system of signs as the basis of their art – was typical for the direction this early reception of Far Eastern dramatic art took. Antonin Artaud brought a new tone into this discussion with his essay on *The Balinese Theatre* (1931). His theories inspired the independents in their search for a theatre which had not been falsified by literary masterpieces. *Enough of the Masterpieces* (1933), Artaud demanded unerringly. The ideological background of this statement was a radical criticism of the Western model of culture.

Thus, in the 1970s it had become virtually an obsession of young people to transcend boundaries – not only the limits of one's own consciousness (with the help of drugs and psychedelic techniques) but also cultural boundaries, especially with respect to Far Eastern cultures. Transculturalism seemed to be the cure-all for the alleged paralysis of Western Art. Thus the opinion of the French director Ariane Mnouchkine, who in any case believed theatre to be "oriental". Furthermore, some Western directors found a source of inspiration for their own artistic work in the spiritualism of Zen Buddhism, an idea which also emerged in the fine arts. The aim was now to tap this spirituality – not least through journeys to the respective regions.

Peter Brook, Ariane Mnouchkine and Eugenio Barba, who had triggered the interest in Far Eastern theatre cultures, systematically researched the anthropological foundations of their dramatic art. Jerzy Grotowski and Eugenio Barba studied the vocal and body techniques of oriental actors in India and Japan. There was a broad consensus in the independent scene that the actor's body and its mechanical possibilities were the actual aesthetic means of dramatic art. With that, it seemed that the traditional acting training which prepared the actor for the "work on the role" (Konstantin Stanislavski), for a "grappling" with the figures in a dramatic piece, had become obsolete. The independent groups practiced the training for this 'other' theatre, usually in the form of workshops. In the independent theatre, this was the beginning of a professionalisation of its own kind. The aim of this training was no longer the character actor of the 'old school' but the authentic 'performer'. In the end, the performer is an individual who must overcome the problems of his everyday life and whose stage appearance is not falsified by any kind of esoteric artistry: the layperson. In this way, for the audience, the aesthetic distance that for a long time aimed to arouse a cognitive process through the events on stage is removed. Instead it professes to present 'life itself', not (just) a mimetic representation of it: a form of hyper-naturalism. The German group Rimini Protokoll referred to this type of performer as "an expert of everyday life". Today, repertory theatres have also long discovered the amateur as a performer. "Authenticity" is the new magic word. Eugenio Barba founded the International School of Anthropology (ISTA) in 1979. However, the reflections on acting techniques and the training methods of Brook and Grotowski in the 1960s had already charted a course in the direction of a 'different' theatre. In this context, Brook even spoke of the "holy theatre" and its "wordless language". This concept of acting differed greatly from the epic way of playing in the didactical theatre of Brecht. It put the relationship of the theatre to the Western literary and theatre traditions into a perspective in which it had certainly previously existed and manifested itself in productions characterised by a faithfulness to the original.

In the 1980/90s, a number of productions of great classical works were staged as 'projects'. The artistic fascination of these productions lay in the synthesis of Western dramaturgy and oriental aesthetics and dramatic art. Thus, Peter Brooks' nine-hour production of episodes from the ancient Indian epic poem, *Mahābhārata* (1985) in a stone quarry near Avignon was one of the artistic highlights of European theatre at the end of the twentieth century (although not without controversy from the point of view of some non-Western critics). The same is true for the great Shakespeare and Atreides cycles which Ariane Mnouchkine staged at the beginning of the 1980s and at the beginning of the 1990s with the Théâtre du Soleil. These productions also combined oriental stylistic elements (in the costumes, the choreography and the music) with the great literary works of European origin. Mnouchkine even advocated translating the works of Shakespeare into a "language of the body". The productions of Brook and Mnouchkine, whose culinary fascination paved the way for a new artistic direction, were performed in many places around the world. Brook´s production of the *Mahābhārata* was also filmed after the tour.

The end of the 1980s and the beginning of the 1990s saw an epochal upheaval which affected almost the entire cultural sphere of the Western industrial countries. The independent theatre movement reacted to this upheaval, too. After the end of the ideological confrontations between 'West' and 'East', it became evident to what extent this had always been a productive factor in art. Furthermore, there were far-reaching changes on the political level, the economic level, and in most of the areas of social life, and not only in the societies of the former Eastern Bloc. The founding of the Polish trade union Solidarnośc in 1980 heralded a new era, and with it the decline of the Eastern Bloc. Five years later, Mikhail Gorbachev announced his policy of "perestroika" – a restructuring of society and the political system in the USSR. The accident at the Chernobyl nuclear power plant in 1986 made a broader public (including those in Western societies) aware for the first time of the possibility of an ecological catastrophe and shook their belief in a secure future safeguarded by technological advancement. The situation for European economies was further exacerbated by an intensified confrontation with the problems of globalisation. Around this time, the populations in Western European societies were becoming more and more aware of the fact that changes had taken place as a result of the increasingly great number of migrants and that, owing to this, conventions from other cultures which 'old' Europe knew only from pictures from its colonial times were becoming increasingly present in everyday life. Reactions to this led to national-conservative resentment in some countries which, in turn, resulted in political unrest. In 1989, the Berlin Wall fell, which for decades had been the symbol of a divided Europe. In all European countries, the economisation of the cultural sector increased drastically, which led to further aggravation of the already precarious situation of the independent theatres. Moreover, not only the independent scene but the theatre in general lost ground. This was presumably a consequence of the mass spread of electronic media in the entertainment sector. At the same time, there was an apparently politically endorsed reduction in traditional educational content which had severe consequences for the institution of "theatre", which up until then had been firmly anchored in the cultural consensus of Western societies. Theoretical discourses which focused on the role of the theatre in rapidly changing societies took place within the artistic sphere. The programmatic writings which had served the independent theatre movement for decades as orientation all dated back to the 1960s. Theatre studies coined the term "post-dramatic" for the newer developments in the theatre, whereby an epoch-making caesura in European theatre culture was evidenced. Apparently, post-dramatic theatre was an attempt to react to these changes and position the theatre in the environment of mass media and pop culture. The American star director Robert Wilson optimally satisfied the needs of the zeitgeist of the 1980/90s with his opulent show pieces, whose texts and images programmatically eluded clear interpretation.

The independent theatre also blazed new trails at the end of the twentieth century. It was indeed a consequence of the changed life experiences of the young people in these decades. Above all, a process of professionalisation gained momentum in the independent scene. Many new groups were founded which no longer primarily defined themselves through their political aspirations. In most European countries, this realm of the theatre was also more or less integrated into the public funding programmes, which had not generally been the case for the independents in previous decades. Only the outstanding internationally active independent theatre companies received subsidies back in the 1970s (e.g., from foundations); some played in permanent venues. Here are a few prominent examples: Ariane Mnouchkine moved into the abandoned halls of a munitions factory, the Cartoucherie in Vincennes, with her Théâtre du Soleil in 1970. The Paris City Council approved this move. In 1979, the city of Amsterdam took over the partial funding of the Mickeryteater. The Berliner Schaubühne, indeed a private theatre yet similar to an independent theatre collective in the orientation of its programme and the circumstances of its founding, received considerable subsidies approved by the Berlin Senate which did everything it could to get the very successful ensemble under the direction of Peter Stein to commit to the city long-term. Peter Brook's CIRT was given a permanent venue with the Théâtre des Bouffes du Nord, a former music hall (and a building which had actually been condemned). This and Mnouchkine's Cartoucherie were both located in working-class districts of Paris. The same was true for the Berliner Schaubühne, which in its beginnings was housed on the Halleschen Ufer in a former multifunctional hall belonging to the Arbeiterwohlfahrt (or Workers' Welfare Association) in Berlin-Kreuzberg, also a working-class district of the city. In 1981, the Schaubühne moved to the Mendelsohn-Bau on the Kurfürstendamm in the centre of the city. At the beginning of the 1980s, a venue for independent theatre groups was opened in the former ironworks of Nagel & Kaemp in Hamburg. Since 1985, the Hamburg Senate has subsidised the theatre programme of this Kulturfabrik GmbH, which is now its official name. There are similar theatre venues in other large European cities.

These few examples demonstrating that it is possible to solve the problem of providing performance venues for independent groups or independent ensembles which do not have their own stage are in no way intended to qualify the fact that the availability of performance venues – the prerequisite for continuous and calculable work – is today still one of the most urgent problems facing the independent theatre, as is the case in all European countries.

Since the 1990s, and more markedly since the beginning of the financial crisis in 2008, financial problems have dominated discussions about the theatre, including within the independent scene. This is particularly true of countries with a theatre scene subsidised by public funding. As a rule, independent theatre groups have to apply for funding for their productions from project to project. The notoriously low level of media attention given to the independent theatre to begin with has adverse effects on willingness to provide public funding, as can be expected. Cleary independent theatre also lacks such charismatic directors, to the extent that they influenced the public image of an 'alternative' theatre from the outset. Many of these directors – whether Peter Brook or Ariane Mnouchkine, Luca Ronconi or Dario Fo – committed themselves with their names and reputations to artistic innovation and a high professional standard of their ensembles. Today, they are quite rightly no longer regarded as representatives of the independent theatre; they are part of a new establishment within the European theatre and have gone their own way in their artistic careers. However, by now new hierarchies have been established in the realm of the independent theatre too, so that the working conditions of individual independent groups or independent productions – on the national as well as on the European level – are no longer comparable.

Yet, today's independent theatre scene is significantly better networked internationally, as well as with repertory theatres, through collaborations as in the 1960/70s. In Germany, for instance, the programme Doppelpass, supported by the Federal Cultural Foundation, finances such forms of cooperation. An extremely active international festival scene has also established itself in the area of independent theatre. However, only a small number of independent groups are actually involved in these two developments. A globally active system of associations and organisations operating on behalf of the independent theatre has also long since developed.

In contrast to the 1960/70s, the influence of US-American groups on the independent theatre in Europe today is of no relevance. One reason for this may be found in the fact that the independent theatre, but not only the independent theatre, remains on the sidelines when it comes to geopolitical areas of conflict. Critics have even remarked that around the turn of the millennium "the distance of the theatre to society" has increased (Peter Iden).

At the interfaces of the fine arts and the theatre, a broad field of hybrid forms has established itself; the same is true for music and dance. In general, the different fields of art have approached each other in their development – a process which today by no means has the features of a rebellion. In the fine arts, theatrical performances have "risen" to the quality of a museum art form. However, the era of happenings and street theatre is over. New formats have come into play.

There does, however, seem to be one constant in the history of the independents from the end of the nineteenth century until today: the ambivalent relationship of the repertory theatres – starting around 1890/96 – to the independent groups or the independent theatre today. This dividing wall between these two realms of the theatre was more permeable than it seemed at first. In practice, this alleged 'rivalry' really only lasted a few years. Although the trend toward the established stages was always recognisable, it was not uncommon for the repertory theatres to adopt innovations, or even copy what was developed in the independent scene, provided it was well received by a wider audience or seemed to fit with the changing zeitgeist. Also remarkable is the fact that directors from the independent stages and the independent scene have moved to the more secure domain of the "permanent stages" – apparently because of better working conditions and the fact that they can remain reasonably true to their artistic standards.

It should in any case be noted that the theatre aesthetics in the final third of the twentieth century have fundamentally changed, and that this development has accelerated since the 1980s/90s. Some productions at leading repertory theatres hardly differ conceptually from projects in the independent scene. Collaborations between independent groups and repertory theatres were made possible through this process of reconciliation but also through changes in the theatre-cultural environment of the "permanent stages". Attending the theatre today is as normal as any other leisure activity, like going to the cinema – and not only for the younger generation.

Once again, here is a brief look at the history of the independent stages:

André Antoine, who was celebrated on tours with his ensemble Théâtre Libre soon after its founding – but who went bankrupt with his theatre in Paris only a few years later (1894) – took over the direction of the then already highly established Théâtre de l'Odeon in Paris, which today is one of the French national theatres. Otto Brahm, who had opened the Freie Bühne in Berlin in 1889 with Gerhart Hauptmann's scandalous play *Before Sunrise*, took over the direction of the most prestigious private theatre in Berlin (the Deutsches Theater at the Gendarmenmarkt) in 1896, after the Freie Bühne had fulfilled its function as a pioneer of the modern stage. With an outstanding ensemble, he was able to continue and perfect his working method. Moreover, the commercially sound financing of the theatre ensured a certain continuity of his work. Eight years after the founding of the Independent Theatre Society, so severely criticised at first, Jacob Grein was honoured with the highest awards for his achievements in renewing the British theatre.

After less than a decade, the erstwhile 'dropouts' or 'rejectionists' had been reabsorbed by the theatre realm from which they had withdrawn only a few years before, and which in its artistic orientation had significantly changed in only ten years. Personalities like Antoine, Brahm and Grein were the forerunners for these changes at the end of the nineteenth century – for the opening up of the theatre to modernity.

The development took quite a similar course not much more than a decade after the theatre rebellion in the years between 1960 and 1970. A considerable number of directors who had developed their 'artistic signatures' in the independent scene now hold positions as theatre managers and artistic directors of the big state and municipal theatres – apparently legitimised by the "political mission" (Christoph Schmidt) which they had in the 1970s. It must, of course, not be forgotten that in the 1960s/70s positions were held at prominent repertory theatres which could hardly be distinguished from those of the independent theatre movement, at least in terms of their aims and their choice of aesthetic means. Examples of theatre people who have 'changed sides' can be found in most European countries. Also the former 'alternative' theatre venues have today long been integrated into the theatre programme of many repertory theatres.

A practice typical of even the early independent theatre which was soon adopted by some of the repertory theatres (at the latest in the 1980s) was the tendency to work on and stage 'projects' rather than producing plays. The motive for the project-oriented work of the independent groups was initially research into social problem areas, a kind of critical field research from whose findings a dramatic plan was then developed – usually collectively. Besides, experimental, artistic intentions also always underlay this manner of working. Similar projects were those on which Peter Brook worked in the early years of the CIRT, often with a scientific and artistic preparation that lasted for years. The first of these projects was *Orghast* (1971), which was first performed in Persepolis in Iran. It was an experiment whose aim was to research intercultural communication based on a new artificial language. Source materials were fragments of Greek and Persian myths; anthropological and neurological research hypotheses concerning language as a system of expression were also included in the project work. Half a decade earlier, Brook and Charles Marowitz, while still in England, staged Artaud's *First Manifesto of the Theatre of Cruelty* under the title *Theatre of Cruelty* together with the experimental independent group Lamda within the context of theatre-aesthetic research.

The projects of the Het Werkteater in Amsterdam had a different objective. In the 1970s, this theatre collective explored areas of which the general public had hardly taken notice: conditions in prisons, in nursing and juvenile homes, and in psychiatric clinics. The collective developed their stage projects based on the researched material. Biographical data, experiences and memories of members of the group were also used as a basis for staged situations. *Ut bent mijn Moeder* (1981) was the most performed project of its kind.

It is essential to mention the production works of Jerzy Grotowski in Wrocław and Tadeusz Kantor in Krakow in connection with artistic project work, because their work is closely associated with the tradition of Polish literary and intellectual history. Together with his dramatists Grotowski developed text collages from different literary sources which served as the dramatic plan. Kantor developed his projects based on fragments of memories from his own biography, poetic texts of his own, and by other authors and his creative work.

Eugenio Barba's ethno-cultural theatre excursions to Southern Italy and to the Amazon region of Venezuela were both artistic and scientific research projects. His own understanding of theatre and what was considered "Western" as a staged representation became very negotiable. On these excursions, the actors from the Odin Teatret were confronted with an audience which had never seen theatre in this sense before. Peter Brook's *Theatre Safari* through Africa, which lasted over 100 days, was a project with similar aims about which John Heilpern published an impressive documentation in 1977.

The Berliner Schaubühne set standards with its projects based on ancient classics (1974 and 1980) just as Ariane Mnouchkine had done with her revolutionary plays (1970 and 1975). In 1977 in Prato, Italy, Luca Ronconi set up the Laboratorio di Progettazione Teatrale in a former cement works, an experimental venue where he and an architect explored the interdependencies of stage production and the space in the factory hall of the former cement works. "The play is the space" was the conclusion Ronconi drew from this experiment.

A distinctive feature of all of these 'projects' was the fact that they only found their artistic form in the process of explorative research work and that, in this process, new theatrical formats were developed. A particular task is now also in store for dramaturgy: the dramaturg has become a quasi-writer. Today hardly any popular classic of world literature escapes stage treatment. These working practices have certainly been facilitated by the widespread flexibilisation of production processes.

For the situation of the independent theatre, the blurring of the boundaries with the repertory theatres has considerable consequences. Few independent groups or independent collectives are now able to develop an artistic profile which is associated with their name and which gives the group a noteworthy or even an internationally recognised position. The two German groups Rimini Protokoll and the performance collective She She Pop, as well as the Belgian group Need Company or the group Forced Entertainment from Great Britain, exemplify how independent collectives which have developed an artistically original, distinctive manner of working and have focused on a specific (and apparently also marketable) format, are quite able to assert themselves successfully.

In the metropolitan theatre centres, the leading repertory theatres offer a varied programme at a highly sophisticated level of artistry for which often directors are responsible who have developed their 'signature' in the independent scene or on stages which were able to allow them comparable artistic freedom. Most independent groups, with their consistently precarious working conditions, are hardly able to function as a sphere of artistic innovation, much less aspire to be avant-garde. And this is not only because of the far better financial resources and technical facilities of the established stages, but also because the development of theatre aesthetics as well as the theatre-cultural environment of the repertory theatre have moved in a direction and changed so that many long-established conventions have been abandoned which had distinguished the independent scene from the repertory theatres. At the same time, however, they have served to deepen the differences within the independent theatre scene itself, to the benefit of those collectives whose professional working methods and potential for artistic innovation allow them to enter into co-operative relationships with town or regional state-funded theatres, or who, because of extensive support, through the public, from the repertory theatres, are capable of competing successfully in the cultural sector's open market.

The festival Theater der Nationen took place in Hamburg in 1979 and invited the German Centre of the International Theatre Institute (ITI) for the first time, as well as eight highly prestigious stages such as the Wiener Burgtheater, the Peking Oper, the Theatron Technis from Athens, the Royal Shakespeare Company from Stratford, England, and the Maxim Gorki Theater from Leningrad, 16 independent groups from around the world, and nine "one-person theatres" including Marcel Marceau from Paris, the clown Jango Edwards from Amsterdam, and Dario Fo from Milan. This was the first time that the "theatre of the world" was present in all its diversity. It was also the first time that professional independent theatre appeared as an intrinsic part of the culture of the grand world theatre as a matter of course.

The emergence of the independent theatre movement in the 1960s – only a decade and a half after the end of the Second World War – was symptomatic of a social and artistic upheaval of epoch-making dimensions whose ideological centre was characterised by a concept of freedom which extended far beyond the field of aesthetic perception. The developments in the following decades – German "Regietheater" (director's theatre) and "Autorentheater" (author's theatre) or "theatre of images" – have not only changed theatre artistically, but changed its perception by the public, including that of the "permanent stages". The development of the independent theatre took place under very different circumstances in the post-socialist countries, since it developed as an autonomous, theatre-cultural sector which had usually sympathised with the political opposition. In some of these countries, independent theatre was linked to an experimental, avant-garde theatre scene which had existed there in the 1920s and until shortly after the beginning of the 1930s. In countries such as the former Yugoslavia, the theatre had much greater freedom than in the Eastern bloc countries. As was the case in the entire cultural sector in the decades prior to the great upheavals in the 1990s, the theatre in all these countries had been exposed to alternating phases of 'political thaws' and rigorous controls by party functionaries during 'political ice ages'. The relationship of the independent groups – if they existed – to the state theatres was organised differently in the individual countries, and the administrative regulations to which independent theatre was subject also differed. This was also true for the times before and after the upheavals in the 1990s. At this time in the post-socialist countries, a confrontation with the immediate past (life under the dictatorship) was the central issue, including for the independent scene. Above all, the problems of adapting to the Western economic system and the restructuring of cultural and everyday life provided a wealth of subjects for the theatre, including the independent theatre.

In any case, in this situation one would expect a greater proximity to current events from the independent theatre than from the repertory theatres, which are normally obliged to uphold the national literary and cultural traditions. The idea of a national theatre stands for this continuity of tradition, which has been respected in almost all European theatre cultures since the nineteenth century. This internationally oriented independent theatre allows its audience to become acquainted with theatre from other countries and other cultures during their festivals more frequently than established stages do. This particularly conforms to the public's interest in some post-socialist countries where this 'pent-up demand' triggered an outright festival boom.

The independent scene has almost exclusively occupied the field of experimental dance – as opposed to dance theatre and stage dance as it is presented by repertory theatres. The circumstances in the field of experimental music are similar. In these areas, the independent international productions are today's avant-garde.

The independent scene is that realm of the theatre – in the artistic area – in which presumably far more people of non-European backgrounds work than is the case at most repertory theatres. These migrants, who have long since belonged to a post-migrant generation, are people of different ethnic backgrounds than mainstream society. Internationality and multiculturalism were always integral aspects of the independent theatre movement. Not least, the more open group and production structures of the independents facilitated the access to work at the theatre for artists with an educational background which did not comply with the conventional requirements for employment at a repertory theatre.

In our research project, Azadeh Sharifi examined the relationship between independent theatre and migration at the European level, as well as the problems experienced by artists whose ethnic backgrounds do not fulfil the expectations which the audience associates with the role. All too often, the ethnic appearance obscures the audience's view of the artistic performance of the actors especially as 'artist of colour'. The independent theatre can counter such expectations in ways the repertory theatres would not dare to attempt. A particular focus of Azadeh Sharifi's research is post-migrant theatre.

Andrea Hensel explored the situation of the independent theatre in the post-socialist countries: the positioning of this realm of the theatre in the overall theatre scene of the respective countries, which have reacted very differently to the changes leading to the collapse of the Soviet confederation of states and the dissolution of the former state of Yugoslavia. She provides an overview of the diversity of subjects and aesthetic directions of the independent theatre in these countries. This is of particular interest, since it was especially this realm of the theatre that played a leading role in more liberal developments in the socialist societies prior to the upheavals in the 1990s.

The study by Tine Koch is devoted to children's and young people's theatre in Europe. Her study reveals that in the European context, particularly in the area of theatre for very young audiences, the most creative conceptual developments in independent theatre are taking place. The established stages, on the other hand, seldom offer a regular theatre programme for this audience. From the political side, which includes UNESCO, although the social importance of children's theatre is always affirmed, it remains underfunded despite this purported significance.

The study by Petra Sabisch presents a picture of the relationships between production conditions and aesthetics in experimental dance, outlines its artistic directions, the most important discussion forums and the current theoretical discourses.

Experimental music is almost exclusively a domain of the independent groups. Matthias Rebstock gives an overview of this scene, discusses the current artistic trends and presents the most important players.

Henning Fülle discusses the theoretical basis for a new post-modern theatre in the context of a 'crisis of modernity' and describes the structural and cultural-political situation in Western European theatre focusing on the new forms of theatre that have developed since the mid-1990s.

Wolfgang Schneider examines the cultural policy for the independent theatre in different European countries and argues that we must adopt a new policy for theatre.

These studies focus on the central areas of work of the independent theatre and its position in the theatre scene in individual European countries. The basis for these studies – in addition to the author's own view – is detailed research with the help of artists working in the independent scene, cultural policy-makers and scientists, and an examination of the relevant research literature.

The increasing consolidation of this area of the theatre since the 1980s/90s has had far-reaching structural and aesthetic consequences for the European theatre culture in general, and has expanded the understanding of theatre and its experimental margins. Thereby, it becomes apparent that the aesthetic and theatre-cultural developments in the independent theatre and the repertory theatres have approached each other.

The independent theatre, however, reflects the social complexity and the change in European societies even more incisively: in its issues, its networks reaching beyond the national theatre cultures and the experimentation with new, more flexible production structures. In keeping with its history, it is still a socio-critical forum of its own kind. It is more open to other, non-European cultures than the repertory theatre can be because of its still largely cultivated orientation toward the national and European literary traditions. By its nature, the independent theatre is ultimately an international community of young artists. This connects – beyond national borders – a certain opposition, at least an uneasiness, with regard to the real system of values in European societies, which has sometimes been deformed by a political pragmatism.

This research project and this publication were made possible through the generous funding of the Fondazione Internazionale Balzan, in compliance with the regulations associated with the presentation of the *Balzan Prize* to me in 2010. The implementation of this research project, whose aim and whose procedures are explained in an additional foreword, was made in close cooperation with the German Centre of the International Theatre Institute (ITI) and with the Universities of Leipzig, Hildesheim and the Freie Universität Berlin.

Manfred Brauneck
Hamburg, March 2016

For a Topology of Practices
A Study on the Situation of Contemporary
and Experimental Dance, Choreography and Performance Art
in Europe (1990–2013)

Petra Sabisch

> '...we can learn to examine situations from the point of view of their possibilities.'
> Isabelle Stengers: 'The Care of the Possible' (Erik Bordeleau in conversation with I. Stengers), Scapegoat 1 (2011), 12.

Introduction

Der Künstler-Report (The Artist Report) by Karla Fohrbeck and Andreas Johannes Wiesand, written in 1975, provides us with the first known comprehensive, method-bundling study examining both the self-conception of artists in the Federal Republic of Germany at the time and the interdependencies characteristic of their working conditions. Their object of investigation amounts, above all, to the social and economic situation, or 'the legal and market situation', with concentration on self-employed and freelance workers.[1]

In this report, the professional scope of the dancer and/or ballet ensemble member is equated with the following professions: 'dancer, ballet dancer, ballet stage manager, ballet master/mistress, ballet director/choreographer, artistic director for ballet, dance educator'.[2]

---

1 | Karla Fohrbeck and Andreas Johannes Wiesand, *Der Künstler-Report: Musikschaffende, Darsteller, Realisatoren, Bildende Künstler, Designer* [The Artist Report: Musicians, performers, realisers, visual artists, designers] (Munich & Vienna: Carl Hanser, 1975), p. 421. Gender differentiation was part of this study's data collection, although the language of the study itself employs the general masculine form, reflecting common usage of the time.
2 | Ibid.

The professional tasks performed by this employment group are outlined as follows:

'Dancers interpret the content and form of ballet music and/or musical dances through the design of dance roles; in this capacity, they contribute to the scenic design of performances of opera, operetta or musicals as well; in some cases they present and/or perform ballroom dances ('Classification of Professions'). Fields of activity can include classical ballet, jazz dance, freestyle dance and Ausdruckstanz, among others. The work of ballet masters and assistants, dance educators etc. is focussed primarily on activities of an instructional/scholastic, planning-oriented and organisational nature; choreographers invent, design and/or work on artistic dances and the staged performances thereof. The labour of ballet dancers is divided into training, rehearsal and performance activities (with the usual course of development from the increasingly automatised control of individual movement sequences to more differentiated artistic depiction and self-determined creative work). Four hours' daily training as well as additional activities as background dancer in the opera and operetta are normal. The strenuous work dancers must execute as well as the stress they must endure is frequently underestimated.'[3]

In view of this description from 1975, it immediately becomes evident that the characteristics of the choreographic, dance and performance profession in the independent sector have since vigorously changed in ways that can be sketched out based on the following self-description of artistic practices, written in 2001:

'Our practices can be described by a range of terminology, depending on the different cultural contexts in which we operate. Our practices can be called: 'performance art', 'live art', 'happenings', 'events', 'body art', 'contemporary dance/theatre', 'experimental dance', 'new dance', 'multimedia performance', 'site specific', 'body installation', 'physical theatre', 'laboratory', 'conceptual dance', 'independance', 'postcolonial dance/performance', 'street dance', 'urban dance', 'dance theatre', 'dance performance' – to name but a few…
Such a list of terms not only represents the diversity of disciplines and approaches embraced within our practices, but is also symptomatic of the problematics of trying to define or prescribe such heterogeneous and evolving performance forms. However, today more than ever, the drive by cultural institutions and the art market alike to fix and categorise contemporary art practices is often in conflict with the fluid and migratory nature of much of our work, as much as with its needs.
Our practices are synonymous with funding priorities in terms of innovation, risk, hybridity, audience development, social inclusion, participation, new cultural discourses and cultural diversity, cultural difference. They offer new languages, articulate new

---

3 | Ibid.

forms of subjectivation and presentation to play with the cultural and social influences which inform us, to create new cultural landscapes. We address issues of cultural difference. [...]
We consider the borders between disciplines, categories and nations to be fluid, dynamic and osmotic.
We produce work that develops partnerships, networks and collaborations, disregards national borders and actively contributes to the local, European and trans-national contexts.'[4]

I have cited this catalogue of contemporary practices endemic to the field of performance art and dance so thoroughly here due to the significance of its source: the *Manifesto for a European Performance Policy*, published in 2002, a declaration addressing the European Commission and their cultural-political representatives. This document was sparked by an initiative by Jérôme Bel, Maria La Ribot, Xavier Le Roy and Christophe Wavelet to hold a self-organised meeting of artists from 13–18 October, 2001 at Tanzquartier Wien, where the manifesto was written and subsequently signed by numerous European artists.[5]

As the text's title conveys, significant changes in the attributes of these professions are to be traced to the qualitative changes the field itself is undergoing (changes which apply to modes of perception or aesthetics, and to organisational structures), the concomitant expansion and transformation of each individual area of activity, and – quite decisively – the internationalisation of relationships in the performing arts, especially those related to dance and choreography.

In today's day and age, the core benchmark which this artist-written, future-oriented self-description endeavours to set can no longer and in no shape or form be equated with the institution of ballet, which seems, should one accept the socio-empirical data, to have been widely instrumental in shaping the profession in Germany in 1975. Indeed, something else lies at the heart of this present-day artistic self-conception: a diversity of varying contemporary and international practices.[6]

---

4 | *Manifesto for a European Performance Policy* (2002), retrieved 21 July, 2013, from http://www.freietheater.at/?page=kulturpolitik&detail=61304&jahr=2002. The manifesto appears in its entirety in Annex 1 of this study, p. 173. Annex 1: Manifesto for a European Performance Policy.
5 | For a list of the manifesto's first signers, see Annex 1, p. 173.
6 | These are likely to overlap only in the rarest cases with the descriptions of the German Stage Association (Deutscher Bühnenverein), whose characterisations of occupational profiles for choreographers and dancers are to be considered outmoded. Cf. http://www.buehnenverein.de/de/jobs-und-ausbildung/32.html?view=7, retrieved 27.7.2013. Practices of freelance choreographers are insufficiently mirrored in this

The practices named include 'innovation' and 'risk', 'hybrid' forms, the engagement with and development of audiences, and the cultivation of new discourses. Participation, social cohesion, differential diversity and the creation of work likewise appear as manifest features of contemporary practices. Of central importance, however, is the desire voiced in the document's introduction: to be self-determined in regard to production resources, and to be instrumental in decisions related to the transparent setting of criteria for, and awarding of, funding grants:

'Contemporary performance artists are increasingly concerned with being able to decide on their means of production independently. As citizens, they also actively take part in decision-making affecting cultural policies. Their demands aim first and foremost at transparency in support policy, and call for such policy to address artists' extremely varied forms of production today.'

What follows is a lucid catalogue detailing different kinds of support:

'We are calling for innovative artistic structures, but also a new social status that would acknowledge new concepts of work that have altered the distinction between so-called 'productive' and 'non-productive' periods.

We claim recognition for our professional artistic activities, including those that will be visible in the future and which will give voice to that which has not yet been articulated. This increased recognition of the social status of the artist will contribute to and emphasise the quality of the social impact of artistic activities, which is the core of any democratic cultural policy.

---

description of activities, prerequisites and educational backgrounds, whilst the developments in international contemporary dance, were one to follow the Association's text, have yet to be devised. For more on this topic, see also Gabriele Schulz' indication that the German Stage Association has not adjusted its fifty-three occupational profiles to societal realities as named in the list of 114 occupational groups employed by the KSK (artists' social insurance) or to the 178 media professions identified in the AIM-MIA portal. Gabriele Schulz, 'Bestandsaufnahme zum Arbeitsmarkt Kultur' [Survey of the cultural labour market], in Gabriele Schulz, Olaf Zimmermann and Rainer Hufnagel, *Arbeitsmarkt Kultur: Zur wirtschaftlichen und sozialen Lage in Kulturberufen* [Cultural labour market: On the economic and social situations in the arts professions] (Berlin: Deutscher Kulturrat, 2013), 29–201, here p. 46–47.

We want the European Community to:

- resource artists as much as art
- invest in the ongoing needs and long-term growth of independent performers
- actively support artists in research, development and in the ongoing process of their practices, in equal measure to the generation and placement of new works
- recognise and enhance the relationships between and across innovative contemporary practices
- facilitate strategies for cross-disciplinary dialogues, collaborations and funding initiatives
- support new strategies for increasing audience awareness and appreciation,
- demonstrate a genuine commitment to innovation, risk and hybridity,
- actively develop, recognise and support a more important number of active, flexible and inventive artistic structures and infrastructures
- and to engage in a dialogue, set up the conditions for a new debate regarding these questions.'

If one places both statements side by side – on the one side, *The Artist Report*, a document of an engaged, comprehensive empirical study containing recommendations for action, and on the other, *The Manifesto for a European Performance Policy*, an artist-initiated appeal voiced by a number of engaged European performing artists – then the question arises, precisely what has actually changed over the course of the thirty years that lie between them, or of the forty years since the writing of the former until today?

Which structural changes have been made concerning a European performance status, concerning innovative cultural politics and the support of the arts, and finally concerning participatory involvement in crucial decision making processes?

The study before you aims to investigate this question, first, by evaluating the situation of freelance artists in the field of European dance and performance art, and second, by doing so against a backdrop of pivotal stations where research and cultural politics have been organised over the past twenty years.

Since, to date, there has yet to exist any systematic, European exploration of the reality of the *artistic working life* of freelance dancers, choreographers and performance artists, such an evaluation can only be understood, as this study's title attempts to articulate, as an initial contribution to the consolidation of European research studies emerging from dance- and performance-specific standpoints.

In view of the exigencies of the artist's present-day situation, however, it seemed crucial to me that I undertake this attempt, which hopefully, despite unavoidable gaps, can play a part in continued discussions. Overall, my evaluation tries to take into account the most recent research literature in particular.

Although one of my concerns was to include many perspectives from varying countries, the first part of this work surely reflects my own sphere of experience as a freelance choreographer and philosopher who has for the most part resided in France and Germany for long stretches of time. This fact, voiced with a desire to frame my own perspectivity in a transparent manner, finds its cause in the necessity I felt to aim for example-based concretisations of essential discussion points and problematic circumstances in specific localities.

A second step shall develop and hone this study's core question, as illustrated in the above, in critical engagement with the current state of research and the evaluation of the situation of artists in the field of dance, choreography and performance, with a focus on structural and aesthetic shifts.

Allow me to anticipate here the direction this question will take: how does the complex interplay between artistic production, work modes and aesthetics in the field of independent, international, experimental and contemporary dance present itself?[7] What does it look like? The background against which this question is posed lies in the – from the viewpoint of an art practice geared to the production of meaning – baffling matter of fact, that most studies break the irreducible interplay of these three areas down into mono-disciplinary islands; a matter of fact that is clearly reflected in the research literature and that reduces the process of art making to a dissociated aesthetic sector. This leaves us with a sum of discrete parts instead of an analysis of the affective relations between and specific intertwining of conditions, approaches and aesthetics.[8] One consequence of this category-specific procedure is a methodologically induced reduction of the agency of the aesthetic dispositive to the 'pure' field of artistic representation.[9]

In contrast, this study seeks opportunities for the more precise analysis of this interplay. To this end, it pursues the hypothesis that aesthetic representational forms of art are not only influenced by material circumstances,

---

7 | Cf. Chapter 1.2 Critique and formulation of the problem, especially pp. 75-90.

8 | At the turn of the millennium, Jacques Rancière thematised this distribution and ascription of that which is considered sensible, or capable of being sensed, and is also perceived as such, cf. Rancière, *The Politics of Aesthetics: The Distribution of the Sensible*, trans. Gabriel Rockhill (London & New York: Continuum, 2006). (Original work *Le Partage du Sensible: Esthétique et politique* published 2000).

9 | The interesting recently published study *Artistic Lives* argues in a similar vein. Here Kirsten Forkert attempts to demonstrate the influence of material conditions on opportunities and possibilities for practising art, using the example of artists in London and Berlin: 'There has been a long-standing tendency within the art field to ignore the social and economic conditions of cultural production, because these issues are seen to be irrelevant to aesthetic discussions.' Kirsten Forkert, *Artistic Lives: A Study of Creativity in Two European Cities* (Farningham: Ashgate Publishers, 2013), p. 3.

resources and methodologies, but that they also play a role in shaping them.[10] As such, an aesthetic, understood here as the intertwining of perception and representation, could be a direct intervention into these circumstances, or else a proposal for their reordering. Only with a suchlike hypothesis in our toolbox can we allow heretofore underexposed modes of inter-affectivity between artistic, social and economic structures to enter our field of vision.

A third chapter will reflect on the 'practice' as an object of research, on its terminological and methodological implications; it will also expound this study's concrete procedure, which is intrinsically based – in addition to document analysis and a statistics on the internationality of the practices discussed – on qualitative interviews conducted in the frame of this study.[11]

The second part of this study addresses the question of relational conditions of affectivity by means of a concrete analysis of five selected practices, or case studies, that correspond to the delimitation of our field of examination to include international, experimental, contemporary, discourse- and context-generating and artist-initiated (or in other words, artistic development-oriented) practices.

As a result, the complexity of these affective relationships shall be unfurled with the help of examples such as Special Issue in France and later on throughout Europe, the Madrid festival In-Presentable (2003–2012), the Double Lecture Series (2011) in Stockholm, the Performing Arts Forum in France (2005–ongoing) and the sommer.bar in Berlin (2006–2011).

---

10 | The role of the aesthetic as a shaping force is also discussed by Andrew Hewitt: 'The historical claims I make in this volume [...] are claims for the historical agency of the aesthetic as something that is not merely shaped but also shaping within the historical dynamic.' Andrew Hewitt, *Social Choreography: Ideology as Performance in Dance and Everyday Movement* (Durham, N.C.: Duke University Press, 2005), p. 2.

11 | The extensive interview material compiled in conjunction with this study offers a diversified, albeit language-based, insight into individual aesthetic manifestations, tendencies and manipulations of style. In my forthcoming companion project, *A Topology of Practices – The Book of Interviews*, these individual perspectives are contextualized and condensed into a fragmentary cultural history of dance in Europe from the nineties until today.

1. On the Situation of International Independent Dance, Choreography and Performance Art in Europe

1.1 Current State of Research

What has happened in European cultural politics?
When we consider the difference sketched out in the introduction, namely, the difference between practices in the professional independent field of dance and choreography from 1975 until today (2013), one becomes aware that diverse European conventions have been instituted, cultural-political studies have been commissioned, and cultural-political recommendations for actions and responses have emerged, not excluding an array of scholarly problematisations regarding the general situation of the artist, especially their social and economic status. In this section, a short overview of the current research will briefly relate some important studies and data collection programmes that have had implications for the field of dance, choreography and performance in the European region.

Of all the international studies on the general standing of the artist in society, UNESCO's wide-ranging proposals in its *Recommendation concerning the Status of the Artist*, adopted in 1980, is particularly worth mentioning.[12] It recognised the arts as an integral component of life in society, whose freedom of expression should not only be encouraged, but also whose material conditions, requisite for the enabling of artistic work, should be brought into being.[13] I shall call to memory some of these extensive demands, which recognised the special nature of artistic practices and demanded changes in existing policies on workers' rights:

'*Recognizing* that the arts in their fullest and broadest definition are and should be an integral part of life and that it is necessary and appropriate for governments to help create and sustain not only a climate encouraging freedom of artistic expression but also the material conditions facilitating the release of this creative talent,

Recognizing that every artist is entitled to benefit effectively from the social security and insurance provisions contained in the basic texts, Declarations, Covenant and Recommendation mentioned above,

---

12 | On European debates and statements on art in Europe, see the website of the European Parliament, http://www.europarl.europa.eu/sides/getDoc.do?type=TA&reference=P6-TA-2007-0236&format=XML&language=EN, retrieved 9.4.2014.

13 | UNESCO, *Recommendation Concerning the Status of the Artist*, adopted by the General Conference at its 21st session, Belgrade, 27.10.1980, http://portal.unesco.org/en/ev.php-URL_ID=13138&URL_DO=DO_TOPIC&URL_SECTION=201.html, retrieved 9.4.2014.

Considering that the artist plays an important role in the life and evolution of society and that he should be given the opportunity to contribute to society's development and, as any other citizen, to exercise his responsibilities therein, while preserving his creative inspiration and freedom of expression,
Further recognizing that the cultural, technological, economic, social and political development of society influences the status of the artist and that it is consequently necessary to review his status, taking account of social progress in the world,
Affirming the right of the artist to be considered, if he so wishes, as a person actively engaged in cultural work and consequently to benefit, taking account of the particular 'conditions of his artistic profession, from all the legal, social and economic advantages pertaining to the status of workers,
Affirming further the need to improve the social security, labour and tax conditions of the artist, whether employed or self-employed, taking into account the contribution to cultural development which the artist makes,
Recalling the importance, universally acknowledged both nationally and inter-nationally, of the preservation and promotion of cultural identity [...].'[14]

The General Conference put forward these recommendations with an appeal that they be submitted to all authorities, institutions and organisations in member states whose resources and circumstances permitted the taking of measures aimed at improving the status of artists and promoting participation in cultural life and cultural development.[15]

Although the UNESCO recommendations were officially embraced by fifty-five member countries by 2011, and although they led to data collection programmes in many of those countries' individual states as well as to unique improvements in social-security law (as in Germany, for example, where the Künstlersozialkasse [Artists' Social Welfare Fund] was established, primarily as a response to the *Künstler Report*) – despite all this, many of the recommendations, such as the qualitative improvement of the artist's occupational situation or the participation of artists in decision-making processes affecting their professional field, remained unfulfilled.[16]

---

14 | For part one of the UNESCO recommendations, see Annex 4, p. 180.
15 | 'The General Conference recommends that Member States bring this Recommendation to the attention of authorities, institutions and organizations in a position to contribute to improvement of the status of the artist and to foster the participation of artists in cultural life and development.' UNESCO, *Recommendations*, p. 4.
16 | UNESCO, *Consolidated Report on the Implementation by Member States of the 1980 Recommendation Concerning the Status of the Artist* (Monitoring Report of the General Conference in Paris) (2011), http://unesdoc.unesco.org/images/0011/0011 40/114029e.pdf#page=144, retrieved 29.7.2013.

This desideratum received widespread attention in France as the result of a 1997 working conference in Kerguéhennec (Brittany) where ca. fifty dancers, choreographers and researchers belonging to the association *Signataires du 20 août* joined and articulated their complaints against France's implemented cultural policies in an open letter to the French Ministry of Cultural Affairs, under the name of Dominique Wallon, the then-director of the DMDTS.[17] This letter criticised the institutional practices of French cultural policy with regard to dance, focussing on its 'choreographic nepotism', its 'sclerotic' rigidity, its increasingly questionable notions vis-à-vis artistic works (e.g., hierarchy of working relationships) and above all its structurally, recurrently non-participatory approach to affected choreographic artists when it comes to discussions surrounding the working conditions in their own professional fields.[18] The disproportionality of the apportionment of funds between dance and theatre was likewise thematised, as was the fact that dance was being subsumed under theatre.[19] The root question – what can be undertaken when

---

17 | This association included Patrice Barthès, Alain Buffart, Thierry Bae, Marion Mortureux-Bae, Christian Bourigault, Laure Bonicel, Hélène Cathala, Boris Charmatz, Julia Cima, Nathalie Collantès, Catherine Contour, Dimitri Chamblas, Fabienne Compet, Fabrice Dugied, Jeannette Dumeix, Laura De Nercy, Matthieu Doze, Hella Fattoumi, Olivia Grandville, Emmanuelle Huynh, Dominique Jégou, Latifa Lâabissi, Catherine Legrand, Eric Lamoureux, Isabelle Launay, Anne Karine Lescop, Samuel Letellier, Bertrand Lombard, Alain Michard, Véra Noltenius, Alice Normand, Julie Nioche, Rachid Ouramdane, Pascale Paoli, Laurent Pichaud, Cécile Proust, Sylvain Prunenec, Annabelle Pulcini, Pascal Quéneau, Fabrice Ramalingom, Dominique Rebaud, Christian Rizzo, Loïc Touzé, Donata d'Urso, Christine Van Maerren, Marc Vincent, Christophe Wavelet, Claudine Zimmer. Previously known as the DMDTS (Division de la Musique, de la Danse, du Théâtre et des Spectacles) until 2007 – the DGCA (Direction Générale de la Création Artistique) is under the control of the French Ministère de la Culture (and former Minister of Culture Cathérine Trautmann).

18 | See Les Signataires du 20 août, 'Lettre ouverte à Dominique Wallon et aux danseurs contemporains' [Open letter to Dominique Wallon and to contemporary dancers], *Mouvement* 3-4 (1999-2000), http://reas.zinclafriche.org/controverses/ressources/99/wallon.html, retrieved 29.7.2012; idem., 'Etat de grève à Kerguéhennec' [A state of strike at Kerguéhennec], *Mouvement* 2 (1999), http://www.mouvement.net/critiques/critiques/etat-de-greve-a-kerguehennec, retrieved 29.7.2012. For an account of these debates, see also Céline Roux, *Danse(s) performative(s): Enjeux et développement dans le champs chorégraphique français 1993-2003* [Performative Dance(s): Stakes and development in the field of French choreography] (Paris: L'Harmattan, 2007), pp. 55-78.

19 | Jean-Marc Adolphe: 'Des moyens pour mieux faire' [Means for doing better], *Mouvement* 4 (1999), 8: 'Entre le théâtre et la danse, les différences restent toujours aussi flagrantes. Là où 45 Centres dramatiques nationaux reçoivent 326,5 millions de

the gap between the logic of institutional structures and the logic of artistic practices develop in increasingly opposing directions – was answered as follows:

> 'If the democratic state and its elected officials have the responsibility to nominate functionaries as well as those in charge of structural decisions, then the responsibility of the profession [dance] is to debate the content of those officials' respective projects. The profession is in fact sufficiently structured, has sufficient expertise at its disposal and is self-aware enough for such contradictory discussions to take place. How can one accept a sort of legitimacy that is based only on political or communicative know-how rather than on contemporary dancers' adhesion to an artistic and political project? Why are opportunities for discussing content-related issues absent to such a high degree from the French dance milieu?'[20]

The open letter by Les Signataires du 20 août provided a platform, using different words than the *Manifesto for a European Performance Policy*, which it preceded by more than a year, for voices who were demanding a participatory democratisation of the field and who were questioning the legitimacy of purely political, non-content-motivated and non-competency-oriented decision-making processes affecting the field's evolvement.

Additionally, in 1997 the UNESCO Observatory on the Status of Artists, conceived as a practical monitoring tool and databank, was set up in connection with the World Congress on the Implementation of the Recommendation concerning the Status of the Artist.[21]

---

francs (soit 7,25 MF en moyenne), les 18 Centres chorégraphiques doivent se contenter de 60 millons de francs (en moyenne 3,3 MF).'

20 | Les Signataires du 20 août: 'Lettre ouverte'. Original French: *'Si l'Etat démocratique et les élus ont la responsabilité des nominations de leurs fonctionnaires et responsables de structures, la responsabilité de la profession est de débattre des contenus de leurs projets respectifs. Elle est en effet devenue suffisamment structurée, suffisamment experte et consciente d'elle-même pour que de tels débats contradictoires puissent avoir lieu. Qu'est-ce qu'une légitimité si elle n'est fondée que sur un savoir-faire politicien et communicationnel, et non sur l'adhésion des danseurs contemporains à un projet artistique et politique? Pourquoi la possibilité de débattre des contenus est-elle à ce point absente du milieu de la danse en France?'*

21 | See http://www.culturalpolicies.net/web/index.php and http://portal.unesco.org/culture/en /ev.php-URL_ID=38716&URL_DO=DO_TOPIC&URL_SECTION=201.html, retrieved 23.7.2013. See also the informational portal, launched in 1998, of the *Compendium of Cultural Policies and Trends in Europe*, created by *the European Institute for Comparative Cultural Research* (ERICarts). With its eighth edition appearing in 2013, the portal describes measures and statistics, profiles individual countries and

In 2001, UNESCO adopted the *Universal Declaration of Cultural Diversity*, which was complemented in 2005 by the binding *Convention for the Protection and Promotion of the Diversity of Cultural Expression*.[22] Both of these emphasised the central issues of cultural diversity, cultural and natural heritage, manoeuvrable intellectual property, and contemporary modes of artistic expression. Those principles and definitions which held – in contrast to the World Trade Organization (WTO) agreement on the liberalisation of the markets, which makes no distinction between everyday goods and artistic activities – that cultural works should *not* be viewed as purely economic goods turned out to be quite crucial to matters of art and culture:

'*Being convinced* that cultural activities, goods and services have both an economic and a cultural nature, because they convey identities, values and meanings, and must therefore not be treated as solely having commercial value.'[23]

Another novelty of the convention text lies in the unambiguous key role it ascribes to cultural diversity in the furtherance of peace, security and social cohesion,[24] not to mention the importance it places on those protagonists who work towards cultural development as a catalyst for progress in society.[25] It was also resolved that in times of globalization, the responsibility of guaranteeing a 'free flow of ideas and works' should rest on member states, resulting in the apparent fact that international agreements and cooperation are indispensable and worth supporting.

---

surveys overarching topics in cultural politics, http://www.culturalpolicies.net/web/compendium.php, retrieved 9.4.2014.
22 | See http://portal.unesco.org/en/ev.php-URL_ID=13179&URL_DO=DO_TOPIC&URL_SECTION=201.html, retrieved 23.7.2013. UNESCO, *Convention on the Protection and Promotion of the Diversity of Cultural Expressions*, Paris, adopted 20.10.2005 (33rd session), http://www.unesco.org/new/en/culture/themes/cultural-diversity/diversity-of-cultural-expressions/the-convention/ convention-text/, retrieved 23.7.2013.
23 | UNESCO, *Diversity of Cultural Expressions*, p. 2.
24 | '*Recalling* that cultural diversity, flourishing within a framework of democracy, tolerance, social justice and mutual respect between peoples and cultures, is indispensable for peace and security at the local, national and international levels. [...] *Emphasizing* the importance of culture for social cohesion in general, and in particular its potential for the enhancement of the status and role of women in society', ibid.
25 | '*Emphasizing* the vital role of cultural interaction and creativity, which nurture and renew cultural expressions and enhance the role played by those involved in the development of culture for the progress of society at large', ibid.

On the European level, this call for an international dimension was met with a number of measures. In 2006, the *Green Paper: Modernising labour law to meet the challenges of the 21st century* was released by the Commission of the European Community.[26] Under the heading 'flexicurity', this report declares the need for a combination of flexibility and social security and indicates the urgency of innovations and changes towards supportive, inclusive and dialogically responsive policies:

'In the context of globalisation, ongoing restructuring and the move towards a knowledge-based economy, European labour markets need to be both more inclusive and more responsive to innovation and change. Potentially vulnerable workers need to have a ladder of opportunity so as to enable them to improve their mobility and achieve successful labour market transitions. Legal frameworks sustaining the standard employment relationship may not offer sufficient scope or the incentive to those on regular permanent contracts to explore opportunities for greater flexibility at work. If innovation and change are to be successfully managed, labour markets will need to address three main issues: flexibility, employment security and segmentation issues. The purpose of this Green Paper is to promote a debate about whether a more responsive regulatory framework is required to support the capacity of workers to anticipate and manage change regardless of whether they are engaged on indefinite contracts or non-standard temporary contracts.'[27]

The Status of Artists in Europe, a study commissioned by the European Parliament published in 2006, is of central significance for artists' living and working conditions.[28] The paper's principal claim is that even though artists do, in fact, constitute a 'considerable share of Europe's labour force', they do not, despite thriving economies, enjoy sufficient guarantees of their social and economic security, let alone participation in the attendant (decision-making) processes:

---

26 | Commission of the European Community, *Green Paper: Modernising labour law to meet the challenges of the 21st century* (2006), http://eur-lex.europa.eu/LexUriServ/site/en/ com/2006/com2006_0708en01.pdf, retrieved 12.8.2013.
27 | Commission of the European Community, *Green Paper*, p. 9.
28 | European Institute for Comparative Cultural Research (ERICarts), Suzanne Capiau and Andreas Johannes Wiesand, in cooperation with Danielle Cliche, with additional contributions by Vesna Čopič, Ritva Mitchell and a network of European experts, *The Status of Artists in Europe* (Brussels, 2006), http://www.europarl.europa.eu/RegData/etudes/etudes/join/2006/375321/IPOL-CULT_ET%282006%29375321_EN.pdf, retrieved 2.6.2013. Study requested by The European Parliament's Committee on Culture and Education. Original language: English; for German translation see http://edz.bib.uni-mannheim.de/daten/edz-ma/ep/06/pe375.321-de.pdf, retrieved 18.8.2014.

'Despite flourishing culture/creative industry markets, their activities are generally carried out in far more precarious circumstances than other occupations. Atypical (project-based) and casual employment, irregular and unpredictable income, unremunerated research and development phases, accelerated physical wear and tear and high levels of mobility are among the key features not taken account of in the existing legal, social security and tax structures.'[29]

Within a context characterised by the 'diminishing role of the State' and the 'globalisation of market economies' along with extensive privatisations, *The Status of Artists in Europe* examines existing (national) parameters and envisages 'innovative national measures' geared to improving artists' circumstances regarding their 'individual working and contract relations; professional representation; social security; taxation; and aspects of transnational mobility'.[30]

Although *The Status of Artists in Europe* inspects the concrete circumstances of artists quite knowledgeably and critically, it de facto comes to the conclusion, based on the results of scenarios it develops as discussion aids, that the recommendation of the European Parliament (2003) to introduce a comprehensive artists' statute in the form of an EU directive should be dismissed on the following grounds: 'This investigation deemed the proposal somewhat unrealistic', due to 'the complexity of the issues, the widely varying work conditions of the two main professional groups studied (i.e., authors and performing artists) and the innovative solutions existing in several EU member states'.[31]

At the same time, the preservation of the current status quo – in other words, atypical, precarious working conditions within a 'project economy' with structural insecurity – is ruled out by the study as an impracticable option,

---

29 | Ibid., iii. According to the 2004 EUROSTAT study (cross-tabulated combined datasets from NACE – statistical classification of economic activities in the European Community – and ISCO – the International Standard Classification of Occupations – *The Status of Artists in Europe* puts the amount of workers employed in the cultural sectors of the EU's 25 countries (in 2002) at 4.2 million, which amounts to 2.5% of the entire workforce. 30% of these are self-employed, freelance 'cultural operators' and 'entrepreneurs/employers (in comparison to 15% for the overall labour market)', ibid., p. 10. See also Gabriele Schulze's analysis of KSK (Artists' Social Welfare Fund) data, which are vastly more informative and precise as regards the classification of artists in cultural occupations: Gabriele Schulze, 'Arbeitsmarkt Kultur: Eine Analyse von KSK-Daten' [Cultural labour market: An analysis of KSK data], in Schulze, Hufnagel and Zimmerman, *Arbeitsmarkt Kultur*, pp. 241–323, here p. 308.

30 | On the critique of the current discourse on mobility, see p. 82.

31 | *The Status of Artists in Europe*, p. iv. The study's terminological differentiation between 'authors' and 'performing artists' is, in my assessment, problematic.

and pleas are made for a new European Parliament resolution together with a pragmatic package of measures (which would provide for a community charter, a white book on mobility, and the establishment of a central online contact point).[32]

Considering the current state of research, some fundamental remarks are necessary here: it can be generally determined on the basis of data gathered from across Europe that a certain amount of statistics is available by this point, yet one is often met with an abyss when seeking comparative material on the past, which makes the long-term, meaningful analysis of socioeconomic developments in artistic occupations relatively impossible.[33]

It must also be noted that a continuous European monitoring in keeping with a differentiated and comprehensible partitioning into specific professions, or occupational areas, is lacking.[34] The inconsistently handled classifications of

---

32 | 'In recent years, the employment status of many groups, including professional artists, has been influenced by a diminishing role of the State and by a globalisation of market economies. For example, the economy of culture in countries of West Europe has been, over the past 20 years, marked by the privatisation of the audiovisual sector, the reduction of State cultural budgets, the opening up and extension of the European public space and the predominant concentration of imported products transmitted via radio, TV, cable, etc. This has deeply altered the conditions for creation and production. Artistic creation finds itself settled into an economy of projects which are more often than not managed by small and medium-sized enterprises whilst, in the distribution sector, large-scale national and international groups dominate the market. While some groups, e.g. literary authors, may be less affected by such changes, others, such as performing artists, experience them as grave interferences with their ideas and professional practices and may even consider changing their work or working status altogether.' Ibid., p. 13. See also ibid., p. 14: 'The majority of artists nowadays share a structural instability in their conditions of engagement, and this instability is generally not compensated.'
33 | Ibid. p. 10: 'Despite this attempt, there remain no European comparative statistics which aggregate the range of artistic professions...'
34 | Despite the fact that the classification of occupations is no easy task, UNESCO's typology is more than unsuitable, from a dance-scholarly perspective, for providing information about activities in the field of dance. On page 26 of the 2009 *Framework for Cultural Statistics* (FCS), written by the UNESCO Institute for Statistics, Montreal, Canada, UNESCO defines the 'cultural domain' *Performance and Celebration* as follows: '*Performance and Celebration* include all expressions of live cultural events. *Performing Arts* includes both professional and amateur activities, such as theatre, dance, opera and puppetry. It also includes the celebration of cultural events – *Festivals, Feasts and Fairs* – that occur locally and can be informal in nature. *Music* is defined in this domain in its entirety, regardless of format. As such, it includes live and recorded musical

occupational groups leads firstly to an inability to fashion precise socioeconomic statements on dance in Europe, since in Europe dance is electively assigned to the occupational group 'performance' (on the same level, according to UNESCO, as music, as well as any sort of 'celebration' or 'festival' whatsoever), and often, on the national level, to 'performing arts' (thus being equated with theatre).[35]

As a result of country-specific investigations and empirical values that confront, for example, variations in gender differentiation between dance and theatre, or levels of internationalisation and mobility, one can immediately discern acute distortions in the representation of both fields (dance as opposed to theatre, or dance as opposed to music or celebration).[36]

Despite the fact that narrow typo-ontological delimitations seem incommensurate not only with the expansion of practices in dance (code phrase:

---

performances, music composition, music recordings, digital music including music downloads and uploads, and musical instruments.' The combination of two art forms, here music and performance – the former being a category that enjoys a strong industry and the latter being entirely without an industry – is in dire need of explanation, as is the paper's determination of professional as opposed to nonprofessional activities. Beyond this, however, the simple tossing together of 'creative, arts, and entertainment activities' (in CPC2 and ISIC4; (see p.52) together with the celebratory aspect of festivals and fairs is noteworthy, and undoubtedly the fault of the economic perspective, from which most of the classifications are derived (p.51). For the narrower area of actual art production, the absurdity of the varying classificatory systems becomes apparent, for example, in the codes of the 2007 'harmonised system' (HS), whereby the selling of bells, for instance (p. 65), falls into domain B, Performance and Celebration, as does any kind of selling of Christmas decorations, according to the current UNESCO classification (p. 70). This renders the actual artistic activities de facto invisible.

35 | For more on this topic, see Céline Roux, who describes the same turn of events in France, events which she links, among other things, to the consolidation of the departments of music, theatre and dance into the DMTDS, in spite of the 'Dix nouvelles mesures pour la danse' [Ten new measures for dance] demanded by Jack Lang in 1984. Céline Roux, *Danse(s) performative(s)*, p. 56.

36 | In contrast to dramatic theatre forms that are bound to a text, nonlinguistic forms of dance and choreography can at least be circulated internationally – without wanting to reduce dance performances to nonverbal practices. Historically speaking, this feature of choreography and dance may have contributed to a portion of the independent dance scene becoming internationally networked and mobile. Another significant reason for the internationalisation of dance lies, in my opinion, in the quite low percentage of venues for the independent dance scene in Europe, which isn't the case with theatre, and the resultant necessity of positioning oneself internationally and thereby financing oneself through tours.

dissolution of boundaries in the arts, or *choreography as expanded practice*[37]) but also with the aesthetic freedom of artistic alliances, there has nevertheless been a need for years for an even roughly suitable differentiation between, firstly, artistic agents and their more broadly culturally associated activities and, secondly, between dance and theatre or dance and music; a need that has left specific evolvements of and concrete interconnections between these fields untraceable and unanalysable.[38]

Due to this absent difference, or in other words because of dance's subsumption under theatre, the deep disparities between dance and theatre in terms of resource endowment become invisible, which becomes evident when considering the fact that Germany boasts little more than a handful of publicly funded houses that more or less exclusively show dance, performance and international guest performances and that do not show only one company.[39] This figure, which should be spelled out more precisely in individual theatres' budgets, can be contrasted to 140 municipal and state theatres funded by the public hand, which often feel in no way obligated, not even by a percentage, to support or show independent dance.[40]

---

37 | On the concept of choreography as expanded practice, see p. 73.

38 | See also the definition of the performing arts as any and all spectacles that contain a live event, including celebrations and fairs, and even music downloads, found in the purely qualitative monitoring, commissioned by UNESCO, in Michael Söndermann: *Kultureller Beschäftigungsmarkt und Künstlerarbeitsmarkt: Kulturstatistische Analyse zum Anhang des Staatenberichts* [The cultural employment market and the artists' labour market: Cultural-statistical analysis for addendum to the States' Report], requested by the German UNESCO commission, http://www.kulturwirtschaft.de/wp-content/uploads/2011/01/DUK-KB-Endfassung_20121104.pdf, retrieved 2.8.2013, p. 8. As the function of Söndermann's monitoring is to test suitability for standard use, its terminology must herewith be objected to urgently. See also executive summary of study in English, http://www.kulturwirtschaft.de/wp-content/uploads/2012/11/DUK-executive-summary_20120330.pdf, retrieved 2.8.2013.

39 | To name some examples: Pact Zollverein in Essen; Tanzhaus NRW in Düsseldorf, which is momentarily threatened with cuts; K3, Zentrum für Choreographie at Kampnagel Hamburg, which offers a residency programme for young choreographers; and Tanzfabrik Berlin.

40 | The Deutscher Bühnenverein [German stage association] sets the number of German stages at 140 publically funded theatres; 200 private theatres; around 130 opera, symphony, and chamber orchestras; ca. 70 festival houses; around 150 theatres and venues without a fixed ensemble; and approximately 100 stages for tours and guest performances without fixed houses. See the Deutscher Bühnenverein's homepage, http://www.buehnenverein.de/de/theater-und-orchester/19.html, retrieved 4.8.2013.

As a contrasting example, there are 18 choreographic centres as well as the Centre National de la Danse in France. And yet even in France, if we read the 2004 report on the future of the 'spectacle vivant', the status of dance is on no equal footing with that of the other arts: 'Dance still lacks the power to establish a relation of equality, and no longer one of dependence – however well-intentioned the latter may be – vis-à-vis the other arts.'[41]

In view of my point regarding specialised venues for dance, one can, in Germany, indeed question whether there is any recognition of the autonomy of dance as an art form of its own.[42]

On the general situation of artists with regard to gender differentiation, I shall here mention the two-phase study by Reine Prat, commissioned by the French Ministère de la Culture, which examines the implementation of the constitutionally anchored equality between genders in the art field in France between 2006 and 2009, with upsetting results.[43]

---

41 | Report by Bernard Latarjet, *Pour un débat national sur l'avenir du spectacle vivant* [For a national debate on the future of the performing arts], Mission report commissioned by the Ministre de la Culture et de Communication, Jean-Jacques Aillagon (2004), http://www.culture.gouv.fr/culture/actualites/rapports/latarjet/rapport_7mai2004.pdf, retrieved 7.5.2004, p. 111.

42 | France as well is experiencing a need for further spaces, especially for working and research. See Delphine Bachacou, 'De nouveaux espaces pour la danse contemporaine d'aujourd'hui' [New spaces for today's contemporary dance], diploma dissertation, Université Lumière Lyon II/ARSEC, http://pre-fassp.univ-lyon2.fr/IMG/pdf/doc-592.pdf, retrieved 10.7.2012, p. 50: 'We could thus think that the new spaces, Ramdam, le TNT, Les Laboratoires and others not yet cited, such as L'Espace Pier Pasolini in Valenciennes, L'Echangeur à Fère en Tardenois (Aisne) or else Mains d'Oeuvres in Saint Ouen, are about to create a new dispositif for creation, parallel to the existing and predominant one. These spaces were established to equalise the general lack in France of work spaces allocated to contemporary dance and contemporary creation. They were also created in order to establish different kinds of functioning, to launch different axes of work than those developed in the institutions, which, according to them, might lead to "sclerotic practices".'

43 | Reine Prat, *Mission EgalitéS. Pour une plus grande et une meilleure visibilité des diverses compo-santes de la population française dans le secteur du spectacle vivant* [Mission EgalitéS: For bigger and better visibility of diverse constituents of the French population in the performing arts sector], esp. Ch. 1: 'Pour l'égal accès des femmes et des hommes aux postes de responsabilité, aux lieux de décision, à la maîtrise de la représentation [For equal access for women and men to leadership positions, to decision-making processes and to representation] Interim report 1, under the auspices of the Ministère de la Culture et de la Communication (MCC) / Direction de la Musique, de la Danse et des Spectacles (DMDTS)' (2006), http://www.culture.gouv.fr/culture/actualites/rapports/

Regarding Germany, the gender-differentiating analyses on income and participation in leadership roles, as well as social security (including retirement provisions) still look equally devastating.[44]

Studies on the socioeconomic conditions of dance-makers in Germany

The current state of data collection for the socioeconomic conditions of artists in the field of dance, choreography and performance art appears a bit more precise on the national level – not until recent years, however, as regards data on Germany.

In 2007, Germany saw the publishing of the *Abschlussbericht der Enquête Kommission Kultur*, which, in difference to the *Künstler-Report*, did not place its primary focus on art and the social situation of the artist, but rather on the entire cultural realm.[45] Despite this general concept of culture, here dance is

---

prat/egalites.pdf, accessed 6.8.2012; idem., *Arts du spectacle: Pour l'égal accès des femmes et des hommes aux postes de responsabilité, aux lieux de décision, aux moyens de production, aux réseaux de diffusion, à la visibilité médiatique* [Performing arts: For equal access of women and men to leadership positions, to decision-making processes, to means of production, to distribution networks and to media visibility] 2: De l'interdit à l'empêchement [From interdiction to prevention], Interim report 2, under the auspices of the MCC/DMDTS, (2009), http://www.ladocumentationfrancaise.fr/var/storage/rapports-publics/094000235/0000.pdf, accessed 6.8.2012. See also Petra Sabisch, 'Changing Matters in the Performing Arts – A feminist Quasi-Survey', in Sigrid Gareis, Georg Schöllhammer, Peter Weibel (Eds.), *Moments: Eine Geschichte der Performance in zehn Akten*, German-English exh. cat., ZKM Karlsruhe / Museum für Neue Kunst (Cologne: Walther König), pp. 331–338.

44 | According to Gabriele Schulz, the annual income for women in the occupational division 'performing arts' was thirty-two percent lower than that of their male colleagues in 2012, a disparity which intensifies with increasing age. This gap is moreover the widest of all the arts: 'Arbeitsmarkt Kultur: Eine Analyse von KSK-Daten' [Cultural labour market: An analysis of KSK data], in Schulz, Hufnagel, Zimmermann, *Arbeitsmarkt Kultur*, pp. 241–322, here esp. pp. 292–294, as well as 'Bestandsaufnahme zum Arbeitsmarkt Kultur' [Survey of the cultural labour market], pp. 27–201, here p. 45. See also Susanne Keuchel, 'Die empirische Studie' [The empirical study], in Fonds Darstellende Künste & Kulturpolitische Gesellschaft (Eds.), *Report Darstellende Künste: Wirtschaftliche, soziale und arbeitsrechtliche Lage der Theater und Tanzschaffenden in Deutschland. Studien – Diskurse – Internationales Symposium* [Performing arts report: Economic, social and labour-legal situation of theatre and dance makers in Germany. Studies – discourses – international symposium] (Essen: Klartext Verlag, 2010), pp. 29–174, here pp. 52–53.

45 | See Deutscher Bundestag [German Federal Parliament], *Kultur in Deutschland: Schlussbericht der Enquête-Kommission des Deutschen Bundestages* [Culture in

considered an autonomous artistic profession in a brief chapter on the 'special circumstances of dance'. The chapter begins by stating that 'dance was and is an indispensable component of our cultural life, an art form of its own, without linguistic or national barriers'.[46]

The Tanzplan Deutschland programme, launched in 2006, for instance, is mentioned, as well as the problem of professional transition. Additionally, the growing gap between the growth of the cultural sector and the recessionary, absolutely desolate income development in the performing arts is highlighted:

'In the eyes of intermediaries and users alike, the art market makes itself out to be stable and prosperous. [...] In the performing arts, actors and dancers have had to tolerate an income loss of ca. 30 to 40 percent, according to the experts. Data shows that the labour market is constricted for everyone, but particularly for those who were not permanently employed by the 'large houses' of the theatre establishment. Assessments of the developments in this area ranged all the way to their characterisation as a 'ruinous clearcutting'.'[47]

Also published in 2007, in conjunction with a symposium on funding structures (January 2006, Berlin), the volume *Freies Theater in Deutschland* took up current problems experienced by internationally active artists, though it did not go into the situation specific to dance.[48]

In 2010, the *Performing Arts Report* (*Report Darstellende Künste*), initiated by the ITI and the Fonds Darstellende Künste, published empirical inquiries into the economic, social and labour law-related circumstances of theatre and dance makers in Germany, including, among other resources, an overview of documents focussed on the rise of internationalisation in the field.[49]

Germany: Closing report of the enquête commission of the German Bundestag] (Regensburg: ConBrio, 2008). See also Olaf Zimmermann, 'Arbeitsmarkt Kultur: Einführung und methodisches Vorgehen' [Cultural labour market: Introduction and methods of procedure], in *Arbeitsmarkt Kultur*, pp. 9–27, here p. 11.

46 | Deutscher Bundestag, 'Sondersituation Tanz', in *Enquête*, Ch. 4.5.4., p. 474.

47 | Ibid. *Enquête*, p. 428–429.

48 | Fonds Darstellende Künste (Ed.), *Freies Theater in Deutschland: Förderstrukturen und Perspektiven* [Independent theatre in Germany: Funding structures and perspectives] (Essen: Klartext, 2007). The article which appears under my name in this volume was developed collectively by a group of Berlin artists including participants such as Xavier Le Roy and Thomas Lehmen, to name just two. Unfortunately I no longer hold the complete list of names, after my appeals for collective authorship fell victim to the blue pencil for 'space reasons', despite repeated protests.

49 | Fonds Darstellende Künste & Kulturpolitische Gesellschaft (Eds.), *Report Darstellende Künste*. See especially Konrad Bach, Thomas Engel, Michael Freundt and

Keuchel's empirical study likewise reaches the conclusion, once again, that the self-employed performing artist's income has worsened intensely, lying significantly lower than that of the general population – and on no account due to the economic crisis, but instead as a steadily regressive factor.[50] Genders are treated differently as regards income in Germany too – an extremely well-known fact – and even in spite of high rates of academic degree completion: women earn 30 to 42 percent less than men; for women, old-age poverty is a preprogrammed reality.[51]

Finally, I would like to address the very recently published quantitative study, released by the German Cultural Council (Deutscher Kulturrat), *Arbeitsmarkt Kultur* (2013), which undertakes a deliberate baseline study of the cultural labour market (Schulz), demonstrates the opportunities presented by socioeconomic panels (Hufnagel), and offers an evaluation of (Schulz) – while furthermore methodologically as well as historically situating (Zimmermann, and Schulz/Zimmermann) – data from the Artists' Social Welfare Fund (KSK).[52]

The merit of this comprehensive report lies not only in its demonstration of the complexity of the cultural labour market, but also in its critical commentary on the position of the arts within the cultural sphere.[53] Here Olaf Zimmermann

---

Dieter Welke, Der Status der Künstler im Bereich der Darstellenden Künste: Recherche des deutschen Zentrums des ITI [The status of the artist in the performing arts: Research of the German chapter of the ITI], in *Report Darstellende Künste*, pp. 243-272.

50 | Keuchel 'Die empirische Studie', pp. 49-51.

51 | Ibid., p. 52.

52 | Hufnagel, Schulz, Zimmermann, *Arbeitsmarkt Kultur*. For Schulz' baseline study, however, the elaboration of an interior differentiation between dance and theatre is urgently required, since the category 'performing arts' allows the singularities of dance and choreography to be overlooked. This becomes particularly noticeable with regard to the proliferation of courses of study in recent years within the fields of dance/choreography and Dance Studies, which Schulz does not designate as such; with regard to the inclusion of Dance Studies as a discrete profession (Schulz seems to view Dance Studies as a subcategory of Theatre Studies) and, most importantly, with regard to disparities in gender differentiation – see p. 120. The KSK data evidences a 173% rise over the last 20 years in individuals insured under the KSK in the performing arts category: http://www.kuenstlersozialkasse.de/wDeutsch/ksk_in_zahlen/statistik/versicherten bestandsentwicklung.php, retrieved 12.8.2013. Instead of verbalising them, Schulz calculates the following results in tabular form: from 1995 to 2010, in the 'direction and choreography' category, the increase in insured parties was 199% for men and 342% for women (p. 287). These figures beg for clarification.

53 | 'Catalysts for a more intensive engagement with issues surrounding the cultural labour market can be found in the form of simultaneously pursued and partially quite conflictive cultural-political debates. On the one side, the economic importance

describes the differentiation between art and culture as a matter that behoves the German Cultural Council, although such distinctions may not seem entirely reconcilable with the report's title:

'When we talk about the cultural labour market, differentiation is crucial. The cultural labour market per se does not exist; the branches and legal structures, the educational programmes and employment circumstances are too varied for this to be the case. One essential objective is to illustrate that the cultural labour market is more than just a labour market for artists. Such an approach would in no way diminish the significance artists have for this market; on the contrary, artists are its precondition. Without artists no contemporary works would be created; without artists no new performances, recordings or interpretations would be possible. Artists constitute the core of the cultural labour market; all further circles therein form around their works and around their labour. An essential objective of this book is thus to differentiate between artistic labour and the artistic professions, on the one hand, and workers who teach, communicate, sell and circulate art, on the other.'[54]

The study before you emphatically underlines the crucial importance of this differentiation, especially for enabling the examination of structural changes and reallocations between the branches of art production, the communication of art, cultural education and other cultural employment milieus.[55]

---

of this branch is accentuated by the "Initiative Kultur- und Kreativwirtschaft der Bundesregierung" (Federal Initiative for Cultural and Creative Economies), which grants it a value ranking between the chemical and automobile industries. It is viewed as a so-called sunrise industry – a comparatively young, fast growing industry with good prospects for future growth – whose competitiveness should be strengthened. On the other side, among committees in the German Cultural Council, the word is that far too many people are being educated for the cultural labour market, and only a fraction of graduates with art-related degrees will actually have a chance in their desired labour market segment. Here, people are talking about a scarcity of educational capacities. And yet, on a third side the significance of cultural literacy is foregrounded with expectations that new chances for artists and others active in cultural professions will arise here. This expectation collides, in turn, with the fourth side: the already existing and partially upcoming financial cuts in municipal (local) budgets affecting the basic state funding of cultural and educational institutions. And posing a contrast to this are temporary large-scale projects like "Kulturagenten für kreative Schulen" (Cultural Agents for Creative Schools) that have a lighthouse effect.' Hufnagel, Schulz, and Zimmermann, *Arbeitsmarkt Kultur*, p. 20.

54 | Ibid., p. 328.

55 | An example that should be named here is the strike by the French Intermittents, which led to the shutdown of the theatre festival in Avignon in 2003. This strike showed

In her critique of neoliberal conceptions of creativity, the New Yorker art critic Claire Bishop draws attention to this ceaseless non-differentiation and the accompanying, more or less practised indifference towards artistic practices within a generalised concept that lumps together culture, entertainment and creativity, as is evidenced, for example, in the 2005 Dutch right-wing cultural-political report *Our Creative Capacity Hollands*. As Bishop states, 'we find that the authors of this paper acknowledge no difference between "creative industry", the "culture industry", "art" and "entertainment"'.[56]

The *Creative Europe Report*, completed in 2002, should also be viewed with scepticism in this regard: the report presents European government measures and modes of partnership for the support of creative concepts. Admittedly, art's 'atypical' employment conditions are acknowledged in the report, and considerations are made regarding the extent to which exceptional legislation may be passed to accommodate. The focus, however, lies on the *governance* of the so-called creative industry, despite all engaged 'voices from the field'.[57]

---

the extent to which the general labour market (not only the cultural labour market) really profits from art production; the estimated financial losses in gastronomy and tourism clearly revealed the severity of non-participation on the part of artists in this 'supply chain'. For more on discussions of this period, see also the journal *Mouvement* (revue indisciplinaire des arts vivants), which itself is also momentarily threatened by cutbacks: 'Qu'ils crèvent les artistes', *Mouvement* 23 (2003); 'L'art d'en sortir', *Mouvement* 24 (2003).

56 | Claire Bishop, *Artificial Hells: Participatory Art and the Politics of Spectatorship* (London & New York: Verso, 2012), p. 15.

57 | Danielle Cliche, Ritva Mitchell, and Andreas Wiesand, in cooperation with Ilkka Heiskanen and Luca Dal Pozzolo (ERICarts Report to the NEF, Network of European Foundations for Innovative Action), *Creative Europe: On Governance and Management of Artistic Creativity in Europe* (Bonn: ARCult Media, 2002), p. 30: 'In comparison with the "typical" groups of professionals and other wage earners or entrepreneurs, professional artists may need – and deserve – special support systems and special legal provisions within the economic and social frameworks protecting their professional rights and guaranteeing social security to employees and entrepreneurs which reflect their "atypical" status. Related and crucial questions are: *how should these special support systems and legislative provisions be designed in a manner that is responsive and impartial to their varying sectoral (art form) needs, local and regional conditions? Could they be easily altered to respond to wider economic and social changes that effect the position and status of the artists/creators throughout Europe?*' http://www.creativeurope.info/, accessed 27.6.2013. For more about the critique of such creative management, see also Luc Boltanski and Eve Chiapello, *The New Spirit of Capitalism*, trans. Gregory Elliott (London & New York: Verso). (Original work *Le nouvel esprit du capitalisme* published 1999). See also Olaf Zimmermann and Gabriele Schulz with the

The sustainable promotion and development of open structures and autonomous landscapes for art and culture, even the opportunity for specialised co-determination and participation on the part of workers – essential for any democratic society – is being overridden, disappearing into a market-compatible, creative potpourri.

Bishop describes the ideology behind the 'discourse of creativity' as an extraction of art's genuine tasks, such as critique and the unfurling of ambivalences:

'What emerges here is a problematic blurring of art and creativity: two overlapping terms that not only have different demographic connotations but also distinct discourses concerning their complexity, instrumentalisation and accessibility. Through the discourse of creativity, the elitist activity of art is democratised, although today this leads to business rather than to Beuys. The dehierarchising rhetoric of artists whose projects seek to facilitate creativity ends up sounding identical to government cultural policy geared towards the twin mantras of social inclusion and creative cities. Yet artistic practice has an element of critical negation and an ability to sustain contradiction that cannot be reconciled with the quantifiable imperatives of positivist economics. Artists and works of art can operate in a space of antagonism or negation vis-à-vis society, a tension that the ideological discourse of creativity reduces to a unified context and instrumentalises for more efficacious profiteering.'[58]

Among further instances of critical and active advocacy for the improvement of the situation of the artist are the activities of the German Cultural Council, which find shape in numerous critical and politicised papers, in a bibliography devoted to the cultural labour market, and in the making of numerous recommendations for action.[59] It is also worth mentioning some initiatives and statements made by professional (development) associations, which are still relatively new to Germany, such as the Dachverband Tanz Deutschland – Ständige Konferenz Tanz (nationwide since 2006)[60], Zeitgenössischer Tanz

---

collaboration of Stefanie Ernst (eds.), *Zukunft Kulturwirtschaft: Zwischen Künstlertum und Kreativwirtschaft* [The future of cultural economy: Between being an artist and a creative economy] (Essen: Klartext Verlag, 2009).

58 | Bishop, *Artificial Hells*, p. 16.

59 | See http://www.kulturrat.de/text.php?rubrik=4, retrieved 4.8.2013.

60 | I would, however, like to critically remark that the Dachverband Tanz, which considers itself a non-profit organisation and resides, like the International Theatre Institute, in Kunstquartier Bethanien in Berlin-Kreuzberg, feels obliged first and foremost to a network of unions and institutions. According to bylaws, individuals such as dance makers are only to be admitted if they are 'personalities' who have rendered outstanding services to dance, which is decided by the governing body following written

Berlin (founded in 2000)[61], and last but not least the Koalition der Freien Szene (2012).[62]

At the time of this study's completion, the Berlin initiative Koalition der Freien Szene was engaged in vehement criticism of cultural politics in Berlin, fighting against 'structures that hinder rather than foster artistic labour and productivity'. Concretely, what the Koalition is referring to here is the 'concentration on institutional survival', which goes hand in hand with the gravely insufficient distribution of funding among independent agents, with the nonexistence of planning security and sustainability', and with a 'robber economy' based on the exploitation of artistic labour power and productivity'.[63]

European studies and documentary resources on dance, choreography and performance

Dance, choreography and performance-related reports, studies and documentary resources from neighbouring European countries will also be included in the scope of this survey, although the spectrum's sheer breadth presents difficulties for any systematic or complete overview.[64] My selection has emphasised recently published literature and studies on structural changes in the arts of dance and performance; furthermore, attention was given to those reports which were compiled with continuous determination in the long-term.

A very good summary of the current landscape of dance in Flanders, Belgium, can be found in the 2013 report *Performing Art Flanders: Perspective Dance*, published by VTI (Flemish Theatre Institute) and the Institute for

---

application and payment of contribution. See http://www.dachverband-tanz.de/pdf/Satzung_DTD_2010-03-06.pdf, retrieved 12.8.2013.

61 | For more on the Dachverband Zeitgenössischer Tanz Berlin – also located on Mariannenplatz in Berlin-Kreuzberg – and comparatively more open structures, see the Dachverband's German-English homepage, http://www.ztberlin.de/, retrieved 23.7.2013.

62 | The Koalition der Freien Szene campaigns in a pan-disciplinary capacity for a new cultural policy and criticises the 'blatant maldevelopment in Berlin's cultural budgeting'. It fights a policy that 'increasingly exposes the arts that exist within open structures to compulsory exploitation and accordingly reveals dynamics of suppression and displacement, thereby damaging the autonomy of the arts and marginalising the social meaning and societal significance of art'. See the Koalition's homepage, http://www.berlinvisit.org/, retrieved 22.8.2013, where the latest press releases and campaigns regarding the provocative 2014/2015 Berlin budget proposal are also published.

63 | See http://www.bbk-berlin.de/con/bbk/front_content.php?idart=2085&refId=199, retrieved 28.8.2013.

64 | See also the European resource Lab for Culture, a networking website that offers access to European funding opportunities: http://www.labforculture.org/, and the information portal on mobility *On the Move*, http://on-the-move.org/, retrieved 4.6.2013.

the Performing Arts in Flanders. It includes interviews, presents a selection of funded artists, lists educational and training opportunities, and profiles intermediary (in other words, dance-promoting) institutions.[65] The study by Joris Janssens and Dries Moreels, *Metamorphoses: Performing Arts in Flanders since 1993*, deals with qualitative changes in the field over the last twenty years.[66]

An important two-part publication for Serbia, the *Raster – Yearbook of the Independent Performing Arts Scene*, published by TKH/Walking Theory in 2008 and 2009 and funded by the Belgrade Cultural Secretariat, pays tribute to Serbia's independent performing arts scene, acknowledging it as a central protagonist in the Serbian cultural landscape, and employs critical thematic reports and an index of selected productions in order to talk about working conditions and problems the scene is facing now. It also contributes to the systematisation of data and the representation of changes in this field.[67]

Here I will also mention the international performing arts journals *Frakcija* and *Maska*, published in Zagreb and Ljubljana, respectively, both of which have been published bilingually for years (*Frakcija* in Croatian and English since 1996, *Maska* in Slovenian and English since 1990), offering a very good survey of international contemporary discussions and transformations in the fields of dance, theatre and performance.[68]

I would also like to mention – and highlight in particular – the attempt at an English-German online magazine titled *Corpusweb*, which grew into an interesting archive through years of individual thematic focuses and cultural-political critique as well as through a continual devotion to the publishing of discussions on individual performances, until cutbacks rendered it nonexistent.[69] Before it too perishes, the Spanish video and discussion platform *tea-tron*, which emerged from the *libre comunidad escénica* (a network-producing

---

65 | See VTi / Institute for the Performing Arts in Flanders, *Performing Arts Flanders: Perspective Danse* (Brussels: VTi, 2013). See also the VTi's online platform, http://vti.be/en, retrieved 31.7.2013.

66 | See Joris Janssens and Dries Moreels, *Metamorphoses: Performing Arts in Flanders since 1993* (Brussels: VTi, 2007), also available for free download at www.vti.be/metamorfose, retrieved 31.7.2013.

67 | See TKH (Walking Theory), *Raster 2008#1 and Raster 2009#2 – Yearbook of the Independent Performing Arts Scene*, Belgrade, 2008 and 2009, http://www.old.tkh-generator.net/en/Raster2008, retrieved 2.8.2013.

68 | See the websites of the performance journals *Frakcija*, http://www.cdu.hr/frakcija/shop/index.php, and *Maska*, http://www.maska.si/ index.php?id=161&L=1, both retrieved 2.3.2013.

69 | See Corpus's homepage, http://www.corpusweb.net/, retrieved 19.8.2013.

community), should be mentioned here, as should its dissemination of blogs, its performance announcements and its interviews and podcasts.[70]

In Austria, the most recent changes (Wiener Theaterreform 2003) are also relatively well documented.[71] In addition to insights into social circumstances, the most recent study on the life and labour of artists in Ireland also provides an in-depth delineation of working conditions and user-defined developmental needs.[72]

Dance Studies: On the situation of dancers and choreographers

Reading Andrew Hewitt's 2005 text on *Social Choreography*, which he defines as the performance of ideology in dance; or Laurence Louppe, who in the second volume of her *Poétique de la danse contemporaine* [The poetics of contemporary dance] addresses the production methods proper to 'new tendencies' in contemporary dance since the nineties; or Bojana Cvejić and Ana Vujanović's 2010 discussion of the exhausting effects of immaterial labour in the performing arts sector, it soon becomes obvious that the vast majority

---

[70] | See TEATRON's homepage, http://www.tea-tron.com/teatron/Portada.do, retrieved 19.8.2013.

[71] | See Christian Schober, Andrea Schmidt and Selma Sprajcer, *Tanz- und Theaterszene in Wien: Zahlen, Daten, Fakten unter besonderer Berücksichtigung der Effekte der Wiener Theaterreform 2003* [The dance and theatre scene in Vienna: Numbers, data and facts, with a special focus on the effects of the Viennese Theatre Reform of 2003], Commission given by the City of Vienna to the NPO Kompetenzzentrum der Wirtschaftsuniversität Wien (2012), http://epub.wu.ac.at/3634/1/bestandsaufnahme_der_tanz-_und_theater szene_in_wien.pdf, retrieved 3.7.2012. Sabine Kock, *Prekäre Freiheiten: Arbeit im freien Theaterbereich in Österreich*, [Precarious freedoms: Employment in the independent theatre field], Ed. IG Freie Theaterarbeit Wien (2009), http://culturebase.org/home/igft-ftp/Prekaere_Freiheiten_IGFT.pdf, retrieved 8.3.2013; Susanne Schelepa, Petra Wetzel and Gerhard Wohlfahrt, in cooperation with Anna Mostetschnig, *Zur sozialen Lage der Künstler und Künstlerinnen in Österreich* [On the social situation of artists in Austria] Eds. Bundesministerium für Unterricht, Kunst und Kultur & L&R Sozialforschung (2008), http://www.kunstkultur.bka.gv.at/Docs/kuku/medienpool/17401/studie_soz_lage_kuenstler_en.pdf, retrieved 3.3.2012. See also Karin Cerny, 'Die Evaluation der Theaterreform ist abgeschlossen' [The evaluation of the theatre reform is complete], *profile online*, 7.7.2012, http://www.profil.at/articles/1227/560/333790/die-evaluation-theaterreform, retrieved 7.3.2013; and http://www.corpusweb.net/die-evaluation.html, retrieved 7.3.2013.

[72] | See Clare McAndrew and Cathie McKimm, *The Living and Working Conditions of Artists in the Republic of Ireland and Northern Ireland*, commissioned by the Arts Council of Northern Ireland and the Arts Council An Chomhairle Ealaíon (2010), http://www.artscouncil.ie/uploadedFiles/LWCA_Study_-_Final_2010.pdf, retrieved 8.3.2013.

of German Dance Studies displays a lack of attention towards the social and economic reality of dance makers, choreographers and performers.[73]

We are aware of a strong French school of art sociology[74], but there is still no established dance sociology to speak of.[75] And yet a handful of recent approaches to research, often inspired by the choreographer Xavier Le Roy, are leading the way towards critical engagement with the concrete circumstances of artistic production while indicating the potential of artistic research as an autonomous, theory-generating alternative to what Husemann criticised in 2009 as a 'typically praxis-shunning academic discourse'.[76]

I would like to name three important symposiums here as examples selected from the meagre amount of positions in Dance Studies concerned with the conditions of production and, accordingly, with the precariousness of artists' circumstances. In 2010 the Cologne-based professor of Dance Studies Yvonne Hardt organised, in collaboration with Friederike Lampert, the symposium *Choreografie und Institution*, which discussed current challenges faced by choreography at the interface between numerous (dance)-market-defining institutional practices and explored possibilities for dance as an institution-critical praxis.[77] The 2012 anthology reader *Prekäre Exzellenz. Künste, Ökonomien*

---

73 | See Andrew Hewitt, *Social Choreography: Ideology as Performance in Dance and Everyday Movement* (Durham, N.C.: Duke University Press); Laurence Louppe, *Poétique de la danse contemporaine, la suite* [The poetics of dance, vol. 2] (Brussels: Contredanse, 2007), p. 8.; and Bojana Cvejić and Ana Vujanović, 'Exhausting Immaterial Labour' (editor's note), *TkH Journal of Performing Arts Theory* 17 (2010), p. 4: In a special issue of *TkH* co-published by the *Laboratoires d'Aubervilliers* titled 'Exhausting Immaterial Labour', Cvejić and Vujanović describe the exhaustion of the performing arts freelancer scene in the face of transformations in the working environment and formulate a necessity for the concretisation and precise observation of processes of change in artistic production conditions: 'What kinds of transformations of labour and production have the performing arts undergone in the past decade and how specifically different are they from other institutional practices or media?'

74 | See Laurent Thévenot, 'Die Person in ihrem vielfachen Engagiertsein' [The person in multilayered engagement], *Trivium* 5 (2010), http://trivium.revues.org/3573, retrieved 6.4.2013; and Laurent Thévenot and Luc Boltanski, 'Sociology of critical capacity', *European Journal of Social Theory* 2:3 (1999), pp. 359-377.

75 | For a German-language introduction to art sociology, see Dagmar Danko, *Kunstsoziologie* (Bielefeld: transcript, 2012).

76 | Pirkko Husemann, *Choreografie als kritische Praxis: Arbeitsweisen bei Le Roy und Thomas Lehmen* [Choreography as critical practice: The working methods of Xavier Le Roy and Thomas Lehmen] (Bielefeld: transcript, 2009), p. 246.

77 | Yvonne Hardt and Martin Stern (eds.), *Choreografie und Institution. Zeitgenössischer Tanz zwischen Ästhetik, Produktion und Vermittlung* [Choreography and institution:

und Politiken des Virtuosen, edited by Gabriele Brandstetter, Bettina Brandl-Risi and Kai van Eikels – as well as the conference of the same name held in June 2010 in conjunction with the research project *Die Szene des Virtuosen* (SFB *Kulturen des Performativen*) at Volksbühne Berlin – probes issues surrounding the nexus of precarious virtuosities and economised strategies of excellence.[78]

In critical reflexion on the last ten years in contemporary dance, Stefan Apostolou-Hölscher and Gerald Siegmund initiated the 2011 international symposium Dance, Politics and Co-Immunity in Giessen. The symposium brought international Dance Studies and political philosophy to the same table. The recently published reader pursuing Paolo Virno's performance artist as a Post-Fordist virtuoso[79] inquires into the ways in which dance and politics can intertwine and how those links can be examined, without simply re-enacting neoliberal job profiles:

'Dance and its artistic communities have indeed become a model for neo-liberal flexibility and self-exploitation. Given these circumstances, how can we think about the relation between dance and politics today without repeating neo-liberal demands and constraints? This volume focuses on recent developments in contemporary dance and the production of new spaces for collaboration and exchange.'[80]

It would therefore seem fitting to stress the pivotal significance of investigations into forms of artistic labour, negotiated a great many times in recent years under key concepts like 'immaterial labour' or 'working methods and forms of collaboration'.[81]

Contemporary dance between aesthetic, production and mediation] (Bielefeld: transcript, 2011). Meanwhile, it must be noted that the Zentrum für Zeitgenössischen Tanz, which was not reformed until 2009, is itself at the present under the acute threat of closing.

78 | See Gabriele Brandstetter, Bettina Brandl-Risi and Kai van Eikels (eds.), *Prekäre Exzellenz: Künste, Ökonomien und Politiken des Virtuosen* [Precarious excellence: The arts, economies and politics of the virtuosic] (Freiburg, Vienna & Berlin: Rombach, 2012).

79 | See Paolo Virno, *A Grammar of the Multitude: For an Analysis of Contemporary Forms of Life* (New York & Los Angeles: Semiotext(e) 2004), p. 52.

80 | Stefan Apostolou-Hölscher and Gerald Siegmund (eds.), *Communications: Dance, Politics and Co-Immunity*, vol. 1 of the series Thinking Resistances: Current Perspectives on Politics and Communities in the Arts (Berlin & Zürich: diaphanes, 2013), p. 8.

81 | See the recently published habilitation by Kai van Eikels: *Die Kunst des Kollektiven: Performance zwischen Theater, Politik und Sozio-Ökonomie* [The art of the collective: Performance between theatre, policy and socioeconomy] (Munich: Wilhelm Fink, 2013);

In addition to these rather isolated explorations of issues related to artists' production conditions, Dance Studies and the aesthetic theory of choreography provide us with newer examinations of artistic working modes, publics and concrete performance analyses, not to mention with a substantial immersion in aesthetic thematics and historical aspects of dance.[82]

However, particularly in reference to this study's guiding question, it must be clearly noted here that works such as Daniel Buren's trailblazing text 'On the function of the studio' are lacking in the dance field, works that more systematically explore the *interrelationship* between forms of production and distribution, between working methods and aesthetics as a co-effective relation.[83]

---

as well as Stefan Apostolou-Hölscher's recently published dissertation *Vermögende Körper: Zeitgenössischer Tanz zwischen Ästhetik und Biopolitik anhand von Parabeln zu Sasa Asentic, Jérôme Bel, Mette Ingvartsen/Jefta van Dinther, Ivana Müller* [Bodies of potential: Contemporary dance between aesthetics and biopolitics in parables on Sasa Asentic, Jérôme Bel, Mette Ingvartsen/Jefta van Dinther, Ivana Müller] (Berlin: bbooks, 2014); and idem., 'Let's work differently! 6 MONTHS 1 LOCATION and the resonances between production, labor, thought, dance, and community', in Joanna Szymajda (ed.), *Communitas and the Other: New Territories of Dance in Europe after 1989* (London & New York: Routledge, 2012). For more on the project *6 months 1 location*, see p. 114.

82 | For more on the question of publics, see Bojana Cvejić and Ana Vujanović, *Public Sphere by Performance* (Berlin: bbooks, 2012). For the question of work modes, see, for instance, Martina Ruhsam, *Kollaborative Praxis: Choreographie. Die Inszenierung und ihre Aufführung* [Collaborative practice: Choreography – the staging and its performance] (Vienna & Berlin: Turia & Kant, 2011); and Simon Hecquet and Sabine Prokhoris, *Fabriques de la Danse* (Paris: Presses Universitaires de France, 2007). For questions of perception, see Geisha Fontaine *Les danses du temps: Recherches sur la notion du temps en danse contemporaine* [Dances of time: Research on the notion of time in contemporary dance] (Pantin: Centre National de la Danse, 2004); Gerald Siegmund, *Abwesenheit: Eine performative Ästhetik des Tanzes* [Absence: A performative aesthetics of dance] (Bielefeld: transcript, 2006); André Lepecki, *Exhausting Dance: Performance and the Politics of Movement* (London & New York: Routledge, 2006); Susanne Föllmer, *Am Rand der Körper: Inventuren des Unabgeschlossenen im zeitgenössischen Tanz* [On the edge of the body: Inventories of the incomplete in contemporary dance] (Bielefeld: transcript, 2009); Gabriele Brandstetter, Franck Hofmann and Kirsten Maar (eds.), *Notationen und choreographisches Denken* [Notations and choreographic thought] (Freiburg, Berlin & Vienna: Rombach, 2010). On dance history, see Carrie Lambert-Beatty, *Being Watched: Yvonne Rainer and the 1960s* (Cambridge, Mass.: MIT Press, 2008).

83 | For more on the questions posed by this study, see Ch 1.2 Critique and formulation of the problem, esp. p. 89; and Daniel Buren, 'The Function of the studio',

Artistic discourse

An important change from the last ten to twenty years concerning literature on dance lies in the increasing number of published works by artists in the field of artistic research, or rather artistic discourse.[84]

Any adequate representation of this field would require a markedly broader frame; here too, unfortunately, I can only highlight an exemplary selection (rather than present a systematic survey) of some collectively written and published works with relevance for this study's area under examination.

One of these is the artist-initiated 2012 symposium *Choreography as Expanded Practice: Situation, Movement, Object*, which took place from 29–31.3.2012 at the Fundació Antoni Tàpies in Barcelona in conjunction with Xavier Le Roy's exhibition *"Retrospective"*.[85] Curated by Mårten Spångberg in collaboration with Le Roy and Cvejić, this conference undertook a revision of the concept 'choreography' against the backdrop of present-day contemporary artistic practices:

'In the last few years the term 'choreography' has been used in an ever-expanding sense, becoming synonymous with specific structures and strategies disconnected from subjectivist bodily expression, style and representation. Accordingly, the meaning of choreography has transformed from referring to a set of protocols or tools used in order to produce something predetermined, i.e. a dance, to an open cluster of tools that can be used as a generic capacity both for analysis and production.
Choreography is today emancipating itself from dance, engaging in a vibrant process of articulation. Choreographers are experimenting with new models of production, alternative formats, have enlarged the understanding of social choreography considerably

---

trans. Thomas Repensek, *October* (fall 1979), 51–58, first published in French in 1971. For a choreographic critique of such functions, see also p. 134.

84 | This can surely be attributed to new, digital tools and print-on-demand procedures, which have become significantly less expensive and more accessible. At the same time, one must note here that these publications unfortunately receive no funding from Germany, because the temporary publication funding instrument put in place by Tanzplan Deutschland, whose target group was dance makers and dance scholars, was unfortunately neither extended nor replaced by another funding programme.

85 | For more on the symposium *Choreography as Expanded Practice*, see the website http://choreographyasexpandedpractice.wordpress.com/, retrieved 28.8.2013. This event was supported by the Stockholm University of Dance and Circus, MACBA, Fundació Antoni Tàpies, Mercat de les Flors, the Swedish Research Council and the Swedish Arts Grants Committee. Participants were Bojana Cvejić, Dorothea von Hantelmann, Graham Harman, Ana Janevski, André Lepecki, Xavier Le Roy, Maria Lind, Isabel de Naverán, Luciana Parisi, Goran Sergej Pristas, Mårten Spångberg, Francisco Tirado und Christophe Wavelet.

and are mobilizing innovative frontiers in respect of [sic.] self-organizing, empowerment and autonomy. Simultaneously we have seen a number of exhibitions concerned with choreography often placed in a tension between movement, situation and objects. Choreography needs to redefine itself in order to include artists and others who use choreographic strategies without necessarily relating them to dance and, at the same time, it needs to remain inclusive of choreographers involved in practices such as engineering situations, organization, social choreography and movements as well as expanding towards cinematic strategies, documentary and documentation and are rethinking publication, exhibition, display, mediatization, production and post-production.'

Another – collectively edited – publication that should be mentioned is *The Swedish Dance History I-IV* (2009–2012), initiated by Mårten Spångberg and Inpex (International Performance Exchange), as well as the resulting internationally influential *Romanian Dance History I-V*, which is characterised in particular by its features on performative interventions.[86]

The Spanish-English journal *Cairon* edited by José Antonia Sánchez, includes contributions by artists as well as works that discuss the problems of artistic research.[87] The works in performance and book form by the international platform *Everybodys* have endeavoured since 2005 to further develop exchange, making it accessible both performatively and discursively.[88]

---

86 | Cf. Inpex, *The Swedish Dance History*, Vols. I–IV (Stockholm: Inpex), whose four issues (2009–2012) were realised in an honorary capacity by a wide rotating board (Inpex) and were often supported by the Swedish Arts Council (Konstnärsnämnden) and the Stockholm University of Dance. These volumes, sometimes in excess of a thousand pages, with black-and-white photos from the field and containing numerous texts by artists, have become a first-rate discursive European platform that is, remarkably, distributed free of charge, yet without receiving sufficient financial support on the international level. For more on *Romanian Dance History*, the 'scandal' of their disruption of the courtly programme at the ImpulsTanz Festival in Vienna, their receipt of the 2012 Berlin Art Prize, and their invitation to the Venice Biennale, see the homepage, http://rodancehistory.blogspot.de/, retrieved 24.8.2012. On the history of *Romanian Dance History*, see also Manuel Pelmus in the interview with Tom Engels that was conducted as part of this study, esp. MP36-37TE.

87 | For more on this, see the bilingual issue of the Dance Studies journal *CAIRON Revista de Estudios de Danza* 14, Ed. Victoria Pérez Royo and Cuqui Jerez, Special issue 'to be continued – 10 textos en cadena y unas páginas en blanco' (2012). For the topic of artistic practice as research, see also the issue edited by Victoria Pérez Royo and José Antonio Sánchez titled 'Practice and Research', *CAIRON* 13 (2010).

88 | Cf. the website and numerous performative dispositifs of the open international platform, founded in 2005, at http://everybodystoolbox.net/, as well as the Everybodys publications by Alice Chauchat and Mette Ingvartsen (eds.), *Everybodys Self Interviews*

This field is of course much more expansive than can be detailed here; it encompasses artists' monographs, discussions on work and working methods, and the increasingly significant resource sector comprising digital platforms, video databanks, social networks and archives.[89]

In general, it can be said that many artists in the field of dance, choreography and performance publicly articulate their individual practices, research orientations and specific working modes, despite the Europe-wide lack of funding for publications in the fields of dance, choreography and performance.[90]

Compared to the catalogue culture of the visual arts, for example, the quantity of artistic publications and research projects in dance and performance is minimal, which, in view of the transitory, evanescent nature of presentational forms of performance, ultimately entails a quite meagre state of affairs as far as documentation is concerned.

1.2 Critique and Formulation of the Problem

This concise insight into the situation of those working in professional independent dance, choreography and performance throws into sharp relief the especially precarious circumstances that span a broad institutional field of European conventions, national and federal legislation, cultural idiosyncrasies, cultural-political institutions, curators and coproducers, funding programmes, venues, scholarship, press and medial documentation, (continued) education, autodidactic learning and, not least, artists' respective scope of possibilities for organising themselves and their work legally (for example, as a small business, a nonprofit, freelance, or with characteristics particular to a jobholder's position).

Not only has the precarious situation of artists' lives been known for years; it has – were one, for instance, to evaluate income development in Germany since the 1970s – even worsened catastrophically in spite of any efforts to achieve the opposite.

(lulu: books on demand, 2008); idem. (Eds.), *Everybodys Group Self Interviews* (lulu: books on demand, 2009); idem. in cooperation with Zoë Poluch, Kim Hiorthøy, Nadja Hjorton and Stina Nyberg, *Everybodys Performance Scores* (lulu: books on demand, 2010); and Mette Ingvartsen, *6 months 1 location (6M1L)* (lulu: books on demand, 2009).

89 | Cf., for example, the videoportal and digital network, founded by Marlon Barrios Solana, at http://www.dance-tech.net, and the project PERFmts (Performance More Than Special) by Jan Ritsema and Valentina Desideri, cf. p. 142.

90 | One very positive exception was the publication funding provided by Tanzplan Deutschland – which, however, no longer exists. Yet it should be noted here that this funding structure too, despite its short life, was institutionalised, so that access to funding originally intended for authors shifted towards publishers.

Wolfgang Schneider, Professor of Cultural Politics in Hildesheim, Germany, pointedly describes the situation as disdainful of (human) rights:

'The conditions regarding income levels have dramatically deteriorated, and this has occurred even though public funding has increased many times over. Where is the more than 2.5 million euros that German taxpayers invest annually trickling down to when we talk about the preservation of a world cultural heritage site known as the theatre-scape? Why do we pay for a system that holds the social in such contempt, for a system shaped and characterised by self-exploitation, that is preached by proponents of the 'art of living' while its living conditions make it unworthy? A system where politicians schmooze about our society's creative potential on every soap box, but where the everyday actions they take seem to kick around artists' (human) rights?'[91]

Despite all constitutional anchorings, profound gender-inequality with regard to both income and the holding of leadership positions in dance and art has been a reality for years, especially in Germany.[92]

We could be incisive by this point: The facts are clear – but nothing has happened – for years.

In view of this disastrous socio-economic inventory and the very real failure of adequate protective measures safeguarding art and culture, measures that would *tangibly*, *structurally* and *sustainably* improve the situation of the artist in society while encouraging artists' development, fundamental questions arise in regard not only to the efficacy and will of policymakers and politicians, but also to the concomitant urgent need for inspection and review of competencies

---

91 | Wolfgang Schneider, 'Es geht um die Zukunft unserer Theaterlandschaft. Eine kulturpolitische Polemik aus gegebenem Anlass' [The future of our theatre-scape is at stake: A cultural-political polemics in light of recent events], in *Report Darstellende Künste*, pp. 21-25, here pp. 21-22.

92 | For more on gender discrimination in the arts in Germany, see Ulrike Knöfel, "Geschlechtertrennung" ['Gender segregation'], *Spiegel* 12 (2013), pp. 138-140, here p. 140: 'Ninety percent of the works purchased by German museums are produced by men, and ten percent by women – which is how Anne-Marie Bonnet, a professor of art history teaching in Bonn, appraises the situation. Bonnet is French. She says Germany is stuck in the fifties when it comes to gender issues. The majority of directorial posts are still occupied by men.' Cf. also Susanne Burri and Sacha Prechal, *EU Gender Equality Law*, Commissioned by the European Commission, Directorate-General for Justice, http://ec.europa.eu/justice/gender-equality/files/dgjustice_eugenderequalitylaw_update_2010_final24february2011_en.pdf, retrieved 8.8.2013; and Marie-Luise Angerer, Yvonne Hardt, and Anna-Carolin Weber, *Choreographie, Medien und Gender* [Choreography, media and gender] (Berlin & Zurich: diaphanes, 2013).

and responsibilities as well as administrative structures and structures for institutional action [Handlungsstrukturen].

This seems all the more advisable when even the legally adopted measures – such as the German Artists' Social Welfare Fund (KSK) or regarding much needed protections safeguarding artistic products from the planned free trade agreement with the USA – are, de facto, continuously called into question regarding lack of effectiveness in their concrete execution. Currently, such a situation is being faced in the case of the KSK. The German Federal Pension Fund's obligation to regularly review businesses for whom payment into the fund is potentially mandatory is simply not being carried out.[93] Far-reaching consequences are also, however, to be feared in the wake of the transatlantic free-trade agreement TTIP (Transatlantic Trade and Investment Partnership) between Europe and the USA, which now finds itself in the fifth round of behind-the-scenes talks, because it threatens to lift protections on artistic products and expose them to being declared commodities. (At the current moment, for instance, the topics up for renegotiation include cultural funding policy and fixed book prices.)

If elected national caucuses continue to be left out of what can be referred to as no small free-trade agreement, and if businesses are able to file lawsuits against governmental decisions in the future concerning endangerment of their own profit margin, then we have a situation, according to the Deutscher Kulturrat, where the 'foundations of democracy' are called into question.[94]

In what sort of regard should one hold a constitutional state when certain bills are passed without question while others die? How can it be that artists pay

---

93 | In an article on the current discussion, Klais Staeck, the re-elected president of the Akademie der Künste in Berlin, comments on this negligence: 'This throws the KSK out of balance and is a signal to all those who may wish to evade their obligation to pay into the insurance. People who needn't fear sanctions any longer, despite unlawful conduct, can even more easily opt out of solidarity with society.' Klaus Staeck, 'Neue Kämpfe um kulturelle Vielfalt' [New struggles for cultural diversity], *Berliner Zeitung*, 20.6.2013, p. 5.

94 | Olaf Zimmermann and Gabriele Schulz, 'Keine Liberalisierung um jeden Preis. TTIP – Ausnahme für den Kultursektor notwendig' [No to liberalisation at any cost: TTIP – needed exceptions for cultural sector], background report by the Deutscher Kulturrat (2014), http://kulturrat.de/pdf/2840.pdf, retrieved 21.5.2014. Cf. also the continuous and well researched coverage by Deutschlandradio Kultur found, for instance, in the article 'Freihandelsabkommen: Kultur als Ware? Was die TTIP Verhandlungen für die kulturelle Vielfalt bedeuten' [Culture as commodity? What the TTIP negotiations mean for cultural diversity], http://www.deutschlandradiokultur.de/freihandelsabkommen-kultur-als-ware.1895.de.html?dram:article_id=285820, retrieved 21.5.2014.

into an unemployment insurance and nevertheless have no claim to services?[95] How can it be that professional development and ways of securing one's existence in the field of independent dance, choreography and performance in Europe are so significantly reliant on the short-term legislative periods of national politics? And how can a state of affairs prevail where the development of the future of art and culture – as per TTIP – is determined by businesses rather than by democratic procedures?

At the aforementioned conference *Dance, Politics and Co-Immunity*, Randy Martin, Professor of Art and Public Policy and Associate Dean at the New York Tisch School of the Arts, summed up the current relationship between dance and politics as follows: 'Politics today suffers a crisis of evaluation.'[96]

Yet what could the reason be for policymakers' and politicians' lack of adequate compliance with their responsibilities and their mandate regarding art and culture? This question should in no way be misunderstood as a critique of legitimate democratic debates, and that these debates seldom prove to be the *ultima ratio* of a streamlining process is another issue. If democracy, however, is to be constantly used to justify the non-implementation of existing laws or binding conventions, then we must once again urgently take up the question posed by the Signataires du 20 août in their call for an evaluation of the modi operandi of institutions as well as all intermediary entities:

'Put differently, if it isn't the *creation process in contemporary dance* that's doing badly, if instead *contemporary dance's mode of functioning* is the thing that's ailing (a mode prevalent since the early 80s), then what actions should be taken in order to close the gap between the logic of institutional structures and artistic dynamics?'[97]

---

95 | Cf. Zimmermann, 'Arbeitsmarkt Kultur: Einführung und methodisches Vorgehen' [Cultural labour market: Introduction and methods of procedure], in *Arbeitsmarkt Kultur*, p. 13; and the Deutscher Kulturrat's statements 'Resolution: Rahmenfrist zum Bezug für Arbeitslosengeld I den Anforderungen des Kulturbereichs anpassen' [Resolution: Tailor the time frame for receiving Unemployment Benefit I to the cultural sector's requirements], 31.05.2006, http://kulturrat.de/detail.php?detail=780, retrieved 8.8.2012; and 'Resolution: Der Deutsche Kulturrat fordert die Bundesregierung zu einer schnellen Änderung der entsprechenden Regelungen des § 123 SGB III (Arbeitslosengeld I) auf' [Resolution: The Deutsche Kulturrat demands of the federal government swift changes to the corresponding provisions in § 123 SGB III (Unemployment Benefits I)], 21.12.2011, http://www.kulturrat.de/detail.php?detail=2186&rubrik=4, retrieved 8.8.2012.

96 | Randy Martin, 'Mobilizing Dance: Toward a Social Logic of the Derivative', in Stefan Apostolou-Hölscher and Gerald Siegmund (Eds.), *Dance, Politics and Co-Immunity* (Zurich & Berlin: diaphanes, 2013), pp. 209-25, here p. 209.

97 | Les Signataires du 20 août, 'Lettre ouverte à Dominique Wallon et aux danseurs contemporains', *Mouvement* 3-4 (1999-2000), p. 2.

At the moment, one can only surmise the outcome, and the question of whether a certain correlation indeed does exist here must also remain open, a correlation with that 'rigidity' particularly locatable in the cultural labour market. That same rigidity which the Deutscher Kulturrat has identified especially in public cultural institutions, and which stands in sharp contrast to the profile that is imposed upon artists: nonstop flexibility.[98]

In a similar vein, Therese Kaufmann and Gerald Raunig of the European Institute for Progressive Cultural Policies criticise European cultural policies' regressive tendency towards 'institutionalisation', or towards the predominant support of institutions (versus independent artists), and they counterpose to this tendency their own attempt at devising European cultural policies with concrete perspectives for the future:

'But while the aforementioned forms of concrete cultural initiatives are based on principles of temporality and change, the corresponding cultural policies seem to be concentrating on the opposite, namely, by tending, regressively, to support institutions and institutionalise initiatives, to bring movement to a standstill. Even though 1968 was often mystified as a momentous shift in (cultural) politics, the changes that have occur-

---

98 | Gabriele Schulz and Olaf Zimmermann, 'Arbeitsmarkt Kultur: Hoffnungsträger oder Abstellgleis – Bewertung und Schlussfolgerungen' [Cultural labour market: Bearer of hope or back burner? – evaluation and argumentation], in Hufnagel, Schulz and Zimmermann, *Arbeitsmarkt Kultur*, p. 330: 'The cultural labour market is partially rigid – a collective ageing among personnel is the result: in some subareas of the cultural labour market, the numbers of young as opposed to old participants are diverging. The portion of workers over fifty years of age is rising. [...] The number of employees from younger-aged cohorts is sinking proportionately. This immediately suggests the supposition that only a small amount of hiring has been done in recent years. As a result, a staff of personnel ages as one. In addition to the rigidification of the labour market in these fields, another outcome results – hardly any transfer of know-how from older and experienced colleagues to later generations of decision makers is possible. At the same time, the institutions lack the proverbial 'fresh air' that young employees bring. In the long run, this circumstance starts to detract from an institution's future viability. This development is especially to be observed in the public cultural sector. The slashing of posts has made itself felt for some time, as has the failure to fill posts anew when employees vacate them. Since many employees will reach retirement age during the next decade and consequently vacate their posts, the crucial test regarding how institutions will handle this change in generation is already underway. In this context, it must also become apparent whether or not sufficiently trained professionals are standing, so to speak, in the 'second row', professionals who are well suited and willing to assume a leadership position. It is possible that the cultural labour market could, despite a brisk influx of university students, see a shortage of qualified personnel, at least in some regions.'

red since then have been of a mere cosmetic nature, as far as public support of cultural nonprofit organisations as opposed to big public institutions is concerned.'[99]

The study before you aims to take steps using the knowledge gained from this debacle of implementation whilst making no further attempt to refresh the evidence in a case of recognized facts. It does not aim to be a follow-up corrective for flawed policies only to execute a task by raising objections and measuring deficits that should be executed by policymakers themselves, and only to remain unheard even in this capacity.

Instead, its goal is to explore artistic practices in the field of dance and choreography that have, despite such a flagrant situation, espoused a content-oriented continued development of the field. These explorations shall include the observation of structural and aesthetic changes, the illustration of contexts and networks, and a deeper exploration of the relational parameters constituting meaningful action in the professional field of dance and choreography.

In the process, this study intends to discursively blaze a trail for a constructive, artist-oriented professional development that is able to participatively co-create its professional field. To this end, an attempt will also be made to locate and watch present-day, concrete problems that are occurring in connection with certain interdependencies specific to artistic professions, and to recognize these problems as challenges.[100]

Before I spell out this particular horizon of research more precisely, I should, with an eye towards the material available to me, first explain the background for my selection of this distinct field, and also illustrate what demarcates this study.

At the beginning of this chapter, I named the relations of tension within which artists move, but what really strikes the eye here are the complex diversity and varying qualities and forms of relation.

This complexity of the fabric of relations within which dance takes place is in no way sufficiently comprehended (e.g., by means of socioeconomic key data and parameters regarding labour law or business law) in its concretisation and – I explicitly underline this – in its effect of concrete, qualitative change for those who participate in it.

---

99 | Therese Kaufmann and Gerald Raunig, *Anticipating European Cultural Policies, Europäische Kulturpolitiken vorausdenken*, commissioned by the European Institute for Progressive Cultural Policies (Vienna: eipcp, 2003), p. 75. For more on the European Institute for Progressive Cultural Policies, see the institute's homepage, http://eipcp.net, retrieved 13.8.2013.

100 | On the concrete approach of this study, cf. Chapter 1.4 On the method of this study', pp. 98-101.

Even though the gathering of socioeconomic data is necessary, it can only be *one component* of an analysis of the current state of labour. The sketching out of determining factors is also imperative. But determining factors shouldn't be mistaken for production conditions, and production conditions aren't congruent with the current labour reality, not to mention with the continued development of the profession.

If there is a (surely incomplete) and yet still partially available body of data on the cultural sector's social and economic situation, then what is it (apart from numerous aesthetic performance analyses) that is so urgently needed?

A short and schematic look at the methodical procedure known as 'static' data collection, or *Augenblicksentnahme*, which is used across a range of socioeconomic analyses, could be revealing: according to definition, practitioners of *Augenblicksentnahme* perform isolated, blink-of-an-eye extractions of data about two different points in time and dismiss (or at least block out) both the period of time lying between those two points and the multifarious relationships between individual parameters that exist therein (and more often therein than thereout); and this ignoring of the in-between is done with the intention of being able to focus more precisely on the relationship between both points in time. In this sense, such 'static' collection of data insufficiently accounts for qualitative relationships between parameters, the emergence of relationships, and the practices that lead to these relationships and parameters.[101] This methodology of sporadic data collection focalizes and pins down a diversity of relationships while reducing the field to search criteria.

---

101 | In my dissertation, I discussed, by reference to the 'static' analysis of movement, the comprehensive critique of the methodology known as *Augenblicksentnahme* (literally 'blink-of-an-eye sampling') and this critique's philosophical background in, for example, Deleuze and Guattari's philosophy and Bergson's concept of duration (itself a critique of the 'méthode cinématographique'). Cf. Sabisch, *Choreographing Relations: Practical Philosophy and Contemporary Choreography in the works of Antonia Baehr, Gilles Deleuze, Juan Domínguez, Félix Guattari, Xavier Le Roy and Eszter Salamon* (Munich: epodium, 2011), p. 184 et al. The critique operates according to the claim that qualitative change cannot be adequately grasped in this way. Brian Massumi has also criticised this subtraction of qualitative change as, in his case, the logical result of a positional analysis, advancing his arguments in the context of the representation of bodily movement: 'The very notion of movement as qualitative transformation is lacking. There is "displacement," but no transformation; it is as if the body simply leaps from one definition to the next. Since the positional model's definitional framework is punctual, it simply can't attribute a reality to the interval, whose crossing is a continuity (or nothing).' Brian Massumi, *Parables for the Virtual: Movement, Affect, Sensation* (Durham, N.C.: Duke University Press, 2002), pp. 3–4.

This means newly appearing circumstances cannot be as adequately detected as given kinds of regularly retrieved search data (like marital status, income, employment situation, etc.). That being said, what is needed – if we're talking about conducting adequate qualitative inquiry into the empirical reality of artists, in parallel, of course, to the regular monitoring of selected search criteria – is an equally regular, continuous examination of new aspects and parameters: one that is geared to the requisites of artistic production. A mere continuation of the customary search criteria would lead to distortions in the depiction of socioeconomic situations and in the focus of the research itself.

One example of this type of distortion by means of adhesion to search criteria can be sketched out here under the keyword 'mobility': in recent years, numerous studies have tried to explore international mobility, particularly in the performing arts sector; to name obstacles and problems; and thus to promote this mobility.[102] This extremely meritorious undertaking, however, transformed into the often unquestioned equating of mobility with a positive value in itself, a value that nowadays turns in part against those agents who were oftentimes pioneers of international professional mobility and a lived Europe.

This turning against happens at precisely the same instant when protagonists are no longer able to co-define and co-steer such developments, and when mobility in a certain sense becomes a dictate: it can be assumed that almost every funded project includes travel as a production condition, whether due to the location of coproducing theatres or to residencies; and what was once a *means* of artistic exploration and cooperation has nowadays become an unavoidable *condition* for involvement in the métier. In turn, this ultra-mobile *workforce* existence naturally affects artists' social, economic and political situation.

Only the evaluation of affected persons' views could prevent future studies from limiting their inquiry in a way that promotes mobility and could prompt them to inquire as well into the extent to which working in a location of one's choice, or in one's city of residence, is even possible at all (which is a situation that produces bizarre kinds of spin-off, such as the fact that it might prove much cheaper and less time-consuming to rehearse in one's town of residence). Such an evaluation would require appropriate instruments that would, firstly, allow for the introduction of a principle of proportionality, secondly, allow

---

102 | Cf. the study by Richard Polacek, *Study on Impediments to Mobility in the EU Live Performance Sector and on Possible Solutions*, published by PEARLE, Ed. Performing Arts Employers Association League Europe (Brussels: Finnish Theatre Information Centre Mobile Home, 2007); and the study by Theatre Info Finland, *Mobility Infopoint Mapping in Finland*, Helsinki (2011), http://on-the-move.org/files/Mobility_Infopoint_Mapping_Finland_lopullinen.pdf, retrieved 8.3.2013.

scientific scrutiny of professional forced migration, thirdly, enable socially and economically conscious pro-worker adjustments to migrational structures and, fourthly, open those structures to redefinition by those who participate in them.

In addition to its reductiveness – which includes the reduction of complex relational conditions to still images and the hardening of search criteria – one can make out the 'static' method's immanent narrowness, which constitutes the basis for much empirical data collection and statistical procedure, and which is also reflected in the kind of available data on artists' socioeconomic situations. This isn't meant as an across-the-board roast of one method, but rather as a simple fact, namely, that every method holds its own perspective and thereby transports specific limits as well.[103] Expressed differently, the merit of the 'static' method lies in its ability to make developments in measurable and quantifiable parameters like income representable.

Finding ourselves before this methodological background, it would seem the appropriate moment to establish that data collection regarding relational fabrics in the professional field of dance, choreography and performance has heretofore only insufficiently reflected co-relational lines of connection and qualitative changes of *complex* relationships. Moreover, the collected data has not, as per its collection method, helped to uncover any previously unknown data arrays.

Qualitative inspection of the research quite concretely reveals that the available data, even when correlating individual datasets, gives hardly any indication of co-dependencies, affective relations or power balances, not to mention of decision-making processes or organisational structures. Even if this surely cannot be traced to the 'static method' alone, one must still bear in mind that the guarantee of freedom of expression must also always include the freedom to organise this expression. The real problems become discernible precisely in organisational processes and decision-making processes, as Félix Guattari established long before the recent upswing of organisation theories.[104]

---

103 | See also Chapter 1.3 Why practices? On methods, p. 90.

104 | Félix Guattari, 'On Capitalism and Desire', in Gilles Deleuze, *Desert Islands and Other Texts, 1953–1974*, Ed. David Lapoujade, trans. Michael Taormina (Los Angeles & New York: Semiotext(e), 2004), p. 264: 'The same goes for traditional political structures. It's always the same old trick: a big ideological debate in the general assembly, and the questions of organization are reserved for special committees. These look secondary, having been determined by political options. Whereas, in fact, the real problems are precisely the problems of organization, never made explicit or rationalized, but recast after the fact in ideological terms. The real divisions emerge in organization: a particular way of treating desire and power, investments, group-Oedipuses, group-super-egos, phenomena of perversion...' On institutional analysis and critique in 1970s France, see also Félix Guattari, *L'intervention institutionnelle* [Institutional intervention] (Paris:

From a scientific standpoint, this omission of the temporal in-between is astonishing, especially regarding the already corroborated socioeconomic grievances and (cultural-)political implementation setbacks. It is, at the very least, in need of explanation. But from the perspective of a democratic society, it raises more wide-ranging questions.

The foremost question is 'what kind of shape is democracy in within the professional field of dance?' If we plug into this central question, the following issues are brought into the arena: What possibilities for participation exist for professional dancers who wish to constructively co-create and co-influence ongoing decision-making processes? What degree of responsiveness exists between freelancers and institutional practices? What interdependencies, what hierarchies exist in the field? How are they organised? To what competencies, to what level of transparency are they tied? What forms of critique are possible? What does the autonomy of dance look like *de facto*? Who are the interlocutors to whom one can submit suggestions regarding content and structure?

In a colloquium conducted in Hamburg as part of this study, Amelie Deuflhard, artistic director at Kampnagel Hamburg and prior to that director of the Sophiensaele in Berlin, positioned herself clearly regarding the question of structural changes in the field by distinguishing a pronounced hierarchisation in comparison to the nineties, which she illustrated by explaining (among other things) how artists submitting applications for project funding are required to provide written confirmation from theatres who pledge to support, show and/or coproduce the project, and how curatorial concepts have increasingly been exercising content-related influence on art.[105] Whereas the theatre was once tasked with caring for individual projects, today the theatres are the ones who not only decide on the selection of projects for a given season, but who also preside over the general allocation of production means.

The growth of these dependencies is treated by the Swedish choreographer Mårten Spångberg in his book *Spangbergianism* (which first appeared as a blog), particularly when he describes the relationship between artists and curators:

Payot, 1980); and idem., *Psychotherapie, Politik und die Aufgaben der institutionellen Analyse* [Psychotherapy, politics and the tasks of institutional analysis] (Frankfurt am Main: Suhrkamp, 1976). For an historical overview of institutional analysis, see Marta Malo de Molina, 'Common Notions, Part 2: Institutional Analysis, Participatory Action-Research, Militant Research', Trans. M. Casas-Cortés & S. Cobarrubias (2004), http://eipcp.net/transversal/0707/malo/de, retrieved 3.2.2011; and Stefan Nowotny and Gerald Raunig, *Instituierende Praxen: Bruchlinien der Institutionskritik* [Instituting practices: Faultlines in institutional critique] (Vienna: Turia & Kant, 2008).

105 | 27.1.2012, *Kampnagel*, Hamburg.

'A dance programmer comes up to me and asks: 'So what do you think about the program?' What can I say? We know that under the regime we live today, it is unthinkable to object. The first rule of the contemporary artist: Don't ever dispute, never get angry, avoid conflict at any price. If I'm in the program, it is obviously perfect and if I'm not, any objection will be understood as narrow-minded or greedy. Metaphorically my answer is always: – 'I'm available' – 'Whatever you propose, I'm in'.'[106]

Spångberg goes on to explain that the 'restrictive budget' argument, which programmers in the dance field usually employ to redirect critics of their programmes towards the extenuating circumstances, doesn't apply equally to artists:

'No way, the artistic act is supposed to exist independently of budgets and if there are any cuts or missing funding, the artist is supposed to come up with some brilliant idea; change the format, fire the producer, save money on costumes [...], hire faster dancers, anything – anything – [...]. But who would expect a programmer to have a brilliant or even acceptable idea: to sack the assistant, change the format, skip the big companies, change the marketing strategy. Or why not double as a ticket girl, work in the bar, or... Hey give up a part of his salary? Programmers are victims of external circumstances, whereas artists only have themselves to blame.'[107]

Besides dance makers' one-sided dependencies on venues, artistic directors and the awarding of guest performance contracts in Germany, one should also mention that the academicisation of art, described by Didier Lesage as a result of the 1999 Bologna Accord, should be more precisely evaluated. Lesage describes this development as the 'obligation to become academic':

'Arts academies were being requested neither to engage in critical self-analysis nor to recall the highlights of their histories. The academies were instead required to listen to their big other, the universities, who in some countries and regions in Europe proposed to tell academies how to become academic. Universities which had no experience of teaching practice-based arts in the many decades or even centuries of their venerable existence supposed that they could assess whether art academies had reached an acceptable academic level in teaching art. Though the universities stressed that the evaluation of teaching and research can only qualify as academic if it is undertaken by peers, they failed to see that university academics without any experience of practice-based arts education or artistic research could not properly be considered as 'peers' of academies on their own terms. The universities, though unqualified as peers, were not about to disqualify themselves as the proper institutions to evaluate the academization

---

106 | Mårten Spångberg, *Spangbergianism* (Gargzdai: Print-It, 2011), p. 21.
107 | Ibid., pp. 22-23.

of academies. Indeed, universities were very happy to be able to evaluate academies, and to play a decisive role in the procedural machine which in time would accredit programmes at academies as being academic. In some countries, universities also took it upon themselves to deliver the newly created doctoral degree in the arts.'[108]

The conditions and results of further content-based development in the performing arts would also have to be examined here, especially in the wake of the implementation of the Bologna Process.

According to Marijke Hoogenboom from the Amsterdam School of the Arts, herein can be detected a major setback for contemporary content-based development, leading to the suppression of innovative art forms rather than to the incentivisation of structural support:

'Beyond Bologna, these research groups have been a response to a worrying development at art schools and universities of applied sciences, which are increasingly defining themselves according to the current labour market and dedicating too much of their application-oriented teaching to concrete vocational training. In theatre, for example, this means that courses in stage direction, acting, dance or dramaturgy become stuck in traditional occupational images, barely contributing to contemporary developments, let alone provoking innovative art forms.'[109]

Looking at these fundamental, still scientifically unresearched, content-based restructurings of the professional field of dance and performance art, as well as at the dependencies expressed therein, it becomes clear that a more comprehensive evaluation is needed – one that, instead of merely examining market viability and the value-added chain of a 'creative' Europe, also examines organisational structures and decision-making structures in all their (inter)dependencies, permeable freedoms and participatory forms.[110] To date, I believe one can say that not a single study looking more systematically in this direction exists in the dance field.

In an article published by the Austrian Cultural Council (Österreichischer Kulturrat), Therese Kaufmann underlines the urgency of the question of democracy, codetermination and participation:

---

108 | Didier Lesage, 'PaR in Continental Europe: A Site of Many Contests', in Robin Nelson (Ed.), *Practice as Research in The Arts: Principles, Protocols, Pedagogies, Resistances* (Houndsmill Basingstoke: Palgrave Macmillan, 2013), pp. 142-51, here pp. 142-143.
109 | Marijke Hoogenboom, 'If artistic research is the answer, what is the question?', in *CAIRON, Revista de Estudios de Danza* 13, pp. 115-124, here p. 117.
110 | On the critique of discourses on creativity, see p. 65.

'The central – hardly addressed – question in this context concerns the relation between culture and democracy, or more concretely, between cultural policy and democratic policy in the EU. What role befits the cultural field as Europe undergoes democratisation? How can we develop strategies against the current tendency to turn cultural policies exclusively into venues for neoliberal governmentality where hippy-ish terms like 'intercultural competence' denote nothing more than business tools on the international market or contemporary mechanisms of control and regulation? What can be undertaken against the reduction of the cultural sector to an experiment-field for the 'creative competitiveness' of post-industrial workforces where artists serve as models for the flexible, self-reliant, independent, project-oriented and trend-setting subject of the New Economy?'[111]

In an interview on his book *Moments politiques*, Jacques Rancière criticises the transformation of representative institutions into complacent agents of free market logic, which, according to Rancière, opens up a double option regarding democracy: either one declares democracy to be a failed mirage, or else it must be exercised anew with another kind of participation in decision-making processes:

'In Europe we have got used to identifying democracy with the double system of representative institutions and those of the free market. Today this idyll is a thing of the past: the free market can be seen increasingly as a force of constriction that transforms representative institutions into simple agents of its will and reduces the freedom of choice of citizens to variations of the same fundamental logic. In this situation, either we denounce the very idea of democracy as an illusion, or we rethink completely what democracy, in the strong sense of the word, means. Democracy is not, to begin with, a form of State. It is, in the first place, the reality of the power of the people that can never coincide with the form of a State. There will always be tension between democracy as the exercise of a shared power of thinking and acting, and the State, whose very principle is to appropriate this power. Obviously states justify this appropriation by citing the complexity of the problems, the need to the long term, etc. But in truth, politicians are a lot more subjected to the present. To recover the values of democracy is, in first place, to reaffirm the existence of a capacity to judge and decide, which is that of everyone, against this monopolisation. It is also to reaffirm the necessity that this capacity be exercised through its own institutions, different from those of the State. The first democratic virtue is the virtue of confidence in the capacity of anyone.'[112]

---

111 | Therese Kaufmann, 'Strategies of (Self-)Empowerment and Spaces of Resistance' (2006), http://eipcp.net/policies/dpie/kaufmann2/en, retrieved 10.8.2013.
112 | Cf. interview by Paula Corrotto with Jacques Rancière on the occasion of the publishing of his book *Moments politiques: Interventions 1977–2009* (Paris: Editions La Fabrique, 2009): 'Democracy is not, to begin with, a form of state', Trans. democracities (2013),

The overall evaluation of the dance field that the existing research currently lacks, and that is so urgently needed, requires an all-encompassing and consistent empirical investigation into European actualities and practices, and it also necessitates focussed examinations (most likely several) on real interdependencies, uni- and multilateral relations and possibilities not only for codetermination, but also for artistically autonomous innovation in dance and performance art.

Against this background, this study can only be a first approach to this desiderat, an approach that characterises the diverse and dynamic interplay between interactions in their complexity as other than purely 'static', and that also expands the socioeconomic search field to include questions of art and the perception of art, artistic working modes and dispositifs, aesthetics and operative relations.[113]

A first step, therefore, is to investigate realities of artistic work. I will pursue the hypothesis that a complex interlinkage between artistic production, artistic working modes and individual modes of perception (aesthetics in the sense of *aisthesis*) exists in artistic labour in dance, choreography and performance, an interlinkage that has heretofore not been systematically explored. This investigation will attempt to make the socioeconomic parameters determining the artist's situation become readable as important additional stones that must be laid in the path towards an account of the primary factor: production conditions. But these parameters are inextricably related to their respective working modes as well as to the intricacy of sensible processes of perception.

In an article on the publication of the *Everybodys* self-interview book, Martina Ruhsam points to this inextricable interconnection, for which she justifiably looks to the ground-breaking significance of Xavier Le Roy:

'The making visible of production conditions and processes in choreographies themselves has become a big issue since performance as an – audience-based, exhibited – artistic end product lost the status of the extra-contextual and the closed, and since it was, as a result, recognised as a staging and as the conditions of a specific working process that leads to certain results while excluding others. The working process seems to be at least as interesting as the result it gives rise to. The widest possible variety of

---

http://democracities.com/2013/08/18/jacques-ranciere-interview-democracy-is-not-to-begin-with-a-form-of-state/, retrieved 23.7.2013. Originally published 2012: 'Hablar de crisis de la sociedad es culpar a sus víctimas', *Publico.es*. (2013), http://www.publico.es/culturas/416926/hablar-de-crisis-de-la-sociedad-es-culpar-a-sus-victimas, retrieved 23.7.2013.

113 | Cf. Claire Bishop's study, which made similar findings: *Artificial Hells*, p. 16. See also Bishop's critique of the instrumentalisation of art as 'social engineering' in British New Labour politics.

methods with which production conditions and processes can be displayed in choreographies have been tried out. To mention an artist who has dedicated many projects to this question, Xavier Le Roy's self-interview (which was originally geared to reflection on E.X.T.E.N.S.I.O.N.S, a research project he initiated; and which could almost be described in today's performance scene as classical), allowed a sort of auto-questioning of self-designed practices to become operative within choreographic processes.'[114]

More precise exploration of this context would require an aesthetic discourse that is capable of understanding and depicting the singularities of the artistic practices of dance, choreography and performance in their sense-building qualities as well as in their contexts, which themselves inevitably exceed the aesthetic; in their methodological, organisational and technical relations; in their historical traditions, and in their political and social dimensions.

The ground being built here should provide a beginning for a – necessarily incomplete – topology of international artistic practices with its gaze firmly fastened onto the concrete *doings* of artists who in recent years have backed the development of the professional field of dance, performance and choreography.

In contrast to a deficiency-seeking inventory of what couldn't be implemented in (cultural) policy and to the numerous unwritten track records in dance history, the motif of this investigation thus consists in demonstrating what has actually come into existence regarding international, contemporary and experimental artistic works and research over the last twenty years.[115] A more exact description, including deliberations on the method and on the concrete field of my investigation, will be set forth in the next chapter.

But to begin with, allow me to concretize the question: how does the relational interplay between artistic production (and distribution), working

---

114 | Martina Ruhsam, 'Everybodys Selbstinterviews: Ein Buch als nutzerfreundliche Kartografie choreographischer Gegenwartspraktiken' [Everybodys Self Interviews: A book as a user-friendly cartography of contemporary practices], *Corpus* (28.12.2009), http://www.corpusweb.net/everybodys-selbstinterviews-4.html, accessed 6.7.2013. See also Everybodys Publications by Alice Chauchat and Mette Ingvartsen (Eds.), *Everybodys Self-Interviews* (lulu: books on demand, 2009).

115 | Due to the much-discussed ephemeral or immaterial nature of dance and choreography work on the one hand and the increasingly short lives of projects and structures on the other, it should be noted here that no exhaustive history of dance can be written through retrospective document analysis alone. Instead, such a history must begin by documenting present-day currents. Today it is possible to state that a divergence in content between artistic documentation and a scientifically composed dance history does exist, a divergence in which the latter risks leaving contemporary changes to be forgotten by overlooking them.

modes and aesthetics within independent, international, experimental and contemporary dance, choreography and performance operate?

Other questions are implicit: What affective relations and interdependencies constitute artistic labour? Which ones allow the development of artistic work? What decision-making structures, responsibilities and possibilities for codetermination exist in the field? What conflicts and concerns? What needs? Is there a responsiveness among individual institutional work practices? How is artistic labour actually organised, and in what relation do these organisational forms stand with institutional structures? Can the existing institutional funding instruments support innovative impulses from dance and performance art, and can they do it promptly, flexibly and unbureaucratically? What meaning do continuity, structure and development hold for contemporary artistic creation processes? How can they be effectively produced, even in view of the increasing exploitation that not only artistic practices are facing? To what extent is critique possible in all levels of decision-making processes? How can concerns and concrete problem areas be located *by artists*?

The aim is therefore to present a qualitative exploration of sense-building practices that enables the relational and dynamic observation of complexity without separating perceptive processes from actions and their surroundings, and without reducing affective relations to cause-and-effect snapshots and thereby advance the instrumentalisation of art.

1.3 Why Practices? On Methods

Aiming the focus of observation at practices is, with regard to method, an urgently advisable, critical corrective to the static method, as it allows us first and foremost to comprehend the concrete dynamics of kinds of doing in their complexity.

Such a practice-oriented method interrogates existing situations as to their *madeness* (as opposed to default, or natural, existence) and thereby as to their changeability. The place where we should analyse those practices that lead to the everyday, repeated maintenance and reproduction of this state of affairs lies exactly where certain things – such as socioeconomic conditions or the partly inadequate adoption of categories by socioempirical data collection – seem unchangeable.

Precisely this impetus for critical reflection also confirms Robert Schmidt's 2012 book *Soziologie der Praktiken*, which, inspired by Bourdieu, Goffmann and Kant, among others, emphasizes the mutual entanglement of theory and empiricism, which has since been nourished by a variety of approaches:

'Practice sociologies claim a unique form of theory. It should be built to meet the empirical with unsureness, irritation and self-revision. This type of theory tries to make sure

For a Topology of Practices   91

that theoretical suppositions (not least those that are included in the collection of data and, consequently, those that determine what at all can even appear as data) are not treated, by means of empiricism, as if they were above question.'[116]

When we examine the institutional practices of an array of *agencies* from the dance and performance field, such a practice-theoretical background proves long overdue, a background that would construct transparent decisions when it comes to the distribution of means, representation, and the appointing of public offices, and that would be capable of making processes of institutionalisation, deficient (or lacking) administration, bureaucratisation, academicisation and gender discrimination visible in the first place. Such an undertaking, however, would vastly exceed the boundaries of the present study.

This study concentrates on artistic practices in the field of dance, choreography and the performing arts in order to lend a counterweight to the imbalance in research on the work reality of dance makers, and in order to push sense-building, complex and dynamic interlinkages between artistic production, work modes, and aesthetics farther into the centre of focus.

In the style of a succinct resume, I shall here provide an overview of my points of access to artistic practices, to practice-oriented and art-oriented theory construction, and to its relevance for a contemporary and critical social analysis, all of which I have discussed more comprehensively as part of my international teaching activities, as part of the *Practice Symposium* (Stockholm, 2012), which I initiated and co-curated, and as part of my current lecture series, *Art and Practical Philosophy*.[117]

---

116 | Robert Schmidt, *Soziologie der Praktiken: Konzeptionelle Studien und empirische Analysen* [Sociology of practices: Conceptual studies and empirical analyses] (Berlin: Suhrkamp, 2012), p. 31. Cf. also Pierre Bourdieu, *Outline of a Theory of Practice* (Cambridge: Cambridge University Press 1977); and idem., *Practical Reason: On the Theory of Action*, Trans. Randal Johnson (Palo Alto, Calif.: Stanford University Press, 1998); Erving Goffman, *Relations in Public: Microstudies of the Public Order* (New York: Basic Books, 1971); and Immanuel Kant, *Critique of Practical Reason* (Cambridge: Cambridge University Press, 1997). Noteworthy among the various approaches existing today are, according to Schmidt, the synthesis-achieving special research project (SFB) named *Cultures of the Performative* at the Freie Universität Berlin, and the 'sub'-project on the performance of society in games, directed by Gunter Gebauer. See Schmidt, *Soziologie der Praktiken*, p. 274.

117 | See the *Practice Symposium*, Stockholm 29-30.9.2012, which I carried out together with Stina Nyberg (Sweden), Zoë Poluch (Canada) and Uri Turkenich (Israel), thanks to the invitation given me by the International Dance Programme of the Swedish Arts Grants Committee (Konstnärsnämnden), or more specifically, from Anna

If the performative turn already suggested a shift in the analysis towards a temporalisation, which according to John Langshaw Austin also brings the conventions of the performative (speech) act onto the scene, then Judith Butler has been able, using the example of gender and materiality, to show how essentialised societal circumstances constitute and perpetuate themselves through performative repetition.[118] However, beyond the simple, ritualised or routine repetition of discursive ascriptions, the power of performative reiteration lies not only in the perpetuation of given circumstances; performative reiteration *generates* reality. Dorothea von Hantelmann stresses this fact in her book *How to Do Things With Art* in order to show, via examples from artworks by Tino Sehgal and James Coleman, the extent to which the artistic avant-garde's classical break with conventions was transformed into the performative utilisation of the same conventions.[119]

If the performative turn directs attention towards the effective carrying out of societal conventions and makes these conventions once again available to society through (re)stagings, then the practice turn, in which Marx's concept of practice and Hannah Arendt's differentiation between labour, work and action resonates, amplifies the focus on concrete relational, material, and societally situated practices through which know-how and practical ability (implicit knowledge) are transferred and shared.[120]

Efraimsson. For more on my lecture series, see Petra Sabisch, 'What Can Practice Mean Today?', lecture 2 in the series 'Art as Practical Philosophy', delivered 23.4.2012 at the Danish National School of Performing Arts. My teaching activities include a substitute professorship in dance studies at the Justus-Liebig Universität Gießen ('Mapping Practices' and 'Experimental Practices', to name two seminars) and my work with students of the B.A. Programme in dance at the Danish National School of Performing Arts in Copenhagen.

118 | Cf. John Langshaw Austin, *How To Do Things With Words* (Cambridge, Mass: Harvard University Press, 1997); Judith Butler, *Gender Trouble* (New York & London: Routledge, 1990); and idem., *Bodies That Matter: On the Discursive Limits of "Sex"* (New York & London: Routledge, 1993). See also Petra Sabisch, 'Was kann performative Philosophie in Zeiten des artistic turns in den Geisteswissenschaften tun?' [What can performative philosophy do in times of the artistic turn in the humanities?], lecture 1 in the series Art as Practical Philosophy, delivered 6.4.2012 at Uferhallen, Berlin, as part of the Performative Philosophy Conference.

119 | See Dorothea von Hantelmann, *How to Do Things With Art: On the Significance of the Performativity of Art* (Zurich & Berlin: diaphanes, 2007).

120 | For a thorough overview of the practice turn and current debates in contemporary theory, see Theodore R. Schatzki, Karin Knorr-Cetina and Eike von Savigny (Eds.), *The Practice Turn in Contemporary Theory* (London & New York: Routledge, 2001). See Hannah Arendt, *The Human Condition* (Chicago: University of Chicago Press, 1999); and

To that extent, the practice turn comprises an empirical turn and allows us to gain focus on embodiment-phenomena and material aspects as well as the 'situative contingency' of practices.[121] A critique of the classical concept of action and reason also applies here in that – owing, for example, to actor-network theory – it includes nonhuman agencies as well (e.g., artefacts and object relations), reflecting on them with regard to their *affordances*.[122]

Practice theory thus combines such highly differing theoretical directions and research approaches without following a unified, standardized basis programme or formulating a common denominator; it instead appears as a heteroform quintessence of differing research orientations.

Although Schmidt lays out an interesting overview of practice sociologies, my access to artistic practices discloses itself more through art itself, as well as against a backdrop provided by the theories of pragmatism (Peirce, James, Dewey), of process philosophy (Whitehead, Stengers) and of assemblage theory, especially that of Deleuze and Guattari.[123] Echoes of Deleuze and Guattari's thought flow into Schatzki's anthology *The Practice Turn in Contemporary Theory*, while in many instances Schmidt's *Soziologie der Praktiken* does not reflect on its consequences for classical sociological formulations of concepts (such as Bourdieu's).

Karl Marx, 'Theses on Feuerbach', Ed. F. Engels, trans. W. Lough, in *Selected Works*, Vol. 1, ed. Karl Marx and Friedrich Engels (Moscow: Progress Publishers, 1845), pp. 13-15.

121 | Schmidt, *Soziologie der Praktiken*, p. 59. Schmidt defines the three basic characteristics of social practices as temporality, bodiliness and materiality. Of particular interest here is the '*Unumkehrbarkeit der Aufeinanderfolge von Geschehnissen*' (the irreversibility of a succession of occurrences) that follows a certain '*sinnbildenden Richtung*' (sense-building direction), Ibid., p. 52.

122 | Ibid., p. 23, 65; and Andrew Pickering, 'Practice and Posthumanism: Social Theory and a History of Agency', in Schatzki, Knorr-Cetina and von Savigny (Eds.), *The Practice Turn in Contemporary Theory*, pp. 163-74, here p. 165; Bruno Latour, *Reassembling the Social: An Introduction to Actor-Network Theory* (Oxford: Oxford University Press, 2005); and the work of Jane Bennett on the material agencies of things, Bennet, *Vibrant Matter: A Political Ecology of Things* (Durham, N.C.: Duke University Press, 2010).

123 | For insights into Alfred North Whitehead's process philosophy, see Whitehead, *Process and Reality: An Essay in Cosmology*, Eds. David Ray Griffin and Donald W. Sherburne (New York: Free Press, 1979). For more on the concept of assemblage in Deleuze, Parnet and Guattari, see for example Gilles Deleuze and Claire Parnet, *Dialogues*, trans. Hugh Tomlinson and Barbara Habberjam (London & New York: Continuum, 1987); 'The Actual and the Virtual' trans. Eliot Ross Albert (London: Continuum, 2006), p. 52; and Gilles Deleuze and Félix Guattari, *A Thousand Plateaus: Capitalism and Schizophrenia*, Vol. 2, trans. Brian Massumi (London: Continuum, 2004), pp. 97-98.

The orientation of a concept of the practice that is carried out within an assemblage of relations towards a pragmatic analysis does, however, have far-reaching implications. The many discussions on whether practices are either collective or individual, whether they are necessarily social (shared practices) or whether they define habit as more of a habitus, routine, ritual or as a productive and transformative force are all questions that such a conception of analysis would not decide in advance.[124] Instead, the fabric made out of heterogeneous parameters and relationships within which practices situate themselves is proposed as a dynamic fabric in which the varying emphasis on, and variation of, individual parameters already has evident effects on how practices manifest themselves.

In 1878, Charles Sanders Peirce wrote that any true distinguishing of the meaning of thought gauges itself by the practical difference that thought makes.[125] From this evolved his famous pragmatic maxim from 1905, which he identified in the following as pragmaticism: 'Consider what effects that might *conceivably* have practical bearings you *conceive* the objects of your *conception* to have. Then, your *conception* of those effects is the whole of your *conception* of the object.'[126]

In *What pragmatism means,* the second lecture in his lecture series *Pragmatism,* William James took this idea up in the sense of a pragmatic method:

'The pragmatic method in such cases is to try to interpret each notion by tracing its respective practical consequences. What difference would it practically make to anyone if this notion rather than that notion were true? If no practical difference whatever can be traced, then the alternatives mean practically the same thing, and all dispute is idle.'[127]

---

124 | See Barry Barnes's argumentation in 'Practice as collective action', in Schatzki, Knorr-Cetina and von Savigny (Eds.), *The Practice Turn in Contemporary Theory,* pp. 17-28; and Joseph Rouse's differentiation between the regular (mainstream) and normative characters of practices in 'Two concepts of practices', Ibid. pp. 189-198.

125 | Cf. Charles Sanders Peirce, 'How To Make Our Ideas Clear', *Popular Science Monthly* 12 (January 1878), pp. 286-302, CP 5.400: 'Thus, we come down to what is tangible and conceivably practical, as the root of every real distinction of thought, no matter how subtle it may be; and there is no distinction of meaning so fine as to consist in anything but a possible difference of practice.'

126 | Charles Sanders Peirce, 'Issues of Pragmatism', *The Monist* 15:4 (1905), pp. 418-499; idem., 'What Pragmatism Is', *The Monist* 15:2 (1905), pp. 161-181.

127 | William James, *Pragmatism: A New Name for Some Old Ways of Thinking* (New York: Dover Publications, 1995), originally published 1907; and idem., *Essays in Radical Empiricism* (New York: Dover Publications, 2003), originally published 1912.

John Dewey develops this pragmatic understanding further in his *Essays on Experimental Logic*, which is instrumental for our examination of artistic practices and shall therefore be sketched out in the following:[128] To begin with, a practical proposition (or, in our context, the artistic proposal, and not only the philosophical-conceptual) is characterised as an answer to an 'incomplete situation' for the adequately pragmatic reason that 'it wouldn't have to be undertaken otherwise'. Here the *proposition* is simultaneously a determining factor for that which ends up taking place as the result of the completion of this situation. According to Dewey, this proposition implies that *how* the situation is carried out, how it is executed, makes an obvious difference to the completion of the situation, so that the *objective utilisation* of the proposition becomes comprehensible.[129] In view of the wide range of possible consequences the proposition may have, the adequacy of the relation between means and goal are weighed. At the same time, however, the validity of the proposition does not become verifiable until empirical evidence becomes available. In that sense, the proposition remains hypothetical until it is tried out.

This backdrop provided by pragmatic theory-formation and method-formation has been a formative influence on the descriptions, accounts and analyses of artistic practices that are to unfold in the following chapters because, methodologically speaking, it stands alone as the only approach that is capable of capturing that inceptive moment when experimental practices have to be *made* in the first place. Methodologically speaking, this moment can be seen with the help of the principally different dimensions of two questions: While the first question (What is available?) aims for a backwards-looking inventory of whatever current 'is'-condition, the benchmark for the second and pragmatic question is the future and development potential. Correspondingly, it asks: *What can be done to enable constructive developments?*[130]

---

128 | John Dewey, *Essays in Experimental Logic* (Chicago: University of Chicago Press, 1916), esp. pp. 335–349. On the significance of this work, see also Petra Sabisch, 'What Can Practice Mean Today?'

129 | John Dewey, *Essays in Experimental Logic*, p. 39: 'The subject-matter implies that it makes a difference how the given is terminated: that one outcome is better than another, and that the proposition is to be a factor in securing (as far as may be) the better. In other words, there is something objectively at stake in the forming of the proposition.'

130 | For more on this methodological difference, which Deleuze worked out with Spinoza, see Petra Sabisch, 'What Can Choreography Do?' in Inpex (Ed.), *Swedish Dance History III* (Stockholm: Inpex, 2011), pp. 82–103.

Peirce refreshed precisely this moment that rebinds perception of the situation to a potential action, and thereby methodologically implies that action as an option, as the force that drives the changing of habits and behaviour.[131]

This proactive moment of initiating and being involved, of sustainable engagement, and not of uninvolved indifference, allows the pragmatic method to gather and comprehend the situative, process-oriented and production-aesthetical, as opposed to reception-aesthetical, perspectives of artistic situations.[132]

In a similar vein, Chrysa Parkinson, dancer and professor of dance at the Stockholm School of Dance and Circus, characterises the concept of practice in her illustrated video essay *Self-Interview on Practice* as, among other things, 'active thought' through which information is processed as if through a filter. At the same time, the practice is the thing you have to try out, the thing that forms habits.[133]

Only this perspective can shed light on artistic practices as sense-building, meaning-generating and engaged navigations throughout a fabric made of the parameters, conditions, relations, decisions, obstacles and possibilities, perceptions and effects found in each respective situation.

As regards artistic practices, there is no alternative to Deleuze and Guattari's challenge *'penser par le milieu'*, for how else other than in the interwoven nature

---

131 | Peirce, 'How To Make Our Ideas Clear', CP 5.400: 'What the habit is depends on *when* and *how* it causes us to act. As for the *when*, every stimulus to action is derived from perception; as for the *how*, every purpose of action is to produce some sensible result.' Cited here from a version available online, http://www.cspeirce.com/menu/library/bycsp/ideas/id-frame.htm, retrieved 2.2.2013.

132 | On the concept of engagement, see also Laurent Thévenot, 'Pragmatic regimes governing the engagement with the world', in Schatzki, Knorr-Cetina and von Savigny (Eds.), *The Practice Turn in Contemporary Theory*, pp. 56–73; L. Thévenot and Luc Boltanski (Eds.), *Justesse et justice dans le travail* (Paris: Presses Universitaires de Paris/Centre d'Etudes de l'Emploi, 1989); as well as the conference *Artistic Practices*, organised by the *Research Network Sociology of the Arts* at the Universität für Musik und Darstellende Kunst Wien (5.–8.9.2012), where primarily sociologists came to an understanding regarding art. Lectures included Nathalie Heinich, 'Practices of Contemporary Art: A Pragmatic Approach to a New Artistic Paradigm', delivered 5.9.2012; and Laurent Thévenot's lecture about a work by Yves Mettler, 'Artists Engaging the Public in Participation: A View from the Sociology of Engagements', delivered 7.9.2012.

133 | Chrysa Parkinson [chrysa parkinson], *self interview on practice* [video file], text, illustrations and performance by Chrysa Parkinson (2008–2009), http://vimeo.com/26763244, retrieved 3.3.2013. See also the print version at the Belgian platform *Sarma* (Laboratory for criticism, dramaturgy, research and creation), http://sarma.be/docs/1336, accessed 21.8.2013.

of the relational fabric, of the milieu, can the actions of different protagonists and the deployment of different kinds of agency – not to mention the obstacles posed through, and effects generated by, other practices – become in any way visible?[134]

In the following five case studies, the issue at stake shall be precisely this *visibility of artistic practices* and their constant involvement in plural publics, critical discursivity and the extra-disciplinary growth of practices.[135]

Having already demonstrated in the above – by reference to the 'static method' of cultural-political (statistical) research approaches regarding the situation of the artist – the extent to which a certain perspective is suited to a certain scientific method, we can proceed to reformulate this pragmatically: *applied methods are research practices.*

Methods are modi operandi of research which, as scientific modes, intersubjectively reflect their own unique, specific perspectives and make them comprehensible. Herein lies yet another advantage of practice theory, one which Michael Lynch aptly describes in favour of the 'logic of practice', in refutation of Garfinkel's description of the problem of practical objectivity, against the horizon of ethnomethodological research:

'The lesson I derive from this example is that it is pointless to seek a general methodological solution to 'the vexed problem of the practical objectivity and practical observability of practical actions and practical reasoning,' because any abstract account of the logic of practice immediately reiterates the problem. The investigative task for ethnomethodology is therefore to describe how the logical accountability of practice is itself a subject of practical inquiry; an inquiry that can involve struggles and fragile agreements.'[136]

---

134 | For more on Isabelle Stengers' concept of environment and involvement, see Stengers, 'Introductory Notes on An Ecology of Practices', *Cultural Studies Review*, 11:1 (2005), pp. 183-196, here p. 187: 'In the same way, I would venture there is no identity of a practice independent of its environment. This emphatically does not mean that the identity of a practice may be derived from its environment. Thinking 'par le milieu' does not give power to the environment. The obstinate work and research of ethologists to discover what kinds of relations with their apes would be the right ones for those apes to learn, whatever they learn is sufficient to lend support to the point that the issue is not one of power but of involvement.'

135 | See Kaufmann and Raunig, *Anticipating European Cultural Policies*, p. 74: 'What counts is not the demand for or the conceptualisation of an individual public [...] but rather the permanent constituting of many publics that are imagined not as static but as Becomings of articulatory and emancipatory practices.'

136 | Michael Lynch, 'Ethnomethodology and the logic of practice', in Schatzki, Knorr-Cetina and von Savigny (Eds.), *The Practice Turn in Contemporary Theory*, pp. 131-48, here p. 147.

1.4 On the Method of this Study

Basing my approach on a practice-based method, I shall here describe how the precise field for study was staked out, which selection criteria were used with regard to the practices examined in the following, and what procedure existed in reference to data material and data collection. Before all else, it must be indicated that this study's focus on artistic *practices* (and not, for instance, performances) is due to the consideration that a performance analysis would only be able to adequately analyse a small number of individual works and would thus run the risk of reproducing the punctual framing and capturing of the 'project economy'. Such an approach would immediately lose focus on those practices that were consciously developed in *difference* to predominant forms of staged presentation, or in other words, that since their very inception have experimented with new formats and have made content-related processes into the object of their work.

That being said, our field of investigation is limited to international, contemporary, experimental and inventive practices in the dance, choreography and performance field which have articulated, reflected and developed (including in a sense-building capacity) the heretofore insufficiently explored connection between production conditions, work modes, and aesthetics.

Additionally, however, this study has striven to comprehend the collective dimension of such artistic practices that – beyond the evolution of one's own oeuvre, and yet with and on the foundation of performances – initiate debates on the sense of choreography and performance art and thereby generate contexts.[137] At the same time, another essential parameter was that these practices were initiated by artists, meaning they oriented themselves according to the requirements and necessities of artistic practice.[138]

In sum, the selection parameters presented themselves to me as a framework composed of international, contemporary, experimental, inventive as well as discourse- and context-generating practices that were initiated by artists or that are closely geared to artistic practice.

---

137 | The idea, therefore, was to find that 'moment of initiation' for each practice, that moment that analyses the situation in the dance field looking from the inside of the practice outward, and that inquires into concrete, sense-building needs and requirements. With Dewey, these practices are definable as *propositions* to whom the way they are executed makes a sensible difference, see p. 95.

138 | Accountability towards the factual circumstance of the self-determination of art should be hereby shown, but without producing narrow identitarian ascriptions. It would be impossible to create fixed labels in any case, especially in view of the multilayered character of artistic practices discussed at the beginning of this study and reflected in the constant change and simultaneous occurrence of roles, not to mention in the intermittent working relations.

Five case studies with varying diachronic and geographic scopes were sought out: first, *Special Issue* in Aubervilliers, France, which began as a performative weekend presented as a 'special issue' and subsequently became a Europe-wide format (2011–2013); second, the Spanish festival *In-Presentable* (2003–2012), which was initiated and directed by the choreographer Juan Domínguez and has been held annually for ten years; third, the one-week *Double Lecture Series* in Stockholm, which was organised in autumn 2011 by Mårten Spångberg and Mette Ingvartsen; fourth, the *Performing Arts Forum*, founded by Jan Ritsema and others in 2005, in St. Erme, France; and fifth, the *sommer.bar*, which took place from 2006 to 2011 as part of the festival Tanz im August and was curated by Kerstin Schroth.

An indispensable methodological prerequisite for the scientific evaluation of the content-related relevance of artistic practices was the participatory observation of each practice and its modus operandi. The risks that accompany my perspectivity in its perception of the situation, which apply equally to all sciences geared to the empiricism of life (this is the aesthetic dimension of empiricism) are, in my opinion, sufficiently thematised. Yet, a pragmatic science, besides fostering an intersubjective comprehensibility and transparency with regard to its own perspective, should also add for consideration the fact that these risks should be put into proportion with the risk of a science that musters no attempt to make a practical difference.

In the case of the following, the explorations of the practices depicted is based on the analysis of documents, on prepared statistics concerning the internationality of each practice, and a qualitative questioning process.[139] For the purpose of the latter, intensive, qualitative interviews with these practices' five initiators (Alice Chauchat, Juan Domínguez, Mette Ingvartsen, Jan Ritsema, and Kerstin Schroth) were conducted and then reflected on within five 'mirror interviews' with artists from the dance, choreography and performance field who participated in said initiatives (Blanca Calvo, Paz Rojo, Christine de Smedt, Valentina Desideri, Hermann Heisig).

Furthermore, another six planned interviews attempted to direct attention towards other regions in Europe – which indeed occurred for the Scandinavian terrain as well as for Romania and Italy. Four of these interviews took place (with Halla Ólafsdóttir, Emma Kim Hagdahl, Manuel Pelmus and Cristina Rizzo). Further planned regions of investigation were the Balkans and Portugal.[140]

---

139 | Cf. Annex 2, 'Statistics on the internationality of the case studies', p. 175.
140 | For the method of citation of these interviews, see the index 'Interviews & abbreviations', p. 172. In this study, manuscript versions of the interviews are the basis for reference.

Instrumental in the explorative interviews was the question of how the complex interplay between artistic production, working mode, and aesthetics in independent, international, experimental and contemporary dance, choreography and performance operates according to the interviewees' perspectives.

The interviews are non-standardised, open, partially structured, and focussed expert interviews that were devised on the basis of a matrix of main questions and that were respectively connected with individual research processes delving into the experiential scope and backgrounds of each particular initiative and person.[141]

Correspondingly, inquiries were made into the specificity and attributes of each project, into its fundamental concerns and resulting decisions, into its connection with respective institutions, into the interlinkage of forms of production and forms of presentation, into concepts of the relation between artistic practices and audience – but also into the specific problems and difficulties, differentiations and personal definitions of the categories applied to my selection; into the state of education and possibilities for continued education; and into the structural and aesthetic changes that have occurred over the last twenty years.

My method for conducting the time-intensive interviews (usually two-and-a-half hours long) consisted of live or Skype-based interviews, written interviews held in the presence of both interviewer and interviewee (ca. eight hours), and the subsequent transcription and editing of a continuous text in consultation with interviewees. The originally spoken interview material transports thoughts and perspectives that are rooted in their respective temporalities.

Faced with its sizeable temporal and material proportions, I decided to conduct this study together with Tom Engels and Bettina Földesi, both of whom I got to know as master's students in the programme *Choreografie und Performance* during my substitute professorship in Dance Studies at the Institute for Applied Theatre Studies at the Justus-Liebig University Gießen. A week of collective work and discussion served to introduce the study and as a time to establish a common footing.

---

141 | Cf. Annex 3, 'Matrix of central questions for the codification of the interviews', p. 178.

The interviews, which the following depictions of practices feed on, turned out to pose such rich, meaningful and convincing material regarding our questions that I decided to produce, in connection with and as a consequence of this study before you, a follow-up study (*A Topology of Practices: The Book of Interviews*) that extends the plural articulations of concrete affective relations in artistic practices that are begun in this work and makes these articulations available for explorations to come.[142]

2. Practices: Case Studies

2.1 *Special Issue/Edition Spéciale* in Aubervilliers and elsewhere (2011-2012)

Figure 1: Program 'Edition Spéciale', 2011. Photograph: Petra Sabisch

---

142 | Cf. Petra Sabisch (Ed.), *A Topology of Practices – The Book of Interviews* (forthcoming, 2016).

Edition Spéciale/Special Issue # Aubervilliers: 29.41.5.2011

Special Issue # Aubervilliers was a weekend initiated by the Laboratoires d'Aubervilliers[143] (France) which took place from 29 April until 1 May in the north of Paris in the town of Aubervilliers. It showed international contemporary performative practices as a 'special issue' in the sense of a printed journal whose paper is replaced by live works.[144]

Initiated by the 'Labo's' team of directors – Alice Chauchat, Grégory Castéra and Nataša Petrešin-Bachelez – this weekend festival emphasised discursive practices and dispositives conceived as performative engagements with artistic labour and as experimental and ongoing developmental processes.

Invitations were accepted by international artists whose professional provenance often lies in the fields of dance and choreography, such as Jennifer Lacey[145],

---

143 | The Laboratoires d'Aubervilliers, located in the northeastern suburbs of Paris, were established in 1993 by the French choreographer François Verret and a group of artists as an answer to the invitation extended by Aubervillier's mayor to utilise the site. From 2001 until 2006 the Laboratoires were under the shared directorship of the art critic Yvane Chapuis, François Piron and the choreographer Loïc Touzé, all of whom jointly designed the project as an artistic laboratory for research and experiment that would include several arts. From 2007 to 2009 Yvane Chapuis assumed directorship together with the choreographer Joris Lacoste; from 2010 to 2012, it was Grégory Castéra, Alice Chauchat and Nataša Petrešin-Bachelez. Until ca. 2015 (and since 2013) the Labos will continue to be directed by a team: Alexandra Baudelot, Dora Garcia and Mathilde Villeneuve. For more history on the Labos, see http://archives.leslaboratoires.org, retrieved 23.10.2013. The dancer (and at the time of Edition Spéciale also co-director of the Labos) Alice Chauchat describes the conception of the laboratories like so: 'Les Laboratoires d'Aubervilliers is a very particular arts centre in the north of Paris. It is non-disciplinary (hosting projects stemming from whichever artistic practice), and it is constantly reorganising itself around the necessities of the artistic projects hosted there (thereby excluding conventional programming systems or the setting of any standard concerning budget, duration, mode of visibility, or concerning any other preconceived parameter for the projects hosted). It was founded by an artist (French choreographer François Verret) and is always directed by several people at a time, including an artist.' Alice Chauchat interviewed by Petra Sabisch, AC1PS.

144 | For the programme of the first edition of *Edition Spéciale* in Aubervilliers, see http://www.specialissue.eu/special-issue-0-program, retrieved 28.6.2013.

145 | Jennifer Lacey invited people to participate in dramaturgical consultation: *Guided Consultations in the Archives of Amateur Dramaturges To Resolve Problems of Life and Creation.*

the group W[146], Everybodys[147], Laurent Pichaud and Rémy Héritier[148], Krõõt Juurak[149], Mårten Spångberg[150], Noé Soulier[151], Juan Domínguez[152] as well as Natascha Sadr Haghighian[153], Bojana Cvejić[154] and art university students (from ENSA Paris Cergy, and the CNEAI).

An essential component of *Special Issue # Aubervilliers* was the series of moderated *tables rondes* during which all participants could discuss specific aspects of this practice. The round tables covered the following topics: 'conception of discursive set-ups', 'performance of discursive dispositives', 'forms of participation in discourse production (listening instead of reading)', 'technique and virtuosity (a space for practices?)', 'a toolbox for discourse production', and the discussion of the documentation of discursive practices.

The concerns and motivations of the presenters are whittled to a fine point in the announcement of this zero-number of *Edition Spéciale*, which describes

---

146 | The discursive practice *The Bloc* consists of a rule-governed, yet improvised real-time conference; see http://www.1110111.org/, retrieved 10.7.2013.

147 | Everybodys was represented through many practices, including the form of collective lecture known as *Co-lecture*, devised by Alice Chauchat, Mette Ingvartsen and Petra Sabisch. Beyond that, the *Impersonation Game* was executed for Juan Domínguez's performance *Blue*, and *Générique* was shown; see http://www.everybodystoolbox.net/, retrieved 12.4.2013.

148 | Inspired by *OuLiPo*, the *Choreographic Games* by Héritier and Pichaud provoke the discursivisation of styles and aesthetics with the aid of excerpts from performance works.

149 | *Scripts for Smalltalk* is a performance in which the audience reads readymade texts that performatively set thought processes and live interferences into motion.

150 | *Double Speak O Field* focuses the discursive uniqueness of the party (*fête*).

151 | *Idéographie in progress* showed an in-progress version of a performance that filters, analyses and performs philosophical lines of thought.

152 | The performance *Blue* (2009) by Juan Domínguez, produced in collaboration with the performers Luis Miguel Felix, Maria Jerez, Arantxa Martínez, Naiara Mendioroz and Emilio Tomé, was relevant for *Special Issue # Aubervilliers* in several respects: it was the point of reference for the *Impersonation Game* by Everybodys as well as for the *Running Commentaries*. For more on the performance, see also Juan Dominguez's website, http://juandominguezrojo.com/?p=44#more-44, retrieved 12.5.2013.

153 | In *Looking Awry*, the German artist Natascha Sadr Haghighian creates the experience of being cross-eyed as a performative perceptional dispositive. For more on the works of Haghighian, see http://www.johannkoenig.de/6/natascha_sadr_haghighian/selected_works.html, retrieved 10.7.2013.

154 | The format known as *Running Commentaries* is a simultaneous live commentary of performances that have been documented in video form, where the audience is free to choose from multiple commenting voices, each audible on individual headphones.

it as a culmination of a collective need to give existing artistic practices a frame in which they can articulate themselves, reflect on their own work, and pay serious attention to performative practices as instruments of theory-building and artistic research:

'While the performative dimension of artistic practices is currently one of the main subjects of theoretical and critical investigation, numerous artists do not always recognize the models of analysis that are applied to them. They end up constructing their own theoretical tools, by means of performance. [...] These observations are at the origin of *Special Issue*, a publication that brings together a series of dispositives for the production of live discourse. It is performed from time to time in varied contexts, is produced by performance practitioners and is dedicated to discourse as produced by performance.'[155]

In an interview, Alice Chauchat described to me the concerns of *Edition Spéciale # Aubervilliers* as an answer to the increasingly voiced artistic need for performative discursivisation, which has received inadequate visibility or institutional support to date:

'My co-directors Grégory Castéra and Nataša Petrešin-Bachelez and I were very sensitive to the existence, in the performing arts field, of various practices that artists were developing out of necessity and without institutional support. These practices are discursive and performative; they structure performance in order to foster discourse as much as structure discourse for the sake of performance. We wanted to find a way of supporting these practices *as an institution*.
The first step was to make them visible, to create an event or a mini-festival where we invited about thirty artists to show and discuss this phenomenon and ways of supporting it further. In order to insist on its function as a place of discourse, we decided to call it a magazine. For three days, about 623 people took part in about fifteen performative setups.'[156]

In the wake of this small festival, in which international discursive performative practices were presented and reflected upon in this way for the first time, the zero-number of *Special Issue # Aubervilliers* spread quickly to become a European project. Upon the initiative of the presenters, further artists and structures were invited to tackle the proposal and to develop new and local formats for expression based on one question: 'How do the performing arts make discourses public today?'

---

155 | http://www.leslaboratoires.org/projet/edition-speciale-0, retrieved 21.5.2013.
156 | AC1PS.

These discussions matured into an EU-funded project with six more Special Issues that included the participation of the following – mostly artist-initiated – structures: the Spanish festival *In-Presentable* in Madrid[157], the *Laboratoires d'Aubervilliers* (France), *Station* (Belgrade), *Mugatxoan* in Donostía (Basque country), *Hybris Konstproduktion* (Stockholm), *BIS* (Istanbul) and once again the *Laboratoires d'Aubervilliers*.[158]

These *Special Issues* took place primarily between June and December 2012. Allow me to briefly introduce each of them here and provide details about the participating structures and their respective practical emphases:

- 20.–22.6.2012 # *In-Presentable festival*, Madrid, Spain: *Emissiones Cacatúa*. *Emissiones Cacatúa* is a radio show with thirteen field recordings by Arantxa Martínez and Nilo Gallego, which first took place as part of the festival *In-Presentable*, created and (co)curated by Juan Domínguez, until it was transformed into *Open Mic Istanbul* as part of *Special Issue # Istanbul (Santiye)*, which was coordinated by Eylül Fidan Akıncı and was organised by Body Process Arts Association. On 1.2.2013, *Open Mic Istanbul* was broadcast as a livestream from the Institut Français.[159]
- 10.–22.9.2012 # *Les Laboratoires d'Aubervilliers*, France: *The Mountain of Aubervilliers*, initiated by Laurent Pichaud and Rémy Héritier, was made up of a fourteen-day performed magazine that produced daily reports from the viewpoint of the research practice in the form of a blog.[160]

---

157 | For more on *In-Presentable*, see the next case study, and Juan Domínguez in conversation with Petra Sabisch. See also the Spanish dancer and choreographer Paz Rojo in conversation with Tom Engels. From 2013 onward, Rojo put together a new frame in Madrid titled *Y si dejamos de ser (artistas)...?* [And if we let go of being (artists)...?], a collective, nonhierarchical event which calls the festival format into question, PR3TE.

158 | See also AC7PS. For a detailed description of both the history and the current situation of the interdisciplinary project *Mugatxoan*, led by Blanca Calvo and Ion Munduate, see Blanca Calvo in conversation with Bettina Földesi, BC3BF, BC9BF. BC11BF, BC22BF. For the festival *Desviaciones*, under the direction of Blanca Calvo with Maria La Ribot and José A. Sánchez, see also p. 116.

159 | The following artists participated: Arantxa Martínez, Nilo Gallego, Eylül Fidan Akıncı, Basak Günak, Volkan Ergen, Seçil Demircan, Erdem Gündüz, Erol Babaoğlu, Berna Kurt, Defne Erdur, Korhan Erel, İlyas Odman, Dilek Champs, Steven Champs, Ekim Öztürk, Gizem Aksu, Mustafa Kaplan, Damla Ekin Tokel, Hande Topaloğlu, and Aslı Bostancı. See http://specialissue.eu/editions/emisiones-cacatua; to download the livestream, go to https://archive.org/details/Emisionescacatuaistambul, retrieved 11.6.2013.

160 | The invited artists were Mathieu Bouvier, Marcelline Delbecq, Anne Kerzerho, OfficeAbc, and Gilles Saussier. See http://specialissue.eu/daily-publications-in-laboratoires daubervilliers, retrieved 11.6.2013.

- 4.–11.10.2012 # *Mugatxoan,* **San Sebastián, Spain:** *A Disembodied Voice, Towards Love,* initiated by Blanca Calvo and Ion Munduate, questions the live aspect of performances and inspects how the perception of a performance can be transferred to an absent viewer.[161] *Special Issue # Donostia/San Sebastián* was made up of a radio broadcast, a publication and two workshops (with Peio Aguirre and Manuel Cirauqui).[162]
- 15.–27.10.2012 # *Magacin,* **Belgrade, Serbia:** A collaborative laboratory on 'The Choreography of Attention' by *Station Service for Contemporary Dance,* a collective initiative by artists and cultural workers that promotes the production and visibility of knowledge in dance.[163]
- 12.–16.11.2012 # *Dilettant,* **Stockholm, Sweden:** *The Public Office,* initiated by the choreographers Anders Jacobson and Johan Thelander from the group Dilettant (formerly Hybris Konstproduktion), with Myriam Mazzoni

---

161 | See http://www.specialissue.eu/editions/a-disembodied-voice-towards-love, accessed 11.6.2013. As regards the idea of the absent viewer and the expansion of the performative milieu, Calvo describes her interest: 'How to shift the perception of performance to another milieu, on how the absent spectator can share from another place (e.g., the radio) what is produced live.' Blanca Calvo (Ed.) *Cuaderno 1: Una voz sin cuerpo, hacia el amor / A Disembodied Voice, towards Love* (Donostia / San Sebastian: Mugatxoan, 2012), p. 106.

162 | See also Blanca Calvo's description of *Special Issue # Donostia/San Sebastián* and the idea of radio, BC6BF: '*Emission 1. A Disembodied Voice, Towards Love* is a radio broadcast that includes performances, lectures, conversations and interventions that are simultaneously performed in San Telmo Museoa and on a free radio station via presentations by the invited artists. [...] What do we perceive from a performance when we don't see it, when we only hear it? [...] We believe that when the displacement between what happens and what one perceives, which normally occurs through sight, is only perceived by way of the sound it makes, it poses interesting questions to the notion of performance. The idea for the radio programme emerged from interviews with the artists who have passed through *Mugatxoan* over the last ten years. These interviews sought to reflect on the places, the positions and the autonomy from which they were working ten years ago up to where they are now. The vocabulary of an encounter quickly emerged, and the terminology was used to depict and express situations. The working processes undergone in each situation were also defined and discussed. This caused us to turn our attention and purpose towards the sound medium, due to its intangibility, while setting up a line of publications tackling the problem of "translating" an artistic process into the written word.'

163 | This laboratory was initiated by Isin Onol, Marko Milic, Katarina Popovic, Maja Ciric, Ljiljana Tasic, Ana Dubljevic, Malin Elgan, Roger Rossell, Larraitz Torres and Mathilde Chénin. See http://www.dancestation.org/ and http://specialissue.eu/laboratory as well as http://specialissue.eu/editions/choreography-of-attention#, all retrieved 11.6.2013.

and Victor Saiz. In this five-day meeting, questions of publicity, discourse and commons were discussed as part of the long-planned 'public offices'.[164]

- **September 2011 to January 2013 (BIS, Istanbul, Turkey)** *Santiye* (translation: construction area) was initiated as an event series by the choreographer Özlem Alkış and the theorist Eylül Fidan Akıncı in order to evaluate performing arts practices in Turkey, further existing discourses (in the festival iDANS, for example), gain practical experiences in workshops, and explore the nexus of production and critique in the still-young history of contemporary dance in Turkey.[165]

Regarded through the lens of this study's main query, it becomes particularly clear that Special Issue displays a unique interlocking of production modes, work modes and aesthetics. The perception (*aisthesis*) of an increased production of discursive practices led, combined with the simultaneous invisibility of this artistic engagement in conventional dance festivals, to the attempt to give those practices a context and visibility in the form of a discourse-generating performative festival (*Edition Spéciale # Aubervilliers*) through which they can publicly coalesce in their uniqueness in exchange with one another.

Thus, out of numerous artistic work modes emerges a specific presentational format that enables a content-related, performative evolution through the (financial) facilitation and production of these practices, a format whose circulation (to France, Sweden, Serbia, Spain, and Turkey) includes concrete engagement with local audiences.

The presentational format *Special Issue* is not, however, based on the repetition of a once-tested standard in yearly festivals. Its basic idea is circulated internationally in diverse forms and with different emphases. It is often linked to independent artistic initiatives, often in cooperation with existing structures, with an orientation to each specific place's contextual requirements, which themselves are, in turn, searching for an experimental mode of expression, for open-content and formally open, artistically sense-building work formats.

Alice Chauchat describes the procedure:

'The way we worked together was rooted in the demand to realise a format that didn't exist, in order to give a concrete answer to an abstract problem. It meant agreeing on a common object, recognising it as potent for our field, and at the same time discarding the first format that had been proposed for its realisation (the three-day showcase) in

---

164 | Cf. http://www.specialissue.eu/editions/the-public-office and http://thepublicoffice.se, retrieved 11.6.2013.

165 | Cf. http://specialissue.eu/editions/santiye#, as well as the website of the dance and performance festival iDANS in Istanbul, which has been in existence since 2007, http://www.idans.info/; and the festival blog: http://idansblog.org/, both retrieved 11.6.2013.

order to try out other forms. This way, it was more or less impossible to repeat something we already knew. Trying and experimenting was more important than success or confirmation.'[166]

In conversation with Bettina Földesi, Blanco Calvo – who directs the project *Mugatxoan* in San Sebastián together with Ion Munduate, and who in this function, subsequent to her participation in *Special Issue # Aubervilliers*, hosted *Special Issue # San Sebastián* – points out the quite open and autonomous construction of the task of holding a Special Issue:

'More than a format, *Special Issue* was, in our eyes, an invitation. It was open, and it was a dialogue starting from the following question: how does performance produce discourse today? It is for this reason that each guest structure – knowing how *Special Issue* developed the number zero as an unconditioned starting point – could answer this question from their own way of doing and formulate a programme. So each frame was implicitly inscribed into the social and cultural context. I mean, there were no rules for fitting a format. From my point of view, this evokes a very rich diversity concerning the results of each programme. We are interested in this diversity of responses, because you learn a lot from watching, from practice and from the conceptual resolution of each collaborating artist in their own context. This is the interesting thing about networking.'[167]

In this way, an international platform evolved that gave space to cooperation with potential structure-building effects amongst highly diverse approaches to artistic work, a platform that takes local needs into account for each new Issue and that generates new contexts and discourses in the interweaving of performative development, specific work modes, perceptual modes and forms of audience address.

How a discourse- and context-generating European platform grew out of a festival is explained by Alice Chauchat:

'By announcing a form that is not yet determined, although it might seem paradoxical, the project of a performed publication allows artists to leave aside, for a moment, the question of medium. For example, the suspension of parameters often understood as constitutive elements of performance, such as co-presence, the visibility of bodies or the determination of a finite temporal framework, makes way to the constitution of custom-made spaces for specific interrogations and affirmations. Indeed, motivations rather than form redefine practice. The very nature of *Special Issue* demands a constant crossing over different scales. The artists engaged with *Special Issue* work across countries and form together a transnational community. This community develops a dis-

---

166 | AC10PS.
167 | BC2BF.

course, a set of questions, notions and articulations that feed and constitute it. In the same time these artists live 'somewhere' and each one's political, economic, social, professional and personal context differs greatly depending of the place they inhabit. The public of each issue, with its expectations and concerns, varies as well. The meeting of practices and concerns that are shared on a transnational level with the particularity of each context informs the very nature of the issue that it hosts.

This back-and-forth movement between forms and stakes of discourse, between local and transnational engagements is the very matter of the experimentations that *Special Issue* puts at play. For we are not interested in stabilizing a structure or assuring the permanence of a new frame; we strive to maintain in a state of questioning the possible lives of a discourse that is produced in public.'[168]

Orientation to artistic development is crucial for *Special Issue*, as are the perception and understanding of artistic practices in the field of dance, choreography and performance; the generation of a specific framework for the production and development of artistic practices that reflects upon its own format and differentially redistributes itself after the event under local and self-determined auspices.

While in other situations artists must fit into existing formats, with *Special Issue* a frame was produced that focuses attention on engagement in artistic debates surrounding individual questions, needs and wishes concerning discursive performative practices:

'Maybe the most important impact of the project was to frame, defend and finance on a larger scale these contemporary forms of performance and discourse production as the main dish, instead of as a by-product or sideshow activity for more 'conventional' productions. Such an attention and support gave artists and structures the capacity to rethink in a radical way what they want to be doing, freeing them from the usual necessity to adapt to existing frameworks and enabling them instead to invent the frameworks that fit their work.'[169]

While in customary production venues the presentational format is often relatively rigid and prescribed (an evening's programme lasting forty to ninety minutes), and thereby quite obviously affects the parameters of aesthetics, work modes and production modes, *Special Issue* took a closer look at current practices and the associate concerns felt by contemporary artists in order to set

---

168 | http://www.leslaboratoires.org/en/projet/edition-speciale-projet-europeen/edition-speciale-projet-europeen, retrieved 22.8.2013.
169 | AC8PS.

the frame according to those practices: 'We all strive to maintain this relation through which the frame derives from a practice rather than the opposite.'[170]

This different orientation to the horizons of artistic sense and to the already-diagnosed need for the development of discursive, performative practices through exchange, performance and presentation and through collective discussion in context and the resulting furtherance of the presentational format – with several Special Issues circulating throughout Europe – explains how *Special Issue* was able to become an inspiring and stimulating example of discourse- and context-generating practices and experimental formats in the international dance and performance art field. Ultimately, Institutions from five European countries as well as artists from fourteen European countries (Brazil, Germany, Estonia, France, Italy, Iran, Croatia, Norway, Austria, Serbia, Sweden, Spain, Turkey, and the USA) were involved in the European project.[171]

2.2 The Festival *In-Presentable* in Madrid (2003–2012)

Figure 2: Program 'In-Presentable', 2012. Photograph: Petra Sabisch

In-Presentable is an international festival initiated by the dancer and choreo-grapher Juan Domínguez Rojo that took place for ten consecutive years, from 2003–2012, in La Casa Encendida, which belonged to a bank in Madrid.[172]

---

170 | http://www.leslaboratoires.org/en/projet/edition-speciale-projet-europeen/edition-speciale-projet-europeen, retrieved 2.4.2013.

171 | Cf. Annex 2: 'Statistics on the internationality of the case studies', p. 175.

172 | For more on Juan Domínguez's work, see the website http://juandominguezrojo.com/ as well as the interview with Domínguez conducted as part of the research project *Escenas Discursivas* by Ana Vujanović and Marta Popivoda (TkH: Walking Theory) on

The embarkment of *In-Presentable* was marked by Domínguez's receiving an invitation, extended by the programme coordinator for performing arts at La Casa Encendida, Laura Gutiérrez Tejón, to show his performance *All Good Spies Are My Age* (2002) and to contextualise this work through a one-week programme of further experimental practices.[173]

While considering this invitation, Domínguez decided at first to invite the project *P5*, which was made by five artists with a background in dance who met regularly to establish an exchange of information about their respective work processes, and then examined the topic of process-as-result in the choreographic context.[174]

Thus, in 2003, under the name *Procesos (Coreográficos)*, the first 'edition' of the festival *In-Presentable* took place, accompanied by a theoretical programme by the dance critic and director of the Aula de Danza Estrella Casero at the University in Alcalá, Jaime Conde-Salazar. Because of the special situation experienced by dance, choreography and performance in Madrid, Domínguez set forth with this – at first unplanned – freelance curatorial work in order to ultimately create a continuous context for artistic practices in Madrid in the form of a festival.[175]

One could get a sense of the essentials of *In-Presentable*'s programme by describing it as an uninterrupted field of interest and engagement in a

---

critical discourses in the Madrid contemporary performing arts scene, held 22.4.2011: http://escenasdiscursivas.tkh-generator.net/2011/04/interview-juan-dominguez/, retrieved 22.6.2013. The festival's website http://www.in-presentableblog.com/ was unfortunately discontinued in June 2013. Regarding the venue of *In-Presentable* in La Casa Encendida, which belonged to a Spanish bank, one should mention here the special history of the Spanish *cajas*, which were obligated, before the banking crisis and the dissolution of Caja Madrid, by a programme known as *obra social* to invest forty percent of their income in social infrastructure, daycare and education, and culture and the environment; see also Domínguez in conversation with Petra Sabisch JD26PS; and La Casa Encendida's current event programme following the transformation of Caja Madrid into a foundation: http://www.lacasaencendida.es, retrieved 2.5.2013.

173 | The 2002 solo performance *All Good Spies Are My Age / Todos los buenos espías tienen mi edad* by Juan Domínguez was coproduced by Espace Pier Paolo Pasolini in Valenciennes, France, and La consejería de Cultura de la Comunidad de Madrid, with the support of *in situ productions*. The piece was part of the P5 project, which was supported by Tanzwerkstatt (Berlin), Podewil (Berlin), Vooruit (Ghent), and Stuk (Leuven). Writings on the piece can be found in Lepecki, *Exhausting Dance*, pp. 36-7; and Sabisch, *Choreographing Relations*, pp. 209-235.

174 | P5 included works by Eva Meyer Keller, Mette Edvardsen, Cuqui Jerez, Alexandra Bachzetzis and Juan Domínguez. See also JD1PS.

175 | Ibid.

yearly and changing, or continually re-questioned, format. In an article in the performance journal *Movement Research*, Christiane Bouger writes:

> 'Since then, every year a different program is conceived. The programs created have no specified content or theme, but a concept that deals with the artistic necessities Domínguez identifies in Madrid and abroad. Even though, Juan Domínguez does not consider himself to be a curator, since *In-Presentable* does not count on budget to cover travel expenses for him to visit festivals in other countries. For this reason, he considers it to be more accurate to think of himself as a programmer. The independence of the European conventional market is another central characteristic of *In-Presentable*.'[176]

With *In-Presentable* Domínguez turned an artistic concern into a programme by allowing artistic issues, necessities, wishes, questions and discourses to take the fore and shape the point of departure and focus for what would be shown in the festival. In connection with a direct dialogue with the artists, *In-Presentable* thus attempted to enable and support each piece, creating a kind of 'support policy', as the Spanish lecturer, dance scholar and cofounder of the independent research group ARTEA, Isabel de Naverán, describes it.[177]

It was also essential to establish this practice-enabling understanding in relation to the audience and to make the artists' concerns accessible through their presentation, as Domínguez outlines:

> 'I try to be in a constant dialogue with the artist, not only about the production of the work, but about the content, about the research, about where the work fits, about what that work means nowadays and how it can be accessible, about the repercussions of the work... This dialogue was very important. Of course, I also invited people with their finished work, but I tried to be very close to the discourse of the artist. I was inviting artists rather than their works.'[178]

---

176 | Christiane Bouger, 'In-Presentable: Where Cross-Cultural Artistic Practices Meet in Madrid', *Movement Research* 34 (2009), p. 31.

177 | See also Isabel de Naverán, 'Reproducing before adulthood. Support policies at *In-Presentable*', in Juan Domínguez (Ed.), *In-Presentable 03–07* (Madrid: La Casa Encendida, 2007), pp. 63–73, here p. 67: 'This policy is not based on establishing specific procedural models, but on promoting encounters between artists, intellectuals, students, spectators and passers-by.' See also Domínguez, JD8PS: '...onsidering the festival as a platform that could help...' For more on the independent research group ARTEA, which is made up of artists and researchers alike and aims not only at the further exploration of art, but also at creating a correspondingly suitable field for the arts, see http://www.arte-a.org, retrieved 15.8.2013.

178 | JD5PS. Cf. JD6PS: 'It was more about the artist's needs and how to make them accessible.'

In opposition to the product-oriented curatorial 'shopping' practices of conventional festivals, the intention here was to generate contexts between artistic practices and between the audience and those practices, to promote a collective exchange and to reflect upon working conditions and modes of operation.[179]

The Spanish dancer and choreographer Paz Rojo, who after being based in Amsterdam for many years participated in the last edition of *In-Presentable*, and who was also interviewed as part of this study as curator of the 'offspring' project *Y si dejamos de ser (artistas)...?*[180], reflects in the following:

'Throughout these ten years, [*In-Presentable*] really built up an audience, and a kind of community of practitioners, performance artists and people from various disciplines I would say. It addressed questions about artistic modes of production. It also facilitated a framework that supported local artists, creating exchanges with contexts from abroad. There was an engagement with experimental practices of various sorts and tools and methodologies that were till then not known by the local scene.'[181]

This shift in emphasis from product to internationally effective and networked practices, from pure distribution to a more complex experimental and discursive occurrence, did not, however, lead to a situation in which performances weren't produced or shown or where the very non-completion of a choreographic process became the aim. Instead, the focus lay on opening up, and, accordingly, on producing, a broader experiential field which Domínguez explains – with astounding simplicity, from my point of view – with regard to the existing practices of a multitude of conventional European dance festivals: '...pieces are not at all the only format of producing experience in the performing arts'.[182]

In addition to this fundamental concern regarding the perception of artistic questions and the different strategies of the festival, Domínguez cites three essential parameters, or vectors, for his curatorial concept: firstly, revealing diverse local and international practices that have not been shown in Madrid before In-Presentable; secondly, the formation of contexts and discursive exchange as well as special support going especially to young artists from Madrid (as many older artists have emigrated away from Spain); and thirdly, the significance of the audience, the exploration of different publics and the programme's accessibility for them.[183]

---

179 | Cf. JD6PS.
180 | For more about *Y si dejamos de ser (artistas)...?* cf. also p. 117.
181 | PR2TE.
182 | JD9PS.
183 | Cf. JD1PS. For more on this, see also Domínguez looking back on the festival's first five years in Domínguez, 'Introduction', in *In-Presentable 03-07*, pp. 9-27, here p. 15:

Paz Rojo describes this approach to revealing local artistic practices as an essential factor in the success of *In-Presentable*: 'What *In-Presentable* did was to gather and give visibility to artists that would have otherwise been unknown, invisible and isolated from each other, which is more than enough actually.'[184]

The nine years that followed were very different and made good on Domínguez's programme of another festival format 'that is flexible enough to change constantly, in relation to what we think is needed'.[185] To help with the collective evaluation of these needs and the distribution of responsibilities, and as part of a movement away from the solitary decision-making role of the curator, Domínguez was supported by the collective El Club, whose 'members' include Amalia Fernández, Bárbara Bañuelos, Cristina Blanco, Emilio Tomé, Fernando Quesada, Ismeni Espejel, Laura Bañuelos, Maral Kekejian, María Jerez and Tania Arias. Many of the artists from El Club were supported during the festival's formative years and cooperated as such, in a 'heterogeneous' way and yet with a collectively shared responsibility in terms of content and organisation.[186]

As examples, I would like to focus on the last editions of *In-Presentable*, such as in 2009, when Domínguez brought Xavier Le Roy's project *6M1L* with a total of seventeen participating artists to Madrid.[187] In 2010, the emphasis

---

'Over these five years, the festival's main activities have focused on: Contextualising and exhibiting small- and medium-format works whose authors bring new tools and possibilities of applying projects to the advancement of understanding and reflection, and who generally have a difficult time entering the market in our country; Creating a space where artists working in different areas (dance, visual arts, performance, theatre, architecture, etc.) can coexist and connect with the intention of creating a critical and generative discourse. Supporting the works of young artists. Establishing workshops that combine the artistic processes of invited artists with those of the participants, while also serving as working references for both. Collaborating with other organisations and festivals that generate projects, encourage exchanges between artists and facilitate resources for creation and promotion. Involving the public in the entire project through seminars and colloquia and encouraging the active participation of spectators/artists in different activities, drawing everyone into the creative processes, thus facilitating an understanding of the new codes and vocabularies and consequently of the contents presented.'

184 | PR6TE.
185 | JD8PS.
186 | See, for example, the interview with Maral Kekeijan, conducted as part of *Escenas Discursivas*, http://escenasdiscursivas.tkh-generator.net/2011/04/interview-maral-kekejian/, retrieved 22.7.2013.
187 | The project *6M1L (6 Months 1 Location)*, initiated by Xavier Le Roy und Bojana Cvejic, took place between July and December at the Centre Chorégraphique National in

was on local Spanish artists. In 2011, an exception was made in favour of the choosing of a theme – 'humour' as a political and innovative perceptional tool – where the very act of choosing a theme was reconsidered, re-questioned and then implemented as a transversal undercurrent that shaped the framework of the festival.

The very last edition of *In-Presentable* took place in June 2012 according to the concept '100 artists, 10 days'. These ten days saw an extraordinary form of international exchange that featured daily artistic practices and numerous events (exhibitions, performances, discussions, lectures) and that actively raised the question of continuity and development in art, which was for many artists quite urgent. The festival ended with the *Black Market for Useful Knowledge and Non-Knowledge*, a format devised by Hannah Hurtzig, licensed here to Juan Domínguez, which gave expression, through months of preceding email discussions with the one hundred involved artists, to a feeling characterised by crisis, a feeling of fundamental structural change and lacking future prospects: 'An encounter at the end of the world as we know it.'[188]

The historical background of contemporary dance, choreography and performance in Spain at the beginning of the twenty-first century is surely also essential to the tension between local and international practices, but also between artistic works and audience relations, between working conditions and forms of exchange and cooperation. Here I'm alluding to the still young Post-Franco Spain, where it wasn't until the eighties that contemporary dance and

---

Montpellier, France, and included seventeen invited artists, of whom nine were in the programme *EX.E.R.CE*. The participants were Sasa Asentic, Younès Atbane, Eleanor Bauer, Kelly Bond, Inès Lopez Carrasco, Juan Domínguez, Luis Miguel Félix, Thiago Granato, Mette Ingvartsen, Gerald Kurdian, Neto Machado, Chrysa Parkinson, Nicolas Quinn, Eszter Salamon, Jefta van Dinther. In her compilation of participants' contributions, Eleanor Bauer describes this project's specific working mode, where each participant 'led one project and participated in at least two others. The working model was designed to challenge the known paradigms in artistic production and education simultaneously. The usual mobility and time efficiency of a performance-making process in the international coproduction scheme was altered by working on several projects at once over an extended period of time in one place', Eleanor Bauer, '6M1L/ EX.E.R.CE 08', in Alice Chauchat and Mette Ingvartsen (Eds.), *Everybodys Group Self Interviews*, p. 34. See also the book by Mette Ingvartsen, *6 months 1 location (6M1L)* (lulu: books on demand, 2009).

188 | For more on the concept and archive of the *Black Market*, see http://www.mobile academy-berlin.com/englisch/copyleft/madrid_2012.html, retrieved 22.7.2013.

choreography emerged, in the wake of an absolute caesura (i.e., without being able to re-engage with points of reference or existing lines of tradition).[189]

Domínguez has recourse to this 'nothing' and to the concomitant isolation of Spain with regard to the artistic development of dance and choreography, and he tells how – after a first generation of some contemporary choreographers in the eighties who often emigrated due to the scarcity of opportunity for practicing one's profession in Spain – a younger generation emerged who, in their lack of relational contexts, were confronted with this absence of structures directly after their education.[190]

Paz Rojo, herself having left Spain, reflects on this act of generating a specific sense-building context with regard to both the educational situation and *In-Presentable*'s audience as being of historical relevance:

'Although [*In-Presentable*] was limited to a specific audience, it made sense historically. It makes sense that there was such an audience, because there was not such an audience before anyway. People in Madrid would study at the conservatory or the drama school, where all of these issues were not treated. This context had to be created, and in that sense *In-Presentable* was necessary and relevant to happen.'[191]

This historical background allows us to measure the significance of both *In-Presentable* and the earlier, equally international and contemporarily oriented festival *Desviaciones*.

Desviaciones was founded in 1997 by Maria La Ribot and Blanca Calvo and continued for five years, until 2001, in collaboration with José A. Sánchez.[192] In the 2007 book *In-Presentable*, a retrospective look at the festival's first four years, Blanca Calvo sketches out the aims of *Desviaciones* as an international

---

189 | JD1PS: 'So there was no real institutional history of contemporary dance and choreography in Madrid. There was a very strong tradition in flamenco, Spanish classic dance and traditional Spanish folk dance.'

190 | JD1PS. See also Paz Rojo's perspective, PR5TE.

191 | PR4TE.

192 | For more on *Desviaciones* and Calvo's simultaneous work with the interdisciplinary Basque residency and artistic project *Mugatxoan*, directed together with Ion Munduate, see Blanca Calvo in conversation with Bettina Földesi (BC13BF, BC14BF) as well as the virtual archives of the artes escénicas [scenic arts], http://artesescenicas.uclm.es/index.php?sec=conte&id=7, retrieved 25.8.2013. The researcher, professor and author José A. Sánchez was also director from 1999 to 2002 of the festival *Situaciones* in Cuenca, Spain; see also Domínguez in conversation with Petra Sabisch, JD3PS. See also José A. Sánchez and U.V.I. (Eds.), *Desviaciones* (Madrid: La Inesperada y Cuarta Pared, 1999); and idem. and Jaime Conde-Salazar (Eds.), *Cuerpos sobre blanco* (Cuenca: UCLM-Desviaciones / Communidad de Madrid, 2003).

contextualisation and implementation of new forms of perception in the wake of changed, contemporary working modes:

'*Desviaciones* was designed with an international focus, primarily because we felt isolated and invisible and we knew that our individual practices were an experience shared by others, although the places and functions in Madrid were all pre-determined. The codes that we proposed were not fully understood, because people did not identify them with dance, and we had to invent a context that would promote a change in the orders of perception.'[193]

Desviaciones was ended in 2001 due to lack of funds.[194] Two years later, *In-Presentable* began making new signs for the future and continued to do so for the next ten years, and in June 2013 Paz Rojo initiated the first 'series of experimental milieus' under the title *¿Y si dejamos de ser (artistas)...?* (*YSDDSA*).[195]

Even though each festival's approach encompasses different artistic and curatorial strategies, all three programmes have at least one thing in common: they were initiated and carried out by choreographic artists, and they have actively furthered, in an inventive spirit, the societal position of contemporary dance and performance art in Spain.[196]

Beyond all this, *In-Presentable* can be understood – and I can say the following at least with regard to *In-Presentable* – as a highly specific response to breaks in tradition and the accompanying isolation of Spanish dance makers

---

193 | Blanca Calvo, 'Nine', in Juan Domínguez (Ed.), *In-Presentable 03–07*, p. 53.

194 | For more on the financing of *In-Presentable* through La Casa Encendida, see Domínguez in conversation with Petra Sabisch, JD3PS and JD22-23PS.

195 | The intention of *Y si dejamos de ser (artistas)...?*, which means 'and if we let go of being (artists)?', lies, according to Rojo, in 'broadening the special, temporal and structural as well as representational borders of a festival for the scenic arts', http://www.ysidejamosdeserartistas.com/pagina-ejemplo/, retrieved 12.6.2013 (website discontinued). On the title's vocabulary, see http://www.ysidejamosdeserartistas.com/vocabulatorio/; on Paz Rojo and Manuela Zechner's 2008 workshop *Vocabulaboratories* at the Amsterdam School for the Arts, see Sher Doruff, 'A Vocabulary of Doing' (27.6.2008), http://old.researchcatalogue.net/upload/data/A%20Vocabulary%20of%20Doing.pdf, retrieved 12.6.2013. For more on Paz Rojo's reflections on *YSDDSA*, which has happened once in this form, see her interview with Tom Engels, PR17TE.

196 | In the interview, Domínguez emphasises that the allocation of funds for *Desviaciones* differed from that of *In-Presentable* (JD3PS) and that this resulted in varying artistic strategies which he differentiates as 'claiming' and 'affirming'. This also evokes a relation vis-à-vis critique, a relation that insists on the insufficiency of critique as mere 'deficit analysis', pleading instead that it be practiced as 'alternative proposal'. See also the interview held with Juan Domínguez on 22.4.2011 as part of *Escenas Discursivas*.

in its rethinking and continuous development of the spectrum of dance, choreography and *artes escénicas* through its context- and discourse-generating programme while attempting to overcome isolation by means of international networks and work-mode-specific contextualisations, without losing sight of the special local situation.[197]

When asked about the significance of the festival with regard to its ten years' continuity, Rojo underlines the following:

'In the last festival's edition he invited many people, and I decided to take part. In Madrid's context it was quite remarkable that an artistic proposal like his could last for such a long time. I must admit that this never had happened before.
In-Presentable supported local artists, especially in the first editions. It introduced the relationship between theory and practice and the understanding of critical artistic practices and discourse. I think one of the most relevant things *In-Presentable* generated was a discursive and artistic research development and experimentation, which at the time was not present in Madrid's performing arts context.'[198]

If in this respect the importance of *In-Presentable* as well as the extent of its reach lay in a discursive, opening, experimental approach that offered descriptions of uncharted territory and also mapped out research-oriented growth for artistic practices, then the importance of the requisite interconnection between continuity and development of artistic practices becomes all too clear.[199]

In our conversation, Domínguez points out this connection repeatedly, explaining that he would have enjoyed – as part of his constant engagement with the festival's form towards the end of its ten-year course – developing it further into another format, a continuous, non-stop laboratory with constant possibilities for development and a different kind of visibility structure. Ultimately, however, this was not possible.[200]

---

197 | On the act of interdisciplinary – and undisciplined – opening, see also Paz Rojo in conversation with Tom Engels, PR8TE: 'For me [*In-Presentable*] belongs to the scheme of other festivals or initiatives in Europe. But in the context of Madrid, of course, it had different resonances, such as the impact of certain methodologies that were unknown, and the crossings between disciplines, theory, practice, visual arts, choreography and performance were made possible. Until then, the dance and theatre community were completely separated and *In-Presentable* could broaden up and entangle these disciplines. Juan also stayed in close relationship with his own artistic processes, for example by inviting fellow participants of *6Months1Location* to join him in the curatorial team.'
198 | PR1TE.
199 | See also the idea of renaming the festival every year: JD34PS, JD35PS.
200 | For more on Domínguez' idea of the laboratory, see JD8PS, JD9PS, JD17PS.

Domínguez refers to the limits of the sporadic nature and 'event' orientation of a festival:

'But for me, the problem lies in the concept of the festival itself. A festival is great, but what happens during the rest of the year? When this knowledge and experience is generating continuity? And when, in a way, this continuity can grow? Festivals have these dynamics: they are goal-oriented, although they can also be trying to give access to other parts of the process. But in the end – even when they offer this openness to the process or other kinds of experience or knowledge that the process can produce – it takes place only in this moment of the festival. That is also what happened with *In-Presentable*. So, the audience also goes there to consume this in a very sporadic way, I think.'[201]

As a response to this emphasis on the isolated moment (which also co-defines a certain form of the perception of art), a plan surfaced in which a working-place[202] that is active all year long would disseminate the visibility of experiments, lectures and artistic practices differently.[203] Such a continuity, according to Domínguez, would have also been capable of generating a change in the habits of aesthetic engagement. In this context, Domínguez, in astonishment, criticises the way many festivals behave in a primarily reactive manner towards existing social customs instead of changing them or wanting to reshape them: 'I think festivals follow social patterns more than proposing new ones. A festival should be part of how we contract reality, not affirming how reality is.'[204]

Especially against the background of the crisis in Spain, where art and culture (and of course other areas of society) have been dealt the harshest of blows through the collapse of the culturally obligated *cajas* (banks), where inconceivably unsocial cutback measures have been aimed at public moneys and where project funding offered by the 'public hand' has become completely inaccessible and untouchable in the category of performance due to absolutely unachievable stipulations; against the background of the fact that the government's entire research budget was scratched and that the value added tax (sales tax) on cultural goods has been raised to three times its former rate of seven percent so that almost all art cinemas in Madrid have had to close their doors; against the background of this unbelievable rationing away of art and

---

201 | JD16PS.
202 | Translator's note: The term 'working-place' has been opted for here in contrast to 'workplace' as connotative of full-time, hierarchy-based employment where decisions are taken on a top-down rather than bottom-up basis.
203 | Cf. JD67PS.
204 | JD17PS.

intellect, it's no accident that Domínguez continually stresses the urgency of continuity in discourse.²⁰⁵

In keeping with its programme, *In-Presentable*'s last edition revolved around one point of emphasis – 'What now?' – be it through its almost crazy endeavour to conduct, in advance of the festival, an email debate with one hundred people; or be it in its numerous discussions with just as many people on site at the festival, discussions in which at least the attempt was made, with unbroken simultaneous Spanish/English translation, to fan out and understand the diverse perspectives of individual artistic positions.

This was not, however, only a question addressed to the future. Instead, for ten years it was a future-oriented dimension of Domínguez' curatorial practice. And this dimension seems still to be reflected in the programme and in the pieces' titles included in In-Presentable's last edition, such as when Xavier Le Roy, after *Project* and *6M1L*, shows his *"Retrospective"*; when in several *Last Minutes*²⁰⁶ artists such as Amaia Urra, Cuqui Jerez, Ismeni Espejel, Emilio Tomé, Sergi Faustino, Uri Turkenich, Rebecca Stillman, Mårten Spångberg, Dario Facal and Lilia Mestre take a stance on the question 'What now?' and on the discontinuity of the situation; when Bea Fernández, Silvia Sant Funk, Aimar Pérez Galí and Jorge Dutor thematise *Paradigma & Crisis*; when Cristina Henriquez presents the *Materia Cris*; when María Jerez shoots *The Movie*, which practiced a continuous passing on of dialogue from one participating artist to the next; when Arantxa Martínez, Lola Rubio and Eduard Mont de Palol perform *The Present*; when Valentina Desideri asks *So What* and Neto Machado shows his piece *Agora*; when Jorge Alenca thematises the *Souvenir* and Mette Edvardsen presents her 'books' in *Time has fallen asleep in the afternoon sunshine*; when Isabel de Naverán and Victoria Pérez Royo perform a dialogue by unlikely means; when Jorge Dutor and Guillem Mont de Palol present their performance *And why Juan Celda?: Globoflexia, Body Painting y Transformismo*; when BADco asks *Is There Life On Stage?*; when Luís Miguel Félix and Sidney Leonie instigate the *War of Fictions* and Eleanor Bauer in her eponymous 2005 solo depicts the contemporary artist's profile as a 'Post-Fordist art-prostitute'; and when – in addition to many other events that I could not attend – Eszter Salamon and Christine de Smedt perform their brilliant *Dance #2*.

In-Presentable opened the genre borders between choreography, dance, performance, film, radio, discursive practice, dialogue, intervention, black market, and so forth, as seen in many works such as the Prado tours by Jaime

---

205 | JD11PS, JD17PS, JD18PS, JD63PS.

206 | Many presentations in *In-Presentable*'s 2012 programme bore the title 'Last Minute', which can refer on the one hand to the ceaseless rush and the 'just-finished-by-a-hair' feeling in performative work processes, and on the other hand – literally – to the experience of a 'last minute' before the end of performing arts.

Conde-Salazar, the works *Sky lab* by Leo França and *Experimentación con una misma* by Alejandra Pombo Suárez, and not least the public radio broadcasts *Emisiones Cacatúa*.[207]

Surely the question of continuity has long since transcended the borders of Spain in case-specific and differently weighted parameterisations of the triad 'production means, work mode, and aesthetic'.

How, in such a situation, can one continue to make art at all?[208]

How can the evolution of issues and the positionings of critique take place also, and especially, against the background of internationally rather disparate production and living conditions?

What interplay between perception and representation, material conditions and working modes would be adequate in view of today's obviously bleak present and future prospects for art resources in Spain?

Since completing his activities with *In-Presentable*, Domínguez has been carrying on with this form of continuity and continued development in choreographic discourse- and context-generating practices, as in the series *Clean Room (Season 1)* and in the *Picnic Sessions* series.[209]

Looking back on ten years of *In-Presentable*, one can easily recognise, however, the magnitude of this one-of-a-kind festival's contribution to the development of content and continuity.

The question of what kinds of continuous structures will grow to maturation out of In-Presentable certainly still remains to be seen. A first step toward continuity was made in 2013 by Paz Rojo, together with a group of thirty local artists, when she collectively re-posed these questions about discursive continuity through the experimental frame of *Y si dejamos de ser (artistas)...?*, connecting, researching and displaying them towards an undisciplined development of art based on the collective's own notions of 'festival as practice'.[210]

---

207 | See also p. 105.
208 | JD40PS, JD43PS.
209 | On the idea of the series *Clean Room, Season 1*, part of Tanz im August, 2012, see http://juandominguezrojo.com/?p=646; see also the weekly series organised by Domínguez *Picnic Sessions (La Odisea del Deseo)*, 23.5-11.7.2013 at the Centro de Arte Dos de Mayo, http://www.ca2m.org/es/picnic-sessions, retrieved 27.4.2013. Cf. also JD63PS.
210 | For the concept of *YSDDSA* see PR13TE, and for the concept 'festival as practice', see PR33TE.

2.3 *The Double Lecture Series*, Stockholm (28.9–2.10.2011)

Figure 3: MDT-Poster 'The Double Lecture Series', 2011. Photograph: Petra Sabisch

The Double Lecture Series is a five-day international event initiated by Mårten Spångberg and Mette Ingvartsen that took place 28.9–2.10.2011 at MDT Stockholm as an extra issue of *Special Issue*.[211]

---

211 | Under the direction of Danjel Andersson, the Stockholm theatre MDT, founded in 1986, has established itself as a leading coproduction platform for contemporary choreography and performance that is open to new artistic practices and, furthermore, offers residencies and facilitates networking according to its own open policies. See http://mdtsthlm.se/, retrieved 15.4.2012.

As an immediate answer to the zero number of *Special Issue* in Aubervilliers, *The Double Lecture Series* once again picked up on the situation of discursive performative practices in dance and choreography. Objects of interrogation included the importance of contemporary dance discourses within today's knowledge society as well as the possibilities and perspectives of discursive and performative dispositives. The programme text introduces this problem:

'Has dance and choreography any place in the knowledge society? Are these practices that operate in parallel with so-called cognitive capitalism? Can performative practices produce specific kinds of knowledge or even disrupt established modes of knowledge production and issue alternative forms of experience? Five evenings with related seminar program, where meetings between movement and production of knowledge will be explored in relation to representation and expression.

Dance in the first place in respect of production of knowledge in front of, or in conjunction with the spectator, i.e. in and through experience. Five internationally renowned choreographers will present their perspectives on what has been called 'performative discursive dispositives', a still weak style that emerged in tandem with phenomena such as artistic research and practice-based choreography.'[212]

The concept of *The Double Lecture Series*, which is the smallest, that is, shortest programme covered by this study, consisted in the invitation of five artists, each of whom in turn invited one other person for the second part of the evening: the *Double Lecture*: 'For each evening, the choreographers have invited an autonomous voice that in the form of a lecture will replicate, comment, continue, listen to the performances and speak from their own discipline.'[213]

In this sense, the type of relation that existed between the two events per evening would remain open, as open as each invited artist's understanding of 'lecture' was (see programme overview, p. 67), not to mention what they wanted to try out based thereon. More decisive was the invitation to approach the lecture format as a choreography and to explore the performativity and movements of discursive parameters.

The Double Lecture Series was rounded out by daily seminars (with, among others, the Berlin Theatre and Cultural Studies scholar Kai van Eikels; Julian Reid, professor of international relations at the University of Lapland (Finland); Petra Sabisch; and also Mårten Spångberg.

---

212 | Excerpt from the programme text, see http://mdtsthlm.se/artists/the-double-lecture-series-curated-by-mette-ingvartsen-and-maarte/, retrieved 17.8.2013.
213 | Ibid.

Program overview: The Double Lecture Series

28.9.2011	Xavier Le Roy: *Product of Other Circumstances*
	Kai van Eikels: *What does Xavier Le Roy make easier for me?*
29.9.2011	Christine de Smedt: *Untitled 4 – Jonathan Burrows*
	Olav Westphalen: *Lecture*
30.9.2011	Mårten Spångberg: *Spangbergianism*
	Julian Reid: Curious Orange: *Paranoid*
1.10.2011	Mette Ingvartsen: *Thoughts for the Future*
	Reza Negarestani: *Skype direct Lecture from Kuala Lumpur*
2.10.2011	Eleanor Bauer: *Severe Tripping in Context/Space Time Continuum*
	Pierre Rubio: SPELLBINDINGSPELLBREAKING

In an interview held as part of *The Double Lecture Series*, Mette Ingvartsen explains her artistic-curatorial interest in experimentation with frameworks: 'Within the lecture-series, we were experimenting with what this format of a *Double Lecture Series* is and I think, that we're in some sort of second or even third generation of how people approach the idea of lecturing about movement.'[214]

When asked, in response, why producing discourse is important to her, Ingvartsen answers:

'Well, I think there are several reasons why this is important. One reason is of course to insist on discourse production in the community, which is extremely important for the field to go further. But then in proposing it as a series and as a festival, there is another reason, one that's about giving visibility to these practices as performative practices and not as something you do next to the real performances. To actually say that this is a form of performance that should be as accepted and normal as any other type of performance. Because even when discourse-performances are shown in other festivals, they're very often shown as an appendix to the main program, like the small thing that is shown in the little theatre – or not even in a theatre, but rather in the foyer. Thus, they are not properly understood as works. You could say, that this type of work that has been developed over the last fifteen years has started to form a sort of movement where language is used and plays an important role without falling into the trap of being dramatic theatre. And the line between discursive and theatrical is a very delicate line to draw.'[215]

From a contemporary dance-historiographic perspective, this engagement with discursive practices and with the performative exploration of their modes of operation is most understandable, especially considering that dance

---

214 | MI21PS_2011.
215 | MI15PS_2011.

has often been defined as nonverbal movement art and that any accusation of conceptuality has often been tantamount (not only in the nineties, and to an extent unrivalled in any other art field) to ontological expulsion from the guild.[216]

Experimental art forms, however, play with the boundaries that have been ascribed to them, questioning them and altering them, and have been doing so since long before Austin's speech act arrived on the scene, illuminating the (embodied) conventions of meaning-production and the effectiveness of its performances. For dance history at the end of the twentieth century, the lecture-performance *Product of Circumstances* (1999) by Xavier Le Roy certainly marks a crucial break that characterises the representational modes of the lecture-performance to date.[217] This break is put into perspective through Le Roy's new choreography *Product of Other Circumstances* (2009), which reassumes, after the artist gained ten years' worth of distance to the preceding performance, this explicit engagement with production conditions and methods. *Product of Other Circumstances* was also shown in *The Double Lecture Series* in Stockholm.[218]

I would like to recall Foucault's definition of 'discursive practice' here, which in no way means just the spoken act, but rather the very conditions for the operation of expressive functions:

'Lastly, what we have called 'discursive practice' can now be defined more precisely. It must not be confused with the expressive operation by which an individual formulates an idea, a desire, an image; nor with the rational activity that may operate in a system of inference; nor with the 'competence' of a speaking subject when he constructs grammatical sentences; it is a body of anonymous, historical rules, always determined in the

---

216 | See also Sabisch, *Choreographing Relations*, pp. 157-166, and for the delayed arrival of this debate to Sweden, see Halla Ólafsdóttir in conversation with Bettina Földesi HO4OBF: 'Not only is the discussion happening twenty years later than in the rest of Europe, but it feels like such a restrictive and uninteresting categorisation. The discussion of 'conceptual choreography', which apparently isn't dance, versus 'dance dance', which apparently is dance, is in my opinion quite descriptive of dividing the field into two teams.' For a broader engagement with the concept in art, see the conference *The Art of the Concept*, which took place as part of Nathan Brown's and Peter Milat's *Conjuncture* series on June 2012 at MaMa, Zagreb: 'The Art of the Concept', in *Frakcija* 64/65 (Winter 2012) and artofconcept.mi2.hr/, accessed 22.3.2013.
217 | See the website of Xavier Le Roy, http://www.xavierleroy.com/, retrieved 20.7.2013.
218 | Ibid.

time and space that have defined a given period, and for a given social, economic, geographical, or linguistic area, the conditions of operation of the enunciative function.'[219]

Demonstrating these conditions for linguistic articulation and experimenting with their conventions, their expressiveness and effectiveness as well as with the simultaneity of saying and showing, or with language and staged occurrence, are examples of *The Double Lecture Series'* deployment of the discursive practices with which it was concerned.

In Mette Ingvartsen's choreography *Thoughts for the Future*, which later was given the title *Speculations* and which plays, in the form of a performance, with projections of a future performance, Ingvartsen utilises reality-generating statements by describing situations and making them performatively coincide in part with the present moment of the performance and then by simultaneously doubling the statement's presence into the fiction of another space and hence another time. In this way, the scenic present opens itself up when Ingvartsen's descriptions of the scene conflict with the real occurrences on stage, inviting the viewer to imagine other scenes and speculate about the future of the performance.

'It's a show that was thought as a preparation for another show, but with the idea of working on it as a public presentation in itself. So, to think of it as another materialisation of the ideas that I am working on for the future, rather than as a work in progress or a less elaborate version of the show to come.
What I did was work a lot on sources and materials that I'm anyway busy with since a while. There are a lot of book references, also references to images from the media, and references to other artworks and so on. The whole performance is built through three different modes of expression: describing, speculating and imagining situations that are not actually there. Most of the situations come from real sources, like a film scene and a book, or from a concrete place. I try to create a fiction with these preexisting materials.'[220]

The second part to Ingvartsen's *Thoughts for the Future* was a Skype-delivered lecture by the contemporary author and philosopher Reza Negarestani, whose 'speculative realism' and especially his theory-fiction *Cyclonopedia* brought him renown.[221] Negarestani's powerfully eloquent theory of nature and his remarks on the function of universalia today created a choreography of theoretical

---

219 | Michel Foucault, *Archeology of Knowledge* (London & New York: Routledge, 2002), p. 131.
220 | MI1PS_2011.
221 | Reza Negarestani, *Cyclonopedia: Complicity with Anonymous Materials* (Melbourne: re.press, 2008).

references and meaning-constructions in its own right, while – when set in relation with Ingvartsen's choreography – making the differences between Ingvartsen's and Negarestani's respective 'scenic concepts' and presentational formats discursivisable.[222]

This 'setting in relation' performed by the *Double Lecture* gave rise to a third level of reflection, which had very specific retroactive effects on each of the two pieces, discursively displaying their heterogeneous relation.

A further example from *The Double Lecture Series* was Christine de Smedt's then-named portrait *Untitled 4 – Jonathan Burrows*, one of a series of four portraits of the choreographers Jonathan Burrows, Xavier Le Roy, Alain Platel, and Eszter Salamon. Today this portrait series is titled *Four Choreographic Portraits*, and all four performances are preferably to be shown together in one evening. Each has a specific title: *I would leave a signature* (for Alain Platel), *The son of a priest* (for Jonathan Burrows), *A woman with a diamond* (for Eszter Salamon) *and Self-Reliance* (for Xavier Le Roy).[223]

In my conversation with Christine de Smedt, it became clear just how much discursive engagement with highly differing choreographic practices and working modes was going on in this series. Although each individual process was originally motivated by the idea of a self-portrait, as time passed each process led to interviews with the choreographers where each artist's personal thinking methods are made visible as a choreography (and thereby also as a staging):

'For me, *Untitled* was a research on the relation between choreographic practices, methods and artistic interests which I explored by having a dialogue or a conversation with colleague choreographers. This research questioned the relation with the concept of the personal. What do you consider as personal? What is related to your history or biography and how do you relate your own artistic work to the idea of the personal? Or don't you do so?
This investigation came along with the understanding that the personal is a very blurry concept to use, but it's also very important, it's related to this idea of authorship, the identity of a person, the author, and the identity of the work itself. The research started from a statement: '"No to" biographic elements in my work'.'[224]

---

222 | Cf. MI27-28PS_2011.
223 | See also the following book on performance, with contributions by Christine de Smedt, Pieter Van Bogaert, Ana Vujanović and Sarah Vanhee: Christine de Smedt (Eds.), *Four Choreographic Portraits: "I would leave a signature", The son of a priest, A woman with a diamond and Self-Reliance* (Brussels: Les Ballets C. de la B., 2012).
224 | CDS5PS.

In her work on Jonathan Burrows, de Smedt applies, for example, the principle of counterpoint (used strongly in Burrows' work) to her own diction as she reads text fragments from the interview so that a mode of thinking is extended into a choreographic rhythm. De Smedt says that 'the whole research is precisely about the liminal point between the choreography and the personal; how the personal is choreographed and how choreography is individuated in ways of thinking.'[225]

What is interesting here is the interplay between production, work mode and aesthetic. In the following, Ingvartsen explains deliberations from the preparative phases of *The Double Lecture Series* in which both curators took the mutual decision to make their own artistic interests the point of departure for the format:

'When Mårten and I spoke about the *Double Lecture Series*, we noted that it responds to a need we both have, also in our practice. It was not only about thinking what other people need to see, but also about what WE would actually like to experience as a curatorial form.

Eventually we both took part in the *Double Lecture Series*, which, at a certain point was, of course, under discussion (as to whether or not it's good when the organisers also take part in the event). But we decided that this engagement in the material in the making is also a good argument for our participation, since the concerns also come out of our own practices and the practices that we observe around us, with colleagues and friends who are closely connected to that kind of approach.

Even though the idea of the whole project was to open up our own approach and think about this relation between two lectures, becoming sensitive towards the field of theory, for instance, or towards other fields (in one case, the second part was done by the visual artist, Olav Westphalen), it was important on the one hand to solidify aspects of our own practices, and on the other hand to consider how we could actually propose a context that could expand our own practices.'[226]

The side programme of *The Double Lecture Series* hence became the production of a difference that connects individuals' own artistic practices with the production of other works in this context; that invents a format that enables a specific, perspective-generating experimentation; and that attracts new ways of working and new engagements and examinations, thereby becoming a discourse- and context-generating programme. Christine de Smedt talks about this complex and sense-constitutive procedural method: 'Of course, that's why I think this *Double Lecture Series* was such a great project. Because it was creating

---

225 | CDS11PS.
226 | MI1PS_2013.

a context, where then, of course in a concentrated way, these formats or these ways of discourse-generating practices could be shown.'[227]

It is crucial here not only that *The Double Lecture Series* was an artist-initiated event, but also that its format constructed a frame that simultaneously opened new perspectives for existing work modes and evoked new experimentations to be performed on one's own practices.

Ingvartsen describes this with regard to the stimulation of new production:

'Sharing doesn't only happen when we do a production in which we need help or comments from friends to realise it; it's also something that we produce. For instance, among the works that were shown in the *Double Lecture Series*, some choreographers had actually made performances within the same type of understanding of lecture performance or expanded lecture performance, whereas others really made up their propositions especially for this context. In that sense, the *Double Lecture Series* was also a way of thinking together about whether this format of lecture performance properly exists, whether it's still relevant, whether there is a common understanding or completely different ones and whether that triggers new works.'[228]

Both Ingvartsen and de Smedt consider exchange with peers as an essential for artistic development, not only discursively but also in the fully concrete physical meeting and creating of a present-day milieu of engagement.[229]

The exchange that the *Double Lecture Series* initiated pointed in this respect far beyond normal festivals, because through its specific frame it provoked a sort of collaborative 'continued thinking' in situ. On a related note, however, the sense-building dimension of the *Double Lecture Series* also attests, with

---

227 | CDS21PS.

228 | MI3PS_2013.

229 | For the significance of the not-only-virtual context, see CDS23PS: 'The context is there, but it's kind of virtual, but if we do these festivals, as you did the *Double Lecture Series*, the fact that you physically come together, is also the fact that you can physically think together. Whether it's reflecting on what you are doing or on what you should do, or will do, or want to do. And that reflects different, political, cultural issues with which you are confronted in the work.' For the experience of an exchange-generating environment, see CDS24PS: 'So, it's also a social thing. A social gathering with artistic intention, which I think produces new thoughts and new developments. You see, this *Double Lecture Series*, the fact that you have seen *Untitled* there, that we are doing this interview now... Yes, for me, these context-generating situations, they produce experience, and not only the experience of looking at a show, but an experience of an environment in which exchange can happen on different levels, in many different ways. And I think that this exchange of thoughts and experience is very important, especially in a life that is so individual and locally disconnected.'

respect to discursive performative practices, to a more open work mode and form of address, which, as Christine de Smedt underlines, reaches far beyond the significance of individual projects, and which could probably never be produced at all by means of such projects alone:

'I think it's important to think about ways of bringing certain works together. Not as festivals are usually composed and programmed – a series of big shots beside some more risky or experimental work and some 'younger' work. Many festivals are of course a presentation of what is available on the market at that moment. But still, differentiation is good. To link different works based on a particular content or format or concern and to allow a discourse to develop in the space between the works – that's interesting. For the work as well as for the viewer. It allows one to go beyond the limit of the singular work and produces thoughts that a singular work maybe cannot produce. Through this mode of exchange between the works, new perspectives and ideas can develop. In visual arts this is more common, and the medium allows for that. With live performances you are confronted with the limitation of time and space. [...] The importance is of showing these pieces together to create reflection in between and to create opportunities for artists to meet and exchange.'[230]

This sort of specific opening up towards a field means contributing to the constitution of that field.

Figure 4: PAF, 2006. Photograph: Petra Sabisch

---

230 | CDS22PS.

2.4 Performing Arts Forum (PAF, St. Erme, France, since 2005)

The *Performing Arts Forum* (PAF) is housed in a former women's convent in northeastern France (St. Erme) which was purchased in 2005 by the Dutch theatre director Jan Ritsema, who, with approximately thirty invited artists and theorists, brought an open, artist-run forum for performing arts into being.[231] The convent consists of a 6,400 m² building and is surrounded by 1.2-hectare grounds and a garden with five peacocks.

In a recently published article in the Austrian magazine *Springerin: Hefte für Gegenwartskunst*, Nicolas Siepen, professor of visual arts at the Academy of Contemporary Art at the University of Tromsø, Norway, describes the experiment of PAF:

'In the *Performing Arts Forum* (PAF), not far from Paris, Ritsema started a risky social experiment in 2005, sharing his entire worldly fortune with a collective that didn't even exist at the time. A virtual investment in the future, a derivative in the form of a beautiful yet run-down convent. Over the course of the last eight years, the gamble and desire of one person has transformed into a temporary autonomous zone, an almost completely self-organised, independent, international, and astonishingly workable structure—a structure which, although one can name its operational rules and the needs it satisfies, cannot be said to guide PAF's current and future sociographic form. In the international art world in general, and on the performance scene in particular, a patently dire need for such a place is observable, a place where the art business's usual laws apply to a limited extent only, a place where it's worth it to collectively invest a share of internationally hard-earned capital. [...] Here we instead have very different and contradictory approaches that combine to form a complex working-place, a place one would have to invent were it not already in existence, a place from which a model could only be derived with reluctance.'[232]

The magnitude of the need, expressed by Siepen in the above, for this sort of independent, non-art-market-oriented structure can only be confirmed with the help of a statistical review, compiled as part of this study, of user development in PAF from 2006 to 2013: over 5,000 people from sixty-four countries have visited PAF since 2006.[233]

---

231 | On the history of PAF's inception, see Jan Ritsema in conversation with Bettina Földesi, JR1BF.
232 | Nicolas Siepen, 'Free Popular Avantgarde: Die ewige Unruhe des Kunst-und-Politik-Zusammenhangs', *die springerin. Hefte für Gegenwartskunst* XIX 2 (2013), pp. 48–51; available online, http://www.springerin.at/dyn/heft.php?id=80&pos=0&textid=0&lang=de, retrieved 22.6.2013.
233 | See Annex 2: 'Statistics on the internationality of the case studies', p. 175.

This worldwide, constantly growing demand proves that spaces like this are needed. When faced with these numbers, one can hardly speak of *one* 'scene'. And yet these numbers seem even more informative when one considers that PAF is neither production house nor subsidy recipient, meaning that the costs for staying at PAF, including travel costs, are often paid out of pocket by visitors themselves:

'Initiated and run by artists, theoreticians and practitioners themselves, PAF is a user-created, user-innovative informal institution. Neither a production-house and venue, nor a research-center, it is a platform for everyone who wants to expand possibilities and interests in his/her own working practice.'[234]

So what makes up this structure? What experiment are we talking about?

A trait highly constitutive of PAF is that it was started and is maintained and run by artists, theorists and practitioners and that it offers a platform for any and all agents who want to reconsider their own working conditions and practices.[235] Even though the referential framework for many participants had to do with dance, choreography and performance in the project's beginnings, PAF has since functioned according to an idea of genre-openness, and has done so steadfastly in the company of constantly expanding categorisations and crossovers among the practices it hosts.[236]

PAF's website describes the forum's self-conception as follows:

---

[234] | http://www.pa-f.net/basics, retrieved 22.3.2006. The current cost of over-nighting at PAF is fifteen euros per night, a rate that sinks as the stay lengthens and that is included in accommodation costs during times when large-scale meetings take place.

[235] | Cf. ibid.: PAF 'is a place for the professional and not-yet professional practitioners and activists in the field of performing arts, visual art, literature, music, new media and internet, theory and cultural production, and scientists who seek to research and determine their own conditions of work. PAF is for people who can motorize their own artistic production and knowledge production not only responding to the opportunities given by the institutional market'.

[236] | For the increasing influence of PAF in the visual arts and in contemporary philosophy and science, see also Valentina Desideri in conversation with Tom Engels, VD2TE, VD5TE. See also Jan Ritsema in conversation with Bettina Földesi: 'The different art fields are slowly coming closer together. It's a very nice development that the boundaries between the arts are dissolving. This might also be a reason why PAF can exist, because PAF isn't only there for dance, although I came from dance. But it has always been there for all the arts, and in addition to that, for scientists and media activists as well. We work in the direction of an increasing overlapping of the arts, which is far more interesting', JR20BF.

'PAF is, firstly, a forum for knowledge production in critical exchange and constant discursive practice; secondly, a place for temporary autonomy and undivided concentration on one's work; thirdly, a machine for the manufacture of means to develop methods, tools and processes in not-necessarily-product-oriented practices; and fourthly, a place for experimentation with otherwise unknown modes of production and modes for the organisation of work, such as open source procedures'.[237]

Before immediately going into the special operational and functional modes of PAF, the more basic question of how this need and this massive self-organised structure is to be explained must be posed. How did this desire to frequent PAF come about, this wish to keep it running and to repeatedly re-form it, even though Europe is replete with residency locations that are often cost free for the artist?

The Belgian author and research coordinator of a.pass (Advanced Performance and Scenography Studies) in Antwerp, Elke van Campenhout, sees in PAF a temporary answer to the 'malaise of an entire generation':

'In a way the self-description above echoes the concerns of the performing arts scene in the past ten years, which has little by little found itself squeezed between governmental compartmentation (through often ill-fitting and politically-motivated subsidy systems) and the seductive call of the enterprise-funded 'creative industries', paving the way for an understanding of the artist as either a well-prepared and policy-aware dossier-writer, or a self-proclaimed entrepreneur totally in line with the neo-liberal ethics of self-realisation, mobility and economic common sense.
Countless artists have expressed the need and the urgency to escape these corsets of survival by pointing out their toxic by-products: the subsidy system in the well-founded European scene has started to create a way of working and an aesthetic that is not primarily based on artistic choice and necessity, but on the possibilities of touring (and reaching your minimum quota of presentations), networking (getting as many as possible prominent arts centres to back up your project), and formatting (ideally a performance should fit as many venues as possible, not be too costly, and be adaptable to the regular programming strategies of the field). The kind of work that escapes these constraints is often overlooked or doesn't find its way into the regular programmation.'[238]

Not only does the above text demonstrate the complexity of parameters and forces across which an artistic praxis stretches; it also brings to light a clear critical stance towards conventional institutional organisational forms in the choreographic arts that tailor artistic modes of production, work and

---

237 | http://www.pa-f.net/basics, retrieved 22.3.2006.
238 | Elke Van Campenhout, 'Spaces as Tools', *sh 2011*, programme book for the performance festival Steirischer Herbst, 23.9-26.10.2011 (2011), p. 88.

expression to their own profiles, selecting those modes that fit well rather than becoming disruptive to one's own modes of functioning and one's structures; formatting them for market-compatibility, connecting them to the corresponding administrative procedures and representational structures, and thereby homogenising artistic work in terms of content and aesthetics, without ever consulting artistic decisions, wishes or ideas that live beyond the artistic product.[239]

The vast degree to which any simple adoption of institutional 'givens' is indeed formative for artistic work modes and aesthetics has been pointed out not only by Daniel Buren, referring in his case to the function of the studio;[240] a contemporary example for a choreographic 'reprint' of this critique of the self-evident 'nature' of conventions can be found in the decision taken by both the choreographer Halla Ólafsdóttir and Emma Kim Hagdahl (curator of the 2012 Reykjavík Dance Festival: A Series of Event) to fully dispense with the renting of theatres for their dance festival.[241]

Even though knowledge regarding the problematics of the influence of institutionalised conventions on art goes back to the sixties at the latest, institutional forms of organisation seem nevertheless to promulgate a kind of engagement with sense-building developments in professional work and with the life realities of artists, as opposed to their products, that rarely constitutes any truly relevant reference parameter for their own respective institutional

---

239 | In her interview with Tom Engels, Paz Rojo offers an interesting description of the structural communication problems that even occur with artist-hosting institutions, cf. PR1TE.

240 | Cf p. 26, fn 83.

241 | For more on this, see Halla Ólafsdóttir in conversation with Bettina Földesi, HO1BF: 'As in most cases, our budget was too small for actually creating a festival, but we decided to rethink the ways of distributing the money that we actually had and then connect it to how we wanted to engage with each other and with an audience. For example, we decided not to spend money on renting a theatre. A theatre always has its own conditions: you are not free to come in and out as you want.' For more on understandings of the festival as a choreography, see also Emma Kim Hagdahl in conversation with Bettina Földesi, EKH5BF: 'We were interested in choreographing an experience and setting a situation in motion where artists and audience activated and became activated by it at the same time. Calling it choreography is a claim and attempt at expanding ideas and perspectives of choreography relating to organization of bodies in a time space. It was also really an attempt to question the assumptions of aesthetics that an audience might have about how a festival looks like, what a performance looks like, how it starts, how it ends, and so on. We tried to alter this perception and start to reconsider a social situation and rethink the interplays happening through the lens of movement and choreography.'

self-conceptions (which isn't the case when one examines their substantial efforts in audience development, in enlarging theatre operation capacity, in honing their theatres' profiles and so forth).

Precisely these work environments and living realities of nomadic project-makers operating on an application-to-application basis are, however, not only existentially formative for many internationally active artists, but also part and parcel of their own experimental artistic engagement, where the means and methods of production are set in proportion to each respective work, to its modus operandi and modus fingendi.

That being said, perhaps this movement towards the self-initiated shaping of other kinds of dynamics and organisational forms, this searching for new and self-organised forms of association, is not, from an artistic (and especially from a choreographic) perspective, such an astonishing matter; although the contexts that emerge from such connections, as Christine de Smedt illustrates in our interview, are mostly of a virtual nature, more like a kind of 'mental space' without physical form. Asked about the significance of contexts in which artistic practices enter into exchange with one another, de Smedt answers:

'The first thing that comes into my mind is that we are travelling all over the world. Actually, our context is not our neighbourhood. Our context actually is a kind of invisible international scene. Somehow, I think, if we make art these days, and in terms of performance, we live in a virtual space: you are in Berlin; this person is in Vienna. I mean, we are living so much apart, geographically, but actually our mental space, in which we relate to other people in our life, is international and virtual. These festivals, they are also not only context-generating, but I think they allow for a physical meeting somewhere, in one place, by gathering, by allowing for the physical meeting of different pieces together in order to reflect on the practices; to meet and allow exchange to happen but also in order to be part of this community.'[242]

With regard to PAF, van Campenhout explains this connection between artistic engagement in production modes, the increasing importance of exchange and practices, and the necessity for artistically and autarkically definable spaces:

'Also, as makers, artists have expressed the need to think of other production systems than the 'typical' career model proposed to the artists in the 1980's. The model of the sole author-artist, inventing his or her own aesthetics, has been replaced by a much more critical and historically-anchored view on how these artists themselves very quickly become commodities in a system that is in constant search for the 'new'. [...]

---

242 | Cf. Christine de Smedt in conversation with Petra Sabisch, CDS23PS.

Whereas the practice of the sole self-created artist was largely concerned with the uniqueness of his production, creating his value on the artist market on the basis of scarcity, newness and shock-value, the artists discussed in this text are rather concerned with the practices of sharing, of questioning themselves as the centre of gravity, of relating to other (historical, political, economic, discourse) realities. In these contexts, the practice becomes as important as the outcome, the way of organising the work as important as the work itself, the way of dealing with collaborators a significant part of the trajectory leading up (or not) to a public moment.

But for this to become a viable artistic practice, another kind of space has to be created: spaces that are no longer governed by subsidy policies or economic (un)common sense, but by artists themselves. Places that are not under the reign of profiling and networking, not dubbed as subsidiary placeholders for artistic merit, but simply places to work, that take into account the simple but pressing needs of the artists and thinkers concerned.'[243]

Against this background, not only does one stand to be impressed by the experiment of PAF in its scale, in its constancy of engagement and in the changeability of its forms of initiative; one must also recognise that it appears to be the only place of its kind worldwide thanks to its relation to a certain idea – and its constant concretion – of openness.[244] Valentina Desideri describes this uniqueness as an opportunity to take part in unplanned exchange:

'There are many places that offer the opportunity to meet, share and exchange, but what's unique about PAF is that it's not an institution. Other institutions would maybe offer the same possibility, but you would have to apply for a program with a project in which you plan to exchange. In terms of having the possibility to have unplanned exchange, I think PAF is unique.'[245]

This scarcity resonates, however, with the difficulty of breaking new ground experimentally when aiming at a collective production of desire.[246]

---

243 | Van Campenhout, 'Spaces as Tools', pp. 89–90.
244 | Jan Ritsema in conversation with Bettina Földesi, JR28BF: 'I know a lot of artist residencies from Royaumont to Schloss Solitude. I have contacts with organisations, like the Association Centres culturels – Monuments historiques. There are eighty-five European artist residencies in monasteries, in chateaus or in industrial monuments, but they are all these instituted ones where you have to write an application and go through a selection process. So I don't know a place with an idea like PAF [...].'
245 | Valentina Desideri in conversation with Tom Engels, VD8TE.
246 | For the engagement between desire-production and institution in the example of PAF, see Petra Sabisch, 'Zur Choreografie der Organisation: Zeitgenössische

So how is PAF specifically composed? What are this 'informal institution's' functional modes?

When pondering how to name PAF's future addressees/users, Jan Ritsema at first spontaneously coined the phrase 'art that thinks', a formula that was soon transformed into three rules: 'Don't leave traces. Make it possible for others. The doer decides.'[247]

These rules, whose concrete application is not always free of contradiction, enables – in interplay with the three further principles of reversibility, exchange and 'fluidisation' of hardened assessments, habits and structures – a space of thought as responsible as it is playful, which one can describe as open, dynamic and mutable.[248]

This open changeability or fluidisation of property lines finds expression, for example, in Valentina Desideri and Jan Ritsema's fundraising project *Objects Without Property*, which enables the purchase of 10,000 catalogued objects that reside in PAF, such as a teaspoon, the lid to a tin, an old urinal or a piano, all of which, however, are to remain in PAF.[249]

Precisely this open alterability of autonomous organisation is important for the continual re-testing and re-questioning of one's own habits and organisational structures in matters ranging from private property to the maintenance of an international platform, not to mention for the repeated inquiry into how these habits and structures measure up in terms of

---

künstlerische Praktiken', in Yvonne Hardt and Martin Stern (Eds.), *Choreografie und Institution*, pp. 35-52, esp. pp. 48-50.

247 | Jan Ritsema in conversation with Bettina Földesi, JR4-5BF. Valentina Desideri elaborates on this in the interview, indicating the fact that *PAF* is a 'self-sustaining', and thus self-borne structure, VD13TE.

248 | Jan Ritsema, 'The gravity of PAF, or how to be fluid', in *sh 11*, pp. 89-90.

249 | Valentina Desideri in conversation with Tom Engels: 'We were thinking about how to translate this principle of making property liquid, with PAF as property. The property of the house was too complicated, so then we thought we could stick to it on a symbolic level by selling all the objects in PAF. But then the owners were required to leave the bought object in PAF, so that it could be used by everybody. We took pictures of 10,000 objects, described 10,000 objects and categorised them [...] It raised some funds, but there are still so many objects to be sold (*laughs*). There are a couple of rooms we managed to renovate with that money. But there's so much more potential left, if you think that there are 10,000 objects and every object costs around ten euros. [...] It's a gesture towards PAF. Because if you bought a spoon, how do you know which spoon is yours? It's always nice because then when you go to PAF, you might be eating with your spoon. There are a lot of jokes about this.' VD37-40TE.

elasticity.[250] Beyond that, this alterable openness in organisation is, however, also decisive in every artistic and intellectual development, because it generates an indeterminate formability that is neither decided in advance nor governable in any real sense.[251] Mette Ingvartsen thematises this link between artistic development, transformative qualities, and unpredictability in self-organised processes:

'The uncontrollability of such types of projects – I think this is a very important aspect of how the art field is developing. It's important that collective artist-organised projects are given a space that is neither about accountability, nor about who's doing what, but that is more about the needs of the people and how they can be fulfilled by the different strategies that have already been developed. And I think that PAF is another example of this: having been initiated in the beginning by just a small group of people, now – though I haven't been there for quite some years – it's flourishing, as I understand. And currently a lot of people from all over refer to it: "Ah but, I heard about that thing during PAF". You know, like, five years later it still exists and it's still going on. I think the transformative qualities that self-organised projects can have, more so than institutional projects, are very valuable. Such an unpredictability is very difficult to achieve in institutional structures, precisely because in institutional structures you have accountability and you have the name who has to sign it. You also have responsibility and budgets that put the pressure in a different direction.'[252]

The spatial dimensions of PAF allow such a form of organisation in which exchange, development and the trying out of projects, of forms of cooperation are possible. Hence, besides the many guest rooms, the numerous studios, the media lab with the priceless archive of PAF users' performance and film DVDs, PAF also houses a comprehensive library reaching far beyond the (performing) arts.

---

250 | For the connecting of private property with self-organisation, see Valentina Desideri in conversation with Tom Engels, VD27TE, VD31TE.

251 | Asked about what the end of the experiment *PAF* would mean for exchange and cohesion in the independent scene, Jan Ritsema emphasises the necessity of constant continued development: 'Yes, [it has a huge impact on how artists can meet]. But in order to make it interesting it has to develop. If PAF would just continue for ten years and not renew itself, it will be over by then. But we also have to keep the principles up all the time, which are not principles that have to be permanent. We can change our principles, we can even do something against them.', JR19BF. And further: 'Maybe PAF is also a symbol for this direction, that the boundaries are unnecessary – another element of openness here,' JR20BF.

252 | MI5PS_2013.

It's also interesting how this spatial generosity – in connection with PAF's remote location and with the otherwise hardly existent link between living and working as a collective experience in one place – creates time. Where the motto 'time is money' has long since regulated the artistic everyday, PAF is like an unbelievably rich oasis precisely because time for working, exchanging and trying out is engendered there, not least thanks to its collective organisation; a time that may take the form of work meetings, yoga sessions, screenings, techno-practices, evening-long discussions, feedback sessions or collective dinners.

The feeling of having time to try something out and explore something beyond immediate valuation relations and market calculus is of inestimable worth for the development of artistic and theoretical work. In interview, Jan Ritsema clearly lays out this connection:

'You have so much time in PAF, that you can try all kinds of things. You can try to do something with someone else you don't know, or you can try to go for a direction with an uncertain result in your own work. But you have the time to try. Therefore you dare to face many more problems instead of escaping them and looking for quick solutions. People dare and have the freedom to try something whose outcome they aren't sure of. You don't have to calculate as much as you usually do when you make a project. Usually, when you enter a working process, you rent a studio for a few hours, you have to bring people together, you have to have results and you have to end the day well – because people leave. Since people have to work efficiently, they have to think things like 'I should not say this, I'd better not try that because I'm not sure enough.' Here you can have a fight, go away for some hours and continue. You can easily go to the studio and work, then stop, maybe take a walk, and re-think what you are doing. There is much more space for real solutions. Not for short-term solutions, but for finding other ways than the one you thought you would take. When you have a problem, you have the chance to talk with others outside your group, which might also open up your work; or you just hear other people saying something that helps or interests you. Consequently the work becomes more substantial.'[253]

Besides these spatiotemporal parameters with their effects on work, PAF's central characteristics are exchange and discourse. From the beginning, one of PAF's points of emphasis has always been on the formation of self-organised, specific forms of knowledge production and the experimental continued development of theories and practices of doing. These forms find activation in events like the Spring Meeting, the Summer University and the Winter Update Meeting.

---

253 | JR15BF.

These events, often themselves experimental in form (the Spring Meeting consists of a seminar marathon initiated by Mårten Spångberg), not only enjoy international attention; they have also discursively produced and concretely fused cross-disciplinary lines of connection between art, philosophy, ethics, new(er) organisation studies, feminism, Cultural Studies, activism, informatics and so forth. They offer forms of independently determined engagement and continued education – such as the Public School in the local village of St. Erme, which was founded soon after PAF's birth, or the 'call for self-education' – within a precise programme of knowledge production that seeks out, in this free environment, its own peers in the wake of Bologna.[254]

Valentina Desideri, who has lived for longer periods of time in PAF, explains clearly in our interview the kind of influence PAF had on her own educational journey:

'First of all, I consider PAF my real education. It's the place where I met most of the people I work with, the place where I first met all the thinking and reading that has influenced me. For me it was very clear. I was shocked that nobody else was living there, since we all share some sort of nomadic existence. Maybe I am a bit hyper-social, but being in this place where you can just go and stay is fantastic. It's a place where it never stops. At that time I had just finished dance education in London, and I didn't want to make dance pieces because I thought I would just copy-paste everything I learned and perpetuate that pain! I wasn't sure what I wanted to do, but I was sure I didn't want to do that. I didn't want to go and work for companies. At that point, I was living in London, so a dance company job was about working with diagonals, or fall on the floor repeatedly and all these sorts of things. Not very interesting to me. I had seen a little bit of European dance, and I wanted to see and get to know it more. And I could develop professionally in PAF and at the same time learn a lot as a person as well.
PAF is like a micro-society, so you really are confronted with yourself and your motivation for doing things all the time. And on top of that, you meet a lot of new people. For me it was an education on all levels. There I found the people that introduced me to certain thinkers, concepts and other collaborations. And I was free to do projects with or without all these people; everything was possible and exciting. Maybe it was a very selfish motivation to live there. It was a fantastic place to be at that moment. It transformed me into something else; during these first years everything was unclear and then slowly it became clearer what I wanted to do.'[255]

Even in hindsight, as a student in the Master's programme for visual arts at the Sandberg Institute in Amsterdam, Desideri realises that no European programme in the field of dance and choreography would have been able to

---

254 | http://www.pa-f.net/program/call, retrieved 22.8.2013.
255 | VD24TE.

offer her anything comparable to her education at PAF: 'I'm pretty sure there's nothing that I could have got out of an MA program that I wouldn't have gotten in PAF. All these programs actually go to PAF.'[256]

And Desideri is right about this: P.A.R.T.S. in Brussels, *ex.e.r.ce* in Montpellier, the MA in Choreography and Performance in Giessen, the many renowned European educational programmes as well as other art institutions and university-based scientific projects – all of these have long since been regular PAF users.

Since its inception, PAF has been interested in the articulation and production of experimental, emancipatory and critical forms of knowledge in art and society, also focussing on developing, sharpening and continually re-challenging the discourse and artistic exchange going on in the field.[257] This idea of discourse as an engagement with varying positions works differently than a consensually regulated or dogmatic understanding of discourse:

'We think more about politics, philosophy and society in relation to the arts. We don't want to talk vaguely about art, but rather processually, analytically and critically. In these terms PAF has an influence. We provide a notion of discourse and we keep it alive. In the dance world there has always been a separatist discussion between the intellectuals and the 'dance-dancers', which has become much more smoothed out. I think PAF has an influence in these ways, because we're not an organisation that takes a position or secludes itself from others in the sense of being an intellectual bastion. PAF is very smooth, which makes it more absorbable for other people. Another huge influence PAF has is that people build networks here. Coming and meeting each other is much easier here. People who never thought they would work together do so. If you're really engaging in relating in PAF, you can make a lot of connections and that can be very profitable.'[258]

As Ritsema's statements convey, here the overlappings of discourse production, exchange and education are fluid. The decisive factor is that they are oriented to the heterogeneity of forms of expression, to positions regarding content and aesthetics, and that they distinguish themselves from run-of-the-mill creativity jargon. As early as the first meeting in PAF in December 2005, this heterogeneity was a central point of engagement, accompanied by the decision that if the collective platform of the experiment PAF were to lead to a standardisation of aesthetics, it would have to be declared a failed project. From

---

256 | VD25TE.
257 | Cf. Petra Sabisch, 'Die Zone und ihre Shareware: das Performing Arts Forum (PAF)' [The zone and its shareware], in Kirsten Maar and Yvonne Hardt in cooperation with Sabine Kaross (Eds.), *Tanz – Metropolis – Provinz*, Jahrbuch Tanzforschung Vol. 17 (Hamburg: Lit Verlag, 2007), pp. 205–212.
258 | JR13BF.

today's perspective this initial worry seems groundless, which is undoubtedly traceable to the proliferation of differentiations in the discourse.[259] Christine de Smedt demonstrates the primeness of PAF's discourse-generating role: 'I feel that, for instance, by not going to the [...] Spring Meeting or the Summer University in PAF – each time that I don't go there [...] I miss half of the discourse happening in the scene. Because I'm not physically there, I will never be able to catch up the potential of such a meeting.'[260]

Another dimension of this 'discourse on eye level' lies in its engagement for mutual exchange and its tangible engagement with a physical counterpart, including the creation of differing publics for such purposes.

As has been implied several times in the text passages I have extracted from the interviews conducted as part of this study, this dimension can only gain importance in times of increasing individualisation qua nomadically and thereby locally deconnected modes of production and existence. As part of this bigger picture, Jan Ritsema describes the idea of PAF as a kind of refuge, one he deems parallel to mountain cabins as places of shelter and escape for wanderers:

'(...) it's a kind of refuge (...) If things don't work in your profession, when you have difficult times, you can always go to PAF and re-tank. Without PAF you would be much more alone. So the professional field is less alone with PAF. This very much works on the level of a mental state. It's not tangible and you are not aware of it. The existence of PAF gives some base.'[261]

It is in this point that artistic discourses, the critique of market-feasible modes of production and treatment, and the challenges of a 'social choreography' overlap. Alice Chauchat also marks this aspect:

'I think free-lance project-hopping activity produces loneliness and dependency on superficial relationships that one needs to multiply and maintain in order to keep constantly as many doors (work opportunities) open as possible. The conventional company model has been criticised for its hierarchical structure, and since its loss of glamour, artists have continuously strived for possible models of solidarity, commitment and sharing. These attempts are located in the tension between market necessities and human/artistic necessities; *PAF* is an example, Everybodys is another, and there are many more.'[262]

---

259 | Cf. VD23TE.
260 | CDS23PS.
261 | JR12BF.
262 | Alice Chauchat in conversation with Petra Sabisch, AC18PS.

For a Topology of Practices   143

Exactly this kind of content-oriented and context-generating network is part of the plan for the recently begun project *PERFmts (Performance More Than Special)*, which disseminates, in a language beyond the market, worldwide event tips for irregularly occurring performances, symposiums, practices and events that could be of interest for an extensive notion of performance.[263]

Taking into consideration this context of worldwide connection, internationality and mobility, Jan Ritsema adds another aspect to the mix when he spontaneously disrupts and redistributes, with reference to the global village, the tripartite order of internationality, city and travel on the one side, and locality and settledness on the other:

'PAF is in the countryside and most people in the arts want to live in a city. But PAF is not a village; it's an international village. It's more exciting than when you live in the big city and go to the same bakery or the same pub everyday. One often makes a village out of the city one lives in. Here it changes all the time. New people come who define PAF differently. In principle, it's very exciting. You don't travel, but the world travels through PAF to you.'[264]

Through this changing interconnection between people and practices, the identity of PAF remains in flux. Or, as Jan Ritsema says, 'The creation creates itself'.[265] This, at the very least, is what the experiment of PAF is about.

---

263 | VD35TE: 'After that project we started to think about *PERFmts*. We thought it would be nice to have some sort of e-flux newsletter for performing arts. We wanted to create a platform where we can develop a way to talk about the performing arts and add a certain language to it. Since PAF has been a crossing place for so many countries and locations, it would be great if we could update each other on different events that are taking place. It took us many years to develop this. [. . .] The things we announce aren't part of a regular program of institutions like, let's say Théâtre de la Ville in Paris; they are events that are more special, that could challenge our understanding of what performance is. So there's also the possibility for announcing something that's probably not a performance as performance. I think it's great to have a tool that lets people know that somebody is organising a symposium. Maybe you're not able to go there, but at least you get a text whose content is full enough and that gives you the feeling of being informed properly. In that sense it's not like regular advertising or newsletters. We can situate the context more specifically.'
264 | JR34BF.
265 | Ibid.: 'I try to make it so that when you have to go home, you cannot easily say what PAF is. That also keeps the openness, and it keeps us away from the question of who the 'we' or the 'I' is. It is more the creation that creates itself. That's also what's going on here; that's what everybody does. Everybody, from the friends in the beginning [...] to the newcomers – they all contribute, maintain and change PAF by doing something.'

2.5 sommer.bar (Berlin, 2006–2011)

Figure 5: Shoulder bag from 'sommer.bar', 2011. Photograph: Petra Sabisch

The *sommer.bar* is a programme conceptualised by Kerstin Schroth which served as a magnet for Berlin's contemporary, international and local choreography and dance scene during the month of August. Administratively positioned within the framework of Germany's largest dance festival, Tanz im August, where Schroth had previously spent four years working as a producer, the *sommer.bar* was in a certain sense a festival within a festival that during its six years not only presented artists from thirty-three countries,[266] but that would also soon develop into a sustainably influential, open and networked site for work and exchange at Podewil in Berlin.[267]

---

266 | For statistical figures, see Annex 2: Statistics on the internationality of the case studies, p. 175.

267 | The Berliner dancer and choreographer Hermann Heisig, who as part of this study looks back in conversation with Bettina Földesi on the *Spiegelinterview* (mirror interview) that took place at *sommer.bar*, describes the importance of Podewil from his perspective: 'In its beginnings Podewil was a very important place, near the end of the nineties, above all for a string of artists like René Pollesch, Thomas Lehmen

In interview, Kerstin Schroth describes the starting point of her deliberations on the concept:

'When in 2005 I proposed the *sommer.bar*'s concept to the festival Tanz im August, I had already worked four years for the festival and five years in Berlin. Enough time to analyse the festival's structure and to realise that it lacks a centre. A place where exchange can happen between the invited artists, the audience and the Berlin scene. One often wouldn't see the artists unless one went to their presentation, since the festival, strictly speaking, has no venue of its own, but instead enters into collaborations with the different theatres throughout the entire city. Another aspect interested me: why are artists from all over the world flown to a two-week festival in a great city with its own lively dance scene without placing an emphasis on interaction between the international artists and the Berlin scene? The artists stayed in the city for a maximum of four days; arriving, setting up, performing, departing seemed to me to be a rhythm that allowed only very superficial exchange and communication.'[268]

Sommer.bar was important in several respects, especially in view of the interplay between production conditions, artistic working methods, modes of perception and aesthetics. Its first formative characteristic consisted in orienting itself to artistic practices. This manifested right from the start, when the first *sommer.bar* in 2006 featured several dance makers, choreographers and artists who examined the performative aspects of the concert. In addition to the opening performance by the American, Paris-based choreographer Mark Tompkins, *Lost and Found*, together with Nuno Rebelo, there were concerts by The Musts as well as the *After Sade* concert by *aisikl* and Mårten Spångberg.[269]

In 2007, this examination of concert-like forms of performance continued in a work by Eszter Salamon and Arantxa Martinez titled *Without you I am nothing*; in *Molly and the Lunchboxes* by Paul Gazzola, Molly Haslund and

---

or Xavier Le Roy, and other visual artists and musicians who worked a lot there. Then Podewil's role was downsized, and it was actually long-since dead by that point. But with *sommer.bar* this spirit was awoken a bit, time after time', HH2BF. The history of Podewil, which is very closely interlocked with the history of independent dance as well as that of art and music, and which was also a work place for choreographers such as Xavier Le Roy and Thomas Lehmen, cannot be explored in detail here. Suffice it to say that Podewil has today become a sad symbol of an unprecedented ousting of independent art production, which was recently the case with the closing of Tesla. For the history, compare the website of Kuturprojekte GmbH, the company which is now inhabiting the building, see http://www.kulturprojekte-berlin.de/ueber-uns/podewil/geschichte-des-hauses.html, retrieved 28.8.2013.
268 | Kerstin Schroth in conversation with Petra Sabisch, KS1PS.
269 | Cf. the 2006 programme pamphlet from 2006.

Catherine Hoffmann; in *Volume* by Vincent Dupont and Thierry Balasse; in *Remake* by Peter Lenaerts, Eszter Salamon, Ephraim Cielen and Your Van Uffelen; and others – not to mention in the minimal, object-narrative-trip-in-concert-form titled *The Monster* (a.k.a. *This is the hello monster*) by the Parisian avant-pop solo band Gérald Kurdian.[270] This aspect of the concert remained until the end with continually changing perspectives, a constant dimension of *sommer.bar*.[271]

In interview, Schroth talks about how she discovered

'that choreographers do not by default only concern themselves with choreography in the form of stage pieces. Instead, they build bridges and link their interests and knowledge with all the other performative, visual and literary arts combined. What's more, every artistic working process has its leftovers, by-products and themes that couldn't be processed any further in a particular piece, although they are present in the space while continuing to haunt people's minds. Mostly by-products for which no space is to be found in a normal festival context or in an ordinary theatre programme. I began getting really interested in these small pieces because they allowed me a totally different view into the artistic work. I had the impression that they completed (in combination with the stage pieces, and beyond conventional artists' talks after performances) my opinion and knowledge of a specific artist's work. All of these aspects considered in connection woke my interest, and so I developed the concept for *sommer.bar*.'[272]

These artistic engagements with concerts and the presentational modes, compositional elements and dramaturgy thereof explored the genre – meaning the perceptual framework and horizon of expectations of the 'concert' – which in turn threw a refreshingly new light on the common perceptual conventions of performances.

Alongside this example, there were many other works – for instance, the by-products presented almost every year in different ways by Manon Santkin and Leslie Mannès at the intersection of fashion and performance, the installation *Abstractions* by Emilio Tomé, the 2010 video installation *Neverland* by Andros Zins-Browne – whose presentational forms consistently managed to defy the format of classical stage performances. This moment stirred an immediate interest among many artists, however, because the usual conventions for showing work were called into question.[273]

---

270 | Cf. the programme pamphlets from 2007 to 2011.
271 | Cf. *The Boys in Concert* by Pieter Ampe and Guilherme Garrido, 2010; Tania Carvalho's, *Mud Lyrical*; and Gérald Kurdian's *Experimental Amateur Choir*, 2011.
272 | KS1PS.
273 | It should be noted that indeed performances did take place in addition to the other events I have mentioned here, such as Tove Sahlin's *Dancing Barefoot* from 2009

Closely connected with this aspect is a second feature that was particularly formative of *sommer.bar*: not only was it devised on the basis of artistic practices; a frame was also created in which experimentation with the format was welcomed. Schroth comments on this point:

'In my opinion, 2006 saw very few festivals that gave space to alternative formats. It's not just about reflecting on the classical stage space. It's also about the more expansive thoughts that apply to factors from the piece's length all the way to the number of viewers. A piece that is, for example, twenty minutes long isn't recognised as being full-length; instead, one always ends up with a double-feature evening. So most often pieces by different artists get combined, frequently very pragmatically and with no attention to content-related considerations. I've always asked myself why people can't simply let twenty good minutes stand alone. Personally, I often much more happily go home after twenty intensive minutes as opposed to sixty half-baked minutes. One-to-one formats, pieces for three viewers, for six viewers, are a rarity in festivals or theatre programmes – from a purely economic standpoint. These pieces can only be seen by a handful of people, which is why programmers would prefer not to show them at all instead of giving a few of them an opportunity.
And a very interesting part of artistic work is thereby made invisible, meaning the artists are indirectly ordered to produce their piece according to theatres' and festivals' conventional, often purely economic perspectives. This excludes any reflection on formats from the very outset, above all among young, still unknown artists whose working lives resound with the fear that the piece won't be shown if it doesn't serve the classical stage format or if it has been produced for a limited number of viewers. Festivals and theatres breed classical formats this way; as a young artist, one is better advised to make solos, or trios at the very most, for a stage space that accommodates one hundred viewers and with a maximum length of sixty minutes. Then the major, long pieces for the large stage spaces with big casts of dancers (lots of dancers please!) come with becoming a well-known artist. The others are the exotics and are often handled as such.'[274]

Hermann Heisig, who was present in *sommer.bar* several times starting in 2008, gives an account of how this concept was showcased:

'So *sommer.bar* definitely made open spaces available and created a context that allowed artists to frame their works differently for a change. In this respect I would say that it was definitely also contemporary in the sense that people don't see only the product

---

and *Roses and Beans*, together with Dag Anderson, 2010; *Undertone* by Sidney Leoni with many guests, 2010; *Shichimi Togarashi* by Juan Domínguez and Amalia Fernández, 2009; *All the way out there* by Guillem Mont de Palol and Mette Ingvartsen, 2010; and *What they are instead of* by Jared Gradinger and Angela Schubot, 2010.
274 | KS4PS.

itself as the artwork; they understand the product's framing as part of it. And *sommer. bar* definitely encouraged artists to take in other ways of seeing or experiment with the framing of their work, which wasn't really a main focus of the main festival, I think. It was also like that when you think of the terms 'centre' and 'periphery'. The *sommer.bar*'s interest in by-products can really also be attributed to the fact that we tried to cancel out the hierarchies a bit, like the hierarchy between artist and audience, who are shown, say, a virtuosic work and are expected to sit there and watch it in amazement. Or also hierarchies between the greater and lesser known artists. Or enabling other presentational formats. It's indeed already the case – although this has changed a bit, too – that the market for dance and performance calls for a certain model of piece, for a certain length, for example. Which is why one does become half-consciously trained to produce products that can also fit into that market. In that sense, *sommer.bar* produced a space for manoeuvering where one can – as part of one's 'opening night', for example – either make a performance that goes for six or seven hours, or a five-minute performance that repeats twenty times.'[275]

This account also elucidates just how successful Schroth's concept, which, as must be noted, took place in combination with performances, proved to be *in realo*.

In addition to this reflection on formats, a third – discursive – factor served as an essential element of *sommer.bar*. Whether it was the *Dialog Demonstrationen* by Janez Jansa, Olga Pona, Xavier Le Roy, Meg Stuart and Gisèle Vienne or the games *Générique* and the *Impersonation Game* by Everybodys, which in the following year took place also in *Tanz im August* subsequent to almost all performances; whether it was an artist's talk, book presentation, the book stand Books on the Move or showings with aftertalks, engagement and discourse were always a crucial component of *sommer.bar*.[276]

---

275 | Hermann Heisig in conversation with Bettina Földesi, HH28BF. For the performances, see the 2008 programme pamphlets; the 2009 opening event *Baden* with Frank Willens; a contact impro in mud (with text) in 2009; or *Just Around the Corner*, together with Elpida Orfanidou, 2011.

276 | See the 2008-2011 programme pamphlets. Books on the Move is a mobile book shop initiated and run by Agnès Benoit that specialises in dance and movement and that made English, French and German books and DVDs more accessible on site at the festival and on the Internet. Artistic books or DVDs in particular, often self-published and/or printed in limited editions, found their audience here. In the presence of its owner, herself well-versed in dance, the bookstand offered several occasions for obtaining information or discussing the history of dance, http://www.booksonthemove. eu/, retrieved 15.8.2013.

Asked about this, Hermann Heisig states, '*sommer.bar* was definitely one of the motors that pushed another kind of speaking about artistic products in Berlin.'[277]

In the following statement, Heisig has recourse several times to *sommer.bar*'s long-since exceptional role:

'*sommer.bar* was important for the contemporary dance and choreography scene. So I do think that it was, and still is, necessary to provide a place where engagement can take place. I mean this in the sense that *sommer.bar* also included quite a lot of conversations and discussions, on the one hand, and quite a few experiments and games with audience discussions. To play, one had to put oneself in the shoes of another choreographer and answer, from the perspective of that choreographer, questions from the audience. One of these was *Générique* by Everybodys, but there was a whole series of these affairs, and *sommer.bar* was a good turf for experimenting with this. [...] I've been in Berlin for quite a while now, but I was also in Montpellier at the Centre Chorégraphique for a year somewhere in there. There was just a completely other form of discourse there, a different kind of engagement with and about pieces, different from what was happening in Berlin at the time. And I think the idea of *sommer.bar* did come from the need to bring the discourse once again onto another level.'[278]

What characterised *sommer.bar* with regard to discursive qualities was that these engagements with performed pieces or other themes didn't stop at the theatre door. They instead proceeded, without any dividing line, to the bar. Intensive conversations and new encounters emerged in a busy and popular meeting place that the Berlin scene had lacked, a lack that went unnoticed by many of the city's presenters. Often many artists also came directly to the bar to utilise the opportunity to partake in exchange on all levels.

Here Kerstin Schroth describes the fourth aspect – the context-generating character of the bar – and how this is linked to her approach of reflecting on the artistic situation:

'It was also really especially about reflecting on our scene – the dance scene is very mobile; we travel to work, almost always; we live in Berlin, Brussels, Paris, work in Rennes, Essen, Zagreb, and perform all over Europe. We seldom meet our colleagues and friends, except when we're working together, which makes any constant exchange impossible. It's a luxury to be able to meet in person, converse and spend an evening together. *sommer.bar* spearheaded this luxury of meeting every evening for two weeks and

---

277 | HH22BF.
278 | HH10BF. See also HH3BF.

placed a high value on the social. Art lives from exchange and communication rather than being something disconnected, outmoded and mothballed.'[279]

sommer.bar and its parties were shaped by the idea of context as a sense-cohesion for the professional field and as a collective exchange inclusive of the possibility for coincidental encounters.

A fifth aspect which already resonates throughout the interview passages in all the case studies included in this report – and yet it may be necessary to cite its importance for *sommer.bar* in particular – was the establishment of networks that spanned international and local scenes. This idea lent the festival its colour and temperature as well.

Extremely revealing in this regard are Heisig's evaluations of the structural changes that have unfolded over the last twenty years and their effects on the dance field in Berlin: shifts in the understanding of internationality that guided the international character of Tanz im August during the festival's first years evolved more through a tendency to import dance and choreography, while today – and not least because of dropping air travel costs and increasing

---

279 | KS6PS. See also KS5PS: 'I really foregrounded the bar idea, the idea of celebration, of partying. But I also zoomed in primarily on finding a frame in which relaxed encounters are possible. I think a bar's the best place for this. My enthusiasm was in creating a frame in which people trip over each other's feet, so to speak, where people are simply able to enter dialogue after the performances. But I also thought of the bar as a frame that provides another atmosphere for talking about pieces that people were seeing. You could encounter the artists there. People keep telling me now that this kind of set frame is lacking. *sommer.bar* was well known in Berlin as a *place*. You could come watch something or just meet for a beer, and you could always bump into people with whom you could converse about pieces you'd seen or were going to see. Everybody went there, local artists, the 'internationals', presenters, the press, the audience. Something like a family reunion with an extremely wide following came into existence over the years, and I had envisioned it that way, too. I like unforeseeable encounters, and it was my goal to create a frame where people don't talk only with ones they know, but with everybody. It was also important to me to create a connector for the widely dispersed venues of Tanz im August. One couldn't catch a glimpse of many of the artists, even as an employee of the festival, if one didn't make it to their performances. The bar was intended to change that. I think a bar like this can be the heart of the festival, and every festival could use this sort of heart in order to anchor itself in the city and in order to anchor individuals in the festival, to be there, be present, to show oneself and offer more than shows. We are, after all, involved with people who come to our city and show something without being in one and the same film together. So in the broadest sense it's also about community, the formation of community, of togetherness, of the collectively experienced and the communication of experience.'

mobility – the Berlin scene has not only experienced international growth, but has also already been working internationally for some time:

'I think this has also changed the role of Berlin drastically over the last fifteen to twenty years. A much more international art community came into existence in Berlin in – not exclusively, but to no small degree – the dance field. Now there are a lot more dancers from many more countries in Berlin. This has led to the milieu of Berlin's contemporary dance scene becoming more and more heterogeneous. This also has to do with Berlin's being cheap back then (now rents are on the rise, of course) and simultaneously with the fact that Berlin offered a rich cultural environment. This has attracted a huge amount of people over the last ten to fifteen years. If I were to imagine a party at Tanz im August in 1995, then surely more German would be spoken there than in 2010. Also, the role of Tanz im August in the 80s or early 90s certainly lay more in the tendency to bring contemporary or modern dance from elsewhere to Berlin. It was definitely also very much a matter of getting the big names from Belgium, the US or from a lot of other countries, ultimately so that we could have an international festival, but one for which productions from outside of Berlin were invited in order to enrich the scene. This differentiation has become more and more fluid. And meanwhile, maybe a lot of artists and participants in the festival have moved to Berlin. So there's no longer such as strong opposition between global and local, and I think these processes are reflected in *sommer.bar*.'[280]

The sometimes explicit formulation of a dissociation from the Berlin scene that has been expressed in recent years by the festival curators of Tanz im August, which caused much confusion and discussions within Berlin's independent dance scene, found willing ears in Schroth's programme:

'I've always considered it important to understand *sommer.bar* as a place of exchange between international artists and the Berlin scene, especially also because the local Berlin artists in the festival Tanz im August played more of an supporting role, and because I thought it was absurd that a festival of this size simply leaves the highly colourful and lively Berlin scene standing out in the cold.'[281]

Scores of connections were established, and new alliances emerged. Schroth's merit lies in her having supported and initiated processes that lend artistic practices a dimension of continuity and development as distinguishable from the shop-till-you-drop model known from so many conventional festivals. Heisig also touches upon this dimension when he outlines how *sommer.bar* became a recurring, structure-generating point of reference that not only

---

280 | HH17BF.
281 | KS2PS.

sustainably affected the scene, but also altered the user-habits of the audience (artists included):

'As I've said, it wasn't so much about competing with the festival Tanz im August as it was about complementing it with a new platform. And I had the feeling that this worked very well in most cases. I mean, the format certainly has its limits somewhere. It's also sometimes important to say that a specific work that one wants to do also needs the presence of a large stage or the attention brought by a festival. That can, of course, be the case. Despite that, however, I think the *sommer.bar* was a sort of incubator. By that I mean that many ideas which were tried out there for the first time later flowed into processes in other pieces. In that sense, *sommer.bar* was definitely visible or perceptible not only when it was happening in Podewil; it also gave impulses that were visible beyond.'[282]

The sixth aspect of *sommer.bar* – this engagement towards the development and continuity of artistic practices – becomes remarkable when viewed in the context of *sommer.bar*'s extremely scant budget, which from year to year never enjoyed any sort of security.[283]

Schroth's own background as a producer, working with Mette Ingvartsen, among others, guides her precise knowledge of the state of affairs from an artistic perspective. When asked about the security she experiences in her

---

282 | HH14BF. See also HH26BF: 'The audience's knowing that a kind of daily programme existed in *sommer.bar* certainly changed the use-habits of the festival, I would say. [...] This is why sustainability definitely helps, in the sense of a repetition – definitely.'

283 | The *sommer.bar*'s budget, which vacillated over the years, amounted to 12,000-15,000 euros. Schroth's personal curatorial and organisational salary amounted to 5,000 euros. For more on continuity, development and sustainability, see KS8PS: 'To me, artistic development possibilities – manoeuvring room and continuity – are, in addition to trust, the most important terminologies as regards the *sommer.bar* as well as my other work. When I decide to work together with an artist, the clincher is of course usually a piece that I saw, or an idea that I heard, a conversation we had. But rather than being interested in this particular work by the artist, I'm quite interested in the development, in what comes after, what came before. For me it was important to build on this continuity with a group of artists in *sommer.bar*, to invite them time and again and follow their development, to continually ask them, 'what do you want to do in this frame? What ideas do you have? I think this is also interesting for an audience; this is how you build audience visibility for an artist. [...] One could say that *sommer.bar* was a place for development. Projects were created here concretely and specifically for *sommer.bar*. There was often only one idea, one thought, one by-product, one wish whose life was developed for *sommer.bar*. Trust played a major role in this context. I had never before seen most of the projects that I showed in the *sommer.bar*. I had only spoken about them with the artists. So I bought the idea, in a manner of speaking.'

own planning as a curator and independent producer, she answers that she understands the main task of her work to be the production of such a planning-security for artists. Here Schroth provides her own sketch of the problems she repeatedly runs into while composing structural plans:

'It's not easy, and I'm flabbergasted time and again how little theatres understand that it is not only important to support projects, new pieces by artists, but that they should also invest in the 'structure'. To date I've found hardly any theatres that want to think with us in this direction. Presenting, yes. Building, sustainability, planning-security, no. What I find interesting is that it indeed always is about interlocutors who, on the one hand, have steady jobs and assume, on the other, that I will jump to answer them any time they want something from me (i.e., Mette Ingvartsen) rather than answering them in regards to individual projects alone.'[284]

One example of *sommer.bar*'s focus on the inseparability and development potential of artistic processes lies in the residencies that Schroth offered increasingly during the festival's final years (and beyond its actual framework) and that complemented and thematised the rather sparely as opposed to fairly paid visibility through quite concrete possibilities for working, developing and encountering.

One should surely view the development of small, special formats for festivals with a healthy amount of criticality, especially considering the general trend of pushing the selling-out of small artistic extra-products in an off-format instead of structurally promoting a qualitatively high-grade work that chooses its own format. The scarcity of resources often turns into a one-sided argument for the crippling of an artistic production that merits serious attention, without any proportionate constriction of theatre profiles or downsizing of festival operations. When the choice in favour of one's own visibility is accompanied by the abandoning of defining one's own working conditions autonomously, this one-sided redistribution of burden often makes independent artists into a kickball for the theatre business.

The boundaries between an initiative that makes something possible with available means and the forcing of a worsening of working situations are oftentimes difficult to draw and to test on a case-by-case basis. Kerstin Schroth was acutely aware of this balancing act:

'Working with an unchanging budget for six years while curating a festival that grew every year and attracted more and more audience became like a shackle at some point. How do you explain to artists that you can only pay them a fee of 250 euros, especially when you're asking them to be housed with friends during the festival? At the same time, however, you would like to show their project three times, and then it turns out that each of the three

---

284 | KS19PS.

events is completely overfilled and that many spectators aren't even able to see them. How is this explainable? *sommer.bar* grew immensely during its six years. [...] At some point its budget was out of proportion with its size and constantly growing success.'[285]

In response to another invitation by the curatorial team of Tanz im August to hold *sommer.bar* again in 2012, Schroth laid out moderate conditions for the increase of the artists' budgets as well as her own honorarium.[286] After a certain amount of procrastination and in openly visible misjudgment of the actual problem, a succinct personal offer was sent to Schroth's which seemed scandalous, considering the far-reaching importance of *sommer.bar* for contemporary dance and the magnitude of Tanz im August's funding.

Logically, Schroth rejected this proposal on political grounds:

'As I already explained, the budget was no longer in proportion to the size and success of *sommer.bar*. Tanz im August is a very well funded festival, and *sommer.bar* became a very lively, very important component of the festival. Yet the festival curators assumed that I would indeed convince the artists to show their work as part of *sommer.bar* for little or no remuneration. 2011 was a really hard year, because shortly before the creation of the programme was completed, one thousand euros were cut from my budget, money that I really needed in order to make good on the invitations I had sent out. So I begged friends and various institutions for a bit of money to get the one thousand euros back. That was an absurd situation, if you visualise the size of Tanz im August. I work with a choreographer, and my main job consists of negotiating good fees for our guest performances so that we can make a living and also make it clear to the theatres that we're not in possession of a regular income from somewhere else, that we in fact live from what we're earning there. With that in mind, 2011 was the year that I swore to myself – never again. I can't fight for an artist on one side and pay artists either badly or not at all for my own events on the other, playing with the fact that they're doing it for me or for *sommer.bar* in exchange for being visible on the other side. For me, 2011 was the last edition of *sommer.bar*.'[287]

---

285 | KS20PS.

286 | KS21PS: 'When I was asked whether I wanted to do another edition in 2012, I said sure, but only under the following conditions: I asked for a 5,000 euro increase in budget for the artists (plus the 1,000 that was cut) and 2,000 euros more for my honorarium – all in all, for good reason. No problem for a festival of this size, right? The curatorial team thought about my proposal for one and a half months and then decided to offer me zero euros more for the artists and 500 euros more for my honorarium. I did not accept. I thought then and I still think that it was right to draw the line and end it then and there. It just can't be – continuity and artistic creation can't be held in such low regard.'

287 | KS21PS.

Independent of which curatorial intentions on the part of the festival direction were originally linked with inviting *sommer.bar*, there was a complete lack of any professional sound judgment regarding the estimation of the qualitative significance and far-reaching implications *sommer.bar* had for the local and international dance scene – a fact that would have necessitated a public cultural-political discussion, but that instead became mute, as is so often the case in the art milieu, in the realm of the private.

The few articles in Berlin's dance press mentioning *sommer.bar* showed a complete ignorance towards the conditions that differentiated it from Tanz im August: the fact that both festivals had different concepts, different curators and two very disparately outfitted budgets.

Against the background of the generally scant situation of documentation in dance, I would like to add that today, two years later, the whole archives of *sommer.bar* as well as that of Tanz im August have already disappeared from online view.[288] A transition period?

In view of this meagre availability of information, which for the ephemeral art of dance and choreography spells nothing less than the disaster of being forgotten, this study can only insist upon the urgency of a contemporary criticism and a dance historiography oriented to the here and now. However, this can only be a second step succeeding a sustainable, experimental, discourse- and context-generating fostering of independent dance and choreography.

3. Conclusion in the Form of a Prolegomenon

A crucial outcome of this first approach to and critical survey of the present situation of internationally active, independent artists in the field of dance, choreography and performance in Europe consists, aside from the disastrous findings on their socioeconomic condition, in the carving out of a desideratum for an innovative and contemporary cultural-political discourse that is oriented to the sense-building complexity of artistic working realities.

Even though all efforts to prepare European data on the underlying socioeconomic conditions of dance and performance makers is to be greeted unanimously here, such data collection cannot replace a cultural policy that aims at professional artistic *development* and is oriented to the current structural needs of vastly diverse artistic productions.

---

288 | Cf. http://www.tanzimaugust.de/2010/seiten/sommerbar.html, website discontinued on 1.9.2013. A part of the *sommer.bar* archive can still be viewed on its eponymous Facebook page, see https://www.facebook.com/pages/sommerbar/307078842271, retrieved 30.8.2013.

In light of this dire situation, I was led by the facts to undertake a new, example-based inquiry into the complex interplay of production conditions, working modes and aesthetics in the context of international, experimental and contemporary dance and choreography, and to portray this interplay in its complexity.

This inquiry unfolded on the basis of analyses of five different case studies that were selected from the consciously delimited field of contemporary, experimental and international dance. These included the initiatives *Special Issue* in France and later throughout Europe; the Madrid festival *In-Presentable* (2003–2012); the *Double Lecture Series* (2011) in Stockholm; the *Performing Arts Forum* in France (2005–ongoing), and *sommer.bar* in Berlin (2006–2011).

The background of this selection lay in my objective not only to discuss a small amount of performances, but also – and more importantly – to take into account those collective dimensions of artistic practices that have been dedicated to the sense-building as well as discourse- and context-generating development of dance and choreography, in spite of current circumstances. Furthermore, a mindfulness of the sheer diversity of spatiotemporal forms and formats was instrumental in this analysis; a diversity that ranges from isolated programmes to pan-European projects, from a structure-fostering forum on the countryside to long-standing festivals in European capital cities.

For this examination, fifteen intensive interviews with artists from Belgium, Denmark, Germany, France, Italy, Iceland, the Netherlands, Romania, Sweden and Spain were conducted in cooperation with Tom Engels and Bettina Földesi. The following people participated in this rich and time-consuming process: Blanca Calvo, Alice Chauchat, Christine de Smedt, Valentina Desideri, Juan Domínguez, Hermann Heisig, Mette Ingvartsen, Emma Kim Hagdahl, Halla Ólafsdóttir, Manuel Pelmus, Jan Ritsema, Cristina Rizzo, Paz Rojo and Kerstin Schroth.

While the interviews brought to light the wide spectrum of the qualitative multiformity of artistic practices in dance and performance, the practices analysed in this report can also be understood as structure-generating initiatives and complex responses to the current state of affairs. Taking into special consideration the increasingly reduced time periods that artists must face when working amidst a project economy within the freelance organisational structures of dance and performance art, where practices pass from sight before they even truly come into being, I am struck by the need for follow-up projects that will not only research the situation but also change it one day.

In this regard, the report before you is to be understood as a prolegomena and plea for a necessarily open topology of practices that takes contemporary experimental choreography and performance art as its point of departure, without exempting itself from opportunities for new alliances and transversal quantum leaps.

Literature and Sources

Adolphe, Jean-Marc. "Des moyens pour mieux faire." In: *Mouvement* 4 (1999), p. 8.
Angerer, Marie-Luise, Hardt, Yvonne and Weber, Anna-Carolin. *Choreographie – Medien – Gender*. Berlin/Zürich: Diaphanes, 2013.
Apostolou-Hölscher, Stefan. "Let's Work differently! 6 MONTHS 1 LOCATION and the resonances between production, labor, thought, dance, and community." In: Instytut Muzyki i Tańca Warszawa (ed.), *Communitas and the Other: New Territories of Dance in Europe after 1989*. London/New York: Routledge, 2014.
Apostolou-Hölscher, Stefan. *Vermögende Körper: Zeitgenössischer Tanz zwischen Ästhetik und Biopolitik anhand von Parabeln zu Sasa Asentic, Jérôme Bel, Mette Ingvartsen/Jefta van Dinther, Ivana Müller* (dissertation). Bielefeld: transcript, 2015.
Apostolou-Hölscher, Stefan and Siegmund, Gerald (eds). *Communications: Dance, Politics and Co-Immunity. Thinking Resistances* (= Current Perspectives on Politics and Communities in the Arts, vol. 1). Berlin/Zürich: Diaphanes, 2013.
Arctor, Fred. *Die Evaluation: 'Tanz- und Theaterszene in Wien' – Eine Studie im Auftrag des Kulturamts der Stadt, erste Begutachtung*. http://www.corpusweb.net/die-evaluation.html (accessed 7th May 2013).
Arendt, Hannah. *Vita Activa oder Vom tätigen Leben*. Munich: Piper, 2002.
ARTE-A (website), http://www.arte-a.org (accessed 15th August 2013).
Artes Escénicas (website), http://artesescenicas.uclm.es/ (accessed 25th August 2013).
Austin, John Langshaw. *How To Do Things With Words: The William James Lectures delivered at Harvard University 1955*. J. O. Urmson and Marina Sbisà (eds). Cambridge: Harvard University Press, 1997.
Bach, Konrad, Engel, Thomas, Freundt, Michael and Welke, Dieter. "Der Status der Künstler im Bereich der Darstellenden Künste. Recherche des deutschen Zentrums des ITI." In: Fonds Darstellende Künste/Kulturpolitische Gesellschaft (ed.), *Report Darstellende Künste* (2010), pp. 243–272.
Bachacou, Delphine. *De nouveaux espaces pour la danse contemporaine d'aujourd'hui, DESS (développement culturel et direction de projet)*. Université Lumière Lyon II, ARSEC 2003–2004.
Barnes, Barry. "Practice as Collective Action". In: Schatzki, T. R., Knorr-Cetina, K. and Savigny, E. v. (eds), *The Practice Turn* (2001), pp. 17–28.
Bauer, Eleanor. "6M1L/EX.E.R.CE 08". In: Chauchat, A. and Ingvartsen, M. (eds), *Everybodys Group Self Interviews* (2009), pp. 34–38.
Bauer, Eleanor. "Eleanor!" *Good Move*, http://www.goodmove.be/ELEANOR (accessed 17th May 2013).

Bennett, Jane. *Vibrant Matter: A Political Ecology of Things*. Durham/London: Duke University Press, 2010.

Berufsverband Bildender Künstler Berlin e.V., http://www.bbk-berlin.de/con/bbk/front_content.php?idart=2085&refId=199 (accessed 28th August 2013).

Bishop, Claire. *Artificial Hells: Participatory Art and the Politics of Spectatorship*. London/New York: Verso, 2012.

Boltanski, Luc and Chiapello, Eve. *Le nouvel esprit du capitalisme*. Paris: Gallimard, 2011.

Books on the Move (website), http://www.booksonthemove.eu/ (accessed 15th August 2013).

Bouger, Christiane. "In-Presentable: Where Cross-Cultural Artistic Practices Meet in Madrid". In: *Movement Research Performance Journal* 34 (2009), pp. 31ff.

Bourdieu, Pierre. *Esquisse d'une théorie de la pratique, précédé de trois études d'ethnologie kabyle*. Geneva: Droz, 1972 [German edition: *Entwurf einer Theorie der Praxis auf der ethnologischen Grundlage der kabylischen Gesellschaft*. Frankfurt a. M.: Suhrkamp 2012.].

Bourdieu, Pierre. *Raisons pratiques: Sur la théorie d'action*. Paris: Editions Seuil, 1996.

Brandstetter, Gabriele, Brandl-Risi, Bettina and Eikels, Kai van (eds). *Prekäre Exzellenz: Künste, Ökonomien und Politiken des Virtuosen*. Freiburg/Wien/Berlin: Rombach, 2012.

Brandstetter, Gabriele, Hofmann, Franck and Maar, Kirsten (eds). *Notationen und choreografisches Denken*. Freiburg/Berlin/Wien: Rombach, 2010.

Brauneck, Manfred. *Die freien Tanz- und Tanztheater-Gruppen in der Bundesrepublik Deutschland: Zweiter Arbeitsbericht zum Forschungsprojekt Populäre Theaterkultur*. Press Office of the Universität Hamburg (ed.). Stade: Krause Druck, 1988.

Brown, Nathan and Milat, Petar (eds). "The Art of the Concept". In: *Frakcija* 64/65 (2012), pp. 6–10 (available online at: http://artofconcept.mi2.hr/, accessed 22nd March 2013).

Buden, Boris, Mennel, Birgit and Nowotny, Stefan. "Europe as a Translational Space: The Politics of Heterolinguality." http://eipcp.net/projects/heterolingual/files/about/ (accessed 11th June 2013).

Buren, Daniel. "The Function of the Studio". Thomas Repensek (trans.). In: *October*, vol. 10 (1979), pp. 51–58 [first published: 1971].

Butler, Judith. *Bodies that Matter: On the Discursive Limits of 'Sex'*. New York/London: Routledge, 1993.

Butler, Judith. *Gender Trouble*. New York/London: Routledge, 1990.

Calvo, Blanca (ed.). *Cuaderno 1: Una voz sin cuerpo, hacia el amor/A Disembodied Voice, Towards Love*. San Sebastián: Mugatxoan, 2012.

Calvo, Blanca . "Nine". In: Domínguez, J. (ed.), *In-Presentable 03–07* (2007), pp. 51–61.
Cerny, Karin. "Die Evaluation der Theaterreform ist abgeschlossen." http://www.profil.at/articles/1227/560/333790/die-evaluation-theaterreform and http://www.corpusweb.net/die-evaluation.html (accessed 7th March 2013).
Chauchat, Alice and Ingvartsen, Mette (eds). *Everybodys Group Self Interviews* (= Everybodys Publications). Lulu: books on demand, 2009.
Chauchat, Alice and Ingvartsen, Mette (eds). *Everybodys Performance Scores* (= Everybodys Publications). In cooperation with Zoë Poluch, Kim Hiorthøy, Nadja Hjorton und Stina Nyberg. Lulu: books on demand, 2010.
Chauchat, Alice and Ingvartsen, Mette (eds). *Everybodys Self Interviews* (= Everybodys Publications). Lulu: books on demand, 2008.
Choreography as Expanded Practice (website), http://choreographyasexpandedpractice.wordpress.com (accessed 28th August 2013).
Cliche, Danielle, Mitchell, Ritva and Wiesand, Andreas. *Creative Europe: On Governance and Management of Artistic Creativity in Europe* (= ERICarts Report to the Network of European Foundations for Innovative Action). In cooperation with Ilkka Heiskanen and Luca Dal Pozzolo. Bonn: ARCult Media, 2002.
Commission of the European Community (ed.). *Green Paper: Modernising Labour Law to Meet the Challenges of the 21st Century*, Brussels, 22.11.2006. http://eur-lex.europa.eu/LexUriServ/site/en/com/2006/com2006_0708en01.pdf (accessed 12th August 2013).
Corpus (online journal for dance, choreography and performance), http://www.corpusweb.net/ (accessed 19th August 2013).
Cvejić, Bojana and Vujanović, Ana. *Public Sphere by Performance*. Berlin: bbooks, 2012.
Cvejić, Bojana and Vujanović, Ana. "Exhausting Immaterial Labour" (editor's note). In: *TKH Journal of Performing Arts Theory* 17 (2010) (= *Exhausting Immaterial Labour*, special edition), pp. 4ff.
Dachverband Tanz Deutschland. "Satzung." http://www.dachverband-tanz.de/pdf/Satzung_DTD_2010-03-06.pdf (accessed 12th August 2013).
Dachverband Zeitgenössischer Tanz Berlin, http://www.ztberlin.de/ (accessed 23rd July 2013).
Dance Station (website), http://www.dancestation.org/ (accessed 11th June 2013).
Dance Station, *Laboratory*, http://specialissue.eu/laboratory (accessed 11th June 2013).
Dance Station, *Choreography of Attention*, http://specialissue.eu/editions/choreography-of-attention (accessed 11th June 2013).
Dance-Tech.net (website), http://www.dance-tech.net (accessed 20th March 2013).
Danko, Dagmar. *Kunstsoziologie*. Bielefeld: transcript, 2012.

Deleuze, Gilles and Parnet, Claire. *Dialogues*. Hugh Tomlinson and Barbara Habberjam (trans.). "The Actual and the Virtual." Eliot Ross Albert (trans.). Forewword by Gilles Deleuze. London/New York: Continuum, 2006 [French edition: *Dialogues*, Paris: Flammarion, 1977].

Deleuze, Gilles and Guattari, Félix. *A Thousand Plateaus: Capitalism and Schizophrenia*, vol. 2. Brian Massumi (trans. and ed.). London/New York: Continuum, 2004 [French edition: Mille Plateaux, Paris: Les Editions de Minuit, 1980].

De Smedt, Christine (ed.). *Four Choreographic Portraits: "I Would Leave a Signature", "The Son of a Priest", "A Woman with a Diamond" and "Self-Reliance"*. Brussels: Les Ballets C de la B., 2012.

Deutscher Bühnenverein (website), http://www.buehnenverein.de/de/jobs-und-ausbildung/32.html?view=7 (accessed 27th July 2013).

Deutscher Bühnenverein, http://www.buehnenverein.de/de/theater-und-orchester/19.html (accessed 4th August 2013).

Deutscher Bundestag (ed.). *Kultur in Deutschland: Schlussbericht der Enquête-Kommission des Deutschen Bundestages*. Regensburg: ConBrio, 2008.

Deutscher Kulturrat (website), http://www.kulturrat.de/text.php?rubrik=4 (accessed 4th August 2013).

Deutscher Kulturrat (ed.). Olaf Zimmermann and Gabriele Schulz. *Keine Liberalisierung um jeden Preis TTIP – Ausnahme für den Kultursektor notwendig*. Background report from 20.5.2014, http://kulturrat.de/detail.php?detail=2840&rubrik=142 (accessed 21st May 2014).

Deutscher Kulturrat (ed.). *Resolution: Der Deutsche Kulturrat fordert die Bundesregierung zu einer schnellen Änderung der entsprechenden Regelungen des § 123 SGB III (Arbeitslosengeld I) auf*, resolution from 21st December 2011.

Deutscher Kulturrat (ed.). *Resolution: Rahmenfrist zum Bezug für Arbeitslosengeld I den Anforderungen des Kulturbereichs anpassen*, resolution from 31st May 2006.

Deutschlandradio Kultur (ed.). "Freihandelsabkommen: Kultur als Ware? Was die TTIP Verhandlungen für die kulturelle Vielfalt bedeuten" (radio report from 19.5.2014). Available at: http://www.deutschlandradiokultur.de/freihandelsabkommen-kultur-als-ware.1895.de.html?dram:article_id=285820 (accessed 21st May 2014).

Dewey, John. *Essays in Experimental Logic*. Chicago: University of Chicago Press, 1916.

Diekmann, Andreas. *Empirische Sozialforschung: Grundlagen, Methoden, Anwendungen* (= Rowohlts Encyclopedia, ed. by Burghard König). Reinbek bei Hamburg: Rowohlt, 2011 [5th edition of the 2007 reprint].

Domínguez Rojo, Juan, http://juandominguezrojo.com/ (accessed 3rd May 2013).

Domínguez Rojo, Juan. *Blue*, http://juandominguezrojo.com/performance/blue-2/ (accessed 17th October 2013).
Domínguez Rojo, Juan. *Clean Room*, http://juandominguezrojo.com/performance/clean-room-4/ (accessed 17th March 2013).
Domínguez Rojo, Juan (ed.). *In-Presentable 03–07*. Madrid: La Casa Encendida, 2007.
Domínguez Rojo, Juan. "Introduction". In: Domínguez, Juan (ed.), *In-Presentable 03–07* (2007), pp. 9–27.
Domínguez Rojo, Juan. "Interview with TkH/Walking Theory, 'Escenas Discursivas'." Madrid, 2nd April 2011. http://escenasdiscursivas.tkh-generator.net/2011/04/interview-juan-dominguez/ (accessed 2nd June 2013).
Doruff, Sher. "A Vocabulary of Doing." 27th June 2008. http://old.researchcatalogue.net/upload/data/A%20Vocabulary%20of%20Doing.pdf (accessed 12th June 2013).
Egeling, Rebecca. *Die Freie Tanzszene: Eine Bestandsaufnahme am Beispiel von Dresden, Frankfurt am Main und Köln*. n.p.: 2012.
Eikels, Kai van. *Die Kunst des Kollektiven: Performance zwischen Theater, Politik und Sozio-Ökonomie*. Munich: Fink, 2013.
Europäisches Netzwerk von Rechtsexpertinnen und Rechtsexperten auf dem Gebiet der Gleichstellung von Frauen und Männern (ed.). *Europäische Zeitschrift für Geschlechtergleichstellungsrecht* 1 (2010).
European Parliament, Committee on Culture and Education (ed.). "Die Situation der Künstler in Europa", by the European Institute for Comparative Cultural Research (ERICarts), Suzanne Capiau and Andreas Johannes Wiesand, in cooperation with Danielle Cliche, additional articles by Vesna Čopič, Ritva Mitchell and a European network of experts. Brussels, November 2006. http://www.europarl.europa.eu/RegData/etudes/etudes/join/2006/375321/IPOL-CULT_ET(2006) 375321_DE.pdf (accessed 2nd May 2013).
European Parliament, Committee on Culture and Education (ed.). "Monitoring der Aktivitäten zu Kunst und Kultur." http://www.europarl.europa.eu/sides/getDoc.do?type=TA&reference=P6-TA-2007-0236&format=XML&language=EN (accessed 9th April 2014).
European Institute for Progressive Cultural Policies (website), http://eipcp.net/ (accessed 13th August 2013).
European Institute for Comparative Cultural Research (ERICarts, Council of Europe). Information website: *Compendium of Cultural Policies and Trends in Europe*, http://www.culturalpolicies.net/web/index.php (accessed 25th August 2013).
Everybodys (website), http://everybodystoolbox.net/ (accessed 9th July 2013).
Föllmer, Susanne. *Am Rand der Körper: Inventuren des Unabgeschlossenen im zeitgenössischen Tanz*. Bielefeld: transcript, 2009.

Fohrbeck, Karla and Wiesand, Andreas Johannes. *Der Künstler-Report: Musikschaffende, Darsteller, Realisatoren, Bildende Künstler, Designer.* Munich/Vienna: Hanser, 1975.

Fonds Darstellende Künste (ed.). *Freies Theater in Deutschland: Förderstrukturen und Perspektiven.* Essen: Klartext, 2007.

Fonds Darstellende Künste/Kulturpolitische Gesellschaft (eds). *Report Darstellende Künste: Wirtschaftliche, soziale und arbeitsrechtliche Lage der Theater und Tanzschaffenden in Deutschland. Studien – Diskurse – Internationales Symposium.* Essen: Klartext , 2010.

Fontaine, Geisha. *Les danses du temps: Recherches sur la notion du temps en danse contemporaine.* Pantin: Centre National de la Danse, 2004.

Forkert, Kirsten. *Artistic Lives: A Study of Creativity in Two European Cities.* Farningham: Ashgate, 2013.

Foucault, Michel. *Archaeology of Knowledge.* London/New York: Routledge, 2002.

Frakcija (performing arts journal), http://www.cdu.hr/frakcija/shop/index.php (accessed 2nd March 2013).

Friebe, Holm and Lobo, Sascha. *Wir nennen es Arbeit: Die digitale Bohème oder intelligentes Leben jenseits der Festanstellung.* Munich: Heyne, 2006.

Goffmann, Erving. *Das Individuum im öffentlichen Austausch: Mikrostudien zur öffentlichen Ordnung.* Frankfurt a. M.: Suhrkamp, 1980.

Guattari, Félix. *L'intervention institutionnelle.* Paris: Payot, 1980.

Guattari, Félix. "On Capitalism and Desire." In: Deleuze, Gilles. *Desert Islands and Other Texts, 1953–1974*, David Lapoujade (ed.) and Michael Taormina (trans.). New York/Los Angeles: Semiotext(e), 2004.

Guattari, Félix. *Psychotherapie, Politik und die Aufgaben der institutionellen Analyse.* Frankfurt a. M.: Suhrkamp, 1976.

Haghighian, Natascha Sadr, Galerie Johannes König website, http://www.johannkoenig.de/6/natascha_sadr_haghighian/selected_works.html (accessed 10th July 2013).

Hantelmann, Dorothea von. *How to Do Things with Art: On the Significance of the Performativity of Art.* Zürich/Berlin: Diaphanes, 2007.

Hardt, Yvonne and Stern, Martin (eds). *Choreografie und Institution: Zeitgenössischer Tanz zwischen Ästhetik, Produktion und Vermittlung.* Papers from a conference held by the Zentrum für Zeitgenössischen Tanz at the Hochschule für Musik und Tanz Cologne. Bielefeld: transcript, 2011.

Hecquet, Simon and Prokhoris, Sabine. *Fabriques de la Danse.* Paris: PUF, 2007.

Heinich, Nathalie. "Practices of Contemporary Art: A Pragmatic Approach to a New Artistic Paradigm." Lecture at the Artistic Practices conference held by the Sociology of the Arts Network at the Universität für Musik und Darstellende Kunst, Vienna (September 5–8, 2012), 5th September 2012.

Hewitt, Andrew. *Social Choreography: Ideology as Performance in Dance and Everyday Movement*. Durham/London: Duke University Press, 2005.
Hoogenboom, Marijke. "If Artistic Research is the Answer, What is the Question?" In: *Cairon – Revista de Estudios de Danza/Journal of Dance Studies* 13 (2010) (= special edition *Practice as Research*, ed. by Victoria Pérez Royo and José Antonio Sánchez, Institut del Teatre de la Diputación de Barcelona y del CENAH de la Universidad de Alcalá), pp. 115–124.
Husemann, Pirkko. *Choreografie als kritische Praxis: Arbeitsweisen bei Le Roy und Thomas Lehmen*. Bielefeld: transcript, 2009.
idans (website), http://www.idans.info/ (accessed 11th June 2013).
idans (blog), http://idansblog.org/ (accessed 11th June 2013).
Ingvartsen, Mette (ed.). *6 months 1 location* (6M1L) (= Everybodys Publications). Lulu: books on demand, 2009.
Inpex (ed.). *The Swedish Dance History*, vols 1–4. Stockholm: Inpex, 2009–2012.
In-Presentable (website), http://www.in-presentableblog.com/ (accessed 22nd June 2013).
James, William. *Pragmatism: A New Name for Some Old Ways of Thinking*. Mineola/New York: Dover Publications, 1995 [first published: 1907].
James, William. *Essays in Radical Empiricism*. Mineola/New York: Dover Publications, 2003 [first published: 1912].
Janssens, Joris and Moreels, Dries. *Metamorphoses: Performing Arts in Flanders since 1993*. Brussels: vti, 2007 (available online at: http://www.vti.be/metamorfose, accessed on 31.7.2013).
Kant, Immanuel. *Kritik der praktischen Vernunft – Grundlegung zur Metaphysik der Sitten*. Stuttgart: Reclam, 1986.
Kaufmann, Therese. "Strategien der (Selbst-)Ermächtigung." 12th September 2006. http://kulturrat.at/debatte/zeitung/politik/kaufmann (accessed 10th August 2013).
Kaufmann, Therese and Raunig, Gerald. *Anticipating European Cultural Policies: Europäische Kulturpolitiken vorausdenken*. European Institute for Progressive Cultural Policies (ed.), commentary by Stefan Nowotny. Vienna: eipcp, 2003.
Kekeijan, Maral. "Interview with TkH/Walking Theory, 'Escenas Discursivas'." Madrid, April 2011. http://escenasdiscursivas.tkh-generator.net/2011/04/interview-maral-kekejian/ (accessed 22nd July 2013).
Keuchel, Susanne. "Die empirische Studie." In: Fonds Darstellende Künste/Kulturpolitische Gesellschaft (ed.), *Report Darstellende Künste* (2010), pp. 29–174.
Knöfel, Ulrike. "Geschlechtertrennung." *Der Spiegel*, 18th March 2013, pp. 138–140.
Koalition der Freien Szene (website), http://www.berlinvisit.org/ (accessed 22nd August 2013).

Kock, Sabine. *Prekäre Freiheiten: Arbeit im freien Theaterbereich in Österreich.* Vienna: IG Freie Theaterarbeit, 2009.
Künstlersozialkasse (website), http://www.kuenstlersozialkasse.de/wDeutsch/ksk_in_zahlen/statistik/versichertenbestandsentwicklung.php, accessed on 12th August 2013.
Kulturprojekte (website) "Geschichte", http://www.kulturprojekte-berlin.de/ueberuns.podewil/geschichte-des-hauses.html (accessed 28th August 2013).
La Casa Encendida (website), http://www.lacasaencendida.es (accessed 22nd June 2013).
Lab for Culture (website), http://www.labforculture.org/ (accessed 4th June 2013).
Lambert-Beatty, Carrie. *Being Watched: Yvonne Rainer and the 1960s.* Cambridge/London: MIT Press, 2008.
Latarjet, Bernard. "Pour un débat national sur l'avenir du spectacle vivant". Compte rendu de mission, on behalf of the Ministre de la Culture et de Communication, Jean-Jacques Aillagon, 2004. (Available online: www.culture.gouv.fr/culture/actualites/.../latarjet/rapport_7mai2004.pdf, accessed 21st June 2013).
Latour, Bruno. *Reassembling the Social: An Introduction to Actor-Network Theory.* Oxford/New York: Oxford University Press, 2005.
Le Roy, Xavier, http://www.xavierleroy.com/ (accessed 20th July 2013).
Lepecki, André. *Exhausting Dance: Performance and the Politics of Movement.* New York: Routledge, 2006.
Les Laboratoires d'Aubervilliers (website), http://archives.leslaboratoires.org (accessed 23rd October 2013).
Les Laboratoires d'Aubervilliers, *Edition Speciale Projet Européen,* http://www.leslaboratoires.org/en/projet/edition-speciale-projet-europeen/edition-speciale-projet-europeen (accessed 2nd April 2013).
Les Laboratoires d'Aubervilliers, *Edition Speziale Zéro,* http://www.leslaboratoires.org/projet/editionspeciale-0 (accessed 2nd April 2013).
Les Laboratoires d'Aubervilliers. "Etat de grève à Kerghuéhennec." In: *Mouvement* 2 (1999), (available online: http://www.danse.univ-paris8.fr, accessed 29th July 2013).
Lesage, Didier. "PaR in Continental Europe: A Site of Many Contests." In: Nelson, Robin (ed.), *Practice as Research in The Arts: Principles, Protocols, Pedagogies, Resistances.* New York/Hampshire: Palgrave Macmillan, 2013, pp. 142–151.
Les Signataires du 20 août. "Lettre ouverte à Dominique Wallon et aux danseurs contemporains". In: *Mouvement* 3–4 (1999–2000).
Louppe, Laurence. *Poétique de la danse contemporaine, la suite.* Brussels: Contredanse, 2007.

Lynch, Michael. "Ethnomethodology and the Logic of Practice." In: Schatzki, T. R., Knorr-Cetina, K. and Savigny, E. v. (eds), *The Practice Turn* (2001), pp. 131–148.
Malo de Molina, Marta. "Gemeinbegriffe, Teil 2: Von der institutionellen Analyse zu gegenwärtigen Erfahrungen zwischen Untersuchung und Militanz". Birgit Mennel (trans.). (available online: http://eipcp.net/transversal/0707/malo/de, accessed 3rd February 2011).
"Manifesto for a European Performance Policy." 2003. http://www.freietheater.at/?page=kulturpolitik&detail=61304&jahr=2002 (accessed 21st July 2013).
Martin, Randy. "Mobilizing Dance: Toward a Social Logic of the Derivative". In: S. Apostolou-Hölscher and G. Siegmund (eds), *Communications* (2013), pp. 209–225.
Marx, Karl. "Thesen über Feuerbach." In: Marx, Karl and Engels, Friedrich: *Werke*, vol. 3. Berlin: Dietz, 1978, pp. 5ff.
Maska (website and Slovenian-English platform and Journal for Performing Arts in Ljubljana), http://www.maska.si/index.php?id=161&L=1 (accessed 2nd March 2013).
Massumi, Brian. *Parables for the Virtual: Movement, Affect, Sensation*. Durham/London: Duke University Press, 2002.
McAndrew, Clare and McKimm, Cathie. "The Living and Working Conditions of Artists in the Republic of Ireland and Northern Ireland". On behalf of the Arts Council of Northern Ireland & the Arts Council/An Chomhairle Ealaíon, 2010. (Available online: http://www.artscouncil.ie/Publications/All/The-living-and-working-conditions-of-artists-in-the-Republic-of-Ireland-and-Northern-Ireland_3051384443/, accessed 12th November 2013).
MDT, http://mdtsthlm.se/artists/the-double-lecture-series-curated-by-mette-ingvartsen-and-maarte/ (accessed 17th August 2013).
MDT (website), http://mdtsthlm.se/ (accessed 15th April 2012).
Mobile Academy, *Blackmarket*, http://www.mobileacademyberlin.com/englisch/copyleft/madrid_2012.html (accessed 22nd July 2013).
Mouvement: Revue indisciplinaire des arts vivants. Journal website, http://www.mouvement.net/ (accessed 5th February 2012).
Naverán, Isabel de. "Reproducing Before Adulthood: Support Policies at In-Presentable." In: J. Domínguez (ed.), *In-Presentable 03–07* (2007), pp. 63–73.
Negarestani, Reza. *Cyclonopedia: Complicity with Anonymous Materials*. Melbourne: re.press, 2008.
Nowotny, Stefan and Raunig, Gerald. *Instituierende Praxen: Bruchlinien der Institutionskritik*. Vienna: Turia & Kant, 2008.
On the Move (website), http://on-the-move.org/ (accessed 4th June 2013).
PAF (website), http://www.pa-f.net (accessed 15th August 2013).
PAF, "Basic Infos", http://www.pa-f.net/basics (accessed 22nd March 2006).

PAF, "Call for Self-Education" (2007), http://www.pa-f.net/program/call (accessed 22nd August 2013).

Parkinson, Chrysa. "Self-Interview on Practice" (June 2009), text, illustrations and performance by Chrysa Parkinson, http://vimeo.com/26763244, accessed on 9th March 2013.

Peirce, Charles Sanders. "How To Make Our Ideas Clear". In: *Popular Science Monthly*, no. 12 (January 1878), pp. 286–302. (Online: http://www.cspeirce.com/menu/library/bycsp/ideas/id-frame.htm, accessed on 2nd February 2013).

Peirce, Charles Sanders. "Issues of Pragmaticism." In: *The Monist* 15 (1905), pp. 418–499.

Peirce, Charles Sanders. "What Pragmatism Is." In: *The Monist* 15 (1905), pp. 161–181.

Pérez Royo, Victoria and Jerez, Cuqui (eds). *to be continued – 10 textos en cadena y unas páginas en blanco*. (= *Cairon – Revista de Estudios de Danza/Journal of Dance Studies* 14), Madrid: Aula de Danza Estrella Casero-Universidad de Alcalá, 2012.

Pérez Royo, Victoria and Sánchez, José Antonio (eds). *Practice and Research*. (= *Cairon – Revista de Estudios de Danza/Journal of Dance Studies* 13, special edition published by the Institut del Teatre de la Diputación de Barcelona y del CENAH de la Universidad de Alcalá), Alcalá: Servicio de Publicaciones Universidad de Alcalá, 2010.

PERFmts (website), http://www.perfmts.net/about.asp, (accessed 28th April 2013).

Pickering, Andrew. "Practice and Posthumanism: Social Theory and a History of Agency." In: Schatzki, T. R., Knorr-Cetina, K. and Savigny, E. v. (eds), *The Practice Turn* (2001), pp. 163–174.

Polacek, Richard. *Study on Impediments to Mobility in the EU Live Performance Sector and on Possible Solutions*. Ed. by PEARLE (Performing Arts Employers Association League Europe). Brussels: Finnish Theatre Information Centre Mobile Home, 2007.

Prat, Reine. "Arts du spectacle: Pour l'égal accès des femmes et des hommes aux postes de responsabilité, aux lieux de décision, aux moyens de production, aux réseaux de diffusion, à la visibilité médiatique." 2: De l'interdit à l'empêchement, Rapport d'étape 2, Ministère de la Culture et de la Communication/DMDTS, May 2009. http://www.culturecommunication.gouv.fr/Actualites/Missions-et-rapports/Acces-des-femmes-et-des-hommes-aux-postes-de-responsabilite-n-2-De-l-interdit-a-l-empechement.-ReinePrat/(language)/fre-FR (accessed 6th August 2012).

Prat, Reine. "Mission EgalitéS. Pour une plus grande et une meilleure visibilité des diverses compo-santes de la population française dans le secteur du spectacle vivant – 1- Pour l'égal accès des femmes et des hommes aux postes de responsabilité, aux lieux de décision, à la maîtrise de la representation." Rapport d'étape 1, Ministère de la Culture et de la Communication/ DM-DTS, May 2006. http://www.culture.gouv.fr/culture/actualites/rapports/prat/egalites.pdf, (accessed on 6.8.2012).

Prat, Reine and Corrotto, Paula. "Entrevista a Jacques Rancière: 'Hablar de crisis de la sociedad es culpar a sus víctimas'." In: *El Publico*, 15th January 2012, pp. 22-25 (online: http://www.publico.es/culturas/416926/hablar-de-crisis-de-la-sociedad-es-culpar-a-sus-victimas, 23rd July 2013, English translation by Democracities, http://democracities.com/2013/08/18/jacques-ranciere-interview-democracy-is-not-to-begin-with-a-form-of-state/, accessed on 12th August 2013).

Rancière, Jacques. *Aisthesis: Scènes du régime esthétiqaue de l'art*. Paris: Editions Galilée, 2011.

Rancière, Jacques. *Le Partage du Sensible: Esthétique et politique*. Paris: Editions La Fabrique, 2000.

Rancière, Jacques. *Moments politiques: Interventions 1977–2009*. Paris: Editions La Fabrique 2009.

Ritsema, Jan. "The Gravity of PAF, or How to be Fluid." In: *sh 11* (2011) (programme for the Steirischer Herbst, 23.9.2011–26.10.2011), p. 89f.

Romanian Dance History (website), http://rodancehistory.blogspot.de/ (accessed 24th August 2012).

Rouse, Joseph. "Two Concepts of Practices." In: Schatzki, T. R., Knorr-Cetina, K. and Savigny, E. v. (eds), *The Practice Turn* (2001), pp. 189–198.

Roux, Céline. *Danse(s) performative(s): Enjeux et développement ds le champs chorégraphique français 1993–2003*. Paris: L'Harmattan, 2007.

Ruhsam, Martina. "Everybodys Selbstinterviews: Ein Buch als nutzerfreundliche Kartografie choreografischer Gegenwartspraktiken." In: *Corpus* (online journal for dance, choreography and performance), 28th December 2009. http://www.corpusweb.net/everybodys-selbstinterviews-4.html (accessed 9th July 2013).

Ruhsam, Martina. *Kollaborative Praxis: Choreografie. Die Inszenierung und ihre Aufführung*. Vienna/Berlin: Turia & Kant, 2011.

Sabisch, Petra (ed.). *A Topology of Practices – The Book of Interviews* (forthcoming 2016).

Sabisch, Petra. *Choreographing Relations: Practical Philosophy and Contemporary Choreography in the Works of Antonia Baehr, Gilles Deleuze, Juan Domínguez, Félix Guattari, Xavier Le Roy and Eszter Salamon*, Munich: Epodium, 2011.

Sabisch, Petra. "Die Zone und ihre Shareware: das Performing Arts Forum (PAF)." In: Maar, Kirsten and Hardt, Yvonne (eds), in collaboration with Sabine Kaross, *Tanz – Metropolis – Provinz* (= *Jahrbuch Tanzforschung* 17, ed. by Gesellschaft für Tanzforschung). Hamburg: Lit, 2007, pp. 205–212.

Sabisch, Petra. "Drängende Veränderungen in der Darstellenden Kunst – Ein feministischer Quasi-Survey." In: Gareis, Sigrid, Schöllhammer, Georg and Weibel, Peter (eds) and Holger Wölfle (trans.), *Moments: Eine Geschichte der Performance in zehn Akten*. Bilingual exhibition catalogue for the ZKM Karlsruhe/Museum für Neue Kunst. Cologne: Walther König, 2013, pp. 331–338.

Sabisch, Petra. Lecture Series on Art and Practical Philosophy I: "Was kann performative Philosophie in Zeiten des artistic turns in den Geisteswissenschaften tun?" Lecture at a conference on performative philosophy, Berlin, Uferhallen, 6th April 2013.

Sabisch, Petra. Lecture Series on Art and Practical Philosophy II: "What Can Practice Mean Today?" Copenhagen, Danish National School of Performing Arts, 23rd April 2013.

Sabisch, Petra. "What Can Choreography Do?" In: Inpex (ed.), *Swedish Dance History*, vol. 3. Stockholm: Inpex, 2011, pp. 82–103.

Sabisch, Petra. "Zur Choreographie der Organisation: Zeitgenössische künstlerische Praktiken". In: Hardt, Y. and Stern, M. (eds), *Choreographie und Institution* (2011), pp. 35–52.

Sánchez, José A. and Conde-Salazar, Jaime (eds). *Cuerpos sobre blanco*. Cuenca: UCLM-Desviaciones/Communidad de Madrid, 2003.

Sánchez, José A. and Conde-Salazar, Jaime /UVI (eds). *Desviaciones*. Madrid: La Inesperada y Cuarta Pared, 1999.

Sarma: Laboratorium für Kritik, Dramaturgie, Forschung und Schaffen, http://www.sarma.be/pages/index (accessed on 25th August 2013).

Schatzki, Theodore R., Knorr-Cetina, Karin and Savigny, Eike von (eds). *The Practice Turn in Contemporary Theory*. London/New York: Routledge/Taylor & Francis, 2001.

Schelepa, Susanne, Wetzel, Petra and Wohlfahrt, Gerhard (eds). *Zur sozialen Lage der Künstler und Künstlerinnen in Österreich, unter Mitarbeit von Anna Mostetschnig, im Auftrag des Bundesministeriums für Unterricht, Kunst und Kultur an die L&R Sozialforschung*. Vienna, 2008.

Schmidt, Robert. *Soziologie der Praktiken. Konzeptionelle Studien und empirische Analysen*. Berlin: Suhrkamp, 2012.

Schneider, Wolfgang. *Es geht um die Zukunft unserer Theaterlandschaft: Eine kulturpolitische Polemik aus gegebenem Anlass*. In: Fonds Darstellende Künste/Kulturpolitische Gesellschaft (eds), *Report Darstellende Künste* (2010), pp. 21–25.

Schober, Christian, Schmidt, Andrea and Sprajcer, Selma. *Tanz- und Theaterszene in Wien. Zahlen, Daten, Fakten unter besonderer Berücksichtigung der Effekte der Wiener Theaterreform 2003, im Auftrag der Stadt Wien an das NPO Kompetenzzentrum der Wirtschaftsuniversität Wien*. Vienna, 2012 (available online: http://epub.wu.ac.at/3634/, accessed on 21st March 2013).

Schulz, Gabriele. "Arbeitsmarkt Kultur. Eine Analyse von KSK-Daten." In: Schulz, G., Zimmermann, O. and Hufnagel, R., *Arbeitsmarkt Kultur* (2013), pp. 241–323.

Schulz, Gabriele. "Bestandsaufnahme zum Arbeitsmarkt Kultur". In: Schulz, G., Zimmermann, O. and Hufnagel, R., *Arbeitsmarkt Kultur* (2013), pp. 29–201.

Schulz, Gabriele and Zimmermann, Olaf. "Arbeitsmarkt Kultur: Hoffnungsträger oder Abstellgleis – Bewertung und Schlussfolgerungen." In: Schulz, G., Zimmermann, O. and Hufnagel, R., *Arbeitsmarkt Kultur* (2013).

Schulz, Gabriele, Zimmermann, Olaf and Hufnagel, Rainer. *Arbeitsmarkt Kultur: Zur wirtschaftlichen und sozialen Lage in Kulturberufen*. Berlin: Deutscher Kulturrat, 2013.

Siegmund, Gerald: *Abwesenheit: Eine performative Ästhetik des Tanzes*. Bielefeld: transcript, 2006.

Siepen, Nikolas. "Free Popular Avantgard:. Die ewige Unruhe des Kunst-und-Politik-Zusammenhangs." In: *Springerin: Hefte für Gegenwartskunst 2* (2013) (available online: http://www.springerin.at/dyn/heft.php?id=80&pos=0&t extid=0&lang=de, accessed on 22nd June 2013).

Söndermann, Michael. *Kultureller Beschäftigungsmarkt und Künstlerarbeitsmarkt: Kulturstatistische Analyse zum Anhang des Staatenberichts*. On behalf of the German UNESCO Commission, published 26th March 2012.

sommer.bar, http://www.tanzimaugust.de/2010/seiten/sommerbar.html (discontinued), 1st September 2013 (partially accessible on https://www.facebook.com/pages/sommerbar/307078842271, accessed on 30th August 2013).

Spångberg, Mårten. *Spangbergianism*, Gargzdai: Print-It, 2011.

Special Issue/Edition Spéciale (website), http://specialissue.eu/ (accessed 11th June 2013).

Special Issue/Edition Spéciale, *Emisiones Cacatúa*, http://specialissue.eu/editions/emisiones-cacatua (accessed 11th June 2013).

Special Issue/Edition Spéciale, download of the live stream *Emisiones Cacatúa*, https://archive.org/details/Emisionescacatuaistambul (accessed 11th June 2013).

Special Issue/Edition Spéciale, *The Mountain of Aubervilliers*, http://specialissue.eu/daily-publications-in-laboratoires-daubervilliers (accessed 11th June 2013).

Special Issue/Edition Spéciale, *A Disembodied Voice*, http://www.specialissue.eu/editions/a-disembodiedvoice-towards-love (accessed 11th June 2013).

Special Issue/Edition Spéciale, *The Public Office*, http://www.specialissue.eu/editions/the-public-office (accessed 11th June 2013).

Special Issue/Edition Spéciale, *Santiye*, http://www.specialissue.eu/editions/the-public-office (accessed 11th June 2013).

Staeck, Klaus. "Neue Kämpfe um kulturelle Vielfalt." In: *Berliner Zeitung*, 20.6.2013, p. 5.

Stengers, Isabelle. "Introductory Notes on An Ecology of Practices" (ANU Humanities Research Centre Symposium, August 2003). In: *Cultural Studies Review* 11 (2005), pp. 183–196.

Stengers, Isabelle. "The Care of the Possible." Interviewed by Erik Bordeleau and trans. by Kelly Ladd. *Scapegoat* 1 (2011). [First published as: "Le soin des possibles", in: *Les nouveaux cahiers de socialisme* 6 (2011)].

Tea-tron, independent online platform for the performing arts, http://www.teatron.com/teatron/Portada.do (accessed 19th August 2013).

The Public Office (website), http://thepublicoffice.se (accessed 11th June 2013).

Theatre Info Finland. *Mobility Infopoint: Mapping in Finland.* Helsinki, 2011.

Thévenot, Laurent. "Artists Engaging the Public in Participation: A View from the Sociology of Engagements." Lecture held at *Artistic Practices* conference, held by the Sociology of the Arts Research Network at the Universität für Musik und Darstellende Kunst Vienna (5th–8th September 2012), 7th September 2012.

Thévenot, Laurent. "Die Person in ihrem vielfachen Engagiertsein." *Trivium* 5 (2010) (available online: http://trivium.revues.org/3573, accessed 21st August 2013).

Thévenot, Laurent. "Pragmatic Regimes Governing the Engagement with the World." In: Schatzki, T. R., Knorr-Cetina, K.and Savigny, E. v. (eds), *The Practice Turn*, pp. 56–73.

Thévenot, Laurent and Boltanski, Luc. *Justesse et justice dans le travail.* Paris: PUF/Centre d'Etudes de l'Emploi, 1989.

Thévenot, Laurent and Boltanski, Luc. "Sociology of Critical Capacity." *European Journal of Social Theory* 2 (1999), pp. 359–377.

TKH (Walking Theory). *Raster 2008#1* and *Raster 2009#2 – Yearbook of the Independent Performing Arts Scene*, Belgrad 2008 and 2009 (available online: http://www.tkh-generator.net/files/raster1eng_0.pdf, accessed 2nd August 2013).

UNESCO (ed.). *2009 Framework for Cultural Statistics* (FCS), Montréal 2009 (available online: http://www.uis.unesco.org/culture/Pages/framework-cultural-statistics.aspx (accessed 28th March 2013).

UNESCO (ed.). *Consolidated Report on the Implementation by Member States of the 1980 Recommendation Concerning the Status of the Artist.* (Monitoring Report from the General Conference held in Paris on 21.10.2011), http://unesdoc.unesco.org/images/0021/002132/213223e.pdf (accessed 29th July 2013).

UNESCO (ed.). *Convention on the Protection and Promotion of the Diversity of Cultural Expressions*, Paris, amended on 20th October 2005 (33rd session), http://www.unesco.org/new/en/culture/themes/cultural-diversity/diversity-

of-cultural-expressions/the-convention/convention-text/ (accessed 12th August 2013).
UNESCO (ed.). *Recommendation Concerning the Status of the Artist*, adopted by the General Conference at its 21st Session, Belgrade, 27th October 1980 http://portal.unesco.org/en/ev.php-URL_ID=13138&URL_DO=DO_TOPIC&URL_SECTION=201.html (accessed 12th August 2013).
UNESCO (ed.). *Universal Declaration on Cultural Diversity*, 2nd November 2001, http://portal.unesco.org/en/ev.php-URL_ID=13179&URL_DO=DO_TOPIC&URL_SECTION=201.html (accessed 12th August 2013).
Van Campenhout, Elke. "Spaces as Tools." In: *sh* (2011) (programme for the Steirischer Herbst, 23.9.–26.10.2011), pp. 87–91.
Virno, Paolo. *A Grammar of the Multitude: For an Analysis of Contemporary Forms of Life*. New York/Los Angeles: Semiotext(e), 2004.
VTI/Institute for the Performing Arts in Flanders (ed.). *Performing Arts Flanders: Perspective Danse*. Brussels: vti, 2013 (available online: http://vti.be/en, accessed on 31.7.2013).
W. (website), http://www.1110111.org/ (accessed 10th July 2013).
Whitehead, Alfred North. *Process and Reality: An Essay in Cosmology*. David Ray Griffin and Donald W. Sherburne (eds). New York: The Free Press, 1979.
World Observatory on the Social Status of the Artist (ed.). http://portal.unesco.org/culture/en/ev.phpURL_ID=38716&URL_DO=DO_TOPIC&URL_SECTION=201.html (accessed 25th August.2013).
Y si dejamos de ser artistas (website), http://www.ysidejamosdeserartistas.com/pagina-ejemplo/ (accessed 22nd July 2013).
Zimmermann, Olaf. "Arbeitsmarkt Kultur. Einführung und methodisches Vorgehen." In: Schulz, G., Zimmermann, O. and Hufnagel, R., *Arbeitsmarkt Kultur* (2013), pp. 9–27.
Zimmermann, Olaf and Schulz, Gabriele (eds), in collaboration with Stefanie Ernst. *Zukunft Kulturwirtschaft: Zwischen Künstlertum und Kreativwirtschaft*. Essen: Klartext, 2009.

Interviews and abbreviations

Alice Chauchat in conversation with Petra Sabisch, June 2013.	ACPS
Blanca Calvo in conversation with Bettina Földesi, May 2013.	BCBF
Christine de Smedt in conversation with Petra Sabisch, May 2013.	CDSPS
Cristina Rizzo in conversation with Bettina Földesi, May 2013.	CRBF
Emma Kim Hagdahl in conversation with Bettina Földesi, June 2013.	EKHBF
Juan Domínguez in conversation with Petra Sabisch, May 2013.	JDPS
Jan Ritsema in conversation with Bettina Földesi, April 2013.	JRBF
Hermann Heisig in conversation with Bettina Földesi, May 2013.	HHBF
Halla Ólafsdóttir in conversation with Bettina Földesi, May 2013.	HOBF
Kerstin Schroth in conversation with Petra Sabisch, May 2013.	KSPS
Mette Ingvartsen in conversation with Petra Sabisch, October 2011	MIPS_2011
Mette Ingvartsen in conversation with Petra Sabisch, June 2013	MIPS_2013
Manuel Pelmus in conversation with Tom Engels, June 2013.	MPTE
Paz Rojo in conversation with Tom Engels, July 2013.	PRTE
Valentina Desideri in conversation with Tom Engels, April 2013.	VDTE

Explanation of citation method

Alice Chauchat in conversation with Petra Sabisch, June 2013.
AC5PS = answer 5 by Alice Chauchat.
ACPS3 = question 3 by Petra Sabisch

Annex

Annex 1: Manifesto for a European Performance Policy
Annex 2: Statistics on the internationality of the case studies
Annex 3: Matrix of central questions for the codification of the interviews
Annex 4: UNESCO Recommendation Concerning the Status of the Artist (excerpt) – 27 October, 1980

Annex 1: Manifesto for a European Performance Policy

Manifesto for a European Performance Policy

We are European
We are citizens
We are workers
We are artists
We are performers
We are independent

Our practices can be described by a range of terminology, depending on the different cultural contexts in which we operate. Our practices can be called: "performance art", "live art", "happenings", "events", "body art", "contemporary dance/theatre", "experimental dance", "new dance", "multimedia performance", "site specific", "body installation", "physical theatre", "laboratory", "conceptual dance", "independance", "postcolonial dance / performance", "street dance", "urban dance", "dance theatre", "dance performance"—to name but a few...

Such a list of terms not only represents the diversity of disciplines and approaches embraced within our practices, but is also symptomatic of the problematics of trying to define or prescribe such heterogeneous and evolving performance forms. However, today more than ever, the drive by cultural institutions and the art market alike to fix and categorise contemporary art practices is often in conflict with the fluid and migratory nature of much of our work, as much as with its needs.

Our practices are synonymous with funding priorities in terms of innovation, risk, hybridity, audience development, social inclusion, participation, new cultural discourses and cultural diversity, cultural difference. They offer new languages, articulate new forms of subjectivation and presentation to play with the cultural and social influences which inform us, to create new cultural landscapes.

We address issues of cultural difference. Our practices have proved to be an articulate platform from which to challenge the dominant post-colonial narratives and traditional representations of the "other".

We consider the borders between disciplines, categories and nations to be fluid, dynamic and osmotic.

We produce work that develops partnerships, networks and collaborations, disregards national borders and actively contributes to the local, European and trans-national contexts.

We are aware of shared anxiety over the loss of "cultural identities" in the European context today but have no fear of the "homogenisation of cultures":

operating on a trans-national level, our artistic practices dismantle such concepts or logics.

We consider dialogue, thinking, research and making as equal constituents of our labour. These activities are not only the search engine for our art and related practices, but also for our societies, for our cultures. We are calling for innovative artistic structures, but also a new social status that would acknowledge new concepts of work that have altered the distinction between so-called "productive" and "non-productive" periods. We claim recognition for our professional artistic activities, including those that will be visible in the future and which will give voice to that which has not yet been articulated.

This increased recognition of the social status of the artist will contribute to and emphasise the quality of the social impact of artistic activities, which is the core of any democratic cultural policy.

We want the European Community to:

- resource artists as much as art,
- invest in the ongoing needs and long-term growth of independent performers,
- actively support artists in research, development and in the ongoing process of their practices, in equal measure to the generation and placement of new works,
- recognise and enhance the relationships between and across innovative contemporary practices,
- facilitate strategies for cross-disciplinary dialogues, collaborations and funding initiatives,
- support new strategies for increasing audience awareness and appreciation,
- demonstrate a genuine commitment to innovation, risk and hybridity,
- actively develop, recognise and support a more important number of active, flexible and inventive artistic structures and infrastructures,
- and to engage in a dialogue, set up the conditions for a new debate regarding these questions.[289]

---

289 | This manifesto was originally signed by Jérôme Bel (Paris, France), Steven de Belder (Antwerp, Belgium), Annabelle Hagmann (Paris, France & Berlin, Germany), Xavier Le Roy (Berlin, Germany), Philippe Riéra (Vienna, Austria), Georg Schöllhammer (Vienna, Austria), Sabine Sonnenschein (Vienna, Austria), Oleg Soulimenko (Vienna, Austria & Moscow, Russia), Christophe Wavelet (Paris, France).

Annex 2: Statistics on the internationality of the case studies

Special Issue
=> institutions from 5 countries
(France, Serbia, Spain, Sweden, Turkey),
=> artists from 14 countries
(Austria, Brazil, Croatia, Estonia, France, Germany, Italy, Iran, Norway, Serbia, Spain, Sweden, Turkey, United States)
in two years

In-Presentable
=> artists from 30 countries in total, over the course of 10 years

2003	from 4 countries (Germany, Norway, Spain, Switzerland)
2004	from 5 countries (France, Italy, Spain, Sweden, United Kingdom)
2005	from 11 countries (Argentina, Belgium, Brazil, France, Germany, Hungary, India, Israel, Spain, Switzerland, United Kingdom)
2006	from 9 countries (Austria, Brazil, Germany, France, Japan, Spain, Sweden, South Africa, United Kingdom)
2007	from 8 countries (Brazil, France, Hungary, Lebanon, Palestine, Spain, United Kingdom, Venezuela)
2008	from 8 countries (Brazil, Croatia, Norway, Portugal, Serbia, Spain, Taiwan, United States)
2009	from 11 countries (Brazil, Denmark, France, Germany, Hungary, Netherlands, Portugal, Serbia, Spain, United States, Morocco)
2010	all from Spain
2011	from 7 countries (Denmark, France, Germany, Italy, Sweden, Spain, United Kingdom)
2012	from 18 countries (Argentina, Belgium, Brazil, Croatia, France, Finland, Germany, Hungary, Italy, Netherlands, Norway, Portugal, Romania, Serbia, Spain, Sweden, Switzerland, United States)

Double Lecture Series
=> artists/lecturers from 8 countries
(Belgium, Denmark, France, Germany, Iran, Sweden, United States, United Kingdom)
in one year

Performing Arts Forum
=> artists from 64 countries in total, over the course of 7 years

2006   from 20 countries
(Australia, Austria, Belgium, Croatia, Denmark, Estonia, France, Germany, India, Lebanon, Netherlands, Norway, Portugal, Serbia, Slovakia, South Korea, Spain, Sweden, United Kingdom, United States)

2007   from 26 countries
(Argentina, Austria, Belgium, Brazil, Croatia, Czech Republic, Denmark, Dominican Republic, Estonia, France, Germany, Hungary, India, Italy, Japan, Netherlands, New Zealand, Norway, Portugal, Romania, Serbia, South Korea, Spain, Taiwan, United Kingdom, United States)

2008   from 34 countries
(Argentina, Australia, Austria, Belgium, Brazil, Canada, Chile, Croatia, Denmark, Estonia, Finland, France, Germany, Greece, Iceland, India, Ireland, Israel, Italy, Japan, Macedonia, Mexico, Netherlands, Nigeria, Norway, Poland, Serbia, South Korea, Spain, Sweden, Switzerland, Turkey, United Kingdom, United States)

2009   from 37 countries
(Argentina, Australia, Austria, Belgium, Bosnia, Brazil, Canada, Colombia, Croatia, Denmark, Estonia, Finland, France, Germany, Greece, Hungary, India, Indonesia, Ireland, Italy, Japan, Morocco, Netherlands, New Zealand, Nigeria, Norway, Paraguay, Poland, Portugal, Russia, Serbia, Slovenia, Spain, Sweden, Switzerland, United Kingdom, United States)

2010   from 42 countries
(Argentina, Armenia, Australia, Austria, Belgium, Bolivia, Brazil, Canada, Chile, Croatia, Denmark, Estonia, Finland, France, Germany, Greece, Hungary, Iceland, India, Ireland, Israel, Italy, Japan, Mexico, Netherlands, Nicaragua, Norway, Philippines, Poland, Portugal, Romania, Russia, Serbia, Slovakia, South Korea, Spain, Sweden, Switzerland, Turkey, United Kingdom, United States, Uruguay)

2011   from 37 countries
(Austria, Belgium, Bolivia, Brazil, Cameroon, Canada, Chile, Croatia, Denmark, Estonia, Finland, France, Germany, Greece, Ireland, Israel, Italy, Lithuania, Mexico, Netherlands, New Zealand, Philippines, Poland, Portugal, Romania, Russia, Slovakia, South Korea, Spain, Sweden, Switzerland, United Kingdom, United States, Uzbekistan)

2012   from 42 countries
       (Australia, Austria, Belarus, Belgium, Brazil, Canada, Chile, China, Croatia, Denmark, Estonia, Finland, France, Germany, Hungary, Iceland, India, Iran, Ireland, Israel, Italy, Japan, Malaysia, Peru, Lithuania, Mexico, Netherlands, Norway, Portugal, Romania, Russia, Serbia, Singapore, South Africa, South Korea, Spain, Sweden, Switzerland, Tajikistan, Turkey, United Kingdom, United States)

sommer.bar

=> artists from 33 countries in total, over the course of 6 years

2006   from 11 countries
       (Australia, Belgium, Brazil, Denmark, France, Germany, Portugal, Slovenia, Sweden, United Kingdom, United States)
2007   from 11 countries
       (Denmark, Belgium, Croatia, France, Hungary, Netherlands, Poland, Russia, Slovenia, Spain, United States)
2008   from 12 countries
       (Australia, Belgium, Brazil, Bulgaria, France, Denmark, Germany, Indonesia, Spain, Sweden, United Kingdom, United States)
2009   from 14 countries
       (Argentina, Congo, Estonia, France, Germany, Italy, Japan, Poland, Portugal, Spain, Sweden, Switzerland, United Kingdom, United States)
2010   from 17 countries
       (Belgium, Denmark, France, Germany, Italy, Macedonia, Portugal, Serbia, Slovakia, South Korea, Spain, Sweden, Switzerland, Turkey, United Kingdom, United States)
2011   from 12 countries
       (Australia, Croatia, France, Germany, Japan, Netherlands, Norway, Slovenia, Spain, Switzerland, United Kingdom, United States)

Annex 3: Matrix of central questions for the codification of the interviews

100	Specificity of the project at the intersection of production conditions, work mode and aesthetics

100.1	specificity of the project/practice at the intersection of production and aesthetics (including motivation, history and (personal) background)
100.2	concern
100.3	format of presentation
100.4	specific core aspects of the project/practice
100.5	decision-making structures/organising structures

101	Categories/concepts/definitions for work modes

101.1	exchange/sharing/role of the social
101.2	discourse-generating (sense 1)
101.3	context-generating (sense 2)
101.4	artist-initiated, artist-led (self-organised)
101.5	continuity & sustainability/development & construction (sense 3)
101.6	experiment & innovation (sense 4)
101.7	contemporary
101.8	international
101.9	(open in format) generating new formats of presentation
101.10	forms of collaboration
101.10a	collective
101.10b	collaborative
101.10c	changing
101.11	development/construction

102	Context of production/interplay between aesthetics and forms of presentation in curatorial concepts and concepts of the audience

102.1	budget
102.2	form of contract
102.3	curatorial concept + aesthetics
102.4	audience
102.5	plannability of the project/practice
102.6	plannability/planning security as artist?

103	**Problems encountered**

104	**Social conditions, conditions of production, aesthetics, and work modes**
104.1	interrelation between production conditions, aesthetics, work modes
104.2	work mode/method
104.3	research
104.4	aesthetics
104.5	social security
104.6	relations/comparison (art and science)
104.6a	in comparison to science
104.6b	in comparison to politics

105	**Education (emancipation/accessibility/remuneration)**
105.1	current situation of dance education
105.2	concerning learning the profession
105.3	concerning impact of qualifications
105.4	role of research
105.5	teaching as a means of sustaining/developing professional life

106	**Participation in decision-making structures – critique and power – dependencies**
106.1	Who are addressees when dealing with problems in the field?
106.1a	as artist
106.1b	as curator
106.2	possibilities to give constructive critique to processes and practices (addressees/dialogue partners)
106.3	evaluation of the impact of a separate contribution to the field in terms of articulation/critique and strengthening of positive effects (possibilities to articulate)
106.4	agency/effects related to artistic status (Do you think that you can have a say as an artist in the professional field/in society?)
106.5	shaping circumstances of production in your professional field
106.6	shaping aesthetic outcome of artistic work process
106.7	evaluation of funding structures
106.8	evaluation of your role in society
106.9	time spent on applications in a year

107	Change/diachrony/genealogy
107.1	structural changes (changes in the circumstances of production) in the professional field over the last ten to twenty years
107.2	aesthetic changes in the professional field over the last ten to twenty years

108	Desire/professional needs/future
108.1	Speculating about the future: What would you like to change/improve (if you could)?
108.2	Which needs of your profession do you think are not yet met?

109	**Other practices with the named categories** (artist-initiated/led, contemporary, experimental, discourse-generating, context-generating, international, self-organised, etc.)

Annex 4: UNESCO-Recommendation Concerning the Status of the Artist (excerpt) – 27.10.1980

"*The General Conference of the United Nations Educational, Scientific and Cultural Organization*, meeting in Belgrade from 23 September to 28 October 1980 at its twenty-first session,

Recalling that, under the terms of Article I of its Constitution, the purpose of the Organization is to contribute to peace and security by promoting collaboration among the nations through education, science and culture in order to further universal respect for justice, for the rule of law and for the human rights and fundamental freedoms which are affirmed for the peoples of the world, without distinction of race, sex, language or relation, by the Charter of the United Nations,

Recalling the terms of the Universal Declaration of Human Rights, and particularly Articles 22, 23, 24, 25, 27 and 28 thereof, quoted in the annex to this Recommendation,

Recalling the terms of the United Nations International Covenant on Economic, Social and Cultural Rights, particularly its Articles 6 and 15, quoted in the annex to this Recommendation, and the need to adopt the necessary measures for the preservation, development and dissemination of culture, with a view to ensuring the full exercise of these rights,

Recalling the Declaration of the Principles of International Cultural Co-operation, adopted by the General Conference of UNESCO at its fourteenth session, particularly its Articles III and IV, which are quoted in the annex to this Recommendation, as well as the Recommendation on Participation by the People at Large in Cultural Life and their Contribution to it, adopted by the General Conference of UNESCO at its nineteenth session,

Recognizing that the arts in their fullest and broadest definition are and should be an integral part of life and that it is necessary and appropriate for governments to help create and sustain not only a climate encouraging freedom of artistic expression but also the material conditions facilitating the release of this creative talent,

Recognizing that every artist is entitled to benefit effectively from the social security and insurance provisions contained in the basic texts, Declarations, Covenant and Recommendation mentioned above,

Considering that the artist plays an important role in the life and evolution of society and that he should be given the opportunity to contribute to society's development and, as any other citizen, to exercise his responsibilities therein, while preserving his creative inspiration and freedom of expression,

Further recognizing that the cultural, technological, economic, social and political development of society influences the status of the artist and that it is consequently necessary to review his status, taking account of social progress in the world,

Affirming the right of the artist to be considered, if he so wishes, as a person actively engaged in cultural work and consequently to benefit, taking account of the particular conditions of his artistic profession, from all the legal, social and economic advantages pertaining to the status of workers,

Affirming further the need to improve the social security, labour and tax conditions of the artist, whether employed or self-employed, taking into account the contribution to cultural development which the artist makes,

Recalling the importance, universally acknowledged both nationally and internationally, of the preservation and promotion of cultural identity and of the role in this field of artists who perpetuate the practice of traditional arts and also interpret a nation's folklore,

Recognizing that the vigour and vitality of the arts depend, inter alia, on the well-being of artists both individually and collectively,

Recalling the conventions and recommendations of the International Labour Organization (ILO) which have recognized the rights of workers in general and, hence, the rights of artists and, in particular, the conventions and recommendations listed in the appendix to this Recommendation,

Taking note, however, that some of the International Labour Organization standards allow for derogations or even expressly exclude artists, or certain categories of them, owing to the special conditions in which artistic activity takes place, and that it is consequently necessary to extend their field of application and to supplement them by other standards,

Considering further that this recognition of their status as persons actively engaged in cultural work should in no way compromise their freedom of creativity, expression and communication but should, on the contrary, confirm their dignity and integrity,

Convinced that action by the public authorities is becoming necessary and urgent in order to remedy the disquieting situation of artists in a large number of Member States, particularly with regard to human rights, economic and social circumstances and their conditions of employment, with a view to providing artists with the conditions necessary for the development and flowering of their talents and appropriate to the role that they are able to play in the planning and implementation of cultural policies and cultural development activities of communities and countries and in the improvement of the quality of life,

Considering that art plays an important part in education and that artists, by their works, may influence the conception of the world held by all people, and particularly by youth,

Considering that artists must be able collectively to consider and, if necessary, defend their common interests, and therefore must have the right to be recognized as a professional category and to constitute trade union or professional organizations,

Considering that the development of the arts, the esteem in which they are held and the promotion of arts education depend in large measure on the creativity of artists,

Aware of the complex nature of artistic activity and of the diverse forms it takes and, in particular, of the importance, for the living conditions and the development of the talents of artists, of the protection of their moral and material rights in their works, or performances, or the use made of them, and of the need to extend and reinforce such protection,

Considering the need to endeavour to take account as far as possible of the opinion both of artists and of the people at large in the formulation and implementation of cultural policies and for that purpose to provide them with the means for effective action,

Considering that contemporary artistic expression is presented in public places and that these should be laid out so as to take account of the opinions of the artists concerned, therefore that there should be close co-operation between architects, contractors and artists in order to lay down aesthetic guidelines for public places which will respond to the requirements of communication and make an effective contribution to the establishment of new and meaningful relationships between the public and its environment,

Taking into account the diversity of circumstances of artists in different countries and within the communities in which they are expected to develop their talents, and the varying significance attributed to their works by the societies in which they are produced,

Convinced, nevertheless, that despite such differences, questions of similar concern arise in all countries with regard to the status of the artist, and that a common will and inspiration are called for if a solution is to be found and if the status of the artist is to be improved, which is the intention of this Recommendation,

Taking note of the provisions of the international conventions in force relating, more particularly, to literary and artistic property, and in particular of the Universal Convention and the Berne Convention for the Protection of Literary and Artistic Works, and of those relating to the protection of the rights of performers, of the resolutions of the General Conference, of the recommendations made by UNESCO's intergovernmental conferences on cultural policies, and of the conventions and recommendations adopted by the International Labour Organization, listed in the appendix to this Recommendation,

Having before it, as item 31 of the agenda of the session, proposals concerning the status of the artist,

Having decided, at its twentieth session, that this question should be the subject of a recommendation to Member States,

Adopts this Recommendation this twenty-seventh day of October 1980:

The General Conference recommends that Member States implement the following provisions, taking whatever legislative or other steps may be required —in conformity with the constitutional practice of each State and the nature of the questions under consideration to apply the principles and norms set forth in this Recommendation within their respective territories.

For those States which have a federal or non-unitary constitutional system, the General Conference recommends that, with regard to the provisions of this Recommendation the implementation of which comes under the legal jurisdiction of individual constituent States, countries, provinces, cantons or any other territorial and political subdivisions that are not obliged by the constitutional system of the federation to take legislative measures, the federal government be invited to inform the competent authorities of such States, countries, provinces or cantons of the said provisions, with its recommendation for their adoption.

The General Conference recommends that Member States bring this Recommendation to the attention of authorities, institutions and organizations in a position to contribute to improvement of the status of the artist and to foster the participation of artists in cultural life and development.

The General Conference recommends that Member States report to it, on dates and in a manner to be determined by it, on the action they have taken to give effect to this Recommendation.

Acknowledgements

For their artistic work, for their interesting and formidable engagement with this study's topics, and not least for their dedication of a sizeable portion of time to the project, I would hereby like to extend my most heartfelt thanks to the interviewees: Alice Chauchat, Blanca Calvo, Christine de Smedt, Cristina Rizzo, Emma Kim Hagdahl, Halla Ólafsdóttir, Hermann Heisig, Jan Ritsema, Juan Domínguez, Kerstin Schroth, Manuel Pelmus, Mette Ingvartsen, Paz Rojo und Valentina Desideri. My deepest thanks also go to Tom Engels and Bettina Földesi for a brilliant collaboration, for their professionalism in conducting interviews, and for their time-consuming work on transcriptions and editing, all of which was indispensable to this research. My special thanks also go to Alice Chauchat for participating in specific research and discussion activities, to João Fiadeiro for his friendly assistance in sending me research material, and to Stéphane Noël for the interesting discussion on the situation in Switzerland. I must also thank all the friends who have supported me in this endeavor. Last but not least, I would especially like to thank Professor Dr. Gabriele Brandstetter, who came to me with the idea for this study and accompanied me along the way; Professor Dr. Manfred Brauneck, who I thank for his role the initiation and execution of this study; and the ITI, which supported engagement with the project through numerous colloquia. Funding from the Balzan Foundation made this work possible.

Independent Theatre in the Post-Socialist Countries of Eastern Europe
New Forms of Production and Creativity in Theatre Aesthetics

Andrea Hensel

1. INTRODUCTION

To this day, Eastern Europe is a 'blank spot' on the map of European theatre. Current research on the theatre scenes in Eastern Europe is, for the most part, meager; the theatres have barely been examined theoretically, much less in view of their practical work. This is true for institutional theatres and, above all, for independent theatres. Neither international experts nor theatre professionals and experts in the countries themselves have given independent theatre much attention. As the Polish curator Marta Keil notes:[1] '[W]e discovered that, despite our common history, we have virtually no common experience. Not only do we have dissimilar development paths and systems, but we also know surprisingly little about each other.'[2] A closer examination reveals, however, that in the past 20 years numerous artistic innovations have been realised in the independent theatre scenes in Eastern Europe. This study examines these developments. It investigates the history and the current situation of independent theatre in the post-socialist countries of Eastern Europe. The study primarily revolves around the former socialist people's republics of Hungary, Poland, the Czech Republic, Slovakia, Romania and Bulgaria, then focuses on the post-Yugoslavian countries of Serbia, Slovenia, Croatia and Bosnia-Herzegovina, and finally considers Russia, Belarus and the Ukraine as former republics of the Soviet

---

1 | The quotations by experts consulted for this study have, in general, been reproduced verbatim in the language chosen by the interviewee (English or German). In many cases, it is not the expert's native language.

2 | Marta Keil, "Preface", in *EEPAP – A Platform for the Development of Performing Arts in Central and Eastern Europe*. Study 2011, see http://www.eepap.org/web/english/eepap.pl, pp 7-8, here p. 7.

Union. Although at first glance these 13 countries seem to have experienced similar socio-political developments, a second look reveals significant differences in history, politics and society which have influenced the culture in the individual countries. These differences are also apparent with regard to the development of independent theatre. The emergence of a new self-image and new artistic working methods for independent theatre is closely linked to the economic, social and political circumstances in the respective countries. For this reason, this study proceeds methodically on the basis of individual analyses. It examines the development and current situation of independent theatre in the respective countries separately. The study also shows to what extent the working methods and production forms described can be viewed as paradigmatic for independent theatre in the post-socialist countries.

The study evaluates research activities which are concerned with independent theatre in Eastern Europe. This work deals with a variety of materials. Thus, there are informative source materials and a great deal of (research) literature on the theatre scenes in Poland, Slovenia and Hungary, but there are little to no public sources and/or examples of English literature available on the (independent) theatres in Bosnia-Herzegovina, Belarus and the Ukraine. Accordingly, the individual analyses here may vary.

Considering the current status of the scope of research, the study of the East European Performing Arts Platform (EEPAP) is particularly noteworthy. This network of theatre makers and theorists published comprehensive reports on the theatre scenes in 17 Eastern European countries in 2011.[3] The reports include analyses of the general conditions of artistic work and the organizational structures of the theatres following the political upheavals.

Furthermore, the following study is based on the author's own on-site research, which was possible as part of the rescarch project. On-site research included attending performances in Poland, Bulgaria, the Czech Republic, Serbia, Slovenia, Croatia and Belarus, together with a great many on-site interviews with theatre makers and theorists. In addition, questionnaires were sent to independent artists and groups, politicians responsible for cultural and educational policies, and theatre critics in the relevant countries, in which they were asked to describe the situation of independent theatre in their country. Seventeen questionnaires were completed and returned, and the responses were integrated into the analysis. Moreover, four extensive interviews took place in Slovenia. The statements made by representatives of independent theatres have also been included in the study. The questionnaires and interviews supplement the information provided by the research literature.

---

3 | The study includes Armenia, Azerbaijan, Belarus, Bosnia-Herzegovina, Bulgaria, Georgia, Croatia, Macedonia, Moldavia, Romania, Serbia, Slovenia, the Czech Republic, Hungary, Slovakia, Ukraine and Kosovo; see EEPAP.

The study is divided into three main areas: The initial focus is on the development of independent theatres in the individual Eastern European countries (Chapter 2). Here the countries are combined according to the different characteristics of their socialist regimes as former socialist people's republics, post-Soviet and post-Yugoslavian states. The study deals with the situation of the independent theatres under socialism as well as their development following the political upheavals at the end of the eighties and at the beginning of the nineties. The chapter also includes an excursus on the independent dance scene because dance plays an important role for the independent theatres.

The next chapter is dedicated to the general conditions of independent theatre work (Chapter 3). The presentation focuses on changes in the cultural policies, in the financial sponsorship of independent theatres and in the production and presentation conditions. In addition, this chapter deals with the issue of restrictions which limit the work of the independent theatres. Finally, the chapter includes descriptions of the professional training and the international networking of independent artists and groups.

The third focal point in Chapter 4 deals with individual productions which feature important working methods and topics which are typical of independent theatre in the post-socialist countries. Even though the analyses are primarily concerned with spoken theatre, or describe performances which emphasise musical elements, these productions are usually transmedial productions which combine different artistic media, such as music, dance and image. Against this background, this study does not assume the usual separation of artistic genres but considers independent theatre as a transmedial practice. This study covers the time up to 2012. Later developments could not be taken into account.

A sensitive approach when dealing with this particular geographical area requires that one first define the term 'Eastern Europe'. It should not be the case that 'the countries of Eastern Europe are all thrown together to form one single region'[4]. In no way was Eastern Europe, even under socialism, a monolithic entity.[5] Former people's republics, like Poland and Hungary, differ from Yugoslavia under Tito, and this, in turn, differs from the republics of the Soviet

---

4 | Larry Wolff, "Die Erfindung Osteuropas. Von Voltaire zu Voldemort", in Karl Kaser, Dagmer Gramshammer-Hohl and Robert Pichler (eds.), *Enzyklopädie des europäischen Ostens, Europa und die Grenzen im Kopf* (Klagenfurt et al.: Wieser 2003), pp. 21-34, here p. 21.

5 | For the history of Eastern Europe see e.g. Ekaterina Emeliantseva, Arié Malz and Daniel Ursprung (eds.), *Einführung in die osteuropäische Geschichte* (Zürich: Orell Füssli 2008); Aron Buzogány and Rolf Frankenberger (eds.), *Osteuropa. Politik, Wirtschaft und Gesellschaft* (Baden-Baden: Nomos 2007); Dieter Segert, *Die Grenzen Osteuropas. 1918, 1945, 1989 – Drei Versuche im Westen anzukommen* (Frankfurt a. Main: Campus 2002); Harald Roth (ed.), *Studienhandbuch Östliches Europa. Geschichte Ostmittel- und*

Union. After the fall of communism, the different countries went their own ways, even if they may exhibit parallel developments in political, social and cultural terms. This study deliberately refrains from assuming a 'one-size-fits-all' perspective of 'Eastern Europe'. However, the study still requires a basis which will enable a comparison of the individual countries. The term *post-socialism* provides such a basis.[6] It refers equally to historical, geographical, ethnic-linguistic and political aspects and stresses the dissimilarity of the historical background and the current situation of the individual countries. It is the aim of this study to present in detail the very heterogeneous history of independent theatre in the individual countries which are still influenced by a socialist past.

To simplify reading, gender-specific differentiation (e.g. he/she) has been omitted.

2. Independent Theatre after the Political Upheavals of 1989/1991

The political developments in the former socialist people's republics and the post-Soviet states included in this study indicate commonalities and differences.[7] In different dimensions, the communist rule in these countries was characterised

---

Südosteuropas (Wien/Köln/Weimar: Böhlau 1999); Jenö Szücs, *Die drei historischen Regionen Europas*, (Frankfurt a. Main: Neue Kritik 1990).

6 | "The term 'postsocialism' does not refer to one type of political system but to many political systems whose development exhibit parallels after the end of communist rule but also important differences"; Anton Pelinka, "Vorwort", in Dieter Segert (ed.), *Postsozialismus. Hinterlassenschaften des Staatssozialismus und neue Kapitalismen in Europa* (Wien: Braumüller 2007), pp. VII-VIII, here p. VII. On post-socialism see also Stanislaw Frącz, *Im Spannungsfeld von Nationalismus und Integration. Zur Komplexität des Transformationsprozesses der postkommunistischen Gesellschaften unter den osteuropäischen Gegebenheiten* (Bonn: Bouvier 2006); Boris Groys, Anne von der Heiden, and Peter Weibel (eds.), *Zurück aus der Zukunft. Osteuropäische Kulturen im Zeitalter des Postkommunismus* (Frankfurt a. Main: Suhrkamp 2005); Klaus von Beyme, *Systemwechsel in Osteuropa* (Frankfurt a. Main: Suhrkamp 1994).

7 | On the history of the former people's republics and the post-Soviet states, see Andreas Wirsching, *Der Preis der Freiheit. Geschichte Europas unserer Zeit* (München: C. H. Beck 2012); Thomas Kunze and Thomas Vogel, *Von der Sowjetunion in die Unabhängigkeit. Eine Reise durch die 15 früheren Sowjetrepubliken. Bundeszentrale für politische Bildung* (Berlin: Ch. Links 2011); György Dalos, *Der Vorhang geht auf. Das Ende der Diktaturen in Osteuropa* (München: C. H. Beck 2009); Henrik Bispinck, Jürgen Danyel, Hans-Hermann Hertle and Hermann Wentker (eds.), *Aufstände im Ostblock. Zur Krisengeschichte des realen Sozialismus* (Berlin: Ch. Links 2004).

by state repression, censorship and a deliberate isolation from the West. Society, education and culture were politicised to the same extent. The political thaw after the death of Stalin in 1953 led to a temporary easing of cultural censorship and the rehabilitation of artists, intellectuals and politicians who had been ostracized. However, after a short time this brief political spring was over. Decades followed in which any attempt at democratisation was put down by force. With the symbolic cutting of the barbed wire on the Austrian-Hungarian border on 27 June 1989, the 'iron curtain' was officially lifted, followed by one political upheaval in the individual socialist people's republics after another. With the dissolution of the Soviet Union in 1991, the communist governments lost their hegemony; the union of socialist states disintegrated, and dramatic transformation processes were initiated. The transformation of the communist dictatorships and planned economies into democracies and market economies was accompanied by a profound orientation and value change.

For the culture, and thus for independent theatre, this meant two things: The state-imposed censorship measures were abolished, and the ending of cultural isolation enabled an international exchange.[8] At the same time, a period of economic instability commenced. The theatres found themselves confronted with a free market economy and were forced to redefine their place in a changing society. The political and societal transformation processes have still not been completed. Despite many commonalities, they took a different course from country to country and thus led to different developments in the independent theatres which will be shown later in the sections dealing with the individual countries.

The political developments in the post-Yugoslavian states differed from those in the socialist people's republics and the republics of the Soviet Union.[9]

---

8 | On the general developments in the theatre scenes in Eastern Europe, see Silvija Jestrovic, *Performance, Space, Utopia. Cities of War, Cities of Exile* (Hampshire i. a.: Palgrave Macmillan 2013); Manfred Brauneck, *Europas Theater. 2500 Jahre Geschichte – eine Einführung* (Reinbek bei Hamburg: Rowohlt 2012); Sonja Arsham Kuftinec, *Theatre, Facilitation and Nation Formation in the Balkans and Middle East* (Hampshire et al.: Palgrave Macmillan 2009); Martina Vannayová und Anna Häusler, *Landvermessungen. Theaterlandschaften in Mittel-, Ost- und Südosteuropa. TdZ Recherchen 61* (Berlin: Theater der Zeit 2008); Manfred Brauneck, *Die Welt als Bühne*. Vol. 5 (Stuttgart/Weimar: Metzler 2007); Norbert Franz and Herta Schmid (eds.), *Bühne und Öffentlichkeit. Drama und Theater im Spät- und Postsozialismus (1983-1993)* (München: Otto Sagner 2002).
9 | See Holm Sundhaussen, *Jugoslawien und seine Nachfolgestaaten 1943-2011. Eine ungewöhnliche Geschichte des Gewöhnlichen* (Wien/Köln/Weimar: Böhlau 2012); Marie-Janine Calic, *Geschichte Jugoslawiens im 20. Jahrhundert* (München: C. H. Beck 2010); Andreas Moritsch and Alois Mosser, *Den Anderen im Blick. Stereotype im ehemaligen Jugoslawien* (Frankfurt a. Main: Peter Lang 2002).

The former Socialist Federal Republic of Yugoslavia was frequently referred to as an 'Eastern bloc country'. This designation is, however, incorrect. The former Yugoslavia was always an independent, socialist state; it was never a member of the Warsaw Pact or the Council for Mutual Economic Assistance. Tito pursued a socialist course which was independent of the Soviet Union. Contrary to the other socialist countries, his regime permitted a certain political, economic and cultural contact with the West. The former Yugoslavian republics were politically equal and only allowed little national autonomy, whereby conflicts between the existing nationalities were allayed by force. The former Yugoslav republics could act somewhat independently regarding cultural issues and were permitted to participate in international networks. Thus, many international festivals emerged, such as the summer festival in Dubrovnik (1950), the theatre festival Sterijino pozorje in Novi Sad (1956) and the Beogradski Internacionalni Teatarski Festival (BITEF), which was founded in 1967 in Belgrade. After Tito's death in 1980, conflicts between the nationalities erupted openly, which foreshadowed the coming breakup of Yugoslavia. The declarations of independence of Slovenia and Croatia in 1991 heralded the end of the Federal Republic of Yugoslavia. The following wars (the ten-day war in Slovenia, the war in Croatia, in Bosnia and the subsequent war in Kosovo) brought a time of violent conflicts, human rights violations, genocide, mass violence, systematic displacements and ethnic cleansing. In this time the theatre almost came to a complete standstill. Only after international interventions such as the Dayton Peace Agreement, the military intervention of NATO and the establishment of the International Criminal Tribunal for the former Yugoslavia in Den Haag did the violence finally come to an end. The severe political, warlike events in the nineties had serious consequences for the transformative processes in the individual post-Yugoslavian states. With the exception of Slovenia, these processes did not begin until about ten years after the other former socialist states. This also had an effect on the development of independent theatre, as will be described in the individual analyses of the post-Yugoslavian states.

In this study, the term 'independent theatre' is also used for the time during the communist regime. It should be noted that the independent groups were not able to act 'independently' in these decades, since they were strongly affected by political restrictions and censorship. However, the independent theatres operated outside the institutional structures and tried to circumvent the guidelines laid down by the state wherever possible.

2.1 Former Socialist People's Republics

On 23 October 1956, there was a 'national uprising' in *Hungary*.[10] The newly appointed Minister President Imre Nagy wanted to lead his country towards democracy and neutrality. Hungary withdrew from the Warsaw Pact. Only a few days later, Soviet troops invaded Hungary and crushed the movement. Imre Nagy was sentenced to death. His pro-Soviet successor, János Kádár, after a period of political severity, took a more liberal political course which became known as "Goulash Communism"[11] in the West. Thus, Hungary assumed a special position among the socialist countries. This also had an impact on the culture, although it still served the socialist system and was subject to state censorship. Yet, contact by artists with the West was permitted. Contrary to the other people's republics, the Hungarian theatre had the possibility to participate in a cultural exchange with international theatre groups and institutions as early as the beginning of the sixties.

In this time period, the first independent theatre groups were founded.[12] University groups such as Szegedi Egyetemi Színház at the Jósef Attila University in Szeged and the University Theatre of the Eötvös Loránd University in Budapest emerged from the amateur theatre movement. The University Theatre became acquainted with new forms of theatre on its first trips abroad, such as Jerzy Grotowski's 'Poor Theatre'. In addition, this group gained attention because of its two founders: Péter Halász, who co-founded the world-famous Squat Theatre in the USA in 1977, and Tamás Fodor, who started the independent theatre Stúdió K. in 1974. Both theatre makers were prominent representatives of the independent scene in Hungary. They dealt with subjects critical of the regime in artistic happenings which frequently took place in private apartments. These working methods had an impact, and new alternative groups continued these traditions at the beginning of the eighties. They includ-

---

10 | For the history of Hungary, see Janos Hauszmann, *Ungarn – vom Mittelalter bis zur Gegenwart*, (Regensburg: Pustet 2004); Paul Lendvai, *Die Ungarn. Eine tausendjährige Geschichte*, (München: Goldmann 2001).

11 | The milder form of communism was referred to as 'Goulash Communism' because it was more strongly oriented towards consumer needs than the Stalinist economic policies; see Jürgen Rahmig, *Ungarns Rückkehr nach Europa. Vom Gulaschkommunismus zu Marktwirtschaft und Demokratie* (Stuttgart: Deutsch-Ungarische Gesellschaft 1998).

12 | For the development of the theatre scene in Hungary, see the questionnaires Hungary I and Hungary II from 30 September 2012 and 7 November 2012; Szakmáry Dalma and Attila Szabó, "Country Report Hungary", in *EEPAP*, pp. 177-200; National Theatre Museum of Slovenia (ed.), *Occupying Spaces. Experimental Theatre in Central Europe 1950-2010* (Ljubljana: National Theatre Museum of Slovenia 2010).

ed the collective Arvisura, the group Utsloó, Artus, the dance company founded by Gábor Goda, and the group Vonal. All of these groups worked in Budapest.

In October 1989, Hungary became a parliamentary republic. Because of the absence of state subsidies, and because of the strong decrease in theatre guests, many of the groups which had existed since the seventies were dissolved, including the theatre Stúdió K. At the same time (the mid-nineties), many young theatre makers and groups stepped into the public light in Hungary for the first time, including Sándor Zsótér, Eszter Novák, Árpád Schilling's independent group Krétakör (which discontinued its work in 2008) and Béla Pintér's company Pintér Béla és Társulata in the Szkéné Theatre of the Technical University in Budapest. The Szkéné Theatre, which has existed since the seventies, and the Trafó Theatre, which was founded by György Szabó in Budapest in 1998, are the most important venues for the independent theatre scene in Hungary today.

These theatre makers are now among the most well-known representatives of the Hungarian independent theatre. With their artistic work, which focuses on social realities, they were not only aesthetic pioneers, but leading figures for many young artists and groups in the first decade of the new millennium. This new generation comprises *Zoltán Balázs*, Kornél Mundruczó, Viktor Bodó and his collective, Szputnyik Shipping Company, Gábor Goda's Artus Company, Pétér Kárpáti's Secret Company, the group founded by Anna Lengyel called PanoDrama, the KOMA Company and the group HoppArt.

Unlike the focus of the collectives, which were founded in the seventies and which opposed the political system and the aesthetic orientation of the established theatres in Hungary, a certain approximation of the independent theatre scene and established theatres has recently occurred. Indeed, there are still big structural and financial differences between these two spheres, but they now influence each other noticeably:

'The two subsystems of established and alternative theatre, though structurally and financially very rigidly separated, in terms of artistic mobility are quite open and very much affecting each other. When the Krétakör, the internationally acclaimed independent theatre, was dismantled in 2008, many of the former actors became part of the National Theatre's company led by Róbert Alföldi. The group Béla Pintér and Company produced *Gyévuska* in cooperation with the National Theatre and performed several times at the studio of the National. The other direction is also common: Viktor Bodó started as an actor and director at the Katona József Theatre, the most acclaimed drama theatre in Budapest, and then decided to found his own independent company, where he could fully develop his specific form of theatre.'[13]

---

13 | Questionnaire Hungary II.

In 2010, the right-wing conservative party in Hungary, FIDESZ, won a two-thirds majority in parliament and Viktor Orbán assumed the office of Minister President for the second time. A year later he oversaw the adoption of a new constitution which called for a reaffirmation of national values. Since then, the freedom of the press and the independence of the judiciary (among other things) have been restricted.

The new regulations have had dramatic effects on public cultural life, and thus on the theatres in Hungary.[14] The government's personnel policy is an important instrument of state control over culture. In state-subsidised institutions, important executive positions are filled for political reasons. Thus, the right-wing actor György Dörner took over as director of the theatre Újszínház in Budapest in February 2012. Róbert Alföldi was removed from his position as artistic director of the national theatre because of 'betrayal of the values and the spirit of the Hungarian nation'. The theatre centre Trafó has also been affected. Its founder and director, György Szabó, was replaced in 2012 by Yvette Bozsik, the so-called 'national choreographer' who is closely linked to the government. Moreover, the cultural policy put the independent theatres under considerable financial pressure, thus robbing them of their flexibility, which is one of the basic premises for their work:

> 'Whereas the political control over the big repertory theatres is exercised by means of the so-called 'selection process' when filling executive positions [...], the independent scene can be controlled by means of drastic budget cuts which are legitimised by the financial crisis.'[15]

In 2012, the government cancelled all subsidies for independent theatres until further notice. The measures are not even directed against individual independent theatre makers but against the entire independent cultural scene. In short, financial support was withdrawn completely. Reports in the media, protests, petitions, demonstrations and public showcases have advocated, and are committed to maintaining, the independent scene in Hungary (so far in vain). Entering into international cooperation or co-productions or dismantling their

---

14 | For the situation of the independent theatre and cultural scene under the government of Victor Orbán, see Keno Verseck, "Zurück zu Blut und Heimat", *Zeit Online*, see http://www.zeit.de/politik/ausland/2013-03/ungarn-verfassungsaenderung-orban; Dorte Lena Eilers, "Achtung Kunst!", in *Theater der Zeit* 12 (2012), pp. 18-19; Lena Schneider, "Das beste Land der Welt. Warum es im Ungarn Viktor Orbáns wenig Platz für unabhängiges Theater gibt. Eine Spurensuche", in *Theater der Zeit* 4 (2012), pp. 33-35.
15 | Andrea Trompa, "Gehen oder bleiben? Die darstellenden Künstler der Freien Szene Ungarns sehen sich vor dem Aus und suchen die Öffentlichkeit", in *Theater heute* 1 (2013), pp. 20-22, here p. 21.

groups are the options open to the artists. They work on the basis of projects (if at all) or see themselves forced to leave the country: 'The result is pretty much that companies are in deep debt, actors are technically unemployed (or decide to work for free), and many times are forced to leave the country – but this time because of economical and not political reasons (at least on the surface).'[16] As in the seventies, independent theatres see themselves in opposition to a political system which poses more and more aesthetic requirements. Whether the independent theatres will survive this precarious situation is uncertain.

In *Poland*, too, the first independent groups appeared at the end of the fifties and at the beginning of the sixties.[17] Unlike Hungary, two directions emerged here which were important for the further development of independent theatre: the *political-artistic* and the *anthropological-artistic* understanding of theatre. Representatives of the *political-artistic* direction continued the student theatre movement of the fifties. In this post-Stalinist time, these included the Studencki Teatr Satyryków (STS) in Warsaw, the Pstrąg Teatr in Łódź, and the group Bim-Bom in Gdańsk. These independent theatres worked as a collective and staged socially critical issues by means of political satire. Their artistic work strongly influenced the sixties and early seventies which were considered the height of political theatre in Poland. Many independent groups were founded. An example of a theatre collective which pursued a political and socially critical approach is the internationally renowned opposition theatre group, Teatr Ósmego Dnia, which was established in Poznań in 1964:

'Theatre of the Eighth Day, founded in 1964, called by the critics 'The Rolling Stones of theatre', is one of the oldest alternative theatres in the world, and it can be still found among the most interesting artistic phenomena. During the times of communism, due to plentiful conflicts with the authorities, the group was perceived as a phenomenon mostly political, it was rare to notice its artistic significance.'[18]

---

16 | Questionnaire Hungary II.

17 | See Berenika Szymanski, *Theatraler Protest und der Weg Polens zu 1989. Zum Aushandeln von Öffentlichkeit im Jahrzehnt der Solidarnosc* (Bielefeld: transcript 2012); Dariusz Kosiński, "Polnisches Theater. Eine Geschichte in Szenen" (Berlin: *Theater der Zeit* 2011); Tadeusz Kornás, *Between Anthropology and Politics. Two strands of Polish Alternative Theatre* (Warschau: The Zbigniew Raszewski Theatre Institute 2007); Kathleen M. Cioffi, *Alternative Theatre in Poland 1954-1989* (London/New York: Routledge 1996).

18 | Joanna Ostrowska, "The rebellion does not fade, it gets settled...", in *Teatr Ósmego Dnia*, see http://osmego.art.pl/t8d/main/en/.

At this time several groups were founded: the group Akademia Ruchu under the direction of Wojciech Krukowski in Wroclaw, the ensemble Scena Plastyczna KUL, led by Leszek Mądzik, the Teatr Provisorium in Lublin, and the Teatr Kana in Szczecin. At the end of the seventies, many of the stages named were institutionalised by permanent state funding. The strict separation of independent theatre and established theatres was gradually dissolved. It is still difficult to make a sharp distinction between the two forms of theatre: 'The formal borders between the repertoire theatre and alternative movement are blurred.'[19]

The impulses for the *anthropological-artistic* understanding of the theatre came from the two most important representatives of the Polish theatre avant-garde: Tadeusz Kantor and Jerzy Grotowski.[20] Kantor founded the Teatre Cricot 2 in Krakow in 1955. Together with Ludwik Flaszen, Grotowski took over the Teatr 13 Rzędów in Opole (known since 1962 as Teatr Laboratorium 13 Rzędów), with which he moved to Wroclaw in 1965. There the theatre was officially awarded the status of a 'Research Institute for Acting Methods'. Kantor and Grotowski not only influenced theatre in Poland, but theatre throughout Europe and in the USA. Grotowski's programmatic essay 'Towards a Poor Theatre' was especially influential. In Gardzienice, a village close to Lublin, Włodzimierz Staniewski founded the Centre for Anthropological Theatre Research and Theatre Practice, Ośrodek Praktyk teatralnych Gardzienice, after having worked with Grotowski in 1977. Inspired by the working methods of Grotowski's Teatr Laboratorium, the Centre Gardzienice concentrated on the anthropological basics of acting. However, it distanced itself from Grotowski's later theatre experiments, which were further removed from performance practice and which were staged in rural areas as so-called 'special projects':

'They tried to re-create the original bond between actors and audience which exists in primitive ritual, and thus to create a more profound sense of community between them. They worked in rural parts of Poland carrying on 'active culture' but not with specially

---

19 | Instytut Polski, Polish Theatre/Dance, see http://www.polishinstitute.org.il/en/polish-culture/theater-dance/33-polish-theatre-of-the-21st-century.html.

20 | For the artistic work of Jerzy Grotowski and Tadeusz Kantor Duzik, see Wojciech Dudzik (ed.), *Theater-Bewusstsein. Polnisches Theater in der zweiten Hälfte des 20. Jahrhunderts. Ideen – Konzepte – Manifeste*, (Berlin: Lit 2011); Jerzy Grotowski, *Für ein Armes Theater* (Berlin: Alexander 2006 /first 1970); Jan Kłossowicz and Harald Xander, *Tadeusz Kantors Theater* (Tübingen/Basel: Francke 1995); Institut für Moderne Kunst (ed.), *Tadeusz Kantor. Ein Reisender. Seine Texte und seine Manifeste* (Nürnberg: Verlag für moderne Kunst 1988); Manfred Brauneck, *Theater im 20. Jahrhundert. Programmschriften, Stilperioden, Reformmodelle* (Reinbek bei Hamburg: Rowohlt 1986).

hand-picked participants such as Grotowski used [...] but with simple people, peasants who, for the most part, were unused to 'artists', unfamiliar with 'theatre'.'[21]

The Gardzienice achieved international acclaim at the beginning of the eighties thanks to impressive productions such as *Żywot Protopopa Awwakuma (The Life of Archpriest Avvakum)*. In the nineties, former members of the Gardzienice founded their own independent groups which furthered the artistic work of the centre. Today, the Gardzienice is one of the most famous alternative theatres in Poland.

In 1980, the economic crisis in Poland led to public unrest and strikes. Lech Wałęsa founded the independent trade union 'Solidarność', which '[became] a symbol of the awakening of the forces of reform in the entire Eastern bloc'[22]. However, revolutionary times did not last long. In 1981, General Jaruzelski imposed martial law in Poland. Strikes were prohibited, intellectuals from the country's opposition were arrested, and the Solidarność was forbidden. The restrictions resulting from the martial law (which lasted until 1983) had a long-term effect on the independent theatres: Grotowski and the group Teatr Ósmego Dnia left Poland. Kantor worked mainly abroad, and the theatre centre Gardzienice did not produce one single play between 1983 and 1990. Thus, the eighties featured the work of young directors such as Jerzy Jarocki and Jerzy Grzegorzewski, who influenced the Polish theatre and the following generations of theatre makers.

After the political upheaval in 1989, a remarkable number of independent theatre groups emerged despite difficult economic circumstances.[23] These groups were often influenced by Grotowsk's theatre or originated from the Centre Gardzienice. Examples are the Studio Teatralne KOŁO, the group SUKA OFF, and the Studium Teatralne, founded by Piotr Borowski in Warsaw in 1995, the group Komuna Otwock near Warsaw, the Teatr Pieśń Kozła in Wroclaw, the Teatr ZAR in Wroclaw and the Instytut Grotowskiego, which was also situated in Wroclaw and which ceased to exist in 2006. Further examples included the group Stowarzyszenie teatralne Chorea in Łódź, the Teatr Węgajty and the theatre school Schola Teatru Węgajty in Węgajty near Olsztyn, the Teatr DADA

---

21 | Kathleen M. Cioffi, *Alternative Theatre in Poland 1954-1989*, p. 206; For the artistic work of Gardzienice, see also Włodzimierz Staniewski and Alison Hodge, *Hidden territories. The Theatre of Gardzienice* (London/New York: Routledge 2012).

22 | Manfred Brauneck, *Die Welt als Bühne*, p. 723. For the political history of Poland, see Klaus Ziemer, *Das politische System Polens* (Wiesbaden: Springer 2013); Włodzimierz Borodziej, *Geschichte Polens im 20. Jahrhundert* (München: Beck 2010).

23 | For the development of the theatre scene in Poland after 1989, see, for example, Tomasz Plata (ed.), *Öffentliche Strategien, private Strategien. Das polnische Theater 1990-2005*, TdZ Recherchen 32 (Berlin: Theater der Zeit 2006).

in Gdańsk which was founded by Leszek Bzdyl and Katarzyna Chmielewska, the theatre research centre Ośrodek Pogranicze – Sztuk, Kultur, Narodów in Sejny in the northeast of Poland on the Lithuanian border and the Teatr Cinema in Michałowice (Piechowice), a small town in Lower Silesia. The independent theatre scene was particularly active in Poznań in the nineties. Following the *political-artistic* movement of the independent theatres in the seventies, the Teatr Biuro Podróży, the Teatr Strefa Ciszy, the group Porywacze Ciał and the Teatr Usta Usta Republika were all founded at approximately the same time. They all still exist and are among the most prominent representatives of the Polish independent theatre scene.

In the nineties, the director and set designer Krystian Lupa had a particularly strong influence on independent theatre in Poland. He understood the theatre as a philosophical-metaphysical experiential space, and he primarily gained recognition because of his adaptations of epic literary works for the stage. He gained international recognition, for example, thanks to his adaptations of *The Brothers Karamasov* by Dostojewski (1990) and *The Man without Qualities* by Robert Musil (1990). Lupa is frequently referred to as the 'master' of the Polish theatre in early post-communist times:

'Lupa opened up a completely new kind of theatre; he caused new strings in our sensitivity for the theatre to vibrate. He allowed himself the luxury of turning his back on politics and the all-powerful journalism, allowed the second circulation [the unofficial circulation of texts or music recordings, author's note A.H.] and the censorship to be forgotten and made it possible for the audience to concern itself with the really important things, like the meaning of our existence which one could easily lose sight of in the tumult of events far-removed from these essential issues.'[24]

Lupa also worked as a lecturer at the Krakow's State Theatre School. There he influenced at least two generations of young directors, such as Krzysztof Warlikowski, Grzegorz Jaryzna, Anna Augustynowicz, Piotre Cieplak, Zbigniew Brzoza and Paweł Miśkiewicz. Known as the 'young talents', they were the main representatives of the Polish independent theatres after the turn of the millennium. They have attained recognition beyond the national borders, which is verified by their many guest performances and invitations to festivals abroad. Furthermore, a new generation of independent groups, such as 52°43'N19°42'E Project, Koncentrat, Towarzystwo Prze-Twórcze and Teatr Bretoncaffe, established themselves in Warsaw in the middle and towards the end of the past

---

24 | Piotr Gruszczyński, as quoted in Tomasz Plata, "Persönliche Verpflichtungen", see above (ed.), *Öffentliche Strategien, private Strategien*, pp. 202-219, here p. 205. See also Uta Schorlemmer, *Die Magie der Annäherung und das Geheimnis der Distanz. Krystian Lupas Recherche "neuer Mythen" im Theater* (München: Sagner 2003).

decade. In 2007, the transmedial internet theatre NeTTheatre was founded in Lublin. Moreover, young theatre makers such as Jan Klata, Marta Górnicka, Maja Kleczewska, Łukasz Kos, Paweł Miśkiewicz, Agnieszka Olsten, Michał Walczak, Aldona Figura, Michał Borczuch and Michał Zadara also made a name for themselves. These groups and artists influence the independent theatre in Poland today. The theatre critic Łukasz Drewniak points out several things which these theatre makers have in common: their 'provocative political incorrectness' as well as their manner of working, in which they concern themselves on the theatre stage with the 'generation of the thirty-year-olds' and develop 'sociological descriptions of Polish reality'.[25]

As in Hungary and Poland, the first phase of establishing independent theatres in the former *Czechoslovakia* began in the late fifties and in the sixties.[26] Experimental theatres especially emerged in Prague, such as the Laterna Magica, Divadlo za branou and Divadlo Na zábradlí. The groups invoked the Czech theatre avant-garde of the twenties and dealt with sociopolitical subjects critically on stage despite censorship and political repression.

From 1989 to 1990, the theatres in Czechoslovakia participated in the political upheaval known as the 'Velvet or Gentle Revolution' by means of their 'persistent criticism of the regime and the system'[27]. In 1993, Czechoslovakia peacefully dissolved, with its constituent states becoming the independent states of the Czech Republic and Slovakia. Nevertheless, as was the case in the other post-socialist states after the political turbulence, drastic changes took place in the field of culture. On the one hand, theatres such as the Divadlo za branou were forced to shut down and prominent theatre makers left the country. These included Pavol Liska, who, together with Kelly Copper, founded the group Nature Theatre of Oklahoma in New York in 1995. On the other hand, the political upheaval gave way to artistic liberties, as was the case in the other post-socialist countries:

---

25 | All quotations from Lukasz Drewniak, " Der Tsunami der Jugend", in Tomasz Plata (ed.), *Öffentliche Strategien, private Strategien*, pp. 95-113, here p. 99. On present-day independent groups see also Aleksandra Rembowska, "Auf der Suche nach Gegenwart. Neue Regiehandschriften aus Polen", in *Theater der Zeit* 4 (2005), pp. 24-27.

26 | For the development of the theatre scene in the Czech Republic, see also the questionnaire Czech Republic dated 2 November 2012; Jakub Škorpill, "Country Report Czech Republic", in *EEPAP*, pp. 147-158; Arts and Theatre Institute, *Czech Theatre Guide* (Prague: Arts and Theatre Institute 2011).

27 | Manfred Brauneck, *Die Welt als Bühne*, p. 719. For the history of the Czech Republic see Markus Mauritz, *Tschechien* (Regensburg: Pustet 2002).

'It brought freedom of expression to theatres. Banned authors could be performed, sidelined artists and emigrants could return, and theatres [...] began freely to create their new era.'[28]

In the nineties, more young theatre makers established themselves. Among them were Petr Lébl, who was known as 'the most dynamic director'[29] in the independent theatre scene in the Czech Republic of that time. Jan Antonín Pitínský, Hana Burešová, Vladimír Morávek, Jan Borna, Michal Dočekal, Jan Nebeský and Jakub Špalek also ranked among the well-known directors. They had already worked in small studio theatres in the eighties and had developed new forms of the Czech theatre. Some of these artists opened their own small theatres in the middle of the nineties; others took over the management of institutionalised theatres. Thus, Petr Lébl moved on to become the director of the theatre Divadlo Na zábradlí in Prague in 1993. The directors Hana Burešová and Jan Borna became directors of the theatre Divadlo v Dlouhé in Prague in 1996; the actor and director Michal Dočekal managed the theatre Divadlo Komedie from 1994 to 2002 and as of 2002 was in charge of the theatre Národní divadlo; the theatre and film director Vladimír Morávek worked at the theatre Divadlo Husa na provázku in Brno from 1898 to 1995 and as of 1995 was artistic director at the theatre Klicperovo divadlo in Hradec Králové. The following generation of independent theatre professionals in the decade of the 2000s differed from them as is described here:

'Here, there is a greater tendency to found independent companies whose members share the same generational background and outlook. These companies often work with the poetics of various (intertwining) theatre genres, most of them emerge from the field of movement and dance theatre, but they also appear in the areas of drama, puppet and even opera and musical theatre.'[30]

After the turn of the millennium, young artists in their mid-thirties primarily influenced the independent spoken theatre. They included Dušan Pařízek, Jan Mikulášek, Daniel Špinar, Jiří Havelka, Jiří Adámek, Martin Kukučka, Lukáš Trpišovský and Rosta Novák. At the same time, a style typified by the New Circus Theatre emerged which is characteristic of the independent scene in the Czech Republic. The Czech theatre had always drawn on circus arts and circus aesthetics as a source for its work. This was already evident in the artistic works of theatre avant-gardists, such as Jiří Frejka, Jiří Voskovec and Jan Werich from the 1920s. The New Circus Theatre now combined circus practices and theatre

---

28 | Questionnaire Czech Republic.
29 | Ibid.
30 | Ibid.

work: 'Czech new circus is not so much based on circus technique as it is on theatre, on a story, on a theme.'[31] In particular, the touring companies Divadlo bratří Formanů and the theatres Divadlo Continuo in Malovice and Divadlo Krepsko in Prague worked with the artistic elements of the New Circus Theatre:

> 'While in traditional circus the artist only stands for himself or herself, the theatre quality of new circus is based on the artist's ability to enact a character, to represent a story, an idea on stage – in front of the audience. The artistic character of new circus is based on the individual's creative potential. The performing artist is the bearer of meaning, the intermediary of communication: it is not the case with the traditional circus performer who is not an actor and who never doubles his or her identity.'[32]

What is more, at the beginning of the new millennium a growing cooperation between independent and institutional theatres becomes apparent. Several groups of artists worked simultaneously or alternately on their independent productions at state-subsidised theatres. This overlapping can frequently still be observed. The independent groups and artists are, above all, active in so-called 'stagione venues': in theatres, associations and clubs which are not used permanently but, like production houses for theatre, as occasional venues. Such locations in Prague include Divadlo Archa, Meet Factory, Palác Akropolis, Experimentální prostor NoD Roxy, Alfred ve dvoře, La Fabrika and Divadlo Ponec. Outside of Prague, these include the theatre Divadlo Konvikt in Olomouc, the venue Club 29 in Pardubice, and the two venues Skleněná louka and Multikulturní centrum Stadec in Brno.

The independent theatre scene in the Czech Republic is characterised by a particularly wide diversity, and not only because of its use of different locations and premises. The artistic working methods are also broadly based. Thus, for instance, Jiří Adámek's group Boca Loca Lab deals with socially critical issues and, in the process, collages the (text) language with musical sounds and song in its artistic productions. The group Handa Gote Research & Development combines installation elements with movement and dance theatre as well as with electronic sounds and live music. The group SKUTR and the Spitfire Company both work on stage with the elements of puppetry, buffoonery, and acrobatics, as well as with text and music. And finally, Miroslav Bambušek relates historical and socio-political themes to each other in his location-specific performances and employs practices taken from artistic reenactment. All the groups mentioned share the practices of using different artistic media

---

31 | *"New Circus in the Czech Republic"*, in *Czech Dance Info*, see http://www.czechdance.info/dance-in-the-czech-republic/introduction/new-circus-in-the-czech-republic.
32 | Ibid.

on the stage and dealing with social problems from the past and the present: 'Independent theatres are more open to contemporary dramatic texts, the problems of the contemporary world, and documentary and social theatre. They often stage original works instead of classic stage plays.'[33]

Figure 1: Pilsen, 2012. Photograph: Andrea Hensel

Many independent theatres have taken this course, the most famous groups among them being mamapapa, Divadlo Vosto5 and Barevný děti in Prague, Bílé divadlo in Ostrava, Divadlo Continuo in Malovice, Divadlo DNO in Hradec Králové und Divadlo Facka in Brno.[34]

In the past 20 years, many organisations with an influence on cultural and educational policies have come together to support the independent theatres in the Czech Republic. These include Jedefrau, mamapapa, the cultural centre

---

33 | Questionnaire Czech Republic.
34 | Other well-known independent groups in the Czech Republic are Cirk La Putyka, Bohinecká divadelní společnost, Décalages – divaldo v pohybu, Depresivní děti touží po penězích, Divadlo Mimotaurus, Farma v jeskyni, Damúza Studio, Stage Code and Veselé skoky in Prague; in Brno the Buranteatr, Divadlo Anička a letadýlko and Divadlo Neslyším; in Braník Divadlo Skelp and in České Budějovice Divadlo Kvelb.

Johan – centrum pro kulturní a sociální projekty, Art Prometheus, Econnect, MOTUS, ProCulture and For a Cultural Czech Republic. All these organisations are based in Prague.

The developments in *Slovakia* followed a course similar to those in the Czech Republic prior to its separation from Czechoslovakia in 1993. One of the first independent theatres, Astorka Korzo, was founded in Bratislava in 1969 at a time when the communist regime was still in power.[35] It was closed after three years for political reasons. After Slovakia had been constituted, young directors produced progressive works in the nineties. The artists included Svetozár Sprušanský, Rastislav Ballek and Martin Čičvák. The independent venue Astorka Korzo was reopened and other independent groups were founded, such as S.T.O.K.A and the theatre Divadlo a.ha in Bratislava. Yet, inadequate attempts at reform led to precarious circumstances in the field of culture. One of the consequences was the fact that a sharp distinction was made between established theatres and independent theatre groups – a distinction which still exists.

Under Minister President Vladimír Mečiar Slovak, nationalism was strengthened in 1994. Culture, and with it the theatre, suffered once again as a result of political instrumentalisation and state regimentation. The activities of the independent theatres virtually came to a standstill. After a change of government in 1998, the necessary cultural reforms that had been hoped for did not materialise; working conditions at the theatres continued to worsen. However, the independent theatres went on working in the years that followed despite the adverse circumstances. They entered into international collaborations, and new independent groups emerged, among them the collectives Divadlo SkRAT and Moje experimentálne divadlo (MED) in Bratislava, which are internationally known today.

Not until 2004, the year in which Slovakia joined the EU, did the country introduce the first reforms in the area of culture. Such cultural reforms are only being put into practice very slowly, but a large number of independent groups and theatres already exist. These include the theatre Radošinské naivné divadlo in Bratislava, the in Nitra as well as the group J.A.eV in Žilina, and the theatre Divadlo z Pasáže in Banská Bystrica. A special feature of the independent theatres in Slovakia is that they largely work as a collective. They

---

35 | For the development of the theatre scene in Slovakia, see the questionnaires Slovakia I and II from 22 November 2012 and from 29 October 2012; Vladislava Fekete, "Country Report Slovakia", in *EEPAP*, pp. 277-286; Johannes C. Hoflehner, MartinaVannayová and Marianne Vejtisek (eds.), *Durchbrochene Linien. Zeitgenössisches Theater in der Slowakei. TdZ Recherchen* 40 (Berlin: *Theater der Zeit* 2007); Slovak Theatre Institute, Independent Theatres, see http://www.theatre.sk/en/homepage/.

usually develop their productions in one rehearsal process in which every actor becomes a co-author of the production. Noteworthy is also the frequent use of music as an important dramaturgical element in productions. Groups such as Divadlo SkRAT, which integrates musical collages on stage and experiments with transmedial elements, and the theatre GUnaGU exemplify this manner of working. In 1985, the latter was founded in Bratislava and remains one of the 'most successful and most popular Slovak theatres'[36] to this day.

The independent groups and venues Štúdio L & S, Divadlo Non.Garde, Tanečné divadlo Bralen and Slovenské divadlo tanca, s.r.o., which are all located in Bratislava, also play an important role.[37] However, independent theatre groups are also active in other cities in Slovakia.

'Independent theatre in Slovakia is definitely the most progressive movement in the Slovak theatrical culture at all. They were the first who reflected new tendencies and forms of theatrical expression they often win prizes in Slovakia and are well accepted abroad.'[38]

The independent theatres in Slovakia have undergone a remarkable development in the past years and still play an important role in the Slovak theatre scene.

The independent theatres in *Romania* can be described in the words of a Romanian theatre maker as 'strong, bold, free, new, fresh, unconventional, open in dealing with all kinds of issues or even taboos'[39]. Yet, their history

---

36 | Juraj Šebesta, "Erfolgsgeschichte mit Hindernissen", in Johannes C. Hoflehner, Martina Vannayová and Marianne Vejtisek (eds.), *Durchbrochene Linien*, pp. 42-58, here p. 47.

37 | Other groups are in Bratislava Teatro Wüstenrot, Asociácia súčasného tanca, Tanečná spoločnosť Artyci, P.A.T., ElleDanse, Arteatro, Biele divadlo, Prešporské divadlo, TANGERE Productions and Divadlo Meteorit; in Košice Staromestské divadlo, Divadlo V kufri, Divadlo Na peróne and Divadlo Maškrta; in Budmerice Teátro Neline; in Pezinok Divadlo PIKI; in Bátovce Divadlo Pôtoň; in Žilina Phenomenon Theatre; in Trnava Túlavé divadlo and Divadelné štúdio DISK Trnava; in Prešov Detské kočovné divadlo DRaK and Portál-komorné divadlo bez opony; in Senica Divadlo oProti; in Svätý Jur Divadlo Na kolesách.

38 | Questionnaire Slovakia II.

39 | Questionnaire Romania I of 4 September 2012. On the development of the Romanian theatre scene see also the questionnaires Romania II and III of 4 October 2012 and 29 October 2012; Julia Popovici, "Country Report Romania", in *EEPAP*, pp. 241-262; Wolf Lamsa, "Transformation und Neubestimmung im Theateruniversum Rumänien. Das rumänische Theater nach 1989", in *gift – zeitschrift für freies theater* 2 (2012), see http://www.freietheater.at/?page=service&subpage=gift&detail=48918&id_text=16; Mari-

differs from the scenarios in the other former socialist people's republics already described here. Whereas in Hungary, Poland and the former Czechoslovakia, free groups were founded under the communist regimes, this was not the case in Romania. The repression under the authoritarian rule of Ceaușescu and his brutal secret police, Securitate, was too strong.[40]

After the country had collapsed economically, a bloody revolution erupted in November 1989 which took a toll of over 1000 deaths and, in the end, succeeded in overthrowing the communist regime. After decades of dictatorship, mismanagement, oppression and isolation, economic changes progressed slowly in the nineties. Even the restructuring of the theatres proved to be a slow process because of the lack of subsidies and reforms:

'The revolution pretty much changed the whole system and deeply affected the theatrical landscape [...]. In short (and maybe a little overly dramatic, but just a little) soon after communism theatre was left with hundreds of jobless actors, not enough spectators and very few to no playwrights (the ones who had worked all their creative life in the communist system, so it was almost impossible to change). It was more and more obvious that theatre needed to change something in order to survive, but it took years before the first change appeared.'[41]

The return of directors who had left the country during the Ceaușescu era marked the beginning of a real change. Theatre makers such as Andrei Șerban, Vlad Mugur and Lucian Giurchescu were 'important reformers from the outside'[42]. They took over the direction of institutional theatres in Bukarest at the beginning of the nineties and encouraged young theatre performers to work experimentally by staging progressive productions. They also strengthened

---

na Mazilu, Marina, MedanaWeident and Irina Wolf (eds.): *Das rumänische Theater nach 1989* (Berlin: Frank & Timme 2011); Ileana Pintilie, "Romanian Artists before and after 1989", *Maska 4* (2006), pp. 122-124.

40 | For the history of Romania see also Thede Kahl (ed.): *Kilometer Null – politische Transformation und gesellschaftliche Entwicklungen in Rumänien seit 1989* (Berlin: Frank & Timme 2011); Kurt Scharr, *Rumänien – Geschichte und Geografie* (Wien/Köln/Weimar: Böhlau 2008); Karl Thede (ed.) *Rumänien. Raum und Bevölkerung, Geschichte und Geschichtsbilder, Kultur, Gesellschaft und Politik heute, Wirtschaft, Recht und Verfassung, historische Regionen* (Wien/Berlin/Münster: Lit 2006); Lucian Boia, *Geschichte und Mythos. Über die Gegenwart des Vergangenen in der rumänischen Gesellschaft* (Wien/Köln/Weimar: Böhlau 2003).

41 | Questionnaire Romania III.

42 | Cristina Modreanu, "Wir haben geniale Ideen, wissen aber nicht, was wir damit anfangen sollen", in Marina Mazilu, Medana Weident and Irina Wolf (eds.), *Das rumänische Theater nach 1989*, pp. 51-58, here p. 51.

the work of the first independent groups and stages in Romania. The nineties marked the beginning of the Teatrul Levantul in Bukarest, which closed in the same year, and the Teatrul ACT, which today is still used under the name Bukarest 'cellar theatre' by independent groups. However, the development of the independent theatre progressed slowly. Because of the precarious circumstances which massively inhibited the work of the independent groups, the Romanian independent scene established itself much later than those other independent theatre scenes already described here. Not until the beginning of the new millennium did the emergence of the independent groups DramAcum and TangaProject in Bukarest mark the beginning of independent theatre in Romania: 'Independent theatre means a new generation of artists who graduated after 1989.'[43] The young directors and theatre makers who now appeared on the scene and who have achieved international recognition today include personalities such as Gianina Cărbunariu, Radu Apostol, Alex Berceanu, Andreea Vălean, Miruna Dinu, Bogdan Georgescu, Vera Ion, Ioana Păun, David Schwartz, Ana Margineanu and Radu Afrim.

All of these artists focused their work on social issues. 'In artistic terms, the most interesting aspects are connected to the emergence of community art, socially committed theatre, political theatre, documentary theatre and site-specific theatre.'[44] This understanding of theatre was pursued by the groups and organisations which emerged in the following years, such as Figura Association in Gheorgheni, Dramafest Foundation in Tîrgu Mureş, The Magic Theatre in Râmnicu Vâlcea, the groups Auăleu Garage, Courtyard Theatre und At4t Association in Timişoara and The Offensive of Generosity (O2G), Theatre without borders, 4Culture Association, Collectiva, Passe-Partout Company and D'AYA Company in Bukarest.

Despite their numbers, the independent theatres in Romania have neither their own stages nor rehearsal rooms. The only exceptions are the Teatrul ACT and Teatrul ARCA in the La Scena Club in Bukarest and the theatres Teatrul 74 und Studio Yorick in Tîrgu Mureş. The drastic lack of space resulted in groups staging their productions in 'everyday places' and in alternative locations, such as bars, galleries, cafés and factories. In Bukarest, such locations used by independent theatre groups for performances include Monday Theatre @ Bar Green Hours, Montage Gallery, Godot Café Teatru and Fabrica.

The political development of *Bulgaria* differs from that of the countries described previously:[45]

---

43 | Questionnaire Romania I.
44 | Julia Popovici: "Country Report Romania", p. 243.
45 | For the history of Bulgaria see also Iskra Baeva and Evgenia Kalinova, *Bulgarien von Ost nach West. Zeitgeschichte ab 1939* (Wien: Braumüller 2009); Georgi P. Dimitrov,

'One should not apply the same standards to Bulgaria as to the other Eastern bloc countries – in our case, after the Soviet model was introduced after 1944, there were never any attempts to overthrow the system. In Bulgaria there were never any forces which could have developed such dynamics like those observed in the Czech Republic, Hungary or Poland.'[46]

Under communist rule, the Bulgarian theatre was not a critical institution. Immediately after the end of communism, many independent theatres emerged. A prominent example is the state-subsidised theatre workshop Sfumato established in 1989 by Margarita Mladenova and Ivan Dobčev. It is still an important meeting point for independent groups and artists. In the first years after the revolution, the following groups emerged: La Strada, founded by Tedi Moskov, the collective Credo founded by Nina Dimitrova and Vasil Vsilev-Zueka, the Triumviratus Art Group founded by Javor Gardev, Georgi Tnev and Nikola Toromanov, and Krasen Krăstev's Aramant Dance Studio. All of the groups were located in Sofia. In addition, independent directors such as Ivan Panteleev, Desislava Špatova, Valerija Vălčeva, Marius Kurkinski, Galina Borissova and Văzkresija Vihărova made a name for themselves. These theatre makers experimented with new ways of working and new dramatic compositions. In doing so, they laid the cornerstone for the development of the independent theatres in Bulgaria: 'The nineties of the past century were the strongest, the most diverse and the most creative period in contemporary Bulgarian theatre.'[47]

In 1997, the worsening economic situation caused the most dramatic national and financial crisis the country had ever experienced. The first signs of a hyperinflation led to mass demonstrations. The government was finally forced to resign. Independent theatres had virtually disappeared. Despite this difficult starting situation, many independent groups were founded at the beginning of the new millennium, and they have been generating trend-setting impulses for the independent theatre scene in Bulgaria to this day. The productions of these collectives focus on a critical view of everyday life in Bulgaria. A great diversity of artistic directions is displayed here, 'from psychological theatre which is based on a text, to performances in which the text is developed by the actors or dancers

---

Kultur im Transformationsprozess Osteuropas. Zum Wandel kultureller Institutionen am Beispiel Bulgariens nach 1989 (München/Berlin: Otto Sagner 2009).

46 | Javor Gardev, quoted in "Das Ende der Ideologie. Neue Regieansätze für eine neue Zeit". An interview with Javor Gardev and Georgi Tenev of the Triumviratus Art Group, in Dorte Lena Eilers, Anna Volkland and Holger Schultze (eds.), *Die neue Freiheit*, pp. 74-83, here p. 77. For the development of the theatre scene in Bulgaria, see also Kalina Wagenstein, "Country Report Bulgaria", in *EEPAP*, pp. 111-124.

47 | Nikolova, Kamelija, "Der Aufstand der verspäteten Modernisten" in Dorte Lena Eilers, Anna Volkland and Holger Schultze (eds.), *Die neue Freiheit*, pp. 54-62, here p. 59.

themselves, from body arts to performance installations"⁴⁸. The most important groups today include the Brain Store Project, 36 Monkeys, the Derida Dance Centre, the group B+, the Garage Collective, the MOMO Theatre Company and the DUNE Dance Company. They are all located in Sofia. An important role for independent theatres in Bulgaria has been assumed by theatre makers, such as Gergana Dimitrova, Mladen Aleksiev, Veselin Dimov, Galina Borissova, Violeta Vitanova, Stanislav Genadiev, Vasilena Radeva, Alexander Georgiev, Dimitar Dimitrov, Martin Vangelov, Petar Todorov and Ida Daniel. It is also important to mention the cultural and political ACT-Organisation, which was established in 2009. It evolved from an association of independent artists who stood up for and supported the independent scene. The working conditions of independent groups are, however, difficult. The financial and artistic gap between the institutional theatres and the independent artists is constantly widening. Rehearsal rooms and stages are not available for independent theatre projects. The production and performance venues of the independent theatre scene in Sofia at this time primarily include art rooms and everyday places such as the Red House – Centre for Culture and Debate, the former swimming pool Poduene, the exhibition room for contemporary art and performance known as The Fridge, the gallery, Industrialna 11, the Pro Rodopi Arts Centre and the Sklada gallery.

2.2 Post-Yugoslavian States

Independent theatre groups in Serbia were first founded in the fifties.⁴⁹ They usually understood theatre as a political medium. A typical representative of these early groups is the avant-garde theatre Atelje 212, which was established in Belgrade in 1956. It worked with censored artistic theatre practices and staged plays which were forbidden, especially plays of the Absurd Theatre. Also noteworthy is the group KPGT,⁵⁰ which emerged at the end of the seventies under the direction of four theatre makers from different Yugoslav republics: Ljubiša Ristić from Serbia, Dušan Jovanović from Slovenia, and Nada Kokotović and Rade Šerbedžija from Croatia. The name of this group, which still exists today, is composed of the first letters of the Croatian, Bosnian, Slovenian and

---

48 | Desislava Gavrilova, "Ausschwärmen und Ausweiten des Feldes", in Dorte Lena Eilers, Anna Volkland and Holger Schultze (eds.), *Die neue Freiheit*, pp. 90-97, here p. 94.

49 | For the development of the theatre in Serbia, see the questionnaires Serbia I and II from 29 September 2012 and 5 September 2012; Andjekla Jankovic, "Country Report Serbia", in *EEPAP*, pp. 263-276; Jadranka Andjelic, "Country Report Serbia", in *IG Freie Theaterarbeit*, see http://www.freietheater.at/?page=europeanoffnetwork&subpage=country_report#13.

50 | KPGT, see http://www.kpgtyu.org/.

Serbian words for 'theatre': kazalište, pozorište, gledališče and teatar. The collective is frequently involved in international projects which have to do with social grievances. This understanding of theatre is also followed by the Teatar Mimart. It was founded by Nela Antonović in Belgrade in 1984 as a nonverbal physical theatre and is today among the most famous independent theatres in Serbia:

'Mimart researches the answers to many axiom questions close to the facts of life, especially in Serbia which had witnessed cultural destruction for the past years. We hold that art educators need to work towards establishing more progressive, non-repressive and non-manipulative ways of interpreting other cultures and other arts. We wish to implant the power of a non-verbal and interactive art process into intercultural communication.'[51]

The wars in the nineties, the destruction of the infrastructure, the economic crises, the ethnic-cultural conflicts, and the international isolation of the country had a strong impact on the situation of the independent theatres in Serbia.[52] Many artists left the country, among them the prominent performance artist Marina Abramović. Subsidies were hardly available to finance even state institutions. Furthermore, they were under pressure to deal with and justify the civil wars in their artistic work. It was practically impossible for independent groups and artists to work. Nevertheless, in the nineties, independent theatre groups were established. One of these was the DAH Teatar – Centar za pozorišna istraživanja in Belgrade, which was founded by Jadranka Anđelić and Dijana Milošević in 1991. The productions of Jagoš Marković and Gorčin Stojanović attracted much attention. The groups and artists dealt critically with the wars waged by their country on stage; they belonged to the artistic opposition in Serbia. They encouraged the creation of further independent theatre collectives which were founded in the middle of the nineties. Even these new groups understood their theatre work in a political sense, such as the groups Ister Teatar, company INTRA for contemporary dance, which was initiated by Dalija Aćin, the group Ad Hoc Lom, the ERGstatus plesni Teatar, the theatre laboratorium Plavo pozorište, the OMEN Teatar, the SVAN Teatar, the Splin Teatar (formerly Popocatepetl), the venue Pozorište Ogledalo and the group Kraft Teatar. All of these groups were located in Belgrade. They laid the cornerstone for the independent theatre scene in Serbia and today are well-known independent theatres. In recent years, young directors such as Bojan

---

51 | Questionnaire Serbia I.

52 | For the history of Serbia, see also Holm Sundhaussen, *Geschichte Serbiens 19.-21. Jahrhundert* (Wien/Köln/Weimar: Böhlau 2007); Katrin Boeckh, *Serbien, Montenegro. Geschichte und Gegenwart* (München: Pustet 2002).

Đorđev, Kinga Mezei and Miloš Lolić established themselves in the scene. The artistic work of the dramatists Maja Pelević and Milan Marković is receiving more and more attention on the local scene as well as internationally.[53]

Figure 2: Belgrade, 2012. Photograph: Andrea Hensel

The independent theatres in Serbia receive support from cultural organisations as well as networks and platforms dealing with cultural policies which, in part, had already been founded in the nineties. These are active in cultural policy-making and are strongly committed to providing support for the independent theatre scene. These organisations include the cultural centres, REX Cultural Center, Dom Omladine and CZKD (Centar za kulturnu dekontaminaciju), the association for contemporary dance called Stanica and the association for independent theatre, NKSS, which was founded in 2011, all of which are located in Belgrade.

Two trends have been evident in the work of the independent theatres in Serbia for some time. The first is the increasing theoretical reflection of their own artistic practice, best exemplified by the theoretical-aesthetic platform Walking Theory, which was created in 2000:

---

53 | In addition, the following independent organisations and groups were founded: BAZAART, DEZ.ORG, MUDRA Teatar and Corpus Artisticum, the DDT kreativni centar za pokret, the Teatar Projekat Objektivna Drama, the Kollektiv SubHuman Teatar, the PoToP (Deluge) Teatar and the SET-Studio, all of which are located in Belgrade. For other groups and artists, see TkH Forum for Performing Arts Critique: RASTER.

'TkH (Walking Theory) is an independent (institutionally non-aligned, extra-academic) platform for performing theoretical-artistic activism. It is initiated and run by the editorial collective TkH whose members are theorists and artists coming from performance theory and practice, theatre, cinema, and visual arts.'[54]

The second trend is the ever-growing importance of dance and performance theatre. Important impulses were provided by the group Mimart in the eighties. Now, young choreographers, performers and groups who primarily experiment with body practices are establishing themselves.

In Slovenia, the centre Križanke, in the capital Ljubljana, is the focus of the independent theatre scene.[55] It is one of the most popular cultural venues in the country. It was built in the 13th century as a monastery for the Knights of the Cross, and later the architect Jože Plečnik rebuilt the ruins at the beginning of the fifties to accommodate the Festival Ljubljana. Since that time, the location has housed an open-air stage and a restored knight's hall (Viteška dvorana), which is used as a venue for experimental theatre. Since the middle of the fifties, independent theatres have performed there: in the early years, Balbina Battelino Baranovič's ensemble Eksperimentalno gledališče, the group Oder 57, Gledališče Ad Hoc, headed by Draga Ahačič, and the children's and young people's theatre, Mladinsko gledališče, which was also newly founded by Balbina Battelino Baranovič and which achieved international recognition in the eighties under the name Slovensko mladinsko gledališče. The groups orient themselves toward non-socialist ideas of theatre:

'As an opposition to the repertoire-driven, soc-realist, traditional theatre of consensus, the experimental theatre consciously staged contemporary, existentialist and absurdist drama, including contemporary politically engaged Slovene plays, and also revolutioni-

---

54 | Walking Theory, see http://www.tkh-generator.net/. For the trends described, see also TkH Forum for Performing Arts Critique, *RASTER – Yearbook of the Independent Performing Arts Scene in Serbia*, Belgrade, *TkH Centre for Performing Arts Theory and Practice* 2009; Miško Šuvaković, "Theoretical Performance", *Maska 1* (2005), pp. 67-72.
55 | For the development of the theatre scene in Slovenia, see the questionnaires Slovenia I and II from 3 November 2012 and 5 October 2012; Tomaž Toporišič, "Country Report Slovenia", in *EEPAP*, pp. 289-294; National Theatre Museum of Slovenia (ed.): *Occupying Spaces. Experimental Theatre in Central Europe 1950-2010* (Ljubljana: National Theatre Museum of Slovenia 2010); Culture from Slovenia worldwide, see http://www.culture.si/en/Category:Theatre.

sed the stage in the sense of Artaud and re-theatralisation. This new theatre did not call itself political but experimental, exploratory.'[56]

The neo-avant-garde performance group Gledališče Pupilije Ferkeverk gained great importance. It was founded at the end of the sixties in Ljubljana. It was not only comprised of professional theatre makers, but included lay performers in its ranks. The collective moved away from literary sources and focused on the relationship between the audience and the actors. Following the movement of the Second Theatre Avant-garde in the sixties and seventies, it hoped to spiritually overcome borders and achieve a(n) (personal) awareness for both actors and audience by means of an anthropological-theatrical process. Tomaž Kralj, one of the founders of the group, commented:

'[I]n our group, the presentation of a text is not the main rule and performances are realised directly through theatrical visualisation which is devoted to theatre and not literature. The final form and consequence of a theatrical situation are not predictable or known in advance; when a situation is theatrically visualised, the simple and the total emerge. The author becomes researcher of his own theatre and research unfolds in practice.'[57]

The group Gledališče Pekarna played an important role among the independent theatres at this time. Lado Kralj, who participated in the independent group Eksperimentalno gledališče Glej at the same time, founded the group in 1972. The concept of the group was based on an intensive occupation with ritual practices in theatre work. The ensemble broke up in 1978.

The independent theatre Eksperimentalno gledališče Glej, mentioned earlier, was founded in Ljubljana by the director and dramatist Dušan Jovanović together with Lado Kralj, Zvone Šedlbauer and others in 1970. It is the oldest non-institutional theatre in Slovenia which until today has had its own permanent venue. The artistic directors – Janez Pipan, Eduard Miler, Nevenka Koprivšek, Matjaž Pograjc, Bojan Jablanovec, Tomi Janežič, Sebastijan Horvat, Diego DeBrea, Jure Novak, Marko (Mare) Bulc and, at this time, Marko Bratuš – still have a strong influence on Slovenian independent theatre. The theatre offers independent theatre makers in Slovenia good conditions for their artistic work. Thus, the theatre is an important venue in the country in which independent

---

56 | Tomaž Toporišič, "Spatial Machines and Slovene (No Longer-)Experimental Theatre in the Second Half of the 20th Century", in National Theatre Museum of Slovenia (ed.), *Occupying Spaces*, pp. 418-468, here p. 423.

57 | Tomaž Kralj, quoted in Tomaž Toporišič, "Spatial Machines and Slovene (No Longer-)Experimental Theatre in the Second Half of the 20th Century", p. 431.

groups can experiment with new methods of working and themes, as former director Marko Bulc describes here:

'Glej always was a new contemporary, a young theatre. It is for directors, who want to get the space in Glej, who want to work in complete freedom, who want to have a lot of free space and some extra production money to do what they want. Glej is not so much focused on the product in the end but mostly we try to focus to think about the process much more than their results. We do also a lot of work-in-progress situations. Mistakes are allowed. [...] We are trying to be a space for new ways of theatre, a space to explore the borders to the media and a space to find interesting stuff.'[58]

Another important venue for independent groups is the theatre Mladinsko gledališče in Ljubljana. Balbina Battelino Baranovič created the first professional children's and young people's theatre here in 1955. In 1978, Dušan Jovanović took over the direction of the theatre and turned the Slovensko mladinsko gledališče, as it was then called, into an internationally recognised stage. Prominent theatre makers such as Ljubiša Ristić, Vito Taufer, Dragan Živadinov, Janez Pipan, Eduard Miler and Tomaž Pandur worked there. In the eighties, they were the most important representatives of Slovenian experimental theatre, and they had a strong influence on independent groups and artists in the country. Today's concept of the Slovensko mladinsko gledališče is described as follows:

'Today, it [the Theatre Slovensko mladinsko gledališče, author's note A. H.] is known for a wide range of innovative poetics of various young directors and the phenomenon of 'ensemble energy' – the [Peter, author's note A. H.] Brook approach, towards acting, which is not based on star hierarchy, but on an acting laboratory connecting individual bravura parts into a strong whole of the acting ensemble. In its performances, the Mladinsko Theatre strives to thematise universal paradoxes of the civilisation, with its programme based on the problematisation of new times and spaces. The Mladinsko Theatre will continue to develop the code of new theatrical practice, new visual paradigms, new views on the classics, modernism and postmodernism. At the Mladinsko Theatre, the actor, director, choreographer, set designer, musician ... all research and develop, risk and create in order to develop a new spectator through their gestures.'[59]

The Slovensko mladinsko gledališče receives state subsidies, has a permanent ensemble and a fixed annual programme. At the same time, it provides a venue for collective performances, alternative dramaturgies and experimental, artistic methods of working.

---

58 | Author's interview with Marko Bulc on 27 May 2012. For artistic work of the Gledališ e Glej, see the theatre's homepage at http://www.culture.si/en/Glej_Theatre.
59 | Slovensko mladinsko gledališ e, see http://en.mladinsko.com/home/.

In 1984, the movement of the artists' collective Neue Slowenische Kunst (NSK) began.[60] The founder quartette consisted of the industrial band Laibach, the painters' collective IRWIN, the graphic and design studio Novi Kolektiviszem, and the experimental theatre group Gledališče Sester Scipion Nasice, which later became known as Kozmokinetični kabinet Noordung. The art of NSK is frequently provocative. In its artistic works, the collective often makes use of symbols, signs, images or icons taken from political-historical contexts, such as the totalitarian systems of the 20th century. These are torn from their original context, reassembled and deconstructed. In addition, at the beginning of the nineties, the collective created a virtual NSK state with symbolic IDs, passports, embassies, consulates and, for a time, a fictional currency. According to reports (although they have not been officially substantiated), it was possible for members of the movement to repeatedly cross international borders using the NSK passport. Because of this critical approach to socio-political and historical issues, the collective was seen as a catalyst for the upcoming independence movement in the country.

Unlike the other Yugoslavian republics, Slovenia already had an extremely active and rich independent theatre scene prior to the break-up of Yugoslavia. Many of the independent groups and artists mentioned are still active today. They are still considered to be important representatives of the independent theatres in Slovenia.

In June 1991, the country detached itself from the former Yugoslavia and declared its independence.[61] Immediately afterwards, there were armed conflicts with the Yugoslavian army. In contrast to the years of war in the neighbouring countries of Croatia and Bosnia-Herzegovina, the fighting ended after ten days. The democratisation and economic development of the country could therefore begin quite soon. This is reflected in the development of the independent theatres. Many young theatre makers appeared in public in the nineties, including internationally known artists such as Matjaž Berger, Vlado Repnik, Davide Grassi (later known as Janez Janša), Igor Štromajer, Marko Peljhan, Emil Hrvatin (later known as Janez Janša, too), Tomi Janežič, Sebastijan Horvat, Matjaž Farič, Jernej Lorenci, Ivica Buljan, Nevenka Koprivšek and Diego de Brea. At the same time, independent theatre collectives formed in Ljubljana, such as Matjaž Pograjc's group Betontanc, the Muzeum Institute,

---

60 | See Alexei Monroe, *Interrogation Machine. Laibach and NSK* (London/Cambridge: The MIT Press 2005); Marina Gržinić, Günther Heeg and Veronika Darian (eds.), *Mind the Map! History is not given* (Frankfurt a. Main: Revolver 2004); Inke Arns, *Neue slowenische Kunst. Eine Analyse ihrer künstlerischen Strategien im Kontext der 1980er Jahre in Jugoslawien* (Regensburg: Museum Ostdeutsche Galerie 2002).

61 | See Peter Štih, Vasko Simoniti and Peter Vodopivec, *Slowenische Geschichte. Gesellschaft – Politik – Kultur* (Graz: Leykam 2008).

the Bunker Institute founded by Nevenka Koprivšek, the internationally renowned Maska Institute, the group Dejmo Stisnt Teater by Mare Bulc, En Knap under the direction of Iztok Kovač, Bojan Jablanovec's Via Negativa and the internationally acclaimed project under the direction of Dragan Živadinov's Kozmokinetični kabinet Noordung. These theatre makers and groups are still active. They are considered pioneers of experimental theatre in Slovenia and primarily influenced young theatre artists with their productions in the first decade of the new millennium. These young artists included Jelena Rusjan and her group Škrip Orkestra, Sebastian Roškarič and Polonka Červek with the group Saltimbanko Magic World, Primož Ekart and his production house Imaginarni Institute, as well as the performance collective Narobov, all of which are located in Ljubljana.[62] The organisation Asociacija, which was founded in 1992, actively supports the independent groups and artists in Slovenia with regard to cultural and educational policies.

Slovenia's independent theatres experienced different phases of development after the political changes in the country. At the end of the socialist era, the starting situation was good compared with the other republics. Today the artistic scope of independent groups and theatre makers is huge. Yet, two conditions limit the work of the independent theatres: the concentration of cultural life in the capital, Ljubljana, and the increasingly difficult economic conditions. Because of the worsening economic situation in Slovenia, theatre makers and independent groups have hardly been able to establish themselves since the middle of the 2000s.

'The theatre and the contemporary dance have been in decline since 2004. The charm of which the Slovenian culture used to be recognised in Ex-Yugoslavia is gone. And NGO sector had been drying out, self-destroying and slowly drowning.'[63]

This is how an independent theatre critic describes the situation of the independent theatres in Slovenia in recent years. How independent theatre will develop in this country in the coming years, and whether new independent groups will emerge under these circumstances, remains to be seen.

The Yugoslavian Republic of *Croatia* experienced the 'Croatian Spring' in the late sixties and early seventies when a broad national-democratic movement

---

[62] | In this context, the following theatre makers can also be named: Sabina Schwenner, Marko Bratuš, Boris Kadin, Peter Kus, Miha Nemec, Mala Kline, Irena Tmažin, Maja Delak, Mateja Bučar, Matija Solce, Andreja Kopač, Katarina Stegnar, Mare Bulc, Jure Novak and Urška Brodar.

[63] | Questionnaire Slovenia I.

called for greater autonomy and more national rights.[64] The Yugoslavian government under state and party leader Tito used force to put down the protest. In this time of political unrest, the first independent theatre groups were founded in Croatia.[65] These emerged from the amateur theatre movement, whose artistic manner of working they continued. The most famous names include the group Kugla glumište (today known as Damir Bartol Indoš) and the student theatre Lero, founded by Davor Mojaš, which were both located in Zagreb, and Nebojša Borojević's 's collective Daska in Sisak. Because there were no theatres available to them, the groups usually presented their productions at festivals in Croatia. By doing so, they received much attention in their own country and beyond its borders. In the eighties, other important theatre groups were founded, such as Romano Bodan's collective Kazališna družina Pinklec in Čakovec, the group Dr. Inat under the direction of Branko Sušac in Pula, Borut Šeparović's performance group Montažstroj in Zagreb, the ensemble, Tranzicijsko-fikcijsko (Trafik) in Rijeka, and the first independent children's and young people's theatre, Mala Scena, which was founded by Vitomira Lončar, Zvjezdana Ladika and Ivica Šimić in Zagreb in 1986. The group KGPT, whose importance has already been mentioned, was also one of the groups founded at this time.

Like Slovenia, Croatia declared its independence in June 1991. In the following four years of the Croatian War, the Yugoslavian army and Serbian paramilitary units forcibly displaced the Croatian population in the areas of the country which they controlled and perpetrated massacres under the banner of ethnic cleansing. In 1995, Croatia ended the war in its favour. The Erdut Agreement regulated the future cohabitation with the Serbian minority. In the years that followed, Croatia implemented many economic, judicial and social reforms.

The work of the Croatian independent theatres was severely restricted during the war. Despite the precarious situation, a few collectives were founded: HKD Teatar by Nenad Šegvić and Lary Zappia in Rijeka and the Teatar Exit in Zagreb. It is important to mention the Pula art Umjetnicki Festival (PUF) in this context. Independent theatre makers such as Davor Mojaš, Nebojša Borojević, Branko Sušac and Romano Bogdan started it in 1994 under the name International Festival for Independent Theatre in Pula: 'PUF was born as a

---

64 | For the history of Croatia, see also Ludwig Steindorff, *Kroatien. Vom Mittelalter bis zur Gegenwart* (Regensburg: Pustet 2001).

65 | For the development of the theatre scene in Croatia, see Jelena Kovačić, "Country Report Croatia", in *EEPAP*, pp. 125-146; Nebojša Borojević, "Country Report Croatia", in *IG Freie Theaterarbeit*, see http://www.freietheater.at/?page=europeanoffnetwork&subpage=country_report#2.

direct commentary on Croatian theatre reality.'[66] The start of this theatre meeting made a considerable contribution to the continuation of the independent theatres in Croatia despite the circumstances of war. However, facilities were reduced to a minimum. The festival still exists, and it is still an important communication platform for independent theatres in Croatia:

> 'PUF functions as a communication channel; revealing the world from a new angle: not monologue and passive communication, but dialogue, frankness, identification, and participation. At the same time, it is obvious that PUF will be a site of encounters between artists who differ in their worldviews and inner necessities, yet not in their marginalized social position.'[67]

In recent years, there have been three outstanding experimental theatres. The Teatar & TD in Zagreb is an important point of contact for independent artists, mainly because of the support programme 'kultura promjene' (culture change) initiated by Nataša Rajković and Marin Blažević. Theatre makers such as Branko Brezovac, Damir Bartol Indoš, Anika Tomić and Oliver Frljić work there. Independent groups, such as the aforementioned performance collective Montažstroj and the group BADco, founded by Goran Sergej Pristaš in 2000, perform in this theatre. The second important venue is the theatre Zagrebačko kazalište mladih (ZeKaeM) in Zagreb. It is headed by the dramatic advisor Dubravka Vrgoč, who has initiated many international projects with a wide spectrum of artistic activities. Finally, the group Teatar Exit, founded by Matko Raguž and Nataša Lušetić in Zagreb, has had its own permanent theatre since 1998. The group's productions are developed on the basis of a collective and process-oriented collaboration of all those involved. The group sees theatre 'as a [...] common [...] workshop, a work in progress with all parties having equal rights with respect to the authorship'[68]. Countless theatre groups and young artists in Croatia adopted this understanding of theatre in the past (e.g., Bobo Jelčić, Nastaša Rajković, Matija Ferlin, Rene Medvešek, Saša Anočič and Lary Zappia). In recent years, other groups have influenced the independent theatre scene in the country. Among them are Boris Bakal's group Bacači Sjenki and the collectives Act Lab, Bumerang, Gustl, Moruzgva, Planet Art, Teatar Rugantino, Teatar Svarog, Kazalište Merlin, Kazalište Hotel Bulić and Studio Kvak. All these groups work in Zagreb. The theatre collectives Room 100, Kazalište Licem u Lice, Play Drama and Malo Splitsko Kazalište were founded in Split.

---

66 | Nebojša Borojević, "Country Report Croatia".
67 | Ibid.
68 | Hrvoje Ivanković, "Zwischen Text und Kontext", in Martina Vannayová and Anna Häusler (eds.), *Landvermessungen*, pp. 63-74, here p. 65.

The free groups Ludens Teatar and Grupa Kugla are situated in Koprivnica near the Croatian-Hungarian border.

The military conflicts in the post-Yugoslavian states in the nineties also devastated Bosnia-Herzegovina. After the declaration of independence of the former Yugoslavian republic in 1992, a three-year war erupted between Bosnians, Serbs and the Croatian minority in the country. After the war ended in 1995, the economic situation in the country was disastrous: residential buildings, industrial facilities and the infrastructure were destroyed, and yet there was no end to the ethnically motivated conflicts.

Given this situation, a collapse of the theatre in Bosnia-Herzegovina in the first half of the nineties would not have been surprising. Yet, the opposite was the case: 'During the four years of occupation, more than a hundred premieres and debut performances took place in Sarajevo.'[69] The theatre Sarajevski ratni teatar (SARTR) in Sarajevo played an important role. It was founded at the beginning of the besiegement of the city by the directors Gradimir Gojer and Dubravko Bibanović, the engineer Đorđe Mačkić, and the author Safet Plakalo. The SARTR was the artistic centre for actors, directors and other theatre professionals whose theatres had been closed in Sarajevo because of the war. It was an important meeting place for many artists and the venue of countless performances. After the war, the theatre was granted the status of a public institution of particular importance for the city.

Some theatre productions which were performed in the occupied city of Sarajevo gained a particular importance because of their political message. One of these was Susan Sontag's *Waiting for Godot*, which was staged in 1993. In the performance, the artist called upon the Western countries to intervene in order to end the war. The performance aroused international attention. This was also true for the performances of *Silk Drums* by the theatre and film director Haris Pašović and the production *In the Country of the Last Things*, an adaptation of the novel by Paul Auster, by the Sarajevo Festival Ensemble. These two performances were among the most famous productions in Bosnia-Herzegovina during the war years. All of the productions mentioned here were of particular symbolic importance because of their political messages: They stood for the survival of the theatre.

---

69 | Almir Bašović, "Theater im Transitbereich oder Dionysos auf Dienstreise", in Martina Vannayová and Anna Häusler (eds.), *Landvermessungen*, pp. 23-30, here p. 24. For the development of the theatre scene in Bosnia-Herzegovina, see also the questionnaires Bosnia-Herzegovina I and II, both from 30 October 2012; Tanja Miletic Orucevic, "Country Report Bosnia and Hercegovina", in *EEPAP*, pp. 95-110; *After the fall. Europa nach 1989. Ein Theaterprojekt des Goethe-Instituts*, see http://www.goethe.de/kue/the/prj/atf/the/sar/deindex.htm.

'In this big area to be covered I can focus the theatre produced during the siege of Sarajevo 1992-1996. Under the inhuman conditions of life (24-hours mortal danger, shelling, snipers, hunger, no electricity, etc.), the artists produced theatre and the audience risked their lives to come to watch the show.'[70]

After the end of the war, the situation changed. The importance of the theatre declined. The country mainly had to struggle with the economic and social effects of the war, which took priority over any cultural matters. There was very little interest in the theatre, and there was hardly any money available.

For many years, until much after the turn of the millennium, there were no independent theatres in Bosnia-Herzegovina. In comparison to the theatre scenes in the post-socialist countries already presented here, an independent theatre scene did not develop until much later. Not until 2005 were there first signs of life, when the director Haris Pašović started the cultural centre East West Centar in Sarajevo.[71] The centre sees itself as an NGO-institution which provides services without generating any profit. It stages its own performances and offers workshops with international theatre makers. Furthermore, it collaborates with independent artists from more than 20 countries. Today the venue is the most famous cultural centre in the post-Yugoslavian states by far. In 2006, the theatre Gradsko pozorište Jazavac was founded in Baja Luka. The venue is not only a children's and young people's theatre, but offers workshops and training programs for acting, dramaturgy and directing. In addition, it is an important meeting place for young theatre makers and groups. Artistically, the productions focus on everyday subjects and deal with the social realities in the country:

'Mission of the Gradsko pozorište Jazavac is to discover and promote young artists and to offer to the public a theatre art as a communication and dialogue on current and everyday topics of their interest, with which they are faced with [sic].'[72]

The theatre centres mentioned here are working to promote the development of the independent theatres in Bosnia-Herzegovina. They are important venues for groups and artists who still find themselves in the very slow process of establishing themselves there.

---

70 | Questionnaire Bosnia-Herzegovina I.
71 | East West Centar, see http://eastwest.ba/.
72 | Gradsko pozorište Jazavac, see http://gpj.ba/.

2.3 Post-Soviet States

The theatre in Russia can look back on a rich history.[73] Theatre reformers such as Vsevolod Meyerhold, Yevgeny Vakhtangov, Alexander Tairov, Konstantin Stanislavsky and Sergei M. Eisenstein had a great influence on the national and international theatre at the beginning of the twentieth century. In the post-Stalin era, directors and theatre makers such as Oleg Jefremov, Georgi Alexandrovitch Tovstonogov, Maria Knebel, Anatoly Efros, Anatoly Vasiliev and Lev Dodin influenced Russian theatre. They mainly worked on experimental stages, such as the internationally reknowned theatre Moskovskiy Hudojestvenny Akademicheskiy Teatr (MChAT), the Teatr na Taganke founded by Yuri Petrovics Lyubimov, the Teatr Sovremennik in Moscow, and the Teatr Mały in St. Petersburg.

After the dissolution of the Soviet Union, severe internal political conflicts erupted in the newly founded Russian state.[74] The privatisation of the economy and attempts to democratise the state and society failed. The industry collapsed; inflation soared, and the gap between the poor strata of the population and the influential oligarchs widened more and more. At the end of the nineties, the country was in a severe economic crisis. Tensions arose in the North Caucasus which led to the two wars in Chechenya. In 2000, Vladimir Putin took over the office of president, which he had already held prior to a four-year interruption between 2008 and 2012. Thanks to tax reforms, capital reflux and the export of raw materials, the economic situation improved. At the same time, Putin had the constitution amended so that the president was given extensive powers.

Despite the difficult political and economic situation, Russian independent theatre continued to develop in the nineties and at the beginning of the new millennium. Especially in Moscow, new stages and collectives emerged, including the Teatr na Pokrovke under the direction of Sergey Artsybashev, the Teatr Kamernaya Scena initiated by Michael Shepenko, the theatre workshop Petr Fomenko Workshop, Alexander Kaliagin's Teatr EtCetera, the Teatr Okolo under Yuri Porgrebnichko and Ludmila Rasumovskaya's Teatr Chevolek.

---

73 | For the development of the theatre in Russia, see also Amy Bryzgel, *Performing the East. Performance Art in Russia, Latvia and Poland since 1980* (London/New York: I. B. Tauris 2013); Robert Laech and Victor Borovsky, *A History of Russian Theatre* (Cambridge et al.: Cambridge University 1999); Theatre Institute Russia, see http://www.teatr.ru/.

74 | For the history of Russia, see Margareta Mommsen, *Wer herrscht in Russland? Der Kreml und die Schatten der Macht* (München: C. H. Beck 2003); Gottfried Schramm (ed.), *Russlands langer Weg zur Gegenwart* (Göttingen: Vandenhoeck & Ruprecht 2001).

Moreover, after the turn of the millennium, the artistic style known as the Novaya Drama emerged.⁷⁵ This development was initiated by the independent theatres. Novaya Drama is represented today by notable groups and artists, including the Teatr.doc, which was founded in 2002 by Michail Ugarov and Elena Gremina, the group CDR – Tsentr dramaturgii i rezhissury of Michail Roshchin und Alexei Kazantsev, the Teatr Praktika founded by Eduard Boiakov in 2005, and the SounDrama under the direction of Vladimir Pankov, also founded in 2005. The groups, which are all located in Moscow, relate their work to the German documentary theatre of the sixties and the British 'in-yer-face' theatre. Their aim is to develop a documentary realism for the theatre which uses authentic source material such as interviews, documents and reports as a starting point. The content of this material is not changed but artistically revised, edited and reassembled. The group Teatr.doc describes its artistic conception of itself in the following words: 'Teatre.doc is a theatre in which there is no acting.'⁷⁶ The movement Novaya Drama is an important artistic direction of the Russian independent theatre. It is also known outside of Russia.

Young directors who made public appearances in recent years include Dimitri Krymov, Ivan Alexandrovitch Vyrypajev, Kirill Serebrennikov, Andrei Mogutschi, Yuri Butusov, Mindaugas Karbauskis and Dmitri Yegorov. The following theatres and collectives are internationally known today: the theatre AKHE of Maxim Isayev and Pavel Semtschenko, the Teatr Oddance and the collective DNEVO, all of which are located in St. Petersburg, and the Studio for Theatre Art of Sergei Zhenovach, the Centre for Dance and Performance, TsEKh and the Teatr Liquid in Moscow.

In August 1991, the Republic of Belarus was constituted.⁷⁷ Since 1994, Alexander Lukashenko has been in power as the head of state. Belarus has a higher standard of living than Russia. Bigger cities such as Minsk, Gomel and Mogi-

---

75 | For the artistic movement *Novaya Drama*, see Dorte Lena Eilers, "Achtung Kunst!", in *Theater der Zeit* 12 (2012), pp. 18-19; Birgit Beumers and Mark Lipovetsky, *Performing Violence. Literary and Theatrical Experiments of New Russian Drama* (Bristol/Chicago: Intellect 2009); Roman Dolschanski, "Kommerz und erfreuliche Ausnahmen", in: *Theater der Zeit* 3 (2006), pp. 23-26; Carola Dürr, "Auf der Suche nach dem verlorenen Helden. Das Festival Neue Dramatik in Moskau", in *Theater der Zeit* 3 (2006), p. 33; Carola Dürr, "Der Aufbruch hat begonnen", in *Theater der Zeit* 3 (2006), pp. 20-22; Nina Belenitskaja, "Kurswechsel. Ein Schlüssel für das Verständnis des Wertekanons in der russischen Gesellschaft", in *Theater der Zeit* 3 (2006), pp. 16-19.

76 | Olga Galachowa, "Archipel Moskau", in *Theater der Zeit* 12 (2012), pp. 12-15, here p. 15.

77 | See Valentin Akudowitsch, *Der Abwesenheitscode. Versuch, Weißrussland zu verstehen* (Berlin: Suhrkamp 2013); Thomas M. Bohn and Victor Shadurski (eds.), *Ein weißer*

lyev project an image of cleanliness, order and security, and there are active subcultures. However, the population lives under a dictatorship. The country is internationally isolated, censorship is harsh, and the omnipotence of the state security organisation, KGB, is intimidating.

Figure 3: Minsk, 2013. Photograph: Andrea Hensel

The state theatres are in a difficult situation.[78] They cannot work independently without fearing repression by the government. Since the beginning of the new millennium, they have only received funding from the state to cover the salaries of artists and operating costs. Furthermore, only those contract productions are subsidised which are considered socially relevant and politically acceptable: 'In this category one can find performances of Belarusian and international classics and plays which deal with Belarusian history.'[79] The state-imposed restrictions limit the founding of independent theatres.

Fleck in Europa...: Die Imagination der Belarus als Kontaktzone zwischen Ost und West (Bielefeld: transcript 2011).

78 | For the development of the theatre scene in Belarus, see the questionnaire Belarus from 22 September 2012; Viktor Pietrow, "Country Report Belarus", in *EEPAP*, pp. 83-94; Fundacja Open Culture (ed.), *A report on the condition of culture and NGOs in Belarus* (Lublin: Episteme 2011), see http://fundacjaopenculture.org/.

79 | Tatjana Komonowa, "Die Welt im Spiegel betrachtet", in Martina Vannayová and Anna Häusler (eds.), *Landvermessungen*, pp. 13-22, here p. 13.

'Experimental theatre and performance and the struggle for performance art, as an experimental art, are forbidden in a political context. An artist and freedom are considered to be contrary to each other, and art as a process is forbidden. Anything that is impossible to be understood by the government is forbidden.'[80]

However, in recent years, more and more independent theatre groups have emerged in Belarus. They work in the underground in private apartments, galleries and cafés. The performances deal with forbidden subjects such as homosexuality, gender issues, mental illness and drug consumption. The theatre makers experiment aesthetically with new, usually censored artistic forms:

'In my opinion, the main peculiarity is the tendency to go beyond the old theatrical style which still dominates in public theatres and to create a kind of new theatrical product according to modern times and today's audience interests. This can be reached in several ways.'[81]

An important artist is Pavel Admatschikow. As an actor and director at the State Academy of the Arts in Minsk, he is considered a pioneer of the movement theatre, which is little known in Belarus. Also the director, Vladimir Petrowitsch, plays an important role in independent theatre. In his works, he motivates the audience to question their own perception and confronts the audience with the social grievances in the country. The director Wladimir Schtscherban is an important representative of the independent theatre. His productions of contemporary Belarusian and international drama have been repeatedly censored or have been dropped from the programme altogether. Since 2005, Schtscherban has been a member of the Belarus Free Theatre, which was founded by the human rights activist Nikolai Khalezin and the theatre producer Natalia Koliada in Minsk in the same year. Because of the restrictions imposed by the government, the group set up a second seat in London in 2011. Their performances, which are staged internationally, deal with the political, social and cultural situation in Belarus. In Minsk, the Belarus Free Theatre is one of the best-known independent theatres. Other independent groups which work in Minsk are the Kornyag Teatr founded by Evgeni Kornyag, Alexander Tebenkow's dance theatre, Gallery, the groups Kryly Halopa, InZest, and Zywaja Planet, the D.O.Z.SK.I Company, the performance groups Jana Try Jon, Petli and Mechaniory Kultury, and the Teatr Psichicznaj neuraunawazanasci. The group Parallels is located in Vitebsk, and the Quadro-Company is situated in Grodno.

---

80 | Viktor Pietrow, "Country Report Belarus", p. 91.
81 | Questionnaire Belarus.

Despite the fact that the groups differ among themselves, they often have an all-encompassing manner of working in common which transcends the usual boundaries which separate art forms. Thus, independent theatre makers cooperate with curators, fine artists, media artists and journalists in the independent scene. New aesthetic formats in unusual venues emerge from this dialogue. Partners of the independent theatre are also culture magazines, galleries and agencies (e.g., the Galerie Ỹ, owned by Valentina Kiselieva, the culture magazine Artaktivist, initiated by Sergei Shabothin, the online magazine, pARTisan, the photo gallery Studio 67, and the concert agency BOpromo in Minsk).

In the Ukraine, independent artists, groups and theatres did not emerge until the beginning of the nineties:[82] 'At that time, ideological restrictions in theatrical and choreographic life were relaxed – after the abolishment of censorship, theatres could finally form their repertoires independently.'[83] In addition to the young directors such as Gregory Hlady, Mark Nestantiner and Yuriy Yatsenko, students of the Russian theatre reformer Anatoly Vasiliev, such as Oleh Lipstyn, Andrij Zholdak and Valerij Bilchenko, made a name for themselves in the independent theatre scene. A renowned venue, the Milodyi Teatr, was established by Volodymyr Kuchynsky in Lviv in 1988; later the theatre became very well-known under the name Teatr Łeś Kurbas and still exists under this name.

After the Ukraine became independent in 1991, the country suffered from economic crises in the nineties; the population was poor and the crime rate high.[84] Nevertheless, new independent theatre groups emerged. Valerij Bilchenko founded the street theatre Kyivisky Teatr Uliczny KET in Kiev at the beginning of the nineties. At the same time, Vitaly Malakhov established the Kyivsky Teatr na Podoli in Kiev. Both theatre groups, together with the Milodyi Teatr, played an important role in the independent theatre scene in Ukraine in the nineties. Their artistic work was primarily influenced by the work of Jerzy Grotowski and Anatoly Vasiliev. However, the difficult economic situation took its toll on the independent theatres. More and more often, well-known theatre makers such as Bilchenko, Oleh Lipstyn, Gregory Hlady, Mark Nestantiner and Yuri Yatsenko worked abroad or left the Ukraine permanently. But new

---

82 | For the development of the theatre scene in the Ukraine, see the questionnaires Ukraine I and II from 28 October 2012 and 11 October 2012; Tina Peresunko, "Country Report Ukraine", in *EEPAP*, pp. 295-348; Fundacja Open Culture (ed.), *A report on the condition of culture and NGOs in Ukraine* (Lublin: Episteme 2012), see http://fundacja openculture.org/.

83 | Tina Peresunko, "Country Report Ukraine", p. 300.

84 | See Winfried Schneider-Deters, *Die Ukraine – Machtvakuum zwischen Russland und der Europäischen Union* (Berlin: Berliner Wissenschaftsverlag 2012).

independent groups and stages were founded, including Vladislav Troitsky's Teatr Dakh and the Tanzlaboratorium in Kiev. Svitlana Oleshko's collective Arabesky and the group P.S. settled in Charkiv. In Lviv, Irina Volytska and Lidiya Danylchuk created the Teatr u Koshyku; the group Verim was established in Dnipropetrovsk, and Vie was established in Zaporishia.

The 'Orange Revolution' in 2004 led to far-reaching political upheavals in the Ukraine. Because of the unstable political situation, the cultural sector – and with it the independent theatres – received little attention from politicians and society in general. Nevertheless, the middle of the 2000s gave rise to new independent groups and venues. These included the stage Budynok aktora and the group Nowa Szena in Charkiv, and the collective Wilna Szena, founded by Dmytro Gogomasov, Anton Ovchinnikov's dance theatre, Black O!Range, the Vilnyi Teatr and the Teatr 19 in Kiev. Together with the groups and directors who had already begun working in the nineties, and with theatre makers of the younger generation such as Maxym Holenko and Igor Ladenko, they are the principal representatives of the Ukrainian independent theatre today.

At this time, the independent theatre in the Ukraine is in dire straits:

'There were more than 200 independent theatre companies in Ukraine in the beginning of the 1990s and now there are just few of them alive [...] mostly they ceased to exist due to lack of funding, lack of space. They did a lot of experiment in the beginning of the 1990s but it didn't change the Ukrainian theatre in general. Ukrainian theatre, as it was in the Soviet Union times, still remains traditional, inflexible, rigid.'[85]

The lack of cultural reforms, antiquated structures in cultural policies, and uncertain economic conditions make the work of the independent theatres difficult in the Ukraine today and have an extremely adverse effect on the development of new groups.

2.4 Excursus: The Independent Dance Scene

With the exception of Yugoslavia, in whose republics culture could develop relatively autonomously, the dance productions in the socialist countries are based on an ideologically charged and politically instrumentalised body image. Dance was used to stage the collective socialist body. This stipulation did not allow any individual body images on stage.

'The collective body in its various hypostases (party structures, workers' unions, local party organisations etc.) was hostile to all manifestations of personal corporeality – distinguishable appearances, sexual or emotional preferences or personal tastes. The

---

85 | Questionnaire Ukraine I.

nation was the 'virtual socialist body', which was not interested in individuality, but encouraged unification and large-scale formations [...].'[86]

Uniformisation and collectivisation characterised the dance productions in the socialist countries. These were obliged to fulfil the aesthetic preconditions prescribed by politics. Classical ballet and folk dance were considered by the government to be the forms of dance with which those prerequisites could best be realised.

Following the political upheavals at the end of the eighties, a lively independent dance scene emerged – especially in Slovenia, Romania, Croatia, Serbia and Bulgaria. To this day, the high level of development in these dance scenes far exceeds anything to be found in other post-socialist countries. 'In the remaining countries contemporary dance is at the beginning of its organisational stage, which can be compared to the Flemish scene in the early 1980s.'[87] This has been noted in the EEPAP study on the development of the dance scene in the other post-socialist countries. In Slovenia, Romania and Croatia, the dance groups received active support through the founding of cultural associations and the establishment of production venues. Examples are the association, Društvo za sodobni ples Slovenije, which was founded in Ljubljana in 1994, the Centrul National al Dansului – Bucuresti (CNDB), founded in Bukarest in 2004, and the Zagrebački Plesni Centar, which was established in Zagreb in 2009. In addition, the practice of reviewing dance performances was promoted. The training of dance dramaturgists also contributed to a professionalisation of the independent dance scene. These three factors enabled the independent dance scene to become firmly established in the cultural landscapes of the three countries.

In Serbia, the emergence of the independent dance scene at the beginning of the new millennium was expedited by groups as well as by individual choreographers and dancers: 'It emerged and evolved mostly within the alternative theatre scene (mainly in Belgrade), as nonverbal, physical, dance theatre, and theatre movement – as well as in various other forms of experimental theatre and performance.'[88]

---

86 | Mira Todorova, *Body, Identity, Community. Dance in Bulgaria after 1989*, 11 pages, no place or date of publication given, manuscript privately owned by the author, here p. 2. For the development of the dance scene in the post-socialist states, see all available questionnaires, all Country Reports in *EEPAP* and Paweł Płoski, "Introduction", in *EEPAP*, pp. 9-62.
87 | Paweł Płoski: "Introduction", p. 37.
88 | Questionnaire Serbia I.

Companies emerged, such as the Dah teatar, the Ister teatar, Placo pozorište, Mimart, Omen and Erg Status. Young choreographers and dancers, such as Boris Čakširan, Ivana Vujić, Bojana Mladenović, Dalija Aćin, Isidora Stanišić, Dragana Alfirević, Dušan Murić, Olivera Kovačević and Saša Asentić gained renown. In a collective process, the body is artistically explored. In doing so, the artistic dance practice is always linked to theoretical reflection. A Serbian choreographer describes the work of the independent dance theatre in her country with these words:

'Open process which creates body declarative art using interactive contemporary arts and interdisciplinary researching way, expanding the borders of theatre. Phenomena are intuitively explored in workshops with body because you can only enter the phenomenon using body. Research using auto-dramaturgy of body brings out new theatre aesthetics of signalise, with risk. [...] Non-verbal theatre transcends all barriers: language, geographic, political, ethical, ethnic, social [...].'[89]

The founding of the association for contemporary dance, Stanica/Station, in Belgrade and the Belgrade dance festival Beogradski *festival* igre in 2001 attracted international attention. They continue to be the focus of international attention, and are therefore in a position to promote the transnational networking of Serbian dance groups. Furthermore, the establishment of the platform Walking Theory in 2000 and the TkH Centre for Performing Arts Theory and Practice in 2002 accelerated the development of the dance scene. Both primarily support international cooperation projects of Serbian independent companies and promote a close connection between theory and practice. In 2005, the Nomad Dance Academy was founded in Belgrade. It contributes to the professionalisation of the independent dance scene and initiates transnational projects. Moreover, it has an influence on cultural and educational policies:

'Its activities have been aimed at creating a strong, recognisable Balkan scene of contemporary dance. NDA is a platform of cooperation, a tool of promotion, a programme of education and creation, and a self-reproducing organisation model.'[90]

Independent dance groups also emerged in Bulgaria. The independent dance groups Ek Studio and Ego Group were formed in the eighties. They combined dance practices which had been unknown in the country until then with the politically prescribed canon of body dramatisation: 'Their performances were marked by the aesthetics of expressionism, and by modernist interpretations

---

89 | Ibid.
90 | Paweł Płoski, "Introduction", p. 38.

of folk motifs, which came to reflect their attempt to 'modernise' dance.'[91] The two companies disbanded after only a few years. Their attempts to open the dance theatre had no aesthetic effect. The choreographer and dancer Krasen Krăstev, who founded the independent group Amarant in Sofia in 1993, was more successful. The company developed its productions in a collective process and entered into international collaborations. The group experimented with new dance practices. In doing so, it contributed to the further development of contemporary dance in Bulgaria:

'They liberated the Bulgarian notion of contemporary dance and its strong dependence on the classical academic position of bodies and body movement from assuming the perfectly trained body and the flawless performance of strict choreography. Free, random, everyday movement started to appear [...], as did chaotic compositions devoid of a single centre. Narration or suggestive metaphors carrying ideas, messages and stories were no longer needed.'[92]

Other young choreographers who became well-known in Bulgaria in the nineties are Mila Iskrenova, Tatyana Sokolova, Albena Atanassova, Galina Borissova and Rossen Mihaylov. They not only worked in Bulgaria, but internationally. At the beginning and in the middle of the 2000s, independent choreographers such as Anna Doneva, Yuliana Siska, Stefan Shterev, Mila Odadjieva and Ivo Dimchev made a name for themselves. Some independent dance collectives were founded at this time, including the group Dance BG, headed by Petya Stoykova and Marga Goranova in Burgas, and the companies Brain Store Project by Iva Sveshtarova and Villy Prager, and the Kinesthetic Project of Violeta Vitanova, Stanislav Genadiev, Diana Papazova, Ognyana Serafimova-Penava and Miroslav Yordanov in Sofia. The productions of these groups were characterised 'by their radicalism, a specific artistic attitude and individualism'[93]. In 2008, the Derida Dance Centre was founded in Sofia, the first and still the only independent contemporary dance theatre in Bulgaria. Its founding is the result of an initiative of the choreographer Zhivko Zhelyazkov and the art manager Atanas Maev. The centre promotes dance training and offers international residence programmes.

The economic situation of the independent dance theatre is difficult in all post-socialist countries. Aside from the fact that there is insufficient funding available, there are also not enough venues. The companies usually work in rented rooms, use cultural centres or cooperate with theatres. However,

---

91 | Mira Todorova, *Body, Identity, Community*, p. 6.
92 | Ibid., p. 7.
93 | Mila Iskrenova, "Nichts soll bleiben, wie es war...", in Dorte Lena Eilers, Anna Volkland and Holger Schultze (eds.), *Die neue Freiheit*, pp. 105-112, here p. 107.

the established cultural institutions are often unwilling to cooperate with independent dance groups. There are few or – in many countries – no funding programmes which include the leasing of premises. Furthermore, contemporary dance receives little mention in cultural and educational policies. 'Contemporary dance is practically absent from cultural policy in most of the countries. [...] Most of the countries still lack a cohesive policy of support for dance despite the constant emergence of new dance companies.'[94]

The inadequate conditions severely restrict the artistic work in the independent dance scene in the post-socialist countries. Companies and artists, therefore, can only establish themselves with difficulty. Yet, as has been described, a positive development of the independent dance theatre can be observed in some post-socialist countries: 'The Eastern European dance scene is evolving slowly. But some developments can be seen on the horizon.'[95]

3. Conditions for Artistic Work

3.1 Cultural Policies and Funding

After the political upheavals at the end of the eighties and the beginning of the nineties, the cultural and educational policies in the post-socialist states changed completely.[96] Everywhere they were given a greater importance and a different function than in the past even though the development was different in the individual countries. Up to that point, culture had served to establish and legitimise socialism. Now the political mission of cultural facilities ended, and with it their economic security. The cultural and educational policies assumed new tasks. The transformation of cultural and educational policies is still impeded, because patterns of thought and behaviour which originated under

---

94 | Paweł Płoski, "Introduction", p. 42.
95 | Ibid., p. 38.
96 | For the entire chapter on cultural and educational policies, see all available questionnaires and all Country Reports in *EEPAP*; Maria Davydchyk, *Transformationen der Kulturpolitik. Kulturpolitische Veränderungen nach dem Zusammenbruch des sozialistischen Systems in Mittel- und Osteuropa* (Wiesbaden: VS 2012); Wolfgang Rauter, *Kulturpolitik und -finanzierung im osteuropäischen Raum* (Saarbrücken: VDM 2008); Deutsche UNESCO-Kommission e.V. (ed.), *Übereinkommen über den Schutz und die Förderung der Vielfalt kultureller Ausdrucksformen. Magna Charta der Internationalen Kulturpolitik* (Bonn: Köllen 2005); Therese Kaufmann and Gerald Raunig, *Anticipating European Cultural Policies. Europäische Kulturpolitiken vorausdenken* (Wien/Linz: European Institute for Progressive Cultural Policies 2003).

socialism continue to exist or a high degree of continuity in terms of personnel prevails.

In all post-socialist countries, two important changes can be observed. Instead of simply implementing the requirements laid down by the state and the party, as in the past, cultural policies now promote cultural diversity and cultural autonomy. Cultural institutions and the stakeholders on the local level are involved in decision-making processes concerning cultural and educational issues. Second, cultural and educational policies face the challenge of finding a 'balance between stability and flexibility, tradition and innovation'[97]. A high degree of flexibility in cultural and educational policies is important to be able to react to the frequent changes in the external conditions. At the same time, a minimum of economic security and cultural-political certainty is necessary. Achieving this balance has proven to be one of the biggest difficulties facing the cultural policymakers in post-socialist countries.

In terms of organisational forms, transparency and the cohesion of cultural policies, the individual post-socialist countries have achieved different levels of development. According to the study by the East European Performing Arts Platform from 2011, the situation at that time could be described as follows: The transformation process in which cultural and educational policies are no longer subordinate to a socialist state but which now represent an autonomous, transparent and stable cultural programme is very far advanced in Slovenia and in the countries of the Visegrád Group (the Czech Republic, Slovakia, Hungary, Poland), or has even reached a level which approximates that of Western European countries. Croatia is also highly developed: 'This group is joined by Croatia, whose cultural system and policy is closest to the achievements of the countries of Central Europe.'[98] The cultural and educational policies of Romania, Bulgaria and Serbia are in the middle of the transformation process. Rigorous state decision-making structures continue to exist, and the networking of cultural institutions has been only partially realised. Both characteristics are carry-overs from the old systems. As has already been described in the individual country analyses, the cultural and educational policies in Russia, Belarus and in the Ukraine are unclear and incoherent. The study characterises them as follows: '[...] a conglomerate of socialist and capitalist tendencies results in a combination of both the good and bad aspects of both systems, including corruption and strong tendency toward introverted self-sufficiency'[99]. In Belarus as well as in Russia there is still a strict censorship; neither is the report positive for Bosnia-Herzegovina. The cultural and educational policies are still influenced by instability, inconsistency and ambiguity, all consequences of the

---

97 | Maria Davydchy, *Transformationen der Kulturpolitik*, p. 37.
98 | Paweł Płoski, "Introduction", p. 12.
99 | Ibid.

hostilities and armed conflicts. For this reason, an independent theatre maker from Bosnia-Herzegovina observes:

'In no country of Europe is cultural policy more important than in Bosnia Herzegovina. Culture is both the cause and the solution to its problems. Cultural arguments were used to divide the country, yet culture might be able to bring people back together again through initiating cultural programmes and activity that increase mutual understanding and respect.'[100]

An important indicator for the democratisation of cultural and educational policies is the question regarding the extent to which theatres are decentrally organised. Here, too, cultural and educational policies in the post-socialist states have advanced to varying degrees. The decentralisation of theatres means an empowerment of regional and local decision-makers. Thus, artistic and administrative decisions do not lie solely in the hands of the central authority of the state, as was the case prior to the decline of the communist systems, but they are transferred to local and regional levels. 'Decentralisation was understood as the state relinquishing direct management of cultural matters and handing them over to lower administrative levels.'[101] This shift to a decentralised structure primarily means advantages for the theatres. They enjoy a greater autonomy. Funding on local and municipality levels increases. Theatres can make decisions regarding programme and financing largely independently, and institutions close ranks with their socio-cultural environment. Decentralisation also holds disadvantages for the theatres: the discrepancies and lack of clarity when the needs and concerns of the theatres are distributed over countless local and regional administrative levels, the lack of consistency regarding theatre-pertinent policies, and the lack of willingness of the political level responsible to administrate and support theatres efficiently. An additional difficulty results from the fact that authorities dealing with cultural and educational issues are usually persons who are mostly unfamiliar with artistic practice: 'It's a pity that cultural policy is increasingly being developed by professional 'culturologists' instead of experts from the individual fields of art.'[102] Lastly, there are communication problems and competition between the different theatre centres.

'Since the authorities resigned their control as a result of decentralization, everyone started looking for artistic freedom on their own, everybody started making their own contacts, their own space. We began to guard our own territory more than before [...].'[103]

---

100 | Questionnaire Bosnia-Herzegovina II.
101 | Paweł Płoski, "Introduction", p. 13.
102 | Questionnaire Czech Republic.
103 | Marek Waskiel, quoted in Paweł Płoski, "Introduction", p. 17.

Whereas the theatres in Slovenia, Croatia, the Czech Republic, Hungary, Poland, Romania, Serbia, Slovakia and the Ukraine are now decentrally organised, centralised and decentralised structures exist parallel to each other in Bulgaria and Bosnia-Herzegovina: 'In Bosnia and Herzegovina, which functions as an asymmetrical confederacy with undefined spheres of competence on the state level, centralist and decentralist tendencies clash with each other.'[104] In Belarus and Russia, on the other hand, centralised structures still prevail. A Belarusian independent director described the situation as follows: 'As for state culture politics – in my opinion, they haven't changed over the last 20 years. The government supports old traditional forms of culture that have existed for years.'[105]

As can be surmised from the individual analyses, the funding of independent theatre groups and artists differs greatly from country to country. The most important possibilities available will be mentioned here: First of all, there is financial support provided by the respective ministry of culture. It consists of project, long-term and short-term funding. Independent theatres and theatre makers can apply, whereby the countries also differ with regard to the prerequisites, the decision-making structures and the use of the funding. Second, financial support is also offered on the municipality or regional level. In this case, too, there are different provisions concerning the prerequisites and decision-making. Third, financial support can be obtained from large companies, such as Telekom, MasterCard and others. Fourth, private financing can also be obtained through individual sponsors, such as Marcel Iures in Romania or Vladimir Filippov in the Ukraine. Fifth, EU programmes such as Culture 2007, Kaleidoskop, Theorem, PHARE and Culture 2000 are also available. The prerequisite for an application is membership in the EU, which is not fulfilled by all of the countries mentioned here (Russia, Belarus, Bosnia-Herzegovina and the Ukraine are not members of the EU). International cultural organisations such as the Goethe Institute and the British Council also offer funding possibilities. Finally, there is the possibility of a partial financing through the sale of tickets. Sales revenues are usually quite low, so only a small supplement to some other form of financing is possible. Finally, international collaborations and networks provide the possibility of obtaining financial support. This form of financing has increased steadily in the past twenty years. It is an important perspective for independent theatres and is one aspect of international cooperation which will be dealt with later in this text.

In addition, three international foundations have been particularly important for the development of independent theatres in Eastern Europe for

---

104 | Ibid., p. 16.
105 | Questionnaire Belarus.

many years.[106] They concentrate their work exclusively on the region of the post-socialist states. The Swiss cultural foundation Pro Helvetia has maintained offices in Poland, Hungary, the Czech Republic and Slovakia since 1992. At first, the foundation was primarily concerned with promoting the democratic restructuring of culture in these countries. Since 1999, it has mainly supported cultural exchange. The Soros Foundation, founded at the beginning of the nineties by the American George Soros, has been coordinated by the Open Society in New York since 1994. The organisation focuses mainly on the Central and Eastern European countries, where the foundation maintains many branches. Besides socio-political and cultural activities, it supports cultural, economic and social reforms. The foundation was among the most important supporters of independent theatres and artists in the post-socialist countries. The Visegrád Foundation has promoted scientific and cultural cooperation among the Visegrád countries since its establishment in the year 2000. This also includes international collaborations. The foundation is an important promoter of independent theatres in the Visegrád Group.

3.2 Production and Presentation Conditions

Despite the existing funding possibilities, the production and performance conditions for independent groups and artists are precarious in all of the post-socialist countries. The established theatres are largely or entirely financed by the state and municipalities. In addition, they have permanent venues. In contrast, all independent theatres are financially unstable. Thus, there is no form of state subsidising available in the Ukraine to this date:

'It becomes worse and worse here in Ukraine. The government and politicians are not interested in the development of culture. They support public theatres very badly. They don't support independent companies at all. And there is no legislation of sponsorship. It is disadvantageous for sponsors to maintain a culture.'[107]

The independent theatres in Belarus have only received state support since 2010: 'In Belarus, private theatres still do not have any legal status, and it was not until 2010 that independent theatres gained some support from the government.'[108] A similar situation can be observed in the other post-socialist states. Thus, one of the responses on the questionnaire regarding the situation in Ro-

---

106 | For international foundations, see the respective homepages of Open Society Foundation, see http://www.opensocietyfoundations.org/; of Stiftung Pro Helvetia, see http://www.prohelvetia.ch/; and of Visegrád Fund, see http://visegradfund.org/.
107 | Questionnaire Ukraine I.
108 | Paweł Płoski, "Introduction", p. 21.

mania reads as follows: 'There is a big discrimination and lack of any support interest in awareness towards the importance of independent theatre from the part of the state and public structures.'[109] With regard to Serbia, one can read: 'Institutional, public theatres have a constant inflow of money, because of the state budget. They do not think about the problems of existence.'[110] The situation in Slovakia is described as follows: 'Independent theatre in Slovakia chronically suffers from underfinancing.'[111] The following is true for Bosnia-Herzegovina: 'We have to work hard on fund-raising, the public theatres don't have to do anything concerning the fund-raising.'[112] The report on Slovenia states: 'In public theatres everybody is getting regular salaries (including cleaning ladies) and they are not dependent on the programme; it is a direct transaction from the state.'[113] The situation in Croatia is described as follows: 'In Croatia the situation is similar: most independent theatres don't have their own space.'[114] The situation in the Czech Republic is equally grim: 'It is difficult for independent theatres to obtain grants. The outlook for independent theatres is therefore very uncertain and their continuous operation is not secured.'[115] The situation in Hungary is no different from that of the other countries: 'Recently the whole scene has been suffocating. The groups look for connections and collaboration to survive and help them out of this situation. But many of them must disappear.'[116]

The working conditions of independent groups and artists are characterised by three drawbacks. The first has already been presented in this chapter as well as in the previous country descriptions: Independent theatres in the post-socialist countries seldom have permanent venues or rehearsal rooms. Leasing premises is seldom a financial option for most groups. Not having their own stage means not being able to maintain regular contact with the audience, and this in turn means receiving far less public attention. This situation has a serious impact on a group's ability to receive funding, since a permanent venue is often a prerequisite for sponsoring. This is well exemplified by the independent theatres in Bosnia-Herzegovina:

'In Bosnia, the theatre policy for the Sarajevo Canton, while recognizing theatres as non-governmental organisations, nevertheless forces them to act under strict and

---

109 | Questionnaire Romania I.
110 | Questionnaire Serbia I.
111 | Questionnaire Slovakia II.
112 | Questionnaire Bosnia-Herzegovina I.
113 | Questionnaire Slovenia II.
114 | Paweł Płoski, "Introduction", p. 22.
115 | Questionnaire Czech Republic.
116 | Questionnaire Hungary I.

strange conditions. For example the policy states that it is necessary for a theatre to have an auditorium with seats fixed permanently to the floor.'[117]

Not having your own venue can also have positive aspects. The groups resort to performing in everyday locations such as cafés, galleries and factories, and in doing so create new space for art. They develop flexible structures, experiment with innovative spatial constellations, and enter into collaborations with other cultural institutions. These developments are characteristic of the independent theatres in the post-socialist countries.

The second drawback regarding the production conditions is the high administrative effort. Independent theatres were constantly forced to request funding, to formulate project applications, and to apply for financial support at home and abroad. Success is far from guaranteed. Often the waiting times are long, requests are refused and payments are delayed, making advanced financing necessary. The pressure on the theatres to continually come up with more and more innovative ideas indeed leads to a constant reflection of their own artistic position, but it also makes on-going work more difficult.

The third drawback related to working conditions concerns state repression and economic restrictions. With the end of socialism, the censorship which had hampered the work of independent theatres in Eastern European countries to varying degrees in the past was supposedly abolished. As a result, the names of authors who had been prohibited reappeared on theatre programmes, and independent theatres could now work with artistic processes and practices which had been forbidden. However, state censorship was not entirely done away with. It is still practiced in Belarus and Russia. In some other countries indirect restrictions are imposed on the work of independent theatres which go beyond the economic limitations already mentioned, and which manifest themselves in the form of censorship. The reason can be found in the strong dependence of independent theatres on their sponsors. A Bosnian independent artist describes the situation thus: 'There was a cultural minister of Canton Sarajevo who I criticized very much in public. The result was that he was cutting our funds for four years. It was another way of censorship.'[118] A Slovenian project, *My name is Janez Janša* (2007), was also affected by political interventions. Three independent artists joined the conservative Slovenian Democratic Party (SDS) and had their names officially changed to that of the incumbent party chairman and minister president, Janez Janša. In doing so, they aroused public interest:

---

117 | Paweł Płoski, "Introduction", p. 22.
118 | Questionnaire Bosnia-Herzegovina I.

'While they renamed themselves for personal reasons, the boundaries between their lives and their art began to merge in numerous and unforeseen ways. Signified as an artistic gesture, this particular name change provoked a wide range of interpretations in art circles both in Slovenia and abroad, as well as among journalists and the general public.'[119]

As part of the project, the artists produced the film of the same name, *My name is Janez Janša*. Although the production ended well, work was problematic because subsidies were not paid due to political pressure. In the words of a Slovenian critic: 'Sometimes the politicians [...] are producing the pressure directly or sometimes just indirectly with the financial procedures.'[120] In Serbia, the lecture performance *They live (in a search of text zero)*, from the year 2012 and performed by Maja Pelević and Milan Marković (and which will be described later) also experienced constraints.[121] The artists were prohibited from performing the piece in an established theatre. Censorship was imposed indirectly by depriving the artists of a venue. In particular, the independent theatres in Hungary are struggling under state repression and politically motivated decisions. As has been described, the measures in Hungary are not only aimed at the independent theatre groups but at the entire independent cultural scene.

3.3 Training

Until 1989/91, the artistic training of actors and directors was under a strong ideological influence.[122] Stanislawski's acting methodology was the most important basis for this training. Its psychological style was accepted from the political side. After the political upheavals at the end of the eighties and the beginning of the nineties, training centres for artists were forced to undergo further development. This did not succeed everywhere: the old hierarchical structures still prevail in some places, instructors still advocate the traditional theatre aesthetics, and experimental ideas regarding the theatre are given little notice. However, there are training centres which have changed their methods and teaching content. A prime example is the New Bulgarian University (NBU) in Sofia, which promotes collective work methods and experimental artistic

---

119 | *My name is Janez Janša*, see http://www.mynameisjanezjansa.com.
120 | Questionnaire Slovenia I.
121 | For the project *They live (in a search of text zero)*, see http://theyliveonline.wordpress.com/.
122 | For acting methodology, see also Manfred Brauneck, *Klassiker der Schauspielregie. Positionen und Kommentare zum Theater im 20. Jahrhundert* (Reinbek bei Hamburg: Rowohlt 1988).

processes. As stated in the chapter on Belarus, the actor and director Pavel Admatchikov provides important impulses for the independent theatres at the Belarusian State Academy of Arts in Minsk by teaching methods used in the theatre of movement. The young director Evgeny Kornyag seized these impulses and acted on them by founding the independent group Kornyag Theatre in Minsk together with students of the academy in 2011. In Prague, the academy Divadelní fakulta AMU v Praze (DAMU) provides a diverse programme which includes a department for experimental forms of theatre in puppetry, the Katedra alternativního a loutkového divadla.[123] In all the countries, there is no difference between the professional training of independent artists and the training of artists who work at institutionalised theatres: 'The separation of artists only comes after graduating.'[124] The majority of independent theatre makers complete a classical artistic training at a drama academy. Many independent theatres offer their own professional training and advanced training courses. The number of courses has increased in recent years:

'Due to the lack of funds and specific policies, professionals in the cultural field where there is a lack of education, are participating in different retraining programmes or courses to improve their professional skills, sporadically, usually under the initiative of foreign donors or NGOs. The programme varies in the quality, genres as well as the length of the education they offer. Shorter educational programmes are organised by many NGOs and have different formats such as: seminars, workshops, coaching's, lectures, talks, discussions. They are programming in the frame of festivals or not.'[125]

The courses give lateral entrants, career changers, newcomers, autodidacts, etc. the opportunity to learn more about artistic processes, to develop their own approaches, and to make new contacts. The workshops, seminars and forums offered by independent groups and artists supplement the usual professional training. Courses such as instruction in technical aspects, seminars on the basics of culture management, and training courses on administration develop skills in those areas which are missing in classical artistic training.

There are also cross-national professional training and advanced professional training projects offered by independent groups or artists. Great importance should be attributed to the project DESANT, initiated by Joanna Wichowska and Goran Injac. The project took place in the Ukraine in 2012 and later in Belarus. Representatives of the Teatr Les Kurbas from Ukraine, the Konfrontacje

---

123 | For all the training centres and initiatives of the Kornyag Theatre, see http://korniag-theatre.com/index.html; NBU, see http://www.nbu.bg/entrance.php?lang=1; Divadelní fakulta AMU v Praze, see http://www.damu.cz/.
124 | Questionnaire Hungary II.
125 | Questionnaire Slovenia I.

Teatralne Festival from Poland, the Slovensko mladinsko gledališče from Slovenia and the theatre Atelje 212 and the Beogradski Internacionalni Teatarski Festival, both from Serbia, offered seminars in Kiev. The subjects dealt with questions relating to the organisation and administration of independent theatre work, networking possibilities, and content concerning art, culture, society and politics. During the second part in Minsk, workshops lasting several days were organised for dramatic advisers, light and sound designers. The project DESANT represents the beginning of a series of training and advanced training programmes whose organisation is supported by the EEPAP. The variety of offers reflects the great importance that independent theatres in post-socialist countries attach to professional training.

'Education is fundamental for the independent theatre work. Being open, curious, imaginative, learning all the time, being well informed about what happens in the market, in the artistic world, makes one's work competitive, a good selling product. So independent work requires a good education and good education is best used in the quality of independent theatre work. As compared to public theatre, independent theatre can't survive if it's not of good quality. So education is a must from all points of view.'[126]

Professional training is considered a prerequisite for artistic work. It is an important quality criterion and is, in the end, a confirmation of one's own professionalism.

3.4 International Networking

The political upheavals in the years 1989-1991 made it possible for independent theatres in Eastern Europe to establish contact with the international theatre scene. As stated previously, up to that point only the Yugoslavian republics had been able to participate in international collaborations and organise festivals with guests from non-socialist countries. Now it was possible to travel abroad, to establish contact with foreign theatres, and to organise international festivals in all the Eastern European countries. Furthermore, a great number of organisations, networks and funding programmes cropped up which support this international exchange. Thus, independent theatres in the post-socialist countries have been able to build up more and more networks across national borders in the past 20 years.

Independent theatre groups and artists are participating more and more often in cultural sponsorship programmes offered by the EU, such as the

---

126 | Questionnaire Romania I.

programme Culture 2007-2013.[127] These programmes primarily sponsor international cooperation projects. However, it is not possible to apply for such support in all the countries. The independent theatres and artists in Romania and Bulgaria can hardly hope for the necessary local co-financing, which makes applying for such EU funding virtually impossible. Those countries, which do not belong to the European Union, are not eligible for such financing. They are only allowed to participate as partner organisations. However, they have taken advantage of the EU cultural programme Eastern Partnership since 2010. This programme supports the reform of cultural institutions and tries to pave the way for participation in regular EU cultural sponsorship programmes.

The networking of independent theatres manifests itself in the ever-increasing number of memberships in international organisations and networks. The International Network for Contemporary Performing Arts (IETM), with particular focus on the platform Balkan Express,[128] the Association Internationale du Théâtre pour l'Enfance et la Jeunesse (ASSITEJ), the Union Internationale de la Marionnette (UNIMA), the International Organisation of Scenographers, the Theatre Architects and Technicians (OISTAT), and the International Festivals & Events Association (EFEA) all represent forums used by independent groups and artists for international exchange. Above all, the frequently mentioned network East European Performing Arts Platform (EEPAP) promotes the development of independent performing arts in the post-socialist countries of Central and Eastern Europe. In 2010, as initiated by the Adam Mickiewicz Institute in Warsaw, the work of the network was focused on three areas: First,

---

127 | The EU cultural sponsorship programme Culture 2007-2013 expired at the end of 2013. Since 2014, the programme Creative Europe has taken over until the end of 2020, and with MEDIA and MEDIA Mundus also supports audiovisual projects. See Claudia Bruell, *Kreatives Europa 2014-2020. Ein neues Programm – auch eine neue Kulturpolitik? Studie des Instituts für Auslandsbeziehungen* (Stuttgart/Berlin: Edition für Kultur und Außenpolitik 2013), see http://www.ifa.de/fileadmin/pdf/edition/kreatives-europa_bruell.pdf.

128 | See IETM – International Network for Contemporary Performing Arts, see http://ietm.org/ietm-balkan-express. IETM is a membership organisation which especially supports the international networking of contemporary performing artists. The task of the organization is to improve the quality, development and general conditions for contemporary performing art. The Balkan Express was initiated by IETM. On this subject, the following can be found on the internet site of the platform: "Balkan Express is a platform that connects people interested in collaboration in and with the Balkans involved in contemporary art and complementary socially engaged practices. Balkan Express is a platform for reflection on the new roles of contemporary arts in a changing political and social environment. It builds new relations; encourages sharing and cooperation and contributes to the recognition of contemporary arts in the Balkans and wider."

the professional training of theatre artists is promoted and the international training programme DESANT is continued. Second, the platform supports the exchange of information among theatres. For this purpose, meetings and workshops are offered by means of the network. This focus also supports the internet site, through which theatre people can contact other members and inform themselves about upcoming events. Third, EEPAP supports international collaborations with its own residence programmes.

The many different international cooperation projects in which independent theatres in the post-socialist countries have participated in recent years not only indicate the great interest in international contacts. The difficult situation in these countries often makes a transnational artistic collaboration essential for survival because it helps them to financially secure their work – at least temporarily. It is important to mention that this is also true for collaborations with established theatres and with other groups in the respective country. The number of such collaborations has increased sharply in recent years. By means of international cooperation projects, the theatres and artists have often attained a greater degree of prominence abroad than in their own countries. This can be said of the directors Árpád Schilling, Kornel Mondruczó and Béla Pintér in Hungary, of the groups Belarus Free Theatre in Belarus and Foreman Brothers in the Czech Republic as well as of the directors Krzysztof Warlikowski and Gregorz Jarzyna in Poland. The international success also contributes to a greater acceptance and visibility in their own countries.

The high degree of international networking is especially evident within the festival culture. Even in the post-socialist countries it is possible to speak of a 'festival boom' that has developed in Europe in the last two decades. This distinctive festival culture is also referred to as a 'festivalisation of the cultural life of cities'[129].

'On the one hand, the multiplication of festivals is the result of the global tendency for this form of cultural activity to expand. On the other hand, authorities have responded to the needs of creators and consumers and consequently have started to support a variety of cultural initiatives. Festivals have proved to be the relatively easiest way to support due to their unique features (a limited and short duration, the accumulation of events) as well as being attractive for the promotion of cities, regions and, last but not least, politicians.'[130]

In the post-socialist countries, the festivals, which often include offers from several different artistic sectors, take place in urban centres as well as in more

---

129 | According to the sociologists John Hannigan, David Harvey, Maria-Louisa Laopoldi, Greg Richards and Julie Wilson, quoted by Paweł Płoski, "Introduction", p. 34.
130 | Ibid.

remote locations. For the independent theatres, they are important platforms on which they can present their artistic work, as can be seen in the following analyses of such performances. At the same time, the festivals are organised more and more often by the independent artists and groups themselves. The ACT Independent Theatre Festival in Sofia, the Mladi Levi Festival in Ljubljana, the INFANT-Festival in Belgrade, the Apostrof Festival in Prague, the KioSK Festival in Zilina, Slovakia, and the PUF Festival in Zagreb are only a few such initiatives. They bring the independent theatres international recognition, transcultural exchange and new networks and collaborations. It is becoming increasingly common for the festivals to include discussion forums and workshops on artistic methods or on the administrative and organisational framework conditions, and this contributes to the artistic quality of the events. Yet, there are also disadvantages which have emerged from this extensive festival culture. The programmes of such events are scrutinised critically. The independent groups and artists depend on the decisions of the respective organisers as to whether they may participate in the festival or not. In addition, the artistic work performed at a festival has almost no sustainable effect, because of the great number of performances staged in a relatively short period of time.

4. Exemplary Analyses

The following chapter presents individual independent groups and performances from different post-socialist countries. An important criterion for the selection of the performances is the artistic significance of the productions in the individual countries and their impact on the respective theatre scene in recent years. The selection is based on the statements made in interviews and in the questionnaires as well as on research conducted on site. The groups and performances presented here show the current spectrum of independent theatre work in the post-socialist countries. Three of the performances place a particular focus on musical elements. All the productions described in this chapter stand for current artistic trends which have developed in the countries. The exemplary analyses focus on presenting these trends in detail based on specific examples. They describe the artistic themes and processes in the productions and filter out the theatre practices which the various independent groups, despite their different socio-political contexts, have in common.

4.1 The Independent Groups *DramAcum* and *TangaProject* – Romania

In 2001, five young dramatists and directors founded the independent theatre group DramAcum (in English, DramaNow). The collective, located in Bukarest, was to make a decisive impact on the independent theatre scene in Romania in the following years. DramAcum is the most influential independent group in the country to this day.

'They were young, and coming with no communist background, bringing a very fresh perspective and way of writing. DramAcum is the first organization formed by directors that appeared with the purpose of finding new playwrights and offering them a place to experience and grow.'[131]

The founders of the group, the theatre makers Gianina Cărbunariu, Radu Apostol, Alex Berceanu, Andreea Vălean and Ana Margineanu, who are now all internationally known, had set an important goal for themselves: They wanted to bring Romanian theatre closer to developments which had taken place in the international theatre scene. The prerequisite for doing so was – according to DramAcum – to transform contemporary Romanian theatre into a theatre that 'depicts a cross-section of reality and neither chokes on metaphors nor hangs on a political hook'[132]. To achieve this goal, new artistic ways of working were necessary. The term 'cross-section of reality' was used by DramAcum to describe the fact that artistic work should be more strongly related to everyday subjects. The group understood its theatre as artistic practice which deals with social issues. With the cooperation of all those involved in the theatrical process, the group primarily addresses social problems and social reality. In addition, one can observe a reassessment of the role and the tasks of the dramatist. He is integrated in the rehearsal process and is also actively involved in designing the performance. His text is not considered a finished product; the finished product emerges out of the common production process.

Another feature of the work of DramAcum is the audience involvement in the happenings onstage. The audience is assigned a 'role' and actively takes part in the theatrical process. At the same time, using networking to make their work known beyond national borders is very important to the group. Thus, DramAcum has organised an internationally oriented competition for playwrights every year since 2002. The winner's text is performed in a

---

131 | Questionnaire Romania III.
132 | Mihaela Michailov, "Theater als Eingriff in den Alltag", in Marina Mazilu, Medana Weident and Irina Wolf (eds.), *Das rumänische Theater nach 1989*, pp. 109-114, here p. 111.

collectively developed production. These competitions help to promote young authors and focus attention on new plays. Furthermore, they make it possible for DramAcum to initiate partnerships with theatres in other countries, thereby establishing transnational networks.

The winner of the DramAcum competition in 2004 was Bogdan Georgescu. The dramatist, social activist and transmedial artist has had a significant impact on the Romanian independent theatre scene to this day. Motivated by the artistic projects of DramAcum, he founded the independent performance group TangaProject in 2005. Its members included the author Vera Ion and the directors Miruna Dinu, Iona Paun and David Schwartz, among others. DramAcum and the TangaProject are two of the most well-known independent groups in Romania.

The projects staged by TangaProject frequently take place in public spaces, using artistic means to point out social problems and initiate critical discussions. The aim of its artistic projects is to change society at its margins and make different strata in the population aware of the socio-political developments in their city. The residents can participate in the theatrical processes; they themselves become co-designers of the group's socio-cultural (city) projects:

'The TangaProject interventions enable a theatre of demonstration and reaction, a theatre that functions directly, that forces reality to discover weaknesses. The artists act as detectors of social problems which they document in order to then scrutinise them.'[133]

The artists pursued this aim in the 25-hour performance of *RahovaNonstop* in 2006. As a site-specific project, the performance was staged in the underprivileged neighbourhood in Bukarest known as Rahova-Uranus. The production dealt with the difficult situation in this part of the city and the lives of its residents. The performance presented the tentative result of research which had lasted one year. The artists had asked the residents to recount their biographies in public places in their neighbourhood. The stories were then documented by the group, rewritten as dramatic texts and then artistically revised and staged. In this way, short documentary performances of approximately ten minutes were produced based on these biographies. They were then presented one after another in the 25-hour performance.

The thematic focus of the documentary-fictional texts and the scenic presentations was the social situation in the Rahova district. During the performance, passers-by could randomly find themselves witness to a public speech being made by the mayor of Bukarest, who was apologising to the residents for the precarious situation in the neighbourhood. The audience reacted angrily with boos and catcalls. In the end, they dragged the mayor off

---

133 | Ibid., p. 113.

the stage. Following that, the TangaProject staged a public discussion to deal with the changes proposed by the residents to improve the living situation in the district. The fictional speech, which was part of the performance and based on the narratives of city residents, was so realistic that bystanders could not distinguish it from actual speeches that had been made by the mayor in the past. The audience's reactions were authentic. The performance and the ensuing discussion brought about the public debate which the director Bogdan Georgescu had hoped to trigger: 'Theatre is for me more than a product that can simply be consumed. With our theatre we create a neutral zone in which we can honestly discuss the really big problems and, at the same time, still enjoy the protection of the theatre convention.'[134]

The performance *RahovaNonstop* was part of the large-scale project *Offensive of Generosity Initiative*, which the TangaProject realised between 2006 and 2009. In those three years, the group organised discussion forums, workshops and artistic work to call attention to the impending eviction of residents in the Rahova district because their apartments had been sold to investors. The residents placed great trust in the group during this time:

'Their sincere interest (interest of the group TangaProject, author's note A.H.) in the lives of the residents which they demonstrated in the search for subjects for their documentary-fictional texts became apparent when one of the young authors was summoned to appear as a witness in the legal proceedings initiated by the residents against the government: Several buildings had been taken over by the state under the communist regime, and the city wanted to have the tenants of those buildings evicted who then, in effect, would have been homeless.'[135]

The socially critical theatre work in the project, *Offensive of Generosity Initiative*, also included improving the quality of life in the neighbourhood by, for example, replanting the Rahova Park. In order to make room for a big event in the mayoral election campaign, all of the trees in the park were cut down in 2005. What remained was a barren area with a few tree stumps which stuck out of the ground like gravestones. There was garbage everywhere. Plastic bottles,

---

134 | Bogdan Georgescu, quoted in Karl Wolfgang Flender, "Die Walnuss-Revolution. Wie die rumänische Theatergruppe TangaProject in Bukarest öffentlichen Raum mit Kunst zurückerobert", in *NEUE STÜCKE AUS EUROPA*, see http://newplays-blog.de/tag/tangaproject.

135 | Cristina Modreanu, "Ankunft im dritten Jahrtausend", in Marina Mazilu, Medana Weident and Irina Wolf (eds.), *Das rumänische Theater nach 1989*, pp. 115-122, here p. 111. For the project described here, see also *Offensive of Generosity Initiative*, see http://ofensivagenerozitatii.blogspot.de/2009/02/rahova-uranus-community-centre-labomba.html.

scrap glass and paper were 'the only spots of colour in front of the dirty grey backdrop of dilapidated urban apartment buildings'[136]. The park was hardly used. 'There isn't any money available to maintain the park, anyway'[137], was the response from city officials. A year later, in October 2006, many of the residents of the district congregated in the park accompanied by members of TangaProject. Residents and artists together began to collect and remove the garbage. They planted walnut trees to replace those which had been cut down by the city. The residents themselves revived the park. They reclaimed it as part of their own urban living space and subsequently used it as a public rehearsal and performance venue for artistic work with TangaProject.

The project *Build Your Community!* also emerged from the undertaking *Offensive of Generosity Initiative*. Following *RahovaNonstop*, the project group once again focused on the situation in the Rahova-Uranus district and its residents in 2007: 'The best part of this kind of work is that the last project always gives rise to the next one. Our group is developing and growing.'[138] The project *Build Your Community!* focused on several social groups in the district. It was about 'inhabitants of apartment buildings covered with advertising banners, the tenants of city-owned buildings, blood donors, the young people in a service project for juvenile delinquents in the district of Bukarest known as Titan'[139]. *Build Your Community!*, as a project in public urban space, used stories from the neighbourhood and reworked them for artistic presentation. In addition, the project included public discussion, drama workshops, creativity workshops for children and a visual archive of that part of the city and the surrounding area.

'TangaProject developed research techniques and procedures which were common to social theatre but which were largely unknown to the Romanian public. TangaProject created a quick-witted style of theatre which takes a clear stand, a theatre which is based on a two-fold joint construction: on the one hand a creative collective (dramatists, directors, actors), whose work requires a team analysis of the target groups, and, on the other hand, a collective which researches the socio-theatrical aspects.'[140]

The project *Build Your Community!* led to a concrete improvement in the quality of life in that district of the city. Shortly after the project ended, a community centre was founded in the neighbourhood. The artistic workshops organised by TangaProject still take place in Rahova.

---

136 | Karl Wolfgang Flender, "Die Walnuss-Revolution".
137 | Ibid.
138 | Bogdan Georgescu, quoted in Karl Wolfgang Flender, "Die Walnuss-Revolution".
139 | Mihaela Michailov, "Theater als Eingriff in den Alltag", p. 113.
140 | Ibid., p. 114.

Besides the socio-cultural projects described here, TangaProject is responsible for other initiatives, such as the programme *Radical Refresh*, which was developed in 2005 to promote young playwrights, or the trans-cultural German-Romanian music and theatre project *Muränien Muränien!* from 2012.[141] In addition, members of the group write and stage plays together, as can be seen in the following comments on the production *Romania! Kiss me!*

4.2 *Romania! Kiss me!* – Romania

Bogdan Georgescu and David Schwartz of the group TangaProject were responsible for the production of *Romania! Kiss me!* in 2010. The play was first performed in the Teatrul Naţional 'Vasile Alecsandri' Iaşi in Bukarest.

The figures in *Romania! Kiss me!* all have the same wish: They want to leave Romania as soon as possible. There is a 20-year-old female student with the boy's name 'Vasile' who would like to continue her studies in the USA with a scholarship from the Soros foundation; the paranoid pensioner, Miss Renata, who has invited herself to stay with her relatives in Germany along with her cat; and the unemployed alcoholic, Mr Neagoe, who has worked illegally to earn enough money to leave the country. The three of them meet by chance in a train compartment. A rivalry develops in which each tries to prove that he or she has the better reasons for wanting to leave Romania. The three figures cite clichés and stereotypes which they immediately recant. Their attachment to their home country clashes with the 'exaggerated utopian vision of a better life in the West'[142]. Their hopes conflict with fear and self-hatred, and everything ends in a tragicomedy. All of them fail in their attempts to leave the country; all three stay in Romania.

An important artistic element in the performance is a chorus-like orchestra which one critic described as follows: 'Five figures dressed in black overalls who, as the text informs us, generate the soundtrack and the 'olfactory framework'

---

141 | For the projects *Radical Fresh, Muränien Muränien!* and *Muränien Muränien!*, see http://muraenien.wordpress.com; Art Act Magazine, see http://artactmagazine.ro/participative-dramaturgy-tangaproject-radical-refresh.html.

142 | Gesellschaft Freunde der Künste, "Drei Rumänen möchten so schnell wie möglich raus - România! Te pup Rumänien! Küss mich", see http://www.freundederkuenste.de/empfehlung/theater-und-premieren/buehne/drei-rumaenen-moechten-so-schnell-wie-moeglich-raus-romania-te-pup-rumaenien-kuess-mich.html. For the play's contents, see also Saviana Stanescu and Daniel Gerould (eds.), *roMANIA after 2000. Five new Romanian Plays* (New York: Martin E. Segal Theatre Center 2007); *NEUE STÜCKE AUS EUROPA 2010*: play description see http://www.newplays.de/index.php?page=archive&content=archive_2010&content_sub=archive_2010_parts&id_event_cluster=542809.

and, quite incidentally, also provide narrative comments on the plot.'[143] The orchestra assumed a number of different tasks. Its sounds accompanied the appearance of the individual figures, the meeting and the failure of the three protagonists. Furthermore, the orchestra was always present. For the audience, the orchestra visually defined the stage area, assumed minor roles, and revealed the theatrical process.

Figure 4: 'Romania! Kiss me!', Teatrul Național, 'Vasile Alecsandri' Iași. Bucharest, 2010. Photograph: Catalin Gradinariu

A separate audience area. An empty stage. Only the 'instruments' of the orchestra could be seen on the ramp: plastic bottles, tin cans, empty canisters, drumsticks, glasses, cups, silverware and kitchen graters. The orchestra sat on the stage, directly facing the audience. The orchestra observed the audience, even stared at the audience, so that the audience could not avoid the stares and the feeling of being watched. It was impossible for the audience to remain passive and uninvolved under the constant scrutiny of the five musicians in black overalls. The tables were turned. The audience was not watching but being watched. A duplicity of looks: seeing and being seen, looking and being looked at. Looking at the orchestra suddenly became, for the members of the audience, the same as looking at themselves.

The appearances of each of the three protagonists were directed by the orchestra. Vasile, Miss Renata and Mr Neagoe stood on rolling pedestals which were pushed to the middle of the stage by a member of the orchestra. The setting for the three protagonists was only suggested by a few props. The actors

---

143 | Jakob C. Heller, "Bis zur letzten Nase", in *NEUE STÜCKE AUS EUROPA*, see http://newplays-blog.de/2010/06/19/bis-zur-letzten-nase/.

themselves remained static on their pedestals while members of the orchestra moved about to position and exhibit them.

The orchestra determined the rhythm and structure of the performance. It influenced the plot by means of the constant interaction with the protagonists and by playing minor roles. Two other sensory elements were also employed: The 'instruments' created noises, sounds, rhythms and melodies, and odours also played a role in the performance. During a scene on the train, two members of the orchestra began cutting garlic, onions and bacon in parallel to the other action on stage. The odours filled the room. One could also smell canned fish, perfume and alcohol. A ventilator carried the mixture of odours to the area where the audience was seated, so they could not escape the smells and were virtually overwhelmed by fascination or disgust. There was no longer a separation of stage and audience, of production sphere and reception sphere. The audience was integrated into the theatrical process. In the process, they were mostly confronted with their own clichés concerning apparently typical Romanian smells. The audience could see (and in this case, smell) the clichés, and this brought about the desired confrontation with the everyday life that was being portrayed on stage. This is what the theatre makers hoped to achieve. In their own words, they wanted to 'create an atmospherically dense, sensory reproduction of everyday life in Romania'[144].

Figure 5: 'Romania! Kiss me!', Teatrul Național,'Vasile Alecsandri' Iași. Bucharest, 2010. Photograph: Catalin Gradinariu

---

144 | Ibid.

The play *Romania! Kiss me!* was conceived as a transcultural performance.[145] Transcultural means a cultural practice which annuls the concept of an alleged 'own' versus an alleged 'other'. The audience realises that what one considers 'one's own' is permeated with what one might consider foreign, and, vice versa, what is foreign may sometimes contain what is 'one's own'. In *Romania! Kiss me!*, transculturality is demonstrated by the acoustic and olfactory elements which make what is 'foreign' a sensory experience which one can then accept as one's own. The constant exchange of visual contact between the orchestra and the audience also contributed to this effect. Looking at the 'other' became a look at oneself.

The successful production was performed many times in translation both in and outside of Europe. In 2010, the group was invited to perform the piece at the theatre biennial Neue Stücke aus Europa in Wiesbaden.

4.3 *Reasons to be Happy* – Slovenia

The performance *Reasons to be happy* premiered in Ljubljana in December 2011. It was performed in the theatre Gledališče Glej, already mentioned in this text as the oldest non-institutional theatre in Slovenia and an important venue for experimentation for independent theatres. The former head of the Gledališče Glej, Jure Novak, developed the production as director together with the performer Katarina Stegnar and the dramatic adviser and translator Urška Brodar. What is remarkable about the performance is the unique concept of space and the unusual way of presenting the figure of the performer and the audience. The performance deals with the subject of depression. It investigates the relationship between the individual's mental illness and society's expectations of the individual.

'It is our duty to be happy. Happy men, women and children on posters and in TV ads constantly show us easy ways to be happy. What is happiness, apart from its chemical makeup? Why is it so high on the ladder of contemporary values? And furthermore – why is happiness the only value that is not called into question that is inherently good? Have you felt bad in the past month, have you felt depressed, sad, tormented or even hopeless? Have you been finding it hard to do things you usually enjoy doing? We have the solution: Jure Novak: Reasons to be happy is a performance about depression, the performance for you. If you buy a ticket now, you will also receive instant gratification. Offer valid while supplies last.'[146]

---

145 | See Günther Heeg, *Das transkulturelle Theater* (Berlin: Theater der Zeit, 2014).
146 | Reasons to be happy. Programme description see http://www.glej.si/en/events/performances/144/128/jure-novak-reasons-to-be-happy.

The performance focuses on the constructed biography of the director, Jure Novak – a kind of 'acting identity'. The figure Jure Novak grew up in Slovenia and was diagnosed with cancer at the age of twelve. Jure Novak can be cured of the illness, but he loses the ability to feel happy. No therapy or other attempts to counteract this have worked. Jure Novak loses his job and social contacts. Subsequently, Jure Novak is completely ostracised. Not until he is treated by the Swiss physician Dr Durani is there hope for improvement. Following the little-researched scientific assumption that emotions are triggered by chemical processes in the body and that these are mechanically controllable, an implant is placed in the emotional centre of Jure Novak's brain. However, the treatment fails, and Jure Novak does not regain the ability to feel happiness. Jure Novak cannot return to the community. Yet, Dr Durani again gives him hope. New medical procedures make it possible to influence emotions extraneously. A device is set so that Jure Novak can decide by pressing a button when he would like to feel positive, negative or neutral. The method is successful. Jure Novak can once again fulfil social conventions; family and friends, his social environment, welcome him back into the fold.

In comparison with other Eastern European countries, Slovenia has an extraordinarily high suicide rate, which can frequently be traced back to depression.[147] There is a lack of therapeutic facilities and psychological counselling. Furthermore, society as a whole suppresses any concern with the illness, which makes treatment difficult. The performance *Reasons to be happy* portrays this pressing problem onstage. It deals with the relationship between the individual and society, between mental illness and social norms. The sociocritical discourse forces the audience to come to grips with this issue.

The artistic process of the performance also challenges the audience to become actively involved. The audience is confronted with a theatre space which does not correspond with the usual arrangement. The separation between audience and stage is eliminated. Audience and actors share the stage with each other. In the middle of the stage, there is a spartanly furnished kitchen with storage shelves containing plates, pots, glasses, pans, seasonings and provisions. Next to it, one can see armchairs and side tables which were apparently bought at the Swedish furniture store Ikea. Articles of clothing and books lie strewn on the floor, among them literature by Sarah Kane, Edgar Allan Poe and Franz Kafka.

---

147 | See European Radio Network: "Hohe Selbstmordrate in Slowenien", see http://www.euranet.eu/ger/Dossiers/Euranet-Schwerpunkte/Depressionen-in-Europa/Hohe-Selbstmordrate-in-Slowenien; Foundation for Depression Relief, see http://www.deutsche-depressionshilfe.de/stiftung/9751.php.

*Figure 6: 'Reasons to be happy', Gledališče Glej, Ljubljana, 2011.
Photograph: Urška Boljkovac*

As the members of the audience, whose number does not exceed 15, enter the room, they are received by Jure Novak. They are greeted with a handshake, kindly requested to put on slippers and asked to take a seat in the armchairs. As 'host' and only actor in the performance, Jure Novak describes his/a fictional life story. While doing so, he does not attempt to portray a role or a figure. He continually refers to his own person and, in doing so, verifies the authenticity of his presentation. Yet, he does not present only himself. He stages himself; he creates an 'acting identity' which is in contrast with reality. The performance is about staging oneself. A state of tension exists between the acting identity and the alleged authenticity. Seemingly authentic, Novak nevertheless remains a performer – a figure in an artistic setting. While speaking, Novak cooks for the audience and involves it in the plot. He asks individual participants for help, distributes questionnaires on the symptoms of depression, sits down next to an audience member and strikes up a conversation with them. Members of the audience cannot withdraw from the happenings, nor can they simply assume the role of observers. In fact, Jure Novak himself becomes a participant who, in the theatrical process, appears simultaneously as a spectator and an actor. As a member of the temporary community, he is assigned an important role. The end of the performance reemphasises this sense of belonging. The audience does not applaud, and the actor takes no bow. Jure Novak takes a seat among the participants as the doors are opened. The discussions continue; the boundaries between player and audience become increasingly blurred.

The production has been performed in Ljubljana for two years and so far has been extremely well received. It has been invited to numerous festivals, such as the PRELET Overflight Theatre Festival 2012 in Ljubljana, the DRUGAJANJE

Contemporary Arts Festival 2012 in Maribor, Slovenia, and the IMPACT International Theatre Festival 2012 in Veles in Macedonia.

4.4 *They Live (in Search of Text Zero)* – Serbia

The lecture-performance *They live (in search of text zero)* came about in spring of 2012 and was based on a concept of the independent Serbian theatre makers Maja Pelević and Milan Marković.[148] Maja Pelević was born in Belgrade in 1981 and studied dramatic writing there. During her doctoral work, she took courses held by Richard Schechner. She still lives in Belgrade and ranks among the leading representatives of contemporary Serbian drama. Her texts have been performed in Germany, Croatia, Slovenia, Russia and Montenegro. The focus of her writing can be described as follows: 'Pelević's post-dramatic texts describe the attitude towards life of a generation which, thanks to modern technologies, is connected to the entire world and has access to all kinds of stimuli – and yet at its core is in danger of being lonely and isolated.'[149] Milan Marković is one of Serbia's most famous young playwrights. He was born in Belgrade in 1978 and has worked as a playwright on German, Slovenian, Croatian and Danish theatre productions. His texts have been translated into different languages and performed in England.

The performance *They live (in search of text zero)* is based on a text which shifts between fact and fiction. The space where fact and fiction mix is the focus of the performance. In February 2012, Pelević and Marković joined the seven largest political parties in Serbia. When registering, they truthfully stated that they were theatre makers:

'[...] Milan Marković and Maja Pelević became members of seven leading parties in Serbia: the Democratic Party of Serbia, the United Regions of Serbia, the Social Democratic Party, the Democratic Party, the Liberal Democratic Party, the Serbian Progressive Party, and the Socialist Party of Serbia.'[150]

As members, they presented a programme for culture marketing to the parties called 'Idea-Strategy-Movement'. It received broad-based support. As gratifying as this positive reaction was at first glance, the more irritating it proved to be at

---

148 | For the biographies and artistic work of both theatre makers, see also Contemporary Performance Network, http://contemporaryperformance.org/profile/Milan Markovic?xg_source=activity; Portrait of Maja Pelevic, in: Nachtkritik/Spielbetriebe, http://nachtkritik-spieltriebe3.de/index.php?option=com_content&view=article&id=128&Itemid=43&lang=de.
149 | Portrait of Maja Pelević.
150 | *They live (in search of text zero)*.

second glance: The programme was not based on the ideas of the two theatre makers. On the contrary, the idea was taken from one of the writings of Joseph Goebbels entitled 'Erkenntnis und Propaganda' (English: 'Enlightenment and Propaganda') which was published in 1928. Pelević and Marković had only changed three words in the text. Instead of 'Adolf Hitler', they had inserted the name of the respective Serbian party chairman. The words 'national socialism' had been replaced by the word 'democracy', and the term 'propaganda' had been replaced by 'political marketing'. Not one single party official noticed the origin of the manifest. In fact, the programme was received with great enthusiasm:

'The leaders of the parties liked the text so much that the two protagonists, who introduced themselves with their real identities, immediately became members of cultural boards and councils in the majority of the selected parties, and in some of them they were even shortlisted for the leading positions in Belgrade theatres.'[151]

The lecture-performance *They live (in search of text zero)* presents this project. It describes how the idea originated, presents excerpts from conversations with party politicians, and shows the reactions of party members. The performance aimed to expose how powerful the political parties in Serbia are and to critically examine their clientelism. Thus, one can read in the description of the performance: 'If you are not a member of a party, you are nothing. Become a member, this is your only chance.'[152]

The significance of this statement can be seen in terms of the performance itself. Indeed, the parties ignored the situation when the project was revealed. However, the public performance of the staged reading proved to be difficult. The premiere was first planned to take place in the Jugoslovensko Dramsko Pozorište, a state-subsidised theatre in Belgrade. A few days before the premiere date, the theatre management cancelled the performance because of an alleged lack of artistic innovation and serious provocation. As a result, the premiere took place in the cultural centre Dom Omladine in Belgrade in April 2012.

'The public reading of They Live was supposed to take place on 17 March, 2012, at the Yugoslav Drama Theatre. On 15 March the authors were informed that the reading was being postponed and they were invited to present the text to the management. After that the reading was cancelled.'[153]

In the following months, the performance was staged in many independent venues, such as the Gledališče Glej in Ljubljana and the Kaserne in Basel, at the

---

151 | Jelesijević, Nenad: "Into the Paradox", in: They live (in search of text zero).
152 | They live (in search of text zero).
153 | Ibid.

annual theatre festival Borštnikovo srečanje in Maribor and at the Beogradski Internacionalni Teatarski Festival (BITEF) in Belgrade. It was at this event that Pelević and Marković were surprisingly given permission to hold the lecture-performance on the premises of the Belgrade city council. On this occasion, the authors added a venue-related prologue and epilogue to their performance.

Figure 7: 'They live (in search of text zero)', Gledališče Glej, Ljubljana, 2011. Photograph: Janko Oven

In the municipal hall, the audience found itself in very prestigious rooms furnished with sparkling chandeliers, marble columns and chairs upholstered in red velvet. For the performance, a table had been placed in the middle of the room so that when seated at the table the performer would face the luxurious interior. Behind the table there were Serbian flags, the municipal coat of arms of the city of Belgrade and two projection screens. Everything seemed to be arranged for a festive event. Maja Pelević and Milan Marković entered the room dressed in black and wearing dark sunglasses. They seated themselves at the table and opened the presentation by reading out the prologue. In it they described the biography of Dragomir Dragi Jovanović, the mayor of Belgrade from 1941 to 1944, who had maintained strong ties to the Nazis. With the figure of Jovanović, they established a connection to the text by Joseph Goebbels. The instructions regarding culture marketing were the focus of the second part of the performance. They were either read out or a recording was played which was highlighted by projected images. Any changes in the original text were indicated. Excerpts from conversations with the politicians and their reactions when they were informed of the true origin of the programme for culture marketing were presented. Finally, the reflections of the two artists were discussed. A text collage emerged which was composed of different voices and different qualities and characteristics of speaking and writing. At the end of the performance, current political measures taken by the Belgrade municipal government and the resulting social grievances were made the subject of discussion. In the epilogue, images and texts appeared on the screens which documented the forced eviction of a Roma settlement in the city, presented its consequences and questioned the political decisions behind it:

'April 2012. The eviction of the Roma near the Belvil estate is coming to an end. Instead of 40 families as announced, the city authorities suddenly evict 250 families located in the range of the access roads. City employees, equipped with hygienic gloves, help the Roma to pack their belongings and enter buses, each of which have one of the five locations written on it. Most of the locations are far away from the places where the residents work, exercise social and health care rights or send their children to school. On top of that, the newly established settlements become targets of attacks by masked Nazis and unmasked neighbours. In the new Jabučki Rit settlement, only a week after the eviction, Roma are attacked by a group of Nazis with baseball bats shouting such slogans as: 'Serbia to the Serbs' and 'Get out'. Regarding the attacks in Resnik, the Mayor of Belgrade declares: 'We are aware that citizens are afraid of the arrival of those who used to steal water, electricity and other things [...]'.'[154]

At the end of the performance, the focus was once again placed on the politicians responsible. A photograph of the incumbent mayor, Dragan Đilas, was shown. In doing so, the presentation closed the circle by returning to the starting point of the performance.

The performance *They live (in search of text zero)* aimed to use artistic means to examine the social, political and cultural reality of the country. The theatre makers first intervened in the political scene and then negotiated this intervention in their presentation. In doing so, they connected historical events in Serbia with current political structures and decisions. The two players wanted to stimulate a broad political discussion. That is why part of their concept included the documentation and public presentation on the internet of the origin and development of the lecture-performance: 'Given the fact, that the presentation is available online – that is, it is freely accessible to anyone – the political image of the event as a whole is completed.'[155]

4.5 *Lili Handel* – Bulgaria/The Netherlands/Belgium

The actor, choreographer, dancer and performance artist Ivo Dimchev is one of the most well-known independent artists in the dance and performance theatre

---

154 | Ibid.
155 | Nenad Jelesijević, "Into the Paradox".

scene in Bulgaria.¹⁵⁶ He was born in Sofia in 1976, studied performing arts at the Dasarts Academy in Amsterdam, and has been an artist-in-residence at the Kaaitheater in Brussels since January 2013. In addition to his artistic activities, Dimchev is also a guest lecturer at the University of Theatre and Film Arts in Budapest, at the Royal Dance Conservatory of Belgium in Antwerp and at the Hochschule der Künste in Bern. In 2004, he founded the cultural organisation NeMe Humarts in Sofia, and annually organises a competition for contemporary choreography under its auspices. Dimchev's performances are characterised by transmedial work methods. He combines elements from dance, theatre, performance, fine arts, music and photography on stage. Dimchev frequently appears as a solo performer. A radical approach to his own body and an almost oppressive closeness of the player to the audience distinguish his work:

'His performances are marked by an intense emotional and personal presence, in his rough and therefore extremely powerful impulses, outbursts, different states that border the human and the animalistic, normalcy and madness. This overwhelming energy is placed on the stage through the highly sophisticated technique of the well-trained body, the cultivated voice, precise choreography.'¹⁵⁷

The performance, *Lili Handel – Blood Poetry and Music from the White Whore's Boudoir,* celebrated its premiere in Stockholm in 2004. The performance centred around the biography of Lili Handel, an ageing diva once famous, popular and loved, who found herself at the end of her career facing old age. The performance not only presented the past life of the diva by means of the spoken word. Instead, the figure used her body to tell the story of her long-outlived glory days. At the moment of decline, the masquerade ended and the figure exposed itself. She recalled individual stages and situations in her life. Physical and temporal transience was demonstrated with a shocking intensity.

Entering the stage area in the House of Dance in Stockholm to watch the 40-minute solo performance, the audience found itself in a conventional setting. Auditorium and stage were clearly separated from each other. The stage was dark and practically empty. Only the silhouettes of individual props and pieces of furniture were visible. In the dim light a shabby old armchair was visible on

---

156 | For Ivo Dimchev and his artistic work, see also the homepage of Ivo Dimchev, see http://www.ivodimchev.com/index.htm; Archiv mime centrum berlin: Ivo Dimchev. Lili Handel – blood, poetry and music from the white whore's boudoir, see http://archiv.mimecentrum.de/video/show/3132; Woetzinger, Julia, "Come on. Do something!", in *Kulturen. Das Online-Magazin der KulturjournalistInnen an der UdK Berlin,* see http://194.95.94.164/wordpress/2012/12/come-on-do-something.

157 | Mira Todorova, *Body, Identity, Community,* p. 9.

which a leather cowboy hat was lying. On the right, the audience could make out the silhouette of a tuba. The remains of a red velvet curtain were hanging on the left side of the stage, reminiscent of an artist's life long past.

Gradually the stage was illuminated. The sound of soft and high-pitched singing whose source could not be identified as male or female could be heard from offstage. The irritation continued when, as the illumination became brighter and the voice became louder and shriller, the figure appeared on the stage: Ivo Dimchev as his 'alter ego' Lili Handel or Lili Handel as a bald-headed naked man – only dressed in a string tanga made of beads and with a beads necklace wrapped around his head – teetered onto the stage in black high heels. The striking masculine face was a mask of white makeup, red lipstick and black mascara. The gender of the figure could not immediately be determined. Since the figure was not wearing anything but a tanga and jewellery, attention was focused on the asexual and faceless body around which the performance centred.

'We are presented with an alien creature whose face looks as artificial as a masque of porcelain, a musician whose only instrument is his own body. We are witnessing the tragic and final outcome of a body that is both naked and helpless, shows signs of emotional torture, yet is beautiful.'[158]

Short individual scenes from the life of Lili Handel followed, but they did not represent a chronological narration of a life story. Up to the end of the performance, the audience did not know who or what was behind the feminine name Lili Handel. Yet, Dimchev impressively portrayed the biography and physical decline using the physicality of his figure. The once-clear voice of the diva could only bring forth croaking sounds reminiscent of eunuchs singing. While play-acting, Lili Handel told of legendary deeds which she claimed to be her own experiences. 'She' put on props, such as a fur coat, a cowboy hat and a wig, only to immediately lay them aside again. The brief phases in costume were quickly followed by a demasking. Lili Handel repeated dance steps, quoted gestures and implied movements which she abruptly broke off. The muscular body reared up once again; it danced, ran and jumped, then suddenly sank into the armchair, fragile, exhausted and breathless. Loud bass tones shook the naked body and caused it to twitch and jerk to the point of exhaustion. The pain and decline of the figure were exhibited. They were not only visible but could actually be felt by the audience, because it was hardly possible for the spectators to escape the proximity and physicality of the figure.

A compelling interplay of seduction, pain and self-obliteration unfolded before the audience. The members of the audience were called on in many

---

158 | Tamal Jaszay, "Lili Handel", in homepage Ivo Dimchev.

ways to subject themselves to a process of (personal) reflection: through the visible physical decline of the figure and its projection on oneself; through the simultaneous meeting of masquerade and exposure, closeness and distance; and finally through the physical transgression of boundaries by the performer. In a review, the curator Renate Klett describes the performance as follows: 'The performance is characterised by a perverse frankness; you can love it or hate it – but you cannot escape it.'[159] During the performance, blood was actually drawn on stage. Lili Handel tied off her upper arm, took a syringe and drew a vial of blood from the vein in the crook of her arm. This was then auctioned off to members of the audience in small doses. By literally selling her own blood, she questioned the (selling) value of art and that of the (aging) human body in society and in today's art scene.

'Ivo Dimchev's powerful solo exposes the body as a multi-expressive reality. It reminds us that the body is not merely a form, to be perceived mainly visually, but that it has a constitutive inside. Dimchev extends this interiority to the audience by all means, voice, movement, speech and even his blood, and engages them viscerally.'[160]

Since its premiere, the production has received numerous awards and invitations for guest appearances in other European countries, such as Belgium, France, Germany, Great Britain, Italy and Switzerland.

4.6 *Szutyok* – Hungary

Béla Pintér is one of the most famous playwrights, directors and actors in the independent theatre scene in Hungary. He was born in Budapest in 1970. Towards the end of the eighties, he worked artistically for the first time as a member of the independent group Arvisura. Pintér had no professional artistic training but started work in the theatre as a lay actor. He established many contacts to other independent groups and artists and founded his own group, Pintér Béla és Társulata (Béla Pintér & Company), at the Szkéne Theatre in Budapest in 1998. Composed of professional and lay actors, the company achieved an international breakthrough at the beginning of the millennium. Since then, they have appeared at countless festivals in Germany, such as NEUE STÜCKE AUS EUROPA in Wiesbaden, euro-scene in Leipzig, the Berliner Festspiele or the Laokoon Festival Kampnagel in Hamburg. The group has also given guest performances in other European countries, such as the Chapter Arts Centre in Cardiff or at the Festival d'automne in Paris.

---

159 | Renate Klett, "Es fließt Blut!", in *Zeit Online*, see http://www.zeit.de/2012/18/KS-Dimchev.
160 | Guru Ertem, quoted in homepage Ivo Dimchev.

Béla Pintér's performances deal with socially critical issues. Artistically, he works with texts, dance elements and music.

'In his plays, Pintér often holds up a mirror to society. With music he is able to open more theatrical dimensions and, for this purpose, uses Hungarian film music from the forties, reminiscences of late-romantic opera, recitatives accompanied by cembalo from baroque operas and very often Hungarian folk music and dances which are used in an unusual and ironic way.'[161]

Music is an important medium in Pintér's work. Its sources can mainly be found in Hungarian folklore, the opera, and film music. Music is not only used as background music or to accentuate what is happening on stage. Pintér uses music as its own dramaturgical medium. He removes pieces of music from their original context and places them – sometimes remixed – in a different context. The music in his performances confounds the audience and loudly interrupts what is happening onstage.

Such is the case in the production of *Szutyok* (*Bastard*) from the year 2012.[162] The play is about a young farmer and his wife, Attila and Irén, from the Hungarian province, who wish to have a child. Because Irén is infertile, the couple decides to adopt. Since the waiting time for a baby seems very long, they decide on the spur of the moment to adopt the 15-year-old Rószi, who is better known in the municipal orphanage as 'bitch'. Rószi can only be adopted together with Anita, a girl of the same age and 'exactly what they did not want: a Roma'[163], as it says in the description of the play. The young parents return to their village with the two teenagers. At first, life together seems harmonious, and music underlines the portrayal of this harmonious co-existence:

'The happenings on stage are accompanied and commented on by a bare-foot flautist who is seated in the background on a perch. There is a lot of singing and music-playing in this play, anyway, folklore by which we should not be fooled: for this is no provincial farce.'[164]

---

161 | *NEUE STÜCKE AUS EUROPA 2012*: Pintér Béla és Társulata, see http://www.newplays.de/index.php?page=events&content=events_program&id_event_cluster=849037.
162 | See Hessisches Staatstheater Wiesbaden (ed.), Béla Pintér, *Miststück*. Play text. Published for the festival, *NEUE STÜCKE AUS EUROPA*, 14 -24 June 2012, pp. 1-104; Theaterformen: Pintér Béla és Társulata – *Miststück*, see http://www.theaterformen.de/Theaterformen_2011/miststueck/.
163 | Romanodialog: Pintér Béla és Társulata, see http://www.romanodialog.org/ZTS%202012%20Bela%20Pinter.pdf.
164 | Esther Boldt, "Gemeinschaft der Verlotterten", in *Nachtkritik*, see http://www.nachtkritik.de/index.php?option=com_content&view=article&id=5819%253Aszuty

However, the seemingly idyllic family life begins to crumble and gives way to reveal the power structures and plight of society. The two girls, initially inseparable, become the worst of enemies. The girls' egotism and greed are now coupled with xenophobia, opportunism and a total lack of empathy for each other. The folk music sounds increasingly twisted and distorted, and is mixed with other musical styles such as pop songs. As in other productions, everyday life is made visible in this performance. It reflects 'the here and now of Hungarian society'[165]. Yet, at the same time, the play could be about any other postmodern society.

4.7 *Magnificat* – Poland

Another example of developments in the independent theatre scene in the post-socialist countries which demonstrates an increased use of musical elements is Marta Górnicka's Warsaw group Chór Kobiet. Górnicka, an independent musician, singer and director, was born in Warsaw in 1986. She completed her studies in vocal music and theatre direction at the Theatre Academy in Warsaw. In 2009, she founded her own women's choir. The Chór Kobiet is made up of 23 women of different ages, backgrounds and occupations. In workshops which began in January 2010 and included intensive movement and vocal training, the group worked out its first performance, *This is the chorus speaking: only 6 to 8 hours, only 6 to 8 hours*. The production celebrated its premiere in Warsaw at the Instytut Teatralny on 13 June 2010 and received the award as the 'Music Theatre Production of the Year 2010' in Poland.

The women's choir deals with three important themes in its performances. The choir occupies itself with old texts, myths and songs: '[...] it recalls Polish songs, forgotten drama texts, as well as chorus songs from ancient dramas'[166]. The choir also experiments with the human voice: '[...] it searches for a chorus voice detached from the language, for example in rhythms, echolalia or in a drone'[167]. A third focus is placed on a presentation of gender issues. The aim of the choir is to give women's voices more strength, and in doing so the choir hopes to stimulate an examination of gender equality in contemporary society. This is clearly demonstrated in the production *Magnificat*, which was developed in January 2011: 'The second project, *Magnificat*, is a statement on the role of women in the power system of the church – and, in the process of making this statement, it completely foregoes using sacred language/holy

---

ok-miststueck-nbela-pinter-schockt-bei-den-theaterformen-mit-zeitgenoessischer-gefuehlsverkommenheit&catid=623%253Atheaterformen&Itemid=99.
165 | Theaterformen: Pintér Béla és Társulata – *Miststück*.
166 | Chór kobiet, see http://www.chorkobiet.pl/en/page/1/.
167 | Ibid.

words. It is a post-opera which makes a polyphonic, pocultural [sic!] Magnificat possible.'[168]

Figure 8: 'Magnificat', Instytut Teatralny, Warsaw, 2011.
Photograph: Marta Ankiersztejn

The twenty-three women in the choir stood facing the audience during the performance of *Magnificat*. They spoke rhythmically, whispered, hissed and broke into sacral-sounding singing. While doing so, they frequently varied their arrangement with each other and their gestures and postures. They recited texts by Elfriede Jelinek, Adam Mickiewicz and Judith Butler. Excerpts from Euripides' 'The Bacchae', biblical quotations, advertising slogans, current newspaper articles and cooking recipes were also recited. A sound emerged which was composed of individual voices with different qualities and characteristics of speaking. This mixture of texts and voices was used to present the role of women in society and in the church.

The performance *Magnificat* received the award from the Polish theatre magazine, Teatr, as the best Polish alternative theatre performance of the season 2010/2011. The choir was invited to perform the production at many theatre festivals throughout Europe, such as the theatre festival Malta in Poznán, the international theatre festival MESS in Sarajevo and the euro-scene in Leipzig.

---

168 | Ringlokschuppen Mülheim an der Ruhr: Programme description Magnificat, see http://www.ringlokschuppen.de/ringlokschuppen/produktionen/bisher-2012/gast spiele-bisher-2012/frauenchor-chor-kobiet-marta-gornicka/.

4.8 *Mŕtve duše* – Slovakia

As a reaction to the difficult conditions for the Slovakian independent theatre, the Association for Contemporary Opera, Združenia Pre Súčasnú Operu, was founded in Bratislava in the year 2000. Young directors, actors, choreographers and composers work on the productions in a team. Every member contributes his experience and skills to the theatrical process and becomes a co-author or co-director of the production. With regard to the conceptual work, the players strive for an intertwining of 'chamber opera and alternative theatre'[169]. They develop musical collages, modify existing compositions and combine them with pop music. The composition of traditional operatic elements and everyday music is used by the group to create a critical parody of artistic conventions. This approach is clearly visible in the performances *Smrt' v kuchyni* (2000), *Okná, brehy, pozostalosti* (2000) and *Čo bude zajtra* (2001).

The Združenia Pre Súčasnú Operu brought forth the group Divadlo SkRAT in 2004. This group continued the work of the association and expanded the artistic practices to gradually include more and more multimedia elements. The more recent performances of Divadlo SkRAT present transmedia collages. Instead of operatic music, electronic noises and sounds are used to rhythmically structure the performances. A good example of this is the performance *Mŕtve duše* (Dead Souls) from the year 2008. The production adopted both the name and contents of the classic 'Dead Souls' by the rock group Joy Division, and Nicolai Gogol's novel of the same name:

'Beside the title, the other thing these Dead Souls have in common with Gogol's novel is that they are a sharp satire of the existing socio-political system. We peep in block of flats on Bratislava's housing estate quarter Petržalka, but it may be on any other such estate in Central or Eastern Europe.'[170]

During the performance, the members of the audience became voyeurs as they observed the residents of different private flats in an apartment building in Bratislava. People could be seen for a fleeting moment: lying in bed, sitting in the bathtub, smoking, drinking, talking on the phone. Silhouettes of a kitchen were discernible; there an ironing board, junk and rubbish. 'Bare highrise apartment buildings, bodies and couples reminiscent of the dark avantgarde post-war photomontages of Heinz Hajek-Halke which communicate forsakenness, unapproachability, chaos,'[171] as was written in one description

---

169 | Juraj Šebesta,"Erfolgsgeschichte mit Hindernissen", p. 50.
170 | Divadlo SkRAT, see http://www.skrat.info/en.
171 | Gabriele Mayer, "Der Voyeur braucht Geduld, um zu fühlen und zu verstehen", in *Mittelbayerische Zeitung*, see http://www.mittelbayerische.de/index.cfm?pid=10022&pk=467515.

of the production. The spectator waited in anticipation of what was to come, whether it be amusement, violence or a breaking down of boundaries. Nothing of the like occurred. Not a single word was spoken, not a note sung. The scenes were filled only with light and music or background noises. Fragments of electronic music could be heard. Fragments of melodies and songs were played, then a hubbub, basses and rhythmic electronic sounds. The sounds highlighted the fragmented picture of a society without interruption and at the same time jolted it. Sound was an important theatrical element of this transmedia performance:

'An exciting, atmospherically dense collage of images, voices, sounds and bits of music, melancholy picutes and magical sounds in pulsating, rapidly changing lighting and sound controls. In the focus: lonely, yearning bodies and dead, lost souls.'[172]

The group gave guest performances at many festivals: in Slovakia at the KioSK Festival in Žilina and the theatre festival Divadelná in Nitra. It was also performed at the Unidram Festival in Potsdam, the DEMOULDY Festival in Olsztyn, Poland, the East Gate Europe Festival in Aarhus, Denmark and the MittelFest Cividale in the city of the same name in Italy.

5. Summary and Outlook

An examination of the individual groups and performances revealed characteristic work practices, aesthetics and dramaturgies of the independent theatres in the post-socialist countries. The main focus was on the productions of independent artists and groups of different backgrounds. The works dealt with different discourses and were the result of different artistic processes and practices. They were based on different ideas of theatre. However, some features became evident which can be considered characteristic of the independent theatres in the post-socialist countries.

What connects the groups and performances described here is a strong focus on everyday themes. The artistic confrontation with everyday realities, with the plight of society, grievances and problems, is often the basis of independent theatre work, whereby theatre is not understood as the mere staging of text but as an artistic process which sharpens the audience's perception of daily life and, in the best case, changes it. This understanding of theatre is shared by

---

[172] | Kunstforum Ostdeutsche Galerie: *Dead Souls. Verlorene Seelen, sehnsüchtige Leiber*, see http://www.freundederkuenste.de/stadtart/regensburg/kunst-veranstaltungen/theater-skrat-aus-bratislava-folgt-einladung-der-donumenta-am-3102009.html.

all the groups included in this study. As has been demonstrated by the artistic approach of the group DramAcum and the community projects of the group TangaProject, the independent theatre work, particularly in Romania, can be considered paradigmatic for this view.[173]

The connection between artistic practice and everyday issues raises the question of the role of the audience. A characteristic of independent theatre work is the involvement of the audience in the artistic events. This need not mean that the members of the audience automatically become active players. By avoiding the usual visual experiences, the audience is already more strongly involved in the theatrical process. This can, for example, be achieved by using unconventional audience-stage arrangements or through a particular presentation by the actor, as in the performance of *Reasons to be happy*. The spectator can not escape the happenings on stage and is called on to take a position on what is being presented.[174]

There are also commonalities in the independent groups' working methods. They often work as a collective, with the individual director taking a step back. Although there are no fixed hierarchies, the groups nevertheless work within defined structures. The focus is placed on the respective skills of the individuals. These are considered to be of equivalent quality and, as such, are integrated into the artistic process. The experience, qualifications and talents of the individual group members enhance the artistic work.[175]

Based on the exemplary analyses, it was evident that independent theatre in the post-socialist countries often cannot be assigned to a particular genre. Although all the individual productions mainly represent spoken theatre, the focus of the performances is usually not placed on the text alone. The independent theatre work can rather be described as a transmedia practice. The independent groups use different genres and media and merge them into

---

173 | See Hans-Thies Lehmann, *Das Politische Schreiben. Essays zu Theatertexten* (Berlin: Theater der Zeit 2002); Hans-Thies Lehmann, *Postdramatisches Theater* (Frankfurt a. Main: Verlag der Autoren 1999).

174 | See Adam Czirak, *Partizipation der Blicke. Szenerien des Sehens und Gesehenwerdens im Theater* (Bielefeld: transcript 2012); Jan Deck and Angelika Sieburg (eds.), *Paradoxien des Zuschauens. Die Rolle des Publikums im zeitgenössischen Theater* (Bielefeld: transcript 2008).

175 | See Jan Deck and Angelike Sieburg (eds.), *Politisch Theater machen. Neue Artikulationsformen des Politischen in den darstellenden Künsten* (Bielefeld: transcript 2011); Hajo Kurzenberger, *Der kollektive Prozess des Theaters. Chorkörper, Probengemeinschaften, theatrale Kreativität.* (Bielefeld: transcript 2009).

a theatrical process.[176] This was particularly evident in the performances of *Lili Handel, Szutyok* and *Mŕtve duše*.

It is important to the independent groups to utilize their collective way of working and the transmedia approach to explore new artistic practices. The centres of independent theatre work resemble laboratories which pursue and modify the intentions of the theatre avant-garde. One of many examples is the theatre centre for anthropological theatre research and practice in Poland, Ośrodek Praktyk teatralnych Gardzienice. Another important direction is the understanding of theatre as a means to research day-to-day life. As has been described in the analyses, social problems and realities are at the heart of this theatre work, and are documented and dealt with artistically in the productions.

Finally, there is a great interest in international cooperation among all the independent groups. It has been shown that independent groups in the post-socialist countries are participating more and more frequently in EU cultural sponsorship programmes. In addition, many international platforms and organisations have been founded and international collaborations have increased. In particular, a transnational festival culture has developed. The international networking not only contributes to a transcultural exchange, to international attention and to a temporary stabilisation of the general conditions. Participating in transnational cooperation projects is much more a survival strategy for the independent theatres. Despite difficult socio-economic conditions, the theatres are able to finance the continuation of their work by means of such international projects:

'For non-commercial art, which has always struggled with the problem of insufficient funding, networks have become an opportunity to raise additional funding without having to abandon ambitious artistic goals. [...] 'Network' and 'networking' have become both a practice and a general philosophy of how to behave in the artistic market, as well as the basic strategy for a group or an institution to survive.'[177]

All independent groups in the post-socialist region are in a precarious financial situation. This not only influences their artistic work but also the social status of the artists. It is responsible for the often hesitant development of new initiatives and makes the establishment of independent groups and artists more difficult. Considerable funding cuts, as have been introduced in Slovenia, Hungary, and in the Ukraine, ultimately mean a substantial worsening of the working conditions. The restrictive structures lead to independent artists' having to

---

176 | Cf. Günther Heeg and Anno Mungen (eds.), *Stillstand und Bewegung. Intermediale Studien zur Theatralität von Text, Bild und Musik* (München: Epodium 2004).

177 | Joanna Leśnierowska, quoted in Paweł Płoski, "Introduction", p. 29.

seek other forms of employment. Many groups have left or are leaving their home countries to settle abroad.

The independent theatre scene in the post-socialist countries has proven to be very flexible. If the political and socio-economic setting changes, the independent theatres adapt to such changes and adjust to the new circumstances. At the same time, it is difficult to formulate a future perspective for the entire independent theatre scene in the post-socialist countries at this point because of the country-specific conditions. As in the past twenty years, the theatre scenes will continue to develop in different directions, and thus the future will hold different perspectives for the independent groups. This is manifested in the answers given on site by the theatre makers, with whose words this study will close. A Slovenian independent critic stated: 'My vision is a bit pessimistic. More and more promising artists will leave the country, which is already happening and quite a few are already struggling with their lack of enthusiasm and are changing their professions.'[178] In contrast, a Slovakian theatre expert commented: 'Independent theatre makers are more and more connected, experienced and educated. More and more they enter into public theatres as guests and influenced them.'[179] A Ukrainian independent theatre critic expressed himself as follows: 'If the government changes nothing, the most of independent theatres can disappear.'[180] And finally, a Hungarian independent director observes: 'Important would be to build a domestic touring network.'[181]

---

178 | Questionnaire Slovenia I.
179 | Questionnaire Slovakia II.
180 | Questionnaire Ukraine I.
181 | Questionnaire Hungary I.

Literature and sources

Questionnaires

The questionnaires returned in the course of the research are in the archive of the International Theatre Institute in Berlin.
Questionnaire Belarus. Received on 22nd September 2012.
Questionnaire Bosnia-Herzegovina I. Received on 30th October 2012.
Questionnaire Bosnia-Herzegovina II. Received on 30th October 2012.
Questionnaire Romania I. Received on 4th September 2012.
Questionnaire Romania II. Received on 4th October 2012.
Questionnaire Romania III. Received on 29th October 2012.
Questionnaire Serbia I. Received on 29th September 2012.
Questionnaire Serbia II. Received on 5th September 2012.
Questionnaire Slovakia I. Received on 22nd November 2012.
Questionnaire Slovakia II. Received on 29th October 2012.
Questionnaire Slovenia I. Received on 3rd November 2012.
Questionnaire Slovenia II. Received on 5th October 2012.
Questionnaire Czech Republic. Received on 2nd November 2012.
Questionnaire Ukraine I. Received on 28th October 2012.
Questionnaire Ukraine II. Received on 11th October 2012.
Questionnaire Hungary I. Received on 30th September 2012.
Questionnaire Hungary II. Received on 7th November 2012.

Interviews by the author

With:
Marko Bulc, former director of the Gledališče Glej theatre in Ljubljana, on 27th May 2012 in Ljubljana, Slovenia.
Tomaž Toporišič, playwright at the Slovensko mladinsko gledališče in Ljubljana, on 28th May 2012 in Ljubljana, Slovenia.
Inga Remata, programme director of the Gledališče Glej in Ljubljana, on 30th May 2012 in Ljubljana, Slovenia.
Andreja Kopač, independent journalist, playwright and performer from Ljubljana, on 31th May 2012 in Ljubljana, Slovenia.
Recordings of the interviews are in the possession of the author.

Monographs and collected editions

Akudowitsch, V. *Der Abwesenheitscode: Versuch, Weißrussland zu verstehen.* Berlin: Suhrkamp, 2013.

Arns, I. *Neue slowenische Kunst: Eine Analyse ihrer künstlerischen Strategien im Kontext der 1980er Jahre in Jugoslawien*. Regensburg: Museum Ostdeutsche Galerie, 2002.

Arts and Theatre Institute. *Czech Theatre Guide*. Prague: Arts and Theatre Institute, 2011.

Baeva, I and Kalinova, E. *Bulgarien von Ost nach West: Zeitgeschichte ab 1939*. Vienna: Braumüller, 2009.

Beumers, B. and Lipovetsky, M. *Performing Violence: Literary and Theatrical Experiments of New Russian Drama*. Bristol/Chicago: Intellect, 2009.

Bispinck, H., Danyel, J., Hertle, H-H. and Wentker, H. (eds), *Aufstände im Ostblock: Zur Krisengeschichte des realen Sozialismus*. Berlin: Ch. Links, 2004.

Boeckh, K. *Serbien, Montenegro: Geschichte und Gegenwart*. Munich: Pustet, 2002.

Bohn, T. M. and Shadurski, V., (eds). *Ein weißer Fleck in Europa...: Die Imagination der Belarus als Kontaktzone zwischen Ost und West*. Bielefeld: transcript, 2011.

Boia, L. *Geschichte und Mythos: Über die Gegenwart des Vergangenen in der rumänischen Gesellschaft*. Vienna/Cologne/Weimar: Böhlau, 2003.

Borodziej, W. *Geschichte Polens im 20. Jahrhundert*. Munich: Beck, 2010.

Brauneck, M. *Europas Theater: 2500 Jahre Geschichte – eine Einführung*. Reinbek bei Hamburg: Rowohlt, 2012.

Brauneck, M. *Die Welt als Bühne*, vol. 5. Stuttgart/Weimar: Metzler, 2007.

Brauneck, M. *Klassiker der Schauspielregie: Positionen und Kommentare zum Theater im 20. Jahrhundert*. Reinbek bei Hamburg: Rowohlt, 1988.

Brauneck, M. Theater im 20. Jahrhundert: Programmschriften, Stilperioden, Reformmodelle. Reinbek bei Hamburg: Rowohlt, 1986.

Bruell, C. *Kreatives Europa 2014-2020: Ein neues Programm – auch eine neue Kulturpolitik? Studie des Instituts für Auslandsbeziehungen*. Stuttgart/Berlin: Edition für Kultur und Außenpolitik, 2013. See also: http://www.ifa.de/fileadmin/pdf/edition/kreatives-europa_bruell.pdf.

Bryzgel, A. Performing the East: Performance Art in Russia, Latvia and Poland since 1980. London/New York: I. B. Tauris, 2013.

Buzogány, A. and Frankenberger, R. (eds). *Osteuropa: Politik, Wirtschaft und Gesellschaft*. Baden-Baden: Nomos, 2007.

Calic, M-J. *Geschichte Jugoslawiens im 20. Jahrhundert*. Munich: C. H. Beck, 2010.

Cioffi, K. M. *Alternative Theatre in Poland 1954-1989*. London/New York: Routledge, 1996.

Czirak, A. *Partizipation der Blicke: Szenerien des Sehens und Gesehenwerdens im Theater*. Bielefeld: transcript, 2012.

Dalos, G. *Der Vorhang geht auf: Das Ende der Diktaturen in Osteuropa*. Munich: C. H. Beck, 2009

Davydchyk, M. *Transformationen der Kulturpolitik: Kulturpolitische Veränderungen nach dem Zusammenbruch des sozialistischen Systems in Mittel- und Osteuropa.* Wiesbaden: VS, 2012.

Deck, J. and Sieburg, A. (eds). *Politisch Theater machen: Neue Artikulationsformen des Politischen in den darstellenden Künsten.* Bielefeld: transcript, 2011.

Deck, J. and Sieburg, A. (eds). *Paradoxien des Zuschauens: Die Rolle des Publikums im zeitgenössischen Theater.* Bielefeld: transcript, 2008.

German UNESCO Commission. *Übereinkommen über den Schutz und die Förderung der Vielfalt kultureller Ausdrucksformen: Magna Charta der Internationalen Kulturpolitik.* Bonn: Köllen, 2005.

Dimitrov, G. P. *Kultur im Transformationsprozess Osteuropas: Zum Wandel kultureller Institutionen am Beispiel Bulgariens nach 1989.* Munich/Berlin: Otto Sagner, 2009.

Dudzik, W. (ed.). *Theater-Bewusstsein: Polnisches Theater in der zweiten Hälfte des 20. Jahrhunderts. Ideen – Konzepte – Manifeste.* Berlin: Lit, 2011.

Eilers, D. L., Volkland, A. and Schultze, H. (eds). *Die neue Freiheit: Perspektiven des bulgarischen Theaters* (TdZ Recherchen 83). Berlin: Theater der Zeit, 2011.

Emeliantseva, E., Malz, A. and Ursprung, D. (eds). *Einführung in die osteuropäische Geschichte.* Zürich: Füssli, 2008.

Frącz, S. *Im Spannungsfeld von Nationalismus und Integration: Zur Komplexität des Transformationsprozesses der postkommunistischen Gesellschaften unter den osteuropäischen Gegebenheiten.* Bonn: Bouvier, 2006.

Franz, N. and Schmid, H. (eds). *Bühne und Öffentlichkeit: Drama und Theater im Spät- und Postsozialismus (1983-1993).* Munich: Otto Sagner, 2002.

Fundacja Open Culture. *A Report on the Condition of Culture and NGOs in Ukraine.* Lublin: Episteme, 2012. See also http://fundacjaopenculture.org/.

Fundacja Open Culture. *A Report on the Condition of Culture and NGOs in Belarus.* Lublin: Episteme, 2011. See also http://fundacjaopenculture.org/.

Gržinić, M., Heeg, G. and Darian, V. (eds). *Mind the Map! History is Not Given.* Frankfurt am Main: Revolver, 2004.

Groys, B., von der Heiden, A. and Weibel, P. (eds). *Zurück aus der Zukunft: Osteuropäische Kulturen im Zeitalter des Postkommunismus.* Frankfurt a. M.: Suhrkamp, 2005.

Grotowski, J. *Für ein Armes Theater.* Berlin: Alexander, 1994 [first edition: 1970].

Hauszmann, J. *Ungarn – vom Mittelalter bis zur Gegenwart.* Regensburg: Pustet, 2004.

Heeg, G. and Mungen, A. (eds). *Stillstand und Bewegung: Intermediale Studien zur Theatralität von Text, Bild und Musik.* Munich: Epodium, 2004.

Heeg, G. and Denzel, M. A. (eds). *Globalizing Areas, kulturelle Flexionen und die Herausforderung der Geisteswissenschaften.* Stuttgart: Franz Steiner, 2011.

Heeg, G. *Das transkulturelle Theater.* Berlin: Theater der Zeit, 2015.

Hessisches Staatstheater Wiesbaden. *Béla Pintér – Miststück*. Play text, 2012. Published as part of the festival *NEUE STÜCKE AUS EUROPA*, 14th–24th June 2012.

Hoflehner, J. C., Vannayová, M. and Vejtisek, M. (eds). *Durchbrochene Linien: Zeitgenössisches Theater in der Slowakei* (TdZ Recherchen 40). Berlin: Theater der Zeit, 2007.

Institut für Moderne Kunst. *Tadeusz Kantor. Ein Reisender: Seine Texte und seine Manifeste*. Nürnberg: Verlag für Moderne Kunst, 1998.

Jestrovic, S. *Performance, Space, Utopia: Cities of War, Cities of Exile*. Hampshire: Palgrave Macmillan, 2013.

Kahl, T. (ed.). *Kilometer Null – politische Transformation und gesellschaftliche Entwicklungen in Rumänien seit 1989*. Berlin: Frank & Timme, 2011.

Kahl, T. (ed.). *Rumänien: Raum und Bevölkerung, Geschichte und Geschichtsbilder, Kultur, Gesellschaft und Politik heute, Wirtschaft, Recht und Verfassung, historische Regionen*. Vienna/Berlin/Münster: Lit, 2006.

Kaufmann, T. and Raunig, G. *Anticipating European Cultural Policies: Europäische Kulturpolitiken vorausdenken*. Vienna/Linz: European Institute for Progressive Cultural Policies, 2003.

Kaser, K., Gramshammer-Hohl, D. and Pichler, R. (eds). *Enzyklopädie des europäischen Ostens: Europa und die Grenzen im Kopf*. Klagenfurt et al: Wieser, 2003.

Kłossowicz, J. and Xander, H. *Tadeusz Kantors Theater*. Tübingen/Basel: Francke, 1995.

Kornás, T. *Between Anthropology and Politics: Two Strands of Polish Alternative Theatre*. Warsaw: The Zbigniew Raszewski Theatre Institute, 2007.

Kosiński, D. *Polnisches Theater: Eine Geschichte in Szenen*. Berlin: Theater der Zeit, 2011.

Kuftinec, S. A. *Theatre, Facilitation and Nation Formation in the Balkans and Middle East*. Hampshire: Palgrave Macmillan, 2009.

Kunze, T. and Vogel, T. *Von der Sowjetunion in die Unabhängigkeit: Eine Reise durch die 15 früheren Sowjetrepubliken. Bundeszentrale für politische Bildung*. Berlin: Ch. Links, 2011.

Kurzenberger, H. *Der kollektive Prozess des Theaters: Chorkörper, Probengemeinschaften, theatrale Kreativität*. Bielefeld: transcript, 2009.

Laech, R. and Borovsky, V. *A History of Russian Theatre*. Cambridge: Cambridge University Press, 1999.

Lehmann, H-T. *Das Politische Schreiben: Essays zu Theatertexten*. Berlin: Theater der Zeit, 2002.

Lehmann, H-T. *Postdramatisches Theater*. Frankfurt am Main: Verlag der Autoren, 1999.

Lendvai, P. *Die Ungarn: Eine tausendjährige Geschichte*. Munich: Goldmann, 2001.

Mauritz, M. *Tschechien*. Regensburg: Pustet, 2002.
Mazilu, M., Weident, M. and Wolf, I. (eds). *Das rumänische Theater nach 1989*. Berlin: Frank & Timme, 2001.
Mommsen, M. *Wer herrscht in Russland? Der Kreml und die Schatten der Macht*. Munich: C. H. Beck, 2003.
Monroe, A. *Interrogation Machine: Laibach and NSK*. London/Cambridge: MIT Press, 2005.
Moritsch, A. and Mosser, A. *Den Anderen im Blick: Stereotype im ehemaligen Jugoslawien*. Frankfurt am Main: Peter Lang, 2002.
National Theatre Museum of Slovenia. *Occupying Spaces: Experimental Theatre in Central Europe 1950-2010*. Ljubljana: National Theatre Museum of Slovenia, 2010.
Plata, T. (ed.). *Öffentliche Strategien, private Strategien: Das polnische Theater 1990-2005* (TdZ Recherchen 32). Berlin: Theater der Zeit, 2006.
Rahmig, J. *Ungarns Rückkehr nach Europa. Vom Gulaschkommunismus zu Marktwirtschaft und Demokratie*. Stuttgart: Verlag der Deutsch-Ungarischen Gesellschaft, 1998.
Rauter, W. *Kulturpolitik und finanzierung im osteuropäischen Raum*. Saarbrücken: VDM, 2008.
Regus, C. *Interkulturelles Theater zu Beginn des 21. Jahrhunderts: Ästhetik, Politik, Postkolonialismus*. Bielefeld: transcript, 2009.
Roth, H. (ed.). *Studienhandbuch Östliches Europa: Geschichte Ostmittel- und Südosteuropas*. Vienna/Cologne/Weimar: Böhlau, 1999.
Scharr, K. *Rumänien – Geschichte und Geographie*. Vienna/Cologne/Weimar: Böhlau, 2008.
Schneider-Deters, W. *Die Ukraine – Machtvakuum zwischen Russland und der Europäischen Union*. Berlin: Berliner Wissenschaftsverlag, 2012.
Schorlemmer, U. *Die Magie der Annäherung und das Geheimnis der Distanz: Krystian Lupas Recherche 'neuer Mythen' im Theater*. Munich: Sagner, 2003.
Schramm, G. (ed.). *Russlands langer Weg zur Gegenwart*. Göttingen: Vandenhoeck & Ruprecht, 2001.
Segert, D. (ed.). *Postsozialismus: Hinterlassenschaften des Staatssozialismus und neue Kapitalismen in Europa*. Vienna: Braumüller, 2007.
Segert, D. *Die Grenzen Osteuropas: 1918, 1945, 1989 – Drei Versuche im Westen anzukommen*. Frankfurt am Main: Campus, 2002.
Stanescu, S. and Gerould, D. (eds). *roMANIA after 2000: Five New Romanian Plays*. New York: Martin E. Segal Theatre Center, 2007.
Staniewski, W. and Hodge, A. *Hidden Territories: The Theatre of Gardzienice*. London/New York: Routledge, 2012.
Steindorff, L. *Kroatien: Vom Mittelalter bis zur Gegenwart*. Regensburg: Pustet, 2012.

Štih, P., Simoniti, V. and Vodopivec, P. *Slowenische Geschichte: Gesellschaft – Politik – Kultur*. Graz: Leykam, 2008.

Sundhaussen, H. *Geschichte Serbiens 19.-21. Jahrhundert*. Vienna/Cologne/Weimar: Böhlau, 2007.

Sundhaussen, H. *Jugoslawien und seine Nachfolgestaaten 1943-2011: Eine ungewöhnliche Geschichte des Gewöhnlichen*. Vienna/Cologne/Weimar: Böhlau, 2012.

Szücs, J. *Die drei historischen Regionen Europas*. Frankfurt am Main: Neue Kritik, 1990.

Szymanski, B. *Theatraler Protest und der Weg Polens zu 1989: Zum Aushandeln von öffentlichkeit im Jahrzehnt der Solidarność*. Bielefeld: transcript, 2012.

TkH Forum for Performing Arts Critique. *RASTER – Yearbook of the Independent Performing Arts Scene in Serbia*. Belgrade: TkH Centre for Performing Arts Theory and Practice, 2009.

Todorova, M. *Body, Identity, Community: Dance in Bulgaria after 1989*. 11 pages of manuscript privately owned by author, no date.

Vannayová, M. and Häusler, A. (eds). *Landvermessungen. Theaterlandschaften in Mittel-, Ost- und Südosteuropa* (TdZ Recherchen 61). Berlin: Theater der Zeit, 2008.

Von Beyme, K. *Systemwechsel in Osteuropa*. Frankfurt am Main: Suhrkamp, 1994.

Wirsching, A. *Der Preis der Freiheit. Geschichte Europas unserer Zeit*. Munich: C.H. Beck, 2012.

Wolff, Larry. "Die Erfindung Osteuropas. Von Voltaire zu Voldemort." In: Karl Kaser, Dagmer Gramshammer-Hohl and Robert Pichler (eds.), *Enzyklopädie des europäischen Ostens, Europa und die Grenzen im Kopf*. Klagenfurt et al.: Wieser, 2003, pp. 21-34.

Ziemer, Klaus. *Das politische System Polens*. Wiesbaden: Springer, 2013.

Periodicals and essays in periodicals

Belenitskaja, N. Kurswechsel. "Ein Schlüssel für das Verständnis des Wertekanons in der russischen Gesellschaft." *Theater der Zeit* 3 (2006), pp. 16-19.

Blaž, L. "The Attitude of the Fourth Generation." *Maska* 4 (2006), pp. 12-19.

Dolschanski, R. "Kommerz und erfreuliche Ausnahmen." *Theater der Zeit* 3 (2006), pp. 23-26.

Dürr, C. "Der Aufbruch hat begonnen." *Theater der Zeit* 3 (2006), pp. 20-22.

Dürr, C. "Auf der Suche nach dem verlorenen Helden: Das Festival Neue Dramatik in Moskau." *Theater der Zeit* 33, 2006.

Eilers, D. L. "Achtung Kunst!" *Theater der Zeit* 12 (2012), pp. 18-19.

Galachowa, O. "Archipel Moskau." *Theater der Zeit* 12 (2012), pp. 12-15.

Pintilie, I. "Romanian Artists before and after 1989." *Maska* 4 (2006), pp. 122-124.

Rembowska, A. "Auf der Suche nach Gegenwart: Neue Regiehandschriften aus Polen." *Theater der Zeit* 4 (2005), pp. 24-27.

Schneider, L. "Bereit zum Sprung". *Theater der Zeit* 3 (2011), pp. 13-15.

Schneider, L. "Das beste Land der Welt: Warum es im Ungarn Viktor Orbáns wenig Platz für unabhängiges Theater gibt. Eine Spurensuche." *Theater der Zeit* 4 (2012), pp. 33-35.

Šuvaković, M. "Theoretical Performance." *Maska* 1 (2005), pp. 67-72.

Trompa, A. "Gehen oder bleiben? Die darstellenden Künstler der freien Szene Ungarns sehen sich vor dem Aus und suchen die Öffentlichkeit." *Theater heute* 1 (2013), pp. 20-22.

Internet Sources

After the Fall: Europa nach 1989. A theatre project by the Goethe Institute. Available at: http://www.goethe.de/kue/the/prj/atf/the/sar/deindex.htm.

Archive Mime Centrum Berlin. *Ivo Dimchev. Lili Handel – blood, poetry and music from the white whore's boudoir*. Available at: http://archiv.mimecentrum.de/video/show/3132.

Boldt, E. "Gemeinschaft der Verlotterten." *Nachtkritik*. Available at: http://www.nachtkritik.de/index.php?option=com_content&view=article&id=5819%253Aszutyok-miststueck-nbela-pinter-schockt-bei-den-theaterformen-mit-zeitgenoessischer-gefuehlsverkommenheit&catid=623%253Atheaterformen&Itemid=99.

Chór kobiet. Available at: http://www.chorkobiet.pl/en/page/1/.

Contemporary Performance Network. Available at: http://contemporaryperformance.org/profile/MilanMarkovic?xg_source=activity.

Culture from Slovenia worldwide. Available at: http://www.culture.si/en/Category:Theatre.

Divadelní fakulta AMU v Praze. Available at: http://www.damu.cz/.

Divadlo SkRAT. Available at: http://www.skrat.info/en.

East West Centar. Available at: http://eastwest.ba/.

Ivo Dimchev. Available at: http://www.ivodimchev.com/index.htm.

EEPAP – A Platform for the Development of Performing Arts in Central and Eastern Europe. *Studie 2011*. Available at: http://www.eepap.org/web/english/eepap.pl.

European Radio Network. "Hohe Selbstmordrate in Slowenien." Available at: http://www.euranet.eu/ger/Dossiers/Euranet-Schwerpunkte/Depressionen-in-Europa/Hohe-Selbstmordrate-in-Slowenien.

Festival Transamériques. Available at: http://www.fta.qc.ca/sites/fta.qc.ca/files/documents/press_kit_fta2012_maudit_soit_le_traitre_en_0.pdf.

Gesellschaft Freunde der Künste. "Drei Rumänen möchten so schnell wie möglich raus - România! Te pup | Rumänien! Küss mich." Available at: http://www.freundederkuenste.de/empfehlung/theater-und-premieren/buehne/drei-rumaenen-moechten-so-schnell-wie-moeglich-raus-romania-te-pup-rumaenien-kuess-mich.html.

Gledališče Glej. Available at: http://www.culture.si/en/Glej_Theatre.

Gradsko pozorište Jazavac. Available at: http://gpj.ba/.

Heller, Jakob C. "Bis zur letzten Nase". *Neue Stücke aus Europa 2010*. Available at: http://newplays-blog.de/2010/06/19/bis-zur-letzten-nase/.

International Network for Contemporary Performing Arts (IETM). Available at: http://ietm.org/ietm-balkan-express.

IG FreieTheaterarbeit. "Country Reports." Avaiable at: http://www.freietheater.at/?page=europeanoffnetwork&subpage=country_report#13.

Instytut Polski. "Polish Theatre/Dance." Available at: http://www.polishinstitute.org.il/en/polish-culture/theater-dance/33-polish-theatre-of-the-21st-century.html.

Klett, Renate. "Es fließt Blut!" *Zeit Online*. Available at: http://www.zeit.de/2012/18/KS-Dimchev.

Kornyag Theatre. Available at: http://korniag-theatre.com/index.html.

KPGT. Available at: http://www.kpgtyu.org/.

Kunstforum Ostdeutsche Galerie. "Dead Souls. Verlorene Seelen, sehnsüchtige Leiber." Available at: http://www.freundederkuenste.de/stadtart/regensburg/kunst-veranstaltungen/theater-skrat-aus-bratislava-folgt-einladung-der-donumenta-am-3102009.html.

Mayer, Gabriele. "Der Voyeur braucht Geduld, um zu fühlen und zu verstehen". *Mittelbayerische Zeitung*. Available at: http://www.mittelbayerische.de/index.cfm?pid=10022&pk=467515.

My name is Janez Janša. Available at: http://www.mynameisjanezjansa.com/.

Nachtkritik/Spielbetriebe. "Portrait of Maja Pelević." Available at: http://nachtkritik-spieltriebe3.de/index.php?option=com_content&view=article&id=128&Itemid=43&lang=de.

NBU. Available at: http://www.nbu.bg/entrance.php?lang=1.

Neue Stücke aus Europa 2012. *Pintér Béla és Társulata*. Available at: http://www.newplays.de/index.php?page=events&content=events_program&id_event_cluster=849037.

Neue Stücke aus Europa 2010. Available at: http://www.newplays.de/index.php?page=archive&content=archive_2010&content_sub=archive_2010_parts&id_event_cluster=542809.

Open Society Foundation. Available at: http://www.opensocietyfoundations.org/.

Ostrowska, Joanna. "The rebellion does not fade, it gets settled... Teatr Ósmego Dnia." Available at: http://osmego.art.pl/t8d/main/en/.

Ringlokschuppen Mülheim an der Ruhr. "Programme description Magnificat." Available at: http://www.ringlokschuppen.de/ringlokschuppen/pro

duktionen/bisher-2012/gastspiele-bisher-2012/frauenchor-chor-kobiet-marta-gornicka/.
Romanodialog. "Pintér Béla és Társulata." Available at: http://www.romanodialog.org/ZTS%202012%20Bela%20Pinter.pdf.
Slovak Theatre Institute. "Independent Theatres." Available at: http://www.theatre.sk/en/homepage/.
Slovensko Gledališče Mladinsko. Available at: http://en.mladinsko.com/about-mladinsko/whos-who/.
Stiftung Depressionshilfe. Available at: http://www.deutsche-depressionshilfe.de/stiftung/9751.php.
Stiftung Pro Helvetia. Available at: http://www.prohelvetia.ch/.
Theaterformen. "Pintér Béla és Társulata – Miststück." Available at: http://www.theaterformen.de/Theaterformen_2011/miststueck/.
Theatre Institute Russia. Available at: http://www.teatr.ru/.
"They live (in a search of text zero)." Available at: http://theyliveonline.wordpress.com/.
TkH. Available at: http://www.tkh-generator.net/.
Walking Theory. Available at: http://www.howtodothingsbytheory.info/about-tkh/.
Verseck, Keno. "Zurück zu Blut und Heimat". *Zeit Online*. Available at: http://www.zeit.de/politik/ausland/2013-03/ungarn-verfassungsaenderung-orban.
Visegrád Fund. Available at: http://visegradfund.org/.

Acknowledgements

This study would not have been possible without the help, energetic support and generous feedback of others. For this, I would like to especially warmly thank:

Nela Antonovic, Tania Arcimovič, Ingrid Beese, Franziska Benack, Urška Brodar, Mare Bulc, Manfred Brauneck, Gianina Cărbunariu, Stefan Çapaliku, Kamila Černá, Gergana Dimitrova, Bojan Djordjev, Annette Doffin, Thomas Engel, Rhonda Farr, Nastasja Fischer, Angelina Georgieva, Maximilian Grafe, Anna Grusková, Günther Heeg, Benno Kaehler, Tine Koch, Elisabeth Kohlhaas, Andreja Kopač, Anna Lengyel, Vitomira Lončar, Mario Lukajic, Atanas Maev, Ana Margineanu, Daniela Miscov, Jure Novak, Tanja Miletić Oručević, Haris Pašović, Ivan Pravdić, Inga Remata, Christiane Richter, Adrian Roman, Petra Sabisch, Kerstin Schmitt, Sara Schöbel, Elisabeth Schwarz, Marianne Seidler, Małgorzata Semil, Elena Seubert, Azadeh Sharifi, Marta Shvets, Viktor Sobiianskyi, Katja Somrak, Peca Ştefan, Anja Suša, Attila Szabó, György Szabó, Alexander Tebenkov, Tomaž Toporišič, Martina Vannayová, Andrea Zagorski, Jasmina Založnik and finally my family.

A Theatre for Postmodernity in Western European Theatrescapes[1]

Henning Fülle

Manfred Brauneck's depiction of (West) European theatre topographies, or theatrescapes, since the Second World War in the fifth volume of his opus *Die Welt als Bühne*[2] recurrently references the emergence of free, independent theatre groups during the 1960s and 70s. Here mention is made mostly of 'free groups' and 'free theatre'[3].

A NEW THEATRE ARISING FROM THE CRISIS OF MODERNITY?

Although most of the youth and student revolts associated with the 'magical' year 1968 do manifest in specific national societies, their attendant processes nevertheless occur in similar patterns, more or less in correspondence to one

---

1 | Rather than being a product of the Balzan Research Project, this essay was commissioned for this anthology as a supplementary perspective and was able to be developed, starting in June 2015, only after completion of the dissertation manuscript (see fn. 5); for this reason, my remarks in the following must remain structurally somewhat akin to a thesis.

2 | [The world as stage], Manfred Brauneck, *Die Welt als Bühne: Geschichte des europäischen Theaters*, Vols. I-VI, Stuttgart and Weimar: J. B. Metzler Verlag, 1993-2007; Vol. 5, *2. Hälfte des 20. Jahrhunderts*, Stuttgart and Weimar: Publisher, 2007, (further citations: Brauneck, WaB/V.)

3 | In the context of his research, the author asks that the German term for the new 'Freies Theater' (and the associated terms 'Freie Gruppen' and 'Freie Szene') be left untranslated in the English text. The self-identification of 'Freies' [free] theatre refers in Germany specifically to theatrical activity that takes place outside the system of state-funded city and regional theatres. This distinction is not necessarily applicable outside Germany, so the literal translation of 'free' or 'libre' holds little meaning. The key feature of this theatrical activity is its independence, therefore 'independent theatre' is the closest translation.

another, and more or less tempestuously and militantly in almost all societies of 'Western'[4] industrial civilization.

Even without recourse to scholarly investigation into the relevant contexts, we can, in the broadest sense, understand the formation of 'free' theatre in West-European societies, or in other words, the formation of production modes, dramaturgies and aesthetic forms of new theatre since the sixties and seventies, as resonant with the moment of these processes of youth revolt.

As regards terminology, however, one must make the point in advance that any talk of 'free theatre' (and its derivatives: the free scene, free groups and so on) comes as a derivative of the German theatrescapes's specificities[5]; it describes the unique circumstance wherein forms and structures of contemporary theatre production in (West) Germany arose only late and in clear contradistinction to the traditional structures of the 'German system'. The term 'free' signifies this dissociation from the structures of state and municipal theatre and is often enough not (correctly) understood in foreign theatrescapes where these structures do not exist, at least not in this all-pervasive monopolistic capacity. Neither The Living Theatre, nor Peter Brook, Ariane Mnouchkine or Georges Tabori (for example) – and to a certain extent also Christoph Marthaler – defined or understood themselves as 'free' theatre, even though their work constitutes central references for what we in Germany have become accustomed to designating as such.

For the emergence of these new forms – of production modes, dramaturgies and aesthetics – one can distinguish two impulse-fields that lend them their character:

- on the one hand, the dynamics of international artistic developments since the Second World War, which have encountered different conditions of realisation in different national cultures and in the corresponding topography of their theatrescapes.
- the second impulse-field consists in – reformist and/or conservative – endeavours on the part of cultural and social politics that, for one, react or are responsive to artistic developments or else make efforts – harnessing, traditionally, the political momentum of the state or emanating from the public hand – to realise certain goals towards development or change by means of classical forms of political and/or administrative (legislative or executive) intervention.

---

4 | Here 'Western' means modern, capitalistically and parliamentary-democratically organized industrial societies – in this sense, also Japan.

5 | Cf., Henning Fülle, *Freie Gruppen, Freie Szene, Freies Theater und die Modernisierung der deutschen Theaterlandschaft (1960-2010)*, dissertation, University of Hildesheim; Hildesheim, Germany, 2015. And Henning Fülle, *Freies Theater. Die Modernisierung der deutschen Theaterlandschaft (1960-2010)*, Berlin 2016 forthcoming.

Figure 1: 'Zelt Schanzenpark', Jango Edwards, Kampnagel, Hamburg, 2001. Photograph: Friedemann Simon

In that regard, it makes little sense, in the international context, – which will also be shown by this essay – to employ the catch-all term 'free theatre' when discussing these forms. This would constitute an illegitimate projection of German circumstances onto other contexts and would furthermore lead to equivocal perspectives and evaluations. 'Independent' is the much more appropriate term for such production modes and products that have produced a new, different theatre – mostly developed by young and new ensembles that frequently understand themselves as 'collectives' – for other audiences, mostly since the end of WW II in the 'Western hemisphere' (which includes, in keeping with the cultural-historical circumstances, Poland, Czechoslovakia, Hungary and the rest of 'Middle Europe').

The term 'free theatre', on the other hand, designates a German phenomenon, whose definition via the term 'free' only becomes systematically and historically coherent against the backdrop of the meaning and constitution of the 'German system', made up of publicly financed state and municipal theatres, and its link to the youth and student revolts of 1967/68. These specificities also explain the continually encountered difficulties in communication between German theatre makers and those from other countries in Western Europe. At issue in the following are almost exclusively the latter – as far as German developments are concerned, reference is to be made to my forthcoming study[6].

As concerns the impact had by the two aforementioned impulse-fields on the formation of developments in diverse theatrescapes, we will adhere to the following guiding hypothesis: the artistic impulses aiming for changes in traditional forms of dramatic text-based theatre are themselves part of the international development of a new phase or era in the evolution of civilisation and culture, an era whose description via the term 'postmodern' has gained broad acceptance.

Postmodernity's backdrop is provided by twentieth-century catastrophes of civilization, by the global mass-medialisation of conditions of communication and by the expiry of the dominance of industrial conditions of production[7], beginning in the regions of capitalistically organised industrial civilisation; in the course of which the teleologico-utopian promise of progress and happiness guaranteed by bourgeois societies since the Enlightenment becomes increasingly obsolete.

When focussing on theatrical-artistic developments since the sixties, one recurrently comes across discussion of Peter Brook, whose work is appreciated as artistic inspiration throughout Western Europe and whose specifics concerning production conditions are regarded as a characteristic impulse for contemporary artistic developments.

In point of fact, Brook's works seem to be of no small importance to the emergence of new, postmodern forms of theatricality precisely because they do not spring from classical theatre discourse.

And yet the detonation of the canonic dramatic theatre of 'Aristotelian'[8] provenance begins much earlier, even in its Enlightenment varieties. I offer the evidence in the following sections while simultaneously taking into account that these developments cannot – even *almost* completely – be accounted for here.

---

6 | Cf. footnote 5.

7 | Just as these regions of the world saw the supersession of dominating agricultural and craftsmanship-realted production conditions by industrial conditions since the second half of the eighteenth century.

8 | Lehmann has aptly shown that the 'Aristotelian' tragedy is an ensemble of rules and forms, a construct that has been embedded, as an adaptation undergoing transformation to this day, in cultural-historical developments in Europe since the Renaissance. Cf. Hans-Thies Lehmann, *Tragödie und dramatisches Theater*, Berlin: Alexander, 2013, pp. 15-32. English translation: *Tragedy and Dramatic Theatre*, London: Routledge, forthcoming (March 30, 2016).

Figure 2: 'Hotel Pro Forma', Kirsten Dehlholm, Kampnagel, Hamburg, 2000. Photograph: Friedemann Simon

SOME HISTORICAL BACKGROUND: THEATRE AS ART

The concepts proper to the fin de siècle 'Theaterreform' (the reformation of the 'German system'), which are linked to the names Craig, Appia, Dalcroze, Moholy-Nagy, Schwitters and others, correspond to those processes of the development of art's self-referentiality, of the shaping of analytical and methodological perspectives like Impressionism, that were triggered both by advances made in the scientific penetration of matter and the world, and by self-reflections on the part of the classical optical and acoustic arts, themselves inspired by the inventions of photography, telegraphy, telephony and phonography.

Ever since the 'Meiningers', continuing through (for instance) Max Reinhardt, Stanislavski, Brecht and Piscator, theatre in Middle Europe develops, starting at the nineteenth century's close, as an increasingly autonomous 'director's art' that stands at least next to embodiment of the drama as core of the staged material; Piscator experiments with the theatre as multimedial political message-spectacle, Brecht with the didactic play as theatrical research process that takes place primarily among the actors and is witnessed and fathomed by the audience – and whichever of the two may be reckoned as the inventor of 'epic' non-Aristotelian theatre will remain undecided here.

If an analytical, self-referential gaze that in a certain sense follows the analytical perspectives of the natural sciences – relativity, quantum physics, psychoanalysis – ensues in the wake of these developments in artistic innovation and reformist concepts until well into the thirties, then already with Dada and the Surrealists themes related to the abdication of sense and enlightenment as the telos of art itself become – as a result of the great catastrophe of civilisation known as World War I – the subject matter as well as the purpose of artistic praxis.

As regards the theatre, in the thirties Antonin Artaud, more than anyone else, comes to mark the watershed in this development: his (admittedly somewhat terminologically diffuse) turn towards a tendentially introspective research-theatre – that also demands of the play the *partager*, the 'sharing' of the experience and witnessing of the interior worlds underneath the varnish of positivist moral philosophies – is, at least theoretically, a central point of departure for the theatre of postmodernity.

Postmodernity in this sense means the rejection of that systematic promise of future, salvation and happiness proper to the self-understanding of bourgeois society, that abdication which emancipated itself from the preestablished divine world orders of any provenance whatsoever and required the system and the teleology in order to counteract the mightiness of theological concepts by means of something approximately equal or similar.

These systems – whether stemming from Lessing, Kant, Fichte, Hegel or Marx – are based, with all the pathos of reason and science in their ultimate justifications, on a principle of belief; but to be precise, it is not the 'acid bath of contingency' so readily quoted by Stegemann, but rather above all the reason-driven reflection itself which – with the Frankfurter School's 'dialectics of enlightenment' being its most elaborated and presumably most bitter modality – notifies us that the abdication of this system is no longer – hardly any longer – negotiable.

The extent to and modality in which artistic and philosophical processes are hence interrelated remains a topic of philological and discourse-hermeneutical research, but this must be set aside at present; yet the writings of Albert Camus and Jean Paul Sartre, John Osborne, Tennessee Williams, Samuel Beckett... can in any event be read for the theatre as reflexes of the increasing rejection of hopes and promises of reason; of the catastrophes of civilisation and the global medialisation of the conditions of communication. After two world wars, the industrial-genocidal efforts to eradicate Europe's Jews, after the appearance of the scientifically elaborated potential for the obliteration of the planet at its inhabitants' own hands, after transportation technologies that were designed to conquer gravitation, it would seem that the heavens are empty and the human being is genuinely free. And yet freedom is no longer a promise; it surfaces instead as a calamity, one spelled out by Sartre and Camus.

As concerns theatre after WW II, in Germany after a brief phase, attempts at new beginnings immediately following war's end in the Bundesrepublik mark the establishment of a tendency towards the restoration of theatre art as vision of the 'conditio humana'. And while the assertion of a theatre of 'Socialist Realism' (and consequently a theatre for the 'scientific age' that carries the 'changeability of the world' in its head) is developed beyond the 'Iron Curtain' in the Soviet Occupied Zone/German Democratic Republic, in Western industrial civilizations the forerunners of artistic engagement with postmodern civilisation begin to show themselves.

The fact that the characteristic influences which are exerted on these forerunners' engagement are emitted by the pioneering development of an autonomous theatre art of modernity practised by protagonists forced into emigration – such as Brecht and Piscator – can only be mentioned here: at any rate, Julian Beck and Judith Malina went through Piscator's Dramatic Workshop in New York before they founded The Living Theatre in 1947. This group's work, which is shown all over Europe during the fifties and sixties, issued some of the most crucial impulses for processes of the contemporary renewal of theatre with respect to production modes, dramaturgy and aesthetics. Much the same can be said for the Bread & Puppet Theatre and the LaMama Group, who mould unique forms of theatre praxis on a foundation of contemporary sociopolitical awareness.

Alongside new forms of production praxis and dramaturgy, a number of authors also embark on new directions in theatre text beyond the drama: with Samuel Beckett as practitioner of the highest degree of radicality, but also with Eugène Ionesco and the French 'absurdists', Jean Genet and the British authors Harold Pinter, Edward Bond and Arnold Wesker; while in Eastern Europe, alongside Socialist Realism, above all in Poland, Jerzy Grotowski and Tadeusz Kantór develop forms of theatre work inspired by Artaud.

Subsequently, in the sixties and seventies this milieu sees the emergence of Peter Brook, Eugenio Barba, Robert Wilson, Ariane Mnouchkine, Luca Ronconi and others who begin afresh to experiment and reflect on theatre for their contemporaries. They found (or take over) research and production institutions in Vienna (Prato (Dramatic Centre)), Paris (C.I.R.T., Bouffes du Nord, Cartoucherie), Holstebro and Opole/Wroclav, where they labour concurrently towards their visions of theatre and towards the continual education and formation of young people.

Their characteristic trademarks: exploratory theatre art for an audience of contemporaries that refers to their time and the Zeitgeist while tackling the demand to treat present-day perception and enable and mediate experiences for their audience. The same way pop culture and pop art devotes itself to the empirical worlds and perceptive modes of the 'masses' – beginning to speak their language and dispensing with pedagogic gestures of improvement and cultivation in the sense of 'higher values' –, each artist of postmodernity assumes the tasks of ushering the traditions of stagecraft into each respective Now, processing stories of political and societal reality and developing the art of perception as a central technique for the evolution of civilisations, and as a vital coping mechanism for postindustrial cultures.

*Figure 3: 'Accions', La Fura dels Baus, Kampnagel, Hamburg, 1986.
Photograph: Friedemann Simon*

THEATERSCHRIFT[9] — REFLECTION AND IMPULSES FOR A THEATRE OF POSTMODERNITY

The quadrilingual – English, French, German and Dutch – periodical *Theaterschrift*, which appeared with a total of thirteen issues from 1992 to 1998, conveys a one-of-a-kind, concentrated overview of the dimensions of postmodern theatre art.[10] It was edited and published by the European production and coproduction network that formed during the late eighties around Hebbel Theater in Berlin, the (new) Theater am Turm in Frankfurt am Main, the Kaai-

---

[9] | Many thanks to Thomas Tylla of the Hebbel Theater Berlin for unbureaucratically borrowing the author a set of the complete edition. Even though in the second issue (October 1992) the chief editor Marianne Van Kerkhoven treats postmodernity as an epoch that is over – 'In the recent period – which is usually labelled "postmodern"' – for the investigations of "new" theatre compiled in *Theaterschrift*, we will adhere to the term "postmodern" – for the mere reason that the history of culture has to this day foreseen no newer epochal designation. [trans. from the German by W.W.]

[10] | An overview of the focuses and authors of all thirteen issues can be found at http://www.archiv.hebbel-am-ufer.de/archiv_hebbel_theater/seiten/archiv/theaterschrift/haupt.html (14.07.2015).

theater in Brussels, Felix Meritis in Amsterdam and the Wiener Festwochen in Vienna.[11]

Already years before the appearance of Hans-Thies Lehmann's opus magnum *Postdramatic Theatre*[12], which gathers these international artistic developments under the same term, here texts and conversations with agents themselves negotiate and refine the dimensions of new contemporary theatre art. The journal is a transcript, as it were, of the search for the formal determinations of these new theatre forms – wherein its special merit and its significance as a source lie. In original essays, interviews and conversations, an indeed rather precise spectrum of artists, theatre intendants, dramaturges and theorists get a chance to speak. These agents' observation and analysis also constitute an informational stock for Lehmann's work.[13] What is more, the greater part of categories into which Lehmann divides postdramatic theatre are treated in this journal series as thematic foci.

The self-determined goal, as described by Marianne Van Kerkhoven, of *Theaterschrift* is 'the study in-depth of dramaturgical work, which accompanies creative work... to place the work of artists in and around the various theatres associated in this project, in a context and in a time'.[14] A 'common basic choice' for all artists who are heard or talked about in these pages is their desire for 'their artistic freedom to be as big as possible and that they reject recuperation through the "system"'[15] Even still, 'not wishing to be locked up in institutes implies that other means have to be sought in order to achieve a consolidation which the work of these artists requires, to which it is entitled.'[16]

Be that as it may, the jumping-off point for *Theaterschrift*'s editorial collective lies in 'institutes' – but ones which 'all stand, to a greater or lesser extent, on the fringes of the theatrical landscape as it appears in their respective countries; so for them *Theaterschrift* is also a way of arriving at a "self-definition"'.[17] The task

---

11 | Later editorial appearances are made by the ATEM-Atelier Théâtre et Musique, Nanterre, das Bayerische Staatsschauspiel with Marstall (starting with issue 7/1994), Kampnagel Hamburg (starting with issue 8/1994) and das ICA – Institute for Contemporary Art, London (issue 10/1995). The editorial location of the 'new edition', with a new size and new graphic layout (issues 11-13, 1997-98), moved to Künstlerhaus Bethanien in Berlin, with an editorial team consisting of Felix Meritis, Kaaitheater, Hebbel Theater, the Festival Theaterformen, the EXPO 2000, Wiener Festwochen and Künstlerhaus Bethanien.
12 | Hans-Thies Lehmann, *Postdramatic Theatre*, London: Routledge, 2006.
13 | Cf. the section titled 'Names' in Hans-Thies Lehmann, *Postdramatisches Theater*, London: Routledge, 2006, p. 23.
14 | Marianne Van Kerkhoven, 'Beyond Indifference', in *ThS* 1 (1992), p. 8.
15 | Ibid., p. 10.
16 | Ibid.
17 | Marianne Van Kerkhoven, 'On Dramaturgy', in *ThS* 5-6 (1994), p.16

at hand for the journal amounts, therefore, to a reflective accompaniment of the artistic working practices employed by both theatre artists and theatre houses.

Figure 4: 'Woyzeck', Pip Simmons, Theater der Welt, Hamburg, 1979. Photograph: Friedemann Simon

These artists' basic initial situation as regards dramaturgy and aesthetics consists in the fact that 'at present, at the close of the 20th century, the theatrical basic code, that is to say, the essential dialectics between fiction and reality – appears to be interpreted in a fundamentally different way than at the start of this century.[18] [...] The relationship between 'real' and 'unreal' in the world becomes one of their important points of attention.'[19]; the 'story of the world can only be told by breaks and jumps', whereas 'one can still feel a desire for a unity'[20]. The 'power of dreaming seems to be the only power which modern art has at its disposal', whereas 'the powerlessness of theatre is almost indiscriminately admitted. [...] the artist does not see him/herself (anymore) as a world reformer'.[21]

---

18 | Van Kerkhoven, 'Beyond Indifference', p. 14.
19 | Ibid., p. 26.
20 | Ibid., p. 28.
21 | Ibid.

As further 'leitmotives'[22] of these new forms of theatre, Van Kerkhoven broaches their a priori European – hence not primarily nationalistic[23] – dimension, the constant togetherness of artistic praxis and theoretical reflection that is consequently 'theory of practice'[24], as well as the goal to convey experiences by means of art:

'[Experience] is considered the (only) way to obtain knowledge about reality. Experience means: "living through something", it means "being touched". [...] Observation is the essential vehicle for this experience and these artists seem to be actually aware of the fact that nowadays this observation is influenced or even manipulated [...]; moreover, they try to use this vehicle in their work'.[25]

What is at stake is hence an approach towards new determinants acting upon the relation between theatre (or theatre art) and the world, and upon the circumstances and phenomena of those theatres and those worlds. To this end, highly diverse suggestions are made throughout *Theaterschrift*:

'The question emerges whether modern theatre, in a context of far-reaching mediatisation, derealisation and fictionalisation of reality (cf. the role of the media during the Gulf War), can still be approached as a "purely fictional" medium. For some time already avant-garde artists within the theatre have felt the need to bring "more reality", "more materiality" on stage. Does this mean that the old paradigm of theatre – to "pretend" within a certain time and space – and the acceptance of this paradigm by an audience is unsettled?'

asks Marianne Van Kerkhoven, in all likelihood rhetorically.[26]
Anatolij Vassiliev makes a statement in near contradistinction:

'During the past few years the process is such that I stopped examining life outside the theatre. I have been concentrating on studying only life in the theatre, life in the art world. [...] Not life itself but the state of the ideas in this life [were of interest to me]. [...]

---

22 | Translator's note: English versions exist for all the texts from the journal *Theaterschrift*, a quadrilingual journal (as mentioned by the author). The author's citations are hence drawn here from these English originals, which in some cases contain linguistic idiosyncrasies. In all quotations from *Theaterschrift* (exception: see fn. 7), the preexisting English versions have been used.
23 | Van Kerkhoven, 'Beyond Indifference', pp. 18/20.
24 | Ibid., p. 18.
25 | Ibid., p. 26.
26 | Ibid., p. 16.

As a consequence, I locked the doors of my theatre. And the more you close the theatre doors, the more it reminds you of a monastery.'

– in any other situation, one would be shut out from the examination of ideas pertaining to society.[27]

In terms of the concept of experience as the centre of theatre's perceptual and effectual potential, Ritsaert ten Cate asserts that 'to my surprise the changes in the world around us have not had such a great effect on my life and work until now.'[28] Your 'experience may be something similar as with the development of CNN: the physical feeling that world news is coming closer, although very superficially.'[29]

Discussing the central point of departure for her work, Laurie Anderson too instances the form of current-events television unfolding in near real time, something relatively new at that point, in its provision of the entire world as live event. Anderson nevertheless accounts for the edited nature of its content and thereby for its fundamental manipulation: 'The whole world is filtered for us by CNN.' Anderson's goal is 'to *look* at things well, not to change them. That's not my job.'[30] And the Performer Tom Janssen formulates the topic thus: 'Television has changed our way of life permanently, as photography did as well.'[31]

The open form of honing observations of and on new forms of theatre art as well as garnering hypotheses on ways of working through conversations with artists, and condensing or expanding on preliminary perceptions or theoretical conceptions, characterises the editorial work of *Theaterschrift*, a work which is also by and large consistently maintained throughout the course of its production; and it is perhaps no accident that the last issue of *Theaterschrift*[32] was published in September 1998, shortly before the 1999 appearance of Lehmann's, in a manner of speaking, canonical concept of 'postdramatic theatre', in comparison to which the 'internal discussion' seems very nearly obsolete.

---

[27] | Analolij Vassiliev, interviewed by Michael Haerdter, 'Theater as monastic community', in *ThS* 1 (1992), pp. 46–78, here p. 64
[28] | Jan Ritsema, interviewed by Marianne Van Kerkhoven, 'So that it remains flexible in itself', in *ThS* 1 (1992), pp. 88–112, here p. 88.
[29] | Ibid., p. 90
[30] | Laurie Anderson, interviewed by Tom Stromberg, 'The speed of change', in *ThS* 1 (1992), pp. 118–132, here p. 120, 124.
[31] | Tom Janssen, interviewed by Elske van de Holst and Marianne Van Kerkhoven, 'We watch with dry eyes and we prepare our soup', in *ThS* 1 (1992), pp. 136–156, here p. 142.
[32] | This issue was published under the theme 'Spirituality: a Utopia?'.

SCENOGRAPHY — 'THE WRITTEN SPACE'

In this open form, thirteen issues handle thirteen discrete aesthetic and dramaturgical thematic clusters on new, postmodern European theatre.

Issue two, titled 'The Written Space', discusses new determinants affecting the relation between theatre art and space, and does so in regard to both the location of work and performance, and the 'stage' in a stricter sense as each work's 'location of occurrence'. Here too it can be viewed as remarkable that Achim Freyer's[33], Robert Wilson's[34] und BAK-Truppen's[35] radical questionings of the central-perspectival Renaissance stage[36] are flanked by a 'Plea for the Italian Stage' by Urs Troller[37].

Troller's plea, however, is anything but conservative orthodox loyalty (or even reactionary, if seen from the perspective of the postmodern artist): 'I think that the question of what theatre can still offer in the context or in the ensemble of all the other media – where is [the thing that] makes it unique among other fields of expression? – can be investigated today at the Italian stage: the box is antinaturalistic and antirealistic.'[38] Even if 'the famous saying of Artaud, that theatre is something quite different from speech which has been written down, and which is then simply supposed to be transposed on stage' were accurate, 'the ritual space that Artaud dreamed of can no longer be restored'; and 'that's not due to our form of theatre, but to the changed – and fundamentally changed – social conditions under which we have to make theatre'[39], formulates Troller against the postmodern efforts to overcome a 'hierarchization of means' in the theatre and supplant language as the 'top of this pyramid'.[40]

Yet all in all, and for the most part, the texts in this issue point towards the development of 'scenography' as opposed to stage design:

---

33 | Achim Freyer, interviewed by Bettina Masuch, 'Looking Behind the Mirror of Appearances', in *ThS* 2 (1992), pp. 114-130.
34 | Robert Wilson, interviewed by Bettina Masuch and Tom Stromberg, 'The Architecture of Theatrical Space', in *ThS* 2 (1992), pp. 102-106.
35 | BAK-TRUPPEN, in *ThS* 2 (1992), pp. 108-112.
36 | 'Our traditional theatres are the heirs of the Renaissance theatre, a space in which all the lines of perspective converged on that one central filled point, the place from which the prince watched the proceedings. Now there is no-one sitting there anymore. "The core of the world is empty." (Italo Calvino).'
Marianne Van Kerkhoven, 'The Written Space', in *ThS* 2 (1992), pp. 6-36, here p. 26.
37 | Urs Troller, interviewed by Gerhard Ahrens, 'Plea for the Italian Stage', in *ThS* 2 (1992), pp. 88-100.
38 | Ibid., p. 92.
39 | Ibid., p. 96.
40 | Ibid.

'When the spatial image in the theatre no longer has to serve to give the audience a faithful and recognisable copy of reality, it can fill itself with inner meanings, external references and abstract connotations. The concern that art should evoke an 'illusion of reality' is completely foreign to the artists present over here. The space which is written or described in this way can be 'read', not as a reference to the world but as an autonomous entity.'[41]

WORLDLINESS AND AESTHETIC EXPLORATION

Both of the first two issues of *Theaterschrift* distinctly show that two currents can be documented as concerns artistic impulses towards the contemporary renewal of the theatre: on the one hand, approaches with which artists react to social, political or cultural developments and proceed to engage with these – the production of 'worldly theatre' –; and on the other, approaches shaped by an aesthetic research that is, so to speak, 'immanent in art'.

The texts in the third issue, under the heading 'Border Violations', circulate within the interface between both tendencies; the task at stake is to identify the momentum that drives these artistic developments: 'How do you describe that inner necessity that takes you to the point of creation? What drives you to go and stand on a stage? So doing, what risks (artistic and otherwise) do you take? To what extent do you have to treat yourself and your audience with 'violence'?'[42] – all these questions are posed 'at the core of the interviews/texts/statements' either by or about the work of Peter Greenaway, Reza Abdoh, René Pollesch, Romeo Castellucci, Hans-Thies Lehmann, Jan Fabre, Marina Abramovic, Truus Bronkhorst, Lloyd Newson, Josse de Pauw, Tom Jansen, Einar Schleef and Ivan Stanev.

These pages include reactions by artists to border transgressions in, for instance, pop culture, where sensational films like *The Texas Chainsaw Massacre* or *The Terminator* violate existing taboos against representations of violence. On this subject, Peter Greenaway says 'that all satisfactory works of art necessarily do have built into them areas of sensitivity and taboo which push the boundaries of human experience to the edges'.[43]

---

41 | Van Kerkhoven, 'The Written Space', p. 16.
42 | Marianne Van Kerkhoven, 'Close to a secret', in *ThS* 3 (1993), pp. 6-20, here p. 8.
43 | Peter Greenaway, interviewed by Brigitte Fürle, 'The exposing of human beings', in *ThS* 3 (1993), pp. 24-42, here p. 26.

Figure 5: 'M7 Catalonia', Els Joglars, Kampnagel, Hamburg, 1979. Photograph: Friedemann Simon

However, Greenaway and the other authors in 'Border Violations' also insist that the breach of boundary and taboo in their work is not a matter of provocation of the audience and its limits of taste (or its voyeurism), but rather of uncompromisingly radical views into the depths of relations of body-politics. Greenaway refers both to cases of alleged or real child abuse and to the advertising campaign of the garment company Benetton depicting 'this naked second-old child, which caused such a furore in England that all the posters had to be taken down'.[44]

Reza Abdoh also makes reference in his work to the then-current events of the first Gulf War and to CNN's coverage thereof as well as to the murders committed by the sex killer Jeffrey Dahmers in the USA[45], and when asked, he confirms that his choice of references to phenomena of social violence is made in pursuit of a concept of catharsis: it's not that he believes so much in catharsis as 'the power of staged atrocity'; he understands it more 'as a celebration of

---

44 | Ibid., p. 38.
45 | Reza Abdoh, interviewed by Hortensia Völckers and Martin Bergelt, 'Violence – Death – Theatre', in *ThS* 3 (1993), p. 48-64.

[emotion]. I don't want to send the audience through purgatory but to create a solemn atmosphere of emotion'.[46]

In the nineties, war, violence, sexuality and pornography are topical public issues to which artists respond; they are also instances of the 'conditio humana' to which the praxis of artistic research turns, especially in the case of Jan Fabre and Marina Abramovic[47], who in their work show real injury and pain in their own bodies as well as the bodies of performers on stage as artistic actions, thereby directing attention towards the unreality of images and enactments of the human being (in the performing arts) which comply with conventions of taste and taboo. Hans-Thies Lehmann explains and defends this artistic praxis in his discussion of Jan Fabre's work:

'Pain, violence, death, and the resultant feelings of fear and compassion, have since antiquity been at the centre of *pleasure in tragic themes*. Nowadays we tend to translate 'eleos' and 'phobos' more as 'misery' and 'horror'. According to Aristotle these were used to evoke 'catharsis' in the audience of an Attic tragedy, designed to purify them of that very state of misery and horror. Whether you understand the latter as release from such feelings, as their mitigation, as their refinement, or as abreaction, the process in any case implies the purification of a form of psycho-physical attack on the audience. The realm of appearance is not cut off from the living world, it is a part of it.'[48]

In such modalities, risky border experiences and the deployment of one's own person into artistic praxis reflect both the radicality of artistic research interests and the situation in which violence and terrorism creep closer as social experiences after the post-1989 years, when a longer period of relative peace prevailing in Western Europe during the Cold War ended.

The pronouncements of these artists reveal two things here: for one, they provide insight into the ideas, thoughts and reflections which initiate and accompany their artistic work and through which they actualise processes of (re)examination; content-wise, they articulate a special quality belonging to these artistic works: they concern themselves with topics and phenomena of the immediate cultural, political or social present – not to mention the present of the audience. 'Tua res agitur' – yours are the subjects of these proceedings – could be the motto which heads these works. The ceaseless flow of real-time news; the breach of taboos against the showing, even exhibiting of violence, death, sexuality; the return of war to Europe; the treatment of diversion and

---

46 | Ibid., p. 56.

47 | Marina Abramovic, interviewed by Ilse Kujkens, 'Catching the moment', in *ThS* 3 (1993), pp. 104-120.

48 | Hans-Thies Lehmann, 'When rage coagulates into form ... On Jan Fabre's "aesthetics of poison"', in *ThS* 3 (1993), pp. 90-102, here p. 92.

entertainment – beyond the embodiment of drama and consequently dramatic literature, these theatre makers take their works directly into conflict with political, social, cultural and communicational relations and conditions, the experience of which they share with their audience. Analysis and orientation within these circumstances are therefore pertinent to their work: perceptual art, experiential art, orientative art.

This holds especially true for issues 4/1993, titled 'The Inner Side of Silence', and 9/1995 on 'Theatre and Music', where the latter in a certain sense reciprocally ponders the ubiquity of noise and music and technologies of sound generation and transmission while also detailing artistic treatments thereof:

'But what really is the purpose of theatre (or dance)? Perhaps to place us in society (in politics) with the aid of work at the fringes of society, by rejecting the terms of the challenge which mass communication imposes (on us), and by looking, instead, for the seeds of a new contract (between the cultural act and society).'[49]

'But also, Sarajevo' – in other words, after the recent Balkan wars is one point of deliberation for a treatment of silence:

'Naturally, there's silence and there's silence. The complicitous silence of politicians. The shameful silence of intellectuals. The resigned silence of public opinion. The media casually mention Sarajevo, only to tell us of our so-called powerlessness, and, in parallel, to inoculate us, perversely, with a feeling of guilt because, in point of fact, we do nothing. Sarajevo is besieged, as we are besieged by sounds, by information which we oppose only with feeble passivity.'[50]

Dramaturgy of the New Theatre

A central locus of interaction for efforts at more precisely apprehending and delineating new forms of theatre art could be found at the symposium *Context 01: Active Pooling, the New Theatre's Word Perfect*, organised by the venue Felix Meritis in Amsterdam, which took place 25–29 August 1993. A series of texts in the *Theaterschrift* double issue 5–6 are extracted from this context.[51]

---

49 | Jean Marc Adolphe, 'Fragments drawn from silence so as not to shut up completely', in *ThS* 4 (1993), pp. 184-202, here p. 194.
50 | Ibid., p. 194/196.
51 | Cf. Marianne Van Kerkhoven, 'On Dramaturgy', in *ThS* 5-6 (1994), pp. 8-34, here p. 14

In her introduction, Marianne Van Kerkhoven summarises the essential facets and tendencies of this dramaturgy for the 'new theatre':

- a 'process-oriented method of working; the meaning, the intentions, the form and the substance of a play arise during the working process, so that the actors often also make a great contribution by means of the material they supply during the rehearsals'.[52]
- 'dramaturgy is no longer a means of bringing out the structure of the meaning of the world in a play, but (a quest for) a provisional or possible arrangement which the artist imposes on those elements he gathers from a reality that appears to him chaotic. In this kind of world picture, causality and linearity lose their value, storyline and psychologically explicable characters are put at risk, there is no longer a hierarchy amongst the artistic building blocks used...'[53]
- 'The "single" individual no longer has the structural means available to master reality's complexity.'[54] This leads to attempts at simultaneity of actions, to circular narrative structure, to the multiple perspectives and also to the next point:
- the need for 'another organisational structure for the performance of repertory theatre with the "leaderless" group De Vere: not the view of one single director or dramaturge of the classical theatre heritage, but a multitude of views, a repertoire in which each actor makes a contribution...'[55]
- 'In this sort of operation production's primary "building blocks" are the participants themselves, and their experience: in this new dramaturgy each actor's personal history gains considerably in importance.'[56]
- 'The individual "writer" of a play is tending to disappear; he is replaced by a collective; but on the other hand this collective has a nature different from the one we remember from the seventies: at that time the groups all tended to rally themselves behind one single (political) conviction; these days the collectives [...] are, rather, made up of the sum of the individuals, expected to provide "many voices".'[57]
- 'The "new dramaturgy" is also looking for a new relationship with its audience: this theatre wants its audience to share in the multiple points of view, or at least alienate from its "normal" way of viewing. [...] In this way the dramaturgy of space and its division also inevitably becomes a drama-

---

[52] | Ibid., p. 18
[53] | Ibid., p. 18 seq.
[54] | Ibid., p. 20.
[55] | Ibid., p. 22.
[56] | Ibid., p. 20.
[57] | Ibid., p. 22.

turgy of the audience and of context in which a performance unfolds. If reality has become an inextricable tangle or a tower of Babel in which all languages are spoken at the same time, then an overview and a spot from which the spectator can obtain this overview are no longer to be achieved.'[58]

This substrate of 'new theatre' dramaturgy – for the description of which Hans-Thies Lehmann proposed (at the aforementioned conference in Amsterdam) the compilation of a thesaurus of sorts, an encyclopaedic 'lexicon' composed of 'terms, notions and components'[59] – is developed in this issue of *Theaterschrift* through texts by Erwin Jans, Josette Féral, Jan Kott, Eda Cufer und Emil Hvratin, Mira Rafalowicz, Marianne Van Kerhoven, Norman Frisch, Elisabeth LeCompte, Robert Lepage, den BAK-Truppen, David Mayaan, Jan Joris Lamers and Alexander Kluge.

Acting – Performance

Now that the building blocks 'stage' (space) and 'sound' (noise, music) as well as the 'dramaturgy' of the 'new theatre' have been examined, it would indeed seem to suggest itself that we turn our attention to the traditional centre of performance – to 'playing' – which is the object of investigation in the seventh issue of *Theaterschrift*[60] under the title 'The Actor'.

Here reference is made to traditions of the conception of acting:

'When we published the very first, exclusively Dutch-language, Theaterschrift 'On Acting' in 1991, we tried to define the new variation of acting that had been developing in Flanders and the Netherlands since the early eighties. In fact we described this form of acting at the time as a Sort of 'third' variation: in contrast to 'the Stanislavski actor' whose work is based on immersion in the character and 'the Brecht actor', who displays his character to the audience, 'the third variation actor' primarily wants to show himself to the audience, whether or not by means of a character.'[61]

---

58 | Ibid., p. 22.
59 | Cf. ibid., p. 14.
60 | June 1994. The issue is dedicated to the performer Ron Vawter of the New Yorker company Wooster Group, who died on 16 April 1994 'high in the air, during his flight from Europe to America'. This new syndrome, which was defined in 1981 as a full-fledged infectious illness, is also a pivotal sociocultural point of reference for the artists of the 'new theatre', not least for Reza Abdoh and his troupe dar a luz. Abdoh died on 12 May 1995 in New York due to AIDS related complications. Cf. Wikipedia, https://en.wikipedia.org/wiki/Reza_Abdoh (14.07.2015).
61 | Marianne Van Kerkhoven, 'The Actor', in *ThS* 7 (1994), pp. 8-30, here p. 10.

This 'third variant', which was first developed mainly with Flemish-Dutch and American exemplars[62] – above all in the work of the Wooster Group – is delved into further in this issue through conversations with a variety of actors, four American, four German, three Flemish, one Dutch, one English and one French[63]. With fodder for reflection provided by Hans-Thies Lehmann and the directors Christoph Marthaler, Jan Lauwers and Gerardjan Rijnders, the image of an actor 'very probably influenced by performance art, among other things',[64] one who 'no longer steps into the character's shoes', who 'allows this imaginary figure to live within' in order that 'the character almost "disappears". "Really existing on a stage" means first of all being oneself, which means that the personality of the actor is more important than his technical capacities: it is not rare for "amateurs" with an interesting stage presence to be integrated into the working process.'[65]

This – and herein lies another perspective on the transformed production modes of the 'new theatre' –

'naturally changes the relationship between the actors and the director. On the one hand, the actor is the "most important material" on the basis of which the director tells his story, and on the other the actor acquires a greater independence as a determining element in the play: he is no longer an interpreter but a co-creator of the piece. This also has its repercussions on the way in which groups of actors come together, or do not, on the way in which actors treat each other on stage and on the way the audience sees this sort of acting.'[66]

And almost secondarily, mention is made of the fact that 'Ron Vawter developed his roles in the plays of Elisabeth LeCompte, which are planned to the last detail. Ron Vawter was pleased to have reached the final version of Frank Dell's *"The Temptation of St Anthony"* after 9 years, while his more traditionally thinking colleague Ulrich Wildgruber feels frustrated and played out when he has to tour the same play for more than three years'.[67]

---

62 | Cf. ibid., p. 14.
63 | Ibid., p. 26; the actors are Ulrich Wildgruber, Hermann Beyer, Margarita Broich, Martin Wuttke, Ron Vawter, Frank Vercruissen, Juliana Francis, Tom Fitzpatrick, Tom Pearl, André Wilms, Viviane de Muynck, Frieda Pittors as well as the dancer and choreographer Wendy Houstoun and the musician Paul Koek.
64 | Ibid., p. 10/12.
65 | Ibid., p. 12.
66 | Ibid.
67 | Ibid., p. 26.

Issue nine from July 1995 on the topic 'Theatre and Music' constitutes de facto the completion of the series of 'workbooks' that explore forms of the 'new theatre'. With little focus on 'theatre music', however, it deals primarily with newer interpretations of the genre 'music theatre' and its relation to opera and opera's tradition.[68] Classical dramaturgical themes for theatre as well as theatre artists are tabled in issues eight, 'Memory'[69], and ten, 'City / Art / Cultural Identity'[70].

And starting with issue eleven, which appears in 1997, not only does the format and the outer appearance of the journal change. The editorial office too shifts from Brussels to Berlin (into Künstlerhaus Bethanien, which itself also joins the circle of co-editors), and Sabine Pochhammer assumes the role of chief editor, replacing Marianne Van Kerkhoven.

Even though its exceptional multilingualism is maintained, even though Hugo de Greef, director of the Kaaitheater, and Tom Stromberg, who meanwhile had moved into the position of director at the cultural programme at *EXPO 2000 Hannover*, assert its continuity and 'guarantee' its 'quality'[71] as compared to the earlier issues, the 'new edition'[72] demonstrates an unmistakable change of course: the gesture of self-exploration and discussion of the 'new theatre' wanes in favour of a scientific and feuilletonistic treatment of dramturgical themes: 'The Return of the Classics?' (with emphasis on Shakespeare), issue 11/1997; 'Time', issue 12/1997 and 'Spirituality: a Utopia?', issue 13/1998, which does not appear until September of that year.

I will engage in no speculation about the end of the journal – whereas a reconstruction of internal discussions occurring at the time would surely be of interest. Suffice it to say that the following is clear: the new artforms' phase of 'self-invention', at least with regard to their 'implementation' and institutional stabilisation in Europe, is to a great extent a settled matter – and to accompany that, the publishing of the canonical work: Hans-Thies Lehmann's *Postdramatic Theatre* is right around the corner.

---

68 | Cf. the essay by Matthias Rebstock in this collection of essays.
69 | December 1994.
70 | December 1995.
71 | Hugo de Greef and Tom Stromberg, Editorial, in *ThS* 11 (1997), p. 8.
72 | As it is called starting with issue 12 (1997).

Theaterscapes and New Theatre in Europe – Cultural-Political Situations and Impulses

A glimpse back on the synopsis of European postmodern theatre's theoretical self-invention reveals its origins in processes of dismantling and reassembling the traditional forms of dramatic-literary theatre as well as the aspiration to go beyond it and utilise the theatre as a medium for artistic engagement with the social and cultural developments of the time: seeking societal, political and cultural relevance, being on eye level with the audience and working towards the formation of medial communication are the most important perspectives proper to the developments that are advanced by artists.

By the middle of the nineties, these new theatre forms – whose designation as 'postdramatic theatre' establishes itself (even before the appearance of Lehmann's work) quite rapidly – are largely consolidated.

At annual international festivals for emerging artists, such as Junge Hunde at Kampnagel in Hamburg (1993–2001), reich und berühmt at Podewil in Berlin (1996–2001) and Hope and Glory at Theaterhaus Gessnerallee in Zurich (1997–2004), one can already discern the next generation of postmodern theatre artists. At the Belgian Kunstenfestivaldesarts, at the Dutch Holland-Festival, the 'Fringe' Festival in Edinburgh, the Zurich Theaterspektakel, but also at the Wiener Festwochen, the Parisian Festival d'Automne and in the programmes of pertinent festivals and production houses from Bergen, Norway, to Zagreb and Polverigi, newer theatre forms are regularly shown and arise within the framework of more or less stable national and international cooperations and coproductions. The Informal European Theatre Meeting (IETM), established in 1981, has since 1989 enjoyed the status of an international nonprofit organisation that represents the interests of supporters of the 'new theatre' in the realm of cultural politics and elsewhere.[73]

Yet the development of these forms, which springs mainly from artistic impulses, is met throughout European theatrescapes with highly varying conditions influencing their creation in varying ways. One must note here that the heretofore illustrated developments in no way comprehensively delineate the field of *new* forms in these theatrescapes. The artists studied in *Theaterschrift* and consulted by Hans-Thies Lehmann are somewhat of an 'avant-garde': leading figures in new production modalities, dramaturgies and aesthetics for a theatre that above all pursues aspirations for the contemporary, for relevance, for authenticity and for a closeness to the audience, thereby distinguishing itself from elite cultural institutions and their productions that representatively display the classic canon of drama. However, apart from the

---

73 | Cf. IETM, https://www.ietm.org/sites/default/files/ietmbrochure_pages.pdf (14.07. 2015).

artists and troupes who find their forum in *Theaterschrift*, during the sixties and seventies stages and theatrescapes across Europe are entered by a wide array of young agents and groups who emulate these avant-gardes or else embark on the creation of new theatre work for new audiences by means of other production modes, employing their own ideas and their own artistic, cultural, political motifs.

The conditions for the formation of new kinds of theatre art in which leitmotifs crystallise are also very different from one nation's theatrescapes to the other – as Manfred Brauneck has shown.

At the same time, his depictions are characterised – and for this reason also become somewhat bewildering and remain rather incomparable as 'theatre landscape paintings' parsed in individual national contexts – by the fact that the elements (structures of the production and presentation of theatre, in connection with its conception, shaping and financing through the public hand on state/provincial and municipal levels) of theatrical-literary and theatrical-artistic productions are handled according to their varying weights in their respective theatrescapes. That being said, Brauneck's descriptions are to be understood under the rather rhapsodic, diffuse term 'theatre sector'.

An overview of the Western-European theatrescapes described by Brauneck shows that in most countries of Western Europe[74], efforts were undertaken to reform and modernise the structures of both state, or 'national' theatre, and bourgeois municipal theatre, both of which had, historically, emerged during the nineteenth and early twentieth centuries. Precisely these reform endeavours determine the conditions of emergence for the new, postmodern theatre forms.

As this process unfolds in all West-European countries[75], impulse-functions lie in store for social protest movements as well as for the emergence of new, independent theatre groups that defected in spirits ranging from critical to rebellious against social, political and cultural circumstances and structures, and against the bourgeois, high-cultural theatre sector.

---

74 | The German situation – the 'German system' consolidated in the Weimar Republic, whose origins in the late eventuation of national unity and the after-effects of a system of small allied states pose a special case to this day – is not discussed in this essay.

75 | Spain and Portugal are not discussed here, since other 'special circumstances' – the dictatorial regimes of Franco and Salazar – prevailed here during the times of late-sixties youth revolt.

MODEL STRUCTURES: THE NETHERLANDS AND BELGIUM

Figure 6: 'Allemaal Indiaan', Victoria & Les Ballets C de la B, Kampnagel, Hamburg, 2000. Photograph: Friedemann Simon

The Dutch model[76] can be considered a special 'type' of theatre sector whose theatrescapes was built into singular structural forms already immediately after the Second World War – and which in turn has also been 'undergoing reform', quite fundamentally and with far-reaching consequences, since 2011.[77]

---

76 | Cf. the chapter on the Netherlands (*Theater in den Niederlanden*) in Brauneck WaB/V. 5, pp. 842–860; Martin Frey, *Creatieve Marge: Die Entwicklung des Niederländischen Off-Theaters*, Vienna and Cologne: Böhlau, 1991 (Institut für Theaterwissenschaft an der Universität Wien (ed.), *Maske und Kothurn: Internationale Beiträge zur Theaterwissenschaft*, appendix 14), and for more recent developments:

77 | 'The Netherlands and Flanders, Theater der Zeit spezial', Berlin: Theater der Zeit, 2013 and Simon van den Berg, 'Mit dem Rücken zum Publikum? Theaterbrief Niederlande (1), Die Subventionskürzungen im niederländischen Kunstbetrieb, http://www.nachtkritik.de/index.php?option=com_content&view=article&id=5815:die-subventionskuerzungen-im-niederlaendischen-kunstbereich&catid=622:theaterbrief-aus-den-niederlanden&Itemid=99 (15.07.2015); and Simon van den Berg, 'Zerstörerische Debatte, Theaterbrief Niederlande (2), Ein halbes Jahr nach den Subventionskürzungen wird das Ausmaß langsam deutlich', http://www.nachtkritik.de/index.php?option=com_content&view=article&id=6687:theaterbrief-niederlande-2-ein-halbes-jahr-nach-den-subventionskuerzungen-im-niederlaendischen-kunstbe

These structures, which in the 1980s and 90s produced the most advanced and successful theatre companies of postmodern European theatre, were based, on the one hand, on the spectacular actions and processes occurring in the course of the 1960s Dutch crisis of modernisation, which brought about radical, lasting changes in the theatre sector built after the war: in the Netherlands, as a country occupied by German forces during the war, where sharp separation from German culture played an important role in post-liberation reorganisation[78], the theatre sector and support system was shaped upon the two discrete pillars of, firstly, ensemble funding[79] – the funding of theatre productions – and secondly, of theatre venues.[80]

On the other hand, the 'Actie Tomaat' – an action on the part of independent artists who protested on 9 October 1969 against the artistic encrustation of Dutch theatre by throwing tomatoes at a performance at the Nederlandse Comedie[81] – has a lasting impact as an impulse for contemporary innovations in funding practices.[82] The new system enabled the incorporation and (financial) support of many groups who were beginning to produce and show another theatre with political and artistic motifs[83] – groups like Publiekstheater, Baal and Het Werktheater in Amsterdam[84] and newer production and presentation venues such as Mickery, Shaffy und Felix Meritis[85].

Without fathoming the advantages and disadvantages of this 'system' here, it undoubtedly offers artists and troupes the opportunity to independently work, form and constantly reinvent themselves according to their own criteria and aspirations; and theatre houses (and festivals) can shape their programmes with distinction and diversity based on their local and regional audiences, not to mention invite guest performances representing a wide variety of approaches.

---

reich-wird-das-ausmass-langsam-deutlich&catid=622:theaterbrief-aus-den-niederlanden&Itemid=99 (15.07.2015).

78 | The decentralised *Holland Festival*, founded in 1947, arose, according to Brauneck, in explicit separation from festivals like Bayreuth or Salzburg. Cf. Brauneck, 'Theater in den Niederlanden', *WaB*/V. 5, p. 845.

79 | E.g. Amsterdams Toneelgezelschap, de Haagse Comedi, Rotterdams Toneel, Nederlandse Comedi and the children's theatre Ensemble *Puck*. Cf. Brauneck, 'Niederlande', *WaB*/V., p. 844.

80 | Cf. ibid., p. 844.

81 | Cf. ibid., p. 842f and Frey, *Creatieve Marge*, p. 33f.

82 | Frey, *Creatieve Marge*, p. 43ff.

83 | Frey gives a rather comprehensive account of the political 'Formingstheater' (ibid., p. 49ff) and the MIME movement (p. 63).

84 | Cf. Brauneck, 'Theater in den Niederlanden', pp. 850-852.

85 | Ibid., p. 849f; and in much more detail: Frey, *Creatieve Marge*, pp. 54-122.

Since 1947, central decisions on the disbursement of structural and financial support are met by a 'Raad voor de Kunst' (council for the arts), which has functioned as an independent organ since 1955. Yet this structure is continually subjected to revisions. For instance, in 1984 funding is limited to four-year periods[86], and yet fundamentally the structure has endured into the immediate present (2015). At the end of the twentieth century, the theatrescapes of the Netherlands consists of 125 municipal stages and 60 studios[87] that show the work of approximately 1,000 producers and combos.[88]

This is the basis for essential artistic innovative developments that radiate across Western Europe[89], especially since the 1994 founding of the theatre school DasArts in Amsterdam by Ritsaert ten Cate and Marijke Hoogenboom[90] and due to international cooperations, coproductions and festivals (see section on *Theaterschrift* above). Since the expansion of Dutch theatre legislation in 1973, all theatres are funded publically, whereas a crucial funding instrument lies in subsidies earned through ticket sales, of which approximately fifty percent are procured by public funding.[91]

Yet a system that enables flexibility and dynamism also makes it possible to cut the ground from underneath the theatrescapes through simple budget measures: 'This Monday, June 27 [2011], the Dutch Parliament will decide on profound cuts to the cultural budget in the Netherlands. The minority government under the liberal VVD and the Christian-conservative CDA, with the support of the right-wing populist PVV (chaired by Geert Wilders), plans to sink the art budget from around 950 to 750 million euros. These cuts are not evenly distributed. The performing arts in particular will be burdened with an approximately 46 percent reduction in budget', writes Simon van den Berg in his June 23 2011 report on the Dutch theatrescapes (1) on Nachtkritik.de.[92]

Since these cuts first went into effect at the end of the four-year allotment period in 2013, many groups evidently had prepared themselves for the shift and began seeking other funding sources to compensate for their losses – in

---

86 | Cf. Brauneck, 'Theater in den Niederlanden', p. 859.
87 | Ibid., p. 859.
88 | Ibid., p. 860.
89 | For example, Hans Man in't Veld, artistic director of Kampnagel Hamburg from 1990 to 1994, comes from the troupe Het Werktheater.
90 | Cf. Brauneck, 'Theater in den Niederlanden', p. 849; and Dasarts – Amsterdams Hogeschool voor de Kunsten, http://www.ahk.nl/theaterschool/opleidingen-theater/dasarts-master-of-theatre/about-dasarts/history/ (15.07.2015).
91 | Ibid.
92 | Simon van den Berg, 'Mit dem Rücken zum Publikum? Theaterbrief Niederlande (1) – Die Subventionskürzungen im niederländischen Kunstbereich'.

any case, the initially feared cultural clear-cutting of 2013[93] seems not to have occurred.

Structures fundamentally similar to those in the Netherlands – albeit with two state-funded national theatres in Brussels and Antwerp for francophone Wallonia and Flanders, respectively – can be found in its neighbour Belgium, which has, above all in its Flemish areas, produced a range of outstanding companies in international postmodern theatre during the last quarter of the twentieth century:[94] Jan Fabre's Troubleyn, Jan Lauwers' Needcompany, the dance company Rosas and most recently the young troupe FC Bergman[95]. And Luc Perceval, who in the late nineties turned to working with municipal theatre ensembles in Germany, initially developed his first works with such a troupe (De Blauwe Mandaag, founded 1984[96]), before his production *Schlachten*[97] opened the way into German municipal theatre in 1999.

Brauneck characterises the 'trend' in Flemish and Dutch theatre in the eighties and nineties thus as follows:

'It was a development that largely gave up on previous decades' ambitions towards theatre work that made – sometimes very direct – reference to current problems in society, in favour of artistic autonomy and issues cut from a more universal cloth. General problems of humanity increasingly came into view, as did a concern with the rudiments of stagecraft itself, with language and the body of the actor. This stance finds expression also in the new production-structures employed by a number of groups. With Jan Fabre's production office Troubleyn as a yardstick, they create their own, mutually cooperating centres. They develop their projects to a great extent outside the established theatre sector and also establish their own educational institutions.'[98]

---

93 | 'There will be no further renewal. The avant-garde is dead and buried,' feared Johan Simons, interviewed by Sebastian Kirsch: 'Was macht das Theater, Johan Simons?' In *The Netherlands and Flanders*, special issue, *Theater der Zeit* (2012), p. 49.

94 | Cf. Brauneck, 'Belgien', pp. 861–872.

95 | Cf. Jörg Vorhaben, 'Arbeiten ohne Regisseur: Zur Geschichte der Schauspielerkollektive in Flandern und den Niederlanden', in *The Netherlands and Flanders*, special issue, *Theater der Zeit*, pp. 30–33, here p. 32.

96 | Cf. Braueck, 'Belgien', p. 865.

97 | Text by Tom Lanoye, premiered in 1997 as *Ten Orloog* in Ghent. Cf. *Schlachten!*, Wikipedia, https://de.wikipedia.org/wiki/Schlachten! (15.7.2015).

98 | Brauneck, 'Belgien', p. 869.

THEATRE (ALMOST) WITHOUT THE STATE: GREAT BRITAIN

Figure 7: 'Enter Achilles', DV8 Physical Theatre, Kampnagel, Hamburg, 1998. Photograph: Friedemann Simon

As a now and again abhorred antithesis[99] to the system of public – federally and locally – funded infrastructure and production praxis in the Netherlands and Belgium, the Anglo-Saxon system is directed, to the greatest possible extent, at governmental diffidence in all things related to the formation of culture and theatre.[100] Britain's overwhelmingly auto-financed theatre sector has certainly 'also prevented [...] that the theatre in England alienated its audience through experiments that went to far'[101], as Manfred Brauneck reckons. At the same time, besides the four state-financed national theatres—the Royal Opera

---

99 | Simon van den Berg writes about the 'ideal of the Anglo-Saxon model—in Great Britain and the USA, the state assumes only a few responsibilities related to the support of the arts, leaving the financing to market dynamics or private sponsors'—which is going to be adopted in the Netherlands. Cf., Simon van den Berg, 'Mit dem Rücken zum Publikum?' Theaterbrief Niederlande (1).

100 | Theatre censorship—i.e., the obligation to submit theatre texts which are to be performed publicly for approval through the Lord Chamberlain—was not, however, done away with until a 1968 Act of Parliament. Cf. Manfred Brauneck, 'Englisches Theater in der zweiten Hälfte des 20. Jahrhunderts: Großbritannien und Irland', *WaB*/V., pp. 873-943, here p. 874.

101 | Brauneck, 'Großbritannien', *WaB*/V., p. 875.

House Covent Garden, Sadlers Wells, the Royal Shakespeare Company and the National Theatre—a large number of regional 'reps' (Repertory Theatres)[102] exist that play much of the time with their own ensembles.

Both Peter Brook, who left England in 1970 and since then has lived and worked in Paris[103], and Peter Zadek[104] had their first practical theatre making experience in this system, which is in fact no stranger to public funding – above all from the Arts Council, founded in 1946[105]. But the same system is nevertheless still quite broadly dependent on private financing and sponsorship, nonetheless boasting, at the end of the twentieth century, an astounding ca. 500 theatres and ca. 300 cultural centres where theatre is also played.[106]

Great Britain in the sixties and seventies also experiences the emergence of a larger number of theatre groups that constitute an 'underground' and also inhabit the 'Fringe'— Edinburgh's major theatre festival. And instrumental production venues like Traverse (founded as early as 1963) and the Open Space (1968) in London come into existence.[107] And apart from Peter Brook, the Pip Simmons Theatre Group, founded in 1968[108], and the troupe Forced Entertainment, which formed in 1984 around Tim Etchells[109], sent out extraordinarily significant impulses for this system's new postmodern theatre.

Here the British *fringe* movement distinguishes itself 'from most alternative theatre groups in theatre centres across continental Europe' by virtue of 'the porousness, from their inception on, of fringe productions as well as of subsidised theatre of literary sophistication such as the Royal Court; but also of commercial stages in London's West End.'[110] In reality, the British system seems to benefit theatre which stages contemporary authors: John Osborne, Edward Bond, Tom Stoppard, Harold Pinter and later, during Margaret Thatcher's time

---

102 | According to Brauneck ('Großbritannien', *WaB*/V., p. 879f), in the thirties there were ca. 50 and in the seventies around 180 houses.

103 | Cf. Oliver Ortolani, *Peter Brook*, Frankfurt am Main: S. Fischer, 1988, p. 20: Brook, together with Micheline Rozan, founds the *Centre International de Recherches Théâtrales (C.I.R.T.)*.

104 | Cf. Günther Rühle, *Theater in Deutschland, 1945-1966, Seine Ereignisse, seine Menschen*, Frankfurt am Main: S. Fischer, 2014, p. 694f.

105 | Cf. Brauneck, 'Großbritannien', *WaB*/V., p. 875.

106 | Cf. ibid., p. 885ff.

107 | Cf. ibid., p. 882ff.

108 | Cf. Wikipedia, https://en.wikipedia.org/wiki/Pip_Simmons_Theatre_Group (15.7.2015).

109 | Cf. Forced Entertainment, http://www.forcedentertainment.com/about/ (15.7.2015).

110 | Brauneck, 'Großbritannien', p. 908.

as Prime Minister, Caryl Churchill, Sarah Kane, Mark Ravenhill, Raoul Walsh and others.

To say the very least, the slightness of state and public 'interference' in the shaping of theatre conditions is plainly not disadvantageous to artistic developments of the contemporary order, even when the artists who are paving the way for the international postmodern avant-garde, or who are to be counted among it (and before mentioning Peter Brook one must absolutely mention the Irishman Samuel Beckett), are finding their focal points outside their home countries – which, incidentally, also applies to Pip Simmons, who worked during the seventies with Ritsaert ten Cate at Mickery in Amsterdam and has, in his home city, Nottingham, managed an office for the German-English collective Gob Squad, which was founded in 1994 and meanwhile lives and works mainly in Berlin, while also showing his work internationally on all continents (apart from Antarctica).[111]

THEATRE CULTURE AS A SERVICE TO THE SOCIAL WELFARE STATE – SWEDEN, NORWAY, DENMARK

Figure 8: 'Planet Lulu', Michel Laub/Remote Control, Kampnagel, Hamburg, 1997. Photograph: Friedemann Simon

An additional type of European theatrescapes – and its significance for the development of alternative contemporary, postmodern theatre forms can be

---

111 | Gob Squad, http://www.gobsquad.com/about-us (18.07.2015).

found in Scandinavia. In the sixties and seventies in these tendentially welfare-state-oriented societies, the state took over primary financial responsibility for the 'provision' of theatre to the population. On the one hand, state-run national theatres are supported; theatres that cultivate the classical traditions and national repertoire in the capital cities. On the other hand, in the three countries of Denmark, Sweden and Norway, relatively similar forms are developed both to be available to the whole land and for population groups who don't stand within any notable proximity to the ideals of the educated middle classes.

In 1963 in Denmark, theatre legislation put into effect the state's responsibility to cover half of Danish theatre's operating costs: in addition to the State Theatre in Copenhagen, which produces works as a repertoire opera, a literary theatre and a ballet, there are also larger municipal theatres in Odense, Arhus and Aalborg as well as a regional travelling theatre.[112] The sixties saw the formation of around 40 free groups that carry as much as 60 percent of the theatre praxis in the country but only have the opportunity to draw on five percent of public subsidies.[113]

In Sweden 'a politics of culture and the theatre [was] a central element' of the social-democratic reformist programme after World War II: 'Hence the sixties and seventies witnessed an enormous expansive development and an obligatory social organisation and design of the entire theatre sector'[114] – not least through Olof Palme, who was the Minister of Culture from 1967 to 1969. The subsidy in full of the theatre sector – besides the state's national theatre, Dramaten, there also exist almost 50 municipal and regional theatres – was simultaneously connected to sociopolitical terms and evaluations whereby even unions engaged in efforts to democratise and reduce ticket prices. Theatre groups without their own venues, which were being founded more and more during the sixties and seventies, received funding and turned ever more intensively to enhancing what they could offer to groups on the outskirts of society.[115] This policy led to a system in which 'the state and municipal theatres, the Riksteatern, the free groups and amateur groups [...] in Sweden form a well-rehearsed cooperative federation, which in turn characterises this theatre culture's profile'[116], a profile which also features a highly elaborate children's and youth theatre, fostered by Ingmar Bergman in his time as artistic director of Dramaten (1963–1966).[117]

---

112 | Brauneck, 'Dänemark', *WaB*/V., p. 859.
113 | Ibid.
114 | Brauneck, 'Schweden', *WaB*/V., p. 809.
115 | Cf. Ibid., p. 810f.
116 | Ibid., p. 813.
117 | Cf., ibid., p. 820.

This system has, to be sure, also been the object – as has welfare state policy in general – of bourgeois-conservative and also artistic critique: Peter Oskarsson, director of the Skanska Teatern, criticises the 'Swedish theatre sector in its institutionalisation and subordination to obligations related to production and pay-scale'; Oskarsson also demands – with reference to Peter Brook – 'an exclusively project-oriented working, in which he saw the preconditions for a renewal of the social meaning of theatre'.[118]

In Norway too, since the mid-1930s, 'the theatre had so convincingly secured its position in cultural and social life that the state subsidy of theatre was considered a cultural-political matter of course.'[119] Since 1960, a subsidy fund has existed for all segments of the performing arts, including children's and youth theatre, and in 1970 the fund was expanded to include independent theatre groups. At the end of the twentieth century, one could speak of a 'supply system' consisting of eleven permanent houses, with three of these in Oslo as well as one in Bergen and one in Stavanger[120], a state touring theatre (Rijksteatret) and theatre available to be seen in the 'Nynorsk' dialect as well as for Sami and Finns, and lastly radio theatre and open-air performances.[121]

Even here, complaints are made regarding a lack of creativity, and Eugenio Barba leaves Oslo in 1967 with his Odin Teatret, which he had built up there in 1960, settling in Holstebro, Denmark[122], where he had been offered better funding and working conditions. But with the Black Box in Oslo, the Avantgarden in Trondheim and the Teatergarasjen in Bergen, centres of artistic modernisation and innovation are erected and also fostered through the festival Bergen Internationale Teater (BIT Festival).[123] In Bergen the BAK-Truppen can establish itself as a group whose name is to be understood as an ironically inverted reference to the demand for an artistic avant-garde, and who tour during the nineties throughout European international festivals and venues for postmodern theatre, which in the nineties is apostrophised and analysed by its supporter Knut-Ove Arntzen as 'post-mainstream theatre'.[124]

On the whole, however,

'theatre in Norway is bound by the subsidy allocation system to a comparatively rigid framework with stipulations on content and institutional structures [...] Jon Nygaard supposes that a pivotal creative momentum would be expected should theatres get

---

118 | Ibid., p. 823.
119 | Brauneck, 'Norwegen', *WaB*/V., p. 831.
120 | Cf. ibid., p. 834.
121 | Cf. ibid., p. 835.
122 | Ibid.
123 | Ibid., p. 836.
124 | Cf. *www.inst.at*, http://www.inst.at/bio/arntzen_knut.htm (16.07.2015).

involved with smaller and locally delimited projects, above all in cooperation with Norway's most highly developed amateur theatre groups'

writes Brauneck.[125]

Well organised and solidly financed theatrescapes have thus formed in the Scandinavian countries, where also niches exist for 'free groups' who initially 'provide' parts of society, for the most part those on the fringes, with theatre productions that take a project-orientated approach. Alongside this feature, an important role beyond purely recreational free-time activities is played by the amateur theatre movement, which has fused to form the North European Amateur Theatre Association (NEATA).[126]

Professionals and Amateurs – Finland

The theatrescapes in Finland[127] only partially matches the 'Scandinavian' model, even though here too the state holds a decisive part in the formation of the theatre sector starting with the country's independence (1917) and on a greater and greater scale since World War II. At the beginning of the 2000s, Finland has 30 Finnish-language and four Swedish-language theatres as well as a total of almost 70 ensembles. 75% of stationary theatres' operating costs are covered by the state or municipalities, as the case may be.[128] In proportion to its ca. 4.5 million inhabitants, Finland boasts 'an extraordinarily dense network of theatres.'[129]

This significance of theatre for the society is strengthened by the 'enormous role played by amateur theatre': there are ca. 6,000 amateur theatre associations of which ca. 150 execute regular performance operations; furthermore, 'until well into the 1960s, several ensembles in subsidised theatre, which in Finland, generally speaking, keeps comparatively small staffs, were composed of professional actors and amateurs.'[130]

However, 'as positive as the explicit engagement of the state and state administration in theatre subsidy is, the theatres are also thereby closely intertwined with the structures and regulations of each respective cultural administration. These administrative bodies have instituted a supervisory

---

125 | Brauneck, 'Norwegen', p. 837.
126 | Cf. North European Amateur Theatre Association (NEATA), http://www.neata.dk/index.htm (16.07.2015).
127 | Brauneck, 'Finnland', pp. 777–785.
128 | Cf. ibid., p. 778.
129 | Ibid.
130 | Ibid., p. 779.

board to which theatres must submit their performance programmes', and which also exert influence on personal and artistic decisions.[131]

Independent groups established in the sixties also turn against these structures, but they soon enough receive public funding: 'The work of independent groups pursues the goal of bringing about a greater relation to the present, by focussing, for instance, on current and social centres of conflict within Finnish society'.[132]

Cultural Modernisation of the 'Grande Nation' – France

Figure 9: 'Aujourd'hui peut-être', Compagnie Maguy Marin, Kampnagel, Hamburg, 1986. Photograph: Friedemann Simon

In France, since the nineteenth century, theatre – like language in general – is endowed with a leading role in the edification and representation of the nation. Here the Théâtre National is conceptualised as the specific bourgeois form that should bridge the social and cultural schism between the aristocracy's courts and the 'people', especially the plebian 'fourth estate'. It maintains its central position well into the twentieth century and is reflected in the development of culture by a central state: the most essential institutions of national culture, thereby also the theatre, are concentrated in the capital city.

---

131 | Ibid., p. 781.
132 | Ibid., pp. 781f.

In this sense, after the Second World War 'the question of theatre's position in society [becomes] a well-nigh mandatory topic in the general renewal debate held amongst the French public after 1944.'[133] A Théâtre National Populaire (TNP) is fostered, although 'the setting of [...] [was] predominantly cultural-political rather than aesthetic. The point was to bring theatre as an institution closer to the majority of the French population as an institution that could make a crucial contribution to the national upheaval so yearned for in the second half of the 1940s.'[134]

Figure 10: Performance 'Jérôme Bel', Jérôme Bel, Kampnagel, Hamburg, 1998. Photograph: Friedemann Simon

Amongst these aims was a demand for the decentralisation of the culture and theatre system, which had previously functioned largely according to a pattern where the products of Parisian cultural institutions were 'exported' into the provinces.[135] Still in the early 1970s, Paris had more theatres than the entire 'rest' of the Republic: only 200 houses in all of France, of which only forty maintain constant operations.[136]

As instruments of decentralisation, at first five regional Centres Dramatiques are set up in Rennes, Toulouse, Aix-en Provence and Strasbourg, amongst

---

133 | Brauneck, 'Frankreich', *WaB*/V., pp. 2-190, here p. 9.
134 | Ibid.
135 | Cf. Ibid. p. 12.
136 | Ibid.

other places; and from 1959 to 1968, six regional Maisons de la Culture are built under the minister of culture André Malraux.[137] Not until 1981 under the minister of culture Jack Lang is the system of the Centres Dramatiques extended to twenty-seven houses, six of which are for children's and youth theatre alone. Additionally, these Centres are constructed such that they are directed by prominent artists who work there with their ensembles ('troupes permanentes') and conduct tour operations throughout the region, basing themselves at the centres: as such, from 1957 to 2002, Roger Planchon, for example, directs the Théâtre de la Cité Villeurbanne near Lyon, which in 1972 is given the title Théâtre National Populaire and from which outstanding aesthetic impulses felt Europe-wide are emitted.[138]

The first Théâtre National Populaire (TNP) under the direction of Jean Vilar, and in the spirit of social integration, is founded in 1951. It should become accessible to workers and convey its bourgeois-elitist character back to the society. Organisational changes are also made in service of this aim, such as the reduction of ticket prices and the rescheduling of performances from the traditional 9 to 8 pm, in order to accommodate the rhythm of life and work of the wageworkers. Vilar gets rid of the proscenium arch stage, the curtain and the proscenium itself, introduces audience discussions – but insists on the highest possible dramaturgical and aesthetic standards for the work: 'The emancipatory effect that, say, performances of classics would have on audiences would result – according to Vilar – from the mere fact that these pieces were made available to them.' Until 1961, Vilar directs the Parisian TNP and founds the Festival d'Avignon in 1947, where he initially shows the most important French stagings of the season.[139]

Especially under Jack Lang – who directed the theatre festival in Nancy from 1963 to 1977 and was the director of the Parisian Théâtre National de Chaillot from 1972 to 1974, assuming control of the Ministry of Culture twice under the presidency of the socialist Francois Mitterand, first from 1981 to 1986 and again from 1988 to 1993 – federal cultural-political and theatre-political reform programmes are developed which open the field in France for artistic modernisation and contribute to its taking root extensively in society. But even as early as the 1970s, France and Paris count, mainly on the basis of state-run programmes, amongst the most important strongholds for the artistic modernisation of theatre in Europe and the world: The Nancy Festival (1962–1983) becomes a meeting place for international theatre avant-

---

137 | Cf. ibid., p. 15.
138 | Ibid. Cf. also Wikipedia, https://de.wikipedia.org/wiki/Roger_Planchon (16.07.2015).
139 | Cf. Brauneck, 'Frankreich', p. 19.

gardes[140]; in 1970 Peter Brook settles in Paris with the Centre International de Recherches Théâtrales (C.I.R.T.) and in 1974 Ariane Mnouchkine founds the Théâtre du Soleil in the Paris Cartoucherie;[141] in addition to the already-existing dramatic centres, in 1984 Jack Lang's administration institutes a number of Centres Chorégraphiques according to a model similar to that of the Centres Dramatiques. Today (2015) 19 such centres are at work.[142]

Besides these, there is also a broad field of independent 'free' theatre troupes – at the turn of the millennium, Brauneck mentions the existence of 1,200 groups whose works are seen by ca. 5 million visitors[143] – who, among other things, flood the city of Avignon annually during the festival.

Thus the French theatrescapes and the impulses related to artistic and structural innovation there are quite massively discharged from the central government and will be carried during the second half of the twentieth century by the reformist endeavours of the socialist government, who make rather large scale investments through public funds towards this goal – which, however, also leads to the 'decentralised', publicly funded institutions' function as relatively elite centres where European and international 'top-notch art' is produced.

THEATRE AS THE EDIFICATION OF CIVIL SOCIETY – SWITZERLAND

Switzerland's theatrescapes provides us with a completely different picture. Here things are organised on the basis of an understanding that 'culture is the business of individuals, of private organisations and municipalities, perhaps of regions', as Brauneck writes.[144] Not until 1975 is a Bundesamt für Kulturpflege (federal ministry for the fostering of culture) established. The support of theatre does not belong traditionally among the duties of the public, but is instead civil society's business. Posing a blatant contrast to Schiller's conception of theatre and culture, Swiss theatre views 'the bourgeois-enlightened notion of the theatre stage as a moral establishment' as a rather foreign idea.'[145]

In that sense, Swiss theatres, without exception, go back to civil activities related to the founding of entities, and are carried – with Lucerne, and since 1992 also Chur as exceptions – by associations, foundations, cooperatives,

---

140 | Cf. ibid., p. 146.
141 | Cf. ibid., p. 145.
142 | Cf. CultureCommunication gouv.france, Danse, http://www.culturecommunication.gouv.fr/Politiques-ministerielles/Danse/Organismes-danse/Creation-Diffusion/Centres-choregraphiques-nationaux (16.07.2015).
143 | Cf. Brauneck, 'Frankreich', WaB/V., p. 137f.
144 | Brauneck, 'Schweiz', WaB/V., pp. 514-536, here p. 514.
145 | Ibid., p. 515.

corporations or theatre societies.¹⁴⁶ And yet this total of 146 professional theatres is meanwhile also supported financially by the municipalities and cantons, albeit in fewer numbers and under requirements to gross higher amounts than in Germany or Austria.¹⁴⁷

Switzerland also sees the emergence of independent theatre groups during the sixties, whose numbers Brauneck calculates in 1990 to equal around 110 groups.¹⁴⁸ They are supported predominantly by the municipalities and cantons. This also holds true for the production houses (Theaterhaus Gessnerallee and Rote Fabrik, Zurich; Kaserne Basel; Dampfzentrale Berne, and later Südpol, Lucerne).

Regardless of independent theatre groups, however, Switzerland is time and again a centre for artistic innovation. With Zurich as the birthplace of Dada during the First World War; the artists' colony on Monte Verità near Ascona; Zurich as the centre for the exiled German-language theatre avant-garde under Kurt Hirschfeld; Frank Baumbauer's tenure as intendant in Basel, when and where Christoph Marthaler (who then himself becomes intendant from 2000 until 2004 in Zurich) produced his first stagings, and Théâtre Vidy in Lausanne, artistic home since 1987 to Maurice Béjart after he left Belgium – all this indicates that the theatre-political public spirit indeed seems to feel responsible for innovation and modernisation of the arts; and in Lucerne, a large, almost comprehensive circle including cultural-political actors has been working since 2013 towards a completely new, integrated model for the municipal theatre – TheaterWerk Luzern – for all genres of the performing arts, which could conceivably begin operations in 2020.¹⁴⁹

AUSTRIA, A CULTURAL STATE

'The cultural marginalisation of the theatre that many countries saw at the end of the twentieth century is hardly imaginable in Austria', Brauneck remarks in reference to the social and cultural significance of this country's theatre system¹⁵⁰, which doesn't especially differ in its structure from the 'German system'. Yet the meaningfulness of theatres in the capital city, and, above all, of the Staatsoper and the Burgtheater, as national theatres is incomparable: in Vienna, where at ca. 1.8

---

146 | Cf. ibid., p. 516.
147 | Cf. ibid., p. 517. Of the 146 theatres, 92 are German-speaking, 48 francophone and 6 Italian-speaking.
148 | Cf. ibid., p. 518.
149 | Cf. Theaterwerk Luzern, http://www.theaterwerk-luzern.ch/#post/15 (16.07.2015).
150 | Brauneck, 'Theater in Österreich', WaB/V., p. 459-513, here p. 459.

million inhabitants you have around one-fifth of Austria's population, 4 million annual theatre goers are counted. As concerns federal as well as municipal funding, the alimentation of the theatre and of the Festspiele[151] are still counted as core responsibilities, even though since 1999 the state has gone through with a plan to release houses from its immediate administration.[152]

This process allots a certain space to alternative production modes and aesthetics: Although in 1956, soon after the end of the Soviet occupation, the leftist, communistically oriented Scala Theater, itself founded in 1950 with the support of the Soviet occupation[153], was denied a license by the social-democratically governed city of Vienna[154] at the time, during the seventies – much the same as in Munich – a structure of independent theatres could establish itself here, a publically funded structure which traces back to the movement of independent groups.[155] These had rapidly 'seized' a range of production venues for the benefit of alternative theatre and had followed through with those venues' funding, after which this structure solidified into a structure of 'middle stages' that – as city-appointed experts criticise – had lost their connection with international developments in 'free theatre'.[156] These expert assessments constitute the beginning of a process known as the Wiener Theaterreform, which alters the funding system and is intended to dissolve the separation between institution/real-estate ownership and artistic theatre direction (the 'rehousing' of free theatre[157]) – which was successful in the case of the group dieTheater, established in 1989 for the work of free groups through the merging of the Künstlerhaus and the Konzerthaus: in 2007 the Viennese coproduction venue known as *brut* joined to work with these other venues once it advertised and filled its open position for director.[158]

---

151 | This concerns chiefly the *Salzburger Festspiele*, the *Wiener Festwochen*, the *Bregenzer Festspiele*, the festival *Steirischer Herbst* in Graz and *Ars Elektronica* in Linz.

152 | Cf. Brauneck, 'Österreich', p. 475.

153 | Cf. Günther Rühle, 'Theater in Deutschland', p. 332ff.

154 | Cf. Günter Rühle, 'Theater in Deutschland', p. 638f and Brauneck, 'Österreich', p. 469.

155 | Cf. Lackenbucher, Mattheiß and Thier, *Freies Theater in Wien, Reformvorschläge zur Förderung Freier Gruppen im Bereich der Darstellenden Kunst*, Vienna, 2003, p.10, http://www.kulturmanagement.net/downloads/theaterstudie.pdf (19.07.2015).

156 | Cf. Lackenbucher, Mattheiß and Thier, *Freies Theater in Wien*, p. 4ff and 9ff; although with regard to artistic innovation, in 1987 the likes of George Tabori settled with his troupe in the Viennese theatre Der Kreis. After this theatre failed in 1990, Claus Peymann brought Tabori to the *Burgtheater*, where he experienced his biggest successes. Cf. Brauneck, 'Österreich', p. 481.

157 | Cf. Lackenbucher, Mattheiß and Thier, *Freies Theater in Wien*, p.10.

158 | Cf. Wikipedia, 'Künstlerhaus Wien', at https://de.wikipedia.org/wiki/K%C3%BCnstlerhaus_Wien (19.07.2015).

Theatreland Italy

'But if one's wish is to follow up on the origins of European theatre construction, one has to repair to Italy. This part of the world witnessed the birth and evolution of this architectural form that would remain determinant for theatre construction until our time,'[159] which is how the description of a 'European road of historic theatre' summarises one side of a paradox; Brauneck formulates the flipside: 'In Italy theatre had no real chance, due to the complete lack of stationary theatres, [...] of establishing theatre in the nineteenth century as an institution with firm roots in the national understanding of culture.'[160]

To be sure, the art form of opera has had a uniquely popular significance in Italy since the eighteenth century, a significance which has not, however, spread to the theatre sector as a whole; Brauneck describes Italy's situation as 'one of a kind in Europe inasmuch as Italy, since the beginning of its more recent history and finally until now, is a theatre landscape of wandering troupes and ensembles'.[161] In the 1990s, he counts 26 *teatri stabili*, which do not, however, dispose of their own ensembles or devise uninterrupted programmed seasons, but rather host the making of two to three productions per year that then tour throughout the other *stabili*; and over 600 theatre groups or cooperatives, which are counted almost exclusively, however, as local urban cultural establishments.[162]

The state financing of this theatre sector is rather modest and remains limited to annually deferred compensation. Productions therefore must, as a rule, be pre-financed through (bank) loans.[163]

The scope of our examination here does not allow us to answer whether it is in spite of, or thanks to, its 'weak constitution' and lack of backing that the Italian theatrescapes produced significant theatre artists who influenced postmodern European theatre substantially – Giorgio Strehler, Lucino Visconti, Federico Fellini, Pier Paolo Pasolini, Dario Fo, Luca Ronconi, Romeo and Claudia Castellucci, and Giorgio Barberio Corsetti.

This outcome could have also been nourished in part by a short period of funding for *ricerca e sperimentazione* ('research and experiment') in theatre, which took up the impulses emitted by the 1968 revolts and whose furtherance was abandoned already as early as the mid-eighties.[164]

---

159 | Kultiversum – Die Kulturplattform, http://www.kultiversum.de/All-Dossier/An-der-Quelle-Die-Europastrasse-Historische-Theater-Teil-7.html.
160 | Brauneck, 'Italien', *WaB*/V., p. 537f.
161 | Ibid., p. 542.
162 | Ibid., p. 542f.
163 | Ibid., p. 545
164 | Ibid., pp. 574f, 584.

It would remain necessary to engage in more precise examination to answer the question of whether indeed the weak shaping of an institutionalised or otherwise-backed theatrescapes in Italy can be traced back to the fact 'that in Italy, more so than in other European countries, film and television quite speedily occupied the market for recreational activities' and 'also tended [...] [to adapt] to the cultural politics of these circumstances'[165], as Brauneck reckons – whereas the early and furious opening of the market to the privatisation of television (in 1976) might possibly have served as a factor of extraordinary significance in culture-political terms.[166]

Post-Postmodernism?

This overview clearly indicates that new forms of postmodern theatre encounter different conditions for evolution and realisation in the different (re)formed theatrescapes of Modernity, determining their influence, their meaning and their feedback-effects on existing systems. It also clearly indicates that they owe their emergence above all to artistic impulses that made their presence known far ahead of the political and social movements of the sixties. These impulses can be read as engagements with the cultural phenomenon of massmedialisation (Mc Luhan) and with the twentieth-century catastrophes of civilisation, which establish massive uncertainty as to the future of Modernity; and with crises of decolonisation – amongst which the Vietnam War must also be counted. These impulses also announce, as it were, the revolt movements against the stewards of the project of an enlightened Modernism.

This almost global connectivity of revolts against the project of Modernism during the 1960s allows one to read them also as revolts against the wellnigh 'excessive' dominating force with which this project's stewards, who simultaneously represented the 68-ers' parents' generation, adhere all the more vigorously to the defence of their value system, itself built on the promise of an enlightened future and motivated by the threat of totalitarianism and of existential dangers to the future. In this sense, the revolts' ousting of teleological ethics in the late 1960s goes together with the needs and praxis of alternative production modes and forms of communication to make their global image as postmodern intelligible.

Meanwhile, however, after roughly fifty years, is this postmodernity possibly nearing its end? If we read the signs in developments in the arts and amongst performing artists, we find, since a relatively brief period of

---

165 | Ibid., p. 541.
166 | Cf. 'Privatfernsehen: Nur noch Volksverdummung?' *Der Spiegel*, 51 (1979): pp. 39-61.

time, forms that point beyond the canon of postmodern theatre as a critical art of perception. Vegard Vinge's *Johan Gabriel Borkmann*, SIGNA's *Schwarze Augen Maria*, Nya Rampen and Institutet, Tino Sehgal, the collectives Cobra, Machina X and others very likely announce, in turn, new production modes, new dramaturgies and new aesthetics in the performing arts which react to the current supersession of the postmodern age of McLuhan's mass media, the atomic age and raging imperialist colonial wars by globalised digital communication, the algorhythmic age, the overcoming of man-made climate change as well as shifts in the international division of labour and in the demographic distribution of humankind across the globe.

Yet the stewards of the project of modernity have in no way, to be sure, really been superseded, and the stewards of postmodernity are just now becoming parents. And the more recent history of culture could teach us about the advantages of very precisely listening to and looking at what these artists have to tell us.

LITERATURE AND SOURCES

The complete collected issues of *Theaterschrift* were examined for this essay:

Kaaitheater, Brussels; Hebbel Theater, Berlin; Theater am Turm, Frankfurt am Main; Felix Meritis, Amsterdam and Wiener Festwochen, Vienna (eds). *Theaterschrift*.
No. 1/1992, *Beyond Indifference*.
No. 2/1992, *The Written Space*.
No. 3/1993, *Border Violations*.
No. 4/1993, *The Inner Side of Silence*.
No. 5-6/1994, *On Dramaturgy*.

Kaaitheater, Brussels; Hebbel Theater, Berlin; Theater am Turm, Frankfurt am Main; Felix Meritis, Amsterdam; Wiener Festwochen, Vienna; ATEM, Paris and Bayrisches Staatsschauspiel, Munich (eds). *Theaterschrift*.
No. 7/1994, *The Actor*.

Kaaitheater, Brussels; Hebbel Theater, Berlin; Theater am Turm, Frankfurt am Main; Felix Meritis, Amsterdam; Wiener Festwochen, Vienna; ATEM, Paris; Kampnagel, Hamburg; Bayrisches Staatsschauspiel, Munich (eds). *Theaterschrift*.
No. 8/1994, *Memory*.

Kaaitheater, Brussels; Hebbel Theater, Berlin; Theater am Turm, Frankfurt am Main; Felix Meritis, Amsterdam; Wiener Festwochen, Vienna; ATEM, Paris; Kampnagel, Hamburg; ICA, London; Bayrisches Staatsschauspiel, Munich (eds). *Theaterschrift*.
No. 9/1995, *Theatre and Music*.
No. 10/1995, *City /Art/Cultural Identity*.

Kaaitheater, Brussels; Hebbel Theater, Berlin; Felix Meritis, Amsterdam; Wiener Festwochen, Vienna; Festival Theaterformen, Hannover/Braunschweig and Künstlerhaus Bethanien, Berlin (eds). *Theaterschrift*.
No. 11/1997, *The Return of the Classics?*
Nr. 12/1997, *Time*.
Nr. 13/1998, *Spirituality: a Utopia?*

An overview of the authors featured in these thirteen published issues is available at: http://www.archiv.hebbel-am-ufer.de/archiv_hebbel_theater/seiten/archiv/theaterschrift/haupt.html.

Further Reading

Abdoh, R. "Violence – Death – Theatre: Reza Abdoh in Conversation with Hortensia Völckers and Martin Bergelt." *ThS* 3 (1993), pp. 48–64.
Abramovic, M. "Catching the Moment: Marina Abramovic in Conversation with Ilse Kujkens." *ThS* 3 (1993), pp. 104–120.
Adolphe, J.-M. "Fragments Drawn from Silence so as Not to Shut up Completely." *ThS* 4 (1993), pp. 184–202.
Anderson, L. "The Speed of Change: Laurie Anderson in Conversation with Tom Stromberg." *ThS* 1 (1992), pp. 118–132.
BAK-TRUPPEN. "Thoughts." *ThS* 2 (1992), pp. 108–112.
Brauneck, M. *Die Welt als Bühne: Geschichte des europäischen Theaters*, vols. 1–6. Stuttgart/Weimar: Metzler, 1993–2007. Especially vol. 5: 2. *Hälfte des 20. Jahrhunderts*. Stuttgart/Weimar: Metzler, 2007.
De Greef, H, and Stromberg, T. "Editorial." *ThS* 11 (1997), p. 8.
Der Spiegel. "Privatfernsehen: Nur noch Volksverdummung?" *Der Spiegel* 51 (1979), pp. 39–61.
Fülle, H. *Freie Gruppen, Freie Szene, Freies Theater und die Modernisierung der deutschen Theaterlandschaft (1960–2010)*. Dissertation, University of Hildesheim, 2015.
Frey, M. *Creatieve Marge: Die Entwicklung des Niederländischen Off-Theaters*. Vienna/Cologne: Böhlau, 1991.
Freyer, A. "Looking Behind the Mirror of Appearances: Achim Freyer in Conversation with Bettina Masuch." *ThS* 2 (1992), pp. 114–130.
Greenaway, P. "The Exposing of Human Beings: Peter Greenaway in Conversation with Brigitte Fürle." *ThS* 3 (1993), pp. 24–42.
Janssen, T. "We Watch With Dry Eyes and We Prepare Our Soup: Tom Janssen in Conversation with Elske van de Holst and Marianne Van Kerkhoven." *ThS* 1 (1992), pp. 136–156.
Lackenbucher, M. and T. *Freies Theater in Wien: Reformvorschläge zur Förderung Freier Gruppen im Bereich der Darstellenden Kunst*. Vienna, n.p., 2003.
Lehmann, H-T. "When Rage Coagulates into Form... : On Jan Fabre's 'Aesthetics of Poison'." *ThS* 3 (1993), pp. 90–102.
Lehmann, H-T. *Tragödie und dramatisches Theater*. Berlin: Alexander, 2013.
Lehmann, H-T. *Postdramatic Theatre*. London: Routledge, 2006.
Ortolani, O. *Peter Brook*. Frankfurt am Main: S. Fischer, 1988.
Ritsema, J. "So That it Remains Flexible in Itself: Jan Ritsema in Conversation with Marianne Van Kerkhoven." *ThS* 1 (1992), pp. 86–113.
Rühle, G. *Theater in Deutschland 1945–1966: Seine Ereignisse – seine Menschen*. Frankfurt am Main: S. Fischer, 2014.
Theater der Zeit. *The Netherlands and Flanders*. Special issue of *Theater der Zeit*, Berlin 2013.

Troller, U. "Plea for the Italian Stage: Urs Troller in Conversation with Gerhard Ahrens." *ThS* 2 (1992), pp. 88–100.
Van Kerkhoven, M. "Beyond Indifference." *ThS* 1 (1992).
Van Kerkhoven, M. "The Written Space." *ThS* 2 (1992), pp. 6–36.
Van Kerkhoven, M. "Close to a secret." *ThS* 3 (1993), pp. 6–20.
Van Kerkhoven, M. "On Dramaturgy." *ThS* 5–6 (1994).
Van Kerkhoven, M. "The Actor." *ThS* 7 (1994), pp. 8–30.
Vassiliev, A. "Theatre as Monastic Community: Anatolij Vassiliev in Conversation with Michael Haerdter." *ThS* 1 (1992), pp. 46–78.
Wilson, R. "The Architecture of Theatrical Space: Thoughts by Robert Wilson Based on a Conversation with Bettina Masuch and Tom Stromberg. *ThS* 2 (1992), pp. 102–106.

ONLINE SOURCES

Berg, S. v.-d. "Mit dem Rücken zum Publikum? Theaterbrief Niederlande (1): Die Subventionskürzungen im niederländischen Kunstbetrieb." *Nachtkritik.de*. Available at: http://www.nachtkritik.de/index.php?option=com_content&view=article&id=5815:die-subventionskuerzungen-im-niederlaendischen-kunstbereich&catid=622:theaterbrief-aus-den-niederlanden&Itemid=99 (accessed 15th July 2015).
Berg, S. v.-d. "Zerstörerische Debatte: Theaterbrief Niederlande (2): Ein halbes Jahr nach den Subventionskürzungen wird das Ausmaß langsam deutlich." *Nachtkritik.de*. Available at: http://www.nachtkritik.de/index.php?option=com_content&view=article&id=6687:theaterbrief-niederlande-2-ein-halbes-jahr-nach-den-subventionskuerzungen-im-niederlaendischen-kunstbereich-wird-das-ausmass-langsam-deutlich&catid=622:theaterbrief-aus-den-niederlanden&Itemid=99 (accessed 15th July 2015).
CultureCommunication gouv.france, "Danse." http://www.culturecommunication.gouv.fr/Politiques-ministerielles/Danse/Organismesdanse/Creation-Diffusion/Centres-choregraphiques-nationaux (accessed 16th July 2015).
Dasarts – Amsterdams Hogeschool voor de Kunsten. http://www.ahk.nl/theaterschool/opleidingen-theater/dasarts-master-of-theatre/about-dasarts/history/ (accessed 15th July 2015).
Forced Entertainment. http://www.forcedentertainment.com/about/ (accesed15th July 2015).
Gob Squad. http://www.gobsquad.com/about-us (accessed 18th July 2015).
Hebbel-am-Ufer. http://www.archiv.hebbel-am-ufer.de/archiv_hebbel_theater/seiten/archiv/theaterschrift/haupt.html (accessed 14th July 2015).
Informal European Theatre Meeting (IETM). https://www.ietm.org/sites/default/files/ietmbrochure_pages.pdf (accessed 14th July 2015).

www.inst.at, "BeiträgerInnen." http://www.inst.at/bio/arntzen_knut.htm (accessed 16th July 2015).

Kultiversum – Die Kulturplattform. http://www.kultiversum.de/All-Dossier/An-der-Quelle-Die-Europastrasse-Historische-Theater-Teil-7.html (accessed 15th July 2015).

North European Amateur Theatre Association (NEATA). http://www.neata.dk/index.htm (accessed 16th July 2015).

Theaterwerk Luzern. http://www.theaterwerk-luzern.ch/#post/15 (accessed 16th July 2015).

Wikipedia "Künstlerhaus Wien." https://de.wikipedia.org/wiki/K%C3%BCnstlerhaus_Wien (accessed 19th July 2015).

Wikipedia, "Reza Abdoh." https://en.wikipedia.org/wiki/Reza_Abdoh (accessed 14th July 2015).

Wikipedia, "Roger Planchon." https://de.wikipedia.org/wiki/Roger_Planchon (accessed 16th July 2015).

Wikipedia, "Schlachten!" https://de.wikipedia.org/wiki/Schlachten! (accessed 15th July 2015).

Wikipedia, "Pip Simmons Theatre Group." https://en.wikipedia.org/wiki/Pip_Simmons_Theatre_Group (accessed 15th July 2015).

Theatre and Migration

Documentation, Influences and Perspectives in European Theatre

Azadeh Sharifi

1. INTRODUCTION

1.1 Position in Context

Many people have migrated voluntarily or involuntarily out of, to or within the European continent in the last centuries. But with the break-up of the colonial empires and the economic rise of Europe, migration to Europe has reached an unprecedented level, particularly regarding the migration of people from former European colonies in the second half of the twentieth century. The fall of the Berlin Wall, the subsequent end of communism, and the expansion of the European Union have contributed to a considerable increase in migration within Europe. In the meantime, refugees from all parts of the world, above all from the so-called "crisis areas", are constantly migrating in the hope and with the idea of settling in Europe, only to discover that today's Europe resembles a well-guarded fortress in many ways.[1]

The hegemony of Western Europe has been challenged by the post-colonial, post-socialistic and Mediterranean migration. The transnational movements have become the driving forces behind a transformation of Europe by creating an "inner" globalization and therefore a "cosmopolitisation"[2] of national Euro-

---

[1] | Regina Römhild, "Aus der Perspektive der Migration. Die Kosmopolitisierung Europas", in: Sabine Hess, Jana Binder and Johannes Moser (eds.), *No Integration? Kulturwissenschaftliche Beiträge zur Integrationsdebatte in Europa*, Bielefeld: transcript (2009), p. 225f.
[2] | Ulrich Beck and Nathan Sznaider, "Unpacking Cosmopolitanism for the Social Sciences: A Research Agenda", in: *The British Journal of Sociology* 57/1, (London, 2006), pp. 381–403.

pean societies.³ Migration has become constitutive for the present social conditions in Europe. Some European countries have acknowledged this fact sooner than others due to their colonial history and confrontations in their post-colonial societies.⁴ Yet, the respective governments do not see migration as a "cosmopolitan force", but rather as a marginal phenomenon taking place on the periphery of society. As a consequence, migration needs to be regulated or partly promoted, culturally integrated or even assimilated with instruments of national and European politics.⁵

The different forms of migration have cast the European cultures into a so-called "flux".⁶ A great number of people, from different geographical locations with different cultural experiences, who have had little or no connection with each other, encounter on European soil and live alongside each other. The migratory movements have triggered a cultural transformation whose traces are also perceptible in the European theatre landscape, although the political conditions of artistic work of these theatre makers are crucial and have an impact on their presence in the respective theatre scenes.⁷ This implies that many immigrant theatre makers are excluded from public subsidies due to their residence status. Despite these systematic reprisals, there is a growing number of immigrant theatre makers who are professionally active in almost every Western European country. This study will examine the influence that these artists actually have on the European theatre scene. It is due to the vision of Manfred Brauneck, who acknowledged sooner than others that the development of theatre and migration has a special focus in his research project. In the early eighties, Brauneck published a study on theatre made by "foreign" theatre professionals in Germany, *Ausländertheater in der Bundesrepublik Deutschland und in West-Berlin* (1983), examining the development of "foreign" theatre makers. The scene, which at that time was only burgeoning, has changed significantly in the last thirty years. Artists of colour and Postmigrant theatre exert a sustainable impact on the structural and aesthetic level of the contemporary theatre scene.

---

3 | Römhild, "Aus der Perspektive der Migration", p. 225f.

4 | Germany, for instance, has only officially declared itself to be a country of immigration since 2005, although migration researchers were already referring to Germany as a "migration country" by the nineties. See also Rainer Münz, Wolfgang Seifert and Ralf E. Ulrich, *Zuwanderung nach Deutschland. Strukturen. Wirkungen. Perspektiven*, (Frankfurt a.M.: Campus Verlag, 1999).

5 | Römhild, "Aus der Perspektive der Migration", p. 225f.

6 | Christina Boswell, *European Migration Policies in Flux. Changing Patterns of Inclusion and Exclusion*, (Oxford: John Wiley & Sons, 2003), p. 1.

7 | Jude Bloomfield, *Crossing the Rainbow. National Differences and International Convergences in Multicultural Performing Arts in Europe*, (Brussels: IETM, 2003), p. 3.

This study attempts to analyze these trends and their importance for social and cultural processes in Europe. It pursues two goals. The first is to present and discuss the questions of the general study concerning the role of independent theatre in the contemporary European theatre scene with a focus on migration: What are the characteristics of independent theatre? What changes in the European theatre landscape have independent theatre groups brought about? And where can processes of artistic changes and changes in cultural policy be found?

The second is to explore the significance of the migration phenomenon for the contemporary European theatre landscape. What shift in production, distribution and reception have artists of colour and the Postmigrant theatre initiated? And how have the state theatres and cultural institutions reacted to it? It is important to mention that no clear distinction will be made in this study between the theatre makers in the independent scene and theatre makers in institutional structures. For a long time, artists of colour were not present in the national and European theatre landscapes; the reasons for this will be presented in due course.[8] Thus, the theatre makers were reliant on working in independent structures. The efforts to achieve recognition and participation in the institutional structures strongly characterize this "scene".[9] If the European Postmigrant theatre scene had not been included in its entirety here, it would not have been possible to present the efforts of the artists as a whole. Therefore, no dividing line has been drawn between the independent scene and institutional structures; instead, a development towards professionalization and institutionalization is presented.

1.2 Theoretical Contextualisation in Existing Discourses

1.2.1 Theatre and Migration

The main focus of this study is migration. Therefore, it is important to define migration and to specify it in the context of theatre. In the following overview, existing discourses will be presented that have taken place simultaneously.

It is important to mention that there is no standard, official definition of migration within the European Union. Migration as a sociological term describes the process in which persons relocate their centre of life across national boundaries. Essentially, all non-European citizens who have immigrated to the EU are considered to be migrants, (i.e., persons from countries not belonging to Western Europe with ethnic origins in Asia, Africa and Latin America). Pri-

---

8 | See also Bloomfield, *Crossing the Rainbow*; Manfred Brauneck, *Ausländertheater in der Bundesrepublik Deutschland und in West-Berlin*, (Hamburg, 1983).

9 | See also Rascheed Araeen, *The Art Britain really ignores. Making myself visible*, (London: Kala Press, 1984).

or to 1990, persons from the so-called "guest worker countries" (Southern and Eastern European countries) were also considered immigrants. Indeed, there is a large migratory movement once again within the countries of Europe which is referred to as internal migration. This has become relevant since the global economic crisis in 2007 and the subsequent European financial crisis, since many people from countries like Greece, Italy, Portugal and Spain migrate within Europe in search of work.[10]

Beyond the purely economic view, migration is understood as a phenomenon with far-reaching social consequences. It not only affects the persons migrating but also those (European) societies as a whole. Consequently, it is a matter of how these societies react to the changes, shifts and diversity of their citizens and how they negotiate living together in these changed circumstances.[11]

In discussions concerning the theatre, migration is not usually dealt with as an issue within theatre structures but as a societal-social phenomenon which happens outside in society. This means that migration is usually assigned to a group of persons who have their own personal experience of migration but are not represented in these institutions. This becomes evident from the fact that migration is often presented as a phenomenon and experience of social peripheries. Images of migrants are created by artists without any migration experience who try to grasp and comprehend the phenomenon without their own involvement. The play *Innocence* by Dea Loher is an example. It presents migration from the perspective of society – as a danger from the outside – and it is only recognised as a socially immanent phenomenon during the course of the play.[12] Not until recent years has this discourse changed by establishing theatre groups and artists of colour.[13] The discourse on making cultural institutions accessible for everyone is taking place all over Europe. However, the emphasis is placed on the side of the audience and not on the artists in the institutions. The state theatres want to create diversity within their audiences – a diversity which does not exist in their own structures.

---

10 | See Béla Galgóczi, Janine Leschke and Andrew Watt, *Intra-EU labour migration: flows, effects and policy responses*, (Brussels: European Trade Union Institute, 2011).
11 | Paul Mecheril, Mario do Mar CastroVarela, Dirim İnci, Annita Kalpaka and Claus Melter, *Migrationspädagogik*, (Weinheim, 2010).
12 | The danger represented by the figures, Fadoul and Elisio, is already apparent in the introduction, where they are already portrayed as "illegal, black immigrants", who, at the beginning of the play, do not try to prevent the suicide of a white woman. The portrayal of the figures, as well as the guilt assigned to them from the outset, identifies them as intruders. See Dea Loher, *Unschuld*, (Frankfurt a. M., 2003).
13 | The term "artists of color" is used in this study and will be explained later.

In addition to the state theatres, there are intercultural[14] and migrant theatres that deal with migration but that are recognized in terms of pedagogical or sociocultural contexts. These theatre groups are usually classified as "lay-theatre" or semi-professional theatres from a theatre-immanent perspective. The limitation of financial, personnel, and aesthetic resources and the strategies for creative implementation under such circumstances are often considered deficient.

Finally, a more detailed discourse on Postmigrant theatre will be presented later in this study.

1.2.2 Theatre and Racism – Is European Theatre White?

Another important discourse in the context of theatre and migration is racism and exclusion of artists of colour in European theatre. This exclusion is in fact intersectional, i.e. overlapping forms of discrimination, the rare presence of female, black or physically or mentally disabled theatre makers. Despite the intersectional discrimination, this paper will focus only on racism.

Racism in this context is used in reference to Stuart Hall's definition. Hall describes racism as the social practice of exclusion which is not based on any distinct theory of "race":

> 'Racism is a social practice whereby the physical characteristics of certain groups in the population are used for the purpose of classification, e.g. if the population is not divided into rich and poor but, for instance, into white and black. In short, in racist discourses physical characteristics function as signifiers, or conveyors of meanings, as signs within a discourse on difference.'[15]

According to Hall, the result is a racist classification system: a differentiation which is based on "racist" characteristics. Racism makes it possible to "produce identity and to safeguard identification". It is a component of the consensus and consolidation achieved by one social group in opposition to another group subordinate to it. In general, this is described by Hall as a construction of the "Other".[16] By stereotyping the "Other", the construction of a society seems homogeneous – a structure into which the "Other" does not fit.

Racist ideologies always arise, says Hall, "when the production of significance is linked to power strategies, and these are used to exclude certain

---

14 | "Intercultural theatre" is not in the sense of the theatre work of Peter Brook, Ariadne Mnouchkine or Robert Wilson, but refers to concepts which, taken from the context of an "intercultural opening", can be defined as "interculture". See Mark Terkessidis, *Interkultur*, (Frankfurt a. M., 2010).
15 | Stuart Hall, "Rassismus als ideologischer Diskurs", in: *Das Argument* 178, (Hamburg, 1989).
16 | Ibid., p. 919.

groups from cultural and symbolic resources".[17] These exclusion practices can often be traced back to a naturalisation, i.e. the depiction of certain cultural or social circumstances as natural characteristics. In this sense, the concept of race is understood as a social construct whose pseudo-biologistic classification structure is based on skin colour and other external characteristics like body shape, hair structure, etc., and is solely used to rationalize and justify unequal treatment.[18]

In the context of theatre, racism is clearly visible in different connections. There is the Europe-wide and much criticised practice of "blackface", in which white actors use black theatrical makeup; there is the practice of casting actors of colour in ethnic roles and characters, but also the practice of contracting artists of colour only for "migrant" theatre productions. Racism strongly influences the subject of theatre and migration on both a structural and an aesthetic level. These influences will be examined and analysed in this paper.

1.2.3 Postmigrant Theatre

In the past ten years, a new category called "Postmigrant theatre" has established itself. Based on the fact that a change in the structure of the population has taken place which is "not only demographic and sociostructural but also identitary and ideological",[19] a moment occurs, at the latest in the second generation of migration in which the identitary "belonging" can no longer be carried out one-dimensionally with respect to the country of origin. Whereas for most first generation migrants a relationship to the country of origin remains because of an active migration experience which, in many cases, is linked to the emotional possibility of return, the relationship to the country of origin in the following generations and the thought of "returning" contain an aspect of "invented tradition".[20] These ethnicised and racially discriminated

---

17 | Ibid., p. 913.

18 | Paul Gilroy describes this in the following way: "For me, 'race' refers primarily to an impersonal, discursive arrangement, the brutal result of the raciological ordering of the world, not its cause." Paul Gilroy, *Postcolonial Melancholia*, (New York: Columbia University Press, 2005), p. 39.

19 | Naika Foroutan, "Neue Deutsche, Postmigranten und Bindungs-Identitäten. Wer gehört zum neuen Deutschland?" in *Bundeszentrale für Politische Bildung: Aus Politik und Geschichte* 46/47 (2010), p. 10.

20 | "Invented tradition" is an ideological concept which was created in 1983 by Eric Hobsbawm and Terence Ranger and introduced in the collection of essays *The Invention of Tradition*. Invented traditions, i.e. traditions constructed in their respective present but projected into a specific past, and which should serve as a historical fiction to solidify and socially legitimise certain norms and structures in the light of an existing pressure to change. Eric Hobsbawm and Terence Ranger, *The Invention of Tradition*, (New York, 1992).

persons are socialised and live not as Germans but as a successor generation of a migrated group in the supposed "country of destination".[21] At the same time, there exist cultural fixations in this group which are strongly fought over by national and hegemonic powers. The use of the term "post-migration" is an attempt to address this situation.

The term has been borrowed from American literature studies; in an analysis of texts written by authors born in Germany, but of immigrant origin, the term "post-migration" is used to indicate that an interpretation of their works should not focus solely on the aspect of migration.[22] It is an attempt to define the heterogeneous phenomenon of migration and, at the same time, to appropriate this discourse by introducing separate terminology which, in turn, should make it possible to establish a common association and thinking space.

Post-migration cannot only be understood in a temporal and periodic sense but as an analogy to the known "post" trends of the twentieth century (postmodernism, post-structuralism, post-colonialism, post-Fordism, etc.) and as a theoretical term which critically and reflexively grapples with that particular phase of migration.[23]

In Germany, the term was first introduced into public and media discourse by the theatre ensemble Ballhaus Naunynstraße. The self-designation "Postmigrant" stands for the "stories and perspectives of those who themselves have not migrated but who have this migration background as part of their personal knowledge and collective memory"[24] and whose artistic achievement is understood as part of the German theatre landscape.[25]

Through the work of the Ballhaus Naunynstraße, the expression spread very quickly in the European theatre scene. In the European project *Europe Now*, which took place from 2011 to 2013, it was used to describe the situation in European society.[26]

---

21 | Ceren Türkmen, *Migration und Regulierung*, (Münster), p.13.
22 | See Nora Marianne Haakh, "Islamisierte Körper auf der Bühne. Identitätspolitische Positionierung zur deutschen Islam-Debatte", in *Arbeiten des postmigrantischen Theaters Ballhaus Naunynstraße Berlin*, (Berlin: Freie Universität Berlin, 2011).
23 | Karin Lornsen, *Transgressive Topographien in der türkisch-deutschen Postmigranten-Literatur*, (Vancouver: University of British Columbia, 2007), p. 211.
24 | Shermin Langhoff,Tuncay Kulaoglu and Barbara Kastner: "Dialoge I: Migration dichten und deuten. Ein Gespräch zwischen Shermin Langhoff, Tunçay Kulaoğlu und Barbara Kastner", in Artur Pelka and Stefan Tigges (eds.), *Das Drama nach dem Drama. Verwandlungen dramatischer Formen in Deutschland seit 1945*, (Bielefeld: transcript, 2011). Quoted from Nora Marianne Haakh, *Islamisierte Körper auf der Bühne*, p. 4.
25 | Ibid., p. 4.
26 | See http://europenowblog.org/about

1.2.4 Artists of Colour – The Use of the Term in this Study

Finding an adequate term to describe the artists and theatre makers who are presented here under the title "Theatre and Migration" poses a real challenge. This is particularly difficult because terms such as "migrant" or "Postmigrant" artists do not cover all persons. The superordinate subject of this study is migration; most of the persons presented, and their families, immigrated to Europe in the 20th and 21st centuries. Yet, the diversity of their origins, including class, cultural traditions, religion, and sex, distinguishes the members of this group from each other more than it connects them. The experiences of these persons are based more on social exclusion and marginalisation than on the reality of migration. Therefore, the term artist of colour is used, which corresponds with the term "person of colour".[27] The expression is also used by the artists to designate themselves as "non-white" and to position themselves in the tradition of the American civil rights movement.

The term people of colour was coined in the United States during the emergence of the Black Power movement in the late sixties. As an anti-racist self-definition, it became a political term which was intended to mobilise and connect racially marginalised groups and their members beyond the boundaries of their "own" ethnic, national, cultural and religious group membership. It does not describe persons based on an ethnic classification but according to racism as it is experienced in its everyday and institutional forms. The orientation of the whole societal and international developments led to a situation in which many people adapted the term people of colour in the motto "all power to the people" in the hope of achieving a worldwide democratisation by committing themselves to the civil rights, women's liberation and anti-Vietnam War movements.[28]

The term people of colour refers to all racialised persons who, to varying degrees, are of African, Asian, Latin American, Pacific, Arab, Jewish or indigenous origin or background. It connects those who are marginalised by the culture of white dominance and collectively degraded by the force of colonial traditions and presence. In this way, an analytical and political space can be created in which differences, commonalities and intersections of different relationships of oppression and exploitation situations involving people of colour can be examined in a post-colonial context. On the one hand, the (ascribed) ethnical, gender-related, cultural and sexual identities and subject positions will be taken into account. On the other hand, this study will go beyond an

---

27 | Rinku Sen, "Are Immigrants and Refugees People of Colour?", in *Colourlines*, (2007). http://Colourlines.com/archives/2007/07/are_immigrants_and_refugees_people_of_Colour.html

28 | Kien Nghi Ha: "People of Colour als Diversity-Ansatz in der antirassistischen Selbstbenennungs- und Identitätspolitik". (Heinrich Böll Stiftung, Berlin, 2009). http://www.migration-boell.de/web/diversity/48_2299.asp

examination of these particular affiliations in order to circumvent a strategy of "dividing and conquering" by attempting to find a common positioning.[29]

1.3 Historical Turning Points of Migration

Throughout the study, a historical turning point will be referred to which is marked by the political upheavals and transitions in the former socialist countries of (Eastern) Europe.[30] However, other factors and historical events will also play a role in the findings presented here.

Globalisation and its consequences mark a turning point for worldwide migration.[31] Globalisation is driven by technological progress but also by political and ideological change. After the fall of the Berlin wall, liberalisation, privatisation, and deregulation of the global market were significant elements of the economic change.[32] These have led to political changes and to a "universalisation of the Western liberal democracy"[33] in the whole world. In another sense, globalisation represents a continuation of imperialism, capitalistic development and expansion, to which researchers from Asia, Africa and Latin America react with post-colonial criticism.[34]

On the one hand, the increasing international and national inequalities, the continuing demand for highly qualified and low-skilled migrant labour

---

29 | Ibid.
30 | For a further explanation I refer the reader to the work of Andrea Hensel. Lepenies points out that the label "Eastern Europe" is rejected by intellectuals from Poland, Czechia, and Hungary who use the term "Central Europe" instead. Wolf Lepenies, *Kultur und Politik. Deutsche Geschichte*, (Bonn, 2006), p. 330.
31 | Globalisation can be defined as "a broadening, deepening and an acceleration of the global interdependence in all areas of contemporary social life". Globalisation should be understood as a technological as well as a political process. Technological change has greatly increased global migration in many respects. On the one hand, travel and communication have been facilitated so that migrant networks and transnational relationships have improved. On the other hand, the access to education and the decreasing illiteracy can be attributed to the technological changes brought about by globalisation. David Held, Anthony McGrew, David Goldblatt and Jonathan Perraton, *Global Transformations. Politics, Economics and Culture*, (Cambridge: Polity Press, 1999), p 2.
Thomas Faist, *The volume and dynamics of international migration and transnational social spaces*, (Oxford: Oxford University Press, 2000).
32 | Joseph Stiglitz, *Globalisation and its Discontents*, (London: Penguin, 2002), p. 67.
33 | Francis Fukuyama, *The end of history and the last man*, (New York: Free Press, 1992).
34 | Arjun Appadurai, *Modernity At Large. Cultural Dimensions of Globalization*, (Minneapolis: University of Minnesota Press, 1996).

in the segmented labour markets of the affluent societies, and, on the other hand, the lack of opportunity, population growth, oppression and violent conflicts in developing countries are factors which expedite the rising migration worldwide.[35] In the last three decades, this has triggered an unprecedented wave of immigration in Europe and to the doors of Europe which has, in turn, given rise to social, political and cultural change in European countries.[36]

Another event which represents a turning point for persons from the Near East and from Islamic countries – regardless of whether they embrace a religious belief or not – was the attack on the World Trade Center and the consequences of 9/11. After 11 September 2001, persons of Muslim faith, or persons from Islamic countries in general, were targeted and became victims of racism.[37] In Europe, the "irreconcilability with Western values "became the focus of the political discussion. Thus, Muslims and persons from Islamic countries are often stereotyped by the media as a homogeneous, deeply religious group which adheres to a fundamentalist Islam.[38] A study which was carried out by the European Union Agency for Fundamental Rights between 2002 and 2005 found that people of colour – in particular, persons of Muslim faith and persons from Islamic countries – were, to a significant extent, subject to discriminatory behaviour. Almost one-third of those surveyed indicated that they saw themselves exposed to discrimination in recruitment and promotion processes or to harassment at work.[39]

It is easier to follow up these general findings by taking a closer look at the individual European countries. For example, the murder of the Dutch filmmaker, Theo van Gogh, in Amsterdam on 2 November 2004, resulted in a strong Islamophobia. Van Gogh was apparently critical of Islam and known for his controversial statements regarding the religion. Among other things, Van Gogh produced a film with the Dutch parliamentarian, Hirsi Ali, on do-

---

35 | Robert Hunter Wade, "Is Globalisation Reducing Poverty and Inequality?" in *World Development* 32(4), (London, 2004), pp. 567-589.

36 | Christina Boswell, *European Migration Policies in Flux*, p. 1.

37 | Whereby animosity towards Muslims and Islamophobia existed in Western countries earlier, see Christopher Allen, "Justifying Islamophobia: A Post-9/11 Consideration of the European Union and British Contexts" in *The American Journal of Islamic Social Sciences*, issue 21, (2004). Not only practicing Muslims are affected by anti-Muslim slurs – the category "Muslim" has been racialised. The terms "Turk" or "Arab" and "Muslim" are used almost synonymously. See Yasemin Schooman, "Islamophobie, antimuslimischer Rassismus oder Muslimfeindlichkeit? Kommentar zu der Begriffsdebatte der Deutschen Islam Konferenz", (2011), http://www.migration-boell.de/web/integration/47_2956.asp#1

38 | European Union Agency for Fundamental Rights, *Muslime in der europäischen Union. Islamophobie und Diskriminierung*, (Vienna. 2006), p. 38.

39 | Ibid., p. 39.

mestic violence against Muslim women which caused a storm among critics. The murderer was a 26-year-old man with a dual Dutch-Moroccan citizenship. Besides the racially motivated acts of violence and arson attacks, Dutch people of colour were exposed to verbal abuse on the street, in public transportation, and at sports events.[40]

In Switzerland, the "minaret controversy" became a public symbol of the existing resentment against persons of Muslim faith. In 2006, Muslim communities in various Swiss cities and towns – including *Wangen bei Olten* in the Canton of Solthurn, Langenthal in the Canton of Bern, and Will in the Canton of St. Gallen – submitted building permit applications for minarets. These applications provoked some fierce reactions in the local population and among politicians, although until that time building permit applications for Muslim prayer rooms had not had any political impact.[41] At first, a parliamentarian initiative in the Canton of Zurich was launched by the Swiss People's Party which was aimed at changing the building laws so that the building of structures with minarets would no longer be approved. After this initiative failed, the Swiss People's Party and the Federal Democratic Union of Switzerland formed the Swiss people's initiative "Against the Building of Minarets".[42] In the referendum carried out in 2009, the Swiss people opted for a ban on minarets.[43] This decision triggered an international debate which resulted in lawsuits before the European Court for Human Rights on grounds of infringement of the basic right to religious freedom and the principle of non-discrimination.[44]

Not only individuals of Muslim faith but also Roma and black Europeans are subject to the anti-Muslim racism described here. A closer look reveals that this involves marginalisation processes in which religion is used as a means to justify collective ascriptions with the purpose of excluding members of minorities.[45]

Globalisation as the catalyst for a global migration movement which, in particular, impacts Western European countries, and 9/11 as a historical point in time at which the racist exclusion of people of colour – and, more specifically,

---

40 | Ibid., p. 92.
41 | Ralph Zimmermann, "Zur Minarettverbotsinitiative in der Schweiz", in *Zeitschrift für ausländisches öffentliches Recht und Völkerrecht (ZaöRV)* 69, (Heidelberg: Beck, 2009), p. 812.
42 | Ibid., p. 813.
43 | http://www.admin.ch/ch/d/pore/va/20091129/det547.html
44 | The law suits have been rejected to date since they have not been filed by so-called "victims". http://www.welt.de/politik/ausland/article13476092/Muslime-scheitern-mit-Klage-gegen-Minarett-Verbot.html
45 | See Schooman,"Islamophobie, antimuslimischer Rassismus oder Muslimfeindlichkeit", (2011).

people of Muslim faith and persons from Islamic countries – becomes most visible, are relevant turning points for those countries considered in this study. They must be seen as the backdrop for the migration policies in the respective countries.

1.4 Overview of the Research

Only one study of theatre and migration in Europe has been published to date; it was contracted by the International Network for Contemporary Performing Arts in 2003. *Crossing the Rainbow – National Differences and International Convergences in Multicultural Performing Arts in Europe* by Jude Bloomfield depicts, on the one hand, the general national conditions for migration and integration in Western European countries and, on the other hand, gives an overview of the "multicultural"[46] theatre and dance scenes in Great Britain, The Netherlands, France, Germany, Austria, Belgium, Italy, Spain, and Portugal. The study shows that racism is, in general, the greatest obstacle which theatre makers of colour encounter in the performing arts.

The work of artists of colour is limited to their ethnical background and is reduced to "social" or "community" art – just not professional art. This downgrading of the artistic quality also takes place on a state level with respect to funding. There is an institutional separation of funding for white artists and artists of colour. The study indicates that this classification – at least in Germany, Austria, and France – is used to justify access to and denial of funds.[47]

The study also shows that certain EU programmes have supported the "intercultural" theatre scene in Europe on local, regional and international levels. However, there is no specific obligation to promote cultural diversity and artists of colour. It is necessary to open the "cultural institutions which are still closed" for artists from the second generation of immigrants and to provide resources for the long-term artistic development of their creativity.[48]

Bloomfield's work is the basis for this study in which she takes up trends and describes them. In general, it can be said that minimal material is available on the individual countries.[49] There is a great need for documentation and contextualisation of the theatre work done by artists of colour in Europe.

---

46 | The term "multicultural theatre scene" is used by Bloomfield without a more precise definition of what is meant. Therefore, the term appears here in quotation marks.
47 | Bloomfield, p. 113ff.
48 | Ibid., p. 115.
49 | A major exception here is Great Britain, where the "Black British" and "Asian British" theatre scenes are well documented.

1.5 On My Own Behalf

I would like to conclude this introduction by positioning myself, defining the subject of this study and an explaining the methodological approach.

As a German theatre and cultural scientist (of colour), I have approached this task from a German perspective. This manifests itself in the use of German literature but also in the German view of the European theatre scene. It seems necessary to mention this fact, since the claim has been made that trends will be examined here in a European theatre dominated by a predetermined Western European perspective. The subject of this study is, therefore, artists of colour and Postmigrant theatre from Germany, Switzerland, Austria, The Netherlands, Sweden, Great Britain, and France. I will return to the choice of countries in the next chapter.

I have collected materials from archives and research literature from the relevant scientific disciplines and have critically analysed existing theatre texts and presented my research for discussion in colloquiums and conferences throughout Europe. Finally, current trends were traced and examined by means of on-site research, interviews with artists and persons from the relevant environment, and participative observation.

In the following chapters, these trends will be described. First, an overview of the national theatre scenes will be presented. In a short summary, historical and political contexts relating to migration in the respective countries will be established, and the political situation and forms of participation and representation will be explained. In addition, in the second chapter, the development of the respective theatre scenes and the most important artists of colour will be described. In an excursus in the third chapter, the "minority theatre" will be presented, and its demands and aims will be contextualised within Postmigrant theatre. In the fourth chapter, structural changes that have been triggered by artists of colour and Postmigrant theatre in the European theatre landscape will be presented in terms of the most important dimensions. In the fifth chapter, the aesthetic means used by artists of colour will be discussed.

This study cannot compensate for the lack of research and archival materials which would be necessary to engrain the subject matter in the collective memory of the European theatre scene. This study attempts to outline the trends in the theatre from a Postmigrant perspective based on structural and aesthetic changes. In the given format, only an overview and an attempt at a contextualisation are possible.

2. Overview of the Countries

The overview of the countries examined and the national Postmigrant theatre scenes is a crucial part of this study. Seven Western European countries were selected: Germany, Austria, Switzerland, France, The Netherlands, Great Britain, and Sweden. The selection resulted from the scientific focus of a German theatre expert whose perspective is influenced by Western European precepts. For this reason, mainly German-speaking theatre scenes were considered. In order to be able to present a coherent picture of trends of the Postmigrant theatre in Europe, it was necessary to include countries whose artists work in cooperation with German and German-speaking theatre makers of colour. It was obvious that collaborations between the Ballhaus Naunynstraße and theatre houses in Sweden, Great Britain, and The Netherlands would also be examined. Another reason was the migration movements in the individual countries and the resulting societal participation which has led to an emancipation and to the Postmigrant theatre scenes. Thus, countries like France, the Netherlands and Great Britain were selected. Because of their colonial pasts, these societies have gone through a long development process in terms of migration. Other countries, such as Austria, Sweden, and Switzerland, have trends resembling those of Germany in terms of development and social debate on migration. By contrasting the countries and their scenes, European trends can be revealed and restricted to countries in Western Europe. A Postmigrant theatre landscape could not be found in Middle and Eastern European countries, since their historical and political history has taken a different course. Finally, the Postmigrant theatre scene, if it can be referred to as such, is relatively small. The included countries with their theatre makers, theatre groups and theatre houses represent the most important players in the scene.

The following chapter will present the historical and political connections in the selected countries with respect to migration and its societal turning points, followed by an overview of the development of the Postmigrant theatre scene in the respective countries. In this context, the most important theatre makers and theatre groups and their work will be set out in brief.

2.1 Germany

2.1.1 Migration in Germany

Germany denied its transition to a country of immigration for a very long time. Despite the immigration of labourers since the fifties and the influx of refugees, German policies on immigration and foreigners were characterised in the past decades by the idea that Germany was not a country of immigration.[50]

From the fifties, the Federal Republic of Germany endeavoured to recruit foreign workers. However, it was intended that the so-called "Gastarbeiter", or guest workers, should only remain in Germany temporarily. Recruitment agreements for labourers were first signed with Italy, Spain, and Greece, and later with Turkey, Morocco, Portugal, Tunisia, and Yugoslavia. As a consequence of the economic recession, the number of jobs for recruited workers decreased between 1966 and 1969. Finally, there was a recruiting stop in 1973 which put an end to the government-organised labour migration. However, at the same time, family members of those workers began to migrate to Germany. Moreover, the number of those persons seeking asylum in Germany increased in the following decades. In the nineties, the idea prevailed in Germany, as in all other European immigration countries, that in the case of continued immigration pressure, a recognisable delimitation to the outside should be the prerequisite for future immigration and integration policies and their acceptance by the indigenous population. After the reunification, racism and discrimination against persons of colour increased in Germany. Acts of violence by right-wing extremists in Hoyerswerda and Rostock-Lichtenhagen were the appalling climaxes of a "partially campaign-like, intensified discussion" on the alleged "mass abuse" of the basic right to asylum anchored in the constitution (Art. 16 GG) by so-called "economic refugees".[51] The volatile climate then led to the so-called "asylum compromise", according to which the basic right to political asylum was radically restricted in 1993.[52]

A paradigm shift did not take place until the beginning of the 21st century, because of the international division of labour, the demographic development in Germany, and the increasing need for foreign workers in German society. Two

---

50 | In 1982 the CDU/CSU and FDP specified in their coalition agreement: "The Federal Republic of Germany is not an immigration country. All humanitarian measures must be taken to prevent the influx of foreigners." See Klaus Bade, *Deutsche im Ausland – Fremde in Deutschland. Migration in Geschichte und Gegenwart*, (Munich, 1992), p. 52.

51 | Carolin Butterwege, "Von der 'Gastarbeiter'-Anwerbung zum Zuwanderungsgesetz", (Bonn, 2005), http://www.bpb.de/gesellschaft/migration/dossier-migration/56377/migrationspolitik-in-der-brd?p=all

52 | The racially motivated attacks led to a mobilisation in the civilian population which primarily took place in the form of demonstrations and chains of lights. The belief that the violence committed by right-wing extremists at that time was over was refuted with the disclosure of ten murders committed by the National Socialist Underground (NSU). The extent of government involvement and structural racism is being investigated to date by a Parliamentary Investigation Committee. See http://www.bundestag.de/bundestag/ausschuesse17/ua/2untersuchungsausschuss/

important legal decisions reflected Germany's new understanding of itself as a country of immigration: A new immigration law was passed, and the German citizenship law was changed. With the reform of the law governing the right to citizenship (which had been in force since 1 January 2000), a considerable step was taken towards recognising the immigration situation long in existence. It ended the one-sided orientation towards the principle of hereditary transmission of citizenship ("ius sanguinis") and its relatively restrictive supplement by which citizenship could be acquired based on a territorial principle through birth in the country ("ius soli"). That was a profound break with ethno-national concepts which could be summarised in the basic principle that one could be a German but not become one. Since then there have been different initiatives on the so-called integration of immigrated persons in Germany. In 2007, a National Integration Plan was published in which the federal government presented a concept for the integration of "persons with a migration background" on all political and social levels.[53]

A special role was assigned to the sectors of society such as media and culture. Cultural institutions were expected to make a particular contribution toward cultural integration. The reason for this request was the finding that the necessary analyses and compilations of data concerning the participation of migrants in the cultural sector were lacking on national, regional and community levels. It was also criticised that migrants were underrepresented "in the audience as well as on the stage". In general, "theatre, opera and museums, often even the music and youth art schools, are said to be institutions which are seldom frequented by foreigners".[54]

2.1.2 The German Theatre Scene

This recognition correlates with the fact that although artists of colour began working in Germany in the sixties and seventies, they did not have access to municipal and state theatres. Erol Boran describes the situation as follows: "The history of Turkish-German theatre projects is almost as old as the history of Turkish migrant labourers in Germany".[55] This history is in no way limited to the guest workers from Turkey but can also be extended to include other groups of immigrants.

---

53 | Integration is described by the German Federal Government as the involvement in the social, economic, intellectual-cultural, and legal structures of the receiving country without forfeiting one's own cultural identity. See *Die Bundesregierung: Der nationale Integrationsplan. Neue Chancen – neue Wege*, (Berlin, 2007).
54 | Ibid.
55 | Erol M. Boran, *Eine Geschichte des Türkisch-Deutschen Theaters und Kabaretts*, (Ohio: The Ohio State University, 2004), p. 3.

Manfred Brauneck's study, *Ausländertheater in der Bundesrepublik Deutschland und in West-Berlin*, was the first research paper on theatre and migration in Germany.[56] Brauneck observes that artistic activities are left to the "personal initiative and self-organisation of the foreigners".[57] According to the prevailing understanding of integration in the eighties, which "aimed at the dissolution of the original national and cultural identity of the foreigners and an all-embracing assimilation",[58] it was initially socio-politically committed institutions which promoted the theatre work of the first generation of immigrants. It provided an opportunity for political, social, and aesthetic articulation which was not to be taken for granted. Thus, the theatre work of immigrants in the Federal Republic of Germany remained virtually unknown until the end of the nineties.[59] Boran analyses that the German reception had little understanding for the cultural productions of immigrants and was extremely narrow. The same applies to the German theatre scene, which was too exclusive and too nationally oriented. It was, in his opinion, a "closed party".[60] This statement is particularly true for municipal and state theatres in Germany. The independent scene was vitalised by artists with diverse migration biographies thanks to its international orientation and its flexibility. Some theatre ensembles were established at this time.

One of the most important theatres founded in Germany in the eighties was the Theater an der Ruhr, established in 1980 by the Italian expatriate Roberto Ciulli and the dramaturg Helmut Schäfer. Ciulli had already been the artistic director of the Globe Theatre in Milan in the sixties. The basic concept behind "Theater an der Ruhr" was to develop a structure which was flexible enough to adapt to the respective needs of the theatre work and the circumstances of the theatre makers. The theatre quickly became one of the most internationally renowned stages; not only was Cuilli himself distinguished for his artistic achievement and as a cultural ambassador, but the Theater an der Ruhr achieved international acclaim as an ambassador for Germany. For this reason, international tours were financed by the German Foreign Office.[61]

In Cologne, the Arkadas Theater was founded in the eighties by the Turkish teacher Necati Sahin, who wanted to give the children of Turkish immigrants the opportunity to learn the Turkish language through theatre. Since then the Arkadas Theater has been renamed the "Bühne der Kulturen", and the German-

---

56 | Manfred Brauneck, *Ausländertheater in der Bundesrepublik Deutschland und in West-Berlin*, p. 6.
57 | Ibid., p. 12.
58 | Ibid., p. 12.
59 | Sven Sappelt, "Theater und Migrant/innen", in Carmine Chiellino (ed.), *Interkulturelle Literatur in Deutschland*. Stuttgart, (Metzler, 2000), p. 276.
60 | Boran, *Eine Geschichte des Türkisch-Deutschen Theaters und Kabaretts*.
61 | See A. Sharifi, *Theater für Alle*, (Frankfurt a. M., 2011), p. 59ff.

Turkish theatre focuses on the diversity of Cologne's population.[62] At the same time, at the end of the seventies, the Turkish ensemble of the Schaubühne Berlin was founded.[63] After the project at the Schaubühne ended at the end of the eighties, the actors of Turkish descent founded the theatre group, Tiyatrom, in 1984.

Tiyatrom is publicly funded by the Senate of Berlin and was founded as a Turkish-language theatre in Berlin-Kreuzberg in 1984. After many years during which the group frequently had to endure criticism from Berlin's Turkish population, the senate set up a commission to evaluate Tiyatrom and to furnish an expert opinion on the group since its work was supposedly neither of an artistic nor of a socio-educational nature.[64] The fight is still going on today. Theatres in Berlin with an "intercultural" focus must compete with each other for subsidies.

The Theaterhaus Stuttgart was also founded in the 1980s and is still an important venue for many immigrant theatre makers. The non-profit-making organisation Theaterhaus Stuttgart e.V. was founded by Werner and Gudrun Schretzmeier and Peter Grohmann in 1984. Since the beginning Werner Schretzmeier has been the artistic director. Many theatre makers and actors of colour, such as Asli Kislal and Emre Akal, have worked for and with Werner Schretzmeier on a regular basis. The Theaterhaus Stuttgart was initially an international venue where internationality was paramount, and the stage language was very often English. As years passed, however, it became clear that not internationality but Germany's multicultural nature should be reflected in the work on the stage.[65] The last very successful production was in 2011, *Twelve Angry Men*, under the artistic direction of Werner Schretzmeier and in which only actors of colour participated.

In the past decade, the theatre scene in Germany has been particularly changed by artists of colour who belong to the second generation of immigrants. In the study "Report on the Performing Arts" (Report Darstellende Künste), commissioned by the foundation for the performing arts (Fonds Darstellende Künste), it was determined that the chance of "persons with a migration background" and other nationalities to find adequate employment in the independent theatre and dance scene increased or decreased in relation to their representation in the overall population. They are employed under the same working conditions and receive remuneration comparable to that of German

---

62 | The Bühne der Kulturen houses a Russian, a Turkish, and a Yiddish theatre ensemble. See http://www.buehnederkulturen.de

63 | Boran, p. 133.

64 | Ibid., p. 133ff.

65 | Werner Schretzmeier in a personal interview.

theatre and dance professionals. Only the Russian and, above all, Turkish theatre makers are underrepresented.[66] Yet persons in Germany with a Turkish or Russian background make up the largest immigrant population. With the recognition that only an institutionalisation could open up the scene and make the theatre makers of colour more visible to the public, the Ballhaus Naunynstraße in Berlin was founded by Shermin Langhoff. Ballhaus Naunynstraße has been used as a venue by migrant theatre groups since 1983, because Kreuzberg is a district of the city with a high percentage of guest workers where "work migration [...] has already left its mark".[67] Since 2004, Shermin Langhoff has worked as a curator for the theatre Hebbel am Ufer in Berlin and for other events such as the festival Beyond Belonging – Migration, which was concerned with art and politics in the context of migration. Due to the great demand on the part of the artists, a permanent platform for Postmigrant cultural practice was established.[68] "The theatre is devoted to Postmigrant theatre work which the artists pointedly call "beyond belonging".[69] The Postmigrant theatre, with its artists of colour, can be seen as an exploratory movement with diverse cultural perspectives which is "nurtured by imagined pasts and visions of the future".

Since the success of the play *Verrücktes Blut*[70] by Jens Hillje and Nurkan Erpulat, the Ballhaus Naunynstraße has been successful. To date, it is the only Postmigrant institution which has established itself in the theatre landscape in Germany. The Ballhaus Naunynstraße is the only institutionalised production venue for Postmigrant theatre in Germany. In autumn of 2013, Shermin Langhoff became the first director of colour of the Maxim Gorki Theater in Berlin. She established the term "migration mainstreaming", which alludes to the fact that diversity is part of the institution in all its parts.

---

66 | Fonds Darstellende Künste, *Report Darstellende Künste. Wirtschaftliche, soziale und arbeitsrechtliche Lage der Theater- und Tanzschaffenden in Deutschland*, (Essen: Klartext-Verlagsgesellschaft, 2010), p. 155.
67 | Website Ballhaus Naunynstraße as of 2008. http://www.ballhausnaunynstrasse.de/HAUS.8.0.html
68 | Azadeh Sharifi, "Postmigrantisches Theater. Eine neue Agenda für die deutschen Bühnen", in Wolfgang Schneider (ed.), *Theater und Migration. Herausforderungen für Kulturpolitik und Theaterpraxis*, (Bielefeld: transcript, 2011).
69 | "Theater kann eine Identitätsmaschine sein", Interview with Shermin Langhoff, in *Nah & Fern*, issue 43, (Karlsruhe: Loeper Literaturverlag, 2009), p. 21.
70 | *Verrücktes Blut* premiered in the Ballhaus Naunynstraße in 2010. In 2011, it was invited to the Berlin Theatertreffen. It received the audience award at the Mülheim Theatertage and was chosen "German-language play of the year" by an independent jury of German-speaking critics in the magazine, *Theater heute*.

2.2 Austria

2.2.1 Migration in Austria

Austria still holds fast to the myth of not being a country of immigration, although historically there was a high degree of migration within the Habsburg Empire and sixty percent of the population of Vienna has a migrant background. Especially after the Second World War, immigration began because of a recruitment agreement (which was also the case in Germany). At the beginning of the fifties, a labour shortage was evident which was exacerbated by the emigration of Austrian workers to Germany and Switzerland. In 1961, the Raab-Olah Agreement was signed, under which the immigration of foreign workers was specified.[71]

The year 1989, and particularly the political upheaval in Romania as well as the subsequent wave of refugees, marked a turning point in Austrian asylum and refugee policies. Influenced by the strongly emotionalised domestic discussions, the right of asylum was dismantled little by little. To "prevent the abuse of asylum", "accelerated court proceedings to determine a person's right to political asylum" were introduced, visa requirements for the countries from which most asylum seekers originated were imposed, and deportations were facilitated. These measures, however, had only minimal influence on the total number of refugees. The collapse of the Yugoslavian state and the ensuing military conflicts in Croatia, Bosnia-Herzegovina, and Kosovo led to the largest refugee movement in Europe since the Second World War. Many of these migrants sought refuge in Austria, if only because of the geographic proximity.[72]

At the beginning of November 2007, 16.3% of all Austrians had foreign backgrounds. The largest group of immigrants are people from the countries of former Yugoslavia, followed by people from Turkey. The third largest group already consists of immigrants from Germany.[73]

2.2.2 The Austrian Theatre Scene

As is the case in Germany, the theatre scene is divided into the independent theatre groups and the state theatres. Also similar to Germany, artists of colour are only active in the independent theatre scene. In a study on the Austrian theatre scene, Kevin Leppek observes that authors of colour as well as "executives in administrative functions of public theatres" with migration background do not exist.[74] This has caused public theatres to begin hiring artists of colour in

---

71 | Werner T. Bauer, *Zuwanderung nach Österreich*, (Vienna, ÖGPP, 2008), p. 5.
72 | Ibid., p. 6.
73 | Ibid., p. 9.
74 | Kevin Leppek, Theater als interkultureller Dialog. Dschungel Wien – Theaterhaus für junges Publikum, (Marburg: Tectum, 2010), p. 162.

recent years. For instance, Asli Kislal staged the play *Verrücktes Blut* by Nurkan Erpulat and Jens Hillje at the Landestheater Linz in 2012. However, such collaboration has only taken place in particular cases.

In the Austrian independent theatre scene, artists of colour have been able to establish themselves. Places like the Werkstätten- und Kulturhaus (WUK) in Vienna were venues for production and presentation. The creation of individual structures strengthened the development. In the meantime, Austria has a small but very productive Postmigrant theatre scene, a development resulting in the appointment of Shermin Langhoff as deputy director and head curator of the *Wiener Festwochen* in 2011, among other things. In the invitation to tender published by the city of Vienna, "concepts to ensure gender mainstreaming, interculture and participation" were requested; "the intercultural structure of Vienna with its historical roots should be reflected in the programme planning for which an active involvement of the cultural scene in Vienna and diverse, 'low-threshold' venues are desired".[75] Shermin Langhoff had to resign from the position for personal reasons in 2012.[76]

The independent theatre groups are primarily located in Vienna. In 1998, the Lalish Theaterlabor was founded by Shamal Amin and Nigar Hasib in Vienna as an experimental centre for the research of rituals and intercultural performance work.[77] In June 2000, they opened their own centre. With the research project *no shadow 2006–2011* and the further investigation of Songs as a Source, the Lalish Theaterlabor devotes itself mainly to the now largely forgotten archaeological search for the human voice, its impact, and its individual and cultural origin.[78]

With the beginning of the season 2009/2010, Harold Posch and Ali M. Abdullah took over the Theater am Petersplatz and renamed it GarageX. They began their collaboration with the project Drama X, which created quite a stir in 2004. The venues were not typical theatre stages, but rather vacant industrial and commercial properties which temporarily – often only for one evening – were used for the theatrical performance. In the Theaterhaus GarageX, Posch and Abdullah set up an artists' negotiation room for socially and politically

---

75 | http://derstandard.at/1304428463416/Hinterhaeuser-und-Langhoff-als-Intendanten-Duo

76 | http://derstandard.at/1336697481118/Designierte-Leiterin-Shermin-Langhoff-zurueckgetreten

77 | See Nigar Hasib, "Lalish-Theaterlabor. Aufbruch zur Quelle der Feierlichkeit", in Monika Wagner, Susanne Schwinghammer and Michael Hüttler (eds.), *Theater. Begegnung. Integration?*, (Frankfurt am Main: Iko-Verlag für Interkulturelle Kommunikation, 2003), p. 221ff.

78 | See http://www.lalishtheater.org

relevant issues in which critical discussions on the present social order in Austria could take place.

In 2004, under the direction of Asli Kislal and a thirty-person ensemble, the art and cultural organisation daskunst was founded, which is closely associated with the Theaterhaus GarageX. daskunst sees itself as a "neo-original Viennese, multi-citizen theatre ensemble"[79] and would like to represent the heterogeneous migrant society in Austria through its artists, through content and its implementation in order to present this perception of reality to an equally heterogeneous audience.

The first piece, *Dirty Dishes*, staged by Ali Kislal, was a social satire about "illegal foreign women" and was performed in Vienna, Graz, and Linz. The first big successes daskunst achieved were at the theatre festival *Spectrum best of(f) Austria* in 2007. In the 2009/2010 season, Asli Kislal took over as artistic director of the Theater des Augenblicks. In the following season, she worked with daskunst as artist in residence in GarageX. With the co-production *Wienerblut, Operette sich wer kann*, which was developed together with 3raum and co-directed by Hubsi Kramer, daskunst attracted a higher degree of media attention. With the festival series *Pimp My Integration*, daskunst and Asli Kislal definitely secured a position in the Austrian theatre scene. The festival was set up as a project series of Postmigrant positions and various artistic positions which examine (post)migrant experiences as well as works which focus on current social reality. Pimp My Integration was performed from the end of October 2011 to the end of February 2012. Asli Kislal, Carolin Vikoler from daskunst, and Ali M. Abdullah and Harold Posch from GarageX were the festival curators. The festival mainly featured international Postmigrant theatre productions, accompanied by sessions in which the opening of Austrian art and cultural institutions was discussed.

The Verein Boem, an interdisciplinary group led by the artist Alexander Nicolic, is also located in Vienna. Alexander Nicolic devotes himself and his projects to the histories of guest workers from all parts of former Yugoslavia, focussing on questions concerning the former common culture and language in relation to Austrian society. These issues are then made manifest in some form in the Vereinsbar, the bar of the club – a local pub which hardly differs externally from other neighbourhood pubs – in the adjacent exhibition rooms or in the WUK. At the *Wiener Festwochen 2012*, the new piece by Alexander Nicolic, *New Bohemian – Gastarbeiter Opera*, which was commissioned by the organisers, was performed as part of the Festwochen Forum. In the play, Nicolic uses lay actors who mainly work in the Vereinsbar Boem as waiters and barkeepers to deconstruct Theodor Adorno's treatment of music in social classes. This contradictory relationship is aesthetically challenged in the *Gastarbeiter Opera* by means of Serbian tavern music.

---

79 | In an interview with Asli Kislal.

God's Entertainment is another independent theatre group in Vienna. Its founders, Boris Ceko, Simon Seinhauser, and Maja Degirmendzic, are mainly concerned with people on the periphery of society. A production which was also shown as part of the *Festwochen Forum 2012* was *Österreicher integriert Euch*. This production, which took place at different locations in the city of Vienna, was inspired by the artistic work Ausländer Raus by Christoph Schlingensief from the year 2000. Prior to the performance, artists interviewed people on the street on the subject of migration, and some of those surveyed gave very prejudicial and racist answers in a kind of camp with lay actors from marginalised groups of the population such as Roma-Austrians, black Austrians, refugees, etc. In the camp it was then possible for white Austrians to "integrate" themselves by means of various activities in order to break down existing resentment.

2.3 Switzerland

2.3.1 Migration in Switzerland

Switzerland has also long denied that it is a country of immigration. With the strong economic upswing after World War II, foreign labour was recruited, and the recruitment of migrant workers largely influenced the second half of the twentieth century. However, not only the needs of the labour market but also xenophobic attitudes influenced the immigration policies, which became more and more restrictive.

After 1950, there were several waves of refugees to Switzerland from different countries: Tibetans, Hungarians, Czechs, Slovaks, and Tamils. Their arrival initiated a series of solidarity movements in the Swiss population. Until the seventies, representatives of business and industry voiced reservations regarding the regulations which only allowed seasonal labour. It was not productive for businesses to have to send workers back home who had been trained to do a particular job only to recruit them again at the beginning of the next season.[80]

The basis for a new integration policy which allowed immigrants to have a better legal status was laid in the seventies. The new policy made it easier for the subsequent migration of family members and improved the right of residence. As a result of the economic crisis in the seventies, however, many immigrants left the country.[81]

Another economic upturn, beginning in the mid-eighties, brought about a rise in cross-border immigration. Although the economy experienced a recession in the nineties, the number of immigrants continued to grow. Between 2000 and 2010, most immigrants to Switzerland had migrated to reunite families or find employment.

---

80 | http://www.bpb.de/gesellschaft/migration/dossier-migration/139678/schweiz
81 | http://www.bpb.de/gesellschaft/migration/dossier-migration/139678/schweiz

In a comparison of European countries, it has been determined that a relatively high percentage of the Swiss population has a migrant background. In 2009, the share of the population of migrant origin amounted to approximately 22.9%. The foreign residential population was mainly made up of immigrants from European countries. The largest group of permanent foreign residents is Italian. The second largest group is German, followed by people from Portugal, Serbia, and Montenegro.[82] As has already been stated, since 2006 there has been a major public debate in several Swiss cantons – a referendum – on the building of minarets. This course of action against people of another faith, although internationally criticised, has recently taken on even greater proportions in the form of sanctions against refugees.[83]

2.3.2 The Swiss Theatre Scene

There is no homogeneous Swiss theatre culture or theatre scene, because of the federal form of government and the multilingualism. Every language region has its own theatres, and these tend to nurture contacts to its same-language neighbours rather than to the other language regions of Switzerland. German-speaking Switzerland looks to Germany and Austria, Western Switzerland to France, and Tessin to Italy. The research on theatre makers of colour in this study focuses on the German-speaking region of Switzerland.

Because of the existing diversity in the theatre scene, deficits can be observed with regard to perception and reflection of demographic change. On the one hand, migration movements and other factors have led to a pluralisation of cultural forms of expression. On the other hand, such influences are not of such importance to the theatre programmes as is assigned them with respect to the active cultural participation of the population in the theatre scene. In the context of the UNESCO Convention, a group of experts composed of Swiss theatre makers was established to formulate proposals to implement the diversity of cultural expression in Switzerland.[84] In the course of the research, few theatre projects could be found which were realised in Switzerland by theatre makers of colour. Some artists are active in Switzerland, but their work is restricted (albeit involuntarily) to the independent scene. This is the case with Diana Rojas, who, after her studies of economics and dance in Bogota, Colombia, studied at the

---

82 | Italians (16.7%), followed by Germans (15.5 %) and Portuguese (12.5%).

83 | A so-called "bathing prohibition" for asylum seekers was issued. The prohibition was justified by authorities in the person of the municipal official, Raymond Tellenbach (FDP) in an interview with the weekly newspaper (WOZ): it was a "precautionary measure to prevent sexual harassment of female pupils and the sale of drugs by asylum seekers." http://www.woz.ch/1332/behoerdlicher-rassismus/ein-amt-schuert-angst

84 | This can be found at the following website: http://www.kulturellevielfalt.ch/visio.php?de,0

École Internationale de Théâtre Jacques Lecoq. Since 2005, Diana Rojas has lived in Zurich and has worked as an actress and performer in the independent scene. She founded the artists' platform "Mandarina & Co." and presented such productions as *"Y tu? Wer bisch du?"* (2007), *"Choco Loco"* (2009), *"Was gisch mer für d'Welt?"* (2010), and *"200mm – thinking about social distance"* (2012) on different stages, including the Schlachthaus Theater Bern, Rote Fabrik Zurich, Theaterhaus Gessnerallee Zurich, and *Züricher Theater Spektakel*. She has no chance to perform in the classical theatres: "I don't speak 'stage German', i.e. I am not accepted in many theatres or I am only cast as a foreigner."[85] Diana Rojas, in her own words, is reduced to her appearance and thus to clichés. In the theatre as well as in films, she is offered the roles of "the sexy Latina, Colombian terrorist, and drug dealer, etc."[86] In a personal conversation, she added that many of her friends and colleagues of colour find themselves in similar situations.

An "intercultural" venue is the Maxim Theater, which is located in Zurich. Work with "immigrants and second and third generation residents"[87] began in 2006, from which an ensemble was established: the Maxim Community, consisting of 150 persons from over 30 countries of origin. Presently, four groups are working at the Maxim Theater and are supervised by two professional theatre directors. The course "Learn German through Acting" is offered in collaboration with a theatre pedagogue and a teacher for German as a foreign language. Theatre productions are developed through improvisations which are presented at least ten times after a six- to eight-month rehearsal period. The fourteen theatre productions and two films which have been produced so far were shown, in part, in very different venues in Zurich. In 2007 and 2009, two youth projects (*Third Eye* I and II) were created, in which over sixty young persons from Switzerland and Bosnia participated. In 2009, the Maxim Theatre participated in the project *"Creating Belonging in Immigrant Cities"* at the Institute for Cultural Studies in the Arts at the Zurich Academy of the Arts.[88]

2.4 The Netherlands

2.4.1 Migration in The Netherlands

In the 17th century, The Netherlands became one of the greatest colonial powers in the world, the largest colony being Indonesia. In the 20th century, Indonesia rebelled against this colonisation. After violent conflicts lasting until long after the Second World War, Indonesia finally became independent in 1949. One of

---

85 | Personal interview with Diana Rojas.
86 | Ibid.
87 | See http://www.maximtheater.ch
88 | http://www.maximtheater.ch

the results of this was the immigration of people from Indonesia and Surinam to The Netherlands after the war.

Until the late seventies, however, the prevailing opinion was that The Netherlands was not a country of immigration. This changed after two periods of immigration. The first wave of immigrants came in the sixties and was comprised mainly of temporary workers from Turkey and Morocco. Although The Netherlands did not consider itself a country of immigration, there were no restrictions with regard to family reunification, as was the practice in other countries, so that in the late seventies the numbers of immigrants rose because of the subsequent immigration of family members.[89] At the same time, there was a second wave of immigrants, mainly from the post-colonial areas of Indonesia, Surinam, and the Dutch Antilles. In addition, in the larger Dutch cities, the number of illegal immigrants "sans-papiers" rose.[90]

The right to citizenship introduced in 1985 automatically granted the third generation of immigrants Dutch citizenship and facilitated the acquisition of citizenship for the second generation. As a result, more than half of the immigrants have a Dutch passport. The Netherlands was long considered one of the most liberal and immigrant-friendly countries in Europe, but the mood changed in the nineties when multiculturalism was strongly criticised and immigrants were accused of being unwilling to integrate. The perspective of society shifted to the different cultures of the immigrants. A different culture was no longer considered an asset but a possible obstacle to integration. A strong Islamophobia developed, and Muslim immigrants were accused of not accepting social values.[91] In recent years, various new laws have been enacted which require immigrants to learn the Dutch language and accept certain liberal and democratic values.[92] The mood changed dramatically when in 2010 a minority government was established which was tolerated by the right-wing populist party, PVV, led by Geert Wilders.[93] This government distinguished itself in the first year through reduced funding to the performing arts, which were hard hit by cuts of up to 40%. The independent scene and its twenty-one production houses were no longer to be subsidised.[94] As is the case in other European countries, artists of colour are primarily active in The Netherlands in the independent scene.

---

89 | Jan Lucassen and Rinus Penninx, *Newcomers: Immigrants and their Descendants in the Netherlands 1550-1995*, (Amsterdam: Het Spinhuis, 1997), p. 149.

90 | Bloomfield, p. 9 ff.

91 | http://focus-migration.hwwi.de/index.php?id=2644

92 | http://focus-migration.hwwi.de/index.php?id=2644

93 | This failed after 18 months. http://www.faz.net/aktuell/politik/ausland/niederlande-grosse-koalition-nimmt-ihren-dienst-auf-11950527.html

94 | http://www.die-deutsche-buehne.de/Magazin/Leseprobe/Euro%20-%20Krisen%20-%20Theater

2.4.2 The Dutch Theatre Scene

One of the few successful artists of colour at a municipal theatre is Jörgen Tjon A Fong, who holds the position of programme director for the area of cultural diversity at the Stadsschouwburg Amsterdam. He founded the theatre group "Urban Myth" in 2002, which works together with classically trained theatre makers. He works with them at the Stadsschouwburg Amsterdam on his own theatre productions.

Another theatre located in Amsterdam which was founded in recent years is the MC Theater. At the beginning they organised theatre workshops in which stories about diaspora and "street" were told. Because of the lack of structures in which artists of colour could work professionally, Marjorie Boston, Maarten van Hinte, and Lucien Kembel joined forces and founded the theatre. Their productions reflect the perspective of today's multiethnic, multicultural, urban Europe. For every project, artists from different disciplines are invited to participate. This approach makes it possible to generate and present innovations, to set up a network of talented artists of colour, and to attract a more diverse and younger audience to the theatre. Besides its artistically innovative concept, the MC Theater has also distinguished itself by trying new structures. The cost cuts which have affected the entire Dutch theatre scene hit the artistic projects with a so-called "multicultural focus" the hardest. Therefore, the founders of the MC Theater decided to run the theatre without public funding.[95] They applied for a one-off start-up grant which would end after four years and which would make it impossible for them to receive further public funding. The financial independence of art has to be achieved through commercial dance and music events. MC Theater has in the meantime been able to establish itself as a venue, and it is regularly invited to present productions at international theatre festivals and theatre houses.[96]

The theatre group Rast Theater from Amsterdam has also made a name for itself through international as well as European co-productions. It was founded by Saban Ol, who stages stories about persons from the periphery of Dutch society. The theatre productions show perspectives of an intercultural public in The Netherlands. The Rast Theater works mainly with young theatre makers and would like to advance the development and promotion of theatre makers of colour. The theatre work has three focal points: it produces several plays annually which are attended by a broad public, it promotes the development of young talents of colour with the programme Jong RAST, and it implements an exchange between Europe and Turkey with RAST International which is organised in international co-productions and workshops during the annual summer theatre academy in Turkey. The Rast Theater has now established an

---

95 | Lucien Kembel in a personal interview.
96 | Ibid.

international profile. It participated in the Europe Now project and produced the play Elsewhere Land under the direction of Saban Ol in connection with this project.

2.5 France

2.5.1 Migration in France

Immigration in France has always been strongly influenced by its colonial history and a long tradition of acquisitioning foreign workers. Immigration has become more and more important and has had a sustainable influence on French society. Although immigration was long considered to be a success, at least from an economic point of view, this perspective has changed (especially in the last three decades) and immigration is now perceived as the cause of social problems. Electoral victories of right-wing extremist parties – particularly the Front National (FN) – underline this fact, as does the unrest which flares up time and again in the suburbs of French cities. With regard to the political development, the French immigration policies have become restrictive in recent years. As is the case in other European countries, French authorities are attempting to control immigration more strongly by criteria based on economic benefit.[97]

Immediately after the Second World War and during the economic boom in the fifties and sixties, France recruited workers mainly from Italy, Greece, Spain, Portugal, Morocco, Tunisia, Turkey, and Yugoslavia. At the same time, immigration from the former colonies increased as a result of the process of decolonisation. Particularly in connection with the Algerian War (1954–62) and the subsequent independence of Algeria in 1962, there was a massive migration to France. In 1964, France entered into an agreement with Algeria regulating the recruitment of Algerian workers. In the economic crisis of the early seventies, France followed the example of other European countries and ended all recruitment agreements for foreign labourers in 1974. The end of the recruitment did not result in immigrants returning to their home countries or to a reduction in the numbers of immigrants. Many stayed in France and had their families follow. Since then, family reunification has become the most common reason to immigrate even though the current trend is falling.

In the late eighties and early nineties, the conservative Minister of the Interior, Charles Pasqua, pursued a zero-immigration policy. Countless regulations were tightened. Especially the "fight" against irregular migration became the centre of attention. The introduction of the so-called "Pasqua Laws" was extremely controversial. Protests reached a peak in 1996 when a church in Paris was occupied by people from several African countries and by refugees from China who had been living in France without a proper residence permit and who hoped to call

---

97 | http://focus-migration.hwwi.de/index.php?id=1231

attention to their precarious situation in this way. Thousands supported the protest actions of the "sans-papiers", people without a legal residence status in France.

The government under Prime Minister Lionel Jospin withdrew or mitigated many of the restrictive regulations and introduced a special immigration status for highly qualified workers. In 1997, a legalisation programme was drawn up for immigrants who were residing in France illegally. Since the election of a conservative government in 2002, there has been a return to more restrictive immigration policies. This course was continued under the administration of Nicolas Sarkozy.

At the beginning of 2008, approximately five million immigrants were living in France. Despite the restrictive policies, immigration to France has steadily increased in the last years.[98] The immigrants of the second and third generations make up a large part of the French population. Estimates for the year 2010 indicate that about 6.4 million persons living in France are members of this group. This amounts to 10.4% of the total population.[99]

A French universalistic concept of integration which still prevails today would like to turn immigrants into "citoyens", since the cultural prerequisites for citizenship are acquired through socialisation rather than inherited. Thus, great importance is attached to language and education. The French national culture is very strongly dominated by "high culture", which is represented and protected by the state. The preservation of cultural traditions and the French language dominated cultural policies for a long time. In the past decade, a shift has taken place towards the promotion of culture for each individual.[100]

---

98 | The influx of foreign students rose from about 50,000 persons in the years 2007 and 2008 to about 60,000 persons in 2010 and 2011. See http://focus-migration.hwwi.de/index.php?id=1231

99 | The composition of the group of descendants of immigrants reflects France's migration history. 3.3 million persons with a migration background had at least one parent who immigrated to France from another European country, especially from Italy, Spain, and Portugal, countries which provided the major share of foreign labour in France during the early phases of the labour migration beginning in the 19th century. Another 1.8 million persons were descendants of immigrants from the Maghreb, former French colonies in North Africa. The remaining 1.3 million persons with migration backgrounds have roots in other regions of Africa and Asia, the countries in which the more recent immigration influx to France originated. http://focus-migration.hwwi.de/index.php?id=1231

100 | Bloomfield, p. 42.

2.5.2 The French Theatre Scene

The republican concept of citizenship is based on the equality of all those born in France and of all those naturalised citizens, but it refuses to recognise ethnic, religious, linguistic or other cultural minorities.[101] Because of these legal framework conditions, it was almost impossible for migrant artists to found their own theatre groups until far into the eighties.[102] In this time, the "friches" – the independent scene in France – represented the only theatrical space in which artists of colour could work. In France – as in other European countries – the "friches" emerged from the socially engaged artists' movement of 1968. Thus, an artistic practice which was embedded in a social context developed which included the artists of colour in their work and relationships.[103]

Now in the last twenty years, some artists of colour have been able to establish themselves, including Moïse Touré and his theatre group "Cie Les Inachevés", which he founded in Grenoble as an amateur ensemble. Touré worked as an assistant to George Lavaudant at the Odéon-Théâtre de l'Europe. From 2000 to 2003, he was active in the Scène Nationale Artchipel Guadeloupe, where he created the basis for a dramatic repertory in the Creole theatre. From 2010 to 2012, Moïse Touré was hired by the National Theatre in Tokyo, where he staged *Quai Ouest* by Bernard-Marie Koltès, and he developed the project *Ville-monde / ville utopique* in San Francisco.

He produced three plays by Marguerite Duras together with his theatre group in Burkina Faso. The ensemble toured with their plays through Vietnam in autumn of 2012 and through France in 2013. The originality of this work lies in the preparation for staging. At every venue, professional actors and amateurs were cast and prepared for the rehearsals in workshops for theatre, singing and dance. Touré calls his actors "acteurs témoins" – active witnesses – because they experience every step of the creative process of staging as well as the participation in the workshops prior to the rehearsals.[104]

Mohamed Rouabhi is an artist from Paris. He dropped out of school when he was fifteen and did odd jobs before he was accepted at the École Nationale Supérieure d'Arts et des Techniques in 1985. He is an actor, director, playwright, librettist, and screenwriter. After first working as an actor, he founded the theatre group "Les Acharnés" together with the director Claire Lasne in 1991. Since then they have produced many plays, including *Les Acharnés* (1993), *Les Fragments de Kaposi* (1994), *Ma petite Vie de Rien du tout* (1996), and *Jeremy*

---

101 | http://www.ericarts.org/web/index.php
102 | Bloomfield, p. 44.
103 | Ibid., p. 49.
104 | http://www.franceculture.fr/emission-sur-les-docks-ouagadougou-guantanmo-sanaa-14-marguerite-duras-en-afrique---i-moise-toure-e

Fisher (1997). Rouabhi's plays were also staged by other contemporary directors in France as well as internationally. From 2007 to 2008, Rouabhi produced the play *Vive la France* in the Théâtre Gérard Philipe, a large-scale production in which more than forty artists are on stage at one point. In 2007, his play *Jeremy Fisher* was adapted as a libretto and performed at the Opéra de Lyon under the direction of Michel Dieuaide.[105]

Another successful contemporary artist is Lazare – writer, director, actor, and improviser. He studied at the École du Théâtre National de Bretagne and named his theatre group "Vita Nova" in reference to Dante's *Divine Comedy*.[106] As of 2008, a hard core of artists formed around Lazare with whom he produced the trilogy *Passé – je ne sais où, qui revient*, followed by *Au pied du mur sans porte* in 2011 – two pieces which were inspired by the works of Pessoas. The last part, *Rabah Robert*, has been completed since then. The trilogy is about the figure "Libellule", an alter ego of Lazare, and his family. It connects the parts of the family history taking place in France and Algeria with Lazare's own biography. Lazare's plays are documentary and utopian at the same time. They are about reality and the dreams of the protagonists. He does not judge his figures, but gives them the fictional space of the theatre to develop their own realities. Lazare and Vita Nova were invited to perform their play Au pied du mur sans porte at the Festival D'Avignon in 2013.[107]

Finally, there is Leyla Claire Rabih. She studied theatre sciences and Romance languages and literature in France and then changed to acting direction at the Hochschule für Schauspielkunst "Ernst Busch" in Berlin. She acquired her first practical experience in Germany municipal and state theatres (Deutsches Theater Göttingen, Staatstheater Cottbus). Her responsibilities included working as assistant director to Thomas Ostermeier. She works mainly on and with texts by young and contemporary authors and publishes the series *Scène – Neue französische Theaterstücke* with Frank Weigand. In January 2007, she took over the direction of the theatre company "Grenier de Bougogne" at the Théâtre Mansart in Dijon. In January 2008, she founded the theatre company "Grenier/Neuf" with the intent of making contemporary theatre more accessible to the public, who had had little contact with this type of theatre before then. She also works in Germany, and staged *Der Schnitt* by Mark Ravenhill in 2008 and *Nordost* by Torsten Buchsteiner in 2009 at the Theater Konstanz.[108]

---

105 | http://www.lesacharnes.com/Mohamed-Rouabhi-Biography.pdf
106 | http://www.franceculture.fr/personne-lazare.html
107 | http://www.festival-avignon.com/en/Artiste/208
108 | Leyla Rabih in a personal interview.

2.6 Great Britain

2.6.1 Migration in Great Britain

Contrary to other European countries, Great Britain's colonial history has caused it to attract many artists and people engaged in culture from member countries of the British Commonwealth. They came to Great Britain because they were seeking artistic freedom and exchange with European artists. Until the sixties, Great Britain did not grant immigrants participation rights. Racist attacks and political exclusions in the sixties and seventies led to a political mobilisation and self-organisation among immigrants. The civil rights movement which emerged in the sixties was the catalyst for black activists and creative artists to initiate a movement of artists of colour in the art and cultural scene in Great Britain.

In the eighties, the neoliberal administration under Margaret Thatcher promoted the privatisation and commercialisation of culture which was referred to as the "Thatcherising of the Arts Council".[109] Under the new social movement against Thatcher's neoliberal administration in which many artists of colour participated, the access to "high culture" was expedited. Festivals were organised which promoted the diversity of the collective memory in Great Britain by featuring artists of colour and supporting cultural institutions.[110] This reactivation of the black art movement was advanced by representatives of the second generation of immigrants who had grown up in Great Britain and were dealing with questions regarding identity and representation in the British society.

The Arts Council England specified "cultural diversity" with a focus on "ethnicity" as one of its major focal points.[111] The reason for this announcement was the publication of the *MacPherson Report* in 1999, after which anti-discrimination measures were introduced in all public institutions. Although the fight against institutionalised racism seems sensible, the measures also provoked criticism. The critics, mostly artists and cultural theorists of colour, considered such measures to be wise and identified noticeable effects on the art scene; at the same time, these measures led to a greater differentiation between artists from the majority society and those from ethnic minorities. The initiative of the Arts Council England did not succeed in nullifying the existing polarisation

---

109 | The term "Thatcherism" is attributed to Stuart Hall, among others. In his essay "Marxism Today", Hall used the term in a cultural-theoretical context. Stuart Hall, "The Great Moving Right Show", in *Marxism Today*, (London, 1979); Wu Chin-tao, *Privatising Culture. Corporate Art Intervention since the 1980s*, (London: Verso, 2002), p. 65.
110 | Helen Jermyn and Philly Desai, *Arts – what's in a word. Ethnic minorities and the arts*, (London: Arts Council England, 2000), pp. 11-12.
111 | See http://www.artscouncil.org.uk/media/uploads/pdf/What_is_the_Creative_Case_for_Diversity.pdf

between ethnic arts and mainstream arts. Another criticism was that the measures did not bring about any change in the national profile but in fact led to generalisations in the discussion on racism in art because of the schism in the art community and what was referred to as "alibi" actions.[112] The artistic director, Jatinder Verma, questions the effectiveness of these "good" intentions: "And will showcasing culturally diverse work – as the Decibel initiative purports to do – help that critic to drop his ethnic lens? I very much doubt it."[113] The Arts Council England places ethnicity and inclusion above the aesthetic importance of art. It is necessary to set aside the Eurocentric view of art which could be made possible by politicians responsible for cultural policies who have cultural competence as well as knowledge of cultural traditions.[114]

Artists of colour have brought about far-reaching changes in the British theatre landscape whose archiving and creating of traditions have been advanced by cultural theorists like Stuart Hall, but also through controversial cultural and political measures introduced by the Arts Council. Nevertheless, the artists still have to fight against the stereotyping and downgrading of their work to their ethnicity.

2.6.2 The British Theatre Scene

There is a long list of theatre groups which have been able to establish themselves in England since the seventies. Tara Arts was the first Asian-British theatre group which became a platform for Asian-British artists. Tamasha, Temba, and Nitro are all theatre groups of colour which have made a name for themselves in the British theatre scene in the last decades.

At this point, however, three theatre houses will be presented, because their international and political theatre productions in recent years are worth mentioning.

One of them is Tara Arts. The artistic director Jatinder Verma is a highly esteemed artist who was the first British-born Asian to stage productions at the National Theatre in London. Verma has no theatrical training; he found his way to art, like many artists of colour, because of the prevailing situation in the seventies.[115] Verma says, "Our impetus at the time was to find a voice".

---

112 | Richard Hylton, *The nature of the beast: Cultural Diversity and the Visual Arts Sector. A study of policies, initiatives and attitudes 1976–2006*, (Bath: Icia Institute of Contemporary Interdisciplinary Arts, 2007), p. 19.
113 | See Jatinder Verma,*The Arts and Cultural Diversity*, (London, 2003). http://www.butterfliesandwheels.com/articleprint.php?num=29
114 | Ibid.
115 | Graham Ley: "Tara Arts 1977-1985", in Sarah Dadswell and Graham Ley, *British South Asian Theatres. A documented history*, (Exeter: University of Exeter Press, 2011), p. 13ff.

Verma thought it was only possible to encounter the voicelessness of the time in a confrontation through the arts on stage. He founded Tara Arts as the first British / South Asian theatre group in Great Britain. In his opinion, there was a need for an independent theatre group of "black artists" with its own aesthetics and self-determined content. Verma wanted to oppose the Eurocentric British theatre scene, which perceived Asian theatre as ethnic art in the sense of folklore and did not leave any space for artists of a non-white background.

After ten years and a hard fight to resist the existing funding structures, Tara Arts finally received revenue funding from the Arts Council. Revenue funding is the ultimate financing for theatre houses in Great Britain since it is granted for three years and thus allows medium-term planning. It can also be renewed again and again. This was the case for Tara Arts from 1986 to 2008, until the funding was reduced and the theatre group was forced to concentrate on a collaboration with the community and schools.[116]

The second important theatre from a Postmigrant perspective is the Arcola Theatre, founded by Mehmet Ergen and Leyla Nazli in 2000. Arcola became known for the diversity of its programme, which comprises both new and classic drama. The group presents its own productions and guest performances by British and international theatre groups. Arcola Theatre played a significant role in the project *Europe Now* and staged the production *Mare Rider*. The play is about Selma, an independent, modern woman who is lying in a delirium after the stillbirth of her child in a hospital in East London. In a surreal nightmare, she is beset by Elka, a mythical figure. In Turkish mythology,[117] Elka hunts down mothers who have just given birth and snatches their children away. She rides through the steppes of Asia and lives out her freedom on horseback. "To me, Elka is a representation of early feminism," says the author, Leyla Nazli. "She represents freedom – to ride horses and get drunk, hunt and do all those things which for thousands of years women were probably forbidden to do."[118] Selma has heard the stories of Elka since her childhood, a subtle indication of her Turkish origins in the play without them being explicitly mentioned. In Mare Rider, migration is presented from a feminist point of view. Leyla Nazli was distinguished as one of England's most important contemporary playwrights by the Royal Court in 2007 (Royal Court Fifty).

Finally, the Bush Theatre is also an important theatre. It has established itself as a theatre house since its founding in 1972. With the appointment of Madani Younis as director in 2012, the focal point of the theatre was placed on the new artists of colour. Younis was previously artistic director at the Freedom

---

116 | Jatinder Verma in a personal interview.
117 | http://hackneycitizen.co.uk/2013/01/15/leyla-nazli-arcola-mare-rider-interview/
118 | Leyla Nazli in an interview. http://hackneycitizen.co.uk/2013/01/15/leyla-nazli-arcola-mare-rider-interview/

Studios in Bradford, Yorkshire. His most successful production was *The Mill – City of Dreams*, which is based on the narratives of local and immigrant mill workers and concerned with the history of the city as well as questions regarding urban life in the future.

The Bush Theatre shows plays which tell contemporary stories from different social perspectives. The theatre's success is particularly evident in the makeup of the audience, which largely consists of persons of colour. Like many other British theatres, the Bush Theatre provides the possibility of direct forms of vocational and advanced training for talented artists of colour.[119]

2.7 Sweden

2.7.1 Migration in Sweden

Sweden has a relatively high rate of immigration; about 200 different nationalities can be found among the 9.4 million inhabitants of the country. 19.1 percent of the inhabitants of Sweden had a migration background in 2010, with the Finns making up the largest group of immigrants. In recent years, the immigrants have come mainly from Iraq, Somalia, and Poland.

The Swedish integration policies were considered to be some of the most liberal and successful in the world for a long time.[14] The Scandinavian welfare model has a large public sector at its disposal which offers extensive social security systems to all inhabitants. Equal opportunity, solidarity, cooperation, and consensus are the key elements of this system, although the system has been repeatedly called into question in recent years.

In the sixties and seventies, immigrants could easily find employment in Sweden. Industry also provided them with accommodation, and trade unions helped with the integration process. In schools, children from immigrant families had the right to be instructed for several hours a week in their native language. The local libraries received funding to purchase dictionaries, newspapers, and books in the languages most commonly used by immigrants. Sweden at that time had a strongly social-democratic orientation, and it was assumed that the immigrants had come to stay. In 1968, the egalitarian approach mentioned above was already anchored in the *Guidelines for Immigration Policies*: Immigrants should have the opportunity to achieve the same standard of living as the rest of the population. In this phase, Sweden began to develop into a multicultural country. In 1975, the government granted immigrants the active and passive right to vote in local elections and in elections for the provincial parliaments.

In the eighties and nineties, when the stream of refugees and their families to Sweden increased, Sweden's image as a country whose immigration policies

---

119 | See http://www.bushtheatre.co.uk/futures/

had been characterised by generosity and equality for years was increasingly seen as a liability. The government felt forced to demonstrate that Sweden was in a position to restrict immigration. Stricter immigration controls were now seen as a prerequisite for a functioning integration process.

In 1991, the populist, right-wing party "New Democracy" (Ny Demokrati) succeeded in gaining representation in the Swedish parliament, and right-wing extremist groups attacked centres which housed asylum seekers and mosques. The image which many Swedes had of Sweden as being an open and tolerant country was tarnished. In order to avoid a right-wing shift in public opinion, new integration policies were introduced. The reduction of social benefits as a countermeasure and a facilitation of processes to recognise foreign educational qualifications were intended to expedite the integration of immigrants into the Swedish employment market. However, anti-discrimination measures and family reunification policies still make up a large part of the integration policies.[120] The bombing in 2010, in which the assassin, an Iraqi-Swedish man, committed suicide and injured two other persons in the centre of Stockholm, had a long-term impact.[121] The bombing and its consequences on Swedish society will be discussed in more detail later.

2.7.2 The Swedish Theatre Scene

The concept of participation was reflected relatively soon in the Swedish art and cultural scene. Over the past ten years, artists of colour have made their way into Swedish cultural institutions. An institution which promoted this development from a very early stage is Intercult, an independent production and distribution institution. Since 1996, the collective around Intercult has worked in Sweden and in Europe as an initiator of collaborative cultural projects and networks. It initiated large-scale co-productions in Europe and connects local and international initiatives. Intercult offers possibilities to share experiences in seminars, conferences, lectures, and mentoring. Chris Torch is Intercult's artistic director and one of its founders.

Rani Kasapi worked for Intercult for a long time until she changed to Riksteatern and took over the area of international collaboration. The national theatre company Riksteatern is the largest theatre company in Sweden and considers itself a national touring company. Under Kasapi's direction, the area of international collaboration has been expanded and many productions by and with theatre makers of colour have been developed. Over the past eight years, many theatre makers have been able to establish themselves in Sweden and attract a public of colour. Rani Kasapi and the Riksteatern played a major role in initiating the European project Europe Now.

---

120 | http://www.bpb.de/gesellschaft/migration/dossier-migration/57839/schweden
121 | See http://www.spiegel.de/thema/selbstmordattentat_stockholm_2010/

An important Swedish playwright is Jonas Hassen Khemiri. In 2003, he attracted attention to himself with his debut novel, *Das Kamel ohne Höcker* (in English, *The Camel without Humps*), for which he received the prestigious Borås Tidnings Debutant Prize. His next novel, *Montecore*, was awarded the Per Olov Enquist Prize in 2006. He first appeared as a dramatist with the play *Invasion!* at the Stockholm City Theatre in 2006. In 2008, Khemiri presented *God Times Five*, his second play. *We Who Are A Hundred* followed in 2009, premiering at the Gothenburg City Theatre and receiving the HEDDA Award for the best play in 2010. In his plays he concerns himself with current social events and features the experiences of people of colour with racism and marginalisation in Swedish society. His plays are performed in many European theatre houses. His most recent play, *I Call My Brothers*, was written as part of the project *Europe Now* and was performed as a co-production with Ballhaus Naunynstraße and the Landestheater Niederösterreich in 2013.

Farnaz Arbabi is a director, dramatist, journalist, and author who works very closely with Jonas Khemiri. She studied acting direction at the Dramatiska Institutet in Stockholm. She stages classical Swedish dramas at state theatres as well as new plays and her own productions from the perspective of persons who have experienced social exclusion in Swedish society. The last joint project with Jonas Khemiri was *I Call My Brothers*, which premiered at the Stockholm Stadsteater.

Another very successful artist is Nasim Aghili, director, author, and performer, who deals with issues concerning racism primarily from a queer-feminist perspective. Her performances, theatre installations, and compositions focus on the experiences of people who have fled to Sweden for political or economic reasons and who now live there in exile. Her pieces are mainly performed in public spaces and focus on the human body and how it is perceived. Her theoretical and practical pieces reflect her perspective of a Swedish woman with a diaspora background. In her own publishing company, Nasim Aghili produces the magazine *Ful*, which has a queer-feminist, and post-colonial orientation and which was named Sweden's best cultural magazine in 2010. Ful is also the name of the theatre group with which Aghili works. One successful production was *Blood Wedding*, which was produced as a sound installation with eleven Iranian-Swedish actors in Swedish and Fasi and which was performed in the Audiorama Stockholm. Another play is *Om vi kunde gå hem till mig* (*If we could go to my place*), which deals with homeless and illegal children in Sweden (some of whom actually participated in the performance of the play). Nasim Aghili is also a member of the Swedish Cultural Council and is active in the steering team which awards grants to independent artists and theatre groups. She is also on the jury of the first Swedish Biennale for Performing Arts.

2.8 Italy

2.8.1 Migration in Italy

For a long time, Italy was a country of emigration; at the beginning of the 20th century many Italians from the South of the country emigrated to the United States, and after World War II many guest workers emigrated within Europe.

The development from a country of emigration to a country of immigration happened in a very short period of time. At the end of the 1970s, more and more immigrants came to Italy. In contrast to the northwestern European countries, the immigration didn't occur in a time of reconstruction and economic growth, but in a time of deep economic crisis marked by increased unemployment.

Migration was not regulated in Italy until recent years. The other countries of the Schengen Area forced to a clear political act, so the government of Italy established the Martelli-Act in 1990, which enforced border controls and made a Visa mandatory. It also implemented the deportation of illegal immigrants. For the first time, Italy took action to measure and regulate immigration, but migration increased in the following years.[122]

In 1998, the Turco-Napolitano Act, Italy's first systematic migration act, was constituted. The laws were intended to reduce the numbers of "clandestiner" (illegalized persons) and impose the return of illegal immigrants to their country of origin. But the law also equated legal migration with the rights of Italian citizens, ensured the family reunion as part of legal immigration, and made it possible for foreigners to apply for permanent residency after living in Italy for five years.

When Silvio Berlusconi became Prime Minister in 2002, the so-called "Bossi-Fini Act" was passed, under which immigration was handled restrictively by limiting legal immigration and enforcing drastic actions for the "fight" against illegal immigration. Therefore, immigration of persons from third countries was only allowed if they had a working contract. [123]

In the following years, because of the global conflict zones in African and Middle Eastern countries, migration to Italy increased drastically: about 400 percent between 2000 and 2010. Today the rate of increase of the immigrated population is one of the highest in the European Union.

The majority of immigrants are refugees and asylum seekers who flee from the Mediterranean Sea to Italy. Through the European border controls, which are regulated by the organisation Frontex, Europe has become a fortress. Frontex is ensuring that refugees will not come close to the European water borders. After several disastrous incidents – especially the drowning of 400 people on the coasts of Italy in the autumn of 2013 – the Italian marine started

---

122 | http://www.bpb.de/gesellschaft/migration/laenderprofile/145487/italien
123 | http://www.bpb.de/gesellschaft/migration/laenderprofile/145487/italien

a rescue mission under the name "Mare Nostrum" in order to help the people until 2014.[124] The Italian government is now demanding more responsibility on the part of refugees from other European countries.[125]

2.8.2 The Italian Theatre Scene

In a classical sense, the Italian theatre scene is intercultural through the work and influence of Eugiono Barba and his intercultural research of theatrical articulation. He evoked the internationalisation and "Europeanisation" of the scene, but because of the political situation it did not produce a scene of artists of colour or artists with migration backgrounds. In contrast to the other northwestern European countries, many different projects with refugees and asylum seekers have been created within recent years.

The project *H.O.S.T. – Hospitality, Otherness*, Society, Theatre – aims to work on the complex dimensions of migration through aesthetic research and artistic praxis. The artistic work which is called "sociological research" is a cooperation between artists from the Eufonia-Astràgali Teatro in Lecce and academics from the university in Salento. The projects intend to give immigrants and refugees a voice to make their experiences through theatrical methods perceptible for other persons, especially persons with the same experiences. The project was funded by the European commission from 2007 until 2013.[126]

The project *Acting Diversity* is being organised by three cultural institutions in Italy, Palestine and the UK. It seeks to work with asylum seekers, immigrants and young adults from around the world in intercultural theatre workshops. The workshop's goal is to create an intercultural dialogue and actively promote diversity in a democratic and inclusive society. They produced two productions where racism, stereotypical ideas on the "Other" as well as migration, citizenship and civil rights were discussed.[127]

"Teatro di Nascosto – Hidden Theatre" is making theatre reportage under the leadership of Annet Henneman. Teatro di Nascosto uses the stage so stories of people without a voice, persons from marginalised communities, can be heard. The theatrical work is being brought between Europe and the Middle East.[128]

---

124 | http://www.ansamed.info/ansamed/en/news/sections/generalnews/2013/10/15/Immigration-Italy-launches-Mare-Nostrum-400-saved_9466386.html
125 | http://www.dw.de/eu-denkt-über-quoten-für-flüchtlinge-nach/a-17985303
126 | http://www.astragali.org/project!20
127 | http://www.annalindhfoundation.org/granted-projects/2012/acting-diversity-project-intercultural-theatre-political-refugees-and-young#sthash.awdclwGJ.dpuf
128 | http://teatrodinascosto.com

Another theatre which deals with refugees and the human rights of immigrants is Teatro Aperto, which was founded during the "Nuovo Teatro Popolare" in 1974 by Guido Ferrarini. At the beginning the theatre focused on the intercultural collaboration of artists, but since then they have concentrated on telling the experiences of immigrants as part of contemporary European history. Since Lampedusa became a symbol of the tragedy of European borders and the Italian programme "Mare Nostrum" was created, the artists of Teatro Aperto feel obliged to make the inhuman European politics visible on stage.[129] The journalist and author Jeff Biggers, who is part of the "Mare Nostrum" Project at Teatro Aperto, has written about their project:

'For Ferrarini and other international members of Teatro Aperto, including myself, the theater – as the stage for Europe's unfolding Mare Nostrum challenges – can at least provide for a safe, healing and creative space, as well as a historical and narrative context, for such stories to be voiced and heard.' [130]

Figure 1: 'Verrücktes Blut', Ballhaus Naunynstraße, Berlin, 2010. Photograph: Ute Langkafel

---

129 | http://www.teatroaperto.it
130 | http://www.huffingtonpost.com/jeff-biggers/beyond-mare-nostrum-itali_b_5634746.html

Theatre and Migration – Documentation, Influences and Perspectives

*Figure 2: 'Verrücktes Blut', Ballhaus Naunynstraße, Berlin, 2010.
Photograph: Ute Langkafel*

*Figure 3: 'Telemachos - Should I stay or should I go?', Ballhaus Naunynstraße, Berlin, 2013.
Photograph: Ute Langkafel*

Figure 4: 'Telemachos - Should I stay or should I go?', Ballhaus Naunynstraße, Berlin, 2013.
Photograph: Ute Langkafel

Figure 5: 'Beg Your Pardon', Ballhaus Naunynstraße, Berlin, 2012.
Photograph: Ute Langkafel

Theatre and Migration – Documentation, Influences and Perspectives 363

Figure 6: 'Jag ringa mina bröder', kulturhuset stadsteatern, Stockholm, 2013.
Photograph: Petra Hellberg

Figure 7: 'Jag ringa mina bröder', kulturhuset stadsteatern, Stockholm, 2013.
Photograph: Petra Hellberg

*Figure 8: 'No Mans Land' Das Kunst, Garage X, Vienna, 2006.
Photograph: Bernhard Mrak*

*Figure 9: 'No Mans Land' Das Kunst, Garage X, Vienna, 2006.
Photograph: Bernhard Mrak*

3. Excursus: Minority Theatre

3.1 Theoretical Considerations

The aim of this chapter is to put minority theatre in context of this study. In the exposé for the research project, the study intended to be an examination of theatre makers with migrant backgrounds and those who belong to a (cultural, religious, ethnic, etc.) minority. In the course of the research, it became clear that it would not be possible to do justice to both subject areas if they were combined, since the interests and identity aspects have to be considered from different perspectives.

First of all, reasons will be given to explain the general importance of a minority theatre. Using three theatres as examples, the diversity of minorities as well as the conditions for and necessity of a minority theatre will be presented. These three examples alone suffice to demonstrate that the framework conditions within could not be more different. Finally, in the last part of this excursus, a comparison will be made with Postmigrant theatre to point out possible differences and common interests.

How can minorities be described? Minorities – whether indigenous or immigrant – can differ from the mainstream population in many ways. The difference can lie in the ethnic origins, in cultural traditions, in the language, the religion or in a combination of these aspects. Different minorities are often falsely thrown into one group and referred to under one label, as, for example, when people from Pakistan, Bangladesh, Morocco, and Turkey are all referred to as Muslims, regardless of their geographical, ethnic, or actual religious backgrounds.

A description of minorities which does not include the attribution of being alien was attempted by Gilles Deuleuze. In *Pour une Littérature Mineure (Towards a Minor Literature)*, Deleuze defines minorities not only by means of their numbers but by means of a certain characteristic: "Its (the minority's) capacity to become or, in its subjective geography, to draw for itself lines of fluctuation that open up a gap and separate it from the axiom constituting a redundant majority".[131] The majority is understood as what is homogeneous, that which requires a normativity to maintain power, to be able to exercise self-control in order to achieve self-affirmation.[132] The so-called "minority" can resist by withdrawing to escape the pressure of homogeneity. The minority can devise lines of flight, interspaces, and "being different" to resist the constraints of the majority. The minority in Deleuze's sense has the strength of variation on its side, as opposed to the constancy and

---

131 | Verena Conley, "Minoritarian", in Adrian Parr (ed.): *The Deleuze Dictionary*, (Edinburgh: Edinburgh University Press, 2005), p. 164f.
132 | Conley, p.164f.

security of status which the majority strives for: "Minoritarian is seen as potential (puissance), creative and in becoming. Blacks, Jews, Arabs and women can only create by facilitating a "becoming", but never through ownership.[133]

The minority is in a state of becoming and has no fixed identity – therefore it cannot be counted: "[A] minoritarian politics does not have a pre-given (or transcendent) measure or norm for inclusion or identity. Each addition to the group changed [!] what the group is".[134] The attributed identity of the minority is always provisional and is constantly changing.

How can subjects related to minorities be dealt with? Contemporary theatre is apparently often selected as a medium to deal with issues (ethnic, cultural, religious, etc.) of the minority, to negotiate social injustice and discrimination or to present topics of general interest for discussion from the perspective of minorities. In minority theatre, the collective memory, among other things, is transported to the stage. Theatre is a privileged place in which traumas of the past can be illuminated, in which the disposition of one's own identity can be explored and challenged. Theatre can contribute to the catharsis (reactivation) of the crisis of the group's collective identity and is thus a crucial space and a chance for minorities to make themselves seen. It is a place in which authenticity can be reaffirmed and in which a different public can legitimise the cultural specifications. Minority theatre is not present or visible in the national theatre scenes, but it addresses important topics like the construction of minorities, the process of exclusion and difference. According to Deleuze, minority theatres can be elements in the process of creating self-awareness in which "a minority consciousness [is transformed into]...a universal-becoming"[135] and a dynamic impulse for change can be set against how the minority is represented. Theatre is also the space in which predefined identities in a historical, economic, social, or cultural context or in the context of colonisation can be contested.[136]

3.2 Roma in European Societies and the Theatre of the Roma

One of the groups most severely affected by racially motivated marginalisation is the Roma. They have a special status as a minority because they have been resident in Europe since the Middle Ages. Their exclusion began in early modern times with the emergence of territorial states, and persecution, expulsion, and

---

133 | Ibid., p. 164f.
134 | Claire Colebrook, *Gilles Deleuze*, (London: Routledge, 2002), p. 117.
135 | Gilles Deleuze, "One Less Manifesto", in Timothy Murray (ed.), *Mimesis, Masochism and Mime. The Politics of Theatricality in Contemporary French Thought*, (Ann Arbor: Univ. of Michigan Press, 1997), p. 256
136 | Madelena Gonzalez and Patrice Brasseur (eds.), *Authenticity and Legitimacy in Minority Theatre. Constructing Identity*, (Cambridge: Cambridge Scholars Publishing, 2010).

discrimination defined their living conditions. Under the National Socialists, the persecution of Sinti and Roma reached a dreadful culmination in the racially motivated annihilation of over five million Sinti and Roma in Germany and occupied Europe. There are currently around nine million members of this group in the population, the largest minority in Europe. They are distributed all over Europe, but most of them have settled in southeastern Europe. In Romania, Bulgaria and Serbia there are over three million Roma.

Sinti and Roma still struggle against massive prejudices. One of the last defamation campaigns against Roma which attracted international attention took place under the government of Nicolas Sarkozy. Sarkozy referred to the alleged illegal Roma communities as "hotbeds of crime".[137] The subsequent mass deportations of Roma met with harsh criticism. The UN Committee on the Elimination of Racial Discrimination demanded an immediate stop to the deportations on the grounds that collective deportations violate human rights. The EU Commission also reacted and accused France of violating the right to freedom of movement of EU citizens which is anchored in the Treaty of the European Union. EU Justice Commissioner Viviane Reding threatened France with criminal proceedings on the grounds of breaching the Charter of Fundamental Rights of the European Union. As a result, France gave in and announced that it would fully comply with EU law.[138]

This brief overview of the political status of the Roma in Europe indicates that the century-long marginalisation of this minority is still continuing in parts of Europe. It is all the more important that individual perspectives and historical accounts on an artistic level are set against these stereotyped images. The most successful theatre group in Europe is Theater Pralipe. Theater Pralipe was first active in Skopje in Macedonia, where their plays dealing with the situation of the ethnic minority led to public opposition and an end to their funding. Roberto Ciulli, the director of the Theater an der Ruhr, granted the theatre group artistic asylum when the war in Yugoslavia broke out in 1991. As part of the Theater an der Ruhr, Theater Pralipe developed its own aesthetic language and staged classic pieces like Shakespeare's *Romeo and Juliet*, Brecht's *Mother Courage and Her Children*, and Lorca's *Blood Wedding* and *Yerma*. As of 1995, the theatre work of Pralipe took on a stronger political dimension by presenting topical fields of interest. Thus, in protest against attacks on the Roma population in the Austrian Oberwald, they were invited to the Burgtheater in Vienna and toured East German cities under the motto "culture against violence" to protest against the racially motivated attacks on residences for asylum seekers in Rostock and Hoyerswerda.[139] Contemporary productions

---

137 | See http://focus-migration.hwwi.de/index.php?id=1231
138 | See http://europa.eu/rapid/press-release_MEMO-10-384_en.htm
139 | http://www.spiegel.de/spiegel/print/d-13687521.html

are intended to present the life of the Roma aesthetically on stage, as in the play *Tetovirime Vogja (Tattooed Souls)* by Goran Stefanovski, which deals with the living conditions of Roma as well as the roots of the Roma culture. It was presented at the Intercultural Theatre Festival in Vienna in 1996. Another of Theater Pralipe's successful plays is *Z 2001, die Tinte unter meiner Haut* (*Z 2001, The Ink Beneath My Skin*), which is about the annihilation of the Sinti and Roma during the National Socialist era.

Despite their international success, financial support for Theater Pralipe was cut by the state legislature of North Rhine-Westphalia as early as 2001. The theatre, heavily indebted, was dissolved.[140] Nedjo Osman, a Pralipe actor and co-founder of the TKO Theater in Cologne in 1996, established the first European Roma theatre in Cologne in 2008 which aspired to cooperate with professional Roma actors from Hungary, Romania, Macedonia, and Serbia. The theatre makers wanted to promote the professionalisation of Roma culture in Europe.[141]

In 2010, an EU-sponsored project entitled *Romanistan – Crossing Spaces in Europe* was set up by the IG Kultur Austria. The project was intended to create a European cultural programme with three Roma self-organisations such as the Roma Cultural Centre in Vienna, the FAGiC in Barcelona and the Amaro Drom in Berlin. *Romanistan* was envisaged as an emancipatory project which would present not only folklore, but also contemporary cultural activities of the Roma. By utilising self-organisation, networking, and sustainable structures and strategies, a greater freedom of action could be created to make the cultural activities of the Roma known and acknowledged in Europe in all their heterogeneity and diversity. Key issues were self-empowerment and self-organisation, networking, and media and public relations. The artistic conceptions included the cultural activities of the Roma in the communities, so that by means of participation they could be transformed medium-term into something ground-breaking. A public discussion on the mechanisms of stigmatisation and discrimination was to be held, in which specific topics like identity, cultural self-determination, opportunities for cultural and political education, the importance of one's own language, participation and empowerment as well as cultural diversity and a re-politicisation of the Roma culture would be dealt with. Roma artists were to be in the foreground, and the focus was to extend beyond the usual ethnicising and romanticising to their artistic approaches and circumstances.

The aim of the two-year project was to organise a cultural festival and to establish a cultural think tank which was to deal with the subject "Roma

---

140 | Bloomfield, *Crossing the Rainbow*; http://www.minderheiten.org/pralipe.htm
141 | http://www.tkotheater.de/logicio/pmws/indexDOM.php?client_id=tko&page_id=roma&lang_iso639=de

and Culture Production" critically and in a multi-disciplinary fashion.[142] In April 2013, the Neue Gesellschaft für Bildende Kunst in Berlin organised a two-day festival at which films, music and dance productions were shown and discussions were held on the creation of space for culture productions which could bring forth and visualise new ways of thinking in the work against stigmatisation and racism.[143] *Romanistan* is considered a starting point and should establish itself long-term as an arena for autonomous culture and discussion.

3.3 German-Sorbian Folk Theatre Bautzen

How different the situation of minority theatre can be becomes apparent when the study turns to the German-Sorbian Folk Theater in Bautzen, which is famous nationwide for its minority theatre. The West Slavic Sorbs have lived in Upper and Lower Lusatia (in Saxony and Brandenburg) since the sixth century. The Sorbian people comprise approximately 60,000 persons and are recognised as a national minority. They have maintained their own identity through the centuries and have successfully resisted all sorts of attempts to be assimilated.[144]

In Bautzen there are two Sorbian theatres: the German-Sorbian Folk Theatre and the Sorbian National Ensemble.

The German-Sorbian Folk Theatre is a bicultural theatre, since productions are staged in both German and in High and Low Sorbian. In 1948, the Sorbian Folk Theatre "Serbske ludowe dźiwadło" was founded, which initially was only a production location because performances took place in inns in Sorbian communities. In 1963, the Bautzen City Theatre and the Sorbian Folk Theatre together became the German-Sorbian Folk Theatre Bautzen, which since then has built up a large repertory of plays and pieces for puppet theatre. The target group is defined as "everyone"; the theatre is a folk theatre with the respective programme and sees itself as the opposite of the "big city expert theatre".[145] The repertory includes classic folk plays such as *Im weißen Rössl* by Ralph Benatzky and subject matter of more local interest such as *Das Volksstück vom Johannes Karasek, genannt der Schrecken der Oberlausitz* by Ralph Oehme.

The Sorbian National Ensemble was founded in 1952 as an initiative of the national umbrella organisation of the Lusatian Sorbs. The ensemble is sponsored by the foundation for the Sorbian people, and it endeavours to preserve,

---

142 | http://www.amarodrom.de/romanistan
143 | http://romanistan-berlin.de/pdf/ROMANISTAN_flyer_web_230313.pdf
144 | http://www.mwfk.brandenburg.de/cms/detail.php/bb1.c.250117.de
145 | See http://www.theater-bautzen.de

maintain, and develop the cultural tradition of the Sorbs in three professional sectors: ballet, choir, and orchestra.

In this self-portrayal, the "living habits and customs of the Sorbian people" are presented as the source and "inspiration for a unique ethnic performing art".[146] Emphasis is placed on the Sorbian language, Sorbian history and local traditions. An attempt to merge the German-Sorbian Folk Theatre and the Sorbian National Ensemble Bautzen at the end of 2003 failed.

3.4 Bimah – Jewish Theatre Berlin

Yiddish theatre developed from the Purim plays, which, like the Christian Passion plays, originated in the Middle Ages. The basic prerequisite for the emergence of the Jewish theatre was reforms by Moses Mendelssohn in the 18th century, which created a new spiritual and intellectual orientation and enlightenment under which restrictions prohibiting costumes, acting and images were relaxed or abolished. Abraham Goldfaden is generally considered to be the founder of the first professional Yiddish theatre company, which was established in Iaşi (Jassy or Iassy) in Romania in 1876 and later moved to Bucharest. While most companies at that time specialised in musical vaudeville and light comedy, Goldfaden devoted himself to relatively heavy operettas with biblical and historical content, especially on a longer tour through the cities of Imperial Russia. The works of Scholem Alechem were also of great significance for the Yiddish theatre. The Yiddish theatre spread to Russia, but many Jewish actors emigrated to the West because the Russian government prohibited theatre performances in Yiddish in 1883. Yiddish theatres were founded in Paris, London, the United States (especially in New York), and South America. In New York, the Yiddish theatre experienced its "golden age" in the first decades of the twentieth century with the plays of Jacob Gordin.[147]

Since Yiddish was spoken mainly in Eastern Europe and many well-known theatre groups were founded there, there were also Yiddish theatres and theatre ensembles. However, they played a relatively minor international role since Jews were usually assimilated into the majority society in Western European countries. However, plays were also developed by theatres in Western Europe which were performed internationally on Yiddish or Jewish stages. Beginning in the thirties, the scene concentrated more and more in New York, where Yiddish film also experienced its heyday. After the end of the Third Reich, Jewish theatre was not performed in Germany for many years.

---

146 | http://www.sne-bautzen.de/index.php?id=2351&L=0
147 | Joel Berkowitz, *Avrom Goldfaden and the modern Yiddish theatre. The Bard of Old Constantine*, (Winter: Hebrew Publishing Company, 2004).

Not until 1996 was the "Verein zur Förderung der jüdischen Kultur und zur Errichtung des ersten jüdischen Kultur- und Theaterhauses in Deutschland e.V." (Association for the Promotion of Jewish Culture and Establishment of the First Jewish Cultural Centre and Theatre in Germany) founded, and with it the first Jewish theatre and cultural centre in Germany in the postwar period, the Theater Michoels. In 2001, the Israeli director and actor Dan Lahav founded the Jewish Theatre Bimah in Berlin. Since autumn of 2011, it has had its home in the Admiralspalast in Berlin. The permanent ensemble is committed to presenting contemporary plays by Israeli, English-language and German-Jewish authors. On the programme one can find such plays as *Bent* by Martin Sherman, *Das Zimmer* by Harold Pinter, or plays like *Das Geheimnis der Pianistin in der 5. Schublade* with strongly autobiographical traits of the director Dan Lahav and content from his Hamburg-Jewish family history. *Esther Glick* is the fictional story of the first Jewish female detective, who gets inspiration while cooking that helps her solve her cases. A great sensation was caused by the production *Eine unglaubliche Begegnung im Romanischen Café*, in which a fictional meeting of Lotte Lenya, Else Lasker-Schüler, Erich Kästner, Kurt Tucholsky, and Friedrich Hollaender is staged on the day before their emigration from Nazi Germany. In *Shabat Shalom*, the audience experiences a Friday evening in a Jewish family.

The theatre is also committed to political and socio-political upbringing and education – a commitment reflected in the support it provides to finance educational and vocational measures for migrants and the police force.[148]

3.5 The Minority Theatre and Postmigrant Theatre

In the presentation of Minority theatre, it is evident that they could hardly be more different because, depending on ethnic, religious, or cultural grouping, the theatres pursue different interests. Commonalities can be found only in the external characteristics and framework conditions. All three theatres of minorities described here consider it very important to define production, distribution, and reception themselves and to represent themselves. Roughly classified, they either deal with issues which concern their own community or issues which are imposed by society. In this way, marginalised positions are visualised aesthetically and the active and complex evolution of their own positions in the society are dealt with on stage.[149] Minority theatre makes it possible to present positions and oneself in a social context which is created by means of an aesthetic space. And it is here that

---

148 | http://www.juedischestheaterberlin.de/Theater.php?Bereich=Geschichte
149 | Madelena Gonzalez, "Introduction. The construction of identity in minority theatre", in Madelena Gonzalez and Patrice Brasseur, *Authenticity and Legitimacy in Minority Theatre. Constructing Identity*, (Cambridge: Cambridge Scholars Publishing, 2010).

one can identify intersections and commonalities with the Postmigrant theatre. The artists are in both cases marked as not belonging to the mainstream; they are artists whose art is ethnicised or related to the biographical context of the authors and who are impacted by exclusion. Artists of colour deal with these mechanisms of social exclusion in their productions.

Nevertheless, differences between a theatre of a minority and a Postmigrant theatre can be identified with regard to expectations and conclusions. In Postmigrant theatre it is understood that there is a migration society in which migration in different manifestations is considered to be the norm. The heterogeneity of the society is reflected on stage and assumed to be a normal state. Their own structures secure artistic positions which are lacking in subsidised structures because of marginalisation and racism. Postmigrant artists find themselves in "transitional stages" with the long-term perspective of producing and performing in established theatres. The heterogeneity of the artists is the main focus. It is paramount to point out specific differences in the overall social context.

Minority theatre should be seen as an independent structure. Its aim is a long-term preservation of its own stories, the perspective of national history, and local traditions and linguistic idioms. Minority theatre deals with community-specific issues, and its ultimate aim is to preserve the homogeneity of the ethnic, cultural, or religious group.

Artists of colour, whether they are assigned to the theatre of a minority or the Postmigrant theatre, share a feeling of solidarity which can be traced back to their experience with racism and structural exclusion. This is illustrated by the regular cooperations between Roma artists and the Ballhaus Naunynstraße.

In this very brief presentation, the different approaches and aims of the minority theatres have been strongly generalised. A study devoted solely to the phenomena and subjects of minority theatre would be necessary to provide a more complete picture.

4. Structural Changes

A debate is taking place in each of the European countries examined here over the institutional – and thus political, social, and cultural – participation of the immigrant population. The necessity to respond to the change in the population by means of structural changes is usually referred to as "intercultural opening".[150] Unfortunately, one can observe an inflationary use of this term; it is now used indiscriminately without considering what it really means and

---

150 | In Germany, Austria, Switzerland, and The Netherlands a discussion has arisen on an "intercultural opening" in almost every sector of society. See Hanspeter Fent, *Die*

what it should achieve. A broad understanding of culture underlies the term "interculturality". Interculturality is not limited to aesthetic dimensions, but includes everyday culturally connoted interactions. Culture is understood as historically context-related and as a dynamic process which is in a constant state of flux and which includes affiliations, delimitations, patterns of interpretation, forms of articulation, as well as realities of life.

Interculturality is not understood, however, in the sense of the intercultural theatre which was primarily set in the seventies and influenced by directors like Ariane Mnouchkine, Robert Wilson, Peter Brook, or Tadashi Suzuki. Put simply, they appropriated "Eastern" theatre traditions in order to transport them to Western stages. Erika Fischer-Lichte described this as follows: "Elements are broken out of the different cultural systems of at least two distinctly different cultures and set in relationship to each other in the theatre production."[151] This appropriation of cultural elements and the one-sided participation in the discourse of theatre was criticised by many theatre makers from post-colonial contexts.[152]

Mark Terkessidis gives the term "interculture" a different twist. For Terkessidis, the term suggests a rethinking of stereotypical attributes and is extended to include a "'culture in between' as structure in flux". His definition refers to the barrier-free access to all possibilities of cultural, political and social participation in a diverse German society. [153]

Intercultural opening can therefore be seen as a process by and between different persons, living beings and organisational forms, in which barriers preventing access to organisations are abolished and segregation mechanisms are dismantled.

The process of intercultural opening has also been promoted by cultural institutions. Policy recommendations have been devised by the state (e.g., the National Integration Plan of 2006).[154] On the administrative level, more and more cultural and political guidelines are being implemented whose aim is to facilitate the participation and representation of artists of colour. The cultural and political guidelines apply equally to state theatres and are now being implemented in various programmes for migrants, such as urban

interkulturelle Öffnung von Verwaltungsdiensten, (Winterthur: Edition Soziothek, 2007); Mark Terkessidis, *Interkultur,* (Frankfurt a. M., 2010).
151 | Erika Fischer-Lichte, *Das eigene und das fremde Theater,* Tübingen 1999. 179f.
152 | See Rustom Bharucha, *The Politics of Cultural Practice. Thinking through Theater in an Age of Globalization.* (Hannover, 2000).
153 | Terkessidis, p. 131.
154 | http://www.bundesregierung.de/Content/DE/StatischeSeiten/Breg/IB/2006-10-27-ib-nationaler-integrationsplan.html

neighborhood projects with lay actors. Artists of colour have mainly achieved structural changes in the European theatre scene through a steady process of institutionalization, and thus of the creation of their own structures. These three areas will be more closely examined in the next chapter.

4.1 Cultural and Political Measures as Exemplified by the Arts Council and its Programme of Cultural Diversity

Cultural and political measures which are initiated by the government as a means of reacting to migration societies can be found in all of the countries included in this study. In this chapter, British cultural policies will be presented in detail and used exemplarily to describe the different stages of confrontation with institutional access barriers and structural segregation mechanisms.

Although artists of colour have long been active in Great Britain, it was not until the seventies that they were officially recognised by the public funding institution Arts Council. *The Arts Britain Ignores* by Naseem Khan, which was commissioned by the Arts Council in 1976, focussed on the "arts of ethnic minorities" for the first time.[155] It was established that since artists of colour lacked access to institutions, their artistic work was not considered professional. This study was, on the one hand, the first official examination of the situation of artists of colour in Great Britain, but it also led to the first controversy, because artists of colour were reduced to their ethnicity. In the eighties, there was a revival of the black art movement. Representatives were mainly immigrants of the second generation who had grown up in Great Britain and were preoccupied with questions concerning identity and representation in British society. They were supported by experts on cultural studies who invoked the ideas of Antonio Gramsci and the Black Movement as well as those of the feminist movement. Antonio Gramsci's[156] concept of cultural hegemony attributed a privileged status to the individual as an artist of colour in the process of cultural production. The artist was no longer to be identified as a member of an ethnic minority but as a black artist whose artistic works reveal individual history and an individual aesthetic approach. The discussion on aesthetics conducted by the theatre

---

155 | Naseem Khan, *The Arts Britain Ignores*, (London: Arts Council England, 1976).

156 | In connection with his concept of cultural hegemony, Antonio Gramsci determined that every person lives in his or her "social class", and although this social class is not consciously perceived, everyone's lives are significant to the social class. See James Martin, *Gramsci's Political Analysis. A Critical Introduction*, (Bristol: Palgrave Macmillan, 1998), p. 161f.

makers of colour followed a course quite contrary to the prevailing colonial discourse.¹⁵⁷

The Arts Council England took the subject to heart and established a subsidy fund for ethnic minority art which was aimed more at social integration than artistic recognition.¹⁵⁸ Theatre makers criticized the fact that their artistic work was reduced to their ethnicity and their individual artistic talent was inadequately acknowledged. The Arts Council reacted to the criticism and introduced the term "cultural diversity" so that the emphasis no longer lay on ethnicity.¹⁵⁹

At the end of the nineties, the focus of funding shifted to "cultural diversity" with "specific reference to ethnicity".¹⁶⁰ The catalyst for this shift was the direct reaction to the publication of the Macpherson Report¹⁶¹ in 1999. According to the Arts Council England, the Macpherson Report marked "a sea change in the understanding of the significance of institutional racism".¹⁶² Anti-discrimination measures were indeed introduced on a compulsory basis in all public institutions. However, the Arts Council England had set itself the objective of introducing cultural and political measures to combat racism. A conference was held at which, together with theatre makers of colour, strategies to fight racism in the English theatre scene were developed.¹⁶³ Recommendations for action were formulated which would create participation and access opportunities for

---

157 | Michael McMillan and SuAndi, "Rebaptizing the World in Our Own Terms. Black Theatre and Live Arts in Britain", in Paul Carter Harrison, Victor Leo Walker and Gus Edwards (eds.), *Black Theatre: Ritual Performance in the African Diaspora*, (Philadelphia: Temple University Press, 2002), pp. 120-121.
158 | See Sharifi, *Theater für Alle?*, p. 222.
159 | See H. Jermyn and P. Desai, *Arts – what's in a word?*, pp. 11-12.
160 | With particular attention paid to ethnicity.
161 | The fatal stabbing of the black British teenager Stephen Lawrence at a bus stop in South London caused a public uproar. Police investigations were initially based on the assumption that the victim had committed a crime. Finally, five suspects were arrested but not convicted. It was assumed that the crime was racially motivated and the boy had been murdered because of the color of his skin. In 1999, the former judge Sir William Macpherson examined the documentation of the police investigations and determined that they had been influenced by an "institutional racism". The public was outraged, and the Macpherson Report has since then contributed to a considerable change in the understanding of institutional discrimination. See http://news.bbc.co.uk/vote 2001/hi/english/main_issues/sections/facts/ newsid_1190000/1190971.stm
162 | See Arts Council, *History of Arts Council*, (London, 2004).
163 | See Stuart Brown, Isobel Hawson, Tony Graves and Mukesh Barot (et al.), *Eclipse Report. Developing Strategies to Combat Racism in Theatre*, (London: Arts Council London, 2001), p. 4.

artists of colour. Beginning in 2003, every publicly financed theatre in Great Britain was compelled to employ artists of colour.[164]

One of the initiatives was the project *Decibel*, designed to address the problem of underrepresentation and to ensure a significant increase in the number of artists of colour in employment.[165] Production, distribution, and reception possibilities were to be increased. The programme comprised three main instruments: *Performing Arts Showcase, Visual Arts Platform,* and *New Audiences Programme.*

The *Decibel Performing Arts Showcase* is an annual festival which has taken place every year since 2003 and which showcases the works of theatre makers of colour.[166] The Visual Arts Platform was active from 2003 to 2004 and financed an artists' programme. This included traineeships and mentoring programmes for future curators as well as one-year scholarships for artists of colour and artists with a migration background.[167] In addition, promotion programmes were created to involve audiences of colour. The New Audiences Programme was financed by the Arts Council England from 1998 to 2003 with the intention of attracting new audiences to the theatre and so-called "non-visitors" and marginalised groups of the population, like children and young persons, the elderly, families, and people with disabilities.[168]

Although the fight against institutionalised racism seemed to make sense in all areas of society, including the theatre, the measures also gave rise to criticism. Artists and cultural critics voiced the opinion that such measures only made sense to a certain extent and had a significant impact on the art scene. They said that they segregated artists from ethnic minorities from those in mainstream society. The initiative of the Arts Council England did not succeed in eliminating the existing polarisation between ethnic art and mainstream art.[169] Some critics even felt that the Decibel programme not only did not lead to any kind of change in the national profile, but that it even trivialised the discussion on racism in art through segregation and "alibi" actions.[170]

Harsh criticism was aimed at the Arts Council's inconsistent designation of African, African-Caribbean, and Asian groups. Critics alleged that old, imperialistic terms which nourished racial discrimination were once again being applied to describe the work of the artists. They were being "ethnically

---

164 | Ibid.
165 | See Arts Council, *Decibel. Performing Arts Showcase*, (London, 2011).
166 | See http://www.decibelpas.com/en/about/decibel.
167 | Hylton, *The Nature of the Beast*.
168 | Ibid., p. 133.
169 | Ibid.
170 | Ibid., p.19.

stigmatised" and thus were not given the space or the right to define themselves and their art.[171]

Another critical aspect was the interpretation of cultural diversity. The Arts Council England interpreted cultural diversity as social integration and the use of art as a kind of social policy. But this would mean that the essence of art would disappear and only a visualisation of the "ghettoised" activities would be in the foreground, causing ethnicity and inclusion to take precedence over the aesthetic importance of art itself. It would be necessary to eliminate the Eurocentric view of art, which could be facilitated by politicians of colour responsible for cultural policies who have the cultural competence as well as the knowledge of black cultural traditions.[172]

The prominent debate between British cultural policy makers, institutions, and artists of colour is examplary for other European countries in which the discussion has not progressed as far. In Germany, the report *Kultur in Deutschland* by the Enquete Commission, which was requested by the German Parliament, was published in 2005.[173] The report also deals with migration and migration society as well as artists of colour. In a special section entitled "Areas of particular importance eligible for funding", there is a chapter which deals with "Migrant Culture/Interculture". Terkessidis criticises that, in the report, artists of colour are apparently not named because of their artistic qualities but only in connection with their contribution to "integration":[174] "Today, for example, many German-Turkish directors or authors are famous representatives who have found specific artistic forms to express the contradictions in integration as a subject matter."[175] In general, Terkessidis points out the inadequate perspective applied when presenting the people of colour in the Enquete Report.[176]

All in all, it can be observed that in the last ten years a public reaction (and therefore a cultural and political one) to the changes in European society has taken place. Special subsidies have been introduced for artists of colour which, as Jude Bloomfield pointed out in her 2003 study *Crossing the Rainbow*,

---

171 | Graves, Deepening Diversity.
172 | Ibid.
173 | Deutscher Bundestag (ed.), *Kultur in Deutschland. Schlussbericht der Enquete-Kommission des Deutschen Bundestages*, (Bonn, 2008).
174 | Terkessidis, p. 179.
175 | Deutscher Bundestag (ed.), *Kultur in Deutschland*, p. 212.
176 | The report refers to the "integration deficits" of persons with migration backgrounds. They have deficiencies in education and vocational training, and they do not have an adequate command of the German language. A study which would substantiate these statements was not named. Terkessidis, p. 180.

separates them from the subsidies for white or mainstream theatre makers. Thus, in all the countries surveyed, there are particular promotion institutions for "intercultural culture projects" whose budget is far lower than those which are allocated to "normal" funding projects. As a result, artists of colour cannot apply to institutions for subsidies other than to those specially established to finance "intercultural" projects. In Bloomfield's study it was pointed out that the artistic work of artists of colour is still assigned to a social sector. Therefore, the work produced by artists of colour is denied the aesthetic quality and thus the significance otherwise attached to art, and this remains one of the greatest problems which limits artists of colour in Europe today.

4.2 Structural Changes in State Theatres

While state theatre houses in all European countries had long been "white", i.e. places in which only white theatre makers worked, not only on but also behind the stage and in the governance structures, there has been a change in recent years. Great Britain has made progress in comparison to many countries, but even here there is still a lack of representation, and theatre makers of colour still encounter existing access barriers in cultural institutions.

In the study published by the Centre for Audience Development in Berlin in 2009, "migrants as an audience group in public German cultural institutions" were examined.[177] For the first time, a representative study investigated the extent to which German cultural institutions deal with the subject of migration.[178] Over 50 percent of cultural institutions which participated said that they deal with this "thematic area", but, as Mark Terkessidis quite correctly noted, "about 70% of those responsible only dealt with the subject to the extent that it was necessary to demonstrate that they 'wanted to make a contribution' to integration."[179] The state theatre houses have actually introduced various programmes for "migrants", and this indicates a certain understanding for the problem. It is not only about artistic positions and positions in ensembles which should be filled by theatre makers of colour but about socio-cultural projects which should primarily motivate the "migrant" with a stereotyped image – from poorly educated social strata, with a poor command of the German language, and living in a "parallel world" – to visit the theatre.[180] These projects usually take place outside the theatre houses

---

177 | Centre for Audience Development, *Migranten als Publikum in öffentlichen deutschen Kulturinstitutionen. Der aktuelle Status Quo aus Sicht der Angebotsseite*, (Berlin, 2009). Online publication.
178 | Ibid.
179 | Terkessidis, p.174.
180 | See Sharifi, *Theater für Alle*, (2011).

in socially disadvantaged districts and which mainly work with "experts from everyday life", or residents from these districts, on stage.

The example described here is a case in which, for the first time in Germany, an urban neighbourhood project was implemented because of a need and the hope to examine and present urban stories. In 2004, the Munich Kammerspiele triggered the first major discussion when they produced *Bunnyhill*, which was staged with residents of the Hasenbergl district.

The project was first developed from the story of the German-Turkish youth called *Mehmet*, who had already committed sixty criminal offences by the time he was fourteen and who was deported to Turkey on the initiative of the city of Munich. The case attracted international attention, because for the first time a child of foreigners legally resident in Germany was deported to the original home country of the family unaccompanied by relatives. The play, *Ein Junge, der nicht Mehmet heißt (A Boy who was not named Mehmet)*, was produced together with youths from the Hasenbergl district, one of the districts in Munich with the highest percentage of migrants and the district with the highest crime rate. Artists used the deportation as a metaphor and starting point for artistic research of German society. The artistic approach of Peter Kastenmüller, Björn Bicker, and Michael Graessner raises the question of whether artistic practice cannot be defined as social practice and vice versa.[181]

The project, *Bunnyhill*, which the artists defined as a "state" and whose national territory was the Neue Haus of the Kammerspiele, became the space in which the urban reality of Munich could be exposed to artistic scrutiny. For eight weeks, the artists from different genres participated in the project and immersed themselves in the phenomenon. For at least two months, the peripheral districts of the city and their inhabitants were the centre of cultural life in Munich.[182]

In his article "Theatre as a Parallel Society?",[183] Björn Bicker self-critically pointed out the danger that the subject could be exploited and degraded to a "voyeuristic migration and diversity peepshow". At the same time, he feels that the search for form which the theatre is undergoing at this time could create the possibility of "playful, political and open discussion" through which "multicultural networking and border-crossing" could be achieved.[184]

---

181 | See Munich Kammerspiele, Programme "Bunnyhill – Eine Staatsgründung", (Munich, 2005).

182 | Ibid.

183 | Björn Bicker, "Theater als Parallelgesellschaft. Über das Verhältnis von Theater und Migration", in Sabine Hess, Jana Binder and Johannes Moser (eds.), *No Integration? Kulturwissenschaftliche Beiträge zur Integrationsdebatte in Europa*, (Bielefeld: transcript, 2009).

184 | Ibid., p. 32.

One of the few examples of a state theatre which has involved itself in the process of urban change (but a very good one) is the Theatre Zuidplein in Rotterdam. The theatre is located in Rotterdam-Zuid, which is primarily inhabited by immigrants. When Ruud Breteler became the new theatre director in 1998, he wanted to encourage people from the surrounding district to participate in the theatre. In his own words, he chose the path of "empowerment".[185] By means of an invitation for applications, he put together a commission of ten people who were to mirror the composition of the population in Rotterdam. The ten commission members had no professional theatre training (some had never been to the theatre before), yet they were asked to create the theatre programme for the new season. A change took place from a theatre based on offers, which prepares productions and then seeks an audience for them, to a theatre of demand in which the audience determines what should be performed.

Thanks to the commission, which consisted of people of different cultural backgrounds, more and more plays by and with persons of non-Western European origin were included in the programme which, at the same time, attracted a more diverse audience. Besides the commission, organisations of people of colour were commissioned to organise "monocultural" festivals.

"Gradually more and more people from the different cultural target groups found their way into the theatre. These different audience groups began to mix as time passed, at first in stand-up comedy and cabaret, later in (world) music and dance performances. The time had come to take leave of the monocultural festivals, but not, of course, from the self-organisations; they remained involved in the theatre."[186] That is one possible reaction to the changing social reality and a reaction to the "intercultural opening" of an institution. The theatre programme of the Zuidplein does not make theatre *for* persons of colour but *with* persons of colour. Even the employees are artists of colour. This is really a rarity because artists of colour are still cast based on their ethnic backgrounds or not cast at all. More and more artists of colour are employed as guests at state theatres, but the cooperation is usually a one-off engagement restricted to productions which deal with "migrant" topics.

4.3 Institutionalisation and Independent Structures

In addition to all the efforts on the part of cultural policy makers and public cultural institutions to enable the participation of theatre makers and a public of colour, the initial structural change can mainly be traced back to the creation of independent structures by artists of colour. This can at least be deduced

---

185 | Lecture at Bundesfachkongress Interkultur Hamburg, 2012. See http://www.youtube.com/watch?v=3BKBNVqfhZ4
186 | Ruud Breteler, (Hamburg, 2012).

based on the examples from the countries included in this study. Discussion platforms were used for relevant topics when artists of colour appropriated them and created their own positions in the respective theatre scene by virtue of their numbers. The so-called empowerment led to a change on the institutional level. Empowerment is the "process in which people who are deprived, disadvantaged or excluded begin to take things into their own hands by becoming aware of their own abilities and developing their power in order to use their individual and collective resources to determine their own lives."[187]

In the light of structural power imbalances in the society, the empowerment concept aims at creating equitable distribution and democratic participation, i.e. at strengthening the involvement of citizens in decision-making processes.

As has already been explained, artists of colour were not present in the national and European theatre scenes for a long time. It was suggested that a lack of artistic quality might be the reason.[188] In order to overcome this, the foundation of independent structures and venues became necessary. The change in Germany would not have been possible without the founding of the Ballhaus Naunynstraße and the theatre maker Shermin Langhoff. Langhoff, who first worked as assistant to Fatih Akin, wanted to use the theatre to show "migrant perspectives and stories".[189] As of 2004, she worked as curator for transcultural festivals at the theatre "Hebbel am Ufer", including *Beyond Belonging*, in which established theatre makers and playwrights like Nurkan Erpulat, Feridun Zaimoglu, Maral Ceranoglu, Neco Çelik, Tuncay Kulaoglu, and Ayse Polat participated. The festival, which was supported by the German Federal Cultural Foundation, led Langhoff to realise the necessity of an independent and permanent theatrical space which could offer young artists the chance to experiment and gain experience. "When I created the *Beyond Belonging Festival* at the Hebbel theatre with productions on the subject of migration, I noticed that we would need much more than only one festival, but rather a forum where we could stage experimental theatre and where a special promotion would be possible."[190]

---

187 | Norbert Herringer, *Empowerment in der Sozialen Arbeit*, (Stuttgart: Kohlhammer, 2010), p. 20.

188 | This experience is shared by all theatre makers *of color* and theatre makers with migration backgrounds. This experience is perceptible in interviews and personal conversations. See Onur Suzan Kömürcü Nobrega, "Alienation in Higher Education. Lived Experiences of Racial and Class Based Inequality in Film and Drama School", in *The Living Archives. Kulturelle Produktionen und Räume, Dossier Heinrich-Böll-Stiftung*, (Berlin: Heinrich-Böll-Stiftung, 2013); Sara Ahmed, *Strange Encounters. Embodied Others in Post-Coloniality*, (London, 2000).

189 | Interview with Shermin Langhoff, *Nah & Fern 43*, p. 18.

190 | Ibid., p. 20.

From the opening of the first "Postmigrant" theatre in the 2008/2009 season to its establishment in the German theatre scene in 2010/2011 with the invitation to the Berlin Theatertreffen, not much time passed. Nevertheless, the artists of colour have to fight hard for the funding of their house. The Ballhaus now has funding until 2014, but must reapply for subsidies.

In addition to the theatre houses, independent production venues or access to institutionalised production venues are very important. People like Rani Kasapi managed to acquire theatrical rooms. Kasapi first worked for Intercult and changed to the Swedish national theatre, Riksteatern, in 2005. She was head of the international department at the Riksteatern, where she was in charge of international collaborations and co-productions. She considered it one of her duties to initiate a debate on and with the Swedish multicultural society and demanded the involvement of theatre makers of colour. Over time, more and more theatre makers, such as Farnaz Arbabi and Jonas Khemiri, could produce their own plays at the Riksteatern and go on tour in Sweden. She used her position not only to internationalise the Riksteatern but also to implement a strategy to empower theatre makers and the public. Many artists of colour are currently active in the Swedish theatre scene.

Together with other European theatre makers of colour, Rani Kasapi founded the project *Europe Now*, in which the artists met to discuss what Postmigrant Europe could mean in an aesthetic context.[191] *Europe Now* was a collaboration of theatre makers of colour who came together under the premise of Postmigrant Europe to create artistic productions. Authors, directors and producers of colour met to work artistically in dialogue with each other. Five theatres from Sweden, the Netherlands, Turkey, Germany, and Great Britain were involved.

The starting point was the premise that the European theatre was dominated by a "white, middle-class elite" which excluded artists and spectators from other cultures or classes, and yet there is a cultural diversity in Europe which is not sufficiently represented. Moreover, migrant artists were being "ethnicised". "Diversity in my view should be interpreted beyond the current fetishism for ethnicity."[192] The *Europe Now* project was intended to reflect precisely this cultural diversity.

Five plays and productions were created which toured in at least two countries in order to reach a larger audience and to create a European mobility and possibilities for Postmigrant theatre makers. The Riksteatern (Sweden) was represented by Rani Kasapi, Farnaz Arbabi, and Jonas Khemiri with the play

---

191 | See http://europenowblog.org/
192 | Özkan Gölpinar, Programme Manager for Cultural Diversity for The Netherlands Foundation for Visual Arts Architecture and Design. See http://europenowblog.org/blog/69

I Call My Brothers. Deniz Altun (author), Lerzan Pamir (director) and Hakan Silahsizoglu (production director) came from the Talimhane Tiyatroso (Turkey), which produced the play *Pippa*. The theatre RAST, from The Netherlands (with Saban Ol and Anouk Saleming), produced the play *Elsewhereland*; the Arcola Theatre London produced *Mare Rider* by Leyla Nazli and Mehmet Ergen. Marianna Salzmann and Hakan Mican Savas from the Ballhaus Naunynstraße produced *Beg your pardon*.

The plays were about reflections on a European society seen through the eyes of figures living in Postmigrant Europe and presented in stories dealing with the same.[193]

The theatre makers did not allow themselves to be assigned to a particular geographical frame of reference and positioned their theatre practice in a transnational context. Since their work was now presented in a European context, it was internationalised at the same time. The rudiments of a Postmigrant European theatre were advanced through the exchange and joint development of ideas.

It is important to mention the importance of theatre festivals in this connection. Theatre festivals are an important format for the distribution of works by theatre makers of colour. The festival series *Beyond Belonging* created a basis for the networking and presentation of Postmigrant theatre from which the necessity of an independent platform for a Postmigrant theatre house in Berlin was born. Another example is the *Europe Now* festival in Amsterdam, which took place in April 2013. A final presentation was the culmination of months of theatre work, and the participating artists were given the chance to exchange ideas and network with other European artists.

The structures developed by the theatre makers of colour in the last twenty years have made production, distribution, and reception of Postmigrant perspectives and plays possible. Without these theatrical venues and aesthetic space, all cultural and political measures and programmes of institutionalised theatres would not make any sense.

4.4 Professional Training

4.4.1 Artistic Training

There seems to be no difference between theatre makers of colour and white theatre makers in terms of vocational and professional training - at least, that is what the study "Report on the Performing Arts"[194] might lead one to believe.

---

193 | Ibid.
194 | Fonds Darstellende Künste, *Report Darstellende Künste. Wirtschaftliche, soziale und arbeitsrechtliche Lage der Theater- und Tanzschaffenden in Deutschland*, (Essen,

The study, which only deals with the situation in Germany, points out that theatre makers and dance professionals in Germany are predominantly highly qualified professionals, two thirds of whom have university degrees. Two thirds of the theatre and dance professionals who have graduated from university have a degree in some area of the arts.[195] This study also included theatre and dance professionals with a migration background. According to the study, there are no differences between theatre and dance professionals in Germany with a migration background and those without.[196]

The results of the study could absolutely be confirmed through talks and interviews with theatre makers of colour, as well as in the other European countries, at least by those artists who were contacted. Many have professional training in some area of the arts; however, acquiring such professional training is considerably more difficult than for their white colleagues. In personal talks, it becomes clear that the theatre makers of colour often encountered more difficulties in completing their secondary school education because of their background.[197] Creative abilities remained unrecognised because of the discrimination experienced early on, a situation typical of almost all the biographies examined. In a face-to-face conversation, Emre Akal, a young actor, author, and director, talked about his early school experiences in which his teachers relegated him to a kind of extended primary school for children up to the age of fifteen because of his Turkish migration background. After finishing school, he completed vocational training before he began his artistic career and was able to attend drama school.[198]

Many artists have experienced such marginalisation prior to fighting their way into drama schools and art academies. Onur Kömürcü Nobrega refers to the important role which drama schools and art academies play for artists of colour.[199] Schools like the Berlin Academy of Dramatic Arts Ernst Busch or the Folkwang University of the Arts have indeed reacted to the need and have at least one to three graduates of colour in every graduating class. At the

---

2010).
195 | Ibid., p. 130.
196 | Ibid., p. 152.
197 | Onur Suzan Kömürcü Nobrega commented on this in her dissertation on "Rasse, Prekariat und künstlerische Arbeit am Beispiel des Ballhaus Naunynstraße. In the article "Alienation in Higher Education: Lived Experiences of Racial and Class-Based Inequality in Film and Drama School", she describes the theatre makers of the Ballhaus Naunynstraße who all come from working class families and have all experienced racism and discrimination in acting school or other institutions offering artistic professional training. O. S. Kömürcü Nobrega, "Alienation in Higher Education", p. 31ff.
198 | In a personal interview. Munich, April 2012.
199 | Kömürcü Nobrega, p. 31.

Folkwang University of Arts, this has also been put into practice with respect to those teaching. Thus, Adewale Teodros Adebisi is a teacher for acting and for special tasks.[200]

Nevertheless, artists of colour are also confronted with racism at drama schools. Onur Suzan Kömürcü Nobrega interviewed Nurkan Erpulat on his experiences at the Berlin Academy of Dramatic Arts Ernst Busch. "It was horrible! After several racist incidents in school, my self-confidence was completely gone, and I thought for a while that I could not continue with my studies until Shermin Langhoff asked me 'Do you want to direct a play at the *Beyond Belonging* festival' and I was like,'Wow, of course I want to'."[201]

In this context, it seems relevant that many artists first completed social and pedagogical-artistic vocational or professional training prior to embarking on an artistic career. Nurkan Erpulat, who had already graduated from a drama school in Turkey, studied theatre education at the University of Arts in Berlin before he studied at the Berlin Academy of Dramatic Arts Ernst Busch in 2003.

In Great Britain, one can observe similar trends. A good example is the Talawa Theatre, which was founded in 1986 by Yvonne Brewster, Carmen Munroe, Mona Hammond, and Inigo Espejel. The aim of the Caribbean-African artists was to help Caribbean-African women to enter the theatre scene and to give them a chance to participate.[202] The position of artistic director was held by Yvonne Brewster, who was the first black artist to attend Rose Bruford College[203] and the Royal Academy of Music. As of 2003, Paulette Randall took over the direction of Talawa. Randall's biography is typical of the path that black artists in the second generation frequently take in the British theatre scene. She attended the Community Arts Course at Rose Buford College, then worked with young people with difficult backgrounds. Thanks to a scholarship from the Arts Council for young directors – the Royal Court Young Writers' Scheme – she found her calling in the theatre. First she worked at the Tricycle Theatre, another contemporary theatre for black artists, and finally became artistic director at the Talawa.[204]

In contrast to Germany, where artistic training is linked to drama schools or universities, artistic training in Great Britain is offered at theatre houses. The Bush Theatre gives young theatre makers from 16–24 years of age the opportunity to start an artistic training in the programme Bush Futures

---

200 | http://www.folkwang-uni.de/de/home/theater/lehrende/detailansicht/?mehr=1&detaildozent=346&cHash=581601ecd3
201 | Kömürcü Nobrega, p. 35.
202 | Keith D. Peacock, *Thatcher's Theatre. British Theatre and Drama in the Eighties*, (Westport: Praeger Frederick, 1999), p.181
203 | The Rose Bruford College of Theatre & Performance is a prestigious drama school in London.
204 | Peacock, p. 182.

Project. Such programmes are also offered at other theatres, such as The Young Vic Directors Program. At the Talawa Theatre, master courses have been held since 1996 in creative writing, performance, poetry, and music to promote young theatre makers, especially those of colour.

4.4.2 Lateral Entrants or Twofold Security

The study "Report on the Performing Arts" indicates that a quarter of the theatre and dance professionals with university degrees have taken up their work in the theatre and dance scenes as lateral entrants.[205] Research and personal interviews show that this percentage is higher among artists of colour.

On the one hand, there are political reasons behind the decision to express oneself through aesthetic means. The racially motivated riots in the sixties and seventies led to the founding of Tara Arts:

'In the summer of 1977, race riots were erupting across the capital. [...]. Everywhere my friends and I looked, it seemed black people, as we identified ourselves, were victims of white oppression. [...]. I set up a theatre company, Tara Arts, with four friends who felt the same way, and who were migrants like me'.[206]

In the summer of 1976, the Sikh teenager Gurdeep Singh Chaggar was murdered in Southall, London, for racist reasons. Jatinder Verma was studying at the time, but not for the theatre. Verma and the other co-founders of Tara Arts found that they could put on theatre productions with rudimentary means to present young "Asian British" in the cultural sector.[207] For them it was about self-determination of their aesthetic concepts. They wanted to be able to decide which subjects should be addressed on the stage and how the contents should be presented. Tara Arts wanted to resist the Eurocentric theatre and cultural scene, which perceived black arts as ethnic art in the sense of an art which is oriented toward the traditional culture of the country of origin and which did not permit non-white artists access to the mainstream.

The fact that the artists of colour as lateral entrants – and not as classically trained theatre makers – took up theatre work can be traced back to an important biographical aspect. For the so-called "lateral entrants", it is important to safeguard their livelihood by taking up a second vocational or professional training and thus ensuring employment in some area. The Swedish author, Jonas Hassen Khemiri, and the young author, Deniz Utlu, who curated a series of readings at the Ballhaus Naunynstraße and has headed the literature workshop with Marianna Salzmann at the Gorki Theatre since the autumn

---

205 | Fonds Darstellende Künste, *Report Darstellende Künste*, p. 131.
206 | http://www.theguardian.com/stage/2008/jan/10/theatre1
207 | Ley, p. 13.

of 2013, both studied economics. The reasons do not differ much from those of white theatre makers. It is not possible to earn a living solely from work in the theatre. However, in the case of many theatre makers of colour, the dual professional background is also a result of their migration history and the need to have a secure professional or vocational training which, if necessary, will allow them to pursue a profession long-term outside their work in the theatre.

4.4.3 Autodidacts

In recent years, there has been a trend in all of the European countries included in this study to try to reach all groups in the population with theatre – even groups which are educationally disadvantaged and remote from the theatre. Traditional professions like those in the area of theatre education or applied theatre have gained in importance, but also new occupational sectors which are related to the theatre have emerged. The participation of people from socially deprived strata in the population should be made possible.

In the last ten years, more and more programmes for different groups in the population have been offered in the institutional theatre houses as well as in the independent scene, including programmes tailored to young people of colour. Almost every theatre group offers work with young people, but very few seem to manage without a paternalistic approach. This would mean not only developing theatre for young people but also finding a language and form together with young people.

The Ballhaus Naunynstraße offered arts education projects right from the start. One very successful project is the *akademie der autodidakten* (academy of the autodidacts). Youths and young adults, mainly with a migration background, who have artistic talent but no academic training, can participate in art and cultural production. Some of the successful graduates of this academy are Neco Çelik, Hülya Duyar, and Tamer Yiğit. The projects of the *akademie der autodidakten* are supervised by directors and artists from the Ballhaus Naunynstraße. Theatre and acting workshops are offered on a regular basis which are open to young persons interested in theatre. By working on theatre and video productions, young participants can learn to deal with different topics in their texts and their own productions and develop their own creative form of expression.

The akademie der autodidakten staged their first successful project in 2007: *Klassentreffen – Die 2. Generation (Class Reunion – The Second Generation)*. The second part of the cycle, *Ferienlager – Die dritte Generation (Summer Camp – The Third Generation)* was produced by Lukas Langhoff and was invited to the Theatertreffen der Jugend in 2010. The third part, *Pauschalreise (Package Tour)*, was a collaboration by Lukus Langhoff and Hakan Savas Mican. Another successful format was initiated by Neco Çelik: *Kiez-Monatsschau – Nachrichten aus der Naunynstraße (Neighbourhood News of the Month – News from the*

Naunynstraße), in which experienced artists from different disciplines offered their support.

One artist who has been very successful in her work with young people is Asli Kislal from Vienna. The co-founder of daskunst also initiated the founding of the club "Echo" with young persons of colour. As is the case in the akademie der autodidakten, the young people are involved in the processes in all the work areas in the theatre. One of the successful young people from Echo is Oktay Güneş, who now works as an actor for daskunst, GarageX, and the children's theatre "Dschungel" in Vienna. Echo received the prize for the best young people's theatre group in Austria in 1995. In a combination of spoken theatre, elements of dance theatre, and acrobatic interludes, plays are developed there which look at society from a young person's perspective. A collaboration with daskunst in 2004 gave rise to the production *Dirty Dishes*, a socio-critical comedy from England which is about the lives of migrants who are illegally employed in the kitchen of a pizzeria. The play is performed in colloquial speech which is announced on the website and in the printed programme with the warning, "Caution: no stage German".[208]

In another production cast with young people from Linz with migration backgrounds, the play *Verrücktes Blut* (*Crazy Blood*) by Nurkan Erpulat and Jens Hillje was successfully staged at the u\hof: Landestheater Linz in 2012. The theatre work, which lasted over three quarters of a year, brought forth highly motivated young actors whose enthusiasm for the theatre was expressed on stage as well as in the interview.

5. Aesthetic Trends and Influences on the European Theatre

What are the aesthetic influences which the artists of colour have exercised in the national and European theatre scenes? Can one even refer to aesthetics of migration?

One of the concepts borrowed from the fine arts which was coined by the cultural theorist Mieke Bal is "migratory aesthetics".[209] Mieke Bal describes migratory aesthetics as an attempt at a theoretical positioning of migration as a metaphor for artistic practice in art.

---

208 | http://www.daskunst.at/dirty%20dishes.html
209 | Mieke Bal, "Lost in Space, Lost in the Library", in Sam Durrant and Catherine M. Lord (eds), *Essays in Migratory Aesthetics. Cultural Practices Between Migration and Art-making*, (New York: Editions Rodopi, 2007), p. 23ff.

She refers to the "relational aesthetics" of Nicolas Bourriaud, the "emphatic aesthetics" of Jill Bennett, and political art, all of which are subject to the idea that a work of art is empty as long as the act of beholding it is not inherent to it. Only through the beholder and his view does a work of art achieve meaning and thus become an expression of a political act.

In migratory aesthetics, the migrant quality should be thought of as an attribute or a modification which refers neither to the migrants, the act of migration, nor the experienced state of migration, but which creates a complex of discrepancy of attribution, ambiguity and vagueness. Migratory aesthetics can open the field of possibilities and become the basis for experiments in order to illuminate the context of migration without reducing it to an association – for example, with the migrant himself as a subject.

In order to better comprehend the nature of migratory aesthetics, Mieke Bal uses an example from her own artistic practice in which she and an Iranian artist developed a video installation on the subject of "home, security, and borders" which included interviews with persons who were or had been refugees. In connection with this project, whose aesthetics were influenced by displacement, shift in meaning, and the appropriation of linguistic and aesthetic space, she describes her concept of migratory aesthetics. One moment in which, according to Bal's descriptions, the idea of migratory aesthetics is manifested in her project was during the interview with an Iranian man who, at the time of the interview, had been an asylum seeker in Germany for several years. The man who had only a limited command of English was only able to adequately express himself – not only linguistically but also sensually and thus in an aesthetic manner – when he spoke in his "own language". When given the chance to speak in his native language, the liberation experienced by the man being interviewed, however, meant a vagueness and discrepancy for the interviewer who, at that moment, did not understand him. However, by accepting the space and acquiescing to a double discrepancy – between language and understanding but also between meaningful and meaningless sounds – migratory aesthetics are created. The man's language defined the aesthetics of the film.[210]

Based on this, she describes the word "migratory" as a constructive view of an aesthetic occurrence which, detached from the certainty of a geopolitical allocation, becomes a vague experience in which self-empowerment and self-representation are the key elements.[211]

How can one deal with the problem of vagueness or, the other way around, how can one proceed in a culturally specific manner in the analyses of cultural processes and works of art without defining the individuals or the works of art

---

210 | Bal, "Lost in Space, Lost in the Library", p. 27.
211 | Ibid., p. 30.

by means of classification to which they no longer belong or to which they no longer feel a sense of belonging?

Mieke Bal suggests, in the absence of a clear cultural identity, to assume a "distinctive multicultural feature" which cannot be assigned to the concept of multiculturalism but which is based on the idea that there is no central culture in the globalised world and that culture has to be defined in particular contexts which, in turn, are inherent to diverse relations.[212] It is only possible by suspending the label of "cultural origin" which describes them as being "foreign" and accepting the synaesthetic whole – the distinctive multicultural feature – of presentation.

Drawn from practice, these theoretical considerations on migratory aesthetics can be transferred in their essence to the aesthetics of artists of colour. As stated above, the "labelling" – the national-cultural classification – is a problem which is continually at the centre of the artistic practice of artists of colour. As expressed in the following section, these are precisely the political demands and contents which are visualised on stage by artists who attempt to manifest migratory aesthetics. In the vagueness and lack of classification, as well as in the fight for aesthetic freedom, trends which reflect Postmigrant perspectives can be identified. They are the perspectives of those marginalised, the obsequious who often speak of racism and discrimination (and thus of cultural stagnation) in the receiving countries and who are confronted with the voyeuristic gaze of mainstream society which is directed at their labelled aesthetic productions.

5.1 Metaphor of Migration, Metaphor of Displacement

The metaphor of migration is an aesthetic figure of speech used to describe a series of shifts in artistic practice for several different purposes: to visualise the increasing fragmentation of subjectivity in the (post-) modern age, to reflect the semantic instability of constructions of (personal/cultural/national) identity, to stress the homology between the experiences of displacement and those of destabilisation of essentialistic ideologies and fixed paradigms and patterns of thought.[213] Migration inevitably leads to the alteration of traditions which make the frame of reference for interpretation and translation of a universal assessment and categorisation impossible and produce incommensurable aesthetics

---

212 | Bal, "Lost in Space, Lost in the Library", p. 32.

213 | Graham Huggan, "Unsettled Settlers: Post-colonialism, Travelling theory and the New Migrant Aesthetics", in Sam Durrant and Catherine M. Lord (eds.), *Essays in Migratory Aesthetics. Cultural Practices Between Migration and Art-making*, (New York: Editions Rodopi, 2007), p. 131.

or aesthetics of incommensurability.[214] The dimension of incommensurability is visualised again and again as a metaphorical construction in the works of artists of colour. The metaphorical constructions can be detected in plays whose subject is migration as a phenomenon or which portray such persons whose subjective experiences become a metaphor for migration and displacement. Subjectivity is often described as a placeholder for structural influence and thus for the phenomenon of migration. Together, the metaphorical interpretations of migration represent the basis of knowledge and changing descriptions of political, social, and cultural views of history. The metaphor of migration and the metaphor of displacement will be explained here with two examples. Both plays and their respective stage productions are concerned with life in a migration society in which individuals are defined by their race, ethnicity, nationality, etc., in which subjects become objects and the subjective perspective or the subjective view is not permitted socially.

5.1.1 *I Call My Brothers*

The Swedish playwright Jonas Hassen Khemiri wrote *Jag ringer mina bröder* (*I Call My Brothers*) based on an incident which took place in Stockholm in 2010. A young Swede of Iraqi origin, Taimour Abdulwahab al-Abdaly, detonated a bomb, thereby committing suicide and injuring two other people. Although only the assassin was killed in the bombing, the events led to a public discussion in Sweden centred around the threat from (and thus the general suspicion directed at) the Muslim population in Sweden.

Khemiri treats this suspicion to which people of colour are subject because of their race, ethnicity, and nationality, in the play *Jag ringer mina bröder* (*I Call My Brothers*), which Farnaz Arbabi produced for the Stadsteater Malmö in 2013. *I Call My Brothers* is about Amor, whose name suggests an Arab background and who uses some Tunisian-Arabic words and speaks of the "second country" in the course of the play. The meaning of this ethnic designation is revealed as the plot develops, since it does not represent any kind of self-perception but is an external ascription which has been internalised. What is disguised as a dialogue, but what is actually a monologue going on in the head of the protagonist, takes place in a period of 24 hours.

Amor calls his brothers on the telephone to tell them about the explosion and the suicide bomber. As the play progresses, it becomes clear that the calls are not to his biological brothers. They are to his brothers in spirit, brothers who share the experience of social exclusion and structural racism.

---

214 | Sam Durrant, "Storytellers, Novelists and Postcolonial Melancholia: Displaced Aesthetics in Chinua Achebe's Things Fall Apart", in Sam Durrant and Catherine M. Lord (eds.): *Essays in Migratory Aesthetics. Cultural Practices Between Migration and Art-making*, (New York: Editions Rodopi, 2007), p. 145.

'I call my brothers and say: Something really sick happened just now.
Have you heard? A man. A car. Two explosions.
In the middle of town.
I call my brothers and say: No, no one was arrested.
No one was suspected. Not yet.
I call my brothers and say: Here goes. Be prepared.'

Supposedly in search of a spare part for an electric drill, Amor walks through the centre of Stockholm which is still in an uproar and full of police. Amor tries to act as normally and inconspicuously as possible.

'I call my brothers and say: Now it's time. The day has come. The hour has struck. Wake up! Hey – wake up! It is time to get up. Get out of your beds. Shave your faces. Put on clean and respectable clothes. Watch out: The clothing must be anonymous. The clothing must not be anonymous. It may not be so anonymous that it is conspicuously anonymous. Exactly. The aim is to blend in. The aim is to be invisible. Leave the Pali scarf at home. Do not carry any suspicious bags. So – now you are ready. Now you can leave your flats. But before you go out, you must arm yourselves. What? No, why that? Take a carving knife with you. Sharpen a screwdriver. Smuggle a razor blade in your wallet. Is that really necessary? Now you are ready to leave your flats. Transform yourselves into representatives. Smile at everything and everyone. The neighbours, The pets. The dummies in the shop windows. Say thank you VERY loudly if someone holds the door open for you. Apologise for being. Whisper in the underground trains. Giggle quietly in the cinema. Transform yourselves into invisible gases.'

But what is normal? And who is a potential suspect? He asks himself what will happen if he becomes the object of the suspicious looks of passers-by, policemen and Swedish society? Amor realises that he outwardly resembles the assassin. He is not white like the rest of society – he is black, he is an Arab. He could be the assassin because he has black hair and dark skin. He is a suspect because he is made a suspect by the public voice. The paranoia of the city becomes his own. In the course of the play, Amor loses hold of himself and doubts his innocence more and more:

'I call my brothers and whisper: Okay. I admit it. It was me.
Pause.
What do you mean?
I did it... the car. The explosions.
What are you talking about? Of course, it wasn't you.
Yes, it was.
But... no, it wasn't you. We know it wasn't you.
But, of course, it must have been me. Everything points to it. I did it.'

And then there are the experiences of his friends and family who have been victims of racist attacks just because they are not white:

'As I came closer, I remembered the policeman who came at Houda's cousin and beat him bloody with the back of his rubber truncheon just because he couldn't keep his mouth shut, and I remembered the policemen who broke Nasim's shinbone and then charged him with attacking a police officer, and I remembered Maribel's sister, who wasn't allowed into the soul club and when she shouted discrimination, the bouncers called the police, and the police came and found a packet of weed in her handbag although she had never smoked grass in her entire life.'

In the end, he loses his "fight" against the hegemonic description of his person, which he finally takes to be his own because of the constant repetition in the mass media and by politicians. The play ends with the words:

'I call my brothers and say: Something really sick happened just now. I was on my way home when I saw a very suspicious person. He had black hair and an unusually large backpack, and his face was covered by a Pali scarf.
Pause.
I call my brothers and say: It only took a fraction of a second until I realised that this was my reflection.'

Even if *I Call My Brothers* was written as an intimate psychological journey of one young man, it is a parable of European societies which does not disclose the "doctrine" of the assassin but the doctrine of society. The metaphor of displacement and marginalisation is revealed in the omnipresence of social (anti-Islamic) racism. The moment of "migratory aesthetics" is the moment in which the attributes which have been created in public discussion are accepted and in which, nevertheless, Amor calls out to his brothers and invokes them to become "visible".

5.1.2 *What Fatima Did*
Another play which deals with a similar phenomenon is *What Fatima Did*, which premiered at the Hampstead Theatre in London in 2009.[215] Fatima's headscarf is a metaphor for an ongoing European debate on the lack of perspective which women who wear headscarves have. It shows how others see them and reveals the prejudices and fears fuelled by this proxy debate.

The main figure is Fatima, a modern, young girl in London who, like all other English girls, drinks alcohol, smokes and parties. Suddenly she decides to

---

215 | In 2011 *What Fatima Did* was produced by Mina Salehpour at the Niedersächsisches Staatstheater in Hannover.

wear a headscarf (the hijab – the traditional headscarf worn by Muslim women to cover their hair). The effects the decision has on her family and friends constitute the subject of the play. The main figure, Fatima, remains unseen and silent throughout the play. She is not present and is either quoted by others or presented in form of written statements. Fatima's decision is discussed in her absence.

For her mother, the headscarf represents a betrayal of her values. The mother, Ruckshana, is a resolute, hard-working woman who likes to drink wine. She tells how she had to fight her ex-husband for the right to wear "Western" clothing and how her mother before her had to fight for the right not to wear a headscarf. On stage she says about her daughter:

"She looks like a bloody fundamentalist postbox, I told her I'd be happier if she'd turned out to be a one-legged, pregnant prostitute than a hijab wearer."

Fatima is not the only Muslim; her best friend Aisha is afraid of the headscarf. For her it is a piece of cloth stained with blood because many women were forced to wear it.

When Fatima's ex-boyfriend George first sees her wearing the headscarf, he complains:

"My girl just came in looking like she'd come from sucking Bin Laden off."

George would like to continue his relationship with Fatima, but his attempt to save it ends in disaster. In desperation, George pulls Fatima's headscarf off. After that, she registers a complaint at school accusing George of racially motivated harassment. Fatima's twin brother Mohammed can't understand why everyone is so upset about Fatima's decision at first, but as the situation in their circle of friends escalates he is forced to take his sister's side. In an argument with his mother, he blames her for giving her children Muslim names and then acting surprised when they "grow into them".

And thus the satirical banter about a piece of cloth – which could not have a greater importance regarding questions of identity in contemporary England – remains unresolved. Fatima does not appear on stage, remaining veiled, invisible, and silent. While others discuss the advantages of wearing the hijab, the only person who really understands is not allowed to explain her own motives.

Atiha Sen Gupta wrote *What Fatima Did* as a reaction to the events of 9/11. The play presents the current public discussion on the headscarf as female attire on the one hand and a form of concealment on the other. Is the hijab a patriarchal form of control, a symbol of political autonomy, or simply a fun fashion statement? In an interview, the author points out that the hijab has always been a political symbol. "Part of the problem is that the hijab and the burka tend to make the wearer visible as a Muslim and invisible as a woman."[216]

---

[216] | http://metro.co.uk/2009/10/21/tales-of-terror-in-what-fatima-did-3438124/

On the other hand, it was important for her to show how the "other" person is marginalised and excluded in the public media discussion. The absence of Fatima as the subject and the absence of her voice on stage refer to the provocative post-colonial thesis in Gayatri Spivak's book, *Can the Subaltern Speak?* Spivak writes about racism and power relationships which expressed themselves in the context of the prohibition of the practice of widow burning in India. She writes that everything which could be discovered about widow burning originated from the British colonial rulers or Hindu leaders but that there was no information from the women who chose to be burned as widows. Spivak mentions the lack of an independent voice in this context in order to contemplate whether the subaltern – the women allegedly deprived of power – would be allowed to have their own opinions, their own voices, in the public discussion.[217] Sen Gupta's Fatima brings this theoretical discussion to the stage and substantiates Spivak's thesis which describes the practice of talking about and on behalf of the subaltern but which does not allow the subaltern themselves to have a voice.

5.2 Postmigrant Perspectives in Theatre

Another aspect of theatre made by persons of colour is the political one. In the reflections on post-dramatic theatre, theatre experts and theatre makers have grappled with the political dimension in theatre. The political is considered part of the theatre, inscribed in the theatre and structurally inherent to it. Jan Deck points out that in the theatre it is possible to physically and symbolically intervene in a real environment by means of specific actions, although the intervention is primarily an aesthetic one intended to change the audience's perception. In this way, the implicitness of societal relations is challenged and socially normed control mechanisms can be undermined. Those who create political theatre intend to make the artistic process a political act.[218] Deck refers to Rancière in this context when the point is to understand the political dimension of the theatre as the creation of space and relationships in order to materially and symbolically re-establish common ground.[219]

Hans-Thies Lehmann suggests that in the case of theatre one should not think "from the centre out to the edges" but "from the edges to the centre". As an example, he refers to the essay written by Jacques Derrida on the occasion of the theatre project *Karl Marx théâtre inédit* by Jean-Pierre Vincent and Bernard

---

217 | Gayatri Spivak, *Can the Subaltern speak? Postkolonialität und subalterne Artikulation*, (Vienna, 2007), p. 214.
218 | Jan Deck and Angelika Sieburg (eds.), *Politisch Theater machen. Neue Artikulationsformen des Politischen in den darstellenden Künsten*, (Bielefeld, 2011), p. 28.
219 | Jacques Rancière, *Das Unbehagen in der Ästhetik*, (Vienna, 2007) p. 32.

Chartreux at the Théâtre des Amandiers in Nanterre. The play is about the situation of the "sans-papiers" (illegal immigrants in France). Derrida writes that "the theatre will make something happen, but not by presenting, imitating or staging a political reality on the stage which otherwise takes place somewhere else in order to pass on a message or a doctrine, but by allowing politics or the political dimension into the structure of the theatre, i.e. by breaking open the present."[220]

Breaking open the present means allowing other voices to be heard in the theatre. According to Lehmann, Derrida speaks in the same context about the necessity of a genuine re-politicising of the theatre which changes "the form, the time, and the space of the theatrical event":[221] theatre that breaks through its aesthetic boundaries by assuming political responsibility, by exposing itself to foreign voices which are otherwise not heard and have no representation in the political order, thereby opening the theatre as a place which can accommodate the "political outside".

In Derrida's understanding, the political dimension can be understood in Postmigrant theatre as a Postmigrant perspective. Postmigrant is then a political dimension through which society is no longer defined by its nationality but understood as a society defined by migration. As Mieke Bal showed in her "migratory aesthetics", a Postmigrant perspective of society would no longer be accepted (or simply tolerated) as the exception, but would be understood as a constant social determinant. In the theatre, this primarily means the representation of "unheard" voices and "unseen" perspectives. The fact that these must first be liberated from discriminatory attributes and racist stereotypes seems to be a continuous element in the theatre work researched for this study.

5.2.1 *Verrücktes Blut*

The two plays already presented here both exhibit perspectives on a theatre which can be described as Postmigrant. In this chapter, the play which made the so-called Postmigrant theatre famous will be presented.

With the play, *Verrücktes Blut* (*Crazy Blood*), Nurkan Erpulat made an international name for the Ballhaus Naunynstraße and attracted international attention to Postmigrant theatre. In an interview which he gave prior to his success and breakthrough, he spoke of the classification of his person and work as "ethnic" or "labelled art":

---

220 | Jacques Derrida, "Marx, das ist jemand", in H.-J. Lenger, J. Sasse and G. Ch. Tholen (eds.), *Zäsuren. E-Journal für Philosophie, Kunst Medien und Politik*, No. 1 (2000), *Ökonomien der Differenz*, p. 65.

221 | Hans-Thies Lehmann, "Wie politisch ist Postdramatisches Theater?", in Jan Deck and Angelika Sieburg (eds.), *Politisch Theater machen. Neue Artikulationsformen des Politischen in den darstellenden Künsten*, (Bielefeld: transcript, 2011), p. 33.

'I will go so far as to claim that I am more familiar with Shakespeare than with stories from the streets of Neukölln [a district of Berlin with a high percentage of foreign residents]. But the theatre directors have, up to now, not had the courage to let me stage such plays.[...] Until this very day, I have been exclusively responsible for intercultural subjects.'[222]

The fact that Erpulat had already enjoyed professional artistic training in Turkey and had graduated in Germany with degrees in theatre education and acting direction seems to have had no influence when production work was commissioned by the artistic directors of the theatre house. His experience shows that only his ethnic background is relevant; a director of Turkish origin seems predestined to direct the *Neuköllner Straßengeschichten*. The play *Crazy Blood* can be seen as an examination of these stereotypes and classifications applied by mainstream society. Erpulat deals with the deconstruction and appropriation of the stage for people of colour.

The story is about a teacher who is insulted and harassed by her pupils who are mostly "visibly of foreign origin". Schiller is on the project plan for the theatre workshop *The Robbers* and *Intrigue and Love*. The teacher talks about Schiller's aesthetics, but no one is listening. The pupils have other problems. Macho posturing and threats fill the room until in a struggle a revolver falls out of a backpack. The gun is real and loaded. The teacher grabs it and becomes an "education terrorist". She takes her pupils hostage and forces them at gunpoint to act on the school stage. In an absurd way, she achieves her mission of aesthetic enlightenment by means of violence.

In the production by Nurkan Erpulat at the Ballhaus Naunynstraße, all of the roles are played by young actors of colour, which was interpreted by most of the audience and the press as "authentic". This interpretation had less to do with what is "authentic" than with the demonstration of precisely those stereotypical attributes. The actors of colour were selected because of their "authenticity" rather than their quality.

At the beginning of the play, the actors are on stage and can be seen dressing for their roles. After they have slipped into their roles, they begin to spit on the audience in the truest sense of the word. At this point the play begins; the audience witnesses a scene in which the pupils humiliate the teacher. This humiliation is presented to justify the "violent" transfer of power in which the teacher acts out the humiliation she has experienced on the pupils – physically and psychologically. The pupils should act out a play by Schiller, true to his

---

222 | Nurkan Erpulat and Patrick Wildermann, "Menschen zu besseren Menschen machen. Der Autor und Regisseur Nurkan Erpulat im Gespräch mit Patrick Wildermann", in *Theater der Zeit. Zeitschrift für Politik und Theater*, issue 11/2010, (Berlin: Theater der Zeit, 2010), p. 48.

maxims on aesthetic education; man is only "an entire being when at play".[223] But as the "play in the play" continues, the roles are increasingly reversed. The roles of Franz and Karl Moor, Amalie, Ferdinand and Luise are broken when usurped by the pupils' reality. The poisoning of Luise by Ferdinand in *Intrigue and Love* is exposed as an "honour killing". In *Crazy Blood*, this scene is not meant to be an identification with the "tradition" of the pupils but as a demonstration of a super-cultural phenomenon. It is not a pupil but Ferdinand, a figure from German Classicism, who commits the murder because his honor has been injured.

As the hostage-taking situation progresses, a slow deconstruction of all supposedly clear identities takes place. Little by little the pupils make the Schiller texts their own in order to describe their own situation. In the process, the classical stage language is repeatedly broken. The "wog gestures"[224] and incorrect pronunciation of the pupils are interrupted by German folk songs sung in "correct German", thereby creating a new order on the stage. The stage is designed as a rectangular fighting arena and supplemented by a prim chorus formation which intervenes between the scenes to give warning and which serves as a connecting element. At the end of the play the teacher seems to have achieved her mission. The pupils are "enlightened", quote Schiller and the maxims of the French Revolution and rebel against psychological and physical violence. But the teacher cannot accept the change in her pupils and wants to continue to wield her power. In the middle of this play for power, the actors drop out of their roles; the teacher outs herself and reveals she is Turkish. She has lost interest in the "wog self-hate act". They all decide to leave the stage together to have a kebab, but one youth who was initially a meek pupil does not want to give up his role as Franz Moor and confronts the audience with the "responsibility" addressed in the "play". He takes the gun and, as a last resort, shoots into the auditorium.

In *Crazy Blood*, the supposed stereotypes of cultural identities fall apart Erpulat turns our view (and thus the focus) away from the stage to the audience which, as the representative of the German society, is the creator of discriminatory classifications. The voyeuristic perspective is unmasked, and the audience is held responsible for discrimination and racism.

---

223 | Friedrich Schiller, *Über die ästhetische Erziehung des Menschen. In einer Reihe von Briefen*, (Stuttgart: Reclam, 2005).
224 | Director's notes by author.

5.3 Formats of Empowerment: Documentary Theatre

5.3.1 *Telemachos*

When asked about the aesthetic orientation of Postmigrant theatre in an interview, Shermin Langhoff said:

'Aesthetically we are oriented towards, among other things, documentary theatre, researching real situations, putting real protagonists on the stage. We go outside the theatre, presenting not only in the theatre but performing, for example, in Anatolian cafés frequented only by men as well as on stage in the Naunynstraße. It's about gaining access to new producers and stories as well as acquiring new recipients. This happens when people can identify with stories, and here we are especially successful with the Ballhaus.'[225]

The means provided by documentary theatre and the research of real circumstances become formats of empowerment in Postmigrant theatre. One theatre project, which was a collaboration between the Ballhaus Naunynstraße and the Onassis Cultural Center in Athens, is *Telemachos – Should I stay or should I go? Telemachos* (English "Telemachus") is documentary theatre in the sense of projects produced by the theatre group Rimini Protokoll, in which the actors playing in the respective events are present on stage and preserve their authenticity as well as the authenticity of their stories within the artistic framework of the theatre.

The framework story of the play is the ancient Greek myth about Telemachus, the son of Ulysses and Penelope. Telemachus is a child when his father leaves home to fight in the Trojan War, and later he cannot prevent Penelope's suitors from plundering Greece. Ulysses' whereabouts are unknown, and his young son Telemachus asks himself, "Stay or go?" The story of Telemachus is linked to the stories of the actors on stage who have asked themselves the same question because of the economic situation in Greece. The German-Greek directing duo Anestis Azas and Prodromos Tsinikoris attempt to present this dilemma on stage together with a number of actors of different generations who spend their lives in a back-and-forth situation between Greece and Germany. Their life stories and the reports on their emigrations, immigrations and remigrations are linked to songs about the wanderings and adventures of Ulysses. In the play one of the actors asks: "If we go to Greece, they say the Germanos is here. The German is here. Well, then... in Germany we are foreigners; in Greece we are foreigners. Where are we not foreigners? Perhaps in Turkey?"

---

225 | Interview with Shermin Langhoff, *Nah & Fern 43*, p. 20.

Another level in the play is shown in a depiction of life in Germany and the story of the Greek guest workers. Two of the actors came to Germany as guest workers in the sixties and seventies. The director Prodromos Tsinikoris, also on stage, is himself a child of immigrant Greek workers and was born in the German city of Krefeld. They describe life in Germany from their perspective.

Telemachos uses self-images and public images to present the current dispute on the crisis in Greece and then uses the subjective stories of the actors on stage to deconstruct those images. It is, however, a format of empowerment, since the artists on stage relate their own stories and present their own perspective on the situation in Greece.

5.4 Influences on Aesthetic Discourses

A study published by the International Network for Contemporary Arts in 2003 found that the theatre of artists of colour developed its own aesthetic orientation from a political and social commitment. Apart from the national differences which have to be taken into account, it is apparent that the artists demonstrate commonalities and share a common path. The most important aspect on which the social and cultural changes are based is the emergence of a theatre scene of the second generation which takes part in the public discussion and has established its own position in the theatre landscape.[226]

This trend has increased in recent years. The importance of theatre makers of colour and their artistic practice for the European theatre scene is growing. In the European independent theatre scene, the topic of migration is omnipresent: in the origin of the persons, in the working language, and in research. As the theatre makers say themselves, the language is no longer in the foreground, but the bodies, the research and the subject.[227]

Yet, the state theatres continue to be closed shops. Günther Heeg puts forward the thesis in his research on "transcultural theatre"[228] that the municipal theatre will in the long-run become part of a transcultural theatre landscape. Transcultural theatre does not originate from demarcated, distinct cultures which must be brought into contact with each other. This holistic cultural concept no longer works in the age of globalisation. Wolfgang Welsch describes this in the following way:

---

226 | Bloomfield.
227 | Mieke Matze in an interview.
228 | GüntherHeeg,FremdheitserfahrungohneExotisierung,(Hildesheim,2013). http://www.nachtkritik.de/index.php?view=article&id=7645%3Ahildesheimer-thesen-xi-die-zukunft-liegt-im-transkulturellen-theater&option=com_content&Itemid=84

'Transculturality wants [...] to point out that today's make-up of cultures lies far beyond their old [...] form and that the characteristics of this difference [...] can be found in all cultures today as cultural determinants so that cultures are no longer defined by a clear demarcation but through interrelationships and commonalities.'[229]

Thus, it can be assumed that cultures do not primarily exist in themselves but only take on form through intercultural contacts. In the "third space" and in the translation of cultural differences, cultures are constituted externally as processes of overlapping and mixing.

Heeg adds that transcultural theatre "begins at the point of experiencing what is foreign inside the cultural phantasms which surround us". It is important that theatre "should not exoticise what is foreign, and that it should not presume to speak for others or to represent them vicariously."[230] Therefore, it is essential for transcultural theatre to rethink forms of presentation and open new possibilities.

One approach would be, for example, to eliminate the prevailing labelling of artists of colour and to consider these artists as a part of the overall existing theatre scene. The labelling makes sense in connection with identity policies[231] but only produces injustice in the context of artistic production. Mieke Bal says that the culturally specific and enduring dominance of the so-called "mainstream", which does not consider the unequal distribution as an intellectual problem, continues colonial historical elements in an age of decolonisation. The exploitation of the "other" goes on when, for example, an exhibition is furnished with a "made in" label so that the meaning of the artwork is not purely conditional on aesthetic aspects.[232] This statement referring to visual art can also be applied to the performing arts. In the debate on blackface, which has cropped up frequently in the last ten years in all the European countries included in this study, it becomes clear how much colonial images are still present in today's theatre scene. For some time now, the racist connotations of the "Zwarte Piet" (Black Peter) have been discussed in The Netherlands every year around St. Nicholas Day. The figure was originally meant to represent the devil, who had no name and was supposed to represent all that is bad. In 1850, the character first appeared in a book by Jan Schenkman as a companion of Sinterklaas and is commonly depicted as a blackamoor: a Moroccan slave. To this day, white Dutch men who play the role of

---

229 | Wolfgang Welsch, "Was ist eigentlich Transkulturalität?", in Lucyna Darowska, Thomas Lüttenberg and Claudia Machold (eds.), *Hochschule als transkultureller Raum? Kultur, Bildung und Differenz in der Universität*, (Bielefeld: transcript, 2010).
230 | Heeg, *Fremdheitserfahrung ohne Exotisierung*.
231 | Mark Terkessidis points out that only by identifying the institutional structure can the deficits in the representation of groups in society with migration backgrounds become visible. Terkessidis, *Interkultur*.
232 | Bal, "Lost in Space, Lost in the Library", p. 25.

Zwarte Piet paint their faces black and their lips red and put on afro wigs. Critics point out the colonial context of blackface. Until now, their criticism has generally gone unheard. This debate has also surfaced in Germany in recent years.[233]

In 2012, the Schlossparktheater in Berlin hung up posters with a blackface to announce its production of *I'm Not Rappaport*, a play by the American playwright, Herb Gardner. This led to a public debate in the theatre community throughout Europe. Critics of this stylistic device, mainly artists of colour, pointed out the racist and colonial connotations in comments and opinions presented in different media.[234]

Blackface also has a long tradition in the German theatre, since white actors wearing blackface can be designated as "foreign". While "white" figures remain unmarked on stage, "black" figures – or figures of colour, whether Asian, African or Aboriginal – are made "visible" with blackface.[235] The aesthetic tradition is based on the assumption that the persons on and behind the stage as well as those in the audience are white, and persons of colour are not present.

Furthermore, blackface on German stages is reminiscent of the theatrical device as it was used in minstrel shows. In American minstrel shows of the 19th century, clichés of black plantation workers were portrayed by white actors wearing blackface and painted thick red lips. This kind of characterisation can be found again and again in German productions in which "black" figures appear.[236]

The Schlossparktheater dismissed the criticism as inappropriate and explained that blackface was used because there was no qualified black actor available.[237] At the same time the theatre formulated a plea for artistic freedom:

'It may be that the feelings of some African-Germans were hurt. However, up to now, running the risk of injuring feelings was justified by the sanctity of artistic freedom. Be-

---

233 | There was also a debate in Sweden about the use of blackface because of a production of Dea Loher's play *Illegal*. Personal interview with Nasim Aghili and Famz Arbabi.
234 | See also http://www.migration-boell.de/web/integration/48_3355.asp
235 | An example is the traditional presentation of Othello.
236 | According to Edward Said, an analysis of the Western construction of the Orient can be helpful. Said refers to the theatrical representation which adopts as its own what is "foreign", the construction of the "Orient" through images and portrayals. "The idea of representation is a theatrical one: the Orient is the stage on which the whole East is confined. On this stage will appear figures whose role it is to represent the large whole from which they emanate. The Orient then seems to be not an unlimited extension beyond the familiar European world, but rather a closed field, a theatrical stage affixed to Europe." Edward Said, *Orientalism*, (London: Vintage, 1977), p. 63.
237 | See "Network community criticises Hallervorden's Schlossparktheater", Nachtkritik 2012. http://www.nachtkritik.de/index.php?option=com_content&view=article&id=6457&catid=126

cause the principle of the theatre is that people there can act as if they were someone else and that in doing so they sometimes show things which do not please everyone.'[238]

This comment denies the fact that the criticism of blackface was expressed in the aesthetic frame of reference of the theatre. The theatre makers and theatre critics of colour are degraded to persons whose "feelings" have been hurt. Their historical and aesthetic knowledge is denied and with it the possibility of formulating aesthetic criticism. The critics retaliated vehemently: not only individual artists criticised the theatre's position but also the initiative Bühnenwatch,[239] an association of artists, theatre makers, political activists and academics. They criticised the racist practice from an aesthetic standpoint in panel discussions, conferences, and public statements.[240] Public interventions of this sort can also be observed in other European countries. Artists of colour enter the discussions on theatre aesthetics and actively influence them with their own positions.

6. Prospects for a European Theatre

6.1 Theatre and Migration: From the Independent Scene to Institutionalisation

The sub-study "Theatre and Migration" observed that in the past decade artists of colour and Postmigrant theatre have evoked structural and aesthetic changes in the independent scene of contemporary European theatre. In each of the countries surveyed in this study, there were artists of colour. Independent structures have formed almost everywhere; either Postmigrant theatre houses have been established or production venues have shifted their emphasis to cultural diversity. And finally, there are funding institutions especially for theatre makers of colour and Postmigrant theatre. There seems to be a trend in which artists of colour are moving more and more into the focus of the theatre scenes, away from the independent scene to institutions and institutionalisation.

As part of this study, a conference entitled "Postmigrant Perspectives on European Theatre" was held in March 2013 with the Goethe Institute in London and with the support of the foundation of the German newspaper *Die Zeit*. Artists, academics, and politicians dealing with cultural policy from Germany, Sweden,

---

238 | Matthias Heine, "Rassismusvorwurf gegen Dieter Hallervorden", *Die Welt* of 10 January 2012 http://www.welt.de/kultur/article13807516/Rassismusvorwurf-gegen-Dieter-Hallervorden.html
239 | http://buehnenwatch.com
240 | *Theater und Diskriminierung. Heinrich Böll Stiftung*, (Berlin, 2012). http://www.migration-boell.de/web/integration/48_3355.asp

Great Britain, and The Netherlands were invited. Postmigrant positions were presented in the forum, and questions concerning representation, cooperation and institutionalisation were discussed.[241]

The outcome of the conference was the conclusion that there is still a need for a social reality in which there are equal access opportunities and equal representation for different narratives. As was established in the study published by the International Network for Contemporary Performing Arts in 2003, "Racism remains the generally unacknowledged barrier to cultural diversity in the performing arts."[242]

The existing social, political, and economic distribution of power makes it unnecessary for those with decision-making authority to consider the issues, experiences and problems of marginalised persons. "The centre doesn't have to think about the periphery."[243] Those who are marginalised, on the other hand, have learned to adopt the perspective of the centre and, at the same time, have not only learned to voice their own cultural perspective but also to take a different view of the existing situation. Thus, the potential which could be derived from stories, experiences and primarily from the artists of colour remains untapped within prevailing production and promotion conditions.

How can the stories, aesthetics and formats which are labelled as being ethnic and which exist on the periphery of cultural events be made visible?

'Just look at what we are doing as theatre makers. By taking refuge in a dream, aided by imagination and a bit of poetic exuberance. When the borders of the political reality no longer play a role, the scene of action also changes, irrevocably, and faster than you could believe. Only then does the viewer regain his freedom, and the awareness returns that theatre is truly magical, that theatre creates life rather than taking it.'[244]

Or to include Chakrabarty's pessimistic view of history which stresses its limitations and impossibility, financial support must have as an objective that the theatre "deliberately makes its own repressive strategies and practices visible which lie in the structure of its narrative forms."[245]

---

241 | See Maximilian Grafe, *I am not a postmigrant artist!* http://azadehsharifi.wordpress.com/2013/04/22/i-am-not-a-postmigrant-artist/
242 | Bloomfield, p. 127.
243 | Hassan Mahamadallie at the conference.
244 | Özkan Gölpinar, Programme Manager for Cultural Diversity for The Netherlands Foundation for Visual Arts Architecture and Design. See http://europenowblog.org/blog/69
245 | Dipesh Chakrabarty, "Europa provinzialisieren: Postkolonialität und die Kritik der Geschichte", in Dipesh Chakrabarty, *Europa als Provinz. Perspektiven postkolonialer Geschichtsschreibung*, (Frankfurt a.M.: Campus Verlag, 2010), p. 65.

It is not only about *what* Postmigrant theatre can bring forth in the theatre landscapes of the individual countries or in Europe with regard to aesthetic and structural changes, but *how* theatrical perspectives can become utopias for societal positions which do not follow the existing political traditions in which ethnicity or race or gender are used as distinguishing characteristics (and thus characteristics of exclusion), and how Postmigrant theatre can use its aesthetic resources to expedite a re-thinking and a re-imagination.

'If the future of the intercultural has to be posited in tangible terms, and not just as an empty fantasy, we will have to open ourselves to those realities that resist being imagined easily.'[246]

6.2 Postmigrant Perspectives for European Theatre

In my final observations, I would like to take up the thoughts of the historian Dipesh Chakrabarty, who criticises Eurocentric historiography and demands an emancipation of (Western) European histories by "provincialising" Europe, i.e. by putting the importance of Europe in relation to global history into the correct perspective. In this connection he expounds the problem of post-colonial historiography: The conceptual instruments like "nation", "revolution" or "progress" of European social and cultural sciences contribute to making European experience a universalistic perspective and prefigure and "Europeanise" the importance of the respective local pasts. He demands a history of a modern age which is able to think through its own repressive foundations, exclusion mechanisms and marginalisations. Chakrabarty adds that "we" all, who, with our different and frequently non-European archives, nevertheless "practice" European histories, should have the possibility of a policy of alliances and an alliance project between the prevailing metropolitan histories and the subaltern pasts from the periphery. The resulting project would be the "provincialising of Europe". It means underwriting the narratives which have been privileged up to now, which are nourished by imagined pasts and visions of the future in which collectivity is neither defined by rituals and European nationalities but only by the "tradition" created by a modern age. Since there are no places in the existing structures in which such "dreams" can be institutionalised, they must continue to recur until the "subjects of nationality and nation state dominate our narratives of a historical transition because it is precisely this oppression of our dreams to which the modern age owes its existence."[247]

Theatre in the migration society could be put into the context of this difference and in the impossibility of the project of "provincializing" Europe. Theatre could open a space which would not be possible in other areas of

---

246 | Rustom Bharucha, *The Politics of Cultural Practice*, p. 162.
247 | Chakrabarty, p. 19 ff.

society. From the position of a "provincialised Europe", in which stories of a new reality are presented on the stages, a new perspective achieved by overwriting European (theatre) histories could be addressed.

Another important element for a societal change of perception is the necessity to rethink the canons of national art. In an essay entitled "Art History as a Common Heritage", the British-Indian artist and publicist Rasheed Araeen deals with the national identity of Great Britain. His aim is to point out that the construction of a national concept of British art has always implied an exclusion of non-white artists. The works of non-white artists have always been appraised from an ethnicised perspective. British post-war art has mainly been influenced by the post-colonial and multiethnic society. Araeen makes a plea for the recognition of the influence of migrant artists on the overall cultural history of the country: "Without a recorded history, nothing else can follow: no celebration of achievement, no development of a common cultural heritage. This results in immigrant populations looking outside these shores for their history and cultural points of reference."[248]

By means of a change of perspective and a paradigm shift on the part of theatre makers, which would mean an acceptance of the social reality in Germany and the diverse cultural histories, the theatre can become a place for all people. This would require that the authority to define art must be reconsidered and new possibilities of self-representation must be created.

---

248 | Rasheed Araeen, *Art History as a Common Heritage*, (London: Third Text Publications, 2009).

LITERATURE AND SOURCES

Ahmed, S. *Strange Encounters: Embodied Others in Post-Coloniality*. London: Routledge, 2000.
Allen, C. "Justifying Islamophobia: A Post-9/11 Consideration of the European Union and British Contexts." *The American Journal of Islamic Social Sciences* 21 (2004), pp. 1–25.
Appadurai, A. *Modernity at Large: Cultural Dimensions of Globalization*. Minneapolis: University of Minnesota Press, 1996.
Appignanesi, R. *Beyond Cultural Diversity: The Case for Creativity. A Third Text Report*. London: Third Text, 2010.
Araeen, R. *The Art Britain Really Ignores: Making Myself Visible*. London: Kala Press, 1984.
Arts Council of England. *Cultural Diversity Action Plan for the Arts Council England*. London: Arts Council England, 1998.
Arts Council of England. *Decibel: Performing Arts Showcase*. London: Arts Council England, 2011.
Azas, A. and Tsinikoris, P. *Telemachos – Should I stay or should I go*. Event programme, Ballhaus Naunynstraße, Berlin. Berlin: Kultursprünge e.V., 2013.
Bade, K. *Deutsche im Ausland – Fremde in Deutschland: Migration in Geschichte und Gegenwart*. Munich: C.H. Beck, 1992.
Bal, M. "Lost in Space, Lost in the Library." In: S. Durrant and C. M. Lord (eds), *Essays in Migratory Aesthetics* (2007), pp. 37–48.
Bauer, W. T. *Zuwanderung nach Österreich*. Vienna: ÖGPP, 2008.
Beck, U. and Sznaider, N. "Unpacking Cosmopolitanism for the Social Sciences: A Research Agenda." *The British Journal of Sociology* 57 (2006), pp. 381–403.
Berkowitz, J. *Avrom Goldfaden and the Modern Yiddish Theatre: The Bard of Old Constantine*. Winter: Hebrew Publishing Company, 2004.
Bharucha, R. *The Politics of Cultural Practice: Thinking through Theatre in an Age of Globalisation*. Hanover: Wesleyan University Press, 2000.
Bicker, B. "Theater als Parallelgesellschaft: Über das Verhältnis von Theater und Migration." In: S. Hess, J. Binder and J. Moser (eds), *No Integration? Kulturwissenschaftliche Beiträge zur Integrationsdebatte in Europa*. Bielefeld: transcript, 2009, pp. 27–32.
Bloomfield, J. *Crossing the Rainbow: National Differences and International Convergences in Multicultural Performing Arts in Europe*. Brussels: Informal European Theatre Meeting, 2003.
Boran, E. M. *Eine Geschichte des Türkisch-Deutschen Theaters und Kabaretts*. Ohio: Ohio State University Press, 2004.
Boswell, C. *European Migration Policies in Flux: Changing Patterns of Inclusion and Exclusion*. Oxford: John Wiley & Sons, 2003.

Brauneck, M. *Ausländertheater in der Bundesrepublik Deutschland und in West-Berlin*. Hamburg: University of Hamburg Press, 1983.

Brown, S., Hawson, I., Graves, T. and Barot, M. *Eclipse Report: Developing Strategies to Combat Racism in Theatre*. London: Arts Council England, 2001.

Chakrabarty, D. *Europa als Provinz: Perspektiven postkolonialer Geschichtsschreibung*. Frankfurt am Main: Campus, 2010.

Chakrabarty, D. "Europa provinzialisieren." In: Conrad, S. and Randeria, S. (eds), *Jenseits des Eurozentrismus: Postkoloniale Perspektiven in den Geschichts- und Kulturwissenschaften*. Frankfurt: Campus, 2001, pp. 283–309.

Chin-tao, W. *Privatising Culture: Corporate Art Intervention since the 1980s*. London: Verso, 2002.

Colebrook, C. *Gilles Deleuze*. London: Routledge, 2002.

Conley, V. "Minoritorian." In: Adrian Parr (ed.), *The Deleuze Dictionary*. Edinburgh: Edinburgh University Press, 2005, pp. 164-165.

Deck, J. and Sieburg, A. (eds). *Politisch Theater machen: Neue Artikulationsformen des Politischen in den darstellenden Künsten*. Bielefeld: transcript, 2011.

Deleuze, G. "One Less Manifesto." In: Timothy Murray (ed.), *Mimesis, Masochism and Mime: The Politics of Theatricality in Contemporary French Thought*. Ann Arbor: University of Michigan Press, 1997, pp. 239–258.

Derrida, J. "Marx, das ist jemand." In: J. Lenger, J. Sasse and G. Ch. Tholen (eds), *Zäsuren: E-Journal für Philosophie, Kunst Medien und Politik* 1 (2000) (= *Ökonomien der Differenz*), pp. 58–70.

Deutscher Bundestag [German Parliament]. *Der nationale Integrationsplan: Neue Chancen – neue Wege*. Berlin: German Parliament Pres and Information Office, 2007.

Deutscher Bundestag [German Parliament]. *Kultur in Deutschland. Schlussbericht der Enquete-Kommission des Deutschen Bundestages*. Bonn: Bundeszentrale für politische Bildung, 2008.

Durrant, S. "Storytellers, Novelists and Postcolonial Melancholia: Displaced Aesthetics in Chinua Achebe's *Things Fall Apart*." In S. Durrant and C. M. Lord (eds), *Essays in Migratory Aesthetics* (2007), pp. 145-160.

Durrant, S. and Lord, C. M. (eds). *Essays in Migratory Aesthetics: Cultural Practices between Migration and Art-making*. New York: Rodopi, 2007.

Erpulat, N. and Hillje, J. *Verrücktes Blut. Frei nach einem Motiv aus dem Film 'Heute trage ich Rock' Drehbuch und Regie von Jean-Paul Lilienfeld*. Berlin: Pegasus, 2010.

Erpulat, N. And Wildermann, P. "'Menschen zu besseren Menschen machen': Der Autor und Regisseur Nurkan Erpulat im Gespräch mit Patrick Wildermann." *Theater der Zeit* 11 (2010), pp. 48–49.

European Union Agency for Fundamental Rights. *Muslime in der europäischen Union. Islamophobie und Diskriminierung*. Vienna: The European Union Agency for Fundamental Rights, 2006.

Faist, T. *The Volume and Dynamics of International Migration and Transnational Social Spaces.* Oxford: Oxford University Press, 2000.

Fent, H. *Die Interkulturelle Öffnung von Verwaltungsdiensten.* Winterthur: Edition Soziothek, 2008.

Fischer-Lichte, E. *Das Eigene und das Fremde Theater.* Tübingen: Francke, 1999.

Fonds Darstellende Künste. *Report Darstellende Künste: Wirtschaftliche, soziale und arbeitsrechtliche Lage der Theater- und Tanzschaffenden in Deutschland.* Essen: Klartext, 2010.

Foroutan, N. "Neue Deutsche, Postmigranten und Bindungs-Identitäten: Wer gehört zum neuen Deutschland?" *Aus Politik und Geschichte* 46/47 (2010), pp. 9-15.

Fukuyama, F. *The End of History and the Last Man.* New York: Free Press, 1992.

Galgóczi, B., Leschke, J. and Watt, A. *Intra-EU Labour Migration: Flows, Effects and Policy Responses.* Brussels: European Trade Union Institute, 2011.

Gilroy, P. *Postcolonial Melancholia.* New York: Columbia University Press, 2005.

Gonzalez, M. "Introduction: The Construction of Identity in Minority Theatre." In: P. Brasseur and M. Gonzalez (eds), *Authenticity and Legitimacy* (2010), pp. ix-xxix.

Gonzalez, M. and Brasseur, P. (eds). *Authenticity and Legitimacy in Minority Theatre: Constructing Identity.* Cambridge: Cambridge Scholars Publishing, 2010.

Gupta, A. S. *What Fatima Did.* London: Oberon, 2012.

Haakh, N. M. *Islamisierte Körper auf der Bühne: Identitätspolitische Positionierung zur deutschen Islam-Debatte in Arbeiten des postmigrantischen Theaters Ballhaus Naunynstraße Berlin.* Berlin: Freie Universität Berlin, 2011.

Hall, S. "Rassismus als ideologischer Diskurs." *Das Argument* 178 (1989), pp. 913–921.

Hall, S. "The Great Moving Right Show." *Marxism Today* (January 1978), pp. 14–20.

Hasib, N. Lalish-Theaterlabor. "Aufbruch zur Quelle der Feierlichkeit." In: M. Wagner, S. Schwinghammer and M. Hüttler (eds), *Theater. Begegnung. Integration?* Frankfurt am Main: Iko-Verlag für Interkulturelle Kommunikation, 2003, pp. 221–242.

Held, D., McGrew, A., Goldblatt, D. and Perraton, J. *Global Transformations: Politics, Economics and Culture.* Cambridge: Polity Press, 1999.

Herringer, N. *Empowerment in der Sozialen Arbeit.* Stuttgart: Kohlhammer, 2010.

Hobsbawm, E. and Ranger, T. *The Invention of Tradition.* Cambridge: Cambridge University Press, 1992.

Huggan, G. "Unsettled Settlers: Postcolonialism, Travelling Theory and the New Migrant Aesthetics." In S. Durrant and C. M. Lord (eds), *Essays in Migratory Aesthetics* (2007), pp. 129-144.

Hylton, R. *The Nature of the Beast: Cultural Diversity and the Visual Arts Sector. A Study of Policies. Initiatives and Attitudes 1976–2006.* Bath: Icia Institue of Contemporary Interdisciplina, 2007.

Jermyn, H. and Desai, P. *Arts – What's in a Word: Ethnic Minorities and the Arts.* London: Arts Council England, 2000.

Khan, N. *The Arts Britain Ignores.* London: Arts Council England, 1976.

Khemiri, J. H. *Ich rufe meine Brüder.* J. Hallberg (trans.). Hamburg: Rowohlt Theater Verlag, 2013.

Kömürcü Nobrega, O. S. "Alienation in Higher Education: Lived Experiences of Racial and Class Based Inequality in Film and Drama School." In: *The Living Archives: Kulturelle Produktionen und Räume* (Heinrich-Böll-Stiftung Dossier). Berlin: Heinrich-Böll-Stiftung, 2013, pp. 31–38.

Langhoff, S., Kulaoglu, T. and Kastner, B. "Dialoge I: Migration dichten und deuten. Ein Gespräch zwischen Shermin Langhoff, Tuncay Kulaoglu und Barbara Kastner." In: Pelka, A. and Tigges, S. (eds), *Das Drama nach dem Drama: Verwandlungen dramatischer Formen in Deutschland seit 1945.* Bielefeld: transcript, 2011, pp. 309–408.

Lehmann, H-T. "Wie politisch ist Postdramatisches Theater?" In: J. Deck and A. Sieburg (eds), *Politisch Theater Machen* (2011), pp. 29–40.

Lepenies, W. *Kultur und Politik: Deutsche Geschichte.* Bonn: Bundeszentrale für Politische Bildung, 2006.

Leppek, K. *Theater als interkultureller Dialog: Dschungel Wien – Theaterhaus für junges Publikum.* Marburg: Tectum, 2010.

Ley, G. "Tara Arts: 1977-1985." In: S. Dadswell and G. Ley (eds), *British South Asian Theatres: A Documented History.* Exeter: University of Exeter Press, 2011, pp. 13–56

Loher, D. *Unschuld.* Frankfurt am Main: Verlag der Autoren, 2003.

Lornsen, K. *Transgressive Topographien in der türkisch-deutschen Post-Migranten-Literatur.* Vancouver: University of British Columbia, 2007.

Lucassen, J. and Penninx, R. *Newcomers: Immigrants and their Descendants in the Netherlands 1550-1995.* Amsterdam: Het Spinhuis, 1997.

Martin, J. *Gramsci's Political Analysis: A Critical Introduction.* Bristol: Palgrave Macmillan, 1998.

McMillan, M. and SuAndi, O. "Rebaptizing the World in Our Own Terms: Black Theatre and Live Arts in Britain." In: P. C. Harrison, V. Leo and W. G. Edwards (eds), *Black Theatre: Ritual Performance in the African Diaspora.* Philadelphia: Temple University Press, 2002, pp. 115-129.

Mecheril, P., Castro Varela, M., Dirim, İ., Kalpaka, A. and Melter, C. *Migrationspädagogik.* Wenheim: Beltz, 2010.

Münchener Kammerspiele. Programme for *Bunnyhill – Eine Staatsgründung.* Munich: Münchener Kammerspiele, 2005.

Münz, R., Seifert, W. and Ulrich, R. E. *Zuwanderung nach Deutschland: Strukturen, Wirkungen, Perspektiven.* Frankfurt am Main: Campus, 1999.
N. A. "'Theater kann eine Identitätsmaschine sein': Interview with Shermin Langhoff." *Nah & Fern* 43 (2009), pp. 18–23.
Peacock, K. D. *Thatcher's Theatre: British Theatre and Drama in the Eighties.* Westport: Praeger Frederick, 1999.
Rancière, J. *Das Unbehagen in der Ästhetik.* Vienna: Passagen Verlag, 2007.
Römhild, R. "Aus der Perspektive der Migration: Die Kosmopolitisierung Europas." In: S. Hess, J. Binder and J. Moser (eds), *No Integration? Kulturwissenschaftliche Beiträge zur Integrationsdebatte in Europa.* Bielefeld: transcript, 2009, pp. 225–238
Said, E. *Orientalism.* London: Penguin, 1977.
Sappelt, S. "Theater und Migrant/innen." In: C. Chiellino (ed.), *Interkulturelle Literatur in Deutschland.* Stuttgart: Metzler, 2000, pp. 275–293.
Schiller, F. *Über die ästhetische Erziehung des Menschen: In einer Reihe von Briefen.* Stuttgart: Reclam, 2005.
Sharifi, A. "Postmigrantisches Theater. Eine neue Agenda für die deutschen Bühnen." In: W. Schneider (ed.), *Theater und Migration: Herausforderungen für Kulturpolitik und Theaterpraxis.* Bielefeld: transcript, 2011.
Sharifi, A. *Theater für Alle? Partizipation von Postmigranten am Beispiel der Bühnen der Stadt Köln.* Frankfurt am Main: Peter Lang, 2011.
Spivak, G. *Can the Subaltern speak? Postkolonialität und subalterne Artikulation.* Vienna: Turia & Kant, 2007.
Stiglitz, J. *Globalisation and its Discontents.* London: Penguin, 2002.
Terkessidis, M. *Interkultur.* Frankfurt am Main: Suhrkamp, 2010.
Türkmen, C. *Migration und Regulierung.* Münster: Dampfboot, 2008.
Wade, R. H. "Is Globalisation Reducing Poverty and Inequality?" *World Development* 32 (2004), pp. 567- 589.
Welsch, W. "Was ist eigentlich Transkulturalität?" In: L. Darowska, T. Lüttenberg, C. Machold (eds), *Hochschule als transkultureller Raum? Kultur, Bildung und Differenz in der Universität.* Bielefeld: transcript, 2010, pp. 39–66.
Zimmermann, R. "Zur Minarettverbotsinitiative in der Schweiz." *Zeitschrift für ausländisches öffentliches Recht und Völkerrecht (ZaöRV)* 69 (2009), pp. 829–864.

Theatre homepages

(accessed 12th September 2013)

http://color.lalishtheater.org
http://europenowblog.org
http://buehnederkulturen.de
http://ballhausnaunynstrasse.de

http://maximtheater.ch
http://bushtheatre.co.uk
http://theater-bautzen.de
http://daskunst.at/dirty%20dishes.html
http://juedischestheaterberlin.de/Theater.php?Bereich=Geschichte
http://tko-theater.de/logicio/pmws/indexDOM.php?client_id=tko&page_id=tko
http://amarodrom.de/romanistan
http://lesacharnes.com
http://teatroaperto.it
Http://sne-bautzen.de/index.php?id=2351&L=0
Http://buehnenwatch.com

Online Sources

(accessed 7th September 2015)

"Acting Diversity: intercultural theatre projects for political refugees and young people, Alexandria, 2013." Available at: http://www.annalindhfoundation.org/granted-projects/2012/acting-diversity-project-intercultural-theatre-political-refugees-and-young#sthash.8JqvfV3A.dpuf

Adebisi, A. T., "Folkwang Universität." Available at: http://www.folkwang-uni.de/de/home/hochschule/personen/lehrende/vollanzeige/?mehr=1&detaildozent=346

Alfree, C. "Tales of Terror in What Fatima Did." 2009. Available at: http://metro.co.uk/2009/10/21/tales-of-terror-in-what-fatima-did-3438124/

Araeen, R. "Art History as a Common Heritage." Available at: http://www.thirdtext.com/wp-content/uploads/2009/03/arthistoryasacommonheritage.pdf

Arts Council. "What is the Creative Case for Diversity?" Available at: http://artscouncil.org.uk/media/uploads/pdf/What_is_the_Creative_Case_for_Diversity.pdf

Biggers, J. "Beyond Mare Nostrum: Italian Theater Launches International Project for Immigration Stories." 30th July 2014. Available at: http://huffingtonpost.com/jeff-biggers/beyond-mare-nostrum-itali_b_5634746.html

Breteler, R. "Vortrag beim Bundesfachkongress Interkultur Hamburg." 2012. Available at: http:// youtube.com/watch?v=3BKBNVqfhZ4

Butterwege, C. "Von der 'Gastarbeiter'-Anwerbung zum Zuwanderungsgesetz." Bonn 2005. Available at: http://bpb.de/gesellschaft/migration/dossier-migration/56377/migrationspolitik-in-der-brd?p=all

Carrel, N. "Dossier Migration Schweiz." Bundeszentrale für politische Bildung, 2012. Available at: http://bpb.de/gesellschaft/migration/dossier-migration/139678/schweiz

"Designierte Leiterin Shermin Langhoff zurückgetreten." *Der Standard*, 21st May 2012. Available at: http://derstandard.at/1336697481118/Designierte-Leiterin-Shermin-Langhoff-zurueckgetreten

"Ein Amt schürt Angst." *Die Wochenzeitung*, 8th August 2013. Available at: http:// woz.ch/1332/behoerdlicher-rassismus/ein-amt-schuert-angst

Ersanili, E. "Niederlande." *Fokus Migration*. Available at: http://focus-migration.hwwi.de/index.php?id=2644

Deutscher Budestag [German Parliament]. *Der Nationale Integrationsplan*. Bundesregierung.de. 2006. Available at:http://bundesregierung.de/Content/DE/StatischeSeiten/Breg/IB/2006-10-27-ib-nationaler-integrationsplan.html

"EU denkt über Quote für Flüchtlinge nach." *Dw.de*, 9th October 2014. Available at: http://dw.de/eu-denkt-über-quoten-für-flüchtlinge-nach/a-17985303

"Euro-Krisen-Theater." *Die Deutsche Bühne* 12, 2012. Available at: http://die-deut-sche-buehne.de/Magazin/Leseprobe/Euro%20-%20Krisen%20-%20Theater

European Institute for Comparative Cultural Research. http://ericarts.org/web/index.php

Fokus Migration. "Länderprofil Frankreich." 2012. Available at: http://focus-migration.hwwi.de/index.php?id=1231

"Gegen den Bau von Minaretten." Petition, 8th July 2008. Available at: http://admin.ch/ch/d/pore/va/20091129/det547.html

Gölpinar, Ö. "How to Address an Imbalance." 2011. Available at: http://europenowblog.org/blog/69

Grafe, M. "I Am Not a Postmigrant Artist!" Available at: http://azadehsharifi.wordpress.com/2013/04/22/i-am-not-a-postmigrant-Artist/

Graves, T. "Deepening Diversity." 13 June 2003. Available at: http://spiked-online.com/articles/00000006DDFF.htm

N.A. "Große Koalition nimmt ihren Dienst auf." *Frankfurter Allgemeine Zeitung*, 5th November 2012. Available at: http://faz.net/aktuell/politik/ausland/niederlande-grosse-koalition-nimmt-ihren-dienst-auf-11950527.html

Ha, K. N. "'People of color' als Diversity-Ansatz in der antirassistischen Selbstbenennungs- und Identitätspolitik." Heinrich Böll Stiftung, Berlin 2009. Available at: http://migration-boell.de/web/diversity/48_2299.asp

Heeg, G. "Fremdheitserfahrung ohne Exotisierung." *Nachtkritik*, 2013. Available at: http://nachtkritik.de/index.php?view=article&id=7645%3Ahildesheimer-thesen-xi-die-zukunft-liegt-im-transkulturellen-theater&option=com_content&Itemid=84

Heine, M. "Rassismusvorwurf gegen Dieter Hallervorden." *WeltNet*, 10th January 2012. Available at: http://welt.de/kultur/article13807516/Rassismusvorwurf-gegen-Dieter-Hallervorden.html

N.A. "Hinterhäuser und Langhoff als Intendanten-Duo." *Der Standard*, 4th May 2011. Available at: http://derstandard.at/1304428463416/Hinterhaeuser-und-Langhoff-als-Intendanten-Duo

"H.O.S.T. – Hospitality, Otherness, Society, Theatre." *Astragali Edizioni – Eufonia Multimediale*, Lecce. Available at: http://astragali.org/project!20

"Immigration: Italy launches Mare Nostrum, 400 more saved." *Ansamed. info*, 15th October 2013. Available at: http://ansamed.info/ansamed/en/news/sections/generalnews/2013/10/15/Immigration-Italy-launches-Mare-Nostrum-400-saved_9466386.html

Länderprofile Migration: Daten – Geschichte – Politik. "Italien." Bundeszentrale für politische Bildung. Available at: http://bpb.de/gesellschaft/migration/laenderprofile/145487/italien

"Marguerite Duras en Afrique – I: Moïse Touré et ses acteurs témoins." Available at: http://franceculture.fr/emission-sur-les-docks-ouagadougou-guantanamo-sanaa-14-marguerite-duras-en-afrique---i-moise-toure-e

"Muslime scheitern mit Klage gegen Minarett-Verbot." *Welt.Net*, 8th July 2011. Available at: http://welt.de/politik/ausland/article13476092/Mulime-scheitern-mit-Klage-gegen-Minarett-Verbot.html

Nazli, L. "Juggling Myth and Reality." *Hackney Citizen*, London 2011. Available at: http://hackneycitizen.co.uk/2013/01/15/leyla-nazli-arcola-mare-rider-interview/

"Netzgemeinde wettert gegen Hallervordens Schlossparktheater." *Nachtkritik*, 2012. Available at: http://nachtkritik.de/index.php?option=com_content&view=article&id=6457&catid=126

N.A. "Overkill der guten Absichten." *Der Spiegel*, p. 170, 1st February 1993. Available at: http://spiegel.de/spiegel/print/d-13687521.html).

Parusel, B. "Dossier Migration: Schweden." Bundeszentrale für politische Bildung, 2009. Available at: http://bpb.de/gesellschaft/migration/dossier-migration/57839/schweden

"Race: The Macpherson Report." *BBC.co.uk.*, 7th May 2001. Available at: http://news.bbc.co.uk/vote2001/hi/english/main_issues/sections/facts/newsid_1190000/1190971.stm

"Romanistan: Crossing Spaces in Europe." Event flyer, Berlin 2013. Available at: http://romanistan-berlin.de/pdf/ROMANISTAN_flyer_web_230313.pdf

"Roma-Theater Pralipe im Zirkuszelt." *Minderheiten.org*. Available at: http://minderheiten.org/pralipe.htm

Schooman, Y. "Islamophobie, antimuslimischer Rassismus oder Muslimfeindlichkeit? Kommentar zu der Begriffsdebatte der Deutschen Islam Konferenz." Heinrich Böll Stiftung, Berlin 2011. Available at: http://migration-boell.de/web/integration/47_2956.asp#1

"Selbstmordattentat in Stockholm." *Der Spiegel*. Available at: http://spiegel.de/thema/selbstmordattentat_stockholm_2010/

Sen, R. "Are Immigrants and Refugees People of Color?" *Colorlines*, 2007. Available at: http://colorlines.com/archives/2007/07/are_immigrants_and_refugees_people_of_color.html

"Sorben in Brandenburg." http://mwfk.brandenburg.de/cms/detail.php/bb1.c.250117.de

"Statement by Viviane Reding, Vice-President of the European Commission and EU Commissioner for Justice, Fundamental Rights and Citizenship, on the Roma situation in Europe." Brussels, 2010. Available at: http://europa.eu/rapid/press-release_MEMO-10-384_en.htm

"Theater und Diskriminierung." Heinrich Böll Stiftung, 2012. Available at: http://migration-boell.de/web/integration/48_3355.asp

"Theatertreffen der Minderheiten." *Theater der Zeit*, 2012. Available at: http://theaterderzeit.de/blog/meldungen/festival/theatertreffen_der_minderheiten_strich_festival_erstmals_für_2014_in_bautzen_geplant/

"Über den Künstler Lazare." http://franceculture.fr/personne-lazare.html

"Untersuchungsausschuss 'Terrorgruppe nationalsozialistischer Untergrund'." http://bundestag.de/bundestag/ausschuesse17/ua/2untersuchungsausschuss/

Verma, J. "The Arts and Cultural Diversity." London 2003. Available at: http://butterfliesandwheels.com/articleprint.php?num=29

Verma, J. "What the Migrant Saw." *Theguardian.com*, 10th January 2008. Available at: http://theguardian.com/stage/2008/jan/10/theatre1

"Vorschläge für die Umsetzung der UNESCO-Konvention über die Vielfalt kultureller Ausdrucksformen in der Schweiz." http://kulturellevielfalt.ch/visio.php?de,0

Zentrum für Audience Development. "Migranten als Publikum in öffentlichen deutschen Kulturinstitutionen: Der aktuelle Status quo aus Sicht der Angebotsseite." Available at: http://www.geisteswissenschaften.fu-berlin.de/v/zad/media/zad_migranten_als_publika_angebotsseite.pdf

Independent Children's Theatre in Europe since 1990

Developments – Potentials – Perspectives

Tine Koch

1. Introduction

1.1 Objectives

The prime objective of this study is to provide an overview of those developments, discourses and paradigms which have influenced independent children's theatre in Europe since 1990 and which are still influencing it today. Drama, comedy, dance and music theatre will be taken into account. In the course of the comparative analysis of exemplary structures, formats, and themes, the countries of Germany, Austria, Switzerland, Belgium, The Netherlands, Italy, France, England, Sweden, Poland, and Russia will be given particular consideration, because they provide notable, innovative impulses on the structural and/or aesthetic level or that their children's theatre scene is distinguished by specific characteristics which are also of interest in the pan-European context.[1]

At the same time, the European perspective on the preconditions for contemporary independent children's theatre with regard to cultural and educational policy, financial, structural, personnel, and intangible factors should help to optimise independent children's theatre wherever it is deemed necessary in order to better exploit its potential in the future.

The main part of the study is divided into two parts: the first part provides an overall view of significant commonalities and differences between independent children's theatre scenes throughout Europe and provides a panorama of current manifestations, tendencies and examples of good practices; the second

---

1 | See also the countries considered in this study in Chapt. I/5: "Limitations of the Study".

part is devoted to a critical reflection of the given circumstances and attempts to point out deficits and problem areas and to question practices which are in place simply as a matter of course.

In the final part of this paper, consequences and demands will be derived from these considerations, and, finally, perspectives and visions for the future will be formulated.

1.2 Methodological Procedure

The overview to be presented is based on a data collection process which was standardised for all the countries in question. Depending on their availability, the existing specialist literature, accessible archive material, and internet sources were exemplarily viewed and evaluated with regard to the specific aspects of the study. Furthermore, the research centred on the continuous exchange with national and international experts and those persons responsible in the children's theatre scene. This was achieved using questionnaires specifically designed for this study, which were sent by email, and also with qualitative, guided interviews. Some of these were done on the telephone, but most took place on-site during festivals and symposia. The insights into the landscapes of European children's theatre acquired in this way could be illustratively deepened through numerous informational and documenting materials which were kindly made available by individual artists and ensembles. Last but not least, the participatory observation of the author provided the basis for the analyses and reflections presented in this paper. All thoughts and theses which are not those of the author are clearly cited as such in the source references.

1.3 Source Material

Europe is severely deficient in its statistical coverage of children's theatre. General data and facts can only be obtained with great difficulty, if at all, and current and complete surveys of children's theatre in individual European countries are not available. According to all national experts questioned, no specific yearbooks, chronicles or professional journals on the subject of children's and young people's theatre are published for the countries relevant to this study, with the exception of Germany and France; statistics are not recorded. "Generally we experience a lack in documentation. This is a political question that our ministry and National Arts Council haven't been able to solve, strangely enough." Thus Niclas Malmcrona (ASSITEJ Sweden) describes the situation of Swedish children's theatre. He goes on to say, "and then the official statistics within this field [sic!] are sadly neglected by the governmental authorities".[2] Paul Harman (ASSITEJ Great Britain) confirmed:

'I repeat that theatre for young audiences in the UK is a free-market, unregulated activity. There is no authority which approves or monitors standards. There is therefore no official body which needs to collect any statistics. As far as Government is concerned, TYP [Theatre for Young People] does not exist.'

It can also be observed that the statistical data coverage in many countries cannot be evaluated for children's theatre, because no distinction is made between children's theatre and "adult theatre", and the available data thus refers to the theatre system in general without distinguishing between target groups. Moreover, artists and ensembles often do not seek a clear affiliation with one or the other group, since it is part of their common practice to regularly work for children and young people as well as for adults.

Even the data on children's theatre made available by the ASSITEJ groups in different countries is not comparable across borders – for one thing, because the members do not distinguish between independent and non-independent children's theatres, and for another, because the number of members in each country is not equal to the total number of artists and groups working for children and young people, especially because the importance of ASSITEJ, and with it the interest of the artists in a membership, varies greatly from country to country.

Finally, the comment made by Willemijn Kressenhof, staff member in the media library of the Theater Instituut Nederland, when asked about the books available on the subject of children's theatre, holds true. He described the situation exemplarily as follows:

'Although we have lots of information about theatre in general, theatre for young audiences is an underexposed area in our library. Most books on this subject [sic!] were written in the 1980's and 1990's.'

There are also significant deficiencies in the coverage and acknowledgement of theatre for children and young people by official sources and researchers. The only positive exceptions here are France and Germany:

The French ATEJ has published *Théâtre en France pour Jeunes Spectateurs* annually since 1963 (!), a comprehensive repertory directory, supplemented by

---

2 | All of the quotations of experts consulted for this study have, in general, been reproduced verbatim in the language chosen by the interviewee (English, French or German). In many cases it is not the native language of the expert.

the *Lettres d'information*[3] which appears regularly and frequently during the course of each year. The German yearbook of the ASSITEJ, *Grimm & Grips*, was known as a standard work of the professional theatre for children and young people even beyond the country's national borders. Besides general information on the ASSITEJ contributions from theory and practice, it contained a chronicle of the season as well as an annual overview bibliography on current publications, thus providing the basis for a comprehensive database on the offerings in the area of children's and young people's theatre in Germany. In 2013, after more than 25 years, *Grimm & Grips* was replaced by its successor, *IXYPSILONZETT*, which appears three times a year as a supplement to the journal *Theater der Zeit* and which, in turn, is supplemented by a yearbook published every January.

Furthermore, the Children's and Young People's Theatre Centre in Germany (Kinder- und Jugendtheaterzentrum in der Bundesrepublik Deutschland), which was founded in Frankfurt am Main in 1989, played an important role as an information and documentation centre. The centre has an extensive library which not only contains plays for children's and young people's theatre but also programmes, posters, photographs, secondary literature, magazines, videos, DVDs and other media documents on the subject which are available to the public. Since 1991, the centre has been home to the International ASSITEJ Archive, in which documentary materials from all the local ASSITEJ groups are collected so that different historical and contemporary theatre archives are compiled in one location.[4]

However, at the same time, Dr. Jürgen Kirschner, researcher in the Frankfurt archive, had to admit that the children's and young people's theatre centre, in the light of the deficits described earlier, did not have a "statistical telescope" for the European region and therefore could not provide complete data for a comprehensive comparative overview.

1.4 Working Definition of the Term "Independent Theatre Scene"

An analysis of all the structural models of children's theatre in Europe and their respective (legal) status within the individual national theatre systems, not to mention a comparison of these models Europe-wide, would be suitable

---

3 | In addition, two comprehensive empirical surveys were carried out in the 2006 and 2008 seasons which presented and compared – if only selectively – the production conditions of the artists in the area of children's and young people's theatre with the help of numerous statistical data (See also *Scène(s) d'enfance et d'ailleurs* (Association nationale de professionnels des arts de la scène en direction des jeunes publics)/Ministère de la culture et de la communication/DMDTS 2009 – For a complete bibliographical reference see also here and in the bibliography appended to this paper).

4 | See also Schneider 2001, p. 247.

as the subject of a research paper devoted solely to this topic and cannot be accomplished in this study. Therefore, for the relevant context of observation within the framework of this study, a purely pragmatic definition of the term "independent" children's theatre will be applied.

If, in the following text, reference is made to "independent" children's theatre in Europe, a professional organisational form is meant which is at home in the performing arts and which a) is not part of the public sector and b) cannot be described as a private theatre with a commercial intent. The author does not contest or ignore the fact that the group of theatre ensembles and artists included in this definition is just as big as it is heterogeneous.

1.5 Limitations of the Study: "Independent Children's Theatre in Europe"?

This study, as the title suggests, is dedicated to the 'independent children's theatre in Europe'. It must first be stressed that the selection of countries included in this study does *not* cover the entire European region and that this was not the author's intention. The fact that primarily the countries of Germany, Austria, Switzerland, Belgium, The Netherlands, Italy, France, England, Sweden, Poland and Russia are taken into account is a necessary prioritisation which came about in the course of the research and which is related to the respective exemplary structures and developments and/or model-like initiatives and impulses which characterise the particular children's theatre scenes. When reference is made in this paper to children's theatre in "Europe", those countries are always meant which are the focus of this study.

Furthermore, the study, as stated in the title, concentrates primarily on theatre for *children*. It concerns those forms of the performing arts which target an audience aged between 0 and 12 years and can be classified as "intended" children's theatre.[5] The two equally common terms, "theatre for children" and "children's theatre" are used synonymously unless otherwise specified. Theatre for youth aged 12 to 18, here referred to as "theatre for young people", is only included at times when a separation of the two sub-systems is not given or does not seem useful.[6] This prioritisation is mainly due to the fact that the boundary between theatre intended for young people and "adult theatre" has become

---

5 | A pragmatic definition of "intended" children's theatre, according to Hans-Heino Ewers, includes "all theatrical productions which – whether by the producers, whether by other instances in the society – are deemed to be a suitable theatrical offering for children" (Ewers 2012, p. 21).

6 | In this case the author refers generally to "theatre for children and young people" or "theatre for young audiences" which, in this context, is understood as an overall system which clearly distinguishes itself from the system of "adult theatre".

increasingly pervious in recent years, and the number of plays and productions which (in the meantime) can be included in the category of "theatre for young persons" has increased exponentially in this regard. Extensive research in this area would thus go beyond the scope of this investigation.

The same is true for the sector of puppet and/or figure and object theatre to which only marginal attention can be devoted in this study.

It was also decided that this study would concentrate on professional theatre. Theatre formats found in schools have been excluded, as well as productions by lay drama groups and children's recreational groups, as long as no professional artists are involved in such programmes. Moreover, this paper will systematically focus on independent theatre work and disregard all collaborations with state, municipal and regional theatres which lead to a temporary, more or less advanced "institutionalisation" of independent theatre professionals. Also these focal points are of a purely pragmatic nature and do not imply any valuation or forming of hierarchies.

Finally, despite the stated aim of pointing out developments and possible future perspectives, this study can be, in the end, no more than a snapshot. As was stressed at "European Audiences: 2020 and beyond", a conference organised by the European Commission which took place in October 2012 in Brussels and was attended by more than 800 experts from the cultural sector, the arts sector is undergoing a particularly rapid change in the united Europe at this time:

'[E]verything and everyone is in flux. No organisation can afford to sit still. Change is likely to be a permanent reality that the sector needs to contend with and embrace, to see and benefit from the opportunities that the world today offers.'[7]

This study is thus subject to the reality of this constant change and the resulting short "shelf life" of the facts which it presents.

1.6 Excursus: Poland and Russia – "No Practice"

The two Eastern European countries, Poland and Russia, which are also included in this study, constitute special cases. Indeed, both countries have a children's and young people's theatre landscape which is rich in tradition and structurally diverse – but neither country has an *independent* children's theatre scene.

Lucyna Kozien, artistic director of the Teatr Lalek Banialuka and publisher of the *Teatr Lalek* magazine, describes the situation in Poland as follows:

---

7 | European Commission 2012, p. 12.

'The theatre for children and young people in Poland is represented mainly by 24 institutional, fully professional puppet theatre companies. [...] Occasionally, their activities are complemented by 62 dramatic theatres, which sometimes include in their repertoire plays for children and young people. They generally do it once a year and their immediate motivation is improving attendance and revenue from [sic!] ticket sales. In what they offer the young audience, although often attractive and produced with a staging flourish, one cannot find titles other than the school obligatory reading list or classics of children's literature.'[8]

In other words, "children's theatre" within the Polish theatre system is still virtually synonymous with "institutional municipal puppet theatre":

'After 1989 the nature of children's theatre in Poland changed as did the social, political and economic situation. The result of the transformation meant the end of supporting national puppet theatres from the state budget. The theatres became the responsibility of local governments. [...] Theatre directors, for the first time in the history of the Polish theatre for children and young people had to start thinking about the market, economic profitability. Theatres had to account not only for the artistic results of their activity, but also for economic indicators, which were often more important. In most cities local governments provide funding for theatres only to cover the costs of the so-called 'base', that is the buildings and companies. [...] Such a change in the way theatres operate, since earlier they had funds for complete maintenance, company and new productions, was revolutionary in Polish conditions.'[9]

A professional independent scene could virtually not develop under these circumstances, even after 1989:[10]

'Hundreds of new theatre companies hoping to thrive in the new reality and subjected to the laws of the market and the dictates of the economy and commerce were forced to discover unfavourable conditions for development. Supported at the onset with subsidies provided by the state and self-government budgets, or by sponsors, and then left to their own devices they ultimately fell silent.'[11]

The greatest structural problem results from the fact that public funding is almost always used to support the institutional municipal theatres, and

---

8 | Excerpt from "The Report on the State of Children and Young People's Theatre in Poland" (2004) – Original manuscript kindly provided by Lucyna Kozien.
9 | See note 9.
10 | The so-called "Theatre for Early Years" is an exception and will be explained in detail later.
11 | Kozien 2011, p. 13.

since they no longer receive long-term overall funding, they also find it necessary to continuously acquisition subsidies in (unequal) competition with any independent theatres, so that there are scarcely any funds left for the independent scene.[12]

In this respect, only the following sobering conclusion can be drawn by theatre professionals with regard to Poland:

'In more than twenty years that have passed since the systemic transformation, Poland [sic!] has been unable to construct solid foundations for the functioning of independent theatres and lacks structural, legal and economic solutions. [...] Poland still has no place for truly independent and non-institutional theatre companies. Apparently, history has made a full circle: we are returning to a pre-1989 state when institutional companies delineated the rhythm of theatrical life.'[13]

In Russia, the situation is hardly different. According to Pavel Rudnev (Moscow Art Theatre), there are many different theatres which very successfully target young audiences – approximately 50 drama theatres and between 80 and 100 puppet theatres; however, all of them are state-controlled and completely institutionalised:

'In Russia till now the Stalin system of state repertoire companies is active. Private companies (especially when they are non-profit and of good quality) are a very rare phenomenon. And also from Stalin time we have got a tradition: If a town has more than 300,000 citizens, the town must have a theatre for young spectators, and if more than 500,000 citizens – a puppet theatre. They are responsible for young audiences. And they are permanent with long-term artists. [...] Each state company must have its own (but state) venue. This is standard. Sure, theatres for young spectators and puppet companies have got less venue than central drama theatre. As usual 400-500 seats venue plus chamber venue with 50-120 seats.'

An independent children's and young people's theatre scene does, therefore, not exist – and, according to Pavel Rudnev, is not desired: 'As you understood, we have got a lot of special theatre for youth (practically in every town). So if some independent theatre for children appears, it will usually be a potboiler.' Much more desirable would be a 'new directing generation that [sic!] is free of Soviet dogmata and came to theatre for children without compulsion'.

The Polish theatre makers, on the other hand, explicitly expressed the desire to draw on the Western European standard of independent children's

---

12 | See Bartnikowski 2011, p. 58.
13 | Kozien 2011, p. 13.

theatre with regard to the structures, aesthetics and dramaturgies – and named the following as the most significant positive trends in their national scene:

- 'openness of programmers/artists/researchers that travel abroad, take part in seminars/festivals/conferences/workshops and promote good quality of children's theatre in Poland' (Alicja Morawska-Rubczak, ASSITEJ Poland);
- 'much wider cooperation with foreign theatre centres – mainly from Germany';
- 'free exchange of ideas and experiences (mainly from Europe, but also by international activity of ASSITEJ) after 1989 when the isolation of our country was over' (Zbigniew Rudzinski, Children's Arts Centre, Poznan).'

In light of the particular situation of the theatre in Poland and Russia, both of these Eastern European countries have been largely excluded from the following observations and reflections. Unless specifically indicated, all of the statements made here regarding commonalities and differences in the European children's theatre landscape, involving developments, problem fields and perspectives, do not refer to the Polish and Russian situations, since these differ too greatly to be included in a study whose focus is the *independent* theatre scene.

2. Manifestations, Discourses, Developments

2.1 Structural Emancipation of (Independent) Children's Theatre

Following the enactment of the United Nations Convention on the Rights of the Child on 20 November 1989, a framework of reference was created on a European level which defined by contract the rights of children to art and culture and proclaimed their participation in cultural and artistic life as an aim worthy of public support. This was indeed a milestone in the history of children's theatre in Europe.

Article 31 of the UN Convention on the Rights of the Child states the following:

'(1) The contracting states recognise the right of the child to rest and leisure, to play and active recreation appropriate to its age as well as to free participation in cultural and artistic life.
(2) The contracting states respect and support the right of the child to full participation in cultural and artistic life, and promote the provision of suitable and equal opportunities for cultural and artistic activities as well as for active recuperation and recreation.'[14]

---

14 | See also http://www.unicef.de/fileadmin/content_media/mediathek/D_0006_Kinderkonvention.pdf

The fact that 193 contracting states have acceded to this convention to date – more than to any other UN convention – underlines how great the prevailing consensus is in this respect, and clearly demonstrates that the interests of children, at least conceptually, should be and have been an integral part of the cultural sector for over 20 years.

A specific look at performing arts for a young audience shows that since the 1990s the scene has not only been continuously developing in artistic terms but has also grown and become increasingly differentiated, and thus has been able to emancipate itself structurally from antiquated traditions! What Ilona Sauer says exemplarily about the current status quo of theatre for children and young people in Germany can be applied to all European theatre landscapes:

'The theatre for children and young people is accepted as an important player in the German theatre landscape. It is no longer seated at a "side table" but is situated right in the middle of things; it has bid farewell to its niche existence and perhaps even to its existence in the "comfort zone" as well [...].'[15]

2.1.1 High Degree of Permeability between the Systems

In general, it can be observed that the boundaries between the system of "adult" theatre and theatre for children and young people, which were clearly delineated at first, are today becoming more blurred and permeable.[16] In particular, there is a lively exchange between both systems in the independent scene; a large number of the independent artists work flexibly for the theatre for children and young people and the theatre for adults, especially in project-specific "production ensembles".[17] In many European countries, independent groups often produce for a young audience, at least in part. Thus, Eline Kleingeld (Vereniging van Schouwburg- en Concertgebouwdirecties) confirmed that in The Netherlands a percentage of 10-15% of the entire programme of independent groups is aimed at children and young people; in Sweden, it is even 70-80% of the productions of publicly funded groups, says Lotta Brilioth Biörnstad (Arts Council Sweden). For Flanders, it could be paradigmatically established that the number of independent artists who move between the two areas rose to at least 41% between 1993 and 2005:[18]

---

15 | Sauer 2013, p. 36.
16 | Exceptions in this context are Great Britain and Austria, where a specialisation of artists, and thus to a large extent a separation of the two systems, is the norm.
17 | See also the comments in Chapt. 3.1.5.
18 | See Anthonissen 2011, p. 2.

'Artistically speaking, adult and youth theatre have more or less kept pace with one another, partly due to the intense movement back and forth between them. For example, developments taking place in one place also occur elsewhere and vice versa.'[19]

The spanning of this gap, which on the whole means an upgrade of (as well as an equal status for) children's and young people's theatre, is facilitated by increasing interest on the part of leading directors and actors from adult theatre in productions for young audiences. This is indicated by Zbigniew Rudzinski's (Children's Arts Centre, Poznan) comment on the Polish scene:

'More and more theatre directors with a very high position in theatres for adults prepare performances for children. [This entails] the presence of performances for children, playwrights, readings of plays during festivals known till now as festivals for adults like Warsaw Theatre Meetings, Festival of First Nights in Bydgoszcz, Festival of Polish Contemporary Plays RAPORT in Gdynia.'

The increasing amount of public and media attention paid to children's and young people's theatre in this way has a positive effect on its position in the overall architecture of the theatre culture and contributes to its structural emancipation.

2.1.2 Increasing the Recipient Group: Adults as Part of the Primary Target Audience

'In contrast to earlier decades in which a clear delimitation between childhood, youth, and adulthood was possible, the boundaries are now blurred'; 'the spaces reserved for each generation [...] are no longer strictly separated but interwoven, the boundaries fluid'.[20] What Carsten Gansel states with regard to the current relationship between generations in (Western) European societies in general is true for children's theatre – perhaps even more so: At least since the 1980s, there has been a tendency within European children's theatre landscapes to appeal to an adult audience on a hitherto unprecedented scale and to see this group as an essential part of the primary target audience. This attempt by the "special theatre" to dissolve its specificity is still continuing today.[21]

This is evident in a purely formal sense in the various renaming processes which have taken place:[22] The "children's theatre"/*Kindertheater/théâtre jeune public* has become the "theatre for all ages"/*Theater für alle/théâtre tout public*,

---

19 | Ibid., p. 7f.
20 | Gansel 2005, p. 364 and p. 365.
21 | See also concerning "blurred boundaries" and the resulting dominance of theatre for young people Hentschel 1996, pp. 31-47 and Hartung 2001, p.120ff.
22 | See also Hentschel 1996, p. 34.

the *Familientheater* or the "theatre for young audiences"/*Theater für ein junges Publikum*. On the other hand, especially with regard to the independent scene – and here, in particular, with regard to performance and installation formats – it can be increasingly observed that productions (and their artists) deliberately refuse to commit themselves to a specific target audience.

Thus, it has almost become a matter of course that at the prestigious independent theatre festivals in Germany, "Impulse" and "Favoriten", besides "adult" theatre, children's theatre productions are regularly included; moreover, the Helios Theater in Hamm has, indeed, already been a prizewinner several times. In addition, children's theatre productions are now increasingly being included in the evening programmes, and, as the initiative *Schönen Abend!* of the Junges Ensemble Stuttgart (JES) proves, even full evening programmes with productions for children and young people are being introduced. This principle, which already has a tradition in countries such as France and which extends back to the 1960s, is of course not an attempt to exclude children from children's theatre, but rather to specifically *include* parents and other adults and thus to appeal across generations, as Maurice Yendt (ASSITEJ France) stresses: 'Les spectacles présentés en soirée ne sont pas exclusivement pour adultes, ils réunissent un public inter-générationnel d'enfants et d'adultes.'

All of this blurring of distinctions may, if nothing else, have a commercial background – for many independent theatre professionals who work for children and young people, however, it is also a matter of upgrading their own art form, says Myrtó Dimitriadou (Toïhaus Theater, Salzburg): 'The idea behind it probably has to do with changing the image of theatre for children – not 'childish' and with an exaggerated focus on what is considered appropriate for children, but little works of art for everyone.'

2.1.3 Extending the Producer Group: Children also on the Stage

'Every artist who receives public funds should be obliged to work with young people' – with this statement Hortensia Völckers, artistic director of the German Cultural Foundation (Kulturstiftung des Bundes),[23] took an unequivocal stand on another fundamental development which has taken place in the European children's theatre landscape in recent years: namely the tendency to see children not only as members of the audience but as partners in the artistic production, to involve them in the production process, and to allow them to perform on stage as "experts on everyday life". More and more often, "children's theatre" in this sense also means "theatre *with* children".

The principle of what is so frequently designated "participation" is not a phenomenon of the nineties per se, but goes back to the impulses provided by the independent scene in the seventies. The "conquest of the theatre landscape

---

23 | Odenthal 2005, p. 108.

by the target group",²⁴ as described by Wolfgang Schneider, Chairman of ASSITEJ Germany and Honorary President of ASSITEJ International, is, however, really something new,²⁵ and manifests itself paradigmatically in the fact that at the renowned *Augenblickmal! Festival* in Berlin in 2013, *9 Leben* by the Junges Ensemble Stuttgart (JES) under the choreographic direction of Iwes Thuwis-De-Leeuw, a production *with* young people was selected by the jury to be included in the regular festival programme and was presented on equal terms with professional productions *for* a young audience.

The motivation and objectives for such theatre projects with children vary from project to project; the spectrum of methodological, content-related and aesthetic forms is broad. The reasons given by the European network for young music theatre, RESEO, (European Network for Opera and Dance Education), for the trend towards participative projects for music theatre with children can also be applied to the field of performing arts in general. According to RESEO, apart from the increasing call for programmes for cultural education from those responsible for cultural and education policies, the following arguments can be put forward from an artistic point of view:

'The presence of children on stage allows young audiences to identify with the young performers;
Young performers provide energy to the project, which has a dynamic effect on the attitude of the spectator;
In this way, children on stage are revalorised, especially when they are involved in professional productions working with professional adults;
Children on stage allow for a more "interactive" exchange between the spectators and the actors (this reinforces the link between the work and the audience);
Young audiences may feel the desire to start learning an artistic discipline themselves. These types of performances show that artistic practice is accessible to everyone;
[...] Audiences are more attentive and more interested;
It appeals to a wider audience (families also attend, widening the audience that attends Opera).'²⁶

Aside from these arguments, there is no denying that there is a purely pragmatic – namely commercial – self-interest on the part of the independent theatre in offering more participation projects. In times in which, according

---

24 | Quoted from an editorial on *IXYPSILONZETT, Jahrbuch 2013*, p. 1.
25 | The trend to make the artistic work *with* children more and more a conceptual component of theatre programmes, projects and proclaimed profiles of many independent groups can no doubt be seen in the light of the general debates on cultural education. See also detailed explanation in Chapt. II/A.1.
26 | RESEO 2009, p. 35f.

to the "EU culture barometer", attending the theatre ranks seventh on a list of possible cultural activities – thus *after* visits to cinemas, libraries, historical monuments, sports events, museums, galleries and concerts – and, of those persons surveyed, the artistic participation in theatre-acting ranks last (!) in the list of arts queried in the survey,[27] it seems more than appropriate to work towards specifically training the "audience of tomorrow". In order to face increasing competition with other art forms and media and acknowledge the frequently noted "ageing of the audience",[28] it is necessary to involve members of the upcoming generation in the artistic work and to allow them to experience the performing arts in a manner which is personally significant to them.[29]

A danger of such participative formats which are closely linked to "audience development" may be detected in the fact that this has a tendency to fulfil, as Carmen Mörsch formulates it, a purely *affirmative* or *reproductive* function: The participation by children in the production processes of artistic work primarily serves to impart what the institutions of high culture produce to an accordingly initiated and already interested audience "as smoothly as possible", or to win over the next – paying – audience generation.[30]

This situation applies to the independent children's theatre scene, albeit under different circumstances: Since independent theatre professionals are seldom interested in the preservation of an institution, of an establishment, a structure per se, affirmative and reproductive functions of participation projects are almost automatically less important. Instead, other functions which Mörsch refers to as *critical-deconstructive* and *transformative* tend to gain in importance: Mörsch recognises a critical-deconstructive function of cultural representation and promotion when the "existing implicitness of high culture and its institutions is questioned, disclosed and adapted" and learners are equipped with knowledge "which makes it possible for them to form their own opinion and to become aware of their own status and circumstances". If one's own preoccupation with art and culture goes beyond such critical scrutiny in that the cultural representation and promotion tries to "influence that which it represents and promotes and, for example, to change it in terms of more

---

27 | According to the survey, only 3.8% of those questioned in the EU population are active in theatre in their free time (See *THE EUROPEAN OPINION RESEARCH GROUP 2002*, no page). However, only persons aged 15 and older were included in the survey.

28 | Schneider 2007, p. 83.

29 | Especially opera houses see themselves, in this context, in acute financial peril: As RESEO ascertained for the music and dance theatre sector by means of an empirical study, at least 81% of the pedagogy departments of opera houses in Europe currently mount stage productions in which children and young people are (also) active (See RESEO 2009, p. 35).

30 | Mörsch 2011, p. 11.

justice, more critical thinking and less social distinction", Mörsch then refers to a transformative process which can bring about social and institutional change.[31]

Against this backdrop, Mörsch develops a set of objectives and functions for the artistic practice *with* children, which may sound like a song of praise but which, at its core, when aptly summarised could and should have the effect that an encounter with the arts would have in the ideal case:

'Understood in this way, it serves the promotion of social emancipation and co-determination and thus the permanent (self-)analysis and transformation of art, of culture and its institutions. It encourages rebelliousness. It stresses the potential of diverse experiences and sets the importance of failure, of searching, of open processes and aggressive uselessness as a disturbing factor against an efficiency-oriented thinking. Instead of offering individuals the will to permanent self-optimisation as the best survival option, it provides space in which – in addition to fun, pleasure, the desire to create and produce, training of perception, communication of knowledge – problems can be identified, named and dealt with. Space in which disputes can take place. Space in which such naturally positive things like love of art or the will to work can be questioned, and a discussion can arise about what the good life is for whom. Space in which it is less about life-long than about life-changing learning. Space in which no one is discriminated because of age, origin, appearance, physical disposition or sexual orientation and in which instead one acts on behalf of others.'[32]

The fact that this potential is not or cannot often be exploited to the maximum and that this is frequently because the initiators of these projects and programmes pursue other, more production-oriented interests, is a different matter.

2.1.4 Increasing International Networking

As is the case with the independent scene in general, independent children's theatre is becoming more and more internationally networked. The factors which have contributed to and promoted this networking are manifold, but overall they are comparable to those which characterize independent theatre in Europe.

Besides the increasing number of international festivals, and the lively import and export of theatre texts which had already led to the creation of a European repertoire of modern plays for children's theatre at the beginning of the nineties, three lines of development are particularly relevant.

---

31 | Ibid., p. 11.
32 | Ibid., p. 19.

First, not only an increase in the number of networks can be observed, but also their growing expansion and use. ASSITEJ, the global umbrella organisation for independent children's and young people's theatre, should be mentioned here to begin with. ASSITEJ held its 17th World Congress in 2011, on which occasion over 1500 delegates, artists and organisers from more than 50 countries met. ASSITEJ currently has members in 85 national centres on all continents and will celebrate its fiftieth anniversary in 2015. The charter of this UNESCO organisation (which was founded in 1965) was signed by the 42 countries then present and reads as follows:

'Considering the role theatre can play in the education of younger generations, an autonomous international organisation has been formed which bears the name of the International Association of Theatre for Children and Young People (ASSITEJ International). [...] Theatre for young people respects its young audiences by presenting their hopes, dreams and fears; it develops and deepens experience, intelligence, emotion and imagination; it inspires ethical choices; it helps awareness of social relations; it encourages self-esteem, tolerance confidence and opinions. Above all, it helps young people to find their place and voice in society. [...] [ASSITEJ International] holds with the belief of the Report of the World Commission on Culture and Development, "Our Creative Diversity", that young people must be given a cultural identity and made visible everywhere in society.'[33]

It speaks for the quality of this charter that its premises and goals have not lost any of their timeliness and urgency to this day.

Secondly, the international and, above all, the European-wide networking of independent children's theatre is promoted by the growing number of guest performances from abroad, which has been noticeable for some years. In the case of France, there are specific figures which confirm this trend exemplarily:

'La création étrangère est de mieux en mieux accueillie en France. Au début des années 2000, elle représentait 2% des programmations jeune public. Au cours des trois dernières saisons (de 2007-2008 à 2009-2010), près de 25% des programmations adressées au jeune public en France présentent des spectacles étrangers.'[34]

France can be said to hold a forerunner position when it comes to children's and young people's theatre in relation to the theatre system in general:

'Le rapprochement avec les chiffres d'ensemble met en lumière une manifeste spécificité de ce secteur en matière d'accueil de spectacle étranger. Entre 2007 et 2010, 25%

---

33 | See http://www.assitej.at/ueber/assitej-international/
34 | ONDA 2011, p. 36.

des programmations adressées au jeune public en France présentent des spectacles étrangers, alors que sur la même période, environ 12% des programmations du réseau labellisé présentent des spectacles étrangers.'[35]

Although respective data from other European countries is not available, it can be noted that independent children's theatre is definitely on a par with "adult theatre" with regard to networking through international guest performances.

Finally, in parallel to this development, the interest of professionals from the independent theatre scene in participating in transnational co-productions and collaborations as well as in residence and exchange programmes is apparently increasing steadily. This form of networking is naturally practiced more frequently between those countries in which similar structures of children's theatre exist.

2.1.5 Increasing Professionalism: Targeted Promotion of Young Talent

In the past decades, independent children's theatre in Europe has emancipated and established itself. All the country experts surveyed have confirmed this, since most artists who are active in this field today have completed artistic training and learned their craft under professional guidance. The number of autodidacts, lateral entrants and amateurs has decreased considerably.

In addition, due to the lack of specific education and training opportunities at state universities and other educational institutions, a certain 'immanent system' to promote young talent has developed within the scene which is particularly aimed at preparing participants for the requirements of producing for children and at creating spheres for experimenting and experiencing in which young artists can undertake their own first projects for this audience.

A prime example in this context is the training laboratory Het Lab in the Dutch city of Utrecht, which is highly regarded in Europe and which for years has operated as a talent factory where young professionals are promoted for independent children's and young people's theatre. "There is no shortage of talented young theatre makers in The Netherlands who can and will work for young audiences. If there is any problem, it is with the continuation of these artists into the world of the professional theatre",[36] says one of the fundamental premises of the Het Lab. An essential characteristic of the 'training' was the long-term and individual support given to the young artists by experienced mentors; 'long-term custom-made partnerships whose ultimate goal was for the artists to obtain a place in professional theatre, either with an existing company or independently':

---

35 | Ibid., p. 37.
36 | Meyer 2012, p. 8.

'During these long-term collaborations over several years we not only supported the artists artistically, but we also focused on cultural entrepreneurship. Developing a long-term view, acquiring an understanding of the business side and the production aspects of the theatre, and audience development were among the subjects we tackled.'[37]

Another aspect of this specific formula for success was the implementation of a target group orientation for children's theatre during the rehearsal and play development process:

'One very important thing Het Lab would focus on, therefore, was simply getting to know the young audience. By just talking to them, working with them, including them in the artistic process at regular intervals. Each artist would have his or her own trajectory with the young target audience: from talks in a classroom to giving workshops centred on the subject of the performance and to discussing rehearsals and tryouts. The children proved inspiring dramaturges. Their concrete experiences and responses would often lead the making of certain decisions. In order to be able to offer this type of research, Het Lab established strong connections with schools and teachers who were interested in working with us.'[38]

Moreover, the continuous expansion of its own scope of training and experimenting in the direction of dance theatre is exemplary and exceptional:

'Although Het Lab Utrecht mainly supported stage directors and playwrights during its earlier years, we have always focused on dance as well [...]. From 2009 onwards the scope for dance increased permanently. The ambition is to give dance for young audiences a similar set of impulses as we have done for theatre.[39]
From 2009 to 2012, [Het Lab] supported over ten productions that have found their way to stages both nationally and internationally. In addition, the house took the lead in initiating the Fresh Tracks Europe network.'[40]

The establishment of its own dance department resulted in an increasing internationalisation of the artistic staff almost automatically;[41] the intercultural aspect of producing together for a young audience became the centre of attention and provided new impulses.

---

37 | Meyer 2012, p. 7.
38 | van den Broek 2013, p. 30.
39 | Meyer 2012, p. 7.
40 | van den Broek 2013, p. 31.
41 | See Meyer 2012, p. 8. See also the following supplementary observation: "We have seen an explosive increase in international, mainly European, attention for our work from the very moment we included dance permanently" (ibid., p. 8).

The central importance of such a multidisciplinary and multicultural training centre as a source of invigoration for the scene was undisputed for years:

'For more than ten years, the production houses have played a crucial role within the Dutch theatre landscape. Within theatre for young audiences, Het Lab Utrecht and Bonte Hond in Almere have carefully devoted their energy to bridging the gap between art schools and professional art practice. Het Lab has focused on text-based theatre and performance/dance; Bonte Hond on site-specific theatre and physically/visually based theatre. A relatively large number of recent graduates have been given an opportunity to work on small-scale projects and experiments with one of the two production houses.'[42]

In 2013, Het Lab was facing closure due to across-the-board, drastic cuts in the cultural sector in The Netherlands.[43] The dramatic consequences this will have for independent children's and young people's theatre can only be supposed at this point in time.

Apart from such exceptional examples, the independent scene is in many places specialised in recruiting and providing continuous training for young artists from its own ranks. A common model in the German independent scene is, in this context, the attempt to support members from participative theatre projects *with* young people or from the theatres' own youth clubs on their way towards becoming professionals by providing rehearsal rooms and technical resources like costumes, stage sets and lighting as well as dramaturgical support.

An example of good practice is the Theater Marabu in Bonn under the artistic direction of Claus Overcamp and Tina Jücker, because the Marabus have launched exemplary initiatives to promote young artistic talent on several levels at the same time. For one, besides the actual Theater Marabu, there is the Junges Ensemble Marabu (Young Ensemble Marabu), which regularly puts on theatre performances *with* young people, whereby the productions of the Young Ensemble have the same importance and thus are given the same amount of rehearsal room time as the professional productions, which do not have a participative orientation. In addition, the so-called experimental field of directing was created especially for members of the Young Ensemble and offers interested young people the chance to work on their own projects under the guidance of mentors from the Marabu team over a period of four to six weeks, a time period in which rooms and equipment are provided and at the end of which the final product can be presented to an audience. Furthermore, the Theater Marabu systematically supports young artists in another format: "Young Directors" is aimed at young graduates of theatre schools who are given

---

42 | Blik 2012, p. 3.
43 | van den Broek 2013, p. 29.

the opportunity to put together their own artistic team with whom they can work out a production under professional conditions. The production is then included in the programme of the Theater Marabu for at least one season.

Apart from such in-house talent promotion programmes of individual independent groups, there is occasional support funding, especially in the form of grants to young artists which are intended as a kind of 'start-up help'. Thus, it is possible for independent young artists in the state of North Rhine-Westphalia to receive a lump sum scholarship of five thousand euros for a period of four months in order to work and do research in connection with an established children's and young people's theatre. Such support programmes do not by any means indicate the presence of any type of structure in this respect, and are not the rule but rather a positive and regionally limited exception.

Figure 1: 'Leonce und Lena', Theater Marabu – Junges Ensemble, Bonn, 2012. Photograph: Ursula Kaufmann

2.1.6 Quintessence

All in all, it can be said that, in the course of the decades since 1990, independent children's theatre in Europe has structurally outgrown its 'baby shoes' and has more and more established itself as an art form with a status equivalent to that of "adult" theatre.

If one takes a closer look at the developments, paradigm changes and newly generated discourses which have influenced the landscapes of children's theatre most conspicuously and most sustainably in the past 20 years, essentially three phenomena or tendencies become evident:

- the newly formulated definition of the function of children's theatre as mirrored in the worldwide debates on cultural education

- the involvement of the target group of the youngest theatregoers (0-3 years) and the establishment of a "theatre for early years"
- the increasing trend to productions which transcend genres and disciplines and with it the dissolution of boundaries between sectors and systems

The following is a more detailed analysis of these three main lines of development within independent children's theatre in Europe since 1990.

2.2 Independent Children's Theatre in Europe is Today ... Cultural Education!

"To be a performing artist in Britain in the next century, you have to be an educator, too". Thus was the prophesy made by Sir Simon Rattle in 1999 during a debate on cultural and educational policy in London,[44] and his prediction turned out to be quite right. Not only in Great Britain but in all of Europe (and beyond), a trend was to emerge which would make "art" and "education" inseparable in people's minds, and which would force a decisive paradigm shift in the arts as well. The key phrase, without which any debate on cultural and educational policy would be unthinkable, is "arts education".[45]

In 1999, the thirtieth General Assembly of UNESCO passed a resolution to promote arts education and creativity in schools. In the same year, the European Commission initiated a new programme named *Connect* to mediate between culture and education and to establish networking between the different spheres,[46] and consolidated the directorates for education and culture. However, only two years later, the question regarding the necessity of arts education became the focus of public attention. "It is even possible to name the exact date when the development acquired a new dynamic", says Max Fuchs about the situation in Germany. "It was 4 December 2001".[47] The keyword here: PISA.

On 4 December 2001, Edelgard Bulmahn, then the German Minister of Education, presented the results of the first PISA study. Since that reform programme of educational policies, which was the most successful of all time internationally, the promotion of arts education has been considered in political

---

44 | Quoted from *All Our Futures: Creativity, Culture and Education*. London 1999, p. 182.
45 | On an international level, in this context, the term "arts education" is used almost everywhere; sporadically one can find the English translation of the German term, "kulturelle Bildung" as "cultural education". (Fuchs 2008, p. 111f.).
46 | See *Pre-Conference Reader on the European conference, "Promoting Cultural Education in Europe: A Contribution to Participation, Innovation and Quality"*, p. 42.
47 | Fuchs 2010, p. 93.

discourse to be one of the most important cross-sectional tasks,[48] as the following statement by the group of experts on the Council of Ministers of Culture of the European Union indicates:

'The reinforcement of synergies between education and culture is therefore considered as a key goal both at national and international [sic!] levels, opening the way for the mainstreaming of artistic and cultural education throughout Europe.'[49]

Not least, the extremely high importance attached to arts education is reflected in the fact that the new millennium has already brought forth two world conferences on arts education initiated by UNESCO (World Conference on Arts Education) in 2006 and 2010, at which about 1000 experts from 100 countries met for several days to discuss questions regarding arts education.[50]

Given this central paradigm shift in the form of an "educational turn" on the macro level of global cultural and educational policies, it is not surprising that, especially in the course of this development, the performing arts for young audiences are now regarded in the context of cultural educational opportunities and examined for their potential in connection with the overriding common goal of promoting arts education: The expectations which the public has set in the potential impact of children's theatre – and this includes theatre *with* children as well as theatre *for* children – could hardly be higher:[51]

---

48 | See also the text by Michael Wimmer at www.bpb.de/gesellschaft/kultur/kulturelle-bildung/60202/europa, which provides an overview of this process and of the fundamentals of educational and cultural policies for the promotional activities of the EU in the area of education. See also regarding the legal framework conditions of arts education on national and international levels (incl. arts education in early childhood) Deutscher Kulturrat 2005 and 2009.
49 | Lauret/Marie 2010, p. 4.
50 | http://www.bpb.de/gesellschaft/kultur/kulturelle-bildung/60187/unesco
51 | See for example the findings on the positive effects of arts education, especially of "educational drama and theatre", which the EU-sponsored project of the DICE Consortium ("Drama Improves Lisbon Key Competences in Education") presented, as presumably the most comprehensive empirical study of this kind to date, according to research in 12 countries on projects in which ca. 4,500 young people participated: "[Young people] are assessed more highly by their teachers in all aspects; feel more confident in reading and understanding tasks; feel more confident to communicate; [...] are better at problem solving; are better at coping with stress; are more tolerant towards both minorities and foreigners; are more active citizens; show more interest in voting at any level; show more interest in participating in public issues; are more empathetic: they have concerns for others; are more able to change perspectives; are more innovative and entrepreneurial; show more dedication towards their future and have more plans;

'With the advent of the "knowledge society", a paradigm change has taken place with regard to theatre and education which has rehabilitated the concept of education and comprehends the theatre in its elemental function in arts education and thus in its function for a socially intact community, thus as an indispensable socialisation factor.'[52]

Accordingly, independent children's theatre in Europe has repositioned itself in the overall social structure; some redefinition was necessary, particularly regarding its function. The consequences are diverse: Whether the expectations resulting from cultural and educational policies were the cause or not, the number of cultural and educational offerings and "educational programmes", declared as such, is increasing rapidly and exponentially;[53] the forms of collaboration between independent artists and schools and other educational institutions are becoming more and more varied; and, above all, theatre *with* children has established itself as an independent area of work for independent artists as never before.

2.2.1 An Attempt at a Definition: Arts Education – Common Denominators in the Relevant Discourses

Despite (or perhaps because of) the worldwide debates about and growing attention paid to arts education by scientific research, no common definition exists on a national level, and even less so on a European one.[54] However, in the relevant discourses, some aspects can be identified as common denominators on which there is broad agreement.[55]

It is widely agreed that educational processes in the arts (and in general) can take place in both formal as well as informal contexts, and are thus not bound to the school as a place of learning.[56]

---

are much more willing to participate in any genre of arts and culture [...]; are more likely to be a central character in class; have a better sense of humour; feel better at home". (DICE 2010, p. 6f.). In conclusion, the consortium stated: "DICE claims that educational drama and theatre supports the targets of the most relevant EU level documents", among them "Europe 2020" and the "Lisbon Key Competences" (See http://publish.ucc.ie/scenario/2011/01/kueppers/12/en).

52 | Editorial on dramaturgy: *Zeitschrift der Dramaturgischen Gesellschaft* 1/2007, p. 1. Thus, it was significant that the motto of the annual conference of the dg 2007 in Heidelberg was "What is the new role of theatre in the knowledge society?".

53 | In Germany, for example, the respective percentage has increased fourfold in the past five years (See Keuchel 2010b, p. 238).

54 | See EDUCULT 2011, p. 37.

55 | See Bamford 2009, p. 48f.

56 | Lauret/Marie 2010, p. 24.

Furthermore, it is clear that arts education, understood as a process and the result of encounters and experiences with art, not only includes its reception but also the initiation of one's own artistic practice:

'Arts Education is not only aiming at ways of an enjoyable or reflected reception, it also fosters a productive and practical approach – guided as well as independent – in all artistic fields of perception, expression, composition, presentation and communication.'[57]

The main goal of arts education is to enable young people to "participate in the cultural life of a society", which, in turn, should encourage "a differentiated contact with art and culture and stimulate creative aesthetic action".[58] Moreover, with respect to the many possible goals of arts education, it is important to distinguish between "extrinsic" (non-artistic) and "intrinsic" (artistic and art-specific) aims.[59]

If the arts serve only (or mainly) as a medium or method with which non-artistic contents can be transported and general educational goals can be pursued (for instance, the acquisition of superordinate key competences such as promoting communication and team skills),[60] Anne Bamford refers to "education through the arts".[61] If, on the other hand, the arts themselves represent the contents of the arts education processes, and if the goals are intrinsically related to the arts themselves, Bamford classifies this as "education in the arts".[62] In this case, it is about learning, experiencing and understanding artistic symbols and techniques, which means

---

57 | Deutsche UNESCO-Kommission e. V. 2009, p. 1.

58 | This formulation can be found under the budget title "Kulturelle Bildung" in the "Kinder- und Jugendplan" of the German Federal Government with reference to § 11 of the "Kinder- und Jugendhilfegesetz. See in this regard Art. 26 of the "Universal Declaration of Human Rights", the "UN Convention on the Rights of the Child" and the following premise of the Swedish Cultural Council: "The Arts Council's basic guiding principle is that all children and young people [...] are entitled to equal opportunity to enjoy a range of cultural and artistic offerings and to engage in creative pursuits of their own". (See www.kulturradet.se/Documents/English/strategy_culture_children_young_people.pdf).

59 | See Lauret/Marie 2010, p. 12.

60 | See also the "Lisbon Key Competences" at http://www.oapee.es/documentum/MECPRO/Web/weboapee/servicios/documentos/documentacion-convocatoria-2008/1394 20061230en00100018.pdf?documentId=0901e72b80004481

61 | Bamford 2009, pp. 21 and 71 et passim.

62 | See note 86.

a) communicating art-specific abilities and skills as 'tools' for one's own artistic activity,
b) imparting knowledge about art, artistic processes and products (and the profession of the artist) so that the different arts can be experienced with their characteristic qualities, and
c) promoting the ability to "read" art and experience the process of an "aesthetic alphabetisation"[63] which includes developing individual tastes and needs with respect to aesthetic events.

The decisive aspect of this dichotomy between "education through the arts" and "education in the arts" is that arts education processes should ideally cover both dimensions; instead, in practice, one can observe that they are often played off against each other, mostly with the intention of promoting extrinsic educational aims:

'*Education in the arts* and *education through the arts*, while distinct, are interdependent and it should not be assumed that it is possible to adopt one or the other to achieve the totality of positive impacts on the child's educational realization.'[64]

When defining arts education, there can be no question that the educational mandate for the arts is fulfilled at the expense of artistic-aesthetic quality. However, there is a broader consensus regarding the fact that pedagogical and aesthetic aims should not be excluded and the educational function is reconcilable with the topos "autonomy of art".[65]

This means that it is not about the theatre as a "service theatre"[66] used for pedagogical purposes or degraded to the status of a supplier of topics for school lessons – and this is especially true of children's theatre. A play imparting useful knowledge about environmental protection, the circulation of money, or piracy, does not do a 'better job' of educating the public than one that gives

---

63 | Mollenhauer 1990, p. 9f.
64 | Bamford 2009, p. 71. See also Bamford 2010, p. 82.
65 | As Reinold Schmücker remarks, the autonomy of art, according to a widespread opinion, manifests itself in its "functionlessness and purposelessness" (Schmücker 2011, p. 109) – a misleading understanding of the autonomy of art which has been deeply rooted in the modern understanding of art since the era of Romanticism (See ibid., p.113). Actually, art is in "many ways functional" and could "serve many different purposes – even those which the artist does not approve of" (ibid., p. 114). Nevertheless, the existing autonomy of art can be found "in the privilege of the artists to define standards which their works should meet" and in "their ability to create laws which can be applied to each one of their works as well as to their oeuvre in total" (ibid., p. 113).
66 | Schneider 2005, p. 117.

the audience intensive aesthetic experiences and impressions – it only educates in another respect. Thus, it should always be the concern of arts education to accept the arts for their own sake and to value them as unique learning material. The superordinate goal should be to equally exploit the extrinsic and intrinsic educational potential immanent to the theatre, and to allow each aspect to unfold in its own way.

2.2.2 On the Quality of Arts Education Programmes: "Parameters of Quality"

Although it can be argued that a dimension of arts education is inherent to a preoccupation with the arts per se, the question regarding the artistic aesthetic and pedagogical quality of such learning opportunities has thereby not been answered. Cultural and educational policies in Europe have frequently taken this circumstance into account in recent years. The focus of the international discourse surrounding arts education has increasingly shifted from the necessity of arts education programmes as such to securing and guaranteeing their quality;[67] the position paper formulated at the second world conference, the *Seoul Agenda*, states the following as one of the three main development objectives in this context: "Assure that arts education activities and programmes are of a high quality in conception and delivery".[68]

The report contracted by UNESCO and presented by Anne Bamford in 2006 provided an important impulse with respect to the quality development and quality assurance of arts education programmes. It was entitled "The Wow Factor. Global research compendium on the impact of the arts in education". The report had already been an important basis for the first world conference and has since gained greatly in importance.[69] From a systematic, empirically based perspective, and for the first time in an international comparison, Bamford identifies the framework conditions necessary to create high-quality arts education programmes in the field of artistic work *with* children. In the course of evaluating the empirical findings and case studies from the 37 participating countries, Bamford worked out a catalogue of so-called "parameters of quality" for participation projects which can be applied universally as success factors, regardless of the different educational contents and intended impacts, which may vary from project to project within the scope of arts.[70]

---

67 | See Keuchel 2010a, p. 39ff.
68 | See http://www.unesco.org/new/fileadmin/MULTIMEDIA/HQ/CLT/CLT/pdf/Seoul_Agenda_EN.pdf
69 | See Liebau 2010, p. 11.
70 | See also Bamford: "It was a somewhat unexpected result of the research that from all the diversity of case studies presented the parameters of quality were so uniform"

A key finding of Bamford's research was that the quality of arts education programmes did not strongly depend on any particular *content* but rather on the interaction between suitable *structures* and appropriate *teaching methods*. "The case studies [...] show that content is of less relevance to quality than method and structure",[71] according to Bamford. Bamford further differentiates the two types of quality parameters as follows:[72]

a) Structural quality parameters:
- Public performance/presentation of results
- Detailed documentation and evaluation of the process and the results
- Permeability of boundaries between artists, school(s) and community
- Continuous further training and development of artists

b) Methodological quality parameters:
- Teamwork and cooperation/flexible organisational structures
- Use of local resources, local environment and local context on the material as well as on the content-related levels / involvement of local community and its particular features
- Process-oriented project work on the basis of artistic-creative research

In particular, the last aspect in the list of methodological quality parameters, namely open-ended artistic experimentation and research, was pointed out repeatedly by Bamford to be of the greatest significance with respect to the quality assurance of arts education activities:

'The most significant aspect of methodology that appeared in the qualitative case studies [...] was the arousal of children's curiosity about the world through problem or pro-

---

(Bamford 2009, p. 88). It is, however, clear that these parameters are not adequate for all situations, but only represent the necessary prerequisites, and, for that reason, additional project-specific quality parameters must be added in an actual individual case. The *Potenzialstudie zu Kinder- und Jugendkulturprojekten*, which was contracted by the PwC Foundation and presented by Susanne Keuchel and Petra Aescht in 2007, pursues a comparable objective. Based on the quantitative and qualitative evaluation of 60 good practice examples in Germany, the authors created a catalogue of 104 quality criteria which can be key factors to the "success" of a cultural project for children and young people. These criteria include those parameters developed by Bamford, but far surpass them in the degree of differentiation described (See Keuchel/Aescht 2007).

71 | Bamford 2009, p. 89.

72 | Ibid., p. 88ff. The criteria listed here represent a selection of the most important parameters developed by Bamford and which are of particular relevance for the independent children's theatre scene.

ject orientated activities. [...] Effective project-based arts-rich education involved the child in investigations of their direct environment and responding to issues around them through their art making process.'[73]

It is important that the joint artistic work effort be actively influenced and shaped by the learners[74] – and that wrong decisions or even a possible failure of the project can also be understood as a constructive experience:

'Quality arts-rich education encouraged the children to take risks and allowed them to make mistakes. "Letting go" of control and being confident to enable children to make mistakes [sic!] was an important part of giving children ownership of their creative processes. Uncertainty surrounds quality arts practice and this is to be encouraged.'[75]

The global significance of these UNESCO quality parameters for processes in arts education is illustrated by the fact that almost all of the criteria listed by Bamford have not only been included in the recommendation section of the "Road Map for Arts Education", which was presented as a follow-up to the first UNESCO World Conference,[76] but also in the "European Agenda for Culture" from the year 2010.[77]

Thus, it is all the more surprising that a blatant disparity exists between such widely accepted quality parameters and the actual working conditions of the artists involved.

2.2.3 On the Unique Educational Potential of the Independent Children's Theatre Scene

According to UNESCO quality parameters formulated by Anne Bamford, high-quality arts education programmes are not primarily characterised by content but, above all, by structural and methodological criteria. If one takes a closer look at these parameters, one cannot ignore the fact that the required

---

[73] | Ibid., p. 94. See also ibid., p. 95 et passim.

[74] | "The children not only engaged in the activities presented, but actively designed the scope and nature of the underpinning projects" (Bamford 2009, p. 95). See also Keuchel/Aescht: "Follow-up projects at the project location occur when young people are involved in decisions during the actual course of the project. The participation of young people in the project organisation promotes the interest in further arts education activities" (Keuchel/Aescht 2007, p. 30).

[75] | Bamford 2009, p. 101.

[76] | See.www.unesco.org/new/fileadmin/MULTIMEDIA/HQ/CLT/CLT/pdf/Arts_Edu_Road Map_en.pdf

[77] | See Lauret/Marie 2010, p. 32.

methodological success factors are largely consistent with the typical production and presentation methods of the independent children's theatre scene in Europe.

Teamwork and cooperation are not only common practice in the collective work processes of the groups and ensembles which are mainly non-hierarchically organised and which operate across systems and sectors, but rather a necessary condition for the process of joint production development.

The use of local resources and the inclusion of the local context have always been of great importance – especially in connection with participation projects – for the independent children's theatre scene. The "reality principle"[78] of the theatre, going out into 'the real world' and initiating direct actions in public places (and thus in the real everyday life of those involved and those addressed) in the form of "site-specific" projects is not only a trend which can be observed in "adult" theatre; it is just as much a focus of many theatre formats with children.

Above all, the principle of strongly process-oriented, open-ended project work on the basis of artistic research, which Bamford identified as the most significant methodological quality criterion, was confirmed by virtually all artists in the independent children's theatre scene who were surveyed as a typical working method and was, furthermore, explicitly desired and generally acknowledged as being constitutive.

Therefore, it can be noted that the independent children's theatre scene in Europe has a unique potential, in view of the 'freedom' it claims for itself regarding the choice of methodological access and the organisation of the artistic work process – namely, the potential to offer particularly high-quality forms of arts education activities in the field of participation formats, and thus to make an important contribution to the aim which is so very important to cultural and educational policies. This potential will lie idle, however, as long as it is not acknowledged and sufficiently financed by the public sector.

2.3 Independent Children's Theatre in Europe Today is also... "A Theatre for Early Years!"

The discovery of the target group of the youngest theatregoers, the age group from 0 to 6 years, can be seen as one of the most important innovations of the independent theatre for children since the 1990s. After the emancipatory boom experienced by children's theatre at the beginning of the 1970s, the process of upward revaluation and (aspired) equality of the target group took another decisive step forward with the establishment of the theatre for the very young. Thanks to the growing knowledge of neurobiology, psychology and educational science, a new image of childhood emerged which required that infants and small children be seen as full-fledged individuals, able and entitled to gain

---

78 | Hoffmann 2011, p. 235.

artistic-aesthetic experience. This assumption is reflected paradigmatically in the title of the biggest network worldwide devoted to theatre for the very young: "Small Size, Big Citizens".

The network, founded in Bologna in 2005 as an initiative of children's theatre, La Baracca – Testoni Ragazzi, in which at first only four European countries participated, today connects twelve theatres from twelve different countries as well as partners from three national micro-networks which promote the structural and aesthetic (further) development of the performing arts in Europe for the target group aged 0-6 years, and which develop joint projects, programmes and initiatives for this purpose. In three consecutive funding periods, each sponsored perennially by the cultural sponsorship programme of the European Commission, the project activities of the "Small Size" network are divided into three different areas. The activities focus on the so-called "production" activities. The aim of those theatre professionals in the network is to develop and financially support new productions and co-productions, especially for the very young. In addition, there is a broad spectrum of training activities: workshops, summer academies, and residences which target artists, teachers, educators, cultural mediators, parents and children and, as the name says, are intended as education and training activities. Finally, the sector of promotional activities is very important for the maintenance and expansion of the network, since this allows new contacts to be made and a platform provided on which knowledge can be exchanged, and it also allows a common database to be maintained which is available to all users. These promotional activities not only include the funding of several publications in the field of theatre for the very young, but also multimedia activities for advertising purposes, the acquisition of new network partners and grants, and the organisation of the "Small Size" festivals and showcases, which feature not only productions by the network partners but also performances for very young audiences by external groups.

The fact that "Small Size, Big Citizens" is the only multiyear project for children that was chosen by the European Commission in 2009 for the funding period 2009-2014 reflects the great importance which even the public sector attaches to this trend in children's theatre – a finding which, without a doubt, can be considered in the light of the debate on arts education for the very young, as was discussed earlier. Therefore, against the background of the EU concept of "life-long learning", arts education logically means starting as early as possible.[79] This apparently seems to be sufficient justification for the existence of a specific art form for the very young. Thus, it was by no means a coincidence that the cooperation project "Parentalité, éducation, culture, art",

---

79 | See Final Report of the Enquête Commission: "Kultur in Deutschland", p. 382 and Deutscher Kulturrat 2009.

realised under the auspices of the French independent group ACTA, which concentrated particularly on the very young, was sponsored by the EU education programme for life-long learning, "Grundtvig".

If, during its beginnings in the nineties, the theatre for the very young was a specialty of Italy and France, it has since more or less established itself in almost all European countries.[80] However, in principle, it is clearly a matter of the independent theatre scene. The institutions, it seems, are still not really interested in producing for the very young – whether it is because the expected revenues would be relatively small or because the necessary production conditions are not really compatible with the working structures of a state and municipal theatre. A positive exception is the Theater der Jungen Generation (Theatre of the Young Generation) in Dresden, whose programme offers productions for the very young all year round.

It is particularly noteworthy in this connection that it is precisely the theatre for the very young which is the area of Polish children's theatre, in which the most striking developments are currently taking place, and in which the otherwise hardly existent independent scene seems to have claimed some scope of action for itself. The beginnings of this movement go back to the initiative network of the global key pioneer in this field: the children's theatre La Baracca – Testoni Ragazzi in Bologna with the Children's Arts Centre in Poznan. In 2006, the Polish Children's Arts Centre included a guest performance from Italy in its programme; this was followed shortly thereafter by guest performances by the Toihaus Theater from Salzburg, Austria, and by the Helios theatre from Germany.

The attempt to use these good practice examples for very young theatregoers as a source of inspiration and initial impetus has apparently succeeded. A number of independent artists were inspired to experiment in this direction and to develop plays for a very young audience; independent groups such as Teatr Atofri or the Studio Teatralne Blum were founded, which are completely dedicated to the youngest theatregoers; "and even a very [sic!] well-known director for adults, Pawl Lysak, directed one piece for babies", said Alicy Morawska-Rubczak (ASSITEJ Poland). In short, a separate little movement came into being, and, thanks to that, the theatre for the very young is present throughout the entire country and has increasingly established itself especially as a working field for the independent scene.[81] This is confirmed by the fact that since 2010 an internationally oriented arts festival has taken place in

---

80 | Switzerland is an exception in this case: This art form has not been able to assert itself so far, according to Sandra Förnbacher (University Bern).

81 | It should, however, be noted that in Poland there is now a national theatre exclusively devoted to the target group of very young theatregoers, Teatr małego widza (The Theatre of the Little Spectator).

Poland which is dedicated solely to the very young: *Sztuka szuka malucha* (Art seeks the Toddler), which is sponsored by the Ministry of Culture and National Heritage and which has grown steadily since its inception.

Professionals active in this area see the inadequate networking within this scene as one of the major development projects still to be realised in the future. Not only are there too few possibilities to cooperate and too few opportunities to exchange information on the national level, since the independent groups working for the very young are scattered all around the country, but there is a lack of contact with other European countries where the theatre for the very young has long been a tradition, a fact particularly bemoaned by artists. In this respect, the next festival for the very young in Poland will, if possible, be organised together with an international symposium with a wide spectrum of participants, so that an end will be put to the niche existence of independent artists working in this field, and the Polish independent scene in general will gain momentum and "visibility" (including on an international level).[82]

In general, it can be said that there is at least one festival for the very young in most European countries, and that it is quite naturally a part of a children's theatre scene which considers itself emancipated: *Visioni di futuro, visioni di teatro* in Bologna, *Premières rencontres* in Villiers-le-Bel in France, *Bim Bam* in Salzburg, *Twee Turven Hoog* in Almere in The Netherlands, *TakeOff* in England, *Starcatchers* in Scotland, *Fratz* in Berlin – the list is long, and it is getting longer day by day because the theatre for the very young is booming!

Demand, too, seems to be immense. As Stephan von Löwis, organiser of the renowned international arts festival *kinderkinder* in Hamburg confirms, the saying holds true: "The younger the target group, the 'more sold out' the performance!" Stephan Rabl (DSCHUNGEL, Vienna) says that if he programmed productions for the very young to correspond with the demand, his programme would consist only of performances for this audience. However, it cannot be ignored that despite the great demand and the general upswing which the theatre for the very young has experienced in Europe in recent years, readiness is still lacking when it comes to sponsoring this art form with public funds or to acknowledging it as an art form at all. "There are [sic!] quite a few that make theatre for [the very young, author's note T. K.], but they have no structural money, so there is not a real infrastructure for this age-group (which is very frustrating)", says the Dutch theatre expert Brechtje Zwaneveld about the situation of artists in The Netherlands; even such prestigious groups with a high standing throughout Europe as La Baracca in Bologna, can, in their own words, only finance their productions for the very young with the help of funds

---

82 | This information and these comments are based on the extensive elucidations of the Polish experts Alicja Morawska-Rubczak (ASSITEJ Poland), Zbigniew Rudzinski, and Barbara Malecka (both from Children's Arts Centre in Poznan).

from the "Small Size" network or through collaborations with institutions. A specific funding from public sources does not exist.

The reason for this may lie in the basic problem of legitimising the theatre for the very young. On the one hand, even its most avid proponents cannot deny that the theatre for the very young must constantly assert itself in competition with other 'common' everyday experiences. To the extent that practices are frequently demonstrated and repeated on stage which children are familiar with in their family environment and in nursery school – playing with materials like paper, wood, wool, metal, experimenting with colours, sounds, smells, etc., the theatre always runs the risk of being replaced as a sphere for experience. This is all the more the case when the performance on stage, in the sense of a post-dramatic performance, no longer has a symbolic reference function and does not take place in the mimetic simulation modus of 'pretend', and actors do not play roles but present and demonstrate their own – childlike? – play with objects. The producers of the aesthetic experience a child has when watching such a performance have to accept the fact that such an experience is inevitably compared with those which a small child makes when, for instance, it sees a rainbow or, even more so, when a child can make its own experiences playing in the sand, with wood, or on the piano.

On the other hand, one must keep in mind that the actual receptive experiences of small children during a theatre performance conceived especially for them have not been researched to date and, presumably, not all will be able to be researched. The thesis that the "theatre for children under three years has special qualities which distinguish it from other activities which can delight a small child" has not been proven up to now.[83] This is also true for the premise "that theatre for under-three-year-olds represents an indispensable component in the aesthetic development of an individual".[84] The danger that a "small child is used as a projection surface"[85] on which to express adult, neo-romantic fantasies of a childlike world of experience is great, whereby a certain concept of "childhood" in the early 21st century is implied but seldom questioned.[86] An inevitable fact with which theatre makers have to live is that a measurable contribution to the aesthetic development of a child by the theatre for the very young has not been empirically proven to date.

---

83 | Viehöver/Wunsch 2011, p. 4.
84 | Ibid., p. 4.
85 | Wunsch 2011, p. 15.
86 | Ibid., p. 14. See also Viehöver Wunsch 2011, p. 6.

Figure 2: 'I Colori Dell'Acqua', La Baracca – Testoni Ragazzi, Bologna, Italy, 2003. Photograph: Matteo Chiura

2.4 Independent Children's Theatre in Europe Today is... Interdisciplinary!

In the course of the past decades, independent children's theatre in Europe did not only emancipate itself structurally. Aesthetically, it demonstrates a growing variety of forms and a constantly increasing spectrum of contents. It has laid claim to all formats, genres and sectors, as well as all manner of appearance of the contemporary independent theatre and has enhanced, so it seems, its image in the areas where it interacts with bordering art forms and disciplines. The German term *vierte Sparte* (fourth discipline), which is used to describe the children's and young people's theatre in state, municipal and regional theatres, is more misleading than ever, since it implies that children's and young people's theatre can be located in a category which is separate from the traditional fields of drama, opera and ballet, and in doing so fails to acknowledge the fact that music and dance theatre have long become part of the spectrum of performing arts for young audiences.

As far as the time period relevant to this study is concerned, it should be noted that the year 1990 does not represent a significant turning point with regard to subject matter and themes for children's theatre in Western Europe.[87] A far-reaching paradigm shift had already taken place at the beginning of the seventies when children's and young people's theatre radically extended its scope of subject matter as part of the general reform of the system of thought and action in the field of children's and youth literature. Since then there have been very few absolute taboo topics, and they are becoming fewer and fewer, or as Maurice Yendt has appropriately summarised it: "Il y a bien sur des tabous sociaux ou moraux mais pas plus que dans le théâtre s'adressant aux adultes". A review of the past two decades indicates that the most significant developments on the aesthetic level have been primarily in the area of forms and formats; the interest of theatre makers has mainly focused on experimenting with new post-dramatic narrative styles.

Probably the most important development in this context is the general trend towards cross-genre and interdisciplinary projects. Therefore, it is not surprising that "children's theatre" in many contexts is called the "performing arts for children", and that "theatre" has become the "performing arts" and "théâtre" the "spectacles vivants". Maurice Yendt regards this trend as a quite natural development:

'Cela va de soi. Depuis Sophocle et Aristophane, le théâtre est un art ontologiquement syncrétique qui a toujours fait appel, pour affirmer son identité artistique, à beaucoup d'autres formes d'art (littérature, musique, danse, arts visuels, etc.).'

However, the increasing frequency with which professionals in the independent children's theatre scene pursue this interdisciplinary approach and its growing importance for their artistic work is remarkable. Three areas in particular must be mentioned regarding the general orientation towards "crossover formats" which have strongly influenced the landscape of children's theatre.

First and most notable is music, and above all the dance theatre scene for young audiences which has been developing rapidly for years, and for which interdisciplinary work and the equal interaction of different arts and forms of expression are obviously necessary.

---

87 | At this point it should again be noted that the countries mainly included in this study are all located in Western Europe; Poland and Russia, as stated earlier, have a special status, not least because of historical and political reasons. The children's theatre of the former GDR is also largely neglected in this context in the general comments regarding developments prior to 1990 and the early 1990s.

Second, the meeting of performing and visual arts is still a popular and recurring phenomenon in the area of children's theatre. The spectrum in this sector is very broad and extends from the staging of art objects and video arrangements, as in the case of the successful production of *Hinter den Spiegeln* (2011) by the Helios theatre in Hamm, to interactive installations which members of the audience can walk through and experience alone (!), without the presence of actors, as has been repeatedly and successfully implemented by the Italian-Swiss collective Trickster.

Third, a crossover format with an atypically artistic discipline is becoming more and more common, namely an opening of children's theatre in the direction of science: "Through the differentiation of sciences, the rapidly increasing amount of knowledge, and the new media, formats have gained in importance which present scientific contents with unconventional means and in which the person of the scientist is visible";[88] and, indeed, this can be increasingly observed in the area of independent theatre for young audiences. In "lecture performances" and other documentary formats which explicitly place themselves in the service of science through presentations which illustrate scientific contents by appealing to the audience's senses, socially relevant topics are narrated rather than acted out in a multimedia approach and with artistic means. More recently, in Germany alone, new plays have appeared on the subject of money (see the production of the same name by the Theater an der Parkaue, 2013 and the *Kinderbank* by the Fundus Theater, 2012), on the scarcity of drinking water (*Durst*, Grips Theater, 2013), on environmental pollution (*Trashedy*, Leandro Kees, 2012) and on the influence and manipulation by media and news (*Der Rest der Welt*, Pulk Fiktion, 2011). That the appearance of these formats is undoubtedly closely related to the general cultural and political interest in the promotion of arts education is one of the central internal dynamics in the system of children's and young people's theatre.

To illustrate the increasing interdisciplinary differentiation of independent children's theatre in Europe, the area of dance theatre will be dealt with in more detail in the following chapter – on the one hand because, as will be demonstrated, a particular importance is attached to it regarding arts education opportunities for children, and on the other because the structural and aesthetic change in the system of children's theatre has perhaps most conspicuously manifested itself and taken hold in the area of dance.

---

88 | Gauß/Hannken-Illjes 2012, p. 962.

Figure 3: 'Die Harmonie der Gefiederten'/'L'Harmonie de la Gent à Plumes', AGORA Theater, St. Vith, Belgium, 2014. Photograph: Willi Filz

2.5 Dance Theatre for Children: The Ideal Way to Arts Education?

"Modern boys want to be dancers rather than firemen"[89] – such was the title of an article which appeared in the British newspaper *The Daily Telegraph* on 17 August 2013 and described a "cultural shift". As was discovered in two empirical studies, the profession of "dancer" ranks third for boys as a career option after "doctor" and "footballer" – and before "fireman". The outcome of this study may be surprising – perhaps positively so – and with a view to the current developments which are taking place in the field of dance theatre in Europe, it seems only logical, since the most fundamental and significant structural changes in the independent children's theatre scene are taking place in this area. The art form of dance, "which until not too long ago was, in many places, without public attention, funds and a political lobby",[90] has managed to establish itself, especially in the area of participative dance formats *with* children and young people, as an essential component of arts education (and thus of social life) and has been able to secure a prominent position for itself within the independent performing arts for young audiences.

---

89 | Seehttp://www.telegraph.co.uk/news/uknews/10242601/Modern-boys-want-to-be-dancers-rather-than-firemen.html
90 | Foik 2012, p. 606.

Networks are being founded all over Europe. First and foremost is the impressively successful, EU-subsidised "Fresh Tracks Europe";[91] the number of dance productions and initiatives is growing steadily, as is the offer of specific dance festivals for children (including the very young). So far, the oldest and largest annual international dance festival for young people worldwide is the *Szene Bunte Wähne* in Vienna, which has existed since 1998.

Although dance theatre for young people has enjoyed a comparably long tradition in a few European countries (e.g., The Netherlands, where its tradition generally runs parallel to that of children's and young people's theatre), the incorporation of the art form of dance into the spectrum of the performing arts for children and young people is really a phenomenon of the late nineties and, above all, the beginning of the 21st century in many other countries, where it has only lately begun to enjoy concentrated public attention and funding policy activities. The Swedish Arts Council initiated special support measures for dance theatre for young people in 2009 and increased the subsidies for new projects as well as for existing initiatives.[92]

Germany can be considered a best practice model for arts education measures when it comes to sponsoring dance for children and young people, since it conceived and successfully implemented a regional and supra-regional

---

91 | At this time there are eleven institutions from eight countries who are members and partners of "Fresh Tracks Europe". One of the core members is the dance and theatre laboratory "Het Lab Utrecht" (NL), whose initiative sparked the founding of the network. Others are the Centre for Performing Arts "Kopergietery" (B), the theatre and dance house "DSCHUNGEL Vienna" (A) and the independent Centre for International Dance Art "tanzhaus nrw" (D). Other partners are the venue for contemporary dance "Dansstationen" (SWE), the agencies for contemporary dance "Soltumatu Tantsu Ühendus" (EST) and "Aabendans" (DK) and the festivals "Imaginate" (UK), "Krokus Festival" (B), "Szene Bunte Wähne" (A) and "Tweetakt" (NL). See also www.freshtracks-europe.com and the comprehensive documentation in English "Fresh Tracks Europe (ed.): Innovation in Dance for Young Audiences 2013".

92 | See also the following extract from the publications of the German Cultural Council: "The interest in both classical and modern contemporary dance has increased markedly in recent years – not least among children and young people. The Government is making a concentrated effort to enable dance to reach a greater proportion of the general public and get more people to discover dance as an art form. House of Dance (Dansens hus) is being given special funds to put high-quality dance in focus, in cooperation with other dance institutes. Children and young people are central target groups for this initiative. The national programme Dance in School, which has been coordinated by the Swedish Arts Council since 2005, has been expanded. The National Dance in School Institute was established at Luleå University of Technology in March 2009 to increase research in the area" (http://www.government.se/content/1/c6/15/21/08/bc7ed630.pdf).

structural development plan, which is unique in Europe to date.[93] The so-called "Tanzplan" of the German Federal Cultural Foundation, which was implemented in June 2004, probably represents the most comprehensive cultural and political impulse for the contemporary dance scene in years.[94]

With the programme "Tanzplan", the German Cultural Foundation, for the first time in the history of the German Federal Republic, specifically earmarked funds to promote dance in order to support artists and next-generation artists, professional dance training, arts education and dance as a cultural heritage, to enhance the public perception of dance as an art form, and to develop a model for longer-term structural funding measures. For this purpose, a total of 12.5 million euros was set aside between 2005 and 2010 to be used in financing a great number of local dance initiatives, training projects, research projects and publications.[95] Thanks to the "match funding principle", which required that the regions and communities provide 50% of the subsidies themselves and the declaration of intent requested of the financers regarding the absorption of costs after the end of the project running time, it was not only possible for those parties involved to guarantee long-term planning, but to invest a total sum of approximately 21 million euros in the dance sector.[96] More than 80% of the initiatives are still running; eight of the nine regional dance plans are still being financed by the regions and communities.[97] Four hundred twenty-six project partners and three hundred eighty-nine choreographers from fifty countries were involved in this gigantic programme. Six hundred eighty-one of the one thousand two hundred seventy-seven dance performances were for and with children and young people;[98] especially in the area of arts education through participation formats, "Tanzplan" has an extremely good record, with approximately 13,000 dance lessons involving over 30,000 children and young people after five years' running time.[99]

However, two things were important: on the one hand, the necessary artistic, personnel and financial prerequisites should be created in order to put on professional dance productions for a young target group and to develop sustainable production structures;[100] on the other hand, many different educational offers, ranging from practical dance instruction to group reception

---

93 | See Foik 2012, p. 605.
94 | Müller/Schneeweis 2006, p. 136f.
95 | http://www.tanzplan-deutschland.de/plan.php?id_language=1
96 | Foik 2012, p. 606.
97 | See Odenthal 2005, p. 108.
98 | See ibid.
99 | See Foik 2012, p. 606.
100 | See Kessel/Müller/Kosubek/Barz 2011, p. 22.

and reflection of dance performances, should be made available which would provide different ways to access dance as an art form. For this purpose,

'in collaboration with elementary schools, secondary schools, pre-schools and youth centres, a basis was developed to communicate and teach the art of dance. In particular, in urban neighbourhoods in which the access to dance was difficult, the collaboration with children´s and youth centres was intended as a continuous cooperation. Together with the institutions involved, ways were found to achieve a long-term implementation in order to make dance an integral part of these facilities.'[101]

A case study with exemplary character for such local "Tanzplan" initiatives is the success story of the programme, *Take-off: Junger Tanz – Tanzplan Düsseldorf,* which was implemented from 2006 to 2010 with the "tanzhaus nrw" as project organiser and which is described here in brief. The facts speak for themselves:

Formats
- 32 different productions
- 12 prizes and acknowledgements for 6 productions
- 43 guest performances from 12 different countries
- 1 annual festival
- 20 dance productions with children and young people
- 237 courses and workshops at partner schools, youth centres and pre-schools
- Advanced training offers for dancers, choreographers, and teachers

Players
- 4 theatres
- 1 concert house
- 160 independent choreographers, dancers, and dance instructors from 15 different countries
- 4 institutions of higher learning, 1 university, 10 schools, 4 youth centres, 2 pre-schools

Partners
- 26 local
- 8 supra-regional
- 11 international

Participants
- 6712 participants in dance projects for children and young people at schools, youth centres, and pre-schools

---

101 | Ibid., p. 21.

- 567 children and young people as dancers in productions
- 9017 hours of instruction at schools, youth centres, pre-schools
- 100,088 spectators[102]

It speaks for the success of this programme that after the end of "Tanzplan" the state of North Rhine-Westphalia and the city of Düsseldorf assumed all costs for subsidising *Take-Off* and for the associated festival which still takes place annually.[103]

The German Federal Cultural Foundation has also continued its commitment after the successful conclusion of its pilot project and has subsidised two new funds, "Tanzfonds Partner" and the "Tanzfonds Erbe" with a sum of 2.5 million euros,[104] whereby the "Tanzfonds Partner" is explicitly aimed at the target group of children and young people and at the development of multiyear alliances between schools and dance institutions (theatres, dance companies, and choreographic centres).[105]

Furthermore, more or less in the wake of this comprehensive structural development programme, many other initiatives and target-group-specific arts education and educational formats have emerged as initiatives of institutions and individuals in the German-speaking region, which, in the tradition of the "community dance" concept, are especially devoted to promoting dance *with* children and young persons:

'In many cities and federal states, different projects were founded with the aim of establishing dance in mainstream schools. The networks between the different initiatives and institutions in this field have grown and have become more structured, not least through the joint foundation of an umbrella organisation: the Federal Association of Dance in Schools (Bundesverband Tanz in Schulen e.V.).'[106]

This association, founded in 2007, which has set itself the aims of establishing contemporary dance as an integral part of arts education in German schools and securing and further developing the quality of respective offers,[107] has in

---

102 | See ibid. p. 24.
103 | See Kessel/Müller/Kosubek/Barz 2011, p. 178.
104 | Foik 2012, p. 606.
105 | See also the informative letter from the German Federal Cultural Foundation at www.tanzfonds.de and www.kulturstiftung-bund.de
106 | Foik 2008, p. 54.
107 | See www.bundesverband-tanzinschulen.org, and also Klinge 2012, p. 4. There exist very good empirical studies in the form of evaluation research which were contracted by the Federal Association for Dance at Schools, see Federal Association for Dance at Schools 2009 as well as the work group Evaluation and Research of the Federal Associa-

its own way strongly invigorated and structurally enhanced the independent scene of dance theatre for young audiences.

The success of this initiative clearly indicates that more and more dance projects with children and young people extend the framework or even go beyond the scope defined by schools – whether because participants rehearse in a professional dance studio off school premises or because performances no longer take place 'only' in a school setting but also in professional theatres or dance institutes or in site-specific contexts.[108] The current efforts of the federal association are in line with the slogan "Tanz in Schulen geht raus!" ("Dance in Schools reaches out!") and are aimed at creating new or enhanced structures which can lead to establishing collaborations between independent dance artists and schools and even informal educational facilities like children's welfare centres, education offices, day care centres, houses of dance and theatres.[109]

Furthermore, the newly initiated programme "Chance Tanz",[110] which is part of the initiative "Culture is Strength – Alliances for Education", is another dance promotion concept especially implemented for educationally disadvantaged children and young people.

One example of a successfully implemented dance programme which has not only helped to create structures, but which can be traced back to the initiative of a single individual, is the good practice model "TanzZeit – Zeit für

tion for Dance at Schools 2009. In order to be able to monitor the existence and development of the projects, the federal association established a project data base at http://www.bv-tanzinschulen.info/30+M5713274d807.html for all of Germany, which is maintained and used by the heads of projects and provides a set of tools with which the different projects can be documented, evaluated and reflected. Recently, the organisation has published quality parameters with recommendations on the implementation, quality development and quality assurance for dance projects at schools by dancers, choreographers and dance instructors. (See www.bv-tanzinschulen.de/qualitaetsrahmen.html).

108 | See Bundesverband Tanz in Schulen 2013, p. 5.

109 | See ibid., p. 4.

110 | See also an extract from the programme description: "`Chance Tanz´ promotes local project activities in which children and young people participate in and actively organise a dance-creative process under professional guidance by dance instructors/educators. The results of the projects are then presented in a small- or large-scale context. Besides the active participation in the dance programme, other activities involving the reception of dance in the form of attendance of performances and rehearsals as well as discussions and meetings with dancers are included. Three different formats are planned, Tanz_Start, Tanz_Intensiv and Tanz_Sonderprojekt, which mainly differ from each other in their defined timeframes (30 and 65-80/100 hours of dance). The projects are led by professional dance artists" (http://www.bv-tanzinschulen.info/30+M557164d6160.html).

Tanz in Schulen" in Berlin, which was conceived by the Italian independent dance artist Livia Patrizi in 2005 and at its outset encompassed 37 school classes, 40 independent dancers and choreographers and a start-up grant of 48,000 euros from the Kultursenat of Berlin.[111] Since then, the project has not only been implemented in Berlin, but is also linked nationwide to numerous cooperation partners and institutions, and can thus offer young dancers professional production conditions in prestigious theatres like the HAU or the Radialystem V in Berlin. The project also aims at establishing dance as a regular weekly part of morning classes for school children.[112] Also in this case, the project was financed by means of a mixed financing strategy: The personnel and material costs of the coordinating office were borne by the Berlin Project Fund for Arts Education; the fees for the independent dance artists for instruction were paid through subsidies to the participating schools, voluntary contributions made by parents, through grants from municipal district authorities and resources from the community management in Berlin, as well as through foundations, patrons and sponsors.[113] Since 2010, the financing of "TanzZeit", backed up by investments from Rotary and booster clubs, has been a fixed item in the budget of the Senate Administration for Education, Youth and Science (Senatsverwaltung für Bildung, Jugend und Wissenschaft), which not only represents an important and reliable financial base, but gives a clear signal that the importance of the facilitation of arts education through dance is gradually gaining in standing.[114] Through support from the public sector, "TanzZeit" has been able to expand steadily since its founding; in the seven years of its existence, over 100 schools and over 11,000 pupils from all districts of Berlin have taken part in the project.[115] Yet, the number of schools interested in becoming project partners far exceeds the available budget.[116]

If time has been taken here to describe in detail all of these exemplary structural measures from and in Germany, this is because they demonstrate what is possible when extensive measures concerning culture and arts education are implemented which involve all the relevant players in a development process and, in contrast to one-off investments in flagship projects, create nationwide structures which offer incentives for local politics to (financially) commit itself long-term in the future.

It is therefore particularly welcome, because the area of dance within the performing arts for children may be assigned a special function which justifies

---

111 | See von Zedlitz 2009, p. 8ff. and p. 88f.
112 | See ibid., p. 68.
113 | Ibid., p. 91.
114 | See Beyeler/Patrizi 2012, p. 603.
115 | See ibid., p. 600.
116 | See ibid., p. 603.

the further systematic funding of independent children's theatre on the whole. In contrast to drama theatre and the theatre of the spoken word, dance – non-verbal, sensually specific, physical, archaic – reaches out to all classes, cultures and age groups (including pre-readers[117]):

'Since the human body as the direct and immediate medium of expression is in the centre of the communication, dance can reach everyone, regardless of age, sex or origin, and can communicate human feelings less on an intellectual as on a sensual-emotional level.'[118]

The relevance of dance is not to be overestimated with regard to the intercultural learning aspect in the area of arts education programmes. Great importance is attached to dance as a non-verbal medium because it transcends language barriers and can thus function as an important means to develop communicative and social competences in children. In fact, empirical studies prove that the "positive resonance of existing" that dance offers is particularly high among pupils from migrant backgrounds.[119]

In addition, particularly in connection with participative dance formats *with* children, an important advantage of dance, as opposed to other performing arts and in accordance with the Community Dance concept, is that everyone can move and dance in her own way without any kind of previous knowledge:

'In this sense "everyone is equal" in dance, - whereby everyone can find his or her individual role and importance within the group. A personal feeling of achievement and feedback from the group enable participants to make positive experiences with regard to dedifferentiation and a sense of belonging. As part of the everyday school routine, dance can promote integration and help to counteract the tendencies toward social exclusion.'[120]

Above all, a particular potential is inherent to dance because it is a physical phenomenon. Children can make their (first) aesthetic experiences which are not conceivable in a comparable intensity with any other art form. Since the human body is a "medium permeable to emotions" through which "experiences in and with the world can be processed and symbolized" as well as a "centre of action which implements experiences, ideas, plans and insights", and which provides the sensual basis from which "resistance, differentiation and learning experiences originate",[121] experience and insight potentials come into play in a remarkable way in dance. "In an exploratory, playful approach to the possibilities given by

---

117 | Suchy 2012, p. 14.
118 | Foik 2008, p. 51.
119 | See Kosubek/Barz 2011, p. 140.
120 | Foik 2008, p. 52 – emphasis in original
121 | Klinge 2010, p. 90.

the movement and expression of one's own body, dance offers the potential of immediate attention and sensitivity",[122] whereby, in relation to other physical activities like sports, a comparably large freedom for individual expression is always given. "Physical activity is enhanced in creative dance by the possibility to express personal emotions, situations, experiences in a reflected and structured manner," Livia Patrizi said at the awards ceremony for the German Prize for Violence Prevention in October 2007. "This movement which is transformed into dance can help children to overcome feelings and thus to experience a kind of liberation".[123] In this respect, dance would appear to have a general potential within arts education as an optimal initiation experience for children.

In summary, the following can be said: If, admittedly, contemporary dance had long led a "Cinderella-like existence among the arts",[124] this Cinderella is now getting the "royal treatment", not only because of its relevance to arts education, but largely because of it. "Dance is the ideal way in arts education to create inclusive communities in schools as well as in social and cultural facilities",[125] as formulated in a thesis of the Federal Association of Dance in Schools (Bundesverband Tanz in Schulen). Now it is up to the European makers of policy on arts education to determine whether things will continue on this course, e.g. maintaining and promoting the structures which have been created and developing them further with independent dance professionals.

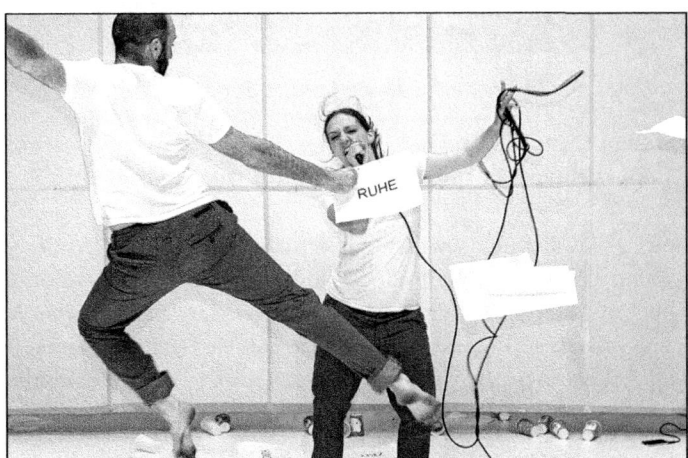

Figure 4: 'TRASHedy', Leandro Kees, Performing Group Cologne, 2012. Photograph: Anika Freytag

---

122 | Klinge 2012, p. 5.
123 | Cited according to von Zedlitz 2009, p. 14.
124 | von Zedlitz 2009, p. 7.
125 | http://www.bv-tanzinschulen.info/30+M551a96f62a1.html

Figure 5: 'Alice', De Stilte, Breda, Netherlands, 2009. Photograph: Hans Gerritsen

2.6 Interim Conclusion I: Risks Involved in the Developments Outlined

Although the developments presented here can generally be considered success stories and describe positive, emancipatory opening and expansion processes in the field of independent children's theatre in Europe, it cannot be denied that, despite all the enthusiasm and respect, some tendencies should be viewed with a critical eye. This is true for the theatre productions *for* children as well as for the participation formats *with* children.

2.6.1 Theatre for Children: Stop under-challenging children! Strive for a complex simplicity!

One of the main dangers of children's theatre, including in the 21st century, is what Holger Noltze termed the "lie of easiness", the danger of "confusing communication with simplification"[126] and of subjecting art to a simplification and disambiguation process in the course of supposed 'communication' – a

---

126 | Noltze 2010, p. 9.

conclusion which can certainly be seen in direct connection with the general trend towards the commercialisation of art:

'Mass media fear complexity. Complexity is feared as an obstacle to mass and broad accessibility of the public. [...] What is true for media on the public marketplace and what seems understandable, has become, in the meantime, also [...] a principle of the systems, "education" and "the cultural sector". Indeed, a "quota" also prevails here, and similar mechanisms of convergence have also come into play here.'[127]

The great taboos of the art (communication) market are thus complexity and effort; conversely, "a strategy of harmonisation" and "dedifferentiation" in terms of "more of the same easily digestible soup"[128] is the order of the day.

This fatal "reductionism" can, according to Holger Noltze, "especially be observed [...] when the child and art meet".[129] This statement is repeatedly confirmed for children's theatre – either because the practical constraints of the market do not (or no longer) allow working methods which do not have a commercial orientation, or because the artists themselves have (too) little faith and confidence in their young audience. Time and again, theatre productions can be seen at prestigious international festivals which tend to confirm clichés about childhood rather than actually deal with children's current living conditions and, possibly, suffering. Children are 'picked up' in their receptive behaviour where adults assume them to be, without basing these assumptions on sound scientific research. Thus, children are regularly under-challenged, and a mistrust in their intellectual and emotional abilities is virtually guaranteed: "It's not only in Poland that the children in contemporary world are changing faster than adults' knowledge (imagination) about that", Zbigniew Rudzinski comments paradigmatically.

It would be more desirable if theatre makers working in the field of children's theatre did not look *down* on their (intended) target group but *engaged them at eye level*, so that by empathising and assuming the target group's perspective, they can enter into a direct communication and direct dialogue with the audience in order to understand its views, interests and needs.

This does not mean that children's theatre should give up its target group orientation and specificity. It has much more to do with the impartial fact that, as a rule, there is a (more or less pronounced) generation gap between producers and recipients, that it is primarily adults who make theatre for children and are thus essentially different from their target group. Analogous to the demand made by Hans-Heino Ewers with regard to literature for children

---

127 | Ibid., p. 233f.
128 | Ibid., p. 104.
129 | Ibid., p. 230.

and young people in comparison to "adult" literature, the aim of children's and young people's literature should not be an identity with adult theatre but solely a separate and equally valid identity. The "differentiation [...] of the subject's perspective" should definitely be maintained:

'In children's literature, the world in which the child lives is the starting point for the development of a common world for children and adults which they, if not exclusively, then primarily, describe in its significance for children.'[130]

In this context, if one speaks of "easiness" or, in general, 'simplicity' of the theatre for children, then one should speak (if at all) of a "complex simplicity"[131] in the sense of an "elementarisation of complex knowledge with the help of a simple, elementary-literary [or genuine theatrical, author's note T.K.] process", says Maria Lypp[132] – and not of a hierarchisation or valuation of whatever kind with regard to the audience orientation. Marcel Cremer, the founder and long-term artistic director of the Belgian children's and young people's theatre group AGORA, from Saint-Vith, exposed the problems behind this demand with regard to the standard practices particularly common to children's theatre:

'In some restaurants there is a page of the menu with children´s dishes. Usually you can find noodles with red sauce, chips with ketchup or mayonnaise, fish sticks with mashed potatoes, sausages with potato salad, often served with a cola or other soft drink free of charge. Careful! Whoever goes to the restaurant to eat what he always eats can save himself the trip. Whoever goes to the theatre in the hope of seeing the old familiar, what is well-known, hackneyed or reprocessed, that person is lacking the most important prerequisite: hunger for something new, unknown, strange. In order to avoid this conflict, some theatre people prefer to sell children and young people fish sticks. I am of the opinion that you should offer them fish and show them how to remove the bones. Fresh fish is much healthier than fish sticks. It contains many vital substances because the creature can still be recognised, and therefore it tells us more about life than fish sticks whose origin and identity have been mutilated beyond recognition.
The pre-requisite is always hunger, hunger for something new.'[133]

To presume that children experience this hunger – and, moreover, to think them capable of being able to deal with something new and unfamiliar

---

130 | Ewers 1995, p. 23.
131 | Jahnke 2001, p. 129.
132 | Lypp 2005, p. 831.
133 | Cremer, Marcel: "Das Sehen lernen." Report as part of the school theatre festival "Spring auf!" in May 2004 in Luxemburg. Unpublished original manuscript, kindly made available by the AGORA Theater in St. Vith, Belgium.

(especially because this is expected of children on a daily basis anyway, not only in the theatre) – could without a doubt help theatre for children to further emancipate itself aesthetically and to ensure increased quality.

2.6.2 Theatre with Children: For whom? How? And why?

In connection with participative theatre formats *with* children, the process orientation of projects is often stressed, to which the players clearly avow themselves and which is even invoked as a necessary condition for joint artistic research. Conversely, however, the concluding public presentation of the result is hardly at issue, but is understood as a constitutive element of the artistic work.

Yet this often gives rise to a problem. If, when working with children, the 'journey is its own reward', and thus the result shown to the public is only relevant with regard to the process from which it arose, then such a project must be open to the question: To what extent is it suited at all to be shown to an audience which itself was not part of the process? The 'process' does not become a 'product' solely by virtue of the performance.

During a discussion with the audience at the end of a performance of a participative music theatre project in Berlin, a member of the audience expressed her feeling of unease in dialogue with the actors: "I like it when an evening of theatre raises questions that I can think about. In your case I had the feeling that you gave me a lot of *answers* which you had found for yourselves during the rehearsals – but I don't know your questions! Somehow I felt left out." The danger is that this feeling of 'being left out' on the part of the audience can result when the process of 'trying things out' and the children involved in this process are paramount. There is nothing wrong with this per se, but in this case one must carefully consider which role the audience should have during the performance and how it can be explicitly involved.

What Manfred Jahnke says about the impossibility of subjecting a purely process-oriented participation format to normal theatre critique can be applied to the question regarding the role of the audience as a whole:

'The tried and tested instruments of a theatre critique can hardly be used in connection with groups which are focused on self-awareness and in which sensibilisation and emancipation of the individual are the most important concerns. On the contrary, such work must be protected from the public which can only be present in the role of a voyeur.'[134]

Thus, it seems necessary to rethink these circumstances with regard to theatre projects with children in order to ensure that the eminently desirable public

---

134 | Jahnke 2001, p. 187.

presentation of participation formats for the players and for the audience is an enriching and pleasant experience in many instances.

Another key question which must be asked and answered anew for every theatre project with children is the question of which role the children themselves play in the course of these formats and in what way they should and can specifically 'participate'. Is it about *doing* or is it about *participating*? Should the professional artists bring their expertise into play and 'stage' and guide the children, or should they help the children to find their own way and just initiate and, if necessary, catalyse the children's own artistic activity?

In the meantime, there are countless examples of both variations – and there are just as many questions that seem poorly thought-out. The result is frequently fraudulent labelling! Whereas such projects are very often promoted to the public with phrases like "self-determination", "artistic self-expression" and "grass-roots democratic participation" of children (and these buzzwords have top priority when it comes to acquisitioning funds), one look behind the scenes usually reveals that the possibilities young players actually have to influence the creation of the project are very limited. There are some quite pragmatic reasons for this. If a project with children is then performed onstage, possibly as part of the evening programme, this implies that the respective product must be 'worth' the normal ticket price – which raises the question regarding the extent to which a project which is performed by lay persons is permitted to be 'amateurish' and 'unprofessional'. There is nothing to be said against the fact that professional artists contribute their professionalism and their experience, but, in contrast, it is desirable that the asymmetry between artists and lay people is used productively and is made fruitful for the children as a learning opportunity. Yet it must be borne in mind that the danger of instrumentalisation is ever present, and the younger the lay persons are with whom the artists are working, the greater this danger. Where children are only 'incorporated' into the plays of adults, without their understanding the overall sense of the play and without their ideas and approaches being taken into account, the term 'participation' borders on the absurd, and the idea of self-determination is turned into the contrary.

One last 'danger zone' can be identified with a view to the current aesthetic developments and trends in the area of children's theatre: the demand for arts education, which is growing increasingly louder. The problem is not the demand itself, but rather the accompanying implied concentration on the area of education *through* the arts as described by Anne Bamford. If one speaks of arts education, what is almost always meant is the communication of knowledge on the level of content; genuinely artistic learning content in the sense of education *in* the arts, which is certainly just as necessary, is neglected or totally ignored. Therefore, the danger of instrumentalisation is lurking here as well, albeit on a different level:

'Precisely theatre for children and young people runs the risk of being instrumentalised and of being used as an extension of educational institutions. Many makers of children's theatre see themselves as imparters of knowledge and educators rather than as artists and researchers. We, makers of children's theatre are often required to focus on specific subjects and problems which fit into the current lesson plan or the general public discourse. Not infrequently, it was about communicating preconceived opinions and approaches, an accepted pedagogical version [...]. The young audience should be able to comprehend, learn and later implement (if not to say, parrot) something in particular.'[135]

Children's theatre seems to be facing this danger all over Europe. Karin Helander (Stockholm University) confirmed this with regard to Swedish children's theatre, which is generally considered highly developed and aesthetically progressive: "Children's culture (and theatre for children) is still very much connected with school culture and concepts like learning and understanding and intelligibility in a rather rigid way".

Against the background of the worldwide debate on arts education, one can also discover a reason for the current trend towards the documentary theatre formats described earlier, which serve to impart knowledge and present scientific findings in a manner 'suitable for children'. However, in this context, other sources of danger and problems result.

For one, children's theatre, if it is primarily devoted to imparting knowledge, puts itself in the rather unfavourable position of being in competition with other media and formats which have the same intention (but which perhaps have the advantage of being able to do it better!). Can theatre for children "explain" complex scientific subjects better than, for instance, the well-reputed German *Programme with the Mouse* (*Die Sendung mit der Maus*)? Is a participation project better suited to encourage children to experiment with materials like metal, wool, wood or trash than a project week at school, or simply a school lesson using action- and production-oriented methods?

In addition, the rediscovered legitimation of art as a source of new, alternative knowledge, as Nikolaus Müller-Schöll explains, almost automatically obliges it to subordinate itself to those other disciplines and to allow itself to be measured by the same criteria as a science – which, in the final analysis, would prove to be unfavorable and unsatisfactory:

'If one looks [..] beyond the much noted showcase examples which are publicised under the mantle of 'artistic research', the suspicion arises that the democratisation of art and

---

135 | Pahl, Silvia: "Da sein – ein Manifest" (January 2013). Unpublished original manuscript kindly made available by the author of "theater 3 hasen oben" from Immichenhain/ Deutschland.

science might sometimes be of pedagogical value and its integrative intention perhaps good, but the actual result is frequently edutainment or arts and crafts, lightweight science and watered-down art. Perhaps it is time to point out that artistic research can only take place where artists are working on their very own questions and issues.'[136]

Even greater than the danger presented in the area of "artistic research" is the risk of children's theatre being usurped by a unilaterally interpreted educational mandate in the area of the so-called "theatre for the very young" – and even more so when especially "keen parents in a state of early education panic"[137] are involved, who take their toddlers to the theatre so they can 'learn' something. In such cases, it is often forgotten that the theatre for the very young is, or should primarily be, the beginning of a theatrical socialisation process.

Since theatre for the very young involves initiation experiences which facilitate the access to theatre for such a very young audience, a performance which communicates the basic characteristics of the art form – theatre – and thus contributes to an education *in* the arts, can hardly be regarded as successful. It cannot suffice simply to fob children off with 'pre-forms' of theatre which (still) do not make use of the theatrical system of signs and symbols and do not genuinely work with theatrical devices. This would be like giving pre-schoolers their first reading lessons using a 'children's alphabet' before teaching them to use the 'real' adult alphabet. So it is also insufficient that the acting of the players on the stage does not differ from the childlike games in nursery school or in the forest playground, and the specific potential of the theatre is not (or is hardly) realised.

Perhaps a change of thinking in this respect, namely in the context of political debates on the legitimation of theatre for the very young, would prove to be helpful.

3. Critical Reflections on the Circumstances

Now that an overview of the particular creative and educational potential of the independent children's theatre scene in Europe has been presented based on central themes of development and exemplary manifestations, the following chapters will be devoted to a critical review of the given circumstances and an examination of deficits and problems. The focus will be placed on the possibilities and limitations of the independent scene and the inherent potential to be developed.

---

136 | Müller-Schöll 2013, p. 39.
137 | Suchy 2012, p. 17.

3.1 Precarious Production and Presentation Conditions

3.1.1 Inadequate Funding of Independent Children's Theatre

In principle, one can say that employment is precarious in the independent scene. The so-called "independent" or "free" scene is, above all, "free" of funds. The discrepancy is particularly striking between what the independent scene offers – and, with respect to the expectations to be fulfilled, *should* offer – and what the public sector accords it in return.

On the one hand, this concerns the comparison of the artist's profession with other professions. In many countries, the wages paid by theatres are considerably lower than what is paid in other occupational sectors;[138] the percentage of those who have a fairly secure job (for which social security contributions are paid) is declining.[139] Almost all the country experts surveyed confirmed that professional artists in the independent scene are generally dependent on a (not necessarily artistic) second job; only in Sweden and France is the situation generally better. In Austria, there are some federal states in which there is hardly a difference in the amount of funding given to amateur theatre groups, according to Barbara Stüwe-Eßl (Interest Group Independent Theatre Work): "A tango club may receive more support than a professional independent group".

In dually organised theatre systems, it is undeniable that there are considerable financial disadvantages for the independent scene compared to institutional state, municipal and regional theatres, as Niclas Malmcrona puts it when describing the situation in Sweden:

---

138 | Thus reports Irène Howald on the circumstances in Switzerland, based on comparisons drawn by ACT, the association of independent theatre professionals: "An actor working an average number of hours earns less, for example, than a social worker. The diploma earned by a graduate in theatre direction from the Zurich University of Arts (ZHdK) or from another prestigious state university is the equivalent of a bachelor's degree in elementary school education. At the beginning of his or her career, an elementary school teacher in the canton Zürich has a gross monthly salary of about CHF 6000.-. An employee with a degree from a technical college and several years of work experience who has a management position at a university in the canton Zürich has a gross monthly salary of approximately CHF 12,000.-. In small theatres and in the independent theatre, wages of circa CHF 4000.- are quite common." In Germany, too, the average annual income for professionals in the independent theatre and dance scene is about 40% of the average income of an employee according to *Report Darstellende Künste* (See Fonds Darstellende Künste 2010, p. 14).

139 | See as an example a current study of the German Cultural Council as presented by Schulz/Zimmermann/Hufnagel 2013, p. 329.

'The main difference is the size and financial situation with the institutional theatres as the "big and rich". Artistically there is no big difference between institutional and independent theatres – the difference is mainly in resources (which sometimes have an artistic outcome...).'

The same can be said of the situation of children's and young people's theatre in Germany. Indeed, the high subsidies for theatres in Germany are internationally unique; however, a very high percentage of these funds go exclusively to institutional theatres. This applies all the more to the area of music theatre, as can be seen in the "Fonds Experimentelles Musiktheatre".

As a common initiative of the "NRW Kultursekretariats" and the "Kunststiftung NRW", the fund which was established in 2005 and which, since recently, explicitly includes music theatre for children and young people, supports experimental music theatre projects in repertory theatres. The aim is to confront the institution of the opera house with other 'independent' work structures in order to relax the standardised production procedures and open the theatres to new impulses from the independent scene. In other words, instead of directly providing the independent scene with more money to enable new experimental music theatre projects, the already highly subsidised theatres and opera houses are given an extra budget, provided they structurally adapt to the production methods of the independent scene and work 'alternatively'.[140]

Finally, the precarious working conditions of independent artists in some European countries such as Germany, Austria, Switzerland and The Netherlands, in particular with a view to children's theatre, are becoming worse and worse. Although children's theatre must fulfill the same criteria in order to be eligible for subsidies and is subject to the same conditions as "adult" theatre, it often receives less funding than theatre in general[141] and, as is the case with dance theatre in The Netherlands, is often hit hardest by cuts

---

140 | See the press release "Förderinstrumente der Stadt Wien entwickeln sich konträr zu erklärten Zielen der Kulturpolitik" ("Subsidies granted by the City of Vienna contradict the professed aims of cultural and educational policies") in the Austrian "IG Freie Theaterarbeit" of 7 June 2013, where one can read: "Thus the circumstances involving subsidies shift in the direction of more money for structures, more for the big and even more for the very big: money is saved on subsidies to small theatres, while in the same reference period, the large institutions – outside the body of reform – can chalk up a significant PLUS" (See http://www.freietheater.at/?page=index&alle=true&detail=19&id_language=2).

141 | See also findings from the year 2006 for funding structures in Austria: "The reality regarding subsidies clearly indicates that performing arts for young (small) people correlates without exception with smaller subsidies" – not even one tenth of the total funding was set aside for the independent groups which produce for children and young people (share: 6.1%); and children's and young people's theatre achieved less than half

in public budgets.¹⁴² "En fait, [...] la mentalité majoritairement adultocentrique de la plupart des décideurs les empêche assez souvent de véritablement s'intéresser aux droits des enfants au théâtre et à la culture en général", thus the explanation given by Maurice Yendt. The fact that artists receive less money for participative theatre projects *with* children than projects *for* children (in Austria, for example) seems all the more incomprehensible in view of the ever-louder calls for arts education programmes.

A special budget reserved exclusively for children's and young people's theatre is nowhere to be found, with the notable exceptions of Sweden, where the "Arts Council" has formulated the aim of investing at least 30% of the total financial resources for culture in programmes and projects for and with children and young people,¹⁴³ and parts of Belgium, where the ministry of culture has established a separate "Conseil du théâtre pour l'enfance et la jeunesse". The subsidies, as Paul Harman from Great Britain explains, are included in the general budgets for the theatres:

'The fact is that the Arts Councils never "officially" funded theatre companies which specialised in TYP – the position adopted by the Arts Councils is that they only fund ART. The audience for which the theatre is made has had no influence on the decision to fund a theatre company – at least in the majority of periods over the last 50 years.'

Only occasionally can one find cultural and political framework guidelines or recommendations aimed at expanding or perpetuating the cultural programme for children and young people so that the theatre for children and young people is indirectly affected (or at least may be affected). In the case of Great Britain, this is a result of an initiative of the British Arts Council and is described by Deborah Stephenson (British Arts Council) as follows:

'[E]ncouraging the participation of children and young people in the arts is a key theme running through all our programmes and we fund many theatres and productions that produce work for young audiences. Achieving Great Art, our strategic framework for the arts, sets out our 5 main goals over the next ten years and goal 5 is "every child and young person has the opportunity to experience the richness of the arts". [...] We have 696 organisations in our National portfolio funding programme (NPO) and of these 64%

---

of the average funding in comparison with the average payment made to those eligible for support (See Stüwe-Eßl 2008).

142 | Akveld 2011, p. 58. In 2009, 5 dance companies were included in the state basic funding (BIS): "Introdans", "Aya", "Meekers", "De Stilte" and "De Dansers". In 2013, these subsidies were eliminated.

143 | See http://www.kulturradet.se/Documents/English/strategy_culture_children_young_people.pdf

are supporting us to deliver goal 5 over the next three years. We do not monitor exactly what proportion of their funding is related to the delivery of this goal, but each organisation will have an activity plan with specific work identified with children and young people and will be expected to report on that work on a yearly basis.'

In all of Europe, there are no targeted initiatives taken by public authorities to support the sector of children's and young people's theatre.

In contrast to this, in the past ten years there has been a rapidly growing number of educational and cultural policy initiatives committed to promoting arts education. These initiatives are, however, focused almost entirely on the public, institutional sector and neglect the independent theatre scene as well as areas not related to formal education in schools:

'The substantial role played by individuals and organisations beyond the public sector is inadequately considered in policy planning and implementation up to now. In practice even a large number of non-education related government and non-government organisations directly contribute to cultural education; a fact which is widely neglected by politicians responsible for cultural education.'[144]

What has been formulated by the "Institute for Art Education" with regard to Switzerland also describes the reality of independent children's theatre professionals in many other European countries:

'Most resources are invested in the cooperation between cultural institutions and schools [...]. While there is money for school projects in many cantons, there is no comparable support for extra-curricular activities by independent cultural educators – and in many places for extra-curricular activities by institutions. Often such projects are passed back and forth between the sectors, culture and education, and in the meantime even social affairs.'[145]

Outside these specific support programmes, independent children's theatre has virtually been unable to profit from the increased attention currently paid to arts education worldwide. For the entire panorama of landscapes of European independent theatre, Maurice Yendt summarises what is indeed only true for the French children's theatre scene but what can easily be applied to the situation of the independent children's theatre in Europe in general:

---

[144] | *Pre-Conference-Reader on the European conference "Promoting Cultural Education in Europe: A Contribution to Participation, Innovation and Quality"*, p. 31.
[145] | Institute for Art Education, p. 176.

'Depuis plus de 10 ans, l'ensemble du secteur théâtral jeunes publics est dans l'attente d'une redéfinition et de la mise en œuvre d'une nouvelle politique de service public en faveur des artistes et de la création théâtrale pour jeunes spectateurs.'

3.1.2 Inadequate Public and Media Attention given to Independent Children's Theatre

The inadequate financial support is still accompanied by a blatant deficit of public recognition. Despite its continuous professionalisation and increased quality, independent children's theatre is seldom taken seriously, if at all, by theatre critics and the media. "A large part of theatre criticism ignores or even disdains children's theatre",[146] says Wolfgang Schneider. With the exceptions of Poland and Russia, whose country experts, Zbigniew Rudzinski and Pavel Rudnev, have confirmed a steady increase in media attention and the existence of a qualified theatre critique (at least in the area of public, institutional children's theatre), independent children's theatre is at a disadvantage in this respect in practically all European countries. This neglect brings about a kind of vicious circle. An area of public life which is not "visible" because it is not given any media attention generally receives less (financial) support. The less the area is supported, the more difficult it is to make itself noticed, and the less attention it receives. The example of private sponsoring has been used to prove this connection. Analyses show

'a clear correlation of quality characteristics in "regional and communal media coverage" to the criterion, "acquisitioning of private sponsors". The reason is obvious. Above all, small companies operating in the vicinity of projects commit themselves as sponsors of such projects, if this is then rewarded with sufficient public attention. And this publicity is more important to medium-sized companies in the area than a superregional presence which is less probable, anyway.'[147]

Therefore, the importance of a qualified theatre criticism and media attention for children's theatre cannot be underestimated, as Cyrille Planson, critic for the French trade journal *La Scène*, specialising in children's theatre, stresses:

'Donc, les retours des médias ont pour nous deux intérêts principaux:
témoigner, grâce à ces retours, de la pertinence de notre démarche auprès des décideurs (directeurs de la culture, politiques...) qui comptent beaucoup sur ces retours de la presse...
porter une parole militante et plus générale portant sur la nature de l'offre culturelle faite aux enfants et à son boom.'

---

146 | Schneider 2005, p. 102.
147 | Keuchel/Aescht 2007, p. 32.

Where there is no qualified public dialogue with the performing arts, severe losses can be expected. Otherwise, as in Switzerland, "unconventional solutions must be found to realise new forms of public confrontation".[148] Such an unconventional solution can be found at the internet website *www.theaterkritik.ch*, which was launched by independent theatre makers and sponsored by the ACT (Association des Créateurs du Théâtre indépendant) and the ASTEJ, and supported by the Swiss Federal Office of Culture (Bundesamt für Kultur) and the Oertli Foundation. Since November 2011, *theaterkritik.ch* has been online as a national platform for theatre reviews through which independent artists and groups can hire up to two critics for their productions against payment, who are then obliged to write a review. Indeed, the fact that theatre professionals contribute to the costs of the project continually leads to questions concerning the impartiality of the reviews;[149] however, there seems to be a broad consensus in the Swiss independent theatre scene that in view of the current predicament, in which the very diverse theatre landscape does otherwise not receive enough media attention, this is the lesser evil. Remarkably, almost half of the almost 20 reviews which appeared before January 2012 were reviews of children's theatre productions. In the opinion of theatre makers, this is a clear sign that there is a particularly great need for critical assessment which the existing media formats do not fulfil at all.

3.1.3 Shortage of Opportunities for Training and Specialisation for Independent Children's Theatre

Despite its increasing structural emancipation – apart from the wider and wider range of offers for courses of studies in the areas of cultural education[150] and theatre pedagogy[151] – as a rule there are no specific training opportunities at state universities[152] in Europe. This also holds true for music theatre: If composing for music theatre only plays a marginal role at most music academies, composing for children plays no role whatsoever. The target group orientation in the area of puppet or figure and object theatre is also neglected. Indeed, most productions in this area are aimed at a young audience, but no particular importance is attached to children's theatre during professional training, as Tim Sandweg reports with regard to the prestigious Hochschule für Schauspielkunst Ernst Busch in Berlin (which has its own course of studies in puppetry). Although experience shows that most graduates work primarily for children and that the market also clearly tends to offer puppet theatre for

---

148 | See *Jahresbericht 12* of astej/Switzerland, February 2013, p. 15.
149 | See *Jahresbericht 11* of astej/Switzerland, February 2012, p. 16.
150 | See Blumenreich 2012.
151 | See Hentschel 2012.
152 | See also Doderer 1993, p. 32ff. and Schneider 2005, pp. 323-330.

pre-school audiences, neither visits to children's theatres nor a respective theoretical analysis is offered during the course of studies[153]. Sandweg explains this desideratum as follows:

'Today, a certain arrogance prevails which leads to the fact that children´s theatre is not considered a form which can really be taken seriously. The aim of the course of studies to establish puppetry as its own serious art could only be achieved by way of the theatre for adults and the respective study plans.'[154]

The question of whether this attitude can be seen as the reason why children's and young people's theatre has still not found its place in the training structures for the performing arts must remain open at this point.

At the same time, there is a great lack of (and need for) professional training for participants in this area in the field of cultural education – the process of professionalisation has only just begun. This is especially true for dance theatre.[155] Although qualification programmes in dance pedagogy are being developed at state universities and in the field of advanced training for professionals, they lack professional training aimed at the dance-specific concerns of work in arts education.[156]

Thus, there is a central and general shortcoming in the area of arts education. This deficiency was described for France in the following way:

'Il faut professionnaliser les acteurs de l'éducation artistique et culturelle. La qualité des formations est un enjeu central" (Jean-Pierre Saëz, directeur de l'Observatoire des politiques culturelles). – L'accord sur ce sujet est large. Plaident en ce sens la plupart des organismes auditionnés [...]. La demande de formations conjointes (acteurs des secteurs culturels, éducatifs et sociaux ensemble) a été fréquemment formulée. Elle est certainement l'une des principales voies de progrès.'[157]

And: "Il est nécessaire de passer du stade de l'expérimentation (parfois de l'incantation) à un véritable développement".[158] In this sense, the training structures would have to be modelled and (to an extent) created from the ground up.

---

153 | See Sandweg 2012, p. 22f.
154 | Ibid., p. 23.
155 | See for example Bundesverband Tanz in Schulen 2012, p. 55.
156 | See Klinge 2012b, p. 882f. and Odenthal 2005, p. 109.
157 | Bouët 2013, p. 24.
158 | Ibid., p. 25.

3.1.4 Lack of Stages

It is one of the particularities of the independent children's theatre scenes in Europe that children's theatre companies do not usually have a permanent venue, much less their own stage. Independent theatre for children is almost synonymous with mobile theatre for children. Almost all country experts confirmed that, besides festival performances and guest appearances in theatre houses and local cultural centres, schools (auditoriums), pre-schools and nursery schools are the main venues for independent children's theatre.[159] A positive exception to be mentioned here is Sweden, where, according to Niclas Malmcrona, approximately 50 independent groups (out of about 100) are equipped with a permanent venue and separate rehearsal rooms. In comparison, in England, of about 170 children's theatre ensembles, only five have a permanent venue, and in The Netherlands it is two out of about 40.

In many cases, this lack of performance opportunities sparks not only the artistically motivated desire, but the necessity to collaborate internationally and organise guest performance tours. As was discussed at the festival *Visioni di futureo, visioni di teatro* in Bologna in 2013, for example, it is extremely difficult for producers of independent children's theatre in Italy to sell their productions in their own country; even the 'festival market' is in such a crisis that it is often difficult for groups – and for new, still not established groups, virtually impossible – to perform a piece in Italy even once. In this respect, networking with other countries is becoming more and more important in order to find a market and venues.

3.1.5 Existing Conditions Complicate the Formation of Ensembles and Hamper Artistic Continuity

Hardly any independent children's theatre group can afford to employ a large, permanent ensemble of actors, much less administrative staff or a special team to document and evaluate their artistic activities. For example, what Paul Harman writes about the children's theatre scene in England can be applied to the personnel situation of many independent groups in most other European countries: "Many of the smaller TYA companies, for example the puppet companies, are just husband and wife teams or extended family groups."

The number of permanent ensembles which produce for children has decreased significantly in the European independent scene in the last few years. Furthermore, it seems that the organisation model, described by Myrtó Dimitriadou as the "production ensemble", is beginning to prevail: a small, permanent core ensemble, frequently consisting only of a director and dramatic

---

159 | An exception in this context is German-speaking Switzerland: According to Sandra Förnbacher (University Bern), independent children's theatre does not usually perform in alternative venues, but always gives guest performances in regular theatre houses.

advisor which hires artists as required by the respective production and for the duration of a project. Long-term cooperation in permanent structures has become a rarity, mainly because the financial modalities make it seem risky, if not impossible, to establish a continuous employment relationship. Long-term planning is far too seldom an issue.

Apart from the fact that the support for independent children's theatre groups in Europe is generally distributed on an application basis and depends on compliance with certain subsidy criteria, very few groups receive public funding which is part of a structural concept (as a rule for three to four years). The great majority, if they get public support at all, depend on one-off project grants which are usually considerably smaller than the structural subsidies.[160] Thus, in 2009 in England, only 42 out of 227 children's and young people's theatres were among those in the RFO or Regularly Funded Organisations which received support over a period of three years; in 2012 in The Netherlands, only eight out of 40 were included in the four-year BIS or Basis Infrastructuur. A positive exception in this respect is Sweden. According to Lotta Brilioth Biörnstad, most independent groups regularly receive national subsidies. In 2011, the Swedish Arts Council awarded SEK 51 million to the independent scene, approximately 50% of which was given to groups that produce for children. As Niclas Malmcrona reports, it is common for permanent ensembles to be created and work together longer-term.

Otherwise, however, the principle of one-off project funding dominates. Work contexts which are severely limited by time and organisational constraints, and within which the growing together – and maturing – of an ensemble is impossible, are the necessary consequence. Despite all the lip service paid to the great importance of arts education, this is also, and especially, true with respect to the reduced number of educational programmes: "In practice it is the sad reality that especially in the area of arts education [...] project promotion with all its drawbacks is more the rule than the exception to it".[161]

The situation in Great Britain is perhaps the most dramatic. There are practically no permanent ensembles in England anymore, says Paul Harman; the artistic team is put together anew for every production and given short-term contracts; every production is – after a rehearsal period of three to four weeks

---

160 | The respective sums vary considerably even on a national level. In Austria, project subsidies are awarded for one project which may vary from €2,000 to €45,000 according to Barbara Stüwe-Eßl from the federal ministry in charge. Even in the different federal states, e.g. the state of Salzburg, the sums for independent groups can vary between €500 and €5,000.

161 | Deutscher Kulturrat 2005, p. 98. Furthermore, initiatives for arts education are often classified as projects – even those which take place in institutions which have a relatively secure funding from the public sector.

– performed *en bloc* in a limited period of time. There is no possibility to go on a longer tour with a production, much less build up a repertory, since within that "small pool of local actors shared with a number of other local companies", every artist is contractually committed to several projects. A collective manner of working or the joint development of a new piece is inconceivable under these circumstances; the actors have accustomed themselves to something else – "to be employees rather than members of co-operative companies; wait for the offer of a job, rather than join with others to follow an artistic and social vision".[162] Rhona Matheson (Starcatchers, Edinburgh) confirms a similar situation with regard to Scotland:

'Whilst the reputation is strong, there is a fragile infrastructure for theatre for children in Scotland. We have only two fully funded children's theatre companies and these are touring companies. There is no centre/building dedicated to children's theatre/arts. The other companies (including *Starcatchers*) are project-funded which gives little security and scope for long-term planning.'

The resulting "lone wolf mentality" which, of course, contradicts any ideas of teamwork and cooperation, is also just as much a part of the precarious and self-defeating conditions of the support system.

3.1.6 Continuous Cuts in the Cultural Sector

At the sixth *Kinder zum Olymp Congress,* held on 13 June 2013 in Hannover, Feridum Zaimoglu, an author of Turkish descent, gave a refreshingly direct and pointed answer to the question concerning success factors for artistic projects with children and young people by saying: 'It is not about the question: 'Does it have quality or not?' but solely about the question: 'Do we have enough money or not?' That, in principle, is the only question.'

The answer to this question for most artists in the independent children's theatre scene in Europe is clear, and an improvement is not in sight.

Since in times of economic and financial crises the cultural sector has to struggle with or is threatened by drastic cost cuts on the national and EU levels,[163] independent theatre for children is also increasingly hard-pressed

---

162 | Harman 2009/2011, p. 13f.
163 | See regarding the planned cuts in the EU budget 2014-2020 the position of the network "Culture Action Europe (CAE)", which, with more than 80,000 member organisations throughout Europe, is the leading European stakeholder group in the field of art and culture: http://www.wearemore.eu/wp-content/uploads/2010/08/CAE_Statement-Council-Agreement_20130211.pdf. The impact of the cost cuts is also being felt on the local level (such as in the production conditions of the independent theatre in Vienna). For years, a prime example of sound cultural funding policies, which continu-

financially, now more than ever. All country experts have said that they have been confronted with continuous budget cuts for at least ten years. Foundations are being used as temporary stopgaps and rescue anchors for basic support everywhere, because the system of government funding has broken down.[164] Maurice Yendt states for the French children's theatre scene: "L'autofinancement devient la règle pour un nombre croissant de compagnies."

In Switzerland, the national ASTEJ might be facing disbandment. The Federal Office of Culture (Bundesamt für Kultur or BAK) has decided to cut the subsidies to the ASTEJ every year by fifty percent in the next funding period between 2013 and 2015. As of 2016, the association will not be subsidised at all. "This degression can only be interpreted in one way," the members themselves say. "The ASTEJ cannot survive without these means".[165] The BAK justifies these measures with the supposed "lack of representativeness of the members",[166] which, in view of the fact that the ASTEJ is the only national theatre association in Switzerland with offices in all four language regions, must seem nothing short of cynical.

Perhaps the hardest hit at this time are the independent theatre professionals in The Netherlands. As part of the dramatically high cuts in the overall theatre system, the budget for national subsidies for children's and young people's theatre, which has been part of the publicly subsidised "Basis Infrastructuur" since 1990, has been virtually cut in half. For individual companies such as the prestigious Toneelmakerij, this will mean cuts of up to 70%. Others, such as the Rotterdam Meekers, the Theatergroep Max, the Theatergroep Siberia or Het nationaal Toneel and Stella in The Hague, might only survive by forming a forced alliance and pooling their resources. Four out of five dance companies are disappearing altogether, and all three production houses for children's and young people's theatre which are known beyond national borders for being talent factories for upcoming young professionals are closing down as well.[167]

---

ously increased the budget for independent theatre for the past ten years until it reached a record high of €25 million, have now also taken a turn for the worse. And contrary to the stated aims of cultural policies, as the IG Independent Theatre Work publicised in a press release of 7 June 2013, the culture department of the city decided to reduce the volume of concept funding by almost half, from €12 million to €6.5 million. Further cuts are planned. (See https://www.wien.gv.at/rk/msg/2013/02/15013.html).

164 | On increasing importance of foundations in the area of arts education, see for example Fleisch 2012.
165 | http://www.astej.ch/?id=2199&L=0
166 | See the respective media release from November 2012 at http://www.astej.ch/fileadmin/images/2012.10/Medienmitteilung_astej_121107.pdf
167 | See Zwaneveld 2011, pp. 43 and 28.

In summary, the independent children's theatre scenes in Europe are so underfunded from the structural prerequisites that they can hardly develop their high creative and educational potential. There are not enough rehearsal rooms and stages, personnel and continuity – and, above all, there is not enough money.

3.2 Economisation

Let us recall: As key methodological and aesthetic quality parameters for high-quality arts education activities, the following three factors were stressed by UNESCO: teamwork, the use of local resources and the involvement of the local context, and particularly the process-oriented work on the basis of artistic-creative research. Yet those success factors are hardly compatible with the prevailing constraints on the theatre market and the eligibility criteria for subsidies. How should professionals work collectively, in a site-specific manner and in an artistic, open-ended, non-result-oriented research process if money, time and long-term planning are not available? How should the experimental freedom be created in which theatre can be oppositional and extraordinary under the increasing pressure from the market?

3.2.1 On the Question of Teamwork and Cooperation

As concerns the question of teamwork and collective, not hierarchically organised collaborative working, it can be observed that not only the trend toward "production ensembles", already described, and the general short-term nature of work structures within the independent children's theatre scene considerably restrict the possibilities of genuine teamwork and ensemble formation. As, for example, Irène Howald (ASTEJ Switzerland) states: Because there are more and more independent companies and at the same time less and less money available, there is an increasing competitive pressure. The struggle for "visibility" and subsidies as well as the constant necessity for self-marketing require rigorously calculated competitive strategies – among the independent companies as well as within a single production team.

3.2.2 On the Question of Location Sensitivity and "Locatedness"

Location sensitivity and the use of local resources, success factors defined by UNESCO, have proven to be particularly important, and not only in connection with arts education programmes for children. In fact, in times of increased pressure on the publicly financed theatre to justify its existence as an economic cost factor, they are generally key factors in creating an individual profile and "theatre development planning", as Wolfgang Schneider explains:

'The theatre which has to do with the respective region or city must be a focus, must search and do research on site, must track down issues and use what seems relevant to the region. That should not only take place in order to attract the regional audience but because one can, in doing so, gain a deeper insight into the society.'[168]

The aim, however, of creating location-specific (cultural) identification offers which are especially directed at local interests and affairs is diametrically opposed to the dictates of the theatre market to produce 'export goods' which are mobile and internationally competitive and which promise a measurable increase in profit through mass distribution.

Lieven Baeyens, artistic director of the Compagnie IOTA in French-speaking Belgium – an independent group which manages without any structural funding – says about the precarious situation which results from having to perform a production as often as possible in as many different venues as possible:

'Pour savoir survivre nous avons besoin d'au moins une centaine de représentations par saison. Pour l'instant nous avons quarante-trois options, c'est très peu sans subventions. Le budget pour le théâtre jeune public n'a pas changé depuis plus de huit ans. Notre indépendance a un prix. C'est une réalité que nous sommes en train d'assumer pour l'instant.'

The consequence of this development on the international market is a 'loss of locality':

'In the European scene – if we not only consider Western Europe – we can observe a process of convergence or approximation of aesthetics and theatre languages in which cultural individuality is at risk of falling by the wayside. Productions are produced with an eye to the European festivals and subsidy programmes and performed in English rather than in the native languages. Less is produced (especially in Eastern Europe) for the local audience than for a market dominated by Western Europe (in the hope of being able to succeed in a Western-dominated global market).'[169]

Analogous to the economic models, European cultural promotion (and therefore also independent children's theatre) brings forth "efficient, innovative productions with mobile resources. What is lost is the [...] distinctiveness, the uniqueness".[170]

If one agrees with Holger Noltze, this trend will be even further promoted by the steadily growing cooperation network within the independent theatre

---

[168] | Schneider 2013, p. 27.
[169] | Hentschel 2012, no page.
[170] | See note 192.

landscapes – too great is the temptation to simply participate "intellectually-conceptionally, almost effortlessly, somehow, somewhere": 'The presentation of some cultural contents create playing surfaces of a common sense whose main striving is to remain as close as possible to the lowest common denominator. That will always work.'[171]

3.2.3 On the Question of Process-Oriented Work Based on Artistic Research

"Education takes place in the active and reflective confrontation with the unexpected, a moment of surprise or difference. Educational processes are not (primarily) aligned to fixed contents or prescribed events".[172] What Martin Stern formulates regarding the necessary openness of educational processes in general can be confirmed even more emphatically with respect to *arts* education processes, since unpredictability, non-standardisation and a certain 'creative chaos' are specific characteristics of what is considered artistic.

Indeed, there is broad agreement with regard to a necessary open-endedness: "Arts education which strives to impart aesthetic insights must at first be experimental, hypothetical, contradictory, vague and fleeting",[173] says Helle Becker. "Aesthetic research only has one purpose – to begin the journey without wanting to achieve a preconceived result. It is a journey with obstacles and an uncertain ending",[174] confirms Helga Kämpf-Jansen. "Arts are characterised by their open, playful and experimental handling of issues and contents and by their way of dealing with discontinuities and ambiguities",[175] says the report "Arts Education – Culture Counts". The European Agenda for Culture from the year 2010 makes the point in the following way:

'Pupils asked to do school exercises are used to looking for a single right answer, which the teacher already knows, and rejecting all other answers, regarded as wrong. On the contrary, involvement in an art project has more in common with research and exploration than with an algorithmic procedure whose stages are marked out in advance. It teaches that there are many right answers possible to the questions we face in seeing the project through. It also teaches us that the result is never known in advance and must always be constructed.'[176]

---

171 | Noltze 2010, p. 190.
172 | Stern 2010, p. 224.
173 | Becker 2011, p. 219.
174 | Kämpf-Jansen 2002, p. 276.
175 | German UNESCO Commission e. V. 2009, p. 1.
176 | Lauret/Marie 2010, p. 12.

The educational opportunities this produces involve discovering new abilities, gaining insights, and opening up a range of behavioural possibilities, so that it is generally easier to tolerate what is unknown, uncertain and ambiguous, since such projects require "a constant discarding, deciding and re-deciding, and accepting of situations" – namely "situations in which, under different circumstances, one would never have found oneself".[177] Understood in this way, the artistic-aesthetic experience becomes a kind of "training programme for an open, creative approach to complexity which is tolerant of resistance and ambiguity".[178]

Furthermore, experiencing a (temporary) failure can be made fruitful by integrating it into the creative process. "To be an artist is to fail, as no other dare fail".[179] This is one of the most frequently quoted sentences from the writings of Samuel Beckett on art theory – and there is a general consensus with respect to education theory that "productive failure" is a key moment in educational processes,[180] since "a diversity of experiences", involving confusion, not being able to, or not knowing how, harbor the potential of expanding, qualifying or changing"[181] existing conditions. Apart from this, errors and detours can lead to new insights and discoveries which could otherwise neither be planned nor foreseen: "With respect to acquiring experience, the shortest way from A to B is not necessarily the best",[182] says Holger Noltze.

In the light of all these insights and findings, the conception and implementation of theatre projects with children should logically always be about allowing an open-ended, research-based artistic work process with a 'license to fail'. Yet the reality of artistic practice in the independent children's theatre scenes in Europe looks different.

On the one hand, it is no secret that independent theatre makers usually work under tremendous time pressure. Faced with short funding periods (and small grants) typical for project promotion, many independent groups are forced to respect the motto "time is money" by producing quickly in order to achieve presentable results within the subsidised time frame, and by realising as many projects one after another in "assembly line" fashion so that a continuous funding is ensured, at least cumulatively. "In many cities the under-financing of independent theatre has paradoxically led to over-production. [...] The primal instinct for survival compels theatres to mass produce".[183] Cecilia Billing

---

177 | Kämpf-Jansen 2002, p. 277.
178 | Noltze 2010, p. 263f.
179 | Beckett 1983, p. 145.
180 | Stern 2010, p. 222f.
181 | Ibid., p. 224.
182 | Noltze 2010, p. 228.
183 | *Evaluation der Freien Theaterszene in Frankfurt am Main*, p. 14.

from Dockteaterverkstan, an independent puppet theatre ensemble from the Swedish city of Osby, describes the production conditions as follows:

'The first problem is to be given the time for development, innovation, building puppets etc. You are under pressure to all the time produce new performances and you must produce in a certain time. (As a touring company we always meet a new audience so we do not have to make new performances all the time. But to get grants you are forced to produce.)'

In addition, there are normally such strict funding criteria and such specific target agreements to which independent groups commit themselves contractually when they receive grants, that a truly open-ended, process-oriented, and experimental working method is hardly possible – to say nothing of failing as a learning experience.

"It would be a wonderful miracle if the independent scene were sponsored so well that the singular theatre experiment can afford to seek and fail without jeopardising its entire existence",[184] says Silvia Pahl from the independent German theatre ensemble "3 hasen oben". However, the real situation is far removed from this 'wonderful miracle'. The cultural and political task of "comprehending theatre promotion as a risk premium", that means "not rewarding what works and is successful in any case but also rewarding the process and the failure", is a funding criterion, as Wolfgang Schneider confirms, which "has been completely neglected"[185] to date. Even the Deutsche Kulturrat in 2005 came to a similar conclusion with regard to European cultural policies in general:

'In principle, especially as part of a pilot project in which, for example, new methods of communicating culture are tried out, failing should be an option because such a project is about experimenting. In reality, it has been the case for years that failure is avoided at all costs because a project owner who has failed hardly has the chance to acquisition for new projects.'[186]

In other words, the problem has long been recognised as such – and no solution or concrete countermeasures are in sight.

Another issue is that a possible failure is normally measured according to whether or not it is a *commercial* failure. For in the end, what stands above everything else in the neoliberal matrix of the economic market, which also controls the 'market' of the independent theatre in Europe, is the principle of

---

184 | Pahl, Silvia: "Theaterblitzlicht". Notes on *Spurensuche* 2012 in Hannover. Unpublished manuscript kindly made available by the author of theater 3 hasen oben in Immichenhain/Germany.
185 | Schneider 2013, p. 28.
186 | Deutscher Kulturrat 2005, p. 98.

usefulness and efficiency – the exploitation and rationality of a cost-benefit calculation. This necessitates "the industrialisation of creative processes which are based on the optimisation of the relationship of effort and yield".[187]

This concerns not 'only' the artistic sector, but that of (arts) education, since the "educational turn" is closely linked with the performing arts for young audiences. And in the area of independent children's theatre, these interactions and dynamics have proven to be especially problematic. In the course of the general commercialisation and economisation of the collective thinking process, educational contents are evaluated more and more according to their profitability: "The educational system is seen today almost exclusively as a supplier for economic processes"[188] and, as a consequence, "education is reduced to a commodity".[189] The aim of most educational processes is employability, and thus the immediate usability of learning contents and competences for the successful creation of work biographies.

'It is only about *qualification* – making people usable in terms of a profitable exploitation. The frequent reference to the importance of the "factor education" for the economy, including the pretty slogan about life-long learning, only reveals what this is really about: not about "educating individuals" but only about "creating capital" by means of tailoring the qualification of subjects to the needs of the potential buyers of the commodity, human labour.'[190]

General postulata about education apply even more to *arts* education. Parallel to the emergence of today's "knowledge societies", a decisive paradigm shift has taken place regarding the weighting of "arts education skills" and the requirements profile for "human capital" on the job market of the future:

'21st century societies are increasingly demanding workforces that are creative, flexible, adaptable and innovative and education systems need to evolve with these shifting conditions. Arts education equips learners with these skills.'[191]

With regard to this, Paul Harman described the changed production conditions of independent artists in Great Britain as follows:

'From the 1950s, UK schools welcomed artists of all kinds to give children direct experience of the arts, as part of a full "education of the whole child". Since the 1980s, pub-

---

187 | Noltze 2010, p. 85.
188 | Ribolits 2004, p. 41.
189 | Ibid., p. 50.
190 | Ibid., p. 48 – emphasis in original
191 | *Road Map for Arts Education*, p. 3.

lic education has been largely reduced to preparing children to serve the economy. They have been graded and tested to show employers how they might be used by business. There is a focus on learning skills of practical use to employers.'

The potential economic usability of arts education initiatives is primarily reflected in the willingness to provide financing and more public funding. For cultural and educational policymakers, the question "Does Mozart Make You Smart?" – the title of a research project sponsored by the German Federal Ministry for Education and Research – is apparently still a crucial, if not the only, criterion for government subsidies.[192] The genuine artistic-aesthetic aspect does not appear as an intrinsically basic right and value, and thus not important enough to merit public support. Grants are always linked to possible non-artistic transfer or "follow-up competences", utility and book values and indirect profitability resulting from knock-on effects.

On the part of the artists and mediators working in the field, this circumstance has been frequently noted and more or less cynically pointed out. Elmar Lampson, President of the Academy of Music and Theatre Hamburg, on the occasion of an awards ceremony for the "junge ohren" Prize 2012, commented: "I am no good at maths. I never was and am still not today. Working with all those numbers – I can´t do it! But I can play a triple counterpoint. Why is that not worth as much?" And Stéphan Vincent-Lancrin, project manager at the Centre for Educational Research and Innovation (CERI) of the OECD, stated in unequivocal terms at a congress on "Perspectives of Research on Arts Education" in June 2013:

'A mathematician would never think about asking whether mathematical skills have positive transfer effects when learning how to play a musical instrument - the other way around, it happens all the time!'

In other words, approaches to arts education are always under pressure to prove their legitimacy. What counts is not arts education itself but its 'barter value'. Social relevance is mainly (or only) attributed to arts education when it is suitable for the acquisition of "key competences" and qualifications which are of interest to the job market.

This can be observed in many places. In 2001, the German Federation for Cultural Youth Education (Bundesvereinigung Kulturelle Jugendbildung e.V.) published an important report on acquiring "key competences through arts education". This report makes clear that for the publishers the acquisition of these key competences refers to the "evaluation and certification of the

---

192 | See also "Macht Mozart schlau – Die Förderung kognitiver Kompetenzen durch Musik" (See http://www.bmbf.de/pub/macht_mozart_schlau_kurfassung.pdf).

educational benefits of arts education for working life" as well as "securing the positive effects of arts education for the individual and making them visible and comprehensible for future employers". The aim is to have young persons "channel these positive effects profitably into their professional careers" and thus be able to document them as a "sustainable resource".[193]

The position of the German Federation for Cultural Youth is also remarkably similar with regard to the "procedure to identify and certify key competences through arts education", implemented between 2001 and 2004, to that of the pilot project sponsored by the Federal Ministry of Education and Research (Bundesministerium für Bildung und Forschung) called Cultural Competence Certificate (Kompetenznachweis Kultur). Young persons achieving this certificate have proven themselves in possession of soft skills which have been organised into 34 sub-competences and which they have acquired through voluntary participation in extracurricular arts education programmes. These are offered in various facilities and projects organised by music and art schools, theatre and dance workshops, literature offices or media centres, in the children's museum and in the children and youth circus. The certification is in the form of a competence passport which when "presented should improve the holder's chances on the job market – and, at the same time, justify the existence of cultural work by presenting 'hard' evidence of its educational impact":[194]

'In a study contracted by the project development department of the German Federation of Cultural Children's and Youth Education, it was determined that young persons who were in possession of a competence certificate could benefit more from their cultural hobby than those youths who did not participate in the certification programme. Employers praise the additional information which is usually not included in CVs and school reports and which is useful in candidate selection processes for apprenticeships or other positions.'[195]

A similar concept with a so-called "Kulturpass" exists in Switzerland.

What manifests itself here is the prevailing collective utilitarian thinking that sees artistic competences primarily in the service of equipping the Me PLC which, in turn, pays off in cash returns in the long run. That education in and with the arts has an immanent worth in itself and for itself, and that education *in* the arts could be desirable as a primary educational goal, is completely forgotten. In other words, even the concept of education is increasingly subjugated to the dictates of the neoliberal market and reduced to

---

193 | Bundesvereinigung Kulturelle Jugendbildung e. V. 2002, p. 5f.
194 | Mörsch, Carmen: Eine kurze Geschichte von KünstlerInnen in Schulen; See: http://kontextschule.org/inhalte/dateien/MoerschKuelnSchGeschichte.pdf
195 | Final Report of the Enquête Commission: "Kultur in Deutschland", p. 388.

"parading readily accessible competences" where its contents are concerned;[196] education's worth and market value, professional (and capital) potential are often inseparable:

'The value of something is a gift given by industry, not a quality of the product itself. Many cultural-political documents refer to a cultural value. In such documents, "value" is a devalued term which is only perceptible from a quantitative perspective, as, for example, in attendance figures with statistical breakdowns which enable the monitoring of social inclusion and provide data on advertising customers and sponsors. In this way the actual worth is subjected to the economic value. The worth which is more valuable than all the others is an economic one [...] The marketability of culture must be guaranteed; Culture is only then valuable when it contributes to the "economy".'[197]

The independent performing arts for children and mainstream education in Europe are finding themselves on the same side of the fence in the struggle against the increasingly strict dictates of the market. Both are under comparable performance, efficiency and marketing pressure resulting from the economisation and commercialisation, in the wake of which they must both justify themselves as an economic factor.

Therefore, the following can be concluded: The methodological-aesthetic quality parameters developed by UNESCO for artistic work processes with children are often neglected in today's labour market, sales market and in prevalent self-marketing processes. It may be that the independent scene, with its own mode of production, is theoretically better able to fulfil the acknowledged conditions for success on this level, but once again the necessary financial resources will be lacking.

3.3 Paradoxical Funding Criteria

The makers of independent children's theatre presently find themselves in a paradoxical situation. The methodological-aesthetic quality parameters defined by UNESCO confirm the necessity of a working method and production aesthetics which are incompatible with the prevailing factual constraints of an increasingly economised art market. Yet a (typically) 'independent' mode of working is expected despite a concurrent, omnipresent absence of freedom and dependence on the part of the independent artists with respect to financial and structural security.

---

196 | See also the essay by Christoph Türcke "Wie das Lernen sein Gewicht verliert" from the *Süddeutschen Zeitung* of 1 Aug 2012, p. 12.
197 | Leslie 2007, p. 57.

Many exemplary cases can be added to this basic perception of what is considered paradoxical. They demonstrate the incompatibility of the criteria used to determine eligibility for funding in the area of cultural promotion with the actual circumstances and possibilities, especially of the independent scene.

Lotta Brilioth Biörnstad of the Swedish Arts Council compiled an incomplete list of general funding conditions for independent groups which included the following criteria:

- High artistic quality
- Development and renewal
- Geographical distribution
- International exchange
- Diversity
- Accessibility
- Gender equality
- Local and/or regional support

Complying with these criteria, however, would require the financial and structural security for which the independent artists first have to apply.

In addition, there are also further funding criteria which are incompatible with the artistic practice of most independent theatre groups; these are described in the following overview.

3.3.1 Permanent Full-Time Employment
As Irène Howald reported on the requirements for granting financial resources in the German-speaking part of Switzerland, one of the criteria for theatre funding is "professionalism", defined as "more than 50% of the activities being performed actively in the theatre". But this is in fact hardly possible, since most of those employed by the independent theatre rely on sideline jobs which need not, but may, be proportionally subordinate to their work in the theatre.

3.3.2 Proof of Venue
Typical of the overall situation is Irène Howald's description of another funding criterion as applied in Switzerland (it also applies to many other countries): proof of venue:

'The (first) performances usually have to be guaranteed, i.e. collaborations have to exist with theatre houses/organisers. [...] More often than in the past, the theatres play an important role in the funding since, more and more, only those productions are subsidised which can show that they have several fixed venues and dates.'

In view of the general lack of theatre venues and performance possibilities for independent groups, this, too, is a requirement which often prevents or severely limits the development of new projects.

3.3.3 Non-Profit Criteria

A country's legal situation, which may favour artists' biographies and the establishment of ensembles and projects more or less, is another important factor in granting subsidies. In this regard, Paul Harmon describes the structural production conditions of independent groups in Great Britain which cannot be separated from the *manner* of production and the production *results* they bring about:

'The great constitutional problem in the UK is the use of Charity law as the basis for registering a non-profit theatre company. Until recently there was no easy way to create a co-operative company which would meet the non-profit criteria demanded by the funders. So the kind of collectives formed after 1969 in Denmark, Germany or Belgium (asbl) were very hard to create in the UK. We had to use a more complex structure which the artists could not run themselves as directors. It works this way:
A registered Charity pays no tax on income or profits and has some other tax advantages. A Charity has to be run by Directors who have no financial interest – so they cannot be paid employees. But to have limited liability if you lose money, you have to be a Company Limited by Guarantee, also having unpaid directors. The Arts Council will normally only fund non-profit bodies set up in this way. So the artists are employed by a group of well-intentioned outside people who have to satisfy the Arts Council funders – and maybe also the Local Authority if they give any money towards the Company's work – that the money is spent only on things the Arts Council approves.
So, after a while, the Arts Council changes its priorities or the Board of the Company decides to do something different and the artistic team changes.
That is a thumbnail sketch but reasonably accurate. [...]
So there is I believe a more direct link between constitutional arrangements and artistic choices. If you can spend six months rehearsing a play, [...] the result will be very different from what you can do in England on three or four weeks rehearsal with actors you recruit for the show on a short contract.'

3.3.4 Employment under an Employee Contract

One problem similar to those of funding criteria and legal situations is that of employment status (in Germany and Austria, for example). The law regulating work in the area of "acting" requires that the employment of actors is based on an employment status subject to social security contributions. While "artists" can generally be classified as self-employed staff and insured with the artists' social insurance (Künstlersozialkasse - KSK), this does not apply to actors who are officially and essentially bound by instructions from an "employer". However, in the artistic practice of independent groups, it is usually impossible to comply with this regulation, which obviously orients itself towards the financial volume of a structurally subsidised state theatre. The social security contribution for employees with permanent contracts would far exceed any (project) budget. Thus, those working in the field of independent theatre have only two options: starting a new 'company' for each project, with its own managing director and in which all participants are personally liable (!) partners – a huge organisational and administrative effort few groups can afford – or giving up their artistic work.

3.3.5 National Interests
One can also observe incongruities in the funding possibilities for promoting national interests and structures, as seen in the criteria for cultural promotion in German-speaking Switzerland:

'In addition to funding from cantons and cities for cultural promotion, the federal government provides subsidies and support exclusively for plans which are of significance for the whole of Switzerland. [...] Since such projects, in general, take place in one location and in interaction with the population in a specific local context, the significance for the whole of Switzerland is difficult to prove.'[198]

Moreover, Irène Howald emphasised the following for the area of children's and young people's theatre: 'In principle, there are big differences between the funding in more rural communities and cantons and in the urban parts of Switzerland. An independent group, working in a small canton, cannot secure its livelihood.'

3.3.6 Innovation
As has been clearly demonstrated based on the criteria from Sweden, development and renewal are still important assessment criteria for the independent theatre scene when it comes to granting financial resources. Apart from that, the frequently cited UNESCO Convention on the Promotion and Protection of the Diversity of Cultural Expression from 2005 refers to the promotion of artistic diversity and specificity as one of the main goals of European cultural policy. A (production-) aesthetic standardisation and producing for the mainstream market are diametrically opposed to these prerequisites.

In reality, however, faced with an increasingly economised art market, the independent groups in particular find themselves under pressure to succeed and to supply productions with passe-partout aesthetics and themes with mass appeal which are internationally competitive, which can be delivered in standardised serial production, and which do not run the risk of being

---

198 | Institute for Art Education, p. 176.

unmarketable. The more important the funding criterion of capacity utilisation becomes, the less the independent theatre makers can afford to experiment, to try out the unconventional, to address taboo and sensitive topics, and the more necessary it is to produce easily 'consumable', purely entertaining 'goods' which guarantee their own marketability.

This trend towards commercialisation and market orientation in the independent children's theatre scenes in Europe was named by all those country experts surveyed, and independent of each other, as one of the most pressing negative developments. Maurice Yendt sums up the situation for France: "Développement quantitatif important en raison de la banalisation des spectacles jeunes publics en tous genres – retour de formes dramaturgiques formatées par les exigences du marché des produits culturels". Karin Helander describes the situation for Sweden as follows:

'Still too many theatres (and adults) are afraid of emotionally strong themes and new innovations. Still a lot of performances for children are based on classical children's literature, fairy tales and well-known figures in very traditional ways. And lack of money too often results in a coward repertoire and poor stagings.'

And Myrtó Dimitriadou added the following comments with regard to independent children's theatre in Austria:

'One problem is surely the financing. Many groups are forced to follow conventional taste, the requirements of the audience, because otherwise they will not have any revenues. This makes it impossible for some to remain consistent and to develop in new directions because they cannot sell the productions. Of course, this is counterproductive for the others.'

Paul Harman describes the following production strategy common in Great Britain:

'Original and contemporary theatre forms are only used by the specialist, independent companies. The larger building-based producing companies largely present conventional adaptations of children's books. This is because there is too great a financial risk in offering an 'experimental' work in a large theatre which has to sell many hundreds of seats to the public.'

For the German-speaking region of Switzerland, Peter Keller from the Theater Arlecchino in Basel reports:

'Since our theatre is not subsidised and we are always on the brink of financial collapse, we are very much dependent on the revenues from ticket sales. We always have to have a programme which will bring in a lot of spectators. Therefore, we specialise in the modern classics of children´s literature. This also distinguishes us from other theatres.'[199]

In other words, the independent groups, especially those which receive only project-related funding (if any), do not usually have the means and possibilities for the (aesthetic) experiments which funding criteria require. Given the dictates of the market, they are more or less forced to play a conventional text and repertory theatre which significantly increases the probability of high ticket sales and full houses because of its mass appeal.

3.3.7 Measurable Interim and Final Results

A basic recommendation made by the European Agenda for Culture in 2010, which can also be found in the structural quality parameters of UNESCO, is the success factor of evaluation and quality assurance:

'[E]valuation is the key to developing and sustaining good work and should be undertaken regularly to contribute to informed decision making and improved action in arts education.
With this in mind, it is proposed: That all projects and programmes should allocate funds from their budgets for evaluation (preferably both internal and external).'[200]

In contrast, the measurable and verifiable, the communicable in general, is *not* really a characteristic feature of artistic processes:

'What is the value of theatre in the lives of children and young people?
Much has been written about the value of the arts, and important work is being done across the globe in researching the powerful effects of the arts on children through studies in neuroscience, neuro-education, developmental psychology and related fields. But as much as we can try to measure the impact of what we do, there is also a level at which the impact of art on its audience remains mysterious and unquantifiable. It is the

---

199 | In the repertory of the Theater Arlecchino, there are adaptations of novels by Astrid Lindgren (Pippi Langstrumpf, Pippi in Taka-Tuka-Land, Ronja The Robber's Daughter, Michel from Lönneberga), Michael Ende (Jim Knopf and Lukas the Engine Driver, Jim Knopf and the Wild 13), Ellis Kaut (Pumuckl), James Matthew Barrie (Peter Pan), P. L. Travers (Mary Poppins), Rudyard Kipling (The Jungle Book) and Lyman Frank Baum (The Wizard of Oz).
200 | Lauret/Marie 2010, p. 31.

profound and unique meeting of the theatre piece with the audience in a particular time and space that makes theatre so unpredictable and exciting.'[201]

Against this backdrop, the evaluation of artistic processes, which in many cases is required of theatre groups to prove their eligibility for subsidies and which can be seen as proof of effectiveness or fulfilment of an educational standard, generates a pressure on said groups to prove their legitimacy which is detrimental and which, in the end, *hinders* or even *prevents* the desired open-ended results and process orientation.

3.3.8 Mission: Arts Education

Finally, certain constraints on independent theatre are specific to children's theatre with regard to the much called-for mission to contribute to arts education. Despite the potential of the independent scene described in this study, funding possibilities focus on the sector of publicly subsidised institutions, leaving only a niche (if anything) for makers of independent theatre:

'The promotion of arts education, which after a long struggle is not financed with resources from the areas of education and culture, often concentrates on schools or collaborations of cultural institutions with educational institutions. Projects which [...] operate outside these funding guidelines in the independent scene, have difficulty acquisitioning funds as long as they do not adapt to the funding criteria. When assessed for cultural funding (which, by far, does not subsidise all the good projects), the artists are lay persons, for social funding the costs are too high for a professional video installation. In both cases it is difficult to think beyond the duration of a project: Innovative projects are desired but seldom follow-up collaborations or even institutional support. Funding stipulations prevent sustainability.'[202]

In summary, Paul Harman states what this means for current developments on the methodological-aesthetic level for the independent children's and young people's theatre scene in Great Britain:

'In the last five years or so, we have seen a greater and greater divide between companies. They fall into roughly three groups. A small group who seek to make art for young audiences. A large group who make entertainment theatre which can attract paying audiences, usually based on known folk tales or adaptations of contemporary picture books for younger children and established titles for older children. The largest group

---

201 | Hardie, Yvette, "President's Message" on the occasion of the World Day of Children's and Young People's Theatre, 20 March 2013; see http://www.assitej-international.org/media/55530/message_2013_yvette.pdf
202 | Berendts 2010, p. 166.

now make overtly 'educational' theatre, which covers a wide range of participatory or didactic products aimed to support aspects of the official curriculum, or to address topics like sex education which teachers assume will be better delivered through dramatised stories or dramatic play.'

The fact that the groups which actually want *and can* produce "art" for children are a minority is one of the crucial absurdities of the art market and the system of cultural funding.

3.4 Interim Conclusion II: Possibilities and Limitations of the Independent Scene

Since the nineties, independent children's theatre in Europe has structurally emancipated itself and aesthetically differentiated and refined itself. It has also successfully repositioned itself in the knowledge society of the 21st century in terms of an explicit educational mandate, giving the independent theatre scene a particular and inherent potential for several reasons.

On the one hand, a particular creative potential can be observed, since certain impulses for the structural change and aesthetic innovation could only emerge under the production and distribution conditions characteristic of the independent scene. The typically 'independent' manner of working alone (i.e., outside predefined structures) has enabled and favoured the development of new formats which have currently influenced and stimulated the children's theatre landscapes in Europe.

The most important factor in this context is the cross-sector and interdisciplinary play development which the majority of independent groups still espouse despite all adversities. In this connection, it is important to bear in mind that the creation of new plays which are perfectly tailored to the talents of the respective artists involved create favourable prerequisites for aesthetic experiments and innovations. In some areas, as in the theatre for the very young and in music and dance theatre for children, the ability to develop separate artistic productions in the group is virtually a necessary condition, because there is to date practically no repertory which artists can fall back on which can be re-enacted one-to-one.

As can be well demonstrated for the sector of music theatre for young people, the flexible structures and production conditions necessary for the development process of new pieces are typical of the independent scene, but not of an institutional opera house: "The team-oriented structures of the independent theatre are much better suited to the character of projects than the hierarchically organised work structures and division of labour which can be found in a [...] municipal theatre",[203] says the so-called "Mannheimer Manifest" on music theatre for young audiences. And what is proclaimed here for music theatre can be generally applied to the principle of separate piece development within the independent performing arts on the whole: 'Independent' work structures are more suitable for piece development.

In addition, it could be shown that the independent children's theatre scene in particular has the potential to fulfil the educational mandate given to the arts. It seems predestined to offer participative activities in arts education of a very high standard, since the compatibility of typically 'independent' production conditions with the quality parameters defined by UNESCO is especially high.

From that point of view, one can say that working artistically *and* 'independently' greatly increases the chances (or is necessary) for both aesthetic innovations and high-quality arts education activities in the area of children's theatre. However, the development of this immanent potential of independent theatre can only take place under certain conditions – conditions which are seldom guaranteed by cultural and educational policies. In fact, independent children's theatre in Europe is still largely neglected in cultural and educational policies, and its potential is disregarded (or underestimated at best).

As has been shown, the lack of financial resources, the constraints and mechanisms of an increasingly economised art market, and the prevailing (and often paradoxical) funding criteria prevent independent groups from being able to work typically 'independently'. Precarious working conditions make it impossible for artists to develop their creative potential in the form of innovations like those prescribed in the UNESCO quality parameters for arts education.

One thing is clear: the makers of independent children's theatre can only use their 'independence' productively and thus be able to develop their potential if they are 'independent' of the constraints of the market – if the independent scene can become an "independent scene with sufficient money and time". This, however, is in the reality of most European countries still a paradox. Independent children's theatre groups normally have neither (sufficient) public funding nor the option of taking enough time to develop a project, and the advancing commercialisation of the market on which art for children is increasingly offered purely as a commodity is making the situation worse.

One of the consequences of these precarious working conditions is the increasing self-exploitation of artists: "If the independent scene [...] claims to be the avantgarde of the theatre, then it has been, in the form of a project-based regime of exploitation, the capitalistic avantgarde for a long time now",[204]

---

203 | From "Mannheimer Manifest zum Musiktheater" (vgl. http://www.assitej.de/fileadmin/assitej/pdf/2009-12-07_Mannheimer_Manifest.pdf), p. 1.
204 | Stegemann 2013, p. 234.

according to Bernd Stegemann. And also the general reflections of Byung-Chul Han on the implicit "structures of subordination and coercion of the neoliberal dictates of freedom"[205] can be transferred almost one-to-one to the working structures of the so-called "independent" theatre scene:

'The call for motivation, initiative and project is more effective for exploitation than whip and commands. As one´s own entrepreneur, the subject of performance is free in that it is not subordinate to the orders and exploitation of others because it exploits itself and of its own volition. The exploiter is the exploited. One is perpetrator and victim in one. The self-exploitation is much more efficient than the exploitation by another because it is associated with the feeling of freedom.'[206]

This mechanism of self-exploitation is also perpetuated by the circumstance that the prevailing hardship in economic circles has been relabelled as a virtue by using the artists as "perfect role models for the economy of the service society"; each is expected to continuously reinvent him- or herself as a "Me Incorporated".[207] In this sense, being 'creative' becomes one of the most urgent "key competences" in a neoliberal exploitation system.

"One could argue that the quality of theatre for children and youth is an indicator of the maturity and sophistication of a theatre culture in any given country, its sense of vision and responsibility, its deliberate investment in the future theatre audience",[208] Dragan Klaic wrote about the importance of theatre for children and young people. In light of this, it must seem completely desirable for independent children's theatre to receive more support in the future to develop its full potential. In order to achieve this, two things must happen as soon as possible:

1.) *"Being an artist means putting up a fight!"*
"The art of being courageous is not losing heart. Keep struggling. Always offering resistance. Against the wind. Counter-current. Always maintaining the balance. Always alert".[209] These are the words which Marcel Cremer (AGORA Theater, Saint Vith) used to describe his general artistic self-perception. On another occasion, he described it as follows:

---

205 | Han 2013, p. 16.
206 | Ibid., p. 15.
207 | Mörsch, Carmen: "Eine kurze Geschichte von KünstlerInnen in Schulen"; see: http://kontextschule.org/inhalte/dateien/MoerschKuelnSchGeschichte.pdf
208 | Klaic 2012, p. 75.
209 | Cremer 2012, no page.

'Being an artist means putting up a fight. The fool and I are one and the same. And the fool generally survives the kings who employ him [...]. An artist is not there to stand up for the powerful or to serve them [...]. We, artists, are on the side of the minorities, especially if we see ourselves as artists of the people [...]. It is part of the biography of an artist that he never puts down his weapons, never refuses to fight for a just cause.'[210]

If one specifically addresses the necessary resistance of the independent artists in the struggle against the usurpation of their art by the mechanisms of the market economy, this can express itself in a deliberate refusal of certain subsidies if the respective prerequisites for funding negatively influence artistic work. Bill Buffery (multi story theatre company) from Great Britain reported on the situation as follows:

'Firstly, we deliberately do not seek revenue funding. This is because, having worked for 23 years within subsidised theatre, we grew weary of the opaque bureaucracy that came with subsidy. We resented the colonisation of our minds and the eroding of our creative time. We found the constraints in terms of what kind of work we could produce and where we could produce it counter-productive.'

The following answer was given by Silvia Pahl from theater 3 hasen oben when asked why she wanted to continue working in children's theatre despite all the difficulties:

'It is very clear to us that our capabilities of exerting any kind of influence on society are (put mildly) limited. With regard to the single individual who comes to the theatre, our influence is, for a short time, a bit greater. We want to use this moment. Even the smallest impulse is worth sending out into the audience – and, thus, into the world. We are idealists, otherwise we would be out of place in children´s theatre.'[211]

There is nothing more to add.

2.) *"A redefinition of public interest in culture!"*
"One should be aware of the fact that saving on culture can only make a small contribution toward balancing a budget. However, the damage done by such

---

210 | Cremer, Marcel: "Jenseits der grünen Wiese". In: *AGORA – Das Theater der Deutschsprachigen Gemeinschaft Belgiens* (ed.): Pieces 8-16. In-house publication 2009 – quoted from: *AGORA 2012*, no page.
211 | Pahl, Silvia, "Da sein – ein Manifest" (January 2013). Unpublished original manuscript kindly made available by the author of "theater 3 hasen oben" from Immichenhain/Germany.

cost-cutting measures is immense".²¹² This statement made by the German Minister of State, Bernd Neumann, indicates a clear direction for European cultural promotion policies: Limit the damage, and, in the best case, *repair* it!

An independent Austrian research institute, EDUCULT, developed and published a cross-section study in 2011 describing the near future of children's theatre in Europe and including the following two horror scenarios:

'Scenario I:
Further budget constrains for public cultural policy and cultural institutions are leading to an even higher concentration on traditional forms of presentation and existing audience. Culture is the final retreat of the diminishing white urban upper class.

Scenario II:
Further budget cuts of public funding are compensated by cultural institutions through a strong market orientation. Besides concentration on traditional forms, cultural offers are identical with entertainment, serving the taste of the audience. Education will be limited to edutainment activities. As a result cultural institutions will no longer have a consistent image, values of culture and the arts will be indicated by quantities of audiences and return on investment.'²¹³

One should also bear in mind that saving should not be an issue when it comes to the quality of such activities, especially in terms of arts education:

'Quality arts education programs have impact on the child; the teaching and learning environment, and on the community, but these benefits were only observed where quality programs were in place. [...] It is of significance to note that a number of case studies indicated that bad and poor quality programs, in fact may be detrimental to children's creative development [...].'²¹⁴

Accordingly, the worst case scenario may be the one pointedly predicted by Paul Harman: "The current austerity measures probably mean that we shall lose most of the improvements in status and public awareness won over the last 30 years."

In order to prevent this catastrophe, politicians must become more active: "Le secteur théâtral jeunes publics français est dans l'attente de la définition et de la mise en œuvre d'une nouvelle politique théâtrale de service public pour jeunes spectateurs au niveau de l'Etat comme des collectivités régionales".

---

212 | Bernd Neumann in an interview with the ver.di-Zeitschrift *Kunst + Kultur*, 14 Dec 2009 (online at: http://www.bundesregierung.de/Content/DE/Interview/2009/12/2009-12-14-bernd-neumann-verdi-kunst-und-kultur.html?__site=Nachhaltigkeit).
213 | EDUCULT 2011, p. 65.
214 | Bamford 2009, p. 101.

Maurice Yendt describes the expectations of children's theatre professionals in France in such a way that most players in the independent children´s theatre scenes in practically all European countries would subscribe to it. Or in the words of Dragan Klaic:

'What is needed in Europe instead of new theatre laws is a redefinition of public interest in culture and the articulation of instruments, criteria, procedures and resources that will implement these interests through the existing and emerging cultural infrastructure, drawing clear demarcation lines between commercial and non-commercial cultural production and distribution. This redefinition cannot be just a matter of national policy but needs strong regional and local anchoring.'[215]

What this can mean for independent children's theatre in Europe in particular, and what steps European cultural and educational policy makers should take in view of the currently prevailing (negative) conditions, will be summarised in the last part of this study.

4. Conclusion: Five Demands on Cultural Policy Makers

What are currently the most important desiderata essential to the well-being of independent children's theatre in Europe which must be addressed to those persons who are and should be responsible for cultural and educational policies? Which measures are urgently needed to ensure a better future for the independent performing artists for young audiences?

4.1 End the Inadequate Financing of Independent Children's Theatre!

As this study showed, the independent groups in Europe, especially in the area of children's theatre, still suffer from a severe shortage of financial support. If public protestations demanding innovation and creativity, the preservation of cultural diversity, and more high-quality arts education programmes are to be more than lip service, then there *must* be more money, and swift and purposeful action *must* be taken on both national and community levels. "Public funding in this area is in the 'public interest'", concludes the German Bundestag's Enquête Commission on Culture[216] – now it is time to turn words into action, not only in Germany but throughout Europe.

---

215 | Klaic 2012, p. 171.
216 | Final Report of the Enquête Commission: "Kultur in Deutschland", p. 381.

This is also true, and should be explicitly emphasised at this point, for the area of arts education:

'There is hardly a greater gulf between what is promised in political speeches and what is actually implemented through day-to-day efforts than in the area of arts education. Leading players from all sectors of society do not hesitate to acknowledge the importance of arts education for the individual and the society; hard and fast consequences for the practice of arts education, however, are often not forthcoming.'[217]

Therefore, in its Road Map for Arts Education, UNESCO designated the following as one of the most urgent developmental tasks in Europe: 'Acknowledging that budgets for Arts Education are either non-existent or insufficient to cover its routine and development needs'.[218]

There is a need for immediate action in order to prevent the gap between expected performance and available funds from widening any further.

4.2 Revamp and Revise Impedimentary Funding Criteria!

The revamping and revision of impedimentary funding criteria is a very broad field about which it is difficult to make general statements, since the cultural funding systems and instances in Europe vary from country to country. There does seem to be a consensus with regard to the following two demands:

First, it is necessary that makers of independent children's theatre are given more possibilities to receive long-term, structural and conceptual support instead of (at best) serial project funding. Only this kind of financial security can enable the long-term planning and continuity which are essential to successful organisational, personnel and quality development.

Second, visionary new funding concepts are needed – in the interest of a continuous stimulation and revival of the scene – which focus on an open-process funding and thus create more room for innovation and experimentation on unfamiliar ground: "Creativity needs a protected space which is free from the dimensions of results-orientation and economic calculability".[219] In this sense, it is to rethink goal agreements and criteria for public promotion for independent children's theatre groups. The scene certainly does *not* need more "efficiency measurements (politely referred to as evaluations)" – what it *does need* is "trust in the experiment [...] and the acceptance of failure".[220]

---

217 | Ibid., p. 377.
218 | http://www.unesco.org/new/fileadmin/MULTIMEDIA/HQ/CLT/CLT/pdf/Arts_Edu_RoadMap_en.pdf
219 | *Evaluation der Hamburger Privattheater*, p. 11.
220 | Hentschel 2012, no page.

4.3 More Venues and Production Houses for Independent Children's Theatre!

The lack of permanent venues for the independent scene has a particularly adverse effect on the system of children's theatre:[221] When independent children's theatre takes place in so-called "alternative" venues, i.e. schools, youth centres or public places, it is seldom aesthetically motivated but occurs for pragmatic, financial reasons – because no other venue is affordable. On the other hand, it must be said that all the independent groups which have their own permanent venue can be designated as "established" and are "visible" in their artistic profile in some way, beyond regional and even national borders, particularly because they are more highly regarded by both the public and the media.

Hence, the order of the day must be to create more venues for independent children's theatre throughout Europe – and, in the best case, to establish more separate theatres for children's theatre. "The future belongs to the theatres!" Wolfgang Schneider proclaimed several years ago and proceeded to describe what a "theatre house" could be:

- 'the place for production and presentation, identification and interaction,
- the model for co-production and cooperation,
- the network of artistic exchange, also with other arts and other cultures,
- the agency for cultural management, for guest performances, festivals, art instruction, for the concerted acquisition of financial resources, sponsoring, fund-raising, public relations and other marketing measures,
- the theatre as a seal of approval for artistic quality. Whoever can participate, is good, guarantees the agency for consumer testing, theatre!'[222]

As a national and/or regional centre, a theatre for a young audience can function as a meeting place, forum and stage for different theatre producers, as an "interdisciplinary, interactive and integrative theatre centre", as a "placement agency, experimental stage, research institute, laboratory" as well as an "idea pool" and "centre for entrepreneurs in the field of independent theatre".[223]

In addition, a theatre house for children, even though it is initiated and run by adults, is a "house and artistic institution for a community of children which

---

221 | The problem is exacerbated in dance theatre; here there are virtually no permanent venues, and thus, despite some exemplary structural and artistic support, hardly any rehearsal and performance possibilities exist for independent dance groups (See Figl 2013, p. 27).

222 | Schneider 2007, p. 90.

223 | Ibid., p. 86.

is created there. It is one of the few possibilities in which children can claim and develop a sphere of their own public space".[224] Therefore, a separate theatre for children not only has an aesthetic importance, but a social significance as well.

The "Frankfurter Perspektivkommission" also stressed the advantages of an unlimited residence at a permanent venue:

'This supports the formation of identity and the anchoring of many ensembles in one location, gives the chance of developing a repertory by providing storage capacity [...] ensures the "owners" rehearsal rooms, allows a diverse artistic programme with even small formats.'[225]

The possible disadvantages of a permanent, or even a separate venue – for example, the stagnation of artistic development, the calcification of entrenched structures or 'stewing in one's own juice' by closing oneself off from the outside world – have so far not been observed in the area of independent children's theatre. Whoever is lucky enough to have their own permanent venue or to operate their own house usually does not stop performing site-specific projects in public space or touring, or networking or opening their doors to other independent groups for guest performances and co-productions. The "innovative potential through theatricality in different locations"[226] is maintained; the essentially desirable and creatively beneficial mobility of the independent theatre is not rejected. Or as Marcel Crème (AGORA Theatre, Saint Vith) once metaphorically described it when his group moved into their new theatre:

'The artist must always seek the unknown. His home is the journey. As soon as the unknown becomes familiar to him, he must move on. What is the Triangel, the new theatre? It is our home port. That's where we are anchored. And we hoist anchor to set out for new horizons. The new destination tells us that we are not nowhere but somewhere.'[227]

The necessary of having a "home port" and "not being nowhere" seems to apply to the independent children's theatre in Europe as well.

---

224 | Richard 1986, p. 63.
225 | *Evaluation der Freien Theaterszene in Frankfurt am Main*, p. 19.
226 | Schneider 2007, p. 86.
227 | Cremer, Marcel: Foreword. In: AGORA – Das Theater der Deutschsprachigen Gemeinschaft Belgiens (ed.): 30 Jahre AGORA. In-house publication 2010 – quoted from: AGORA 2012, no page.

4.4 No Disproportionate Preferential Treatment for Participative Formats!

In light of the global debates on this topic, much (public) funding is now being made available to promote arts education for children. However, an imbalance is becoming more and more evident inasmuch as a disproportionately large share of these subsidies is used to finance educational and participative formats and thus only a small select area of arts education programmes is profiting. The promotion of professional theatre *for* children tends to be neglected.[228] This can be demonstrated by taking a closer look at the current cultural funding guidelines for the city of Hamburg for the year 2012, in which one can read the following statement:

"While, in recent years, there has been an expansion and an increase in quality of the education and training programmes in the area of cultural education Germany-wide, the programmes in the artistic sector seem to be stagnating on a rather low level".[229] Yet no countermeasures are planned; in fact, the actions planned by the senate are aimed almost exclusively at the promotion of formats which derive from the area of theatre pedagogy or "theatre and school".[230] A prime example of this is the stated intention, "on the part of the Hamburg Staatsoper, to intensify the targeting of children and young people by means of specific educational offers and projects" which should be organised analogous to the successful TuSch Programme which has been in place in Hamburg for years.[231] As positive as the implementation of this plan may seem, it is all the more absurd that there is no music theatre for young audiences in Hamburg at this time and that this fact does not seem to merit any kind of attention in this context.

Similarly, Paul Harman describes the recent cultural and political measures in England, stating that they unfairly discriminate and show undue preference towards cultural *education*:

'The Labour Government 1997-2010 spent a large amount of money on Creative Partnerships, by which artists were invited to help teachers develop and use more creative

---

228 | Particularly in the area of dance theatre, there is a great deficit. Although the number of independent groups which produce for children and young people has significantly increased in recent years, it still cannot be said that there is a continuous offer of activities for young people as a matter of course.
229 | *Rahmenkonzept Kinder- und Jugendkultur in Hamburg 2012* (Framework Concept for Children and Youth Culture in Hamburg 2012), p. 15.
230 | See ibid., p. 32.
231 | Ibid., p. 17.

methods to deliver the same utilitarian objectives. Theatre performances by professionals could play no part in this.'

The narrow interpretation of the concept of arts education and the preferential treatment given to participative formats disregards the fact that arts education processes are not only initiated through "learning by doing" but just as much through "learning by *viewing*"; it is often forgotten that watching is also a form of participation – namely on the level of our imagination – and is in no way to be classified as a passive process. Thus, theatre projects *with* children as a means to the end of arts education cannot suffice. Arts education includes practicing art as well as art reception and a "programme of aesthetic alphabetisation":[232]

'In an era in which we are bombarded with signs every day, it makes sense to train the art of seeing. And the best method still seems to be in arousing interest in what can be seen. The theatre offers [...] the possibility of integrating seeing into a communication process which codes and decodes the signs of the time between actors and so-called "spect-actors".'[233]

The "Announcement on the Financing of Culture 2012-2015" (Botschaft zur Finanzierung der Kultur 2012-2015) stresses the importance of the *reception* of the arts:

'Arts sharpen the perception and develop awareness. There is no better school of contemplation, of attention, of differentiation than art. Precise and critical listening, looking, thinking makes people attentive, expressive and discerning.'[234]

The necessity of training and practicing the ability to observe is possibly more important today than ever before, as Ulrich Khuon explains:

'Precisely because the subject and his perceptions are bound to a merciless personal inner-worldly obligation to be present and to participate, and because it hardly seems possible to distance oneself from this obligation or even to dispense with it, the retreat from the strenuous constant presence in the world which we perceive could be a chance for the arts. The observer can watch something without being directly involved; he is meant without having to react immediately. Art could help us to observe more exactly because we wish to continue the perception in this unencumbered state.'[235]

---

232 | Mollenhauer 1990, p. 9.
233 | Schneider 2013, p. 30.
234 | Institute for Art Education, p. 124.
235 | Khuon 2010, p. 47.

Therefore, since an elective course on creative writing in school cannot be a full-fledged substitute for reading literary texts, and most certainly not for reading the classics, theatre work *with* children can be usefully integrated into a professional programme *for* a young audience – and can receive at least the same amount of public funding!

4.5 Fight the Usurpation of Art and Culture by the Mechanisms of the Market Economy!

Another difficulty concerning public funding policies results from a one-sided interpretation of the concept of arts education – this time in the direction of an "education *through* the arts", meaning an education through and in the medium of the arts which has as its aim the imparting of knowledge and promoting the acquisition of non-artistic transfer competences. All too often, and, as it seems, with an increasing trend, the dimension of "education *in* the arts" is neglected, although UNESCO deemed this aspect equally important. Encountering the arts is itself the content and aim of arts education, according to the principle of "education *in* the arts". As has been shown, the strong pressure of legitimisation which is often cited in the public discourse in connection with the high social relevance of arts education programmes can usually be assigned to the categories of "secondary effects", "subsequent benefits" or "positive knock-on effects". "One thing should not be forgotten," according to the warning voiced by the Deutscher Kulturrat in 2013. "The job market, culture, is a unique job market. [...] If art is regarded only from an economical point of view, it loses its magic and dies".[236]

Therefore, perhaps the most important demand on European cultural and educational policies with regard to public funding for arts education for children is the acknowledgement of the specific *intrinsic value* of art and culture. That this intrinsic value is increasingly neglected and, in the course of the progressing economisation of arts, is constantly in danger of being reduced to a level which corresponds with other factors in discussion, is something which has been repeatedly confirmed by independent children's theatre professionals.

Bill Buffery (multi story theatre company) from Great Britain, when asked about the most important demands in the area of professional theatre for children, pointed out the pressure to justify itself in the face of other media, which leads to a situation in which the theatre no longer has faith in its own abilities and instead tries to imitate its "competitors":

---

236 | Schulz/Zimmermann/Hufnagel 2013, p. 333.

'The serious problems are related to [this]: basically a lack of faith in what theatre has to offer and a scrabbling around to grab what is cool from other entertainment models – TV, video, PC, smartphones or whatever. Theatre starts to apologise for not being the new kid on the block and does its very best to appear light and fluffy and eager to please. And so loses its essential seriousness and sense of purpose. And runs the risk of becoming irrelevant.'

This trend leads to a loss of identity within the theatre which denies the children that special potential, that intrinsic value, which only the theatre has to offer: '[Children] don't need theatre to do what their PC does – their PC does that better. They need theatre to do what theatre does – which is to celebrate the transformative power of the human imagination.'

Silvia Pahl of the German independent group theater 3 hasen oben describes her artistic conception of herself as a purposeful attempt to create an "antipole to the prevailing climate" by means of her work in the theatre:

'We live in a society which, it seems, is almost entirely permeated by a materialistic view. Everything that we think and do, everything that we teach and learn, everything we strive for, has one sense: usability. Nearly everything that we do has goals or at least intentions. Even on toys for the youngest children (e.g. HABA toys), there is a recommended age group printed on the package and the skills which the child can acquire with the toy. It seems to me that not one of our actions may be without intention because we think that it would then be useless [...] Every day we miss out on simply being. Our children and we forget how to play just for the sake of playing, telling stories for the sake of inventing, dancing, singing, crying. We unlearn and forget all that, and we do not have any time left, alongside our appointments, for our personal optimisation.'[237]

If the concept of arts education should not be subjugated to the dictates of the market, then when decisions are made with regard to providing public funding, the criterion should not be whether a theatre project for children imparts usable 'knowledge', but the genuinely artistic, aesthetic quality of the project must be the most relevant factor: the extent to which the children watching and/or participating are given the opportunity of making a specific aesthetic experience.

Such an aesthetic experience is, in contrast to the perceptive experiences made in everyday life, by definition "free of every primary connection to external tasks, functions and goals":

---

237 | Pahl, Silvia: "Da sein – ein Manifest" (January 2013). Unpublished manuscript kindly made available by the author of theater 3 hasen oben in Immichenhain/Germany.

'The relationship which we establish to objects when making aesthetic experiences is not subject to any one-sided goal or purpose orientation, but the sense and purpose lie solely in the experience itself.'[238]

This, however, does not mean that aesthetic experiences *do not* fulfil a function. In fact, for many reasons, it is possible to attest because

'[aesthetic experiences] are anchored in the sensuality of perception, but need reflexive processing without, at the same time, losing the touch with physicality. In aesthetic experiences we experience ourselves and the world at the same time and are animated to different kinds of interplay: between sensuality and reflection, between emotionality and reason, between the conscious and the subconscious, between materiality and sign characters, between the speakable and the unspeakable, between the certain and the uncertain. Perhaps the basic openness which makes this interplay possible is, in general, exemplary for human experience and recognition.'[239]

The cultural and educational policies which neglect the funding of education *in* the arts are thus in every respect unacceptable, especially in times in which any remaining oasis which gives us the chance to withdraw from the pressures of everyday life should be preserved and used. The theatre can still be such a refuge – perhaps more than ever before. A different time prevails here: a timeout. And a playing space is opened in which efficiency and exploitation are suspended and the utilisation principle can be thwarted. "The more oppressive we perceive our commitment to the norms of our everyday lives – maximisation, mainstream, deprivation – the more we need to experience something else", says Holger Noltze. "Having once made the experience that this place exists, changes our perspective".[240]

'The very word education comes from the Latin word "educo", to lead out (not to cram in), and this is where the arts come in, with their unique ability to develop communication skills and moral and social awareness, to inspire creativity and self-expression, to instil a sense of self-esteem, self-confidence, achievement and hence identity. To produce rounded, responsible future citizens of the world. To question our assumptions and prejudices and reaffirm our basic values and our shared humanity. To crucially give the lie to the idea that nothing really matters any more except money.'[241]

---

238 | Brandstätter 2012, p. 175.
239 | Ibid., p. 180.
240 | Noltze 2010, p. 265.
241 | See the remarks by Michael Attenborough on 2 May 2013 at http://www.thestage.co.uk/features/analysis-opinion/2013/05/letters-week-may-2-2013

In this sense, the arts can be turned into "launching pads from which we can be sent off into other orbits. And they will work because they defy the control of the prevailing principles".[242]

Providing support for this unique quality of the arts, and thus for independent children's theatre, would not only mean an increase in the quality of arts education activities, but in the final analysis would increase the quality of *life* in all those children who are given the chance to make such aesthetic experiences in and with the arts. And wouldn't that be the best conceivable aim of arts education?

---

242 | Noltze 2010, p. 264.

Literature and Sources

AGORA – Das Theater der Deutschsprachigen Gemeinschaft Belgiens. *Das Engagement der Agora*. Sankt Vith: Agora Theater, 2012.

Akveld, J. "Beste Leerling krijgt zwaarste Klappen." In TM and TIN (eds), *Terugblickken: Theaterseizoen 2010-2011* 15 (2011), pp. 58ff.

Anthonissen, P. *Outline of the Children's and Youth Performing Arts Landscape*. Brussels: VTi, 2011.

Arbeitsgruppe Evaluation und Forschung des Bundesverband Tanz in Schulen e. V. *Empirische Annäherungen an Tanz in Schulen: Befunde aus Evaluation und Forschung*. Oberhausen: Athena, 2009.

Bamford, A. "In Her Own Words: Anne Bamford on Making Arts Education Meaningful." *UNESCO Today 1: Arts Education for All: What Experts in Germany are Saying*, pp. 82-83, 2010. Available at: http://www.unesco.de/fileadmin/medien/Dokumente/Kultur/Kulturelle_Bildung/_FINAL_Unesco_today_1_2010.pdf.

Bamford, A. *The Wow Factor: Global Research Compendium on the Impact of the Arts in Education*. Münster: Waxmann, 2009.

Bartnikowski, M. "Independent." *Teatr Lalek 103-104* (2011), p. 58.

Becker, H. "Mut zur Freiheit! Demokratie lernen in der Kulturellen Bildung?" In: H. Bockhorst (ed.), *KUNSTstück FREIHEIT: Leben und lernen in der Kulturellen Bildung*. Munich: Kopaed, 2011, pp. 217ff.

Beckett, S. "Three Dialogues." In: Ruby Cohn (ed.), *Disjecta: Miscellaneous Writings and a Dramatic Fragment*. London: Grove Press, 1983, pp. 138-145.

Berendts, C. "Tanz für alle: Wie der Community Dance Kultur für alle realisiert – und warum die Kulturpolitik Schwierigkeiten damit hat." In: W. Schneider (ed.), *Kulturelle Bildung* (2010), pp. 159-170.

Beyeler, M. And Patrizi, L. "Tanz – Schule – Bildung: Überlegungen auf der Erfahrungsgrundlage eines Berliner Tanz-in-Schulen-Projekts." In: H. Bockhorst, V. -I. Reinwand and W. Zacharias (eds), *Handbuch Kulturelle Bildung* (2012), pp. 600-603.

Blik, H. "The Beauty of Experiment." In: Het Lab Utrecht, *Magazine* (2012), p. 3.

Blumenreich, U. "Das Studium der Kulturvermittlung an Hochschulen in Deutschland." In: H. Bockhorst, V.-I. Reinwand and W. Zacharias (eds), *Handbuch Kulturelle Bildung* (2012), pp. 849-854.

Bockhorst, H (ed.). *KUNSTstück FREIHEIT: Leben und lernen in der Kulturellen Bildung*. Munich: Kopaed, 2011.

Bockhorst, H., Reinwand, V.-I. and Zacharias, W. (eds). *Handbuch Kulturelle Bildung*. Munich: Kopaed, 2012.

Brandstätter, U. "Ästhetische Erfahrung." In: Bockhorst, H., Reinwand, V.-I. and Zacharias, W. (eds), *Handbuch Kulturelle Bildung* (2012), pp. 174-180.

Broek, M. v.d. "Young Choreographers on the Rise – Het Lab Utrecht." In: *Fresh Tracks Europe, Innovation in Dance* (2013), pp. 29-33.
Bundesverband Tanz in Schulen. *Tanz in Schulen geht raus ... Wie kann außerschulisch kooperiert werden?* Cologne, 2013.
Bundesverband Tanz in Schulen. *Tanz in Schulen in NRW: Ein empirischer Blick in die Praxis.* Bonn, 2009.
Bundesverband Tanz in Schulen. *Tanz in Schulen: Theorie und Praxis.* Cologne, 2012.
Bundesvereinigung Kulturelle Jugendbildung e. V. *Schlüsselkompetenzen durch kulturelle Bildung: Grundlagen. Sachstand. Positionen.* Remscheid, 2002.
Cremer, M. "Courage. AGORA." In: *Das Engagement der Agora*, 2012.
Cremer, M. "Vorwort: AGORA – Das Theater der Deutschsprachigen Gemeinschaft Belgiens." In: *30 Jahre AGORA*, in-house publication, 2010.
Cremer, M. "Jenseits der grünen Wiese." In: *AGORA – Das Theater der Deutschsprachigen Gemeinschaft Belgiens*, parts 8-16, in-house publication, 2009.
Deutscher Kulturrat. "Kulturelle Bildung: Aufgaben im Wandel." Berlin 2009. Available at: http://www.kulturrat.de/dokumente/studien/kulturelle-bildung-aufgaben-im-wandel.pdf.
Deutscher Kulturrat. *Kulturelle Bildung in der Bildungsreformdiskussion (= Konzeption Kulturelle Bildung* vol. 3). Berlin 2005. Available at: http://www.kulturrat.de/dokumente/studien/konzeption-kb3.pdf.
Doderer, K., Knauer, M. and Windisch, A. *Berufsperspektive: Theaterspielen für junge Zuschauer. Eine Untersuchung zum 'Kinder- und Jugendtheater im Rahmen der Ausbildung von Schauspielerinnen und Schauspielern'* (= Deutsche Bühnenverein publications series, vol. 8). Frankfurt am Main: dipa-Verlag, 1993.
Editorial. *Dramaturgie: Zeitschrift der Dramaturgischen Gesellschaft* (2007), p. 1.
Editorial. *IXYPSILONZETT Yearbook* (2013), p. 1.
Ewers, H.-H. "Kinderliterarische Erzählformen im Modernisierungsprozess: Überlegungen zum Formenwandel westdeutscher epischer Kinderliteratur." In: G. Lange and W. Steffens (eds), *Moderne Formen des Erzählens in der Kinder- und Jugendliteratur der Gegenwart unter literarischen und didaktischen Aspekten.* Würzburg: Königshausen & Neumann, 1995, pp. 11-24.
Ewers, H.-H. *Literatur für Kinder und Jugendliche: Eine Einführung.* Paderborn: UTB, 2012.
Figl, J. "Welche darstellerischen Formen brauche ich?" In: *IXYPSILONZETT Yearbook* (2013), p. 27.
Fleisch, H. "Förderung der Kulturellen Bildung durch Stiftungen." In H. Bockhorst, V.-I. Reinwand and W. Zacharias (eds), *Handbuch Kulturelle Bildung* (2012), pp. 399-402.

Foik, J. *Tanz zwischen Kunst und Vermittlung: Community Dance am Beispiel des Tanzprojekts 'Carmina Burana' (2006) unter der choreographischen Leitung von Royston Maldoom*. Munich: Kopaed, 2008.

Foik, J. "Zehn Jahre Tanzfieber: Eine Zwischenbilanz." In: H. Bockhorst, V.-I. Reinwand and W. Zacharias (eds), *Handbuch Kulturelle Bildung* (2012), pp. 604-607.

Fonds Darstellende Künste. *Report Darstellende Künste: Wirtschaftliche, soziale und arbeitsrechtliche Lage der Theater und Theaterschaffenden in Deutschland*. Berlin, 2010.

Fresh Tracks Europe. *Innovation in Dance for Young Audiences*. 2013.

Fuchs, M. *Kulturelle Bildung: Grundlagen – Praxis – Politik (= Kulturelle Bildung*, vol. 10*)*. Munich: Kopaed, 2008.

Fuchs, M. "Qualitätsdiskurse in der kulturellen Bildung: Entwicklungslinien der letzten zwanzig Jahre und aktuelle Herausforderungen. Bundesvereinigung Kulturelle Kinder- und Jugendbildung." In: *Studie zur Qualitätssicherung in der kulturellen Bildung*, Remscheid 2010, pp. 91-95. Available at: http://www.bkj.de/fileadmin/user_upload/documents/Qualitaet/BKJ_Studie_Qualitaet_web.pdf).

Fuchs, M. "Was ist kulturelle Bildung? Wege zur Begriffsklärung." In: *Politik und Kultur: Zeitung des Deutschen Kulturrates* (2007), pp. 10-11.

Gansel, C. "Der Adoleszenzroman: Zwischen Moderne und Postmoderne." In: G. Lange (ed.), *Taschenbuch der Kinder- und Jugendliteratur*, vol. 1: *Grundlagen – Gattungen*, Baltmannsweiler (2005), pp. 359-398.

Gauß, E. M. and Hannken-Illjes, K. "Vermittlung von wissenschaftlichen Erkenntnissen in künstlerischer Form." In: H. Bockhorst, V.-I. Reinwand and W. Zacharias (eds), *Handbuch Kulturelle Bildung* (2012), pp. 961-964.

Han, B-C. *Agonie des Eros*. Berlin: Matthes & Seitz, 2013.

Harman, P. *A Guide to UK Theatre for Young Audiences*. London: Aurora Metro, 2009.

Hartung, K. *Kindertheater als Theater der Generationen: Pädagogische Grundlagen und empirische Befunde zum neuen Kindertheater in Deutschland (= Kinder-, Schul- und Jugendtheater: Beiträge zu Theorie und Praxis*, vol. 11*)*. Frankfurt am Main: Peter Lang, 2001.

Hentschel, I. "Hildesheimer Thesen IX: Die Rolle des Theaters in und für Europa." *Nachtkritik*. Hildesheim 2012. Available at: http://www.nachtkritik.de/index.php?view=article&id=7574%3Ahildesheimer-thesen-ix-&option=com_content&Itemid=60.

Hentschel, I. "*Über Grenzverwischungen und ihre Folgen: Hat das Kindertheater als Spezialtheater noch Zukunft?*" In: A. Israel and S. Riemann (eds), *Das andere Publikum: Deutsches Kinder- und Jugendtheater*. Berlin: Henschel, 1996, pp. 31-47.

Hentschel, U. "Theaterpädagogische Ausbildung." In: H. Bockhorst, V.-I. Reinwand and W. Zacharias (eds), *Handbuch Kulturelle Bildung* (2012), pp. 879-881.
Hoffmann, K. "Kultur und Künste als Spielraum der Freiheit." In H. Bockhorst (ed.), *KUNSTstück FREIHEIT* (2011), pp. 223-238.
Institute for Art Education at the Zürcher Hochschule der Künste. *Zeit für Vermittlung: Eine online Publikation zur Kulturvermittlung.* On behalf of Pro Helvetia, results of the 'Kulturvermittlung' Research Programme, 2009-2012. Available at: http://www.kultur-vermittlung.ch/zeit-fuer-vermittlung/download/pdf-d/ZfV_0_gesamte_Publikation.pdf.
Jahnke, M. *Kinder- und Jugendtheater in der Kritik: Gesammelte Rezensionen, Porträts und Essays (= Kinder-, Schul- und Jugendtheater: Beiträge zu Theorie und Praxis*, vol. 10). Frankfurt am Main: Peter Lang, 2001.
Kämpf-Jansen, H. *Ästhetische Forschung: Wege durch Alltag, Kunst und Wissenschaft – Zu einem innovativen Konzept ästhetischer Bildung.* Cologne: Tectum, 2002.
Kessel, M., Müller, B., Kosubek, T. and Barz, H. (eds). *Aufwachsen mit Tanz: Erfahrungen aus Praxis, Schule und Forschung.* Weinheim/Basel: Beltz, 2011.
Keuchel, S. "Monitoring and Evaluating Arts Education. The Shift to Focusing on Quality." In: *UNESCO Today* 1 (2010): *Arts Education for All: What Experts in Germany are Saying*, pp. 39ff. Available at: http://www.unesco.de/fileadmin/medien/Dokumente/Kultur/Kulturelle_Bildung/_FINAL_Unesco_today_1_2010.pdf.
Keuchel, S. "Von kulturellen Allesfressern und hybriden Kunstformen. Kulturelle Bildung im Spiegel empirischer Forschung." In: W. Schneider (ed.), *Kulturelle Bildung* (2010), pp. 231-243.
Khuon, U. "Das Wesen von Kultur." *Theater Heute* 8/9 (2010), pp. 46-47.
Klaic, D. *Resetting the Stage: Public Theatre between the Market and Democracy.* Bristol/Chicago: University of Chicago Press, 2012.
Klinge, A. "Bildungskonzepte im Tanz." In: M. Bischof and C. Rosiny (eds), *Konzepte der Tanzkultur: Wissen und Wege der Tanzforschung.* Bielefeld: transcript, 2010, pp. 79-94.
Klinge, A. "Zum Stellenwert von Tanz und kultureller Bildung in der Schule." In: *Schulpädagogik Heute* (= *Körper, Bewegung und Schule*, special edition, vol. 3), n.p., 2012. Available at: http://www.bv-tanzinschulen.info/filead min/user_upload/content-aktuell/A_Klinge_Stellenwert_Tanz_KB_2012. pdf.
Kosubek, T. and Barz, H. "Take-off: Junger Tanz im Spiegel der Forschung." In: M. Kessel, B. Müller, T. Kosubek and H. Barz (eds), *Aufwachsen mit Tanz* (2011), pp. 101-164.
Kozien, L. "The Theatre Today: Remarks on the Contemporary Puppet Theatre in Poland." *Teatr Lalek 103-104* (2011), pp. 11ff.

Leslie, E. "Mehr Wert für die Inhalte: Die Verwertung der Kultur heute." In: G. Raunig and U. Wuggenig (eds), *Kritik der Kreativität*. Vienna: Turia & Kant, 2007, pp. 56-64.

Liebau, E. "Der Wow-Faktor: Warum künstlerische Bildung nötig ist." In: A. Bamford, *Der Wow-Faktor: Eine weltweite Analyse der Qualität künstlerischer Bildung*. Münster: Waxmann, 2010, pp. 11-19.

Lypp, M. "Die Kunst des Einfachen in der Kinderliteratur." In G. Lange (ed.), *Taschenbuch der Kinder- und Jugendliteratur*, vol. 2. Baltmannsweiler: Schneider Verlag Hohengehren, 2002, pp. 828-843.

Meyer, D. "Focus on the artist! How to Support Young Theatre Makers." In: Het Lab Utrecht, *Magazine* (2012), pp. 5-8.

Mörsch, C. "Watch this Space! Position beziehen in der Kulturvermittlung." In: M. Sack, A. Rey and S. Schöbi (eds), *Theater Vermittlung Schule: Ein Dialog*. Zürich: Museum für Gestaltung, 2011, pp. 8-25.

Mollenhauer, K. "Die vergessene Dimension des Ästhetischen in der Erziehungs- und Bildungstheorie." In: D. Lenzen (ed.), *Kunst und Pädagogik: Erziehungswissenschaft auf dem Weg zur Ästhetik?* Darmstadt: Wissenschaftliche Buchgesellschaft, 1990, pp. 3-17.

Müller, L. and Schneeweis, K. (eds). *Tanz in Schulen: Stand und Perspektiven. Dokumentation der 'Bundesinitiative Tanz in Schulen'*. Munich: K. Kieser Verlag, 2006.

Müller-Schöll, N. "Das künstlerische Forschen." *Theater heute* 7 (2013), pp. 36-39.

National Advisory Committee on Creative and Cultural Education. *All Our Futures: Creativity, Culture and Education*. London, 1999. Available at: http://sirkenrobinson.com/skr/pdf/allourfutures.pdf.

Neumann, B. "Interview." *Kunst + Kultur*, 2009. Available at: http://www.bundesregierung.de/Content/DE/Interview/2009/12/2009-12-14-bernd-neumann-verdi-kunst-und-kultur.html?__site=Nachhaltigkeit.

Noltze, H. *Die Leichtigkeitslüge: Über Musik, Medien und Komplexität*. Hamburg: Körber Stiftung, 2010.

Odenthal, J. "Tanz als Pflichtfach: Johannes Odenthal im Gespräch mit der Künstlerischen Leiterin der Kulturstiftung des Bundes, Hortensia Völckers." In: Johannes Odenthal (ed.), *Tanz, Körper, Politik: Texte zur zeitgenössischen Tanzgeschichte* (Theater der Zeit Recherchen 27, 2005), pp. 108ff.

Rahmenkonzept Kinder- und Jugendkultur in Hamburg 2012. Mitteilung des Senats an die Bürgerschaft, issue 20/4450, 12th June 2012.

Ribolits, E. "Vom sinnlosen Arbeiten zum sinnlosen Lernen." In: E. Renner, E. Ribolits and J. Zuber (eds), *Wa(h)re Bildung: Zurichtung für den Profit*. Vienna: Schulheft, 2004, pp. 40-52. Available at: http://www.schulheft.at/fileadmin/1PDF/schulheft-113.pdf.

Richard, J. "Schau-Raum, Aktions-Raum oder Lern-Raum oder ...? Überlegungen zur theatralen Grundsteinlegung eines Theaterhauses für Kinder." *Theater-ZeitSchrift* (= *Kinder- und Jugendtheater* special edition, 1986), pp. 48-64.

Sandweg, T. "Spiel-O-Mat: Einige Gedanken anlässlich des 40. Geburtstags der Abteilung 'Puppenspielkunst'." *IXYPSILONZETT* 3 (2012), pp. 22-23.

Sauer, I. "Quer gelesen: Ein kritischer Blick auf kulturjournalistische Beiträge zum Kinder- und Jugendtheater." *IXYPSILONZETT Yearbook* 2013, pp. 36-40.

Scène(s) d'enfance et d'ailleurs (Association nationale de professionnels des arts de la scène en direction des jeunes publics), Ministère de la culture et de la communication and DMDTS. "Photographie d'une dynamique fragile: Etude sur les conditions de production et de diffusion des spectacles adressés au jeune public en France." *Saisons 2006/2008*, Paris 2009.

Schmücker, R. "Die Autonomie des Künstlers und die Bildungsfunktion der Kunst." In H. Bockhorst (ed.), *KUNSTstück FREIHEIT* (2011), pp. 109-119.

Schneider, W. (ed.). *Kulturelle Bildung braucht Kulturpolitik: Hilmar Hoffmanns 'Kultur für alle' reloaded*. Hildesheim: Universität Hildesheim, 2010.

Schneider, W. *Theater für Kinder und Jugendliche: Beiträge zur Theorie und Praxis*. Hildesheim/Zürich: Olms, 2005.

Schneider, W. (ed.). "Von A wie Aufführung bis Z wie Zuschauer: Ein Alphabet des Kindertheaters." In: E. Lippert (ed.), *Theater Spielen*. Bamberg: C.C. Buchner, 2001, pp. 238-259.

Schneider, W. "Von Projekt zu Projekt – am Katzentisch der Kulturpolitik?" In: Fonds Darstellende Künste (ed.), *Freies Theater in Deutschland: Förderstrukturen und Perspektiven*, Essen: Klartext, 2007, pp. 82-90.

Schneider, W. "Wuppertal ist überall! Die kulturpolitische Krise der Dramatischen Künste offenbart Reformbedarfe in der deutschen Theaterlandschaft." In: E. Mittelstädt and A. Pinto (eds), *Die Freien Darstellenden Künste in Deutschland: Diskurse – Entwicklungen – Perspektiven*. Bielefeld: transcript, 2013, pp. 21-31.

Schulz, G., Zimmermann, O. and Hufnagel, R. *Arbeitsmarkt Kultur. Zur wirtschaftlichen und sozialen Lage in Kulturberufen*. Berlin, 2013 Available at: http://www.kulturrat.de/dokumente/studien/studie-arbeitsmarkt-kultur-2013.pdf.

Stegemann, B. *Kritik des Theaters*. Berlin: Theater der Zeit, 2013.

Stern, M. "Tanz als Möglichkeit ästhetischer Bildung in der Schule." In: Y. Hardt and M. Stern (eds), *Choreographie und Institution: Zeitgenössischer Tanz zwischen Ästhetik, Produktion und Vermittlung*. Bielefeld: Transcript, 2010, pp. 209-232.

Stüwe-Eßl, B. "Kleine Menschen – kleine Produktionskosten? Politischer Wert von Kunst für junges Publikum." *Gift – Zeitschrift für Freies Theater* 2008, pp. 37ff. Available at: http://culturebase.org/home/igft-ftp/gift0108.pdf.

Suchy, M. *"über null."* Tanz 1 (2012), pp. 14-18.
Türcke, C. "Wie das Lernen sein Gewicht verliert." *Süddeutsche Zeitung*, 1st August 2012, p. 12.
Viehöver, V. and Wunsch, S. "Zweieinhalb Gedanken zum Hype ums U3-Theater." *Das andere Theater* 77/78 (2011), p. 4f.
Wunsch, S. "Kleiner Prinz 2.0." *Das andere Theater* 77/78 (2011), pp. 14-15.
Zedlitz, S.v. *Auf der Bühne seid ihr Tänzer! Hinter den Kulissen von TanzZeit – Zeit für Tanz in Schulen: Eine Dokumentation.* Munich: Kopaed, 2009.
Zwaneveld, B. "Jeugdtheater bloeit in het buitenland." In TM and TIN (eds), *Terugblickken: Theaterseizoen 2010-2011* 15 (2011), pp. 42-45.

Online Sources
[Accessed 30 July 2015]

Bouët, J. (ed.). "Consultation sur l'éducation artistique et culturelle, 'Pour un accès de tous les jeunes à l'art et à la culture'." January 2013. Available at: http://www.culturecommunication.gouv.fr/Politiques-ministerielles/Consultation-education-artistique-et-culturelle/Resultats-de-la-consultation.
DICE (Drama Improves Lisbon Key Competences in Education) Consortium. "The DICE has Been Cast: Research Findings and Recommendations on Educational Theatre and Learning." 2010. Available at: http://www.dramanetwork.eu/file/Policy%20Paper%20long.pdf.
EDUCULT. *European Arts Education Fact Finding Mission: Final Report 2011.* Available at: http://www.educult.at/wp-content/uploads/2011/09/Report_Fact_Finding_Mission_EDUCULT.pdf.
European Commission. "European Audiences: 2020 and beyond – Conference conclusions." 2012. Available at: http://ec.europa.eu/culture/news/documents/conclusions-conference.pdf.
Evaluation der Freien Theaterszene in Frankfurt am Main, Abschlussbericht der Perspektivkommission im Auftrag des Kulturamtes der Stadt Frankfurt am Main. March 2012. Available at: http://www.kultur-frankfurt.de/portal/de/Kulturdezernat/AbschlussberichtderPerspektivkommissionzurEvaluierungderFreienTheaterszeneinFrankfurt/1291/2370/67661/mod1947-details1/11.aspx.
Müller-Wesemann, B. et al. *Evaluation der Hamburger Privattheater Hamburg 2008.* Available at: http://www.hamburg.de/contentblob/263646/data/privattheater-evaluation.pdf.
German UNESCO Commission. "Arts Education – Culture Counts: A Contribution from European Experts to the Seoul Process." Berlin, 2009. Available at: http://www.unesco.de/fileadmin/medien/Dokumente/Kultur/Kulturelle_Bildung/100120_Berlin_Contribution_FINAL.pdf.

Hardie, Y. "'President's Message' anlässlich des Welttages des Kinder- und Jugendtheaters." 20th March 2013. Available at: http://www.assitej-interna tional.org/media/55530/message_2013_yvette.pdf.

Keuchel, S. and Aescht, P. *Hoch hinaus: Potenzialstudie zu Kinder- und Jugendkulturprojekten.* 2007. Available at: http://www.pwc.de/de/engagement/as sets/PwC_Stiftung_Potenzialstudie_2007.pdf.

Lauret, J-M. and Marie, F. (eds). *Working Group on Developing Synergies with Education, especially Arts Education, Final Report.* European Agenda for Culture, Open Method of Coordination, 2010. Available at: http://ec.europa.eu/culture/key-documents/doc/MOCedu_final_report_en.pdf.

"Mannheimer Manifest zum Musiktheater." Available at: http://www.assitej. de/fileadmin/assitej/pdf/2009-12-07_Mannheimer_Manifest.pdf.

Mörsch, C. "Eine kurze Geschichte von KünstlerInnen in Schulen." Available at: http://kontextschule.org/inhalte/dateien/MoerschKueInSchGeschichte. pdf.

ONDA. *Théâtre, danse, arts de la rue, marionnettes et cirque: Les échanges entre la France et l'Europe.* April 2011. Available at: http://www.onda.fr/_fichiers/documents/fichiers/fichier_42_fr.pdf.

Pre-Conference-Reader for the European Conference 'Promoting Cultural Education in Europe: A Contribution to Participation, Innovation and Quality'. Graz, 2006. Available at: http://portal.unesco.org/pv_obj_cache/pv_obj_ id_131DB701EFAA1B32D091B05B25CF640B70350A00/filename/Pre-Con ference-Reader_Promoting+Cultural+Education+in+Europe+%2833%29-web.pdf.

RESEO (European Network for Opera and Dance Education). *Overview: Productions for Young Audiences in Europe.* Brussels, 2009. Available at: http://www.reseo.org/project/overview-productions-young-audiences-europe-0.

Schlussbericht der Enquête-Kommission Kultur in Deutschland. Issue 16/7000, 11th December 2007. Available at: http://dip21.bundestag.de/dip21/btd/16/070/1607000.pdf.

The European Opinion Research Group. *Europeans' Participation in Cultural Activities: A Eurobarometer Survey Carried out at the Request of the European Commission.* Eurostat, 2002. Available at: http://ec.europa.eu/culture/pdf/doc967_en.pdf.

UNESCO. "Road Map for Arts Education." Available at: http://www.unesco. org/new/fileadmin/MULTIMEDIA/HQ/CLT/CLT/pdf/Arts_Edu_Road Map_en.pdf.

UNESCO. "Seoul Agenda: Goals for the Development of Arts Education." Available at: http://www.unesco.org/new/fileadmin/MULTIMEDIA/HQ/CLT/CLT/pdf/Seoul_Agenda_EN.pdf.

Unpublished manuscripts

Cremer, M. *Das Sehen lernen*. Paper for the Schools Theatre Festival, *Spring auf!* Luxembourg, May 2004. Unpublished original manuscript, kindly made available by *AGORA* Theatre, Saint-Vith, Belgium.

Pahl, S. *Da sein – ein Manifest*. January 2013. Unpublished original manuscript, kindly made available by the author, theater 3 hasen oben, Immichenhain, Germany.

Pahl, S. *Theaterblitzlicht*. Notes for 'Spurensuche'. Hannover, 2001. Unpublished original manuscript, kindly made available by the author, theater 3 hasen oben, Immichenhain, Germany.

List of experts from the arts, politics and research interviewed for this study

Abel, Gilles (Université de Namur, Belgium)
Allen, Beccy (Halfmoon Theatre, United Kingdom)
Amsden, Meg (UNIMA, United Kingdom)
Andrist, Tanja (ASTEJ, Switzerland)
Baanstra, Jan (De Stilte, the Netherlands)
Barkey, Kirsten (Pro Helvetia, Switzerland)
Baeyens, Lieven (Compagnie IOTA, Belgium)
Ben-Horin, Oded (Stord Haugesund University College, Norway)
Beran, Henrike (Le Nuvole, Italy)
Beyeler, Marie (TanzZeit – Zeit für Tanz in Schulen, Germany)
Billing, Cecilia (Dockteaterverkstan, Sweden)
Björklund, Staffan (Dockteater, Sweden)
Bobrova, Tatiana (King Festival, Russia)
Bral, Filip (Pantalone, Belgium)
Brilioth Biörnstad, Lotta (Kulturrådet, Sweden)
Brogi, Luciano (Istituto Addestramento Lavoratori dello Spettacolo, Italy)
Brooks, Sarah (Office for National Statistics, United Kingdom)
Brown, Dan (Big Brum Theatre in Education, United Kingdom)
Buchwald, Dorota (IT, Poland)
Buffery, Bill (Multi Story Theatre Company, United Kingdom)
Burggrave, Evert (Introdans, the Netherlands)
Burgschuld, Kolja (ASSITEJ, Austria)
Calmant, Sandrine (Dwish Théâtre, Belgium)
Cannon, Ryan (DCMS, United Kingdom)
Castang, Emmanuelle (THEMAA, France)
Chaffaut, Brigitte (ONDA, France)
Choi, Young Ai (National University of Arts, South Korea)
Collard, Paul (CCE, United Kingdom)
Coppens, Erin (Oorkan, Belgium)

Cowan, Chris (Loudmouth Theatre, United Kingdom)
Dalla Rosa, Antonella (La Baracca, Italy)
dan Droste, Gabi (Theater der jungen Welt, Germany)
Debefve, Jean (Théâtre de la Galafronie, Belgium)
Decroos, Martine (Studio Orka, Belgium)
Delaunay, Léonor (Société d'Histoire du Théâtre, France)
de Roo, Ruben (Performing Arts School RITS, Belgium)
de Lathauwer, Dirk (Fabuleus, Belgium)
Dethier, Brigitte (Junges Ensemble Stuttgart, Germany)
de Waal, Bianca (TIN, the Netherlands)
Dimitriadou, Myrtó (Toïhaus Theater, Austria)
Dosch, Verena (Verlag für Kindertheater Weitendorf GmbH, Germany)
Dostal, Helga (ITI, Austria)
Dupont, Laurent (ACTA, France)
Engel, Thomas (ITI, Germany)
Fangauf, Henning (kjtz, Germany)
Fechner, Meike (ASSITEJ, Germany)
Fee, Amy (Dansens Hus, Sweden)
Fichtner, Antonia (University of Hamburg, Germany)
Fischer, Petra (Junges Schauspielhaus Zürich, Switzerland)
Fogel, François (ASSITEJ, France)
Förnbacher, Sandra (University of Bern, Switzerland)
Franceschini, Bruno (Franceschini, Droste & Co, Germany)
Franke, Martin (Het Houten Huis, the Netherlands)
Galbiatia, Cristina (Trickster-p, Switzerland)
Galli, Claudia (ACT, Switzerland)
Gardaz, Sophie (Le petit théâtre, Switzerland)
Geerlings, Paulien (De Toneelmakerij, the Netherlands)
Grassl, Stefan (Theater Barfuß, Austria)
Gruber, Helga (Toïhaus Theater, Austria)
Gustafsson, Lena (Teatercentrum, Sweden)
Haddon, Anthony (Theatre Blah Blah Blah, United Kingdom)
Hakkemars, Frans (UNIMA, the Netherlands)
Hardie, Yvette (ASSITEJ International)
Harman, Paul (ASSITEJ, United Kingdom)
Hart, Simon (UNIMA, United Kingdom)
Heid, Katherine (RESEO, Belgium)
Helander, Karin (Stockholm University, Sweden)
Hendriks, Marielle (Boekman Foundation, the Netherlands)
Hoffmann, Christel (Hochschule Osnabrück, Germany)
Horstmann, Tanja (Teatro Due Mondi, Italy)
Howald, Irène (ASTEJ, Switzerland)

Idzikowska, Beata (Central Statistical Office, Poland)
Jeschonnek, Günter (Fonds Darstellende Künste, Germany)
Jücker, Tina (Theater Marabu, Germany)
Karinsdotter, Anna (Royal Swedish Opera, Sweden)
Karr, Ina (Oldenburgisches Staatstheater, Germany)
Kees, Leandro (tanzhaus nrw, Germany)
Keller, Peter (Theater Arlecchino, Switzerland)
Kettlewell, Sara (Playtime Theatre Company, United Kingdom)
Keuppens, Veerle (CJSM, Buelgium)
Kirschner, Jürgen (kjtz, Germany)
Kjellkvist, Mia (Teater Eksem, Sweden)
Kleingeld, Eline (Vereniging van Schouwburg- en Concertgebouwdirecties, the Netherlands)
Knecht, Nina (Figura Theaterfestival, Switzerland)
Kölling, Barbara (HELIOS Theater, Germany)
Komlosi, Emmi (Annantalo Arts Centre, Finland)
Krans, Anja (TIN, the Netherlands)
Kressenhof, Willemijn (TIN, the Netherlands)
Kroonen, Cali (CTEJ, Belgium)
Kucharska, Katarzyna (TASHKA, Poland)
Kożuchowski, Hubert (Studio Teatralne BLUM, Poland)
Lachenmeyer, Juliane (Verlag für Kindertheater Weitendorf GmbH, Germany)
Langenegger, Nicole (PhiloThea Figurentheater, Austria)
Laureyns, Joke (Kabinet K, Belgium)
Lemke, Anja (HELIOS Theater, Germany)
Lewis, Linda (Puppet Centre, United Kingdom)
Loncar, Vitomira (Mala Scena, Hungary)
Malecka, Barbara (Children's Arts Centre, Poland)
Malmcrona, Niclas (ASSITEJ, Sweden)
Mansson, Eva (Unga Klara, Sweden)
Marples, Dempster (DCMS, United Kingdom)
Matheson, Rhona (Starcatchers, United Kingdom)
Mayer-Müller, Katharina (MÖP Figurentheater, Austria)
Melano, Graziano (Fondazione TRG, Italy)
Metsälampi, Katariina (Annantalo Arts Centre, Finland)
Meyer, Anke (Deutsches Forum für Figurentheater und Puppenspielkunst, Germany)
Mikol, Bruno (DRAC Île de France/Service du Théâtre, France)
Morawska-Rubczak, Alicja (ASSITEJ, Poland)
Müller, Linda (NRW Landesbüro Tanz, Germany)
Norquist, Elin (Kulturrådet, Sweden)
O'Hara, Marie (Hurricane Theatre, United Kingdom)

Ostertag, Sara (makemake Produktionen, Austria)
Overcamp, Claus (Theater Marabu, Germany)
Pahl, Silvia (theater 3 hasen oben, Germany)
Peters, Sibylle (Fundus Theater, Germany)
Pfeiffer, Gerlinde (Kinderkommission des Deutschen Bundestages, Germany)
Pfyl, Roger (luki*ju Theater, Switzerland)
Plank-Baldauf, Christiane (Ludwig-Maximilians-Universität München, Germany)
Poiteaux, Didier (INTI Théâtre, Belgium)
Pothen, Kurt (AGORA-Theater, Belgium)
Planson, Cyrille (La Scène, France)
Rabl, Stephan (DSCHUNGEL, Austria)
Ratkiewicz-Syrek, Anna (Gdansk Theatre, Poland)
Rauzi, Maria (Teatro Telaio, Italy)
Richers, Christiane (Theater am Strom, Germany)
Riedl, Gerlinde (Büro des Stadtrates für Kultur und Wissenschaft Wien, Austria)
Rofina, Tanya (ASSITEJ, Poland)
Rosenfeld, Arthur (Maas, the Netherlands)
Rosiny, Claudia (Bundesamt für Kultur, Switzerland)
Rudnev, Pavel (Moscow Art Theatre, Russia)
Rudzinski, Zbigniew (Children's Arts Centre, Poland)
Schade, Jörg (Pyrmonter Theatercompagnie e.V., Germany)
Schappach, Beate (Institut für Theaterwissenschaften Universität Bern, Switzerland)
Schneeberger, Christian (Schweizerische Theatersammlung, Switzerland)
Schneider, Wolfgang (ASSITEJ, Germany)
Smits, Jan (Koninklijke Bibliotheek, the Netherlands)
Sobczyk, Justyna (IT, Poland)
Socha, Ela (ASSITEJ, Poland)
Stasiołek, Katarzyna (POLUNIMA, Poland)
Staudt, Rivka (Ministry of Education, Culture and Science, the Netherlands)
Stephenson, Deborah (Arts Council, United Kingdom)
Stüwe-Eßl, Barbara (Interessensgemeinschaft Freie Theaterarbeit Österreich, Austria)
Tacchini, Barbara (Junge Oper Stuttgart, Germany)
Takei, Yutaka (Compagnie Forest Beats, France)
Terribile, Roberto (Fondazione AIDA, Italy)
Timmermans, Jack (De Stilte, the Netherlands)
Turner, Jeremy (Cwmni Theatr Arad Goch, United Kingdom)
Ullrich, Christoph (Laterna Musica, Germany)
Unseld, Melanie (University of Oldenburg, Germany)

van de Water, Manon (ITYARN, USA)
van den Eynde, Bart (a.pass: advanced performance and scenography studies, Belgium)
van der Meulen, Jamilja (Centraal Bureau voor de Statistiek, the Netherlands)
van der Mieden, Otto (Poppenspelmuseum, the Netherlands)
Vanthienen, Annemie (FARO – Vlaams Steunpunt voor Cultureel Erfgoed, Belgium)
Venturini, Davide (Compagnia TPO, Italy)
Verbrugge, Flora (Theater Sonnevanck, the Netherlands)
von Löwis, Stephan (kinderkinder, Germany)
Wallebroek, Veerle (Het Firmament, Belgium)
Wartemann, Geesche (University of Hildesheim, Germany)
Weber, Brigitta (Theater Eiger, Mönch und Jungfrau, Switzerland)
Wellens, Nikol (VTI, Belgium)
Werdenberg, Ursula (ITI, Switzerland)
Wettmark, Ellen (Kulturrådet, Sweden)
Wischnitzky, Eva (Theater Fallalpha, Switzerland)
Yendt, Maurice (ATEJ, France)
Zagorski, Andrea (ITI, Germany)
Zeeman, Pieter (Fonds Podiumkunsten, the Netherlands)
Zini, Carlotta (La Baracca, Italy)
Zwaneveld, Brechtje (Theatermaker, the Netherlands)

Varieties of Independent Music Theatre in Europe[1]

Matthias Rebstock

Hans-Jörg Kapp begins his essay on independent music theatre in German-speaking Europe with the following sentence: 'It exists, the "independent music theatre scene"'.[2] It is typical for this type of theatre that one would feel the need to point out its very existence. With an eye towards independent music theatre in Germany, I too have argued that there is certainly a vibrant scene, although – unlike independent dance theatre, for example – it is not yet really present to the general public.[3] Its manifestations seem too heterogeneous to enjoy recognition as a cohesive whole, and they often vanish into the expansive categories of an interdisciplinary or multimedia theatre that, as an effect of the traction gained by postdramatic and boundary-crossing works, already deals with all possible materials and media, music being one of them.

What holds true for German-speaking Europe applies to Europe in general: independent music theatre has heretofore not managed to emancipate and establish itself to the same degree as independent dramatic theatre and dance theatre, neither in terms of scholarly discourse nor in the public eye. To name some circumstances amongst many which evince this fact, few extensive studies on the topic have emerged, no empirical inquiries into protagonists working in the field or into audience structures can be said to exist, hardly any activity on the part of international associations and organisations takes place, and if it does, it occurs only in particular areas within this vast field.

---

1 | In the German original the term 'Freies Musiktheater' is used throughout the text. To the different meanings of ‚independent music theatre' and 'Freies Musiktheater' see 1.2

2 | Hans-Jörg Kapp, 'Vom Bestellen lokaler Klangfelder: Freies Musiktheater im deutschsprachigen Raum', in: Eckhard Mittelstädt and Alexander Pinto (eds.), *Die Freien Darstellenden Künste in Deutschland*, Bielefeld: transcript, 2013, pp. 183-194.

3 | Matthias Rebstock, 'Musiktheater: Spielräume schaffen!', in: Wolfgang Schneider, *Theater entwickeln und planen*, Bielefeld: transcript, 2013, pp. 299-314.

Before anything else, independent music theatre must be made accessible as a cohesive field of study.[4]

Against this backdrop, it should only seem logical that the publication before you afford independent music theatre only a side note rather than a full-length study. Correspondingly, my essay concentrates on formulating perspectives for future research projects that would have to devote more thorough and systematic attention to discrete international, national and regional traditions, to culture-political conditions as well as to protagonists, practices and aesthetics. Such an endeavour would be extremely worthwhile, since independent music theatre bears enormous potential for artistic innovation. In this respect, Eric Salzman and Thomas Desi even consider music theatre 'the most central performance art form of the post-modern world'.[5]

I like most of the other authors who occupy themselves with the independent performing arts, operate with the fundamental assumption that a correlation between structures, working processes and aesthetics exists, and that the innovative potential of independent music theatre should be sought within this interrelationship. A thorough study would therefore have to take this cir-

---

[4] | To be sure, there are numerous papers on individual artistic positions. Amongst those which stem from musicology, one observes the preponderance of a work-oriented perspective: the investigation is geared mainly to compositions, or rather scores, and thereby to the segment of the field known as new music theatre, or else new opera (see 1.3). Both the performance as a totality in terms of its music-theatrical form as well as aspects concerned with the processes, production conditions or structural frameworks are usually excluded. Although these topics are indeed addressed by Theatre Studies, independent music theatre receives only marginal attention from it. A Music Theatre Studies would have to achieve a balancing act here. The following are important works that at least partially take this field into account:

Matthias Rebstock and David Roesner (eds.), *Composed Theatre: Aesthetics, Practices, Processes*, Bristol: Intellect Ltd., 2012; Jörn Peter Hiekel (ed.), *Neue Musik in Bewegung: Musik- und Tanztheater heute*, Mainz: Schott, 2011; Eric Salzman and Thomas Desi (eds.), *The New Music Theater*, Oxford: Oxford University Press, 2008; Frieder Reininghaus and Katja Schneider (eds.), 'Experimentelles Musik- und Tanztheater', Vol. 7 of Handbuch der Musik im 20. Jahrhundert, Laaber: Laaber, 2004; Siegfried Mauser, *Musiktheater im 20. Jahrhundert*, Vol. 14 of Handbuch der musikalischen Gattungen, Laaber: Laaber, 2002.

A noteworthy example is the anthology of interviews *Fragen an das Musiktheater*, edited by Jury Everhartz and Kristine Tornquist (Vienna: edition atelier, 2012) in which fourteen independent music theatre ensembles talk about their work, providing for the first time a bundled perspective on the separate activities of Viennese ensembles and thereby constituting what one could call *the* Viennese music theatre scene.

[5] | Salzman/Desi, *The New Music Theater*, cover blurb.

cumstance into account. For what follows, however, I will take a more narrow approach and will concentrate on diverse artistic practices (i.e., on working processes and different fields of artistic engagement that seem to characterise independent music theatre's innovative potential). Societal and culture-political frameworks in individual countries, funding systems and the highly diverse historical traditions can only be touched upon.

If I accent the innovative potential of independent music theatre in the following, I do so in an attempt to pose a double differentiation: the established international opera métier constitutes one frame of reference. Yet discursive use of the term 'opera' usually involves two entirely disparate aspects – on the one hand, 'opera' signifies a certain structure, especially the financing and working modes proper to public opera houses, on the other hand it also signifies a certain repertoire of pieces: that maximum of fifty – or in many countries fewer – operas which define season schedules, being limited for the most part to operas of the eighteenth and nineteenth centuries.[6] My study therefore attempts to pursue the potential that arises when one takes a position beyond this concept of opera. The occurrence of contemporary innovations and the unleashing of new potentials within the established structure of opera, with regard to both modi operandi and the pieces performed, should in no way be denied; these innovations and potentials simply do not enter into the subject matter of this text, since they do not fall under the concept of independent music theatre. They merited scrutiny by another study.

Independent theatre provides a second frame of reference. Were one to conform to the conventional division of the performing arts into text-based dramatic theatre, music theatre and dance theatre, then independent text-based dramatic theatre would be meant here. Yet since independent theatre has, in the course of the postdramatic theatre, bid farewell to the idea of a traditional text-based dramatic theatre, I shall speak only of 'independent theatre' in the following. Many of the issues related to independent music theatre, as well as analyses undertaken more deliberately below, characterise independent theatre in general; typically, they manifest in music theatre with a certain temporal delay, whether one is referring to artistic engagement with new spaces or new formats, or to reflection on one's own artistic working conditions. Hence, my central question reads as follows: how do these issues and topics in independent music theatre set themselves apart from those in independent theatre, and to what extent does the privileging of music give rise to a more specific set of factors?

---

6 | Cf. Arnold Jakobshagen, 'Musiktheater', www.miz.org/static_de/themenportale/einfuehrungstexte_pdf/03_KonzerteMusiktheater/jacobshagen.pdf (last accessed 24.3.2015).

The range of projects and protagonists discussed in detail below cannot be considered a representative selection. It simply follows from the information and materials I have available as well as the knowledge and experiences I have gathered as a director and scholar in this field. A more systematic research in the whole field of independent music theatre in Europe would yet need to be done. The selection, however, is characteristic in the sense that it contains relevant positions in the contexts of the issues or fields of innovation discussed below.

My perspective has essentially been shaped by German-speaking countries, departing from there into international spheres. This perspective's indisputably subjective orientation comes to light in the following for example through my exclusion of Eastern-European regions.[7] In order to get a truly European perspective which could do justice to specific contexts and agents in individual countries from my point of view it would be necessary to include the participation of international researchers.

My own research was accompanied by a research seminar I conducted during the 2013 summer semester at the University of Hildesheim. During this seminar, the participating students and I developed a questionnaire which acted as a basis for holding and evaluating interviews with representatives from various ensembles. The findings gathered from these interviews constitute a vital source drawn upon by the following report.[8]

Hence, the target of this report is to develop approaches for ways one could map the field of independent music theatre in Europe. Depending on which point of view one inhabits while interrogating this field, particular phenomena come to the foreground and others slide to the background. In the first main section, I will attend to the concept of independent music theatre; after that, I will turn my attention towards lines of tradition (genres), and finally towards agents and structures one meets in this field. The second main section revolves around artistic practices, their characteristic strategies and questions as well as their innovative potential.

---

7 | The relatively high number of Berlin-based ensembles and projects whose voices are heard in this investigation is less a result of the subjectivity of my position than a by-product of the fact that Berlin together with Vienna and the scene in the Netherlands and Flanders is one of the centres of independent music theatre in Europe.

8 | My gratitude goes to my students Hannah Ehlers, Mariya Kashyna, Sina Leuenhagen, Mireia Ludwig, Carola Michaelis, Gregor Pellacini, Hans Peters, Ines Schmitt, Johanna Seyffert, Patrick Walter and Edgar Wendt.

1. Terms and Structures

1.1 What Does 'Music Theatre' Mean?

The difficulty of examining independent music theatre in Europe already begins with the term itself, or more specifically, with the different meanings the term has in different languages and countries. For instance, the terms 'Musiktheater', 'music theatre' and 'théâtre musical' don't really mean the same. Their attendant terminologies have varying histories, are integrated in different ways into the lexical fields of their respective languages and are linked to different conceptions. One can, however, discern two distinct meanings that determine the international discourse:

1. 'Music theatre' serves as an umbrella term for all forms of theatre for which music plays constitutive role. Those genres which fall under this term include opera, operetta and the musical,[9] in addition to a spectrum of diverse genres like new music theatre, experimental music theatre, instrumental theatre, staged concerts, concert installations, musical performance and so forth.[10]

This term's outer edges are necessarily blurry and overlap with other terms and their respective fields. Furthermore, such a determination of the term 'music theatre' according to the sum of differing genres is limited when dealing with musicalized forms of theatre, such as in the work of Einar Schleef, Robert Wilson, Jan Fabre or Christoph Marthaler.[11] Hans-Thies Lehmann ascribes a fundamental musicalisation to the forms of theatre he gathers under the term 'postdramatic'. Yet as evidence of such a musicalisation, he cites works by Heiner Goebbels, Meredith Monk and others – prominent examples from the field of *music* theatre. Thus, the relation between the terms 'postdramatic theatre' and 'music theatre' remains unclear at first.[12]

---

9 | Jacobshagen even describes dance as a music theatre genre. Cf. loc. cit.

10 | Cf. also Wolfgang Ruf: 'Besides literary opera and politically engaged music theatre, several varieties of avant-garde music theatre unfolded, types for which no generic term exists, only a series of designations such as 'musical theatre' (Stockhausen, 1961); 'visible music' (Schnebel, 1966); 'visual music', 'audiovisual music', 'staged music' (Dahlhaus) or 'media composition' (H. R. Zeller).' Wolfgang Ruf, 'Musiktheater', in: Ludwig Finscher (ed.), *Musik in Geschichte und Gegenwart*, Vol. 6 of *Sachteil*, Kassel: Bärenreiter, 1997, column #1705.

11 | Cf. David Roesner, *Musicality in Theatre*, Farnham: Ashgate, 2014; and idem., *Theater als Musik. Verfahren der Musikalisierung in chorischen Theaterformen bei Christoph Marthaler, Einar Schleef und Robert Wilson*, Tübingen: Gunter Narr, 2003.

12 | For more on this topic, see 1.3. Instead of a definition or terminology for the sum of varying genres, a systematic way of accessing the term presents itself: accordingly,

Yet it can already be grasped here that 'music theatre' should not be understood as a fixed category. The undermining of established terminological boundaries, categories and genres belongs to the most characteristic features of the arts since the beginning of the twentieth century. Their real métier is the in-between: that which evades unambiguous ascription. Hence, 'music theatre' sometimes becomes more of a perspective from which one can glimpse phenomena. These phenomena, when observed from this perspective, display features which would elude scrutiny were one to observe them using another terminology. Therefore, in my view, a discussion concerning whether for example Christoph Marthaler's works are or are not music theatre is less fruitful than a discussion which concerns what one learns about the works *when* regarded as music theatre – and what reasons there are for doing so. Similar thinking would apply to works by Xavier Le Roy or Sasha Waltz. With good reason, they too would be viewable as music theatre *and* as dance theatre, each moniker allowing the uncovering of other aspects and the referencing of other discourses.

2. Aside from its broader sense, the term 'music theatre' is often used in a narrower sense, namely as a term which poses a contrast to 'opera'. It is important to see that *this* concept of music theatre is not a pure genre designation, but instead goes along with an aesthetic claim (at least in the context of the German state and municipal theatre system): 'music theatre' claims to be more progressive, flexible and up to date than 'opera', the latter still being considered stodgy and aesthetically retrograde.[13] Equally typical of this contrasting of 'opera' to 'music theatre' is an intermingling of aesthetic and institutional aspects. For instance, 'opera' is associated as much with the plot carrying role of the singing parts as with the large orchestra apparatus (referring to the piece's personnel and at the same time to the structure upheld by an institution) and the publicly funded opera house itself; contrariwise, 'music theatre' stands for a smaller form, for the more flexible apparatus and for the giving of equal importance to all the employed theatrical means, which can even lead to the complete absence of singing in music theatre as, for example, in many pieces by John Cage or

---

music theatre would be that form of theatre for which music plays a constitutive role as concerns the production of sense or structure, or where music possesses a dimension relevant to the work's action (*Handlung* meaning 'action' and 'plot'). For more on the concept of action-relevance (*Handlungsrelevanz*), cf. Christiane Plank-Baldauf, 'Erzählen mit Musik – Erzählte Musik', in: *Das Magazin* no. 5, Oldenburg: Oldenburgisches Staatstheater, 2012/13. In practice, however, such a definition encounters its own limits.

13 | The innovative tone exuded over a long period of time by the expression 'music theatre' has admittedly faded to a large extent. Cf. also H.-J. Kapp, 'Vom Bestellen lokaler Klangfelder', p. 184.

Mauricio Kagel. Viewed through an historical lens, this meaning of 'music theatre' draws on decisive impulses from 1960s music theatre, which, as part of a shifting terminology, is defined as 'new' or 'experimental music theatre', or 'instrumental theatre' (for more on this, see 1.3).

However, within the field of pocket opera companies – which do not espouse this radical turn away from the opera, electing instead to adhere to the traditional features of the opera-genre – one can also discern an oppositional position vis-à-vis the traditional opera-institution. Free pocket operas distinguish themselves from the big apparatus and from the restricted programmes of a standardised repertoire, and favour another model for staging works – one characterised by closer cooperation between conductors and directors, for example.

Further differences exist beyond these two fundamentally divergent meanings of 'music theatre' depending on the theatre traditions in respective language regions and pointing to different lines of theatre-historical development.

In the German-speaking part of Europe, for example, a third usage of the term 'Musiktheater' exists that is charged with another aesthetic claim. It opposes 'Musiktheater' to 'Oper' and again implies institutional aspects. When used in this way, 'Musiktheater' stands for the aspiration to create sophisticated and challenging, contemporary theatre. Walter Felsenstein, founder and chief director of Berlin's Komische Oper after World War II, was instrumental in shaping this understanding of 'Musiktheater'. This meaning of the term conveys a specific image of opera staging that lays the typical heirloom gestures of the singer to rest and strives to be taken seriously as theatre. So today, also a number of opera houses such as the Komische Oper Berlin define themselves as 'Musiktheater'.

In the English-speaking world, the term 'music theatre' is far less established than in German-speaking countries and is associated more strongly with musicals: 'Ambitious modern musicals with a pretence to do more than merely entertain are as likely to be designated "music theatre" as anything else.'[14] The tradition of musicals is, in fact, much more sturdy in Great Britain than anywhere else in Europe, which goes not only for Broadway musicals but also for the tradition of sparsely cast, aesthetically advanced musicals. In contrast, the field of the musical in German-speaking Europe, for instance, is left primarily to large commercial productions. For the German discourse about 'Musiktheater' the musical plays a subordinate role.[15]

---

14 | Salzman/Desi, *The New Music Theater*, p. 5.
15 | The musically sophisticated musicals of Stephen Sondheim play a unique role in Great Britain. In Germany, the Neuköllner Oper in Berlin counts as an exception. This house has made a name for limited-size, contemporary and critical musicals, thanks in particular to the productions of Peter Lund. In Holland, the production house M Lab in Amsterdam can be named as an example of independent musical production.

In their book *The New Music Theater*, Salzman and Desi likewise distinguish the two meanings of 'music theatre' sketched above, defining them as 'inclusive' and 'exclusive':

'The inclusive meaning of the term can encompass the entire universe of performance in which music and theatre play complementary and potentially equal roles. In this sense, *opera* can be seen as a particular and historical form of music theatre [...] However, when we say *new music theatre* in this book, we use the term in a way that is almost always meant to exclude traditional opera, operetta and musicals.'[16]

According to Salzman and Desi the 'exclusive' meaning of 'new music theatre' is meant to cover the entire spectrum of forms between operas and musicals – the two excluded. It is worth noting that the inclusive meaning of 'music theatre' already evinces a deeper foundation in performances while the German discourse is still more focused on pieces or works. On the other hand, it seems clear that Salzman and Desi's identification of the term 'new music theatre' is coined more expansively than the German-language variant 'Neues Musiktheater'. They include, i.e., small-scale operas[17] while the German term 'Neues Musiktheater' is descriptive of a narrower field and is primarily characterised by the theatricalisation of New Music since the 1960s.

The French term 'théâtre musical' also knows two variant forms: a superordinate umbrella term and a genre that embraces a future-oriented approach by setting itself apart from opera. As an example, in 1980 a French Ministry of Culture commission defined the general term as follows: 'a theatre spectacle whose dramaturgy is essentially controlled by a musical project and has meaning only in relation to it'.[18] In the more specific sense (in contrast to opera) the term underwent formation in the mid–1970s, when a number of free 'ateliers de théâtre musical' were founded in the wake of the '68 movement and in opposition to the established opera houses.[19] Since its founding in 1976 by the composer Georges Aperghis, ATEM in Bagnolet has become the most

---

16 | Salzman/Desi, *The New Music Theater*, p. 5.

17 | Ibid., p. 4.

18 | '*Spectacle théâtral dont la dramaturgie est essentiellement commandée par un projet musical et n'a de sens que par rapport à celui-ci*', quoted in Daniel Durney, 'Théâtre et Musique. France – Annees 80', in: *Les Cahiers du CREM* No. 4-5 (1987): p. 14.

19 | E.g., l'Atelier lyrique du Rhin, founded in 1974 in Colmar; l'Atelier de Théâtre et Musique (ATEM), founded by Georges Aperghis in Bagnolet in 1976, or Péniche-Opera in Paris, 1982 (cf. D. Durney, 'Théâtre et Musique', p. 11).

influential 'atelier'.[20] In contrast to German 'Musiktheater' and English 'music theatre', the French term 'théâtre musical' is hence more narrowly defined, being bound to forms of contemporary music theatre and corresponding more to what is understood under the designations 'Neues Musiktheater' or 'new music theatre'.

1.2 'Frei' or 'Independent'?

When looking at the phenomena of independent music theatre in Europe from a German point of view as I do it in this article we encounter another terminological difficulty: the term 'Freies Musiktheater' carries other implications than the term 'independent music theatre' and, like the term 'Freies Theater' in general, can only be understood in the context of the theatre system of German-speaking countries and the historical situation of the 1970s. This theatre system occupies a special position in Europe, as explained by Henning Fülle:

'The German theatre-scape is unique amongst theatre-scapes worldwide. This favourite assessment amongst cultural policy makers and columnists is symptomatic of the 'German system': around 150 theatre houses with full-time and salaried artistic ensembles and continuous repertoire operations in all sectors of the performing arts, in public (municipal and state) hands. And yet another kind of uniqueness can be found in the parallel structure of 'Freies Theater' ('free theatre'), which began to take shape in the late 1970s and has since established itself so durably that its importance as well as the urgency of its funding are acknowledged favourably.'[21]

The impulse that spurned the development of a suchlike 'parallel structure' of a Freies Theater in the 1970s came from societal and political aims arising after the '68 movement. These aims were achievable only 'outside the institutional systems of the authoritarianist-governed temple of the educated middle class',[22] thus necessitating a *freeing* of the theatre from these institutions and its repositioning outside those confines. It is only in these terms – not in terms

---

20 | For a thorough rendering of ATEM's work and principles, see Matthias Rebstock, '"Ça devient du théâtre, mais ça vient de la musique": The Music Theatre of Georges Aperghis', in: Rebstock/Roesner, *Composed Theatre*, pp. 223-242.
21 | Henning Fülle, 'Freies Theater – Worüber reden wir eigentlich?' [Free theatre – What are we really talking about?], November 2012, www.festivalimpulse.de (last accessed 1.6.2013).
22 | Ibid.

of freedom from financial constraints or the like – that the newly emerging theatre forms were *free*.[23]

Music theatre played little to no role in this liberating process. Although the Fluxus movement (which initially considered itself a musical movement) and the antiauthoritarian "happenings" and actions of John Cage since the late 1950s had great influence on the theatre world, music theatre developed hardly any institutional approaches of its own. Most works of new or experimental music theatre in the 1970s were performed within structures that New Music had built, especially in the milieu surrounding radio broadcasting institutions. Initially, not many structures evolved parallel to the opera houses.[24] The foundation of free opera ensembles did not set in until the 1980s, gaining a further impetus in 1990s Vienna and Berlin.[25] As opposed to Freies Theater, the formation of a Freies Musiktheater was hence less political and less societally or socioculturally motivated; at issue instead was the performance of a repertoire

---

23 | In his book *Labor oder Fließband?: Produktionsbedingungen freier Musiktheaterprojekte an Opernhäusern* (Berlin: Theater der Zeit, 2013), Rainer Simon offers another examination of the concept of Freies Musikheater. In contradistinction to the remarks of Arnold Jacobshagen in his handbook *Praxis Musiktheater*, (Laaber, 2002), Simon emphasises that the freedom of Freies Musiktheater is not to be equated with a 'presuppositionlessness', as Jacobshagen would have. Without intending to further pursue Simon's reading of Jacobshagen's definition here, it is perfectly obvious that no form of theatre lacks presuppositions, either socially or economically. The conclusion Simon draws from this statement is problematic, however: the freedom would be only a 'relative' freedom regarding both municipal and state theatre as well as Freies Theater (p. 15). We are therefore to understand 'works that are independent, that is, free, from certain conventions regarding production which traditional opera performances are based on' (ibid.) as Freies Musiktheater, regardless of whether they are produced in opera houses or in the field of independent music theatre. This interpretation also recognises the existence of 'free music theatre productions' in state opera houses. Not only does Simon lose sight of historical relations by proposing this definition, he also ignores all the political, financial and institutional differences between public opera houses and the independent music theatre scene.

24 | Amongst the exceptions here are the Neuköllner Oper, Berlin, which was formed in 1972 and has existed since 1977 as a registered association, and the Pocket Opera Company in Nuremberg, which was founded in 1974 by its director Peter B. Wyrsch as opernstudio nürnberg e.V. The Theater am Marienplatz in Krefeld was also founded in 1976.

25 | The following ensembles were amongst those newly founded: Zeitgenössische Oper Berlin (1997); a rose is, Berlin (1997); Wiener Taschenoper, Vienna (refounded in 1999); ZOON Musiktheater, Vienna (1994); Neues Wiener MusikTheater, Vienna (1999); Musikwerkstatt Wien, Vienna (1999). Cf. also H.-J. Kapp, 'Vom Bestellen lokaler Klangfelder'.

of pieces that was not covered by opera houses, the use of a lighter, more flexible apparatus, and themes closer to the present day and to people's lives. In keeping with this orientation, a focus lay from the outset on new pieces and premiere performances.

Freies Theater in German-speaking countries has obviously undergone constant change since these early years. Today a wide array of theatre forms fall under this heading, ranging from the lay group without funding to internationally active, decidedly professional ensembles such as She She Pop or Rimini Protokoll. This applies similarly to today's scene of Freies Musiktheater, whose spectrum ranges from productions by young collegiate artists to those for example by Heiner Goebbels with Ensemble Modern and to international festival productions that tour throughout Europe or worldwide. Whether all these forms of theatre, or music theatre, can be gathered under the collective term 'Freies Theater', or 'Freies Musiktheater', is a subject for further discussion.[26] It is, however, clear that the German versions of these terms are deeply informed by history and cannot be used apart from it.

In the international context, which is not typified among other ways by competition amongst these theatre systems, the term is less charged with a future-oriented outlook and can be conceived more pragmatically: in the following, therefore, 'independent music theatre' means all forms of music theatre on a professional level that are not produced in publically funded houses and that do not pursue purely commercial interests.

1.3 Genres and Discourses

As our discussion of the term 'music theatre' has shown, the delineation of varying genres within the field is a thorny task, and at first glance is rather unproductive for our analysis. Even so, it is typical of music theatre that the varying genres also go along with varying sites of production, channels of distribution and audience groups as well as both public and professional discussions; that is to say, they are part of varying discourses – or, to put into different words, they are affiliated with varying 'cultural systems' or 'scenes'. One of the reasons why independent music theatre does not appear as a distinct scene is that it is split amongst separate cultural systems that have little contact with one another. In light of this circumstance, a process of subdivision into distinct genres would provide us with little insight, but a subdivision into those genres' attendant discursive fields would prove quite illuminating. My

---

26 | Cf. Annemarie Matzke, 'Das "Freie Theater" gibt es nicht: Formen des Produzierens im gegenwärtigen Theater', in: W. Schneider (ed.), *Theater entwickeln und planen*. See also www.festivalimpulse.de (last accessed 1.6.2013).

observation is that three such discursive fields can be distinguished and can be differentiated by reference to certain genres:[27]

The first field is formed by the performance of small-scale operas and musicals as well as adaptations of repertoire operas. Small-scale operas include both baroque opera, which the independent scene has endowed with crucial momentum,[28] and chamber operas (especially those of the early twentieth century) that are generally played rather seldom or have only been recently rediscovered.

I understand 'opera adaptation' as including productions whose self-determined task is to use a small and flexible apparatus in order to 'tell' operas, well-known ones in particular, in novel ways. This can happen through new arrangements of the music, by shifting the story to other contexts, through incorporation of other texts or music, and the like. This approach, which allows a freer treatment of the materials and compositions than was (and is) the case in opera houses, was an important catalyst in the founding of several pocket operas and still figures strongly in the profiles of many independent opera ensembles.[29] Despite its success amongst audiences, this approach encounters difficulties, according to my observations, in carving out its own niche within opera and theatre discourses.

The second field takes shape around new opera and new music theatre.[30] Even though both of these genres were, and for some still are, almost diametrically opposed to one another from historical and aesthetic standpoints, I have associated them here because they share a common discourse: that of New Music. New music theatre is situated in the tradition of the 1960s and is linked to composers like John Cage, Mauricio Kagel, Dieter Schnebel, Vinko Globokar or György Ligeti. This form of music theatre arose, in short, out of a theatricalisation, that is, a performatisation of music-making itself, and out

---

27 | This thesis would need to be verified by corresponding discursive analyses, which I am unable to perform here.

28 | A number of ensembles specialise in both baroque operas and new operas, or in new music theatre. Examples include Muziektheater Transparant in Antwerpen or Musikwerkstatt Wien. For more on the latter, cf. Everhartz/Tornquist, *Fragen an das Musiktheater*, p. 55f. Likewise, several festivals display this contrast between Old and New Music (or Music Theatre): the Schwetzinger Festspiele, for example, or Schlossmediale Werdenberg, Switzerland, founded by Mirella Weingarten in 2012.

29 | E.g., Neuköllner Oper, Berlin; Pocket Opera Company, Nuremberg; Berliner Kammeroper; das andere opernensemble, Munich; Totales Theater, Vienna; or Tête à Tête Opera in London.

30 | For reasons of clarity, I use the term 'new music theatre' here as a superordinate term that includes other forms such as experimental music theatre, instrumental theatre and others. These terms cannot be sharply separated, either historically or systematically (see above).

of an expansion of the concepts of material and composition to include extra-musical, visual realms – and thus out of a position of independence from, and implicit rejection or open criticism of,[31] the bourgeois art form of opera.

New opera did not regain significance in German-speaking Europe until the 1980s and 90s, and did so in connection with the currents of new subjectivism, neotonality or new simplicity in New Music. Literary opera in particular flourished.[32] These new operas fundamentally adhered to opera's form (e.g., the plot-carrying role of singing, the separation between singers and instrumental ensemble, and the centralisation of the singer-actor).

Nowadays, the ideological debates between new opera and new music theatre can be considered a thing of the past. A straightforward categorisation seems difficult, or has become somewhat senseless, and yet specific traditions in which composers stand can still be clearly discerned. Both new opera and new music theatre experience the highest degree of public attention within the vast field of independent music theatre. This sphere has the best structures at its disposal and enjoys a relatively gleaming reputation, even in regions where music theatre is only weakly rooted. However, both forms are well integrated into the discourse surrounding New Music. Amongst their crucial distributors are festivals for New Music that focus on premiere music performances and the role of the composer. In theatre discourse, on the other hand, these forms are only marginally visible. At the same time, one cannot claim that certain venues for independent theatre never show this sort of music theatre production (e.g., Kampnagel in Hamburg or sophiensaele and HAU in Berlin). That being said, the terrain of new music theatre and new opera remains on the outskirts of independent theatre discourse, a situation which is expressed, for instance, by the meagre status accorded to it by theatre journals or Theatre Studies publications.

Finally, one can discern a third sector of music theatre, which, to be sure, is rooted less in music discourse than in theatre discourse. This category is inhabited by forms of musicalised theatre that are largely determined by directors and do not necessarily stand in any relationship with New Music. Historically, this area is positioned in the tradition of theatre practitioners and theoreticians – Appia, Meyerhold, Artaud or Moholy-Nagy – who each in their own way demanded a liberation of theatre from the dominance of the text, proclaiming

---

31 | This calls to mind, for example, the scandal surrounding the 1970 premiere performance of *staatstheater* by Mauricio Kagel at the Staatsoper Hamburg.

32 | The Munich Biennale for New Music Theatre, founded in 1988 by Hans-Werner Henze, became the most important forum for new opera. In countries where the 1950s and 60s avant-garde played no meaningful role, the evolution of new opera followed different paths. In Great Britain, for example, an unbroken tradition of such new chamber operas has existed since Benjamin Britten.

instead the organisation of theatrical elements according to the model of musical compositions (i.e., scores). It is crucial to our context that we see how the aforementioned new music theatre of the 1960s appealed to this tradition in its search for new forms of music theatre beyond opera. Hans-Thies Lehmann, in turn, sees John Cage and the Fluxus and Happening scenes Cage inspired as vital points of reference for postdramatic theatre, which he comprehends as being characterised through 'simultaneity', a 'dehierarchisation of theatrical means', and a fundamental, all-encompassing musicalisation of the material – each of which are facets pertinent to the music theatre of the 1960s.[33] As pointed out earlier, Lehmann's analyses rely on music theatre artists such as Heiner Goebbels, Meredith Monk or Christoph Marthaler.[34] Today Marthaler is succeeded by musicians/directors such as Ruedi Häusermann or David Marton. The distinctive thing about these directors is that, although they began their careers in independent theatre, today they almost exclusively work in dramatic theatre houses, working only in exceptional cases in opera houses.[35] Furthermore, they are discussed primarily within theatre discourse.

In view of the historical and aesthetic connections existing between new music theatre and postdramatic, musicalised theatre, David Roesner and I introduced the term 'composed theatre', intending it to cast light on common characteristics of aesthetics and working processes despite these discourses' customary separation.[36] 'Composed theatre' is to be understood as an umbrella term for theatre forms that feature the use of compositional processes and strategies and are essentially characterised by a musical thinking. It distinguishes itself using specific practices and fundamental aesthetic convictions: by granting equal importance to the elements of text, music, action, image and their musical-compositional organisation, or by dissolving a sequential form of production (libretto, composition, staging) – par for the course in opera – and instead developing pieces and collaborative production structures in which each practice (music, text, scene) works directly towards the performance event. New concepts of the work and of authorship are linked with this approach.

The theatrical concert (or 'staged concert') has recently joined the ranks of the three fields discussed above, each of which presently belongs to a different

---

33 | Lehmann, *Postdramatisches Theater*, p. 139ff., trans. W.W.

34 | For the special significance of Marthaler for independent music theatre in Germany, see also H.-K. Kapp, 'Vom Bestellen lokaler Klangfelder', p. 184f.

35 | Häusermann's *Kanon für geschlossene Gesellschaft* came out in the year 2000 at the Munich Opera, and *Randolphs Erben* in 2009 at the Stuttgart Opera; Christoph Marthaler is, however, also active as an opera director, but his importance for independent music theatre lies in his interpretations of pieces, which he has shown in houses for dramatic theatre.

36 | Cf. Rebstock/Roesner, *Composed Theatre*.

discourse. This genre is about breaking open the traditional concert form and enabling other ways of listening through diverse forms of staging. The music clearly holds central importance and normally amounts to concert music (music that was not originally written for a theatrical context). Theatrical concerts, though, have heretofore played more of a subordinate role in discourse. Amongst practices of staging, it would have to be grouped under composed theatre, yet it more often appears in the context of new ways of presenting and communicating music (*Musikvermittlung*) and the reformation of the standard concert format.[37]

1.4 Protagonists and Structures

Important access to the field of independent music theatre can be gained by asking questions about the agents who are active in this field and the structures in which they are active: Who are the 'makers' involved in artistic production? How are they organised? Where and how are the pieces presented? What structures of production and distribution exist, and what do channels of reception or feedback into a more general music theatre discourse look like?[38]

1.4.1 Music theatre ensembles and production teams

In comparison to independent theatre, when one considers the agents engaged in the artistic production of independent music theatre, it becomes apparent that the production form of the collective plays scarcely any role here. While the collective verges on trademark status throughout the spectrum of independent theatre and amongst independent theatre's top ensembles – one need only think of Forced Entertainment, Gob Squad, She She Pop, Need Company and so forth – in independent music theatre, very few ensembles have worked in the long-term with fixed casts and equitable decision-making structures. On the one hand, this may have to do with the (historically speaking) relatively late and primarily aesthetically motivated emergence of independent music theatre, which, in terms of its original self-conception, was less sustained by an anti-bourgeois, emancipatory and anti-elitist impulse than was the case with independent theatre. In purely practical terms, on the other hand, it has to do with the fact that music theatre productions frequently demand a larger apparatus (instrumental ensembles, singers, conductors, etc.), hence ruling out the intimacy of a collective. Ultimately, however, continuously varying concepts

---

37 | Cf. Martin Tröndle, (ed.), *Das Konzert: Neue Aufführungskonzepte für eine klassische Form*, Bielefeld: transcript, 2009.

38 | As I explained at the outset, I will not go into detail regarding cultural-political frameworks and financial conditions, although these aspects would be essential to a comprehensive description of the field.

of professionalism amongst musicians and theatre-makers play a role as well: From the viewpoint of their education (and often of their self-conception), musicians are more readily considered specialists, while a certain generalism is customary in independent theatre.[39]

The ensemble Die Maulwerker in Berlin holds a special position in this regard. It was founded in 1977 by Dieter Schnebel but has worked since the late 1990s as an autonomous ensemble in which all artistic decisions are made collectively and all members appear on stage. The personnel has remained virtually constant over the years. In larger music theatre productions, the responsibilities of direction, stage design and costume are assumed by people within ensemble circles.[40] Outside of the Maulwerker, the form of the collective seems to be practiced only in smaller formations, such as the Berliner trio schindelkilliusdutschke and the ensemble Musiktheater bruit.

By contrast, independent music theatre typically features ensembles that are organised around a few central figures and that do not have permanent personnel. Within structures that operate more like networks, each group's respective director (or team of directors) has flexible recourse to a more or less stable pool of artists, depending on the project's dimensions. The leading figures are predominantly directors who work together with a team of stage and costume designers. According to each project, they work with particular composers and engage musicians or ensembles with whom they already have a long-standing working relationship. Examples of such groups are theatre cryptic with Cathy Boyd in Glasgow, Veenfabriek with Paul Koek in Leiden, or Totales Theater with Markus Kupferblum in Vienna. In some cases, these production teams also include conductors or musical directors, such as with the opera company Novoflot[41] or the Zeitgenössische Oper Berlin.[42] Even more rarely, composers belong to the team of directors. This is the case with liquid

---

39 | I cannot go deeper into this aspect here. A certain change in the self-conception of musicians has, in fact, been observable in recent years. Cf. also Falk Hübner, *Shifting identities: the musician as theatrical performer*, Amsterdam: International Theatre & Film Books, 2014.

40 | For example, in the production *Songbooks Complete* as part of the 'visible music' series at Stadttheater Bielefeld in 2001, with direction by Chistian Kesten and Henrik Kairies and scenography by Steffi Weissmann. These three ensemble members also performed in the piece.

41 | The Berlin based company Novoflot was founded in 2002 by the director Sven Holm, the conductor Vicente Larrañaga and the performance artist and dramaturg Sebastian Bark.

42 | Between 1997 and 2007, Zeitgenössische Oper Berlin worked under the artistic direction of Andreas Rocholl, with a stable team consisting of members Sabrina Hölzer (direction), Mirella Weingarten (scenography) and Rüdiger Bohn (musical direction).

pinguin in Saarbrücken, for example,[43] or with Teatr Weimar in Malmö.[44] Only in exceptional cases are ensembles directed by performers. Here one could name electric voice theatre with the vocalist Francis Lynch in London or Micro-Oper in Munich, founded and directed by the singer Cornelia Melián.

1.4.2 Composers

Substantial segments of independent music theatre are conditioned by the special role played by composers in the working process. The fields of both new opera and new music theatre can be described as 'composers' theatre': the public's attention is directed towards the compositions and composers (e.g., in premiere performances during new music festivals, for instance). It is they who are expected to yield innovative value. Existing systems of production and reception display a relatively traditional, opera-oriented notion of theatre where this is concerned – a notion which adheres to a clear separation between the work (here the composition) and the staging. Here (music) theatre is not contemplated in terms of an experiential dimension, which is not composite but rather holistic and synaesthetic, or in terms of a constitution of meaning which only emerges in the totality of the interplay of theatrical means. Instead, the supratemporally fixed score is understood as work and essence that can be interpreted one way or another.

Be that as it may, a sizeable amount of new music theatre composers take on responsibility for direction themselves, or rather comprehend the entirety of theatrical elements as the field of their composition. The very separation of composition and staging just mentioned above is subverted by such methods. Counted amongst practitioners who deploy this type of understanding are Heiner Goebbels, Georges Aperghis, Manos Tsangaris, Daniel Ott,[45] Michel van der Aa, Julian Klein, Leo Dick, Jennifer Walsh, François Sarhan or Simon Sten-Andersen. One could also name the aforementioned music theatre collectives, as well as a number of teams who have developed forms of cooperative work,

---

43 | Katharina Bihler (direction) and Stephan Seibt (composition).

44 | Jörgen Dahlquist (text and direction) and Kent Olofson (composition). At the same time, Teatr Weimar is not only a music theatre ensemble; it also produces text-based dramatic theatre. In a statement of artistic intent, it describes itself as 'the leading collective of playwrights, directors and actors in Sweden', www.teatrweimar.se/eng/index.htm (last accessed 9.4.2015). So the directorial work of Dahlquist and Olofson only refers to Teatr Weimar's music theatre productions.

45 | In recent years, several works have come into existence in cooperation with the director Enrico Stolzenburg (e.g., *Blick Richtung Süden*, performed at the Wittener Days for New Chamber Music, 2009).

such as the collaboration between Hannes Seidl and Daniel Kötter[46] or between Elena Mendoza and myself.[47]

1.4.3 Vocal and instrumental ensembles

In addition to music theatre ensembles and composers, free instrumental and vocal ensembles are increasingly vital as agents in the field of independent music theatre. I refer here to ensembles whose focus lies in (contemporary) concert music, but who appear with increasing frequency as initiators and producers of music theatre projects. For example, Neue Vocalsolisten from Stuttgart regularly launch music theatre projects, and ensembles such as 2e2m from Champigny-sur-Marne, Phace from Vienna or the Berliner Solistenensemble Kaleidoskop perceive this sort of performative orientation as integral to their profile. Close cooperation between ensembles and composers is standard here, calling to mind the long-term collaboration between Heiner Goebbels and Ensemble Modern or between Georges Aperghis and the Ictus Ensemble. This type of long-term cooperation is practiced also by Trond Reinholdtsen and the ensemble Asamisimasa from Oslo or by Stefan Prins and the Nadar Ensemble from Flanders. Outside of new music theatre, these ensembles are usually regarded as leading proponents of theatrical concerts.

1.4.4 Production venues

If one examines production and performance venues, one is struck by the fact that a rather slim amount of production houses exist in independent music theatre and that they are less internationally interconnected than in independent theatre. Anyone searching within the music theatre field for a network resembling the cooperation between sophiensaele, Berlin; Kampnagel, Hamburg; Theaterhaus Düsseldorf; Gessnerallee, Zurich; and brut, Vienna, for example, will emerge empty-handed. What's more, here we once again encounter a problem: production houses active in music theatre represent differing segments of the heterogeneous music theatre field and are therefore able to cooperate only restrictedly.

---

46 | See 2.7.

47 | The two music theatre compositions *Niebla* (premiered at Hellerau, Dresden, 2007) and *La Ciudad de las Mentiras* (premiered at Teatro Real, 2017) were created under a collective authorship. For more on this, cf. also David Roesner and Clemens Risi, 'Die polyphone Werkstatt', *Theater der Zeit* (January 2009): p. 28f.; Thomas Betzwieser, 'Von Sprengungen und radialen Systemen: das aktuelle Musiktheater zwischen Institution und Innovation – eine Momentaufnahme', in: Arno Mungen (ed.), *Mitten im Leben: Musiktheater von der Oper zur Everyday Performance*, Würzburg: Königshausen & Neumann, 2011; and Albrecht Wellmer, 'Musiktheater heute', in: Jörn Peter Hiekel (ed.), *Neue Musik in Bewegung*, 2011, p. 28f.

Neuköllner Oper in Berlin has evolved into the most important production house for independent music theatre in Germany and one of the most vibrant in Europe. Each season, it produces approximately ten premieres and runs continuous performance operations with 250 shows annually.[48] It has traditionally emphasised adaptations and new versions of repertoire operas as well as premiere performances of operas that embrace contemporary references or subjects. Moreover, during Peter Lund's tenure as artistic director (1996–2004), Neuköllner Oper made a name for small-scale, German-language musicals. Under the artistic directorship of Bernhard Glocksin (since 2004), it has expanded its spectrum of forms considerably. Simultaneously, however, it maintains its mission to work for a broad audience 'beyond self-referential expert circles'.[49]

In comparison, through its long-term cooperation with the composer Mauricio Kagel, Theater am Marienplatz (TAM) in Krefeld has placed its focus more on instrumental theatre and new music theatre. Other areas of concentration are Beckett's works and authors such as Ernst Jandl or Gerhard Rühm. Gare du Nord in Basel, brought to life in 2002 by Desirée Meiser (who is also its director), views itself as a 'train station for New Music'. An experimental venue for New Music in general, not especially for music theatre, it nevertheless mounts at least one in-house production of music theatre per season. T&M in Paris, whose origins lie in Georges Aperghis' ATEM in Nanterre, outside of Paris, dedicates itself fully to 'théâtre musical et lyrique contemporain',[50] although in recent times it has carried out relatively few own productions. As a member of the network Reseau Varèse (see below), it shows predominantly international high-grade productions.

As far as guest performances, co-productions and (inter)national networks are concerned, production houses in Holland or Flanders – in the motherland of independent production houses, so to speak – are much more versatile and active than those in German-speaking countries, for instance. Veenfabriek in Leiden is currently one of the largest and most successful music theatre groups in the Benelux countries. Directed by percussionist and theatre director Paul Koek, Veenfabriek arose in 2004 out of the legendary Theatergroep Hollandia, founded in 1985 by Johan Simons and Paul Koek. But actually it comes close to a theatre company in its own right since it always works with a fixed ensemble and under the artistic direction of Paul Koek (although it maintains numerous co-operations with other groups). Muziektheater Transparent in Antwerp, in comparison, has the run of a more open structure: Wouter Van Looy and Guy

---

48 | Cf. www.neukoellneroper.de/#profil.
49 | Ibid.
50 | See www.theatre-musique.com (last accessed 28.3.2015).

Coolen being the artistic directors they present work of guest directors as well as those led by its regular director Wouter Van Looy.

1.4.5 Festivals

Although festivals have become the most important producers of independent music theatre (as well as in the realm of independent theatre and New Music), festivals dedicating themselves exclusively to music theatre are rare.[51] Usually, contemporary music festivals programme music theatre in addition to concerts,[52] or they cover the entire range of the performing arts, such as the Festival d'Avignon, the Edinburgh Festival or the Holland Festival. The music theatre genres outlined above are delineated within this rich festival-scape.

Festivals for New Music focus on new music theatre *compositions*, in keeping with New Music's generally standard practice of giving priority to premiere performances and individual works. Hence, new opera or new music theatre is highlighted (see above). In contrast, for the realm of opera adaptations or those forms of musicalised theatre oriented towards postdramatic theatre, only a handful of festivals or presentation platforms exist.[53] The number is even lower for festivals that present the whole gamut of music theatre. A prominent role is played in this regard by Operadagen Rotterdam, where this year an adaptation of *Figaro* by the Belgian group Comp.Marius will be shown, along with *King Size* by Christoph Marthaler and Annelies Van Parys' work from the world of new opera, titled *Private View*.[54]

---

51 | Examples of large festivals include the Munich International Biennale for New Music Theatre and the Operadagen Rotterdam. For smaller festivals, see Tête a Tête Opera Festival, London; Festival d' Òpera de Butxaca, Barcelona (last held in 2007); Taschenopernfestival in Salzburg; or Musiktheatertage Vienna, which first took place in 2015. Between 1992 and 2007, the Almeida Theatre in London also held, under the name Almeida Opera, a summer season for new music theatre as well as New Chamber Opera.

52 | E.g., Wien Modern, Warsaw Autumn, Ultima – Oslo Contemporary Music Festival, Huddersfield Contemporary Music Festival, musicadhoy in Madrid, the Salzburg Biennale, Donaueschinger Musiktage, Maerzmusik in Berlin, and the Borealis Festival in Bergen.

53 | At the same time, however, these forms are hardly ever presented at the free theatre platforms in question. To date, only one music theatre production could be seen at the Impulse Festival – David Marton's theatrical concert *Fairy Queen oder Hätte ich Glenn Gould nicht kennen gelernt* (after Henry Purcell) in 2007.

54 | A Muziektheater Transparant production with *the Asko/Schönberg Ensemble* and Neue Vocalsolisten Stuttgart. It premiered on 13 May 2015 at the Vlaamse Opera, Antwerp, in coproduction with Concertgebouw, Bruges, Deutsche Oper, Berlin, Nationaloper, Bergen, and Les Théâtres de la Ville de Luxembourg.

For German-speaking countries, Gerard Mortier inspired a first-rate music theatre uncoupled from the premiere-performance-driven operations of New Music. During his founding directorship at the Ruhrtriennale (2002–2004), Mortier made 'creations' the official focus: the development of pieces between theatre, music and dance, without insisting that the music belong to the category of New Music. Amongst the inaugural stagings was a theatrical version of Schubert's *Die schöne Müllerin* under the direction of Christoph Marthaler.[55] In spite of this, however, there is still a lack of platforms for such 'creations' of musicalised, postdramatic theatre and for productions of free opera and music theatre that work with pre-existing pieces.

1.4.6 Networks and platforms

On the whole, independent music theatre is less well-networked than independent theatre. This goes for international music theatre scenes, but also for most national ones. The most significant and financially robust network for music theatre on the international level is the Réseau Varèse, an 'alliance of large European festivals and presenters for the promotion and dissemination of musical creations'.[56] The network's membership comprises internationally renowned European festivals such as Wien Modern, Warsaw Autumn, the Holland Festival, Klangspuren Schwaz, Maerzmusik Berlin, the Huddersfield Contemporary Music Festival, and Ultima Oslo Contemporary Music Festival, but also smaller production houses like T&M in Paris or Casa de Musica in Porto. Although it supports and enables the international dissemination of a relatively large amount of music theatre productions, Réseau Varèse is not intended as a special instrument for the promotion of music theatre. As we have seen with the festivals I have discussed, central promotional importance is given entirely to New Music, and to music theatre only when it constitutes a segment thereof.[57] Thus, it also tends to be the case here that a mere portion of the broader field of music theatre is cushioned, that portion being new opera and new music theatre.

Relatively little international networking exists below this upper-level network. We can note, for example, a lack of international associations like reseo or ASSITEJ in the children's and youth theatre sector. Between 1992 and

---

55 | The directors Johan Simons and Paul Koek were also represented in the 2002 programme with several pieces. When Johan Simons, as the new director of the Ruhrtriennale, now reclaims the 'creations' concept, not only a programmatic but also a personal circle is completed.

56 | Cf. statement of intent at www.reseau-varese.com. (last accessed 23.3.2015).

57 | Examples of funded projects in the music theatre field include *Luna Park* by Georges Aperghis, 2011, *Kafka-Fragmente* by György Kurtág under the direction of Antoine Gindt, 2007, and *Eraritjaritjaka* by Heiner Goebbels, 2004.

2004 – a time of growth for independent music theatre – a network brought to life by Dragan Klaic from the Netherlands Theatre Institute known as NewOp/NonOp existed. It organised individual annual meetings in different locations together with respective local partners, meetings that facilitated exchange, discussion and networking amongst agents in the 'Small-Scale Contemporary Music-Theatre and Opera' field.[58] The list of the forty-nine participating companies from throughout Western Europe and Canada alone gives one a feeling of independent music theatre's potential at that time. The last of these meetings took place in Barcelona and was presented by Festival d'Opera de Butxaca. No further meetings took place.[59]

What independent music theatre urgently needs, in addition to networking amongst producers and internal exchange amongst the different ensembles and artists, is greater visibility and the creation of its own discourse. The International Theatre Institute (ITI) is striving to respond to this need through its internationally operative competition Music Theatre Now. The competition, held triennially since 2008, awards prizes in various categories such as 'first productions of new works, which were professionally created anywhere in the world'.[60] Simultaneously, the institute facilitates guest performances within key festivals for at least a portion of the award recipients, so that the productions can then be presented to the public anew as prize winners that have garnered significant attention.[61]

The new directors of The Munich Biennale, International Festival for new music theatre, Daniel Ott and Manos Tsangaris, are also vigorously setting their sights on the internationalisation of the field. Concurrently, they wish to orient the Biennale more strongly towards young artists, thereby rekindling the idea of its founding father, Hans Werner Henze. Besides inviting specifically targeted artists, their concept's core idea lies in the establishment of international platforms where production teams (composers, directors, and musicians) can present themselves through concepts and initial results of working processes. These presentations occur in the form of workshops guided by artistic advisors, making it possible for teams to obtain qualified advice for their continued work on the projects in question. At the same instant, Daniel Ott and Manos Tsangaris can form a picture of the projects at an early stage and finally select those which exhibit the quality requisite for an invitation to Munich. Daniel Ott's and Manos Tsangaris' efforts are pointing to new ways of confronting the basic problem of festival programming: innovative projects should be initiated,

---

58 | This was the network's original name. Cf. www.notnicemusic.com/NewOp.html.
59 | An attempt was made under the name 'C-Opera listserv' to continue the discussion in the form of an e-mail list. Cf. www.notnicemusic.com/C-Opera.html.
60 | www.musictheatrenow2015.iti-germany.de/index.php?id=88.
61 | Prizes in the current competition will be awarded at the Operadagen Rotterdam.

but projects which receive commissions ought not to fail, as this would go on the books as the festival's failure. This frequently means that festival commissions are awarded with a low tolerance for risk, by continually inviting the 'already arrived'. The Munich Biennale's concept allows for risk control by other means, which in turn allows – and this must prove itself starting in 2016 – for a more risk-friendly programming with high quality standards. What's more, a new model for cooperation between artists and festival directors is being initiated. Directors put their decisions up for discussion at the forefront, distribute them over multiple shoulders and, above all, open themselves up to discussion with production teams, including those who are not invited to Munich. This enhances transparency in the decision-making process.

Last but not least, this approach favours a certain working method: from the start, the focus lies on cooperation between composers, directors, musicians and so forth. The perspective shifts from the commissioned composition (as 'work'), which is also staged in the second step, to collectively conceived and produced performance events (see 2.1).

As concerns the degree of networking and the available structures, the individual situations in various national contexts are naturally quite different. In the Benelux countries, where touring belongs to the basic understanding and mission of independent theatre, the degree of networking is comparatively high. The Dutch system was also equipped with substantial subsidies, at least until the cultural clear-cutting of 2013.

Independent music theatre in Great Britain, on the one hand, has no such networks at its disposal. Nonetheless, the Opera & Music Theatre Forum (OMTF), for example, has existed since 1993 as a 'network of companies working to create an environment in which opera and music theatre can flourish'.[62] OMTF maintains a website where events and projects by members are publicised and formally introduced. The Forum thereby offers an overview – although one limited to OMTF members – of what is happening in the world of British independent music theatre. Beyond this, the Forum assumes lobbying responsibilities and offers member workshops devoted to topics such as promotion and audience development.

In countries like Portugal, Spain or Greece, on the other hand, where no stable tradition of independent music theatre has evolved, the situation has markedly worsened since 2008 due to the economic crisis. Lighthouse projects like the festival musicadhoy in Madrid, which was counted for years amongst top-notch festivals, has had to discontinue the music theatre series operadhoy almost completely.[63] The festival Opera d'Butxaca was also forced to throw in the towel in 2008, although it continues operations as Òpera de Butxaca

---

62 | www.omtf.org.uk.
63 | The festival consequently withdrew from the network Réseau Varèse.

i nova creacío on a project-to-project basis and by means of international co-productions (with Theater Basel and Neuköllner Oper Berlin, et al.).⁶⁴

Italy constitutes a special case in this regard, because in the fifties, sixties and seventies it was amongst the European centres of New Music⁶⁵ and boasted a series of interesting music theatre composers.⁶⁶ Since the economic crisis, however, New Music in Italy has almost ground to a halt. The Italian composers who are still very present on the international music theatre scene celebrate their success almost exclusively outside of Italy.⁶⁷

In light of the particular theatre system in German-speaking countries, an exceptional debate over stronger networking has developed here. As is the case with independent theatre, recent years have seen an increased effort to foster and try out different forms of cooperation between independent theatre and municipal or state theatre. An important funding instrument serving this purpose is the German Federal Cultural Foundation's Doppelpass Fund, an investment in partnerships between independent groups and public performance venues in Germany. Out of the twenty-two currently funded tandems, three are from the field of music theatre.⁶⁸

The Nordrhein-Westfalen Fonds Experimentelles Musiktheater (Experimental Music Theatre Fund) is another body which sponsors such co-operations. Each year, a jury selects one project to be realised by a municipal theatre in the region.⁶⁹ Finally, I should mention some initiatives by individual houses here which cooperate with independent music theatre (or more specifically, offer it a platform). Deutsche Oper Berlin, for instance, created a discrete performance venue, opening the Tischlerei in 2012, which is intended to give space to

---

64 | |Cf. e-mail interview with Dietrich Grosse, OPNC director since 07.11.2013.
65 | Specific centres were Rome and the milieu surrounding Nuova Consonanza; the studio of RAI in Milan, which was founded in 1955 by Luciano Berio and Bruno Maderna; or the festival Settimana internazionale di nuova musica in Palermo, where the Cologne and Darmstadt avant-garde gathered in its entirety.
66 | One thinks, for example, of the music theatre works of Luigi Nono and Luciano Berio, but also of lesser-known composers such as Domenico Guaccero or Egisto Macchi. Cf. Raymond Fearn, *Italian Opera since 1945*, Amsterdam: Harwood, 1997.
67 | E.g., Salvatore Sciarrino, Lucia Ronchetti or Giorgio Battistelli.
68 | Komische Oper Berlin and Gob Squad, LOFFT Leipzig and Oper Dynamo West, as well as Dock 11 and Jo Fabian Department.
69 | In recent years, Theater Bielefeld, for example, or the Musiktheater im Revier in Gelsenkirchen have participated. Starting in 2015, the funding concept will undergo some modifications. The funding will be oriented less towards developing a premiere performance, but will be understood as a residency – a funding period during which a team of artists can explore and 'transpose' particular themes in cooperation with a municipal theatre using music-theatrical means.

such experimental encounters. The Staatsoper Hamburg's experimental stage, opera stabile, has cooperated (at least in phases) with the free ensemble opera silens, which originated in 1995 from the environment surrounding the degree programme 'Directing Music Theatre' in Hamburg.[70] Be that as it may, opera houses will not truly open up towards experimental music theatre formats and begin productive partnerships with independent music theatre until the opera houses are prepared to furnish such venues with budgets of their own. If projects must be financed via external subvention funds established for independent theatre, then the opening up of the houses, though indeed welcome, remains questionable in a cultural-political sense.[71]

2. Lines of Innovation in the Field of Independent Music Theatre

In accordance with the heterogeneity and diversity of the field I attempted to sketch in the first main section, it is clear that agents' artistic practices are also highly varied, and that each belongs to specific traditions and depends on the given structural situations within which the artistic work is carried out. Nevertheless, it appears possible to mark certain questions or thematic fields related to artistic engagement that characterise the aesthetic practices of independent music theatre and within which the most sizeable innovative potential is currently to be found. Each of these will be loosely sketched out in the following and briefly expanded upon by way of examples in the form of concrete projects. These discrete examples were chosen not because they were representative of their respective area, but because they take *one* concrete, relevant artistic stance within it. As stated at the beginning, public opera houses and the independent theatre scene serve as the frames of reference for our selection.

2.1 Working Processes

Independent music theatre offers the opportunity to shape the processes by which individual pieces emerge, and do so independent of the well-rehearsed routines and structural constraints of traditional opera houses. Obviously, this is not a case of limitless freedom (see above). On the contrary, any room

---

70 | Cf. www.operasilens.de.
71 | A successful example of a long-term cooperation between a municipality (i.e., a municipal theatre) and independent music theatre is the collaboration between *Veenfabriek* Leiden and Schauspielhaus Bochum at the beginning of Anselm Weber's tenure as director (2010–2013).

to manoeuvre depends on the financial, structural and personnel-related conditions under which productions are brought to life. In spite of this, such relative autonomy is the reason why many professional music theatre makers have opted to develop a project in the independent realm.

The great potential of independent music theatre hence consists in inventing the working process *at the same time* as the project idea, in other words, deriving processes from necessities occasioned by project ideas and from participants' individual needs and working methods. A salient point is that amongst the eighteen free ensembles of the Viennese music theatre scene who were interviewed by Jury Everhartz und Kristine Tornquist,[72] all but one emphasised that they adhere neither to a fixed method nor an unchanging procedure, but design the process differently from project to project.

In relation to his own work, Georges Asperghis encapsulates this aspect when he says, 'Your prior experiences don't help you. [...] I want to dive into new adventures, more difficult ones as there is no experience'.[73]

The eschewing of the use of only one methodology is directly related to his fundamental interest in the unmistakable uniqueness which 'his' musicians transport as individuals. Similarly, his compositions are often musical portraits of the musicians themselves, and challenge them to exceed the boundaries of their own previously estimated faculties: 'Often, when they receive the score, they are excited yet afraid at the same time of its difficulty.'[74]

Hence, many of his music-theatrical pieces actually emerge during rehearsal. What Aperghis, for example, composes during the pre-rehearsal preparatory phase of pieces like *Machinations* (2000) or the children's music theatre work *Le Petit Chaperon Rouge* (2001) amounts to no more and no less than material, just as text or video material might exist. In *Le Petit Chaperon Rouge*, for instance, the composed music consisted of twenty-three short pieces: isolated moments that were not composed expressly for the project and that did not imply a particular formal arrangement, dramaturgy or order. Not until rehearsal, which occurred simultaneously with the staging process, were these fragments fully assembled into a large-scale form. One could describe this as a kind of situational composing, because the musical-theatrical composition takes place within the complexity of all the piece's participant elements. The score, which was finally published to enable further performances of the piece,

---

72 | Loc. cit.

73 | 'Les expériences les plus anciennes ne te servent pas. (...) Je veux me lancer dans des aventures nouvelles, plus difficiles parce qu'il n'y a pas une expérience.' (Georges Aperghis in an interview with Matthias Rebstock in: Rebstock/Roesner, *Composed Theatre*, p. 239).

74 | Georges Aperghis in: Catherine Maximoff and Georges Aperghis, *Storm Beneath a Skull*, DVD documentation, Juxta Productions, 2006.

did not emerge until afterwards. Rather than being the starting point of the musical-theatrical development process, it is its ending point. Although this process was obviously directed by Aperghis, he designed this direction to entice his players to creatively insert their own personalities into the development process, both musically and theatrically.[75] Through this special working method, no difference between piece (composition) and staging (collectively developed musical/theatrical totality) surfaces at first. The status of a musical work represented by the score – which in the case of *Rotkäppchen* contains no stage directions – is only attained retrospectively. Many earlier pieces for which this last step did not occur have in fact become lost to the ephemerality of performances.[76]

In his music theatre, Heiner Goebbels likewise relies wholly on creativity and free exchange amongst the participants. Unlike Aperghis, he follows a more or less standardised structure. Approximately one year before a music theatre work premieres, he conducts a workshop in which everyone 'works using all, even if only thinkable, means', and in which every person involved in the project convenes, regardless of whether they ultimately operate on or off-stage. 'In this try-out time, this time of experimentation, there is a relatively autonomous kind of activity amongst all the forces connected to the theatre.' Since the choice was made that this phase accommodate the initiative of all participants, 'actually vastly more than what I can imagine emerges, even though I've come up with the criteria'[77].

Here Goebbels strongly emphasises that all theatrical elements of a piece must be available during these workshops. With costumes, light and video, for instance, this also pertains to elements that in traditional rehearsal processes do not come into play until quite late and hence cannot exceed an 'illustrative' role or become elementary to the grammar of a piece: 'Anything which comes late in the process is only going to be illustrative; it does not have the power to change anything else which has already been established during the rehearsal period'.[78] Then, following the workshops and the phase of open and

---

75 | Cf. here Markus Gammel's documentation of the rehearsal process in *Rotkäppchen ist der Wolf: Kreativität im Musiktheater von Georges Aperghis*, Master's thesis, Humboldt University Berlin.

76 | This applies in particular to earlier works by Aperghis at ATEM. For example, only isolated players' notations of the piece *Enumerations* (1990) still exist; however, the piece was produced as a film, and has at least been thus preserved.

77 | Heiner Goebbels interviewed by Wolfgang Schneider in: idem., 'Ein synergetisches Ausprobieren. Heiner Goebbels über kollektive Kreativität, Inspiration und Inszenierungsprozesse', in: Stephan Porombka, Wolfgang Schneider and Volker Wortmann, (eds.): *Kollektive Kreativität*, Tübingen: Francke, 2006, p. 116.

78 | Heiner Goebbels in: Rebstock/Roesner, *Composed Theatre*, p. 116.

associative experimentation, comes a phase during which Goebbels withdraws and composes the piece from start to finish, determining the total form. In other words, and in contrast to Aperghis, the musical form is decided upon by Goebbels alone and is then practised during the final rehearsals.

It is certainly no accident that both of these most prominent exemplars of collective development processes in music theatre are composers with whom the musical and the theatrical processes are carried out by one and the same person. But also many artistic teams show great interest in the collective development of pieces, in intensive exchange beyond the confines of professional competency categories and in the concomitant subversion of classical hierarchies. Here independent music theatre adopts techniques endemic to independent theatre and dance theatre. The English term 'devised theatre' has taken root to describe such approaches; a German equivalent is lacking. Even still, a 'devised music theatre' poses a complex field of research, because in such a field, classical concepts like 'work', 'performance', 'score', 'composition', 'direction', 'authorship' and classical concepts of professionalism become fluid and undergo redefinition by necessity.

2.2 Other Places and Spaces

Very few independent music theatre ensembles can call a venue their own. This is usually due to practical resources. And yet many ensembles feel that always playing in new locations and creating new spaces is crucial to their artistic engagement.[79] Thomas Desi from ZOON Musiktheater in Vienna makes the following remark:

'My projects for ZOON are made with the intention of using nontheatrical spaces for theatre. Not in order to conceal the poorness of this theatre, nor to underline the rootlessness of these projects, but rather to introduce the element of the authenticity of the here and now.'[80]

Making such everyday nontheatrical places into theatre sites implies a theatre that attempts to destabilize the threshold between art and the everyday, that desires to exit the 'cultural temple' and step 'out towards people'. As such, an

---

79 | In the following, I use 'places' or 'sites' when referring to geographic localities, and 'spaces' to mean spaces for action or specific atmospheres. Cf. here, for instance, Michel de Certeau, *Kunst des Handelns*, Berlin: Merve, 1988 (originally published in 1980), p. 218f, and Henri Lefebvre, 'Die Produktion des Raums', in: Jörg Dünne and Stephan Günzel (eds.), *Raumtheorie*, Frankfurt a.M.: Suhrkamp, 2006, p. 330ff.
80 | Thomas Desi, 'ZOON Musiktheater', in Everhartz/Tornquist, *Fragen an das Musiktheater*, p. 43.

impulse is carried further here, one already emitted by the free theatre of the seventies, one whose effects continue to be felt when performances take place, for example, at old coal mining complexes during the Ruhrtriennale.[81] Aside from that, however, such places quite concretely offer possibilities for different ways of staging, for characteristic actions, performative materials or situations that can be incorporated into stagings and that do not exist in stage spaces. Beyond this, spaces that are most often sought out already transport a certain atmosphere of their own. Besides public places, places normally inaccessible to the larger public are therefore often chosen (mines, bunkers, old factory buildings, casinos, hotels, harbour installations, etc.), places charged with associations, expectations and a certain aura simply by virtue of their identity. And finally, such places are often accompanied by another relation between players and audience, thanks, for instance, to spatial constriction, to unusual spatial placement of the audience or to unusual seating arrangements resulting from site-specific circumstances, and so forth.

Playing music theatre in such atypical places is essential to the core profile of the Nuremberg-based Pocket Opera Company, which celebrated the fortieth anniversary of its existence last year: *Shooting Stars* is a reworking of *Freischütz* and is playing in the Nürnberger Volksfest; Wagner's *Flying Dutchman* was once performed in a city bus and then in a launderette (*Air Bus Adventure*, 2001; and *Wash House Adventure*, 2012) and Verdi's *Macbeth* resounded on the Reichsparteitagsgelände (1995). Typical of such POC stagings is that the sites are not always an obvious pick, sometimes being employed instead as a contrast. In this vein, the love story between Venus and Adonis in the Peruvian baroque opera *La Púrpura de la rosa* was played in a rather prosaic former bus depot.[82] The POC has intensified its inclusion of popular theatre elements as well: as such, the parcours artists *Crap Movements* played the old Montagehalle in the aforementioned staging; fire artists appeared in *One charming night* (2004), a combination of Purcell's *Fairy Queen* and Bussotti's *La Passion selon Sade*; and in *pocs space enterprise* from 2010, itself also a collage, this time of Monteverdi, Purcell, Schumann and Saint-Saens, the breakdance company Bounce! assumed a central role.

---

81 | Here too, independent music theatre basically only re-enacted what had already started in the 70s in independent theatre and visual art under the heading 'site-specific theatre' or 'site-specific art'. Be that as it may, music theatre's engagement with space has also blazed its own trails, to the extent that it thematises, in particular, perspectives of listening and sound.

82 | *La Púrpura de la rosa* by Tomás de Torrejon y Velasco (music) and Pedro Calderón de la Barca, 2014.

Figure 1: 'La púrpura de la rosa', German première, IGMIV-Halle in Nuremberg/ Schweinau, 2014. Photograph: Herbert Liedel

The music of these operas consistently conveys a strongly reworked sound, in new instrumentations and for a chamber ensemble. As much as each separate staging is inspired by its selected site, the music remains untouched by the place; in other words, the music could, in principle, be played in other spaces and is not based on the acoustic possibilities presented by a space.

Another treatment of spaces is shown in the works of Oper Dynamo West, which is not concerned with setting pieces in a certain space, but with developing pieces in respect to text, performance and music on the very basis of a space:

'We inspect and explore places, we hold interviews and collect materials. We interweave the resulting research material with fictive elements and show our pieces on site or bring them into the theatre. We work with the architecture and history of our performance sites. We influence and transform urban structures; we "go behind their backs". The music for our stagings, too, emerges as part of a research process; it arises out of the sounds and noises of a place and its people, or out of previously known compositions that suddenly sound different in an actual, material context.'[83]

Currently Oper Dynamo West is a team of seven theatre makers who work together on varying projects in constantly varying constellations and with differing functions.[84] Oper Dynamo West is therefore not an ensemble, but rather more a production group recognisable by a specific approach to music

---

83 | www.operdynamowest.org.

84 | Oper Dynamo West is run by Janina Benduski (dramaturgy/production/PR), Janina Janke (direction/stage), Soo-eun Lee (stage/costume/performance), Johannes Müller

theatre instead of a specific artistic handwriting.[85] In *Das Wort haben die Benützer* (The users have the floor) from 2012, sound research serves as the central starting point. Janina Jansen took on the role of director in this project and collaborated with the American composer Bill Dietz. Together they surveyed two apartment buildings in Berlin and Marseille, both built by Le Corbusier and nearly identical in design. Jansen and Dietz gathered image and sound material in the buildings, made recordings of the acoustic surroundings and conducted interviews with the inhabitants, asking them about their favourite music. Then Dietz converted these field recordings and interview tapes into a composition that was played during the performances (or more specifically, during the theatrical tours through the building) on inhabitants' private stereo systems and visitors' mobile listening devices.[86] The dramaturgy of this sort of music theatre is no longer carried by the music, the text or a plot, but rather by the places and spaces themselves. It must be 'walked through' by each viewer; it remains fragile, momentary and fragmentary.

Figure 2: 'La Parole est aux usagers', art project by Bill Dietz and Janina Janke, Marseille 2013. Photograph: Benjamin Krieg

(direction), Andrea Oberfeld (production), Julie Rüter (stage/costume) and Frederike Wagner (communications design).
85 | Cf. interview by Mireia Ludwig with Andrea Oberfeld and Johannes Müller on 24.6.2013.
86 | Cf. www.operdynamowest.org. Musiktheater bruit works with a similar approach underpinned by sound research and interviews in their project *Klangexpedition Ural*, Ballhaus Ost, Berlin, 2013, as do Gordon Kampe, Ivan Bazak and Katharina Ortmann in their project *Plätze Dächer Leute Wege. Musiktheater für ein utopisches Bielefeld*, funded by Fonds Experimentelles Musiktheater, by spending two years initiating and composing Bielefeld inhabitants' utopias for change in their city (premiered 29.4.2015, Theater Bielefeld).

2.3 Other Forms and Formats

What stands out here is an intensive search for other performance formats in independent music theatre. One notable tendency is a turn towards installation-based forms. Here the music frequently takes on the task of unfurling spaces of sound (that is, spaces of listening) rather than limning them as temporal or dramatic arcs of tension. In comparison to the traditional understanding of an ephemeral time-based art, music is understood here more in terms of its materiality, its bodily dimension and its immediate relation to space – space being the very thing that enables it to resound in the first place. Experiences with repetitive music and minimal music as well as sound art and sound installation manifest within such forms.[87]

In the same spirit, Berthold Schneider invested in the consistency of music's spatial character in his version of *Einstein on the Beach* by Phillip Glass and Robert Wilson. He dissolved opera's basic classical and frontal situation and transformed it into a walk-through installation.[88] For the piece's site, Schneider chose the Parochialkirche in Berlin for its characteristic rounded base construction that thwarts any implication of a spatial separation between performers and audience. There were various objects and visual stations spread across the space; even the musicians were dispersed, or rather, they moved throughout. The viewers could likewise move freely within this opera installation, able to determine their distance from the musicians autonomously and freely choose the length of their stay at individual stations. However, the decisive impression was that it was the sound of the music itself, its material quality that generated the installation's space.

In a completely different tenor, the composer and installation artist Georg Nussbaumer has worked for many years on music theatre installations by continually tackling components and stock motifs from the inexhaustible Wagner cosmos. In *Ringlandschaft mit Bierstrom*[89] he shatters the score of the

---

87 | This change in perspective is currently strengthened in particular by Sound Studies, and by Cultural Studies' engagement with audio cultures. Cf., for instance, Holger Schulze (ed.), *Sound Studies: Traditionen – Methoden – Desiderate*, Bielefeld: transcript, 2008; Jonathan Sterne (ed.), *The Sound Studies Reader*, London: Routledge, 2012 or Christoph Cox and Daniel Warner (eds.), *Audio Culture: Readings in Modern Music*, New York: Continuum, 2004.

88 | Premiered in 2005. Furthermore, Berthold Schneider directed the *staatsbank berlin* together with Susanne Vinzenz from 1999 to 2003. This was the only production house for music theatre in Berlin that consistently committed itself to new and experimental forms of music theatre.

89 | Together with the Solistenensemble Kaleidoskop, Donaueschinger Musiktage and sophiensaele Berlin, 2013. Other examples: *Milchstrom, Fragebett, Gralsmaschinen –*

Ring entirely and turns it into a grab bag of material for a sixteen-hour installation where allusions and associations from the Wagner cosmos repeatedly surface acoustically as well as visually and then drift away as an immense acoustic entity. The musicians in the Solistenensemble Kaleidoskop act in spatial – but not musical – separation within diverse installations that quarry the very basis of the Wagner legend by means of Nussbaumer's drastic signature fantasy. In a certain way, these music theatre installations by Nussbaumer are inner spaces of association or resonance, turned inside out to become physical spaces through which an audience can wander, spaces where Nussbaumer's Wagner obsession can reverberate.

Such spatio-installative forms, like those displayed nowadays in the opera installations of Schneider, Nussbaumer and many others, are the consequence of a specific disposition regarding content and music. They are not, say, 'directorial gags' or mere staging strategies; they ensue from a transmuted understanding of music (Schneider), or they let arise music and scenery – space of hearing and space of seeing – in unmediated interrelation with one another (Nussbaumer).

Figure 3: 'Ringlandschaft mit Bierstrom – ein Wagner-Areal', (world première) St. Johannes-Evangelist-Kirche, Berlin 2013. Photograph: Karin Haas

The forms and formats presently evolving throughout the diverse sectors of independent music theatre throw similar essential features into relief, features that are characteristic of the development of theatre in general and that can only be roughly sketched with bywords such as the performativity and

Ein Lohengrin-Gelände, Kunstfest Weimar, 2013; *Die Jaffa Orangen des Richard W. – ein israelisches Rheingold*, Radialsystem V Berlin and Operadagen Rotterdam, 2012.

'eventness' (*Ereignishaftigkeit*) of theatre, the emphasised role of bodily and material enactments and processes, or, as already described, the act of working with atmospheres and spaces. Within this broad scenario of contemporary theatre aesthetics music theatre must define its position in each case based on the relation between music and action, or put differently, between hearing and seeing. In its fundamentally nonlinguistic, performative and emotional character, music is a predestined element of today's theatre – text-based dramatic theatre not excluded. But the fundamental interrogation and composition of the relation between hearing and seeing is within the purview of music theatre in particular. Against this backdrop, those directions in independent music theatre that orient themselves not first and foremost narratively, but rather phenomenologically, that is when they directly investigate specific perceptive circumstances and situations.[90]

With *winzig. Musiktheaterminitaturen – Musiktheater für ein Haus* (1993/98),[91] Manos Tsangaris has invented such a format, which he has since steadily cultivated in a series of pieces with consistently new elements.[92] *winzig* consists of a series of music theatre miniatures, each of a few minutes length, each based on a highly specified constellation regarding how viewers and musicians relate to one another and to the space. According to the principle of the show booth, a limited number of viewers are able to see a miniature, whereupon another group is granted entry and the piece is repeated. Besides this, there are pieces that are constructed as installations and played for the entire duration of the

---

90 | Cf. Matthias Rebstock, 'Im Fluchtpunkt der Sinne. Musiktheater als Arbeit an einer Phänomenologie des Hörens', in: Christa Brüstle, Clemens Risi and Stephanie Schwarz (eds.), *Macht Ohnmacht Zufall*, Berlin: Theater der Zeit, 2012.

91 | Premiere: Alte Feuerwache, Cologne, 1993.

92 | Further stages of the concept of *winzig* are *Die Döner-Schaltung. Stationentheater für großes Ensemble*, Bühnen der Stadt, 2004; *Drei Räume Theater Suite. Stationentheater für großes Ensemble*, Donaueschinger Musiktage, 2004; *Diskrete Stücke. Stationentheater. Hörszenen für einzelne Betrachter*, WDR, Musik der Zeit, 2007; or *Batsheba. Eat The History! Installation opera für Schauspieler, Sänger, Chor und Orchestermäander*, Donaueschinger Musiktage and Magazin der Staatsoper unter den Linden, 2008/2009. The cultivation of the concept consists, amongst other things, in Tsangaris' crossing his 'phenomenological', abstract concept of *winzig* with content-driven and narrative aspects, thereby deriving a new narrative form from this hybridisation. For more on this, see also Matthias Rebstock, 'Vom Erzählen im Neuen Musiktheater', *positionen* 55 (May 2003). For Manos Tsangaris' Stationentheater, see also Jörn Peter Hiekel, 'Erhellende Passagen', *Musik und Ästhetik*, vol. 52 (October 2009): pp. 48–60; and Julia Cloot, 'Gesamtkunstwerk und multimediales Musiktheater', in: Udo Bermbach, Dieter Borchmeyer and Hermann Danuser (eds.), *Wagner und die Neue Musik*, Vol. 2 of wagnerspectrum (2010), Würzburg: Königshausen & Neumann, 2010, p. 130ff.

performance without interruption. Here the audience decides on the length of their stay. Peculiar to all these pieces of limited length is their commencement out of complete darkness and their precisely and thoroughly composed lighting dramaturgies, which, just like the actions or instrumental and vocal parts, are set forth in the score.

For instance, the piece *winzig* from the *winzig* cycle is written for a classical concert situation. Six musicians sit on the stage, and seven people form the audience. Amongst these seven, three other musicians are intermingled as members of an 'artificial audience'[93] who, at the beginning of the performance, crumple candy wrappers, make comments and engage in other typical concert rituals. During the piece, they 'play' their seatmates directly on the ears, thus superimposing an intimate, close-range hearing space over the public space of the on-stage 'concert'.

In *Sessellift*, the situation's intimacy is engendered in a different way: here, two viewers sit across from a 'lift operator'. The piece lasts for the duration of a lift ride to the top and then back to the bottom floor. During the ride, the lift operator executes small instrumental actions of a seemingly ritual nature. One can see a shrine of sorts, or a mini-stage, upon which 'a figure-like sheaf, a little pocket torch, a little bone'[94] are visible in the half-light. At the turning point of the lift ride, the doors open and one looks through a window onto passers-by making their way to another piece with no suspicion of being watched. In the window hang two taxidermy animals: 'a bird and a fish'.[95]

winzig employs such means to question the relation between audience and 'stage'; it rings the changes through highly diverse constellations of seeing and hearing and transfers the viewers into each constellation's respective concrete perceptional situation, to which they must actively respond in one way or the other. The safeguarded, and in this sense impartial, passive observer position associated with the concert, or with the opera house, is unswervingly subverted.

2.4 Interactivity and Intermediality

Since its inception, the music theatre of the sixties was closely linked to technological developments of the time. This calls to mind *Variations V* (1965) by John Cage, where different photo cell systems translate dance movements into sound, or his experiments with record players or radio sets (*imaginary landscape No. 5* and *radio music*),[96] Alvin Lucier's experiments with amplified brain waves (*Mu-*

---

93 | Manos Tsangaris, *winzig* (score), Cologne: Thürmchen, 2006, trans. W.W.
94 | Ibid.
95 | Ibid.
96 | Cf. Hans Rudolf Zeller, 'Medienkomposition nach John Cage', in: Heinz-Klaus Metzger and Rainer Riehn (eds.), *John Cage I* (Musikkonzepte: special volume), Munich: List, 1990.

sic for Solo Performer, 1965) or the live electronic music theatre works of Gordon Mumma or Robert Ashley in the ONCE group.[97] At the same time, music theatre always gained essential stimuli through developments in the field of electronic music and computer music. In contrast to theatre, highly funded institutions already existed in this realm, where artists and technicians or programmers inspired one another to innovate.[98] These studios for electronic music or computer music were at first located mainly within radio broadcasting institutions,[99] but today they exist mostly as independent institutions[100] or facilities in universities[101] where software and interfaces, some of which are relevant to the music theatre field, are developed. Yet here we are moving within a border area adjacent to a broader field spanning from what is usually designated as music theatre, fields like 'media art', 'intermedia' or 'multimedia' (with their aggregate thematics of 'human/machine' and 'extended bodies'[102]), and dance theatre.

This link is revealed, for instance, in the work of Theater der Klänge in Düsseldorf, founded in 1987 by the composer Jorg U. Lensing, who still directs the group. At quite an early date, Lensing was already engaging with possibilities of how movement, music and video could be interlinked via computer. The 2010 *Suite Intermedial* is one of these works. It is a sort of résumé of all these experiences, allowing the theatre space itself to become a complex instrument. The performers – Lensing works predominantly with dancers – move in order to intentionally trigger specific sounds to which they can respond through movement. Such a feedback loop affects movement as well as video. The piece's individual parts were developed by means of spatial improvisations and ongoing refinement of the programmed Max/msp patches. There is no score. The performance's precision is achieved by the exactitude of the dancers' movement sequences. Since none of the space's complex wiring is visible to the audience, the piece's impression is more of a dance performance.

---

97 | Cf. Ralf Dietrich, 'Unzensierte Simultaneität der Stimmen. Robert Ashleys Frühwerk', *MusikTexte* 88 (Februar 2001): pp. 63–80.

98 | Cf. Steffen Scholl, *Musik-Raum-Technik. Zur Entwicklung und Anwendung der graphischen Programmierumgebung "Max"*, Bielefeld: transcript, 2014.

99 | E.g., the WDR Cologne studio or the studio of RAI in Milan; other early studios that were not linked to broadcasting stations were e.g. the Siemens-Studio for Electronic Music in Munich or the Institute for Sonology, Utrecht.

100 | E.g., IRCAM in Paris, STEIM in Amsterdam oder ZKM in Karlsruhe.

101 | E.g., the Institute for Sonology in Utrecht that moved to the University of Den Haag in 1986, or the Studio for Electronic music at the Technische Universität Berlin.

102 | E.g., www.medienkunstnetz.de/themen/cyborg_bodies. And Steve Dixon, *Digital Performance: A History of New Media in Theater, Dance, Performance and Installation*, Cambridge, Mass.: MIT Press, 2007.

As far as the method and way of thinking is concerned, however, it all boils down to a form of composition, or composed theatre.[103]

Besides this type of interactive media deployment, a number of works currently investigate media boundaries through the realisation of specific 'cross-transferrential' projects in diverse media. The work of the liquid penguin ensemble,[104] for example, is noteworthy in that its pieces can enter into distinct aggregate states. In so doing, they move between New Music, music theatre, installation and radio play. *Gras wachsen hören*, for instance, began as an installation with sounds governed by plants. Three versions followed, each of which took shape through an invited guest: concertante with the percussionist Dirk Rothbrust, a dance performance through a collaboration with the dancer Annick Pütz and a theatre performance with the actor Bernd Neunzling. The texts of this last version served as the germ cell for the radio play *Gras wachsen hören*. *Bout du Monde* also exists both as music-theatrical performance and as radio play.

Whereas the above pieces deal with the successive translation of a theme into varying medial formats, the Dutch composer and director Michel van der Aa works with the friction generated between film and live performance. In *Up-Close*, a thirty-minute 'film opera',[105] the cellist Sol Gabetta steps into an imaginary dialogue with her alter ego: an old woman (played by Vakil Eelman). On the stage is a string orchestra. The soloist sits where the conductor normally stands. A video projection screen is placed to the side, and in front of it is a section of empty stage. The film alternates between two settings: we see the old woman in a forest, and later in an abandoned house. She writes enigmatic codes on small slips of paper, which she then sticks into preserve jars in the house. But then we suddenly see her in the same space in which the concert is taking place. The orchestra's chairs are visible and their stand lamps are on, but the space is vacant. The old woman on this abandoned stage in the film seems to be watching the young soloist play on the real stage. The two temporal levels of the film and the stage reality come into contact. Later, parallel actions emerge: both women carry a large floor lamp through the space simultaneously, but they do not encounter one another. The temporal levels remain in a state of surreal simultaneity. Nonetheless, there is an apparently causal link between the two 'worlds': mid-piece, we see in the film how the old woman switches on a machine which can apparently decipher the codes on the slips of paper. When the machine is turned on, the string orchestra, after a long pause, strikes up again as if the film reality were causally connected to the stage reality and could

---

103 | For a comprehensive account of this working mode, see Rebstock/Roesner, *Composed Theatre*, pp. 155-168.
104 | The liquid penguin ensemble was founded in 1997 in Saarbrücken by the director Katharina Bihler and the composer Stefan Scheib.
105 | Tim Rutherford-Johnson, DVD booklet.

'power on' the orchestra. In his works, Michel van der Aa sophisticatedly plays with topoi of film music. Whereas the film at first seems to accompany the cello concert, it later becomes its 'actual' reality and, accordingly, its 'meta-physical' condition. The media engage in dialogue with one another in new ways; their realities infiltrate and reflect one another.

Figure 4: Vakil Eelman in 'Up Close'.
Photograph: Michel van der Aa

2.5 Embodied and Disembodied Voices

It is plain to see that the examination of the voice is a central concern and constant challenge for independent music theatre. Here I will discuss three traditions which appear to me particularly interesting today.[106]

---

106 | In recent years, a contribution has likewise been made by Theatre Studies' and Media Studies' deepening interest in the issue of the voice, whereby the voice in music theatre has also been repeatedly thematised. Cf. Doris Kolesch et. al. (eds.), *Stimm-Welten*, Bielefeld: transcript, 2009; Brigitte Felderer (ed.), *Phonorama. Eine Kulturgeschichte der Stimme als Medium*, Berlin: Matthes & Seitz, 2005; Friedrich Kittler, Thomas Macho

For the new music theatre as well as experimental music theatre of the 50s and 60s, a material-oriented approach initially served as a defining factor, an approach which, in its engagement with the phonetic research of the time, understood and composed vocal utterances as abstract sound material. In the process, the field of the expressive was also examined in its extremes, though generally without any relation to situations or scenarios which would have motivated such emotions. At issue were, for example, the scream, crying or laughter.[107] At the same time, this field almost completely dispensed with traditional opera singing.[108]

In the 70s, a new mode of singing beyond opera appeared on the scene with the emergence of a new generation of vocal performers. Artists such as Meredith Monk, Joan La Barbara and Laurie Anderson and composers such as Robert Ashley turned to archaic or ritual functions of the voice and song (e.g., storytelling in oral cultures or non-Western singing techniques from cultic contexts). The probing of pop and jazz singing also played a significant role in this newly manifested vocal performance, for example in the music of Pamela Z.

In both cases, the broadening of vocal possibilities went hand in hand with the exploration of the newest technological possibilities, which were opened up by the microphone, and since the 80s by real-time sound processing. While the primacy of traditional opera singing went unbroken in opera houses, independent music theatre intensively delved into these new possibilities. Here particular attention is focussed on the relation between body and voice, that is, on phenomena of the disembodied voice and the tendency inscribed in techniques of audio reproduction to re-embody the voice.[109] Through the vital

---

and Sigrid Weigel (eds.), *Zwischen Rauschen und Offenbarung. Zur Kultur- und Mediengeschichte der Stimme*, Munich: Akademie, 2002; Matthias Rebstock, 'Drama der Stimmen. Zum Verhältnis von Körper und Stimme in David Martons Wozzeck', in: Stephanie Schroedter (ed.), *Bewegungen zwischen Hören und Sehen. Denkbewegungen über Bewegungskünste*, Würzburg: Königshausen & Neumann, 2012, p. 325ff.

107 | Reference pieces include *Aventures* und *Nouvelles Aventures* (1962-1965) by György Ligeti, *Anagrama* (1957/1958) by Mauricio Kagel and *Aria* (1958) by John Cage. Cf. Werner Klüppelholz, *Sprache als Musik. Studien zur Vokalkomposition bei Karlheinz Stockhausen, Hans G. Helms, Mauricio Kagel, Dieter Schnebel und György Ligeti*, Friedberg: Pfau, 1976.

108 | Exploring extremes in vocalism and song did, however, play a role in the field of new opera. For example, Eric Salzman and Thomas Desi refer in this respect to the expanded voice techniques of the English singer Roy Hart and their influence on composers like Peter Maxwell Davies, Hans Werner Henze or Harrison Birtwhistle. Cf. Salzman/Desi, *The New Music Theater*, p. 275.

109 | Cf. Thomas Macho, 'Stimmen ohne Körper. Anmerkungen zur Technikgeschichte der Stimme', in: Doris Kolesch and Sybille Krämer (eds.), *Stimme*, Frankfurt a.M.: Suhrkamp, 2006.

role of corporeality and gesture, such performances must inevitably be inclined towards theatre.

The composer and vocal performer Alex Novitz has, for instance, developed a system together with the studio STEIM in Amsterdam that enables him to process his own vocal sounds by using two Wii controllers. Harnessing certain movements, he can sample sounds, loop them through other movements, modulate their pitch, filter them and so forth. He can thus give rise to complex structures on the basis of his own sounds and through a specific repertoire of movements and gestures. In the eyes of the recipient, this exact bond between sound and gesture, between hearing and seeing, remains cryptic in a productive way. For example, in one moment correlations materialise between isolated sounds and sudden jerky movements; in another moment these layers diverge, each developing its own self-determined progression. Here the bodily movements often seem like a peculiar visual music, similar to how the movements of a conductor without an orchestra evoke certain musical events in one's imagination.[110] This visible 'body music' and the music actually emitted by the loudspeakers assume a frictional relation to one another. And finally, the directly generated vocal acts form another, third layer in combination with their own unique corporeality.

Miguel Azguime, composer and director of the miso Ensemble in Lisbon, also uses technical possibilities to project the voice into a theatrical space. In his music theatre piece titled *Salt Itinerary: Für Stimme, live-electronic und multimedia* (2003/06), his point of departure is the hybrid nature of the word: the word is just as much a phonetic form as it is a written character, and thus connects the acoustic with the visual. Azguime himself acts as performer on stage, which is furnished with only a table and chair as well as a large projection surface. He delivers exhaustively musicalised phonetic poems of his own penning, which in turn control the video images on the projection surface, producing in one scene, for instance, an animated landscape of letters that Azguime, as performer, appears to be attacking and that ultimately blanket him completely and 'erase' him. His physical presence vanishes into the thicket of letters he himself initiated, and into a sound cloud that has, thanks to electronics, long since detached itself from the body which had 'conjured' it. Here too, technical feedback blurs the boundaries between cause and effect, action and reaction, physical space and technologically generated spaces.

In addition to both spaces named above, the rediscovery of choric elements is vital to musicalised, postdramatic theatre. The chorus appears on the scene as an acoustic and visual unit of bodies from which single bodies and voices can step forth, and yet it also suspends voice as expression of individuality, consolidates it into a 'new chorus-voice uncannily bestowed with a life of its

---

110 | Cf. Dieter Schnebel, 'Nostalgie, Solo für einen Dirigenten' (visible music II), 1962.

own that is neither individual nor even abstractly collective'.[111] Besides the thematic nexus comprised of voice, individuality and (collective) body touched upon here, another point of heightened interest for our context lies in the musicalisation of language, which is part and parcel of choric speaking. As mentioned previously, one can hardly overestimate the influence of Christoph Marthaler's choric theatre on independent music theatre in German-speaking countries. His techniques for musicalising language, his method of building a piece's dramaturgy on musico-compositional, collage-like principles,[112] and the central role played by choral a cappella song all provided a range of ensembles with points from which to embark on their own distinct explorations.[113]

2.6 Musician as Performer

In the chapter on working processes, I indicated the shifting of classical role and competency distribution through changes in these processes and through independent-theatre-oriented rehearsal techniques. We see actors who sing, dancers who speak and sing, and musicians who execute more than just musical performance. While opera – and this pertains to a wide array of independent opera productions – typically separates the singer-performers on stage from the instrumental ensembles in the orchestra pit (or rather, in a place outside the stage), independent music theatre often seeks to dissolve this partition. Falk Hübner has developed a systematisation in various forms for how musicians can fulfil other performative functions.[114] On one end of this spectrum stands the theatricalisation of the instrumental music making itself; initially the musicians do nothing more than play their instruments. The effects of a theatricalisation, which takes shape in the eye of the viewer, are created, for instance, by the use of different kinds of instruments, through uncommon playing techniques,[115] through staged parallel actions, and other devices. Furthermore, the range of possibilities includes forms in which musicians carry out additional actions, simple forms for the embodiment of a theatrical role, and finally ends with forms in which performers appear as both actors and singers: Jörg Kienberger or Clemens Sienknecht from the 'Marthaler family', Marie Goyette and Jan Czajkowski from the 'David Marton

---

111 | Lehmann, *Postdramatisches Theater*, p. 235, trans. W.W.
112 | For musical dramaturgy, cf. Roesner, *Musicality in Theatre*, p. 212f.
113 | E.g., Musiktheater bruit, schindelkilliusdutschke or the ensemble leitundlause.
114 | F. Hübner, *Shifting Identities*. Hübner's discussion relies here on Michael Kirby's categories between 'not-acting' and 'complex acting'. Cf. Michael Kirby, *A Formalist Theatre*, Philadelphia: University of Pennsylvania Press, 1987.
115 | Cf. Dieter Schnebel, 'Sichtbare Musik', in: idem., *Anschläge – Ausschläge. Texte zur Neuen Musik*, Munich: Hanser, 1993 (1966), pp. 262-300.

family', Sir Henry at Volksbühne Berlin, Françoise Rivalland or Jean-Pierre Drouet in the milieu around Georges Aperghis, or Martin Hägler in the pieces of Ruedi Häusermann. No boundaries are drawn around intermediate forms. Admittedly, Mauricio Kagel had already systematically explored and played through these possibilities in his 1960s instrumental theatre work.[116] But the novelty today rests in the openness with which musicians and ensembles respond to such performative tasks.

It is also remarkable that a field between music theatre and dance theatre has presented itself thanks to choreographers' having displayed an increasing interest in music making as a procedure of bodily movement.[117] One of the most well-known examples is the project *Movements für Lachenmann* (and later *More Movements für Lachenmann*), which the French choreographer Xavier Le Roy carried out with different musicians of the groups Kammerensemble Neue Musik Berlin and Klangforum Wien, among others.[118] Für Lachenmann's *Salut für Caudwell*, Le Roy asks two guitarists to perform the movements of the score precisely – but without instruments. The music is then played by two other guitarists behind a black wall, synchronised with the players' lacking instruments.[119] The movements, which are normally only functional and serve to create sound, become the main attraction and a choreography, and allow the musicians' consummate economy and precision of movement sequences internalised over decades to come to the fore and enter into dialogue with Lachenmann's music. Simultaneously, one hears Lachenmann's music in an entirely new way, for one can no longer optically tie the sounds to their acoustic creation, as is normally the case in concerts.

2.7 Conceptualisation, Interrogation of Reality, Research

Today, independent dramatic theatre and dance theatre are highly self-referential, and through their work on formats, perceptive patterns and media boundaries, they continually question the conditions under which their own work unfolds. Furthermore, an exceptional interest in working with nonprofessional performers and a tendency towards the documentary and the political have

---

116 | Cf. Matthias Rebstock, *Komposition zwischen Musik und Theater. Das instrumentale Theater von Mauricio Kagel zwischen 1959 und 1965*, Hofheim: Wolke, 2007.

117 | Cf. here also Petra Sabisch's study in this volume. In chapter 2.5, she refers to the concert as a thematic focus of the sommer.bar, which took place from 2006–2011 in conjunction with Tanz im August.

118 | In a production of the taschenoper wien, 2005, and of Le Kwatt, Montpellier, 2008, respectively.

119 | With Gunter Schneider, Barbara Romen, Tom Pauwels and Günther Lebbing.

been noticeable for a decade now.[120] These developments have long since gained ground in municipal and state theatre houses as well, not least because the most influential agents in independent theatre are meanwhile also active there. Many of these agents understand this work as research. In light of debates surrounding artistic research held vehemently in academia since the Bologna reforms, on the one hand, and sociological and science-theoretical discourses on new forms of knowledge, on the other, one can no longer assert that a solely metaphorical parlance is at issue here.[121]

Because opera houses eschew everything except the established repertoire and advocate a doctrine of faithfulness to the original work, new approaches can hardly find room to manoeuvre there, at least not on the main stages.[122] In contrast, independent music theatre offers a whole range of these approaches. The central question here is how the specific thrust of music theatre, namely to work using musical means, can be made productive both conceptually and as a research instrument. In this arena one often encounters methods that refer back to musique concrète or to Murray Schafer's soundscape research. A research phase foresees the gathering of concrete sound material, which then serves as the starting point for the compositional work.[123]

The composer Hannes Seidl and the video artist Daniel Kötter have made a name for themselves in recent years with their conceptually structured music theatre productions. In a series of collective works, they engage with everyday life as experienced by specific groups of people and then bring this to the stage.[124] They accompany their subjects' day-to-day lives with a camera and extract the basic material for Seidl's compositions from the video's soundtrack.

---

120 | In German-speaking Europe, these contiguities are exemplified by the work of Rimini Protokoll, Gob Squad, She She Pop, God's Entertainment, Hans-Werner Kroesinger or the theatre projects of the International Institute for Political Murder. Cf. also Jan Deck and Angelika Sieburg (ed.), *Politisch Theater machen. Neue Artikulationsformen des Politischen in den darstellenden Künsten*, Bielefeld: transcript, 2011.

121 | For the discussion on the confluence of the sciences and the arts, see, for instance, Dieter Mersch and Michaela Ott (eds.), *Kunst und Wissenschaft*, Munich: Wilhelm Fink, 2007; Elke Bippus (ed.): *Kunst des Forschens. Praxis eines ästhetischen Denkens*, Zurich: diaphanes, 2009; Martin Tröndle and Julia Warmers (eds.), *Kunstforschung als ästhetische Wissenschaft. Beiträge zur transdisziplinären Hybridisierung von Wissenschaft und Kunst*, Bielefeld: transcript, 2012.

122 | Many houses lack smaller venues where such approaches could be put to the test. Cf. M. Rebstock, 'Musiktheater. Spielräume schaffen!'.

123 | Another example can be found in the work of Oper Dynamo West, see 2.2.

124 | E.g., in *Falsche Freizeit. Elektronische Arbeitsplätze für den Ruhestand*, sophiensaele, 2010, or in *Falsche Arbeit. 4 konzertante Selbstdarstellungen*, Sommer in Stuttgart festival, 2008.

In Freizeitspektakel[125], however, Neue Vocalsolisten Stuttgart appear instead of lay performers. Kötter and Seidl accompanied them over the course of one day, from eight o'clock in the morning until eight o'clock in the evening, until the beginning of a concert performance. We see the five singers busy with everyday actions; we see them singing baroque arias – in articulately staged situations; we see how they prepare for a concert, until we arrive at the last film sequence, the moment immediately before the singers take to the stage at eight p.m. Finally, the evening of music theatre is composed of a concert with the five vocal soloists performing Hannes Seidl's music. Directly next to each singer stands his or her corresponding film portrait appearing life-size on an oblong projection surface. That which is visually discrete and runs in parallel becomes linked to the music in that Hannes Seidl takes the films' soundtracks as the point of departure for his vocal compositions, frequently doubling the soundtrack through vocal sounds. We therefore discern a blurring of the borders between the singers' private and public realities, which are visually depicted as largely disconnected.

Whereas Kötter's and Seidl's works are underlain by a documentary, reality-probing stance, the Berlin ensemble a rose is, directed by the composer and director Julian Klein, has explicitly resorted to the sphere of artistic research. In 2009, together with Radialsystem V and former members of the Junge Akademie at the Berlin-Brandenburgische Akademie der Wissenschaften, a rose is founded the Institut für künstlerische Forschung (*Institute for Artistic Research*). Since then, a number of projects have arisen which were conducted mostly in cooperation with university institutes. The goal is the intermingling of scientific and artistic strategies and the establishment of a mode of research no longer reserved for the sciences alone. In the 2010 project *Do birds tango?* a rose is cooperated with the behavioural biologist Constance Scharff, director of an interdisciplinary research group at the Freie Universität Berlin dedicated to the topic of birdsong. They collectively developed a music theatre project on the rhythm and emotionality of the zebra finch's song. To this end, several musicians lived for an extended period of time with young zebra finches, raising them and playing musical patterns for them three times daily. From the scientific perspective, these measures were aimed at an experimentation with the birds' behaviours of learning and communication. From the artistic perspective, one could experience a music theatre evening about bird voices, birdsong and the domestic coexistence of humans and animals.

---

125 | *Freizeitspektakel. Für die Neuen Vocalsolisten Stuttgart*, Venice Biennale, 2010.

Figure 5: 'Freizeitspektakel', Stuttgart 2010. Photograph: Roberto Bulgrin

2.8 Opera as Material

The perception of text works as material, the deconstruction thereof, their hybridisation with other texts or materials, their reconfiguration in new ways – such are some of the many techniques of director's theatre which have long since been implemented in the realm of text-based dramatic theatre. In opera houses, however, even the tiniest intervention in the musical score stirs up fierce controversies and debates surrounding loyalty to the original, debates that are replete, should one be witnessing them from the vantage point of more progressive artforms, with a vastly incomprehensible emotionality, as if to uphold the imperative of hindering a final breach of taboo. There is hardly a more urgent question in the field of opera than that of how we can treat the special cultural legacy these repertoire operas represent, and how we can manage to live up to the demand they address to us, namely that we meet them head on.[126]

The possibility of unrestricted interpretation in the staging and musical rendering of repertoire operas constituted one of independent music theatre's

---

126 | And the question becomes that much more pressing when we consider that the innovative impulses emitted since the mid-seventies by director's theatre in the opera of directors such as Hans Neuenfels or Ruth Berghaus are popularly viewed as obsolete or spent. These positions formed the basis for the research project *Zukunft der Oper* (The Future of Opera) conducted by Barbara Beyer at the Kunstuniversität Graz, to name one example. Within this framework, three trailblazing versions of Mozart's *Così fan tutte* were realised. For more on this, see Barbara Beyer, Susanne Kogler and Roman Lemberg (eds.), *Die Zukunft der Oper*, Berlin: Theater der Zeit, 2014.

foundational motivations from the start (see 1.3). Even so, this scarcely ventured farther than more or less expansive arrangements. However, when we say that an opera score becomes material – even if the borders cannot be clearly distinguished – we mean to describe an attempt that approaches opera material and composition as a starting point, a referential foil, a field of material; that understands itself, however, as a new composition or a new piece. What is performed is not the operas – however rigorously they are re/arranged – but rather unique creations that engage with and examine operas, similar to the engagements we know from forms of postdramatic theatre or from Frank Castorf's deconstruction of theatre texts. David Marton, who, tellingly, became especially known in the field of postdramatic theatre but does not stage works in opera houses, describes this approach in a nutshell: 'I make theatre, musical theatre, and for this I often use opera material.'[127]

Veenfabriek in Leiden, for example, works with an analogous approach. In their 2010 production *Orfeo naar Monteverdi*, they use madrigals from Monteverdi's *Orfeo*, superimposing them with electronic sounds, minimal music, pop songs and experimental, freely improvised elements. We are not met with a telling of the story of Orpheus and Eurydice, but rather with that story's climate of longing, despair and desire. At the centre stands the actor and singer Jeroen Willems, accompanied by an instrumental ensemble. His position in this concert setting is that of the singer, the star and hence that of Orpheus, but he does not embody him; or he at least remains himself at all times, exhibiting his own idiosyncratic brand of hypnotic stage presence.

Figure 6: 'Orfeo naar Monteverdi', Leiden at Scheltemagebouw, 2009. Photograph: Jochem Jurgens

127 | David Marton in *Theater der Zeit* (March 2012): p. 13.

3. Conclusion

My remarks have striven to open up questions and a range of topics that in my view can be viable tools for an in-depth engagement with independent music theatre in Europe. Such research would have to do justice – more vigorously than I have been able to do here – to all relevant individual theatre-historical and culture-political backgrounds. It would have to concern itself with each background's respective 'culture of independent music theatre', with the existence and consistency of its societal roots, with funding systems and production structures, with the demand brought about by an audience and the structures by which reception and then recirculation into a public discourse are organised. The artistic practices and processes take place within this atmosphere; they arise in reaction to surrounding conditions, which they simultaneously have a hand in forming. Since independent music theatre enjoys a broad-based cultural anchoring in only a few European countries, its future likely lies in international networking and the synthesis of an international perspective.[128] A more detailed, internationally compiled research project on independent music theatre in Europe could make a vital contribution towards such endeavours.

---

128 | The Neuköllner Oper Berlin has already drawn its own conclusions in this regard. With the festivals open op! Europäisches Festival für anderes Musiktheater, 2010, and Move op! Festival für Musiktheater unter prekären Bedingungen, 2013, Neuköllner Oper has set the tone in this regard and has since been continually initiating international coproductions.

Literature and Sources

Betzwieser, T. "Von Sprengungen und radialen Systemen: das aktuelle Musiktheater zwischen Institution und Innovation – eine Momentaufnahme." In: A. Mungen (ed.), *Mitten im Leben: Musiktheater von der Oper zur Everyday Performance*. Würzburg: Königshausen & Neumann, 2011.

Beyer, B., Kogler, S. and Lemberg, R. (eds), *Die Zukunft der Oper*. Berlin: Theater der Zeit, 2014.

Bippus, E. (ed.), *Kunst des Forschens: Praxis eines ästhetischen Denkens*. Zürich: Diaphenes, 2009.

Certeau, M. De. *Kunst des Handelns*. Berlin: Merve, 1988 [first edition 1980].

Cloot, J. "Gesamtkunstwerk und multimediales Musiktheater." In: U. Bermbach, D. Borchmeyer and H. Danuser (eds), *Wagner und die Neue Musik* (= *Wagnerspectrum* vol. 2). Würzburg: Königshausen & Neumann, 2010, pp. 130ff.

Cox, C. and Warner, D. (eds). *Audio Culture: Readings in Modern Music*. New York: Continuum, 2004.

Deck, J. and Sieburg, A. (eds). *Politisch Theater machen: Neue Artikulationsformen des Politischen in den darstellenden Künsten*. Bielefeld: transcript, 2011.

Dietrich, R. "Unzensierte Simultaneität der Stimmen: Robert Ashleys Frühwerk." In: *MusikTexte* 88 (2001), pp. 63–80.

Dixon, S. *Digital Performance: A History of New Media in Theater, Dance, Performance and Installation*. Cambridge, Mass.: MIT Press, 2007.

Durney, D. "Théâtre et Musique. France – Annees 80." *Les Cahiers du CREM*, no. 4–5, (1987).

Eilers, D. L. and Raddatz, F. "Angriffe aus der Gegenwelt: Die Regisseure David Marton und Sebastian Baumgarten über Musik, Theater und die Zukunft der Oper." In: *Theater der Zeit* (3/2012), pp. 13–18.

Everhartz, J. and Tornquist, K. (eds). *Fragen an das Musiktheater*. Vienna: Edition Atelier, 2012.

Fearn, R. *Italian Opera since 1945*. Amsterdam: OPA, 1997.

Felderer, B. (ed.). *Phonorama: Eine Kulturgeschichte der Stimme als Medium*. Berlin: Matthes & Seitz, 2005.

Gammel, M. *Rotkäppchen ist der Wolf: Kreativität im Musiktheater von Georges Aperghis*. Masters thesis, Humboldt University, Berlin.

Hiekel, J.P. "Erhellende Passagen." In: *Musik und Ästhetik* 52 (2009), pp. 48–60.

Hiekel, J.P. (ed.). *Neue Musik in Bewegung*. Mainz: Schott, 2011.

Hübner, F. *Shifting Identities: The Musician as Theatrical Performer*. Amsterdam: International Theatre & Film Books, 2014.

Jacobshagen, A. *Handbuch Praxis Musiktheater*. Regensburg: Laaber, 2002.

Kapp, H.-J. "Vom Bestellen lokaler Klangfelder: Freies Musiktheater im deutschsprachigen Raum." In: E. Mittelstädt and A. Pinto (eds), *Die Freien Darstellenden Künste in Deutschland*. Bielefeld: transcript, 2013, pp. 183–194.

Kirby, M. *A Formalist Theatre*. Philadelphia: University of Pennsylvania Press, 1987.

Kittler, F., Macho, T. And Weigel, S. (eds). *Zwischen Rauschen und Offenbarung: Zur Kultur- und Mediengeschichte der Stimme*. Berlin: Akademie Verlag, 2008.

Klüppelholz, W. *Sprache als Musik: Studien zur Vokalkomposition bei Karlheinz Stockhausen, Hans G. Helms, Mauricio Kagel, Dieter Schnebel und György Ligeti*. Friedberg: Pfau, 1976.

Kolesch, D., Pinto, V. and Schrödl, J. (eds). *Stimm-Welten*. Bielefeld: Transript, 2009.

Lefebvre, H. "Die Produktion des Raums." In: J. Dünne and S. Günzel (eds), *Raumtheorie*. Frankfurt am Main: Suhrkamp, 2006, pp. 330–342.

Lehmann, H.-T. *Postdramatisches Theater*. Frankfurt am Main: Verlag der Autoren, 2005.

Macho, T. "Stimmen ohne Körper: Anmerkungen zur Technikgeschichte der Stimme." In: D. Kolesch and S. Krämer (eds), *Stimme*. Frankfurt am Main: Suhrkamp, 2006, pp. 130–146.

Matzke, A. "Das ‚Freie Theater' gibt es nicht: Formen des Produzierens im gegenwärtigen Theater." In: W. Schneider (ed.), *Theater entwickeln und planen* (2013), pp. 259–272. (Available at: http://www.festivalimpulse.de, accessed 1st June 2013).

Mauser, S. *Musiktheater im 20. Jahrhundert* (= *Handbuch der musikalischen Gattungen* vol. 14). Regensburg: Laaber, 2002.

Mersch, D. and Ott, M. (eds). *Kunst und Wissenschaft*. Munich: Wilhelm Fink, 2007.

Plank-Baldauf, C. "Erzählen mit Musik – Erzählte Musik." In: *Das Magazin* 5 (2012/13), pp. 56–63.

Reininghaus, F., and Schneider, K. (eds). *Experimentelles Musik- und Tanztheater* (= *Handbuch der Musik im 20. Jahrhundert* vol. 7). Regensburg: Laaber, 2004.

Rebstock, M. "Ça Devient du Théâtre, Mais ça Vient de la Musique: The Music Theatre of Georges Aperghis." In M. Rebstock and D. Roesner (eds), *Composed Theatre* (2012), pp. 223–242.

Rebstock, M. "Drama der Stimmen: Zum Verhältnis von Körper und Stimme in David Martons Wozzeck." In: S. Schroedter (ed.), *Bewegungen zwischen Hören und Sehen: Denkbewegungen über Bewegungskünste*. Würzburg: Königshausen & Neumann, 2012, pp. 325–336.

Rebstock, M. "Im Fluchtpunkt der Sinne: Musiktheater als Arbeit an einer Phänomenologie des Hörens." In: C. Brüstle, C. Risi and S. Schwarz (eds), *Macht Ohnmacht Zufall*. Berlin, Theater der Zeit, 2011, pp. 172–182.

Rebstock, M. "Musiktheater: Spielräume schaffen!" In: W. Schneider (ed.), *Theater entwickeln und planen*. Bielefeld: transcript, 2013, pp. 299–314.

Rebstock, M. *Komposition zwischen Musik und Theater: Das instrumentale Theater von Mauricio Kagel zwischen 1959 und 1965*. Hofheim: Wolke, 2007.

Rebstock, M. "Vom Erzählen im Neuen Musiktheater." *Positionen* 55 (2003), pp. 18–21.

Rebstock, M. and Roesner, D. (eds). *Composed Theatre: Aesthetics, Practices, Processes*. Bristol: Intellect, 2012.

Roesner, D. *Musicality in Theatre*. Farnham: Ashgate, 2014.

Roesner, D. *Theater als Musik: Verfahren der Musikalisierung in chorischen Theaterformen bei Christoph Marthaler, Einar Schleef und Robert Wilson*. Tübingen: Gunter Narr, 2003.

Roesner, D. and Risi, C. "Die polyphone Werkstatt." *Theater der Zeit* (1/2009), pp. 28-31.

Ruf, W. "Musiktheater." In: L. Finscher (ed.), *Musik in Geschichte und Gegenwart, Sachteil* vol. 6, col. 1705. Kassel: Bärenreiter, 1997.

Salzman, E. and Desi, T. (eds). *The New Music Theatre*. Oxford: Oxford University Press, 2008.

Schnebel, D. "Sichtbare Musik." In: Schnebel, D. *Anschläge – Ausschläge: Texte zur Neuen Musik*. Munich: Hanser, 1993 [1966], pp. 262–300.

Schneider, W. "Ein synergetisches Ausprobieren: Heiner Goebbels über kollektive Kreativität, Inspiration und Inszenierungsprozesse." In: S. Porombka, W. Schneider and V. Wortmann (eds), *Kollektive Kreativität*. Tübingen: Francke, 2006, pp. 115–126.

Schneider, W. (ed.). *Theater entwickeln und planen*. Bielefeld: transcript, 2013.

Scholl, S. *Musik – Raum – Technik: Zur Entwicklung und Anwendung der graphischen Programmierumgebung "Max"*. Bielefeld: transcript, 2014.

Schulze, H. (ed.). *Sound Studies: Traditionen – Methoden – Desiderate*. Bielefeld: transcript, 2008.

Schroedter, S. (ed.). *Bewegungen zwischen Hören und Sehen: Denkbewegungen über Bewegungskünste*. Würzburg: Königshausen & Neumann, 2012.

Simon, R. *Labor oder Fließband? Produktionsbedingungen freier Musiktheaterprojekte an Opernhäusern*. Berlin: Theater der Zeit, 2013.

Sterne, J. (ed.), *The Sound Studies Reader*. London: Routledge, 2012.

Tröndle, M. (ed.). *Das Konzert: Neue Aufführungskonzepte für eine klassische Form*. Bielefeld: transcript, 2009.

Tröndle, M. and Warmers, J. (eds). *Kunstforschung als ästhetische Wissenschaft. Beiträge zur transdisziplinären Hybridisierung von Wissenschaft und Kunst*. Bielefeld: transcript, 2012.

Wellmer, A. "Musiktheater heute." In: J. P. Hiekel (ed.), *Neue Musik in Bewegung* (2011), pp. 28–39.
Zeller, H. R. "Medienkomposition nach John Cage." In: H.-K. Metzger and R. Riehn (eds), *John Cage I (Musikkonzepte-Sonderband)*. Munich: text+kritik, 1990.

Online publications

C-Opera listserv. http://www.notnicemusic.com/C-Opera.html (accessed 24th October 2015).
Fülle, Henning. "Freies Theater – Worüber reden wir eigentlich?" November 2012. Available at: http://www.festivalimpulse.de (accessed 1st June 2013).
Jakobshagen, Arnold. "Musiktheater." Available at: http://www.miz.org/static_de/themenportale/einfuehrungstexte_pdf/03_KonzerteMusiktheater/jacobshagen.pdf (accessed 24th March 2015).
Medien Kunst Netz. http://www.medienkunstnetz.de (accessed 24th October 2015).
Opera & Music Theatre Forum. http://www.omtf.org.uk (accessed 24th October 2015).
Oper Dynamo West. http://www.operdynamowest.org (accessed 24th October 2015).
Réseau Varèse. http://www.reseau-varese.com (accessed 24th October 2015).
Teatr Weimar. http://www.teatrweimar.se/eng/index.htm (accessed 9th April 2015).
T&M. http://www.theatre-musique.com (accessed 24th October 2015).

DVDs

Maximoff, C. *Georges Aperghis: "Storm Beneath a Skull"*. DVD documentary, Juxta Productions, 2006.
Rutherford-Johnson, T. *Up-Close*. DVD and booklet, Disquiet Media, 2011.

Towards a Theatrical Landscape
Funding the performing arts: cultural policy considerations

Wolfgang Schneider

'What if we gave cultural policy a shake up?' asks the Deutsche Bühne, in a booklet produced as part of its 2011–12 evaluation.[1] Theatre commentators are more than disillusioned with the powers that be: politicians see theatre only in terms of its price tag; absurd savings targets set by local authorities in response to the financial crisis will result only in closures and mergers; the devaluing of the arts and the erosion of the cultural sphere will have lasting repercussions. The journalists are prepared to shoulder some of the blame, lamenting 'the absence of debate about the future of the arts in our feature pages.'[2] Coverage of theatre in print media, radio and television remains healthy: productions continue to be reviewed, critics continue to dispense their opinions on theatre-makers. What's missing is an engagement with the politics or a challenge to the status quo. That status quo is Berlin, Salzburg, Bayreuth; the Kammerspiele, the Thalia and the Schaubühne theatres. A closed shop of the same institutions exchanging the same personnel, a theatrical Champions League. We should not wait for calls for reform to come from the feature pages: better to look online. 'Impulse.de' publishes analytical viewpoints on the theatre scene, www.theaterpolitik.de unites, as its title indicates, the theatrical and the political, and www.nachtkritik.de leads the field in cultural news and policy analysis.

Our theatrical landscape remains unmapped. The dominance of the big players means not enough collaborative projects are nurtured and ideas are rarely pooled. This was recognised by the German government's 2007 inquiry into 'German Culture.' Its report urged regional and local authorities 'to institute regional theatre development plans, invest in the middle-term, and also to provide long-term support to enable theatre, music and opera companies

---

1 | Detlef Brandenburg, in 'Complete Theatrical Works,' Deutscher Bühnenverein (Ed.): The German Stage, No. 8 (2012), Pg. 26–35, here p. 35.
2 | Ibid.

to pursue education projects, and to reach as wide an audience as possible.'³ The report drew attention to the huge number of existing alliances, networks and models, and recommended that they be strengthened. But the will is lacking.

Local authorities complain about empty coffers and tiny culture budgets, and fixate on outputs and square metres of useable space. Structural change is not on their radar. Every year, regional authorities fund what they've always funded. A refreshing of their approach is long overdue. Despite its lack of expertise, national government engages with arts policy indirectly through its national cultural foundation, its Performing Arts Fund and its City Cultural Fund. Without these bodies, Germany would have no arts policy at all. Politicians and cultural commentators would do well to recognise and reflect on this. In the last federal reforms, the regions cemented their cultural supremacy, but theatre reform was left to central government, which left it to the foundations.⁴

The national cultural foundation plays a major part in shaping the theatrical landscape. The 'Heimspiel' ['Home Match'], 'Doppelpass' ['One-two Pass'] and 'Wanderlust' funding programmes go to the city theatres and attest to the issues seen to be most pressing: the decrease in theatre's traditional middle class audience, the exclusion of the wider population, the self-centredness and inward-looking 'German-ness' of the performing arts. The foundation's vision is for city theatres that genuinely serve their whole city, as well as for an internationalisation of ensembles and repertoires, international co-productions and collaborations with the independent theatre sector.

'The 'Doppelpass' Fund is specifically for collaborations between independent groups and permanent building-based theatre and dance companies, to provide the additional time and space needed for the exploration of new models of joint working and artistic production methods. This framework is intended to facilitate new experiences and perspectives for both partners: theatres can offer independent groups performance opportunities, an established infrastructure and organisational and artistic expertise. Independent groups can offer alternative thematic and organisational approaches to help the institutions enrich their practice and reflect on their own working forms, methods and content.'⁵

---

3 | German Parliament (Ed.), Report of the Enquiry into Culture in Germany, ConBrio Publications, Regensburg 2008, Pg. 117.
4 | Wolfgang Schneider: 'Wuppertal is Everywhere! The cultural policy crisis in the performing arts reveals the need for reform to the German theatrical landscape'. In The Independent Performing Arts in Germany: Discussions – Developments – Perspectives, Erkhard Mittelstädt, Alexander Pinto (ed.), Bielefeld, 2013, pp. 21–32.
5 | Government Cultural Funds (Ed.), http://www.kulturstiftung-des-bundes.de

Why is this fund necessary? The scandal is not that central government funds are also going to local and regional theatre organisations, but that government has to provide them before the above can happen.[6]

Germany's theatrical and musical heritage has been recognised by the country's UNESCO Commission, which awarded it World Cultural Heritage status in its first list for the Federal Republic. This was influenced to some degree by the directors of town and regional theatres, together with their funders, who lobbied mayors and culture ministers following a resolution on the subject at their 2013 conference in Kiel.

The dpa [the German Press Agency] often quotes the then-president's plea that the theatre landscape be protected, 'so that in ten or 15 years it is not completely unrecognisable.'[7] But is that not exactly what we want it to be? In order to make the performing arts sustainable, we need a re-design, with new networks and new structures. We need practical ideas with a conceptual basis: ideas drawn from theory, an understanding of history, current experience and our vision for the future. We need a cultural development strategy, a SWAT analysis, discussions that include all stakeholders, clear aims and implementation strategies. Most of all, we need the will to undertake reform.

PLANNING AND DEVELOPING THEATRE

The University Institute for Cultural Policy organised a lecture series in the winter term of 2012–13, in which culture and theatre academics undertook took to test, analyse and evaluate theoretical positions on the aesthetics and dramaturgy of the performing arts from the perspective of the politics of theatrical administration.

Annemarie Matzke, professor and performance artist, offered the provocative opinion that there is no such thing as independent theatre. She highlighted problems with the concept, as well as opportunities offered by it, and linked it historically with the appearance of new theatre forms. Rather than being an aesthetic or political definition, she finds the term to be descriptive of new methods of production and working practices distinct from those found in state-funded theatres. The multiplicity of these new forms, however, means a blanket definition of 'independent theatre' is impossible. Matzke emphasised that she was interrogating the concept, rather than questioning its aesthetic or social relevance. She described current tendencies as reflective of social plu-

---

6 | Wolfgang Schneider: Provocations for the System: the performing arts need cultural policy. In Theatre Platform: the performing arts in flux, contributions to cultural education, Genshagen Foundation (ed.), 2013, pp. 38-45.
7 | Stuttgarter Nachrichten [Stuttgart News], May 24 2013.

rality, informed by increased flexibility on the one hand and new forms of collective production on the other. An investigation into the changing nature of theatre is for Matzke also a collective theatre form in itself.

For Heiner Goebbels, Professor and President of the Theatre Academy in Hessen, the contemporary performing arts have always engaged in a critique of institutions. The performing arts, however, unlike the fine arts, have trouble escaping aesthetic convention: theatre, opera and concert houses are constrained by their architectural structures and organisational hierarchies. The training organisations follow rigid ideological traditions: far from being the exploratory laboratories Goebbels would like them to be, they serve the market. He calls for independent performance spaces unencumbered by demands to deliver effectiveness, optimum space-utilisation, or an uninterrupted repertory. These should not have in-house orchestras, choirs, acting or dance companies, but should be financially supported just like opera houses, city theatres and regional theatres.

Thomas Oberender, Director of the Berliner Festspiele theatre, understands theatrical developments in the context of the deregulation occurring at every level of society. Public funding of the performing arts follows market-based criteria: activity is supported only if it is evaluable and measureable. Oberender charts on the one hand an increase in political power over the arts, through funding and endowment programmes, and on the other, a situation in which artists have become project managers. This new cultural mood has led to the emergence of a 'new type of institution.' He asks pointedly: what do we want to support in the future: the picnic or the Proms, the project or the institution?

Thomas Schmidt, Professor of Theatre Management at the University for Music and the Performing Arts in Frankfurt am Main, describes the current theatrical landscape as rugged, productive, innovative and discursive. However the publicly-funded theatre system is undergoing its most radical upheaval since the Second World War. Schmidt outlines some of the difficult questions theatres are currently asking. Their answers, he suggests, will form the basis for crisis management tactics and models for reform. The idea of what constitutes success in theatre will need to be re-imagined. Schmidt sees collaborative working between institutionalised and independent theatre as one solution, a re-organisation of the funding structure to allow for a fairer distribution of resources another.

Alexander Pinto, independent theatre practitioner and research assistant at the HafenCity University in Hamburg, sees independent theatre as a breeding ground for new ideas, a niche it has carved in response to the near-monopoly of the state-funded theatres. In independent theatre, standard working conditions do not exist. The economic disparity between the two systems has, however, allowed some independent theatre to choose to invest in artistic development, while town theatres groan under financial pressures. Independent theatre remains critical of any institutionalising tendencies of its own, and keeps abreast of directions taken by other theatres around it. As a consequence, the creation of spaces for development and exchange that will be so important to revitalising theatre in towns and cities is likely to be spearheaded by the independent sector.[8]

THEATRICAL COLLABORATION: A EUROPEAN TENDENCY

There are European theatre festivals, networks, grants, prizes, exchange programmes and productions. Europe and theatre have a long history, our theatres perhaps the secular cathedrals of our cultural identity. Few other art forms operate so successfully across borders. There are historical reasons for this. Theatre did not emerge fully-formed, but wrested itself free of its archaic origins through cultural processes to become drama: the drama of human existence itself, whether expressed through stories of gods in the ancient Greek, religious belief in the Spanish, internal conflicts in the Elizabethan, guilt in the classical enlightenment, or society, the individual, nothingness and absurdity in the modern age. The ancient form of the play evolved in Homeric Greece, with roots in both the dance and sacrificial ceremonies and the worship or competition-focussed public games. Tragedy was first recognised as an art form in 534BC, when the famous actor Thespis, from Ikara, was invited to manage the cult of Dionysus celebrations. This cultural event signalled the emergence of European theatre. It proceeded to be moulded by Greek and Roman dramatists, Spanish and French directors, English and German producers. The theatre texts and their stagings travelled throughout Europe, sparking the first dialogues that allowed European artistic relationships to develop.

Europe didn't invent theatre, but it was united by it. Today's classical repertoire attests to this: Euripides and Aristophanes, Shakespeare and Molière, Goethe and Schiller, Chekov and Ibsen, Büchner and Brecht wrote the texts still seen on stages all over Europe. But no European theatrical landscape is like another. While the same plays can be seen in different stagings from Oslo to Madrid, London to Bucharest, theatrical systems differ widely. That, too, is the nature of Europe. Theatrical landscapes might be dominated by powerful leaders with a mandate to represent a broad public, by citizen involvement, the cult of individual artists, and/or by commercial markets. They feature a variety of playing spaces: regional and city theatres, rural stages, theatre agencies, independent and privately-owned theatre, musical theatre venues, venues with

---

8 | Wolfgang Schneider (Ed.): Developing and Planning Theatre: cultural policy concepts for the reform of the performing arts, Bielefeld, 2013.

or without in-house companies, institution-based or project-oriented, with programmes played in repertory or in sequence.

Whatever its form, European theatre has a tendency to be mobile. It travels to different regions, rural areas, other European countries. The hosting of the visiting company is an established principle. This exchange can influence artists, and, occasionally, cultural policy. Theatre practitioners have a need to communicate: with the public, but also amongst themselves. They disseminate not only their stories, but elements of our cultural discourse: they are the voices in an ongoing pan-European dialogue. European theatre is elemental, alive and enlivening; it allows us, through its cross-border co-productions, festivals and networks, to continually re-discover our continent through dialogue and exchange. An analysis of the European theatrical landscape reveals platforms for debate and the sharing of work at every level: we are woven together by theatre. Despite language differences, there is a high level of geographical mobility amongst artists, and despite the different structures in different countries, communal creation is widespread. Festivals are important points of contact, embracing the full diversity of performing arts activity. This mobility and flexibility is made possible by a huge number of organising groups, alliances and networks, which are recognised and supported by cultural policy makers.[9]

Very recently in theatrical history, innovative performing arts projects that united artists from all over Europe and toured all over Europe began to receive financial support. Hugo Greef's Kaaiteater in Brussels, Tom Stromberg's Theater am Turm in Frankfurt am Main, Nelle Hertling's Hebbel-Theatre in Berlin, the Vienna Festwochen [Festival Week], the Avignon Festival, the Theater in der Gessnerallee in Zürich and the Kampnagel in Hamburg all benefitted. European 'centres of production' for the contemporary arts emerged. A European funding information and networking initiative at the Künstlerhaus Mousonturm in Frankfurt am Main even bore that name. Lecture and discussion programmes supplement performances. Usually the more avant-garde the staging, the more alternative its methods of production. These artist-led buildings are worlds away from the traditional theatre houses. They work flexibly, adapting production methods to artistic requirements. They have become the model for the contemporary municipal theatre. They point to a future theatrical landscape composed of interdisciplinary, interactive, integrative performance centres; places that combine production, distribution and reception, and see themselves as experimental stage spaces, research institutions and laboratories for new performance styles.

---

9 | Wolfgang Schneider: Theatre (En)live(n)s Europe: cultural policy in the performing arts: co-productions, festivals and networks. In Cultural Policy Yearbook 2007: European Culture, Institute for Cultural Policy of the Cultural Policy Society (ed.), pp. 303-312.

THEATRE AND INTERCULTURALITY

Academic studies have researched, analysed and reflected on the role of independent theatre. Many focus on theatrical aesthetics, but cultural policy developments have also been mapped, along with production conditions and processes. Consultations have highlighted areas of funding need. Two examples serve to make the cultural policy argument.

One of the greatest social and political challenges in a globalised world is integration, the need to ensure that people of all ethnic backgrounds, religious orientations and cultural traditions are able to participate equally in society. Instrumental to this is the nurturing of respect for cultural diversity in a multi-ethnic and multicultural context. Cultural policy can play a part in this, contributing to the recognition and understanding of cultural difference. Interculturality is a key concept in the identification of appropriate policy and practice to facilitate integration.

In societies characterised by cultural diversity and fast-paced change, efforts towards equal participation will only bear fruit if ideas around cultural identity and artistic activity are understood as process-driven, and if serious, critical questioning of our conceptions of borders and thresholds is recognised as a motor for social change. In the context of cultural multiplicity, discourses around societal forms and the understanding and treatment of difference transcend multiculturalism to become 'transculturalism'. An equalities-based framework is important, and of self-evident practical value, in the implementation of intercultural actions in conceptual and policy arenas, in agenda-setting, especially for collaborative decision-making, in the fair redistribution of cultural funds and in the internal restructure of arts organisations. Infrastructure, network-building and access criteria are key to successful intercultural practice. Possibilities must be created for broad participation, to allow for the forging of relationships based on empathy for the new rather than fear of the strange.

Three major aspects need attention if the theatrical landscape is to be reorganised along intercultural lines. The first and most fundamental area for action is that of cultural education. Unless society can provide a broader cultural training within the compulsory education system – a 'school for life' – large parts of the population will continue to remain excluded from cultural offerings and, in the best case scenario, new forms of cultural expression will eke out a meagre existence beyond the pale of mainstream cultural policy. We must demand a commitment from policy-makers to make good the rhetoric of annual government education reports and regional plans and recognise cultural training as a social responsibility. As mentioned as a dissenting opinion in the Culture Inquiry report, this could be achieved through the inclusion of cultural training in the educational curriculum, as a subject taught from kindergarten to adult education level. Training policy would emphasise culture as a core aspect of lifelong learning.

The second working area is that of audience development, understood as an integrated component of cultural management. This is a cross-cutting issue for all institutions that aspire to a holistic practice: it can inform their creative and organisational methodology and allow them to grow alongside their changing public, as well as to nurture that public. Only a self-imposed commitment to cultural diversity by the entire arts industry will lead to a culturally diverse public. Traditional marketing methods, focussed on the maximisation of profits and the selling of an existing product to an existing customer, are not equal to this task. In order to plan, position, communicate, disseminate and sell cultural offerings to diverse target groups, audience development needs to work in tandem with arts marketing, PR, research, education and training.

The concept of audience development emerged in the Anglo-Saxon world in the 1990s. It is embedded in an understanding of cultural management that takes the central reference point for the cultural organisation to be its public. This is a departure from the supply-based model traditional in Germany. It is important to understand that a demand-based model does not necessarily lead, as Bourdieu has claimed, to a reduction in artistic quality.

Equality of participation, the democratisation of culture, and the dismantling of elitist structures are amongst the most important aims of audience development. Alongside these socio-cultural perspectives are other considerations. Cultural policy-makers have the right to demand to see a wide social cross section of the public in state-funded institutions, based on the belief that art can have a sustained and enriching effect on people's lives, and can strengthen communication, identity and sense of community. The benefits to just one participant can justify the public money invested.

The belief that the arts are intimidating, boring or difficult to understand can only be combated through increased accessibility and education. The public should be engaged in a lively debate with culture. For this to happen, it must be provided with the knowledge and tools to crack cultural codes. In the short term, this can be achieved through direct education provision within cultural institutions themselves, through media-based interpretation aids, such as audio guides, dialogue-based tours or creative discussions in workshops. The quality of the intermediary is of paramount importance in this regard.

A structured, long term cultural training strategy orientated towards the whole population is essential. Increased collaboration between cultural organisations and associations, facilities used for out of school activities and the schools themselves will help. Only such an approach can guarantee that early engagement with art and culture is available to all, and, in particular, is not dependent on a child's social background. Short and long term engagement activity should understand cultural training as intercultural training.

The content of training should be developed with a view to strengthening intercultural perspectives.

The third working area is the nurturing of the community-focussed and mandated cultural hubs that have sprung up throughout Europe, but remain fragile in terms of their financial sustainability and capacity for long-term planning. They contribute to an overall move towards participation in the arts by a wider spectrum of society: people of different ages, ethnic backgrounds or social classes living in the vicinity of the institutions are beginning to include them in their day-to-day lives without needing to be explicitly targeted. Sociocultural institutions are tried and tested places for intercultural communication and participation, and are increasingly also sites for the performing arts, including visiting independent productions and participative theatre work.

CHILDREN AND YOUNG PEOPLE'S THEATRE

The government's 'German Culture' Inquiry presented its report at the end of 2007. Its recommendations have been widely discussed and variously interpreted since then. The report presents the government's policy position and its agenda for the reform of the German cultural landscape. It says:

'theatre for children and young people plays an important role in the German theatre system. As projects within town and regional theatres, autonomous stages or independent theatres of their own, children and young people's theatres are committed to their target group, reflect the realities of young people's experience through texts and staging, and take their educational role seriously. Cultural education contributes towards empowerment and life skills. Theatre for young audiences must focus on the perspectives of young people and help them to negotiate society and develop abstract thought and creative ability.'[10]

Contemporary societies make complex demands on their citizens. Young people must begin at an early age to engage critically with their own development and perspectives on the future. They need both the confidence and the organisational skills to negotiate constant decision-making and change. They can acquire these in the family, at school, or through a range of other activities that promote personal empowerment, cultural training being one. Involvement with the arts develops the key competencies of literacy and the understanding of abstract language, alongside discipline, flexibility and team working skills. The ability to judge and evaluate both newly-acquired knowledge and the behaviour of oneself and others is honed. Cultural training

---

10 | German Parliament (Ed.), Final Report, p. 109.

is however more concerned with self-development than with the transmission of knowledge. As well as producing the above outcomes for young people, it also impacts positively on the cultural sphere itself, bringing young blood in the form of new creators and consumers of art. It contributes to the on-going critique and preservation of the German cultural legacy. Cultural idiosyncrasy and participation are decisive elements in the socialising of young people and must be safeguarded at both national and international level. Article 31 of the UN Convention on the Rights of the Child states, on participation in cultural and artistic life:

'1. States Parties recognise the right of the child to rest and leisure, to engage in play and recreational activities appropriate to the age of the child and to participate freely in cultural life and the arts. 2. States Parties shall respect and promote the right of the child to participate fully in cultural and artistic life and shall encourage the provision of appropriate and equal opportunities for cultural, artistic, recreational and leisure activity.'[11]

All European states have ratified this convention. Germany, as a 'cultural nation,' has promised special protection and long-term state and local authority funding to cultural education. The basic conditions have thus been created, but implementation remains problematic: there is still much to be done to make cultural participation, whether productive or receptive, equally accessible to all young people.

Alternative play areas beyond schools, youth theatres or outdoor spaces should be critically considered. Theatre for pre-school children would benefit from well-equipped performance spaces too. Why not a children's theatre building, a third space for young people alongside family and school? Another part of the inquiry report warns against allocating disproportionate resources to education and participation activity. Theatre offers not only the personal experience of rehearsing for life by treading the boards, but also another kind of personal experience through its consumption. 'Learning by doing' is one side of the coin, 'learning by viewing' the other. In some cultural education formats, the weighting is skewed towards theatrical activity by children and young people themselves. The school subject of drama tends to privilege theatre as a creative workshop, unlike art, in which the teaching of drawing is only one part of the curriculum, or music, in which children learn more than just how to sing. A final demand in this context should be for a union of art and culture, particularly where society's youngest citizens are concerned.

---

11 | German Ministry for Families, Older People, Women and Children: Convention on the Rights of the Child, verbatim report with materials, article 31, p. 23.

The intrinsic value of theatre must be enhanced, not just its products. Theatres should become 'go to places' for 'time out' in a 'playing space'.[12]

Theatre is a special event, a happening that allows the everyday to be turned on its head, the usual rules to be re-written. It provides an experience unlike that usually associated with learning, which can forge strong connections, create profound experiences and transmit varied knowledge. It can provide orientation and overview, and allow for individual evaluation of learned material and its application to real-life contexts. At its best, theatre for children and young people provides an aesthetic experience that has multiple possible meanings, a celebration of the pleasures of life, and a space for new experiences that frees the mind for play.

There is a real opportunity for theatre for children and young people outside formal educational spaces to enhance school-based provision. It could partner with schools to become an integral part of the curriculum. School has a manifest need for what theatre can provide. Both sides could benefit from closer collaboration. This already exists in the form of theatre outings for pupils, special offers for school groups and drama workers in schools and theatres planning activities with both contexts in mind. Artistic training is crucial for social sustainability; children's and young people's theatre can provide it.

According to neuroscientists, a large proportion of essential human social interaction is non-verbal. Non-spoken communication competencies need to be developed and refined. Children and young people's theatre companies have known this for decades. Exposure to their multi-dimensional visual storytelling can contribute to the development of artistic taste and sophisticated skills of perception and judgement.

INDEPENDENT THEATRE NEEDS CULTURAL POLICY

There are many reasons to adopt a new definition of the performing arts. Reform of the theatre landscape to reflect the population being served are long overdue – a view that seems to be gaining only gradual acceptance. In a democracy, the performing arts should cater for everyone, and should play a social role. In order to realise this potential, cultural policy measures must prioritise participation. They must recognise that at present, not everyone is willing and/or in a position to seek non-material benefits from cultural experience, not everyone feels at home in the world of the arts, or necessarily values or aspires to what they can provide in terms of questioning the meaning of life, seeking intellectual fulfilment or even just having fun.

---

12 | Wolfgang Schneider (Ed.): Theatre and Schools: a handbook for cultural education, Bielefeld, 2009.

The first chapter of the 'Culture in Germany' report is titled 'the meaning of art and culture for individual and society.' It states:

'the arts also have indirect meaning for [these people], however, through media and publicity, and as a sub-sector of wider culture. Art is uniquely placed to explore and champion the freedom and dignity of the individual, to portray this in all its contradictoriness, to symbolise it in ways that can be translated into thought and action. Art interrogates individual identity and social bonds. In this sense it has a broad effect over social communication as a whole and impacts on people's day to day decision-making and analysis. Cultural policy must therefore also be understood as social policy. It should enable, defend and help shape art and culture', 2008.[13]

Exposure to ideas that were previously hidden, or that we were afraid to entertain, can help us engage with the changing world and find answers to the questions that concern us. The concept of contingency awareness, identified in cultural research, describes the human quest for ways to shape experience in order to better understand the future. Art questions and refreshes contemporary reality. Some academic studies consider it the most sensitive seismograph of an approaching crisis for humanity. Art introduces us to new subjects, perhaps allowing us to see the world in different ways, perhaps allowing us to deal with it differently.

The performing arts can intervene in the public realm and influence social and political decision-making. Theatre can stimulate thought and debate. It can alter our day to day behaviour and our perception of the world around us. In ideal conditions, theatre can re-animate spaces and present the everyday in a new light, offering surprising, stimulating associations, irritations, even provocations. Embracing new ideas makes the future seem less daunting. The huge variety of artistic modes of expression means there are different opportunities to suit individual issues and needs. Independent theatre, in particular, uses its experimental starting points to critique basic assumptions, equipping us to confront the future with more confidence. At their best, the performance arts can help us to identify connections and can sharpen our ability to judge what is most important in life.

A policy for nurturing the performing arts could serve as a blueprint for concept-based cultural policy as a whole. What would that mean for our theatrical landscape? First, we need to take stock. The Köln 'Werkstatistik' [statistics about theatre activity] are a useful starting point, but knowledge about amateur and independent theatre must be expanded. It would be useful to have a performing arts yearbook that justified its name, alongside a theatre development plan that thinks holistically and across sectors, uniting the

---

13 | German Parliament (Ed.), Final Report, 2008, p. 50.

'Champions League' and the amateur dramatics society, the national opera house and the woodland amphitheatre, the theatre education centre and the independent theatre space. The time is right for concept-based cultural policy.[14]

Even the local lobbies are now aware of the current situation, in which 'because of the reduced share of the national budget, in terms of total expenditure, allocated to culture, only restricted budgetary impact is achievable, and even minor cuts can often lead to irreparable damage to the cultural infrastructure'[15]. The Director of Culture for the German Congress of Municipal Authorities now speaks in terms of collaborations, mergers and even – albeit 'cautiously' – reforms to local culture policies and the need for new structures. The new chair of the government's Culture Committee, Siegmund Ehrmann, has said the public funding of culture should be critically examined: 'there must be a public debate about what types of support are meaningful and in what contexts, and about what we want them to achieve. Perhaps an improvement in quality will result.'[16] Funding models are yet to be evaluated in terms of their real impact, so this is a legitimate demand.

Germany has a long way to go to achieve 'Culture for All.' Only a 'happy few' regularly take part in traditional arts activity. State support is principally for infrastructure, increasing institutionalisation at the expense of project and process-oriented activity. Funding goes to a core group of cultural organisations mainly found in urban centres. The management and upkeep of buildings and equipment consume public cultural funds, using the taxes of all citizens to benefit a few. Production is better resourced than reception, with cultural education getting the leftover crumbs.

This situation represents an opportunity for independent theatre practitioners. Who is making work on the ground, in the diaspora, in the non-funded no man's lands? Who is creating access-routes into communities, working towards culture for all through cultural education? Where are the true 'people's stages'? Participation is currently being re-discovered as a theatrical output in itself, and the patent for the practice belongs to independent theatre.

---

14 | Wolfgang Schneider: The Future of our Theatrical Landscape: a topical cultural policy polemic. In Performing Arts Report: economic, social and employment conditions for theatre and dance practitioners in Germany, Funding the Performing Arts (ed.), Essen, 2010, pp. 21–25.
15 | Klaus Hebborn:'Culture in Germany from a Local Perspective,' in Cultural Policy Reports, Journal for Cultural Policy of the Cultural Policy Society: European Capital of Culture, vol. 127 (2009), pp. 8–10, here p. 8.
16 | TAZ [news website], http://www.taz.de/1/archiv/print-archiv/printressorts/digi-artikel/?ressort=ku&dig=2009%2F12%2F15%2Fa0028&cHash=ba9c0cf4e9ddc01db2d4ed7a6dba88ba.

The goal must be more theatre for more people, as part of a theatrical landscape that features multiple structures able to support diverse forms of practice.

Independent theatre will have to evolve too, if only because of global developments and changes in demographics. Dismissal of the amateurs by the professionals, and vice versa, will have no place in a world in which collaboration will be key. No theatre is an island: however strong our pride in our own artistic traditions, a glimpse beyond our own noses can only do us good.

Theatre Funding: European Comparisons

Those discussing good practice in theatre funding inevitably look to the north. Cultural policy-makers in the Scandinavian countries know that through highs and lows, during economic prosperity or recession, whether social democrats or conservatives hold the balance of power in government, the performing arts must remain high on the agenda. The best sustainable funding practice can be found in children and young people's theatre.

In March 1998, in Stockholm, UNESCO held a conference and launched a report to mark the end of its international decade of world culture. 'The Power of Culture' conference was an 'intergovernmental' gathering on the subject of 'cultural policy and development.' Around 5,000 people of varying degrees of seniority took turns on a political dancefloor. 150 countries were represented, 70 culture ministers spoke, experts presented papers, diplomatic officials, and official diplomats, gathered the material into a 'draft action plan' for cultural policy. The conference produced about ten kilogrammes of paper, which eventually became the 'Convention on the Protection and Promotion of the Diversity of Cultural Expressions' (2005). A fair result, particularly as the document includes an appendix on 'culture for children and young people.' [17] Written by Britt Isaksson of the Swedish Department for Cultural Affairs, it argues over 14 pages for the right of children and young people to have access to art and to be integrated into cultural life. For communication skills to be developed to their fullest, Isaksson argues, creativity must be nurtured early on. The challenge to global media dominance cannot be left to the market, but should centre on local, regional, national and international influencing initiatives. Definitions of cultural education are explored using the example of children's libraries. Isaksson concludes that without imagination, society regresses. She urges that art, in all its variety, be harnessed as part of lifelong learning. In Sweden, support for theatre for children and young people is

---

17 | Britt Isaksson: Culture for Children and Young People, 1998, UNESCO (Ed.): http://unesdoc.unesco.org/Ulis/cgi-bin/ulis.pl?catno=111819&set=005630BB37_3_378&gp=0&lin=1&ll=1.

enshrined in an education act: each year all pupils have the chance to attend the theatre twice. Two million children and young people means a need for four million seats at performances. That means public investment in theatrical productions, funding for touring theatre groups in every region, and flexible playing forms.

The picture is similar in Denmark. Children and young people's theatre groups travel the country in fleets of vans, trailers and minibuses. They drive to the next location, unload, put up then take down the set, move on. It's a strenuous business, but the only way to make their business work. In late April, they converge at a national festival, in a different location every year. The festival has been running since 1971, and is of increasing importance. Audiences include librarians in charge of booking productions, teachers planning for the following year and civil servants from cultural departments putting together their programmes. The bearded old chairman of the Roskilde Theatre Company can be seen chatting with the young, blonde youth theatre manager from a Copenhagen suburb. Audience members can come just for the weekend and choose from an incredible 200 performances in two days. Plays happen in every possible and impossible space. Entire schools are occupied: classrooms become mini auditoria, a story-telling session takes place in the biology lab. In the assembly hall, the theatre groups tout their wares. In the sports hall, up to eight stage sets are played on, one after the other. The whole thing is an organisational tour-de-force with an important cultural policy aim: to provide state support to theatre distribution as well as to its production.

Decentralisation is an important element of Finnish cultural policy too. Comprehensive schools, serving one area in a larger town or the whole of a smaller town, are also cultural centres for the whole community. Finland consistently tops the PISA rankings, a comparative study of educational standards in OECD countries, and anyone who's ever visited a school there can see the reasons in their architecture, conception and practice. At the centre of every school is a media studio with a black box theatre, regularly played in by independent theatre companies.

In Norway, a 'cultural school satchel' combines general education with theatre arts and ensures that from the first to the tenth class, all pupils can see and practice theatre. Independent theatre is financed through measures including a voucher system.

The public funding of theatre in Europe is managed through local and regional political structures using funds from national programmes; local and national policy-makers and occasionally also cultural affairs departments share responsibility. In France, Spain, Italy and many other countries in central and Eastern Europe, theatre funding is the domain of cultural ministries. In the UK, Ireland and the Nordic countries, the funds are administered by Arts Councils, independent from government, following an 'arm's length' principle.

In every national context, however, an increasing gulf is visible between regularly or permanently state-funded organisations and the independent sector. Differences between artistic and business models are also evident, as is an on-going debate about the cultural marketplace and the economics of private funding. In Greece, Spain, Portugal and Italy, independent theatre has fallen victim to national austerity programmes. Only some regions and richer local authorities are able to provide project funding to ensure performing arts provision beyond the big opera houses.

In Belgium, three organisations are active in funding theatre. The country is divided according to regional territories and its three languages. In Flanders, culture is the responsibility of the Flemish government, through a Ministry for Culture, Youth, Sport and Media. Its policy is based on a parliamentary resolution, the so-called arts decree (adopted in 2004, coming into force in 2006, following the 1993 performing arts decree and the legislative decision to enact a theatre decree in 1975). The arts decree aims to support integrated practice for all professional fields in the arts through a long-term support framework. Funding is also available through four and two year grants, project grants, grants for individual artists and for international cultural organisations with a base in Flanders. The change of government in 2012 resulted in uncertainty about the future of these budgets. Most of the money increasingly goes on long-term funding, while smaller project funds have been cut. On its website, The Flemish Theatre Institute calls the arts decree 'a good starting point.' [18] Development, production, presentation, participation and reflection have all been funded. The challenge for cultural policy is how to harness the enormous productivity of the performing arts, to bring new theatre groups and artists into the system and to nurture them so they can achieve the highest standards of practice.

The Netherlands Theatre Institute was seen for many years a model of cultural policy, independent from state, regional and local authorities. Figures like Dragon Klaic, long-term director of the Amsterdamer Zentrale, were able to create artistic momentum and lead innovation. The new conservative government has, however, implemented drastic cuts to the culture budget, ending this era of cultural engagement and artistic autonomy. The Theatre Institute closed in 2013. Only the Theatre Collection remains, a library and archive now housed at the University of Amsterdam. A performing arts fund is still in place, available five times a year, for theatre productions taking part in major international festivals or tours. These funds generally cover travel and transport costs, more rarely also workshops, masterclasses or seminars. The budget for 2014 was only €940,000. There is also a new fund for cultural participation, to support people to play a more active role in artistic activity.

---

18 | Flanders Arts Institute, http://www.vti.be

It prioritises close working relationships with local partners, the support of cultural training institutions, discussion forums and research as well as the exchange of experience and knowledge in amateur arts and popular culture. Since 2009, €14 million has been made available annually by the state for the accreditation of cultural training, €3.5 million for innovative amateur arts, and €3 million for talent and event development. Independent theatre is supported if it meets the criteria of the trustees.

Detailed information about theatre funding in Europe is available on 'Fund-Finder', an online publication by the IETM, the International Network for Contemporary Performing Arts (formerly the Informal European Theatre Meeting). It lists international and interdisciplinary funding programmes.[19] As well as the well-known European Union cultural funds, such as 'Creative Europe,' projects like "Horizon 2020,' the 'European Regional Fund' and 'Interreg' are also featured, all possible avenues of support for independent theatre given its frequent focus on social concerns, urban development and/ or intercultural dialogue. Project funds are of course time-limited, as is also the case with sources like Crowdfunding, social enterprise start-up funds and festival funding. The focus is always on the mobility of practitioners across Europe and on opportunities for artistic exchange.

MODELS OF THEATRE DEVELOPMENT PLANNING

Theatre policy is all too often just funding policy, as an overview of the funding of independent theatre in Germany indicates. Theatre is supported in every region, whether the focus be on the 'innovative and experimental' (Nordrhein-Westfalen)[20], 'the preservation of diversity' (Saarland)[21] or 'artistic quality, originality and capacity to serve as models' (Baden-Württemberg)[22]. Medium term funding may come through 'concept funds', or a 'top-level fund', seen as a 'stamp of quality' (Baden- Württemberg)[23], and may be limited to two, three or four years (Hamburg, Niedersachsen). 'The state, together with local

---

19 | Cf. IETM, http://www.ietm.org
20 | Nordrhein-Westfalen Regional Authority for the Performing Arts, http://www.nrw-landesbuero-kultur.de/index.php?article_id=10
21 | Saarland. Artists and Artist Development, http://www.saarland.de/10104.htm
22 | Baden-Württemberg Association for Independent Dance and Theatre Artists Ltd, 'Cultural Training' Project, http://www.laftbw.de/foerderinstrumente/projektfoerderung_kulturelle_bildung
23 | Baden-Württemberg Association for Independent Dance and Theatre Artists Ltd, 'Cultural Training' Project, http://www.laftbw.de/foerderinstrumente/projektfoerderung_kulturelle_bildung

authorities, also takes responsibility for the resourcing of non-state theatre in Bayern' (Bayern)[24]. Independent theatres such as 'Mummpitz' and 'Pfütze' in Nürnberg are given institutional support, so that an adequate theatre offering is guaranteed in all parts of the region' (Styria)[25].

All the regions also contribute to funding for the independent theatre festivals 'Impulse' (Nordrhein-Westfalen), 'Made in Hessen' (Hessen) and '100 Grad' (Berlin). Funding of theatre means valuing of theatre, so theatre awards are also supported as cultural policy initiatives. These may include prize money and also 'the premiere production of a new play' (Nordrhein-Westfalen)[26], funds towards the next production (Niedersachsen) or for artists or companies in recognition of unusual talent and impressive management (Bayern, Baden-Württemberg, Mecklenburg-Vorpommern). There is also support for productions which have already been produced using public funds to have a longer life. Touring theatre funding goers to organisers, artists and groups (Nordrhein-Westfalen, Mecklenburg-Vorpommern, Hamburg). Additional production and re-staging funds are available 'to stage productions of a play in the home region'[27] and 'to re-stage high expenditure productions' (Baden-Württemberg)[28].

Stipends are another aspect of funding for independent theatre. These may be for work, travel or accommodation (Brandenburg), 'for the artist to devote themselves intensively to their work for a specific period' (Mecklenburg-Vorpommern)[29], or for international exchanges and co-productions (Hamburg). The government and the Goethe Institute are the most active institutions in terms of the dissemination of national cultural policy. Both provide artistic development opportunities for independent theatre in a European and international context. This translates into a commitment to the development of the self-organising skills of independent theatre, to strengthen artists as part of civil society. Networks, regional associations and the Federal Association

---

[24] | Bayern State Department for Training, Education, Science and Arts, Funding for non-state theatre, http://www.km.bayern.de/kunst-und-kultur/foerderung/foerderung-nicht staatlicher-theater.html

[25] | Ibid.

[26] | Nordrhein-Westfalen Frauen Kultur Büro [Women's Culture Department], http://www.frauenkulturbuero-nrw.de/index.php/foerderrecherche/theater/

[27] | Baden-Württemberg Association for Independent Dance and Theatre Artists Ltd, Performance Funding, http://www.laftbw.de/foerderinstrumente/auffuehrungs foerderung

[28] | Baden-Württemberg Association for Independent Dance and Theatre Artists Ltd, Re-staging Funding, http://www.laftbw.de/foerderinstrumente/wiederaufnahme foerderung

[29] | Mecklenburg-Vorpommern Ministry for Education, Science and Culture, Artists Stipends, http://www.regierung-mv.de/Landesregierung/bm/Kultur/Künstlerstipendien

of Independent Theatres offer advice, information-sharing and advocacy on behalf of the sector. In that sense the regions and central government support both lobbying and service provision.

THE TOP TEN OF INDEPENDENT THEATRE FUNDING

- Project funding
- Concept funding
- Funding of institutions
- Funding of festivals
- Funding through theatre prizes
- Funding for young people's projects
- Funding for touring, productions and re-staging
- Funding through stipends
- Funding of international exchanges
- Funding of advocacy

All of these aspects should be included in an over-arching, concept-based cultural policy, which could take the form of a theatre development plan. The focus could be local relevance. Theatre projects with connections to a town or region should be actively engaged in on-the ground research, discovering the themes that resonate with residents, with the aim not only of attracting local audiences, but of achieving a deeper understanding of society. Diversity should be preserved through the nurturing of a variety of theatrical forms and structures.[30]

An appropriate cultural policy approach would be to understand theatre funding as a risk premium, awarding process and failure rather than only that which is known to work. This element of funding has been completely neglected to date. If a theatre director's show flops, they lose their job faster than a football coach in the German league. The fact that independent theatre must evaluate and evidence all its activity can be seen in a positive light. Why is this not the case for all theatre? Why are the town and regional theatres not regularly asked what they've done to develop new audiences or to take theatre into schools?

An important element of a theatre development plan would be interdisciplinary working. The current system is completely out-dated in this regard.

---

30 | Wolfgang Schneider: From Project to Project - on the side-lines of cultural policy? The role of independent theatre in a future theatrical landscape. In Independent Theatre in Germany: funding structures and perspectives, Funding the Performing Arts (ed.), Essen, 2007, pp. 82–70.

Why do we still speak of 'spoken word theatre'? Why is musical theatre still a hermetic entity, along with ballet, dance, puppetry and theatre for children and young people? The avant-garde has always worked across disciplines. The town and regional theatres do too. Our society is intercultural: so should our performing arts be. Dance theatre at present is particularly international in its focus. People have communicated across state borders through theatre for thousands of years. Internationality must be part of theatre development planning.

Cultural policy positions relate to production, distribution and reception, but currently 90% of funding goes to production. There is an expectation that a book, a musical composition, a play or an exhibition must result. Performances, however, are often only staged eight or ten times. Why can these pieces not reach new markets through touring or other funding?

We must ask ourselves again who all this is for: the 'happy few,' or everybody? What would a universal theatre service look like, and how could it be achieved? Which structures must be created to ensure the arts reach as many people as possible? An existing example is the TUSCH programme, an alliance between theatres and schools that operates in many German towns. The school curriculum, however, remains unchanged, as if PISA had never happened. Once again, we lag far behind other countries in reading skills. When will education policy-makers react, and when will politicians wake up to the fact that cultural and educational institutions belong together? Both are publicly funded, both have a social role. It's not just the schools, with their 'Wandertag' [hiking day] and their reduction in lesson-lengths of 45 minutes, which stand in the way of collaborative working. Theatre companies, too, busy negotiating their packed performance schedules, seem content with the status quo.

The development and support of the performing arts must happen within the context of an investigation into national, European and international independent theatre infrastructure and networks. This could be facilitated through an archive of independent theatre, an initiative proposed by the Impulse Theatre Biennale festival in 2013 (www.theatrearchiv.org).[31] It is described as including

'material covering the whole genre, information on production methods and documented practice, text-based drama and physical and visual theatre, international examples, records, artefacts and discovered objects, the mass produced object as well as the theatre marketing video.'

The mission statement says:

---

31 | Impulse Theatre Biennale (Ed.), 2013, Project Description, http://www.theater-archiv.org

'a unique tradition has grown up. It is now a matter of improving its operational conditions so it can develop beyond the town theatre structure. In comparison with other artistic fields, the conditions experienced by independent theatre are problematic and often precarious: short-term funding, constant pressure to evidence the legitimacy of any artistic work that takes place outside established companies and repertory theatres, and an unwillingness to recognise emerging alternatives to the theatrical canon.'[32]

The Department for Culture and Media has now funded the Institute for Cultural Policy at the University of Hildesheim to conduct a 'feasibility study for the establishment of an independent theatre archive.'

Theatre is more than the curtain going up every evening. Theatre policy should not lose sight of the societal meaning of the art form. With philosophy, it may have begun thus: perhaps the first philosopher stubbed their toe on a stone. This accident led them to ponder on why the stone was there, why there was anything there rather than nothing, why the stone was so hard, what the essence of stone-ness was. Why did they trip on the stone, and what should they do about it? Was there something wrong with their eyes, and what is seeing anyway? No one knows how these questions were answered back then, but we do know that not everyone who looks also sees. Seeing is also 'overseeing', 'seeing to' and 'foreseeing.' 'Looking' is perhaps our attempt to make the obscure transparent, to see what usually goes unseen. How should we look, in order to be able to see? In an age in which we are assaulted by symbols, it makes sense to teach seeing. The best method seems to be to awaken interest in what is being seen. In my opinion, theatre offers the opportunity to integrate seeing with communication, to learn to code and decode our world through a dialogue between those playing on the stage and those playing in the audience. Of course the performance must be interesting enough, must stimulate curiosity, must have something meaningful to offer. It needs a sense of purpose in order to engage our attention beyond the superficial, move us, preoccupy us, urge us to action, initiate a relationship with us based on what psychologists call mutual dependency. It needs substance, brilliance and relevance in order to care about itself and to express itself. Once we put our minds to reforming the cultural politics of our theatrical landscape, theatre will be able to achieve all of this.

---

32 | Ibid.

Literature and sources

Deutscher Bundestag (ed.). *Kultur in Deutschland*. Final report by the inquiry commission. Regensburg: ConBrio Verlag, 2008.
Brandenburg, D. "Gesamtkunstwerk Theater." In: Deutscher Bühnenverein (ed.), *Die deutsche Bühne* 8 (2012), pp. 26–35.
Hebborn, K. "Kultur in Deutschland aus Sicht der Städte." In: *Kulturpolitische Mitteilungen* 127 (2009), pp. 8-10.
Pinto, A. (ed.). *Die freien Darstellenden Künste in Deutschland: Diskurse – Entwicklungen – Perspektiven*. Bielefeld: transcript, 2013.
Schneider, W. "Es geht um die Zukunft unserer Theaterlandschaft. Eine kulturpolitische Polemik aus gegebenem Anlass." In: Fonds Darstellende Künste (ed.), *Report Darstellender Künste: wirtschaftliche, soziale und arbeitsrechtliche Lage der Theater- und Tanzschaffenden in Deutschland*. Essen: Klartext, 2010, pp. 21–25.
Schneider, W. "Nadelstiche für's System: Theaterkunst braucht Kulturpolitik." In: Genshagen Stiftung (ed.), *Plattform Theater – Darstellende Künste im Umbruch. Beiträge zur Kulturellen Bildung* Genshagen: Stiftung Genshagen, 2013, pp. 38–45.
Schneider, W. "Theater (be-)lebt Europa. Die Kulturpolitik der Dramatischen Kunst mittels Koproduktion, Festivals und Netzwerken." In: Institut für Kulturpolitik der Kulturpolitischen Gesellschaft (ed.), *Jahrbuch für Kulturpolitik 2007: Europäische Kultur*. Essen: Klartext, 2007, pp. 303–312.
Schneider, W. (ed.). *Theater entwickeln und planen: Kulturpolitische Konzeptionen zur Reform der Darstellenden Künste*. Bielefeld: transcript, 2013.
Schneider, W.: *Theater für Kinder und Jugendliche. Beiträge zu Theorie und Praxis* (2nd draft and expanded edition), Georg Olms Verlagsbuchhandlung, Hildesheim, 2012
Schneider, W. (ed.). *Theater und Migration: Herausforderungen für Kulturpolitik und Theaterpraxis*. Bielefeld: transcript, 2011.
Schneider, W. "Umsturz? Umbruch? Umgestaltung? Überlegungen zur Neustrukturierung der deutschen Theaterlandschaft." In: Institut für Kulturpolitik der Kulturpolitischen Gesellschaft (ed.), *Jahrbuch für Kulturpolitik 2004: Theaterdebatte*. Essen: Klartext, 2004, pp. 237–247.
Schneider, W. "Von Projekt zu Projekt – am Katzentisch der Kulturpolitik? Die Rolle des Freien Theaters in einer zukünftigen Theaterlandschaft." In: Fonds Darstellende Künste (ed.), *Freies Theater in Deutschland: Förderstruktur und Perspektiven*. Essen: Klartext, 2007, pp. 82–70.
Schneider, W.: "Wuppertal ist überall! Die kulturpolitische Krise der Dramatischen Künste offenbart Reformbedarfe in der deutschen Theaterlandschaft." In: E. Mittelstädt and A. Pinto (eds), *Die freien Darstellenden*

Künste in Deutschland: Diskurse – Entwicklungen – Perspektiven. Bielefeld: transcript, 2013, pp. 21–32.
Schneider, W. (ed.). *Theater und Schule: Ein Handbuch zur kulturellen Bildung*. Bielefeld: transcript, 2009.

Online publications and sources

Compendium: Cultural Policies and Trends in Europe. Available at: http://www.culturalpolicies.net (accessed 27th October 2015).
Culture Action Europe. Available at: http://www.cultureactioneurope.org (accessed 27th October 2015).
Bavarian Ministry of Education and Culture, Science and the Arts. "Förderung nichtstaatlicher Theater." Available at: http://www.km.bayern.de/kunst-und-kultur/foerderung/foerderung-nichtstaatlicher-theater.html (accessed 27th October 2015).
Bundesverband Freie Theater. Available at: http://www.freie-theater.de (accessed 27th October 2015).
Flanders Arts Institute. Available at: http:// www.vti.be (accessed 27th October 2015).
Frauen Kultur Büro NRW. Available at: http://www.frauenkulturbuero-nrw.de/index.php/foerderrecherche/theater/ (accessed 27th October 2015).
IETM. Available at: http://www.ietm.org (accessed 27th October 2015).
Impulse. Available at: http://www.impulse.de (accessed 27th October 2015).
Impulse Theatre Biennale. "Project description." 2013. Available at: http://www.theaterarchiv.org (accessed 27th October 2015).
International Theatre Institute (ITI). Available at: http://www.iti-worldwide.org (accessed 27 October 2015).
Isaksson, B. "Culture for Children and Young People." UNESCO, 1998. Available at: http://unesdoc.unesco.org/Ulis/cgi-bin/ulis.pl?catno=111819&set=005630BB37_3_378&gp=0&lin=1&ll=1 (accessed 27th October 2015).
Kulturstiftung des Bundes. Available at: http://www.kulturstiftung-des-bundes.de (accessed 27th October 2015).
Landesverband Freie Tanz- und Theaterschaffende Baden-Württemberg e.V. "Aufführungsförderung." Available at: http://www.laftbw.de/foerderinstrumente/auffuehrungsfoerderung (accessed 27th October 2015).
Landesverband Freie Tanz- und Theaterschaffende Baden-Württemberg e.V. "Konzeptionsförderung." Available at: http://www.laftbw.de/foerderinstrumente/konzeptionsfoerderung (accessed 27th October 2015).
Landesverband Freie Tanz- und Theaterschaffende Baden-Württemberg e.V. "Projektförderung 'Kulturelle Bildung'." Available at: http://www.laftbw.de/foerderinstrumente/projektfoerderung_kulturelle_bildung (accessed 27th October 2015).

Landesverband Freie Tanz- und Theaterschaffende Baden-Württemberg e.V. "Wiederaufnahmeförderung." Available at: http://www.laftbw.de/foerder instrumente/wiederaufnahmefoerderung (accessed 27th October 2015).

Ministry for Education, Science and Culture of Mecklenburg-Vorpommern. "Künstlerstipendien." Available at: http://www.regierung-mv.de/Landesre gierung/bm/Kultur/Künstlerstipendien (accessed 27th October 2015).

Nachtkritik. Available at: http://www.nachtkritik.de (accessed 27th October 2015).

NRW Landesbüro Freie Darstellende Künste. Available at: http://www.nrw-landesbuero-kultur.de/index.php?article_id=10 (accessed 27th October 2015).

Artists and culture promotion Saarland. Available at: http://www.saarland.de/10104.htm (accessed 27 October 2015).

TAZ (newspaper). Available at: http://www.taz.de/1/archiv/print-archiv/print ressorts/digi-artikel/?ressort=ku&dig=2009%2F12%2F15%2Fa0028&c Hash=ba9c0cf4e9ddc01db2d4ed7a6dba88ba (accessed 27th October 2015).

Theaterforschung. Available at: http://www.theaterforschung.de (accessed 27th October 2015).

Theaterpolitik. Available at: http://www.theaterpolitik.de (accessed 27th October 2015).

Theaterportal. Available at: http://www.theaterportal.de (accessed 27th October 2015).

Authors

Emeritus Professor Dr Manfred Brauneck studied literature, art history, theatre arts and philosophy at the University of Munich, graduating in 1965 and receiving his professorship in 1973. Since 1973 he has taught Contemporary German Literature at the University of Hamburg, focusing on theatre and media. In the same year, he was also appointed Professor at the University of Hamburg, with a chair in social research, and later in theatre research. Brauneck has curated a number of exhibitions, including 'Humans and Human Machines: Experimental Theatre in Europe, 1910 to 1933', with Barbara Müller-Wesemann (1978), which appeared in Hamburg, Sofia, Washington and other US states. He has researched amateur theatre and independent theatre, in particular migrant theatre. From 1986 to 2003, he was director of the Centre for Theatre Research and the Theatre Collection at the University of Hamburg, and from 1989 to 2005 leader of the university's theatre directing course, which he developed together with Jürgen Flimm. He has held many guest professorships since 1973, in the USA (where he has also had a number of theatrical productions), Poland and Bulgaria. His main research interests are the history and theory of theatre and frontiers between theatre and the visual arts. His most important publications on theatre include the following: *Literatur und Öffentlichkeit im ausgehenden 19. Jahrhundert: Zur Rezeption des naturalistischen Theaters in Deutschland* (1974); *Theaterlexikon* vol.1 (1986, extended 5th edition 2007), vol. 2 (2007); *Naturalismus: Dokumente zur deutschen Literatur 1880-1900* (with C. Müller) (1987); *Theater im 20. Jahrhundert: Programmschriften, Stilperioden, Reformmodelle* (1982, extended 5th edition 2009); *Klassiker der Schauspielregie: Positionen und Kommentare zum Theater im 20. Jahrhundert* (1988, 1996); *Theaterstadt Hamburg* (with the Zentrum für Theaterforschung) (1989); *100 Jahre Deutsches Schauspielhaus Hamburg* (with M. Giesing et al) (1999); *Die Welt als Bühne: Geschichte des europäischen Theaters*, 6 vols (1993-2007); *Europas Theater. 2500 Jahre Geschichte - eine Einführung* (2012); *Kleine Weltgeschichte des Theaters* (2014). In 2010, Manfred Brauneck received the Balzan Prize for theatrical research.

Dr Henning Fülle is a cultural researcher. He has also been a freelance dramaturg for independent theatres since 2001. Since 2007, he has been a researcher and teacher at the Karlsruhe School of Design and the University of Hamburg. From 1995, he worked as a dramaturg and curator, including for Kampnagel Hamburg (1997-2001) and a variety of other projects, artists and institutions including the Berliner Festspiele and the Berlin-Brandenburg Academy for the Arts. He researches cultural policy and publishes on independent theatre in Germany. He is currently part of the working group for 'Performing the Archive – An Archive of Independent Theatre' and a research associate for its pilot study. His thesis, *Independent Groups, Independent Scene, Independent Theatre and the Modernisation of the German Theatrical Landscape* (supervised by Professor Wolfgang Schneider at Hildesheim University) is completed and will be published shortly.

Andrea Hensel is a research associate at the Institute for Theatre Studies at the University of Leipzig. She studied there from 2007 to 2013, on the BA and MA theatre arts programmes, and worked from 2008-2013 as a student and graduate assistant. Since 2013 she has been working on her thesis as part of the DFG research project 'The Theatre of Repetition' (University of Leipzig, led by Professor Dr Günther Heeg), about the relationship between historiography and historical artistic practice, using the example of theatre historicism in the nineteenth century. Further research interests include the analysis of independent theatrical forms and the relationship between new production methods and theatrical aesthetics and creativity in the post-socialist states of (eastern) Europe.

Dr Tine Koch read Germanic Studies, Romance Studies and Education at the University of Hamburg. After completing her first qualification to teach in secondary schools, she did a doctorate in Germanic Studies, on the subject of the tropes in world theatre and the role of play in the dramatic works of Samuel Beckett and Thomas Bernhardt. She lectured at the University of Hamburg between 2012 and 2014, as well as developing her research involvement in the field of children and young people's theatre. She completed the second state teaching qualification in the subjects of German, French and Theatre Studies in the summer of 2015. Since then she has been a research associate in the Faculty of Education at the University of Hamburg, working on the project 'Didactics of German language and literature.' She is active in both teaching and research and also teaches theatre at a grammar school in Hamburg. Her research interests are literature for children and young people, literary socialisation and learning, aesthetic training, the didactics of drama and theatre and theatre education.

Prof Dr Matthias Rebstock is Professor of Music Theatre at Hildesheim University. He investigates ways of staging music, in particular the various forms of music theatre, musicalised theatre and opera, as well as the history and aesthetics of new music. His latest publication is *Composed Theatre. Aesthetics, Practices, Processes* (with David Roesner), Bristol, 2012. He also works as a director of new music theatre, including developing pieces that cross the boundaries of music and theatre, and directing new works, from staged concerts to new operas. Directing projects include: *Utopien (Utopias)* by Dieter Schnebel, première by the Munich Biennale for New Music Theatre with new vocal soloists, Munich 2014, *Expedition Freischütz (The Freischütz Expedition)*, with Michael Emanuel Bauer, Staatsschauspiel Theatre Dresden 2014, *Neither* by Morton Feldman, Bern Theatre 2013, *Fernweh. Aus dem Leben eines Stubenhockers (Wanderlust: from the life of a couch potato)*, with Hermann Bohlen and Michael Emanuel Bauer, Neuköllner Opera 2012, *Die Geisterinsel (The ghost island)*, première of the opera by Ming Tsao, Stuttgart Town Opera 2011, *Lezioni di Tenebra*, première of the music theatre piece by Lucia Ronchetti, Berlin Concert House and Parco de la Musica, Rome 2011.

Dr Petra Sabisch is a choreographer and philosopher (research interests include choreography and dance studies, aesthetic theory, methodology and practical philosophy). She teaches in arts colleges and institutions all over Europe, including the University of Dance in Stockholm, the Cologne College of Music and Dance, the Co-operative Education Centre in Berlin, the Department of Dance at the University of Paris 8 and the Institute for Applied Theatre Studies at the University of Gießen. In 2011, she was awarded the NRW Dance Studies Prize for her thesis *Choreographing Relations: Practical Philosophy and Contemporary Choreography in the works of Antonia Baehr, Gilles Deleuze, Juan Dominguez, Félix Guattari, Xavier Le Roy & Eszter Salamon* (epodium, Munich 2011). For this work she also received a PhD in London and a grant from Tanzplan Deustschland, a German Government Cultural Fund initiative.

Prof Dr Wolfgang Schneider is the Director of the Institute for Cultural Policy at the University of Hildesheim, holder of the UNESCO Chair in Cultural Policy for the Arts in Development, a member of the International Theatre Institute and the German UNESCO Commission, Chair of the charity ASSITEJ, and President of the International Union for Children and Young People's Theatre. He was founding director of the German Federal Republic's Children and Young People's Centre, Chair of the Theatre Advisory Council for Niedersachsen, member of the Goethe Institute's Advisory Committee for Dance and Theatre and specialist member of the German Government's enquiry commission on 'Culture in Germany', a writer for the chapter 'Cultural Training, Sociology and Theatre'. He has produced many publications, including, as author: *Theatre for*

Children and Young people: contributions to theory and practice (2nd draft and expanded edition)', Hildesheim, 2012; as editor: *Theatre and Schools: a handbook for cultural education,* 2009; *Theatre and Migration: challenges for cultural policy and theatre practice,* 2011; *Developing and Planning Theatre: cultural policy concepts for the reform of the performing arts,* 2014 (all Bielefeld); and *IXYPSILONZETT* a yearbook and a magazine for children and young people's theatre (part of *Theater der Zeit,* Berlin).

Dr Azadeh Sharifi read Germanic Studies, Philosophy and Law at the Ruprecht-Karls University in Heidelberg. She is doing her doctorate at the Institute for Cultural Studies at the University of Hildesheim. Her research interests are post-migrant theatre and racism and post-colonialism in theatre. From 2014 to 2015, she was a fellow at the international research symposium on 'Interweaving Performance Cultures' at the Independent University of Berlin. Her thesis *Theatre for everyone? Participation by post-migrants in the theatres of Cologne* was published in 2011.